EXTREME PREJUDICE

The Terrifying Story of the Patriot Act
And the Cover Ups of 9/11 and Iraq

The Ultimate Conspiracy to Silence Truth

BY SUSAN LINDAUER

CONTENTS

DEEPEST THANKS

My life has been blessed by a number of individuals who profoundly impacted the course of my direction and adventures. For every burden I have faced, there has been a partner in fortune to master the challenge.

All my thanks go to my beloved friend and companion, JB Fields, for his courage to fight unbeatable forces. To activist Janet Phelan, blog journalist extraordinaire Michael Collins, and all time best radio host Michael Herzog, for championing my story and defending Constitutional liberties for all Americans. You are truly awake and vigilant.

To my heroic Uncle Ted Lindauer, for fighting bare knuckled to win my release from Carswell. To Brian Shaughnessy and Tom Mattingly, for recognizing the strengths of my legal defense and carrying my dirtied banner when others dismissed my claims. To Parke Godfrey and Kelly O'Meara, for daring to speak Inconvenient Truths. To the women of M-1 at Carswell—Nancy Zaia, Sharon, Jessica, Renee, Toie and Karen—for reminding me always of the power of transcendence. To Sarah Yamasaki for singing on the rooftop of M.C.C. as if all of our lives depended on your songs—which they did.

Above all, I send my greatest love to Paul Hoven and Dr. Richard Fuisz, whose exuberance and vision launched me on the greatest quest of discovery to create my own life. Whatever happened afterwards, these men encouraged my passion and endurance for almost a decade, challenging me to stand strong for my values and face what I must.

To you most of all, for sharing my greatest adventures, Carpe diem!

FORWARD

My law firm defended Ms. Susan Lindauer against federal charges of acting as an unregistered Iraqi Agent in conspiracy with the Iraqi Intelligence Service. I assure you that Ms. Lindauer's story is shocking, but true. It's an important story of this new political age, post-9/11.

As her attorney, I maintained very high legal standards for validating Ms. Lindauer's claims that she worked as a U.S. Intelligence Asset, supervised by members of the CIA and the Defense Intelligence Agency. Before agreeing to represent her, I took steps to corroborate her story through independent sources that I considered to be extremely high caliber. Those included former Congressional staff, international journalists, and several U.S. and Scottish attorneys involved with the Lockerbie Trial at The Hague. I know some of these people socially and professionally. Ms. Lindauer's story checked out. She has an extraordinary personal history, and I believe it's true.

Vetting her story was much simplified by the extensive records available in her legal discovery. Those included original documents and transcripts from FBI wire taps of 28,000 phone calls; 8,000 emails; and hundreds of captured faxes that are date and time stamped to prove transmission. When, for example, Ms. Lindauer claims that her CIA handler, Dr. Richard Fuisz, paid her $2,500 in October, 2001 for her work on the 9/11 investigation, she's got the personal check to prove it. When Ms. Lindauer claims to have delivered papers on Iraq's probable lack of illegal weapons to the home of Secretary of State Colin Powell, who lived next door to Dr. Fuisz, she's got the FBI photo copy of the manila envelope to vouch that she did it. She's also got copies of the original papers with handwritten notes to the Secretary, provided by the FBI for her prosecution.

Her portfolio smartly repudiates claims that Intelligence Assets made no attempt to correct faulty intelligence on Capitol Hill before the War. Indeed, FBI records show that she worked night and day around the clock to do just that. When Republican leaders decided to invent a new story about the 9/11 warnings, Pre-War Intelligence and Iraq's contribution to the 9/11 investigation, Ms. Lindauer's activism and her reputation for truth-telling, vis a vis Lockerbie, got in their way. For the deception to succeed, they had to take her down.

In my opinion as her attorney, Ms. Lindauer was always competent to stand trial, only the Justice Department wanted to avoid embarrassing revelations from her case.

Brian Shaughnessy July 1, 2010

CHAPTER ONE:

THE WAR ON TRUTH

He who tells history must tell it for all, not only for himself.
–Arab saying

Voice or no voice, the people can always be
brought to the bidding of the leaders.
That is easy. All you have to do is tell them they are being attacked, and
denounce the pacifists for lack of patriotism and exposing the country to danger.
It works the same in any country.
Herman Goering. The Nuremberg Trials 1946

"Hey kid, remember— When they come to kill you, scream your head off."
It was an eerie premonition, those last words by my intelligence handler, Paul Hoven, in the doorway of his apartment. Or perhaps it was a matter of fate, predestined and unalterable. Had we all seen the eventuality of this day, and laughed our way to the other side of its meaning? Like an outlaw from the old West who understands that eventually he's got to hang for robbing those trains. Or a spy who knows his life has memorialized too many inconvenient truths.

Yet when the day arrived, it caught me fully off guard. I heard the heavy pounding on my door early that morning. I wrapped myself in a bathrobe and hurried to the window. A crowd of men in flak jackets had gathered on my front porch. I could see more federal agents in the yard.

"Susan Lindauer— FBI. Open the door. We have a warrant for your arrest."

1

For a few crucial moments, I was too stunned to act.

"Open this door immediately. This is the FBI."

Actually I couldn't. Quite mysteriously, the door jamb had broken about three weeks earlier. The door swung on the air, so that I had no choice but to barricade it shut with plywood and nails.[1] Among friends, I speculated that federal agents cracked the door frame during one of those warrantless searches on the Patriot Act that Congress was so jazzed about.

Suddenly my paranoia did not appear so irrational after all. I pointed to the other side of my house, and started to back out of my living room. I needed to get dressed.

That made them very, very angry.

"WE ARE THE FBI. OPEN THIS DOOR OR WE WILL BREAK IT DOWN."

"What? You already broke it. You're going to break it again?" I shook my head at the FBI agents staring back through my window. "No! You have to come to the side door."

I turned on my heels and fled. A stampede of agents raced to the door off my bedroom as I cautiously pulled it open. A whole team of feds forced their way inside. Now I started shaking.

"What exactly are you doing here? May I see some identification?"

"Susan Lindauer, I am Special Agent Chmiel. You are under arrest on the Patriot Act. You have the right to remain silent. Anything you say, can and will be used against you in a federal court of law—"[2]

The FBI's presence in my bedroom hit me like a dirty punch in the gut. At the mention of the Patriot Act, however, I knew this was serious trouble, and it could be scary trouble. Still, I had no idea my arrest was connected to Iraq or my Pre-War Intelligence activities. I had no inkling what illegal actions the government had clocked against me. I was waking up to make coffee. I was not a bank robber, a drug dealer, or a murderer. I had a couple of minor speeding violations. That's it.

Actually, my arrest would prove distinctive in two critical ways.

First, I was one of only three U.S. Assets covering the Iraqi Embassy at the United Nations before the War, granting me vast primary knowledge of Pre-War Intelligence, as a direct participant in some of the events. I would soon discover that all three of us got arrested as "Iraqi agents" when Congress and the White House decided to cook the intelligence books.

Second, along with Jose Padilla, I was one of the very first non-Arab Americans to discover the slippery and treacherous legal terrain of the Patriot Act. By invoking the Patriot Act against me, the Justice Department used the same tools to smash political dissension against Republican policy that Congress enacted to break terrorists. The message was simple. Oppose the Grand Old Party and you become an "Enemy of the State."

It was especially ironic because my line of specialty, for almost a decade, was anti-terrorism.

The FBI hustled me to a sedan in handcuffs, and we drove off towards Baltimore, gambling it would be out of range of the Washington media. I kept it light, joking about the fingerprint machine that scanned thumb prints straight onto a computer screen. Pretty cool technology, I guffawed. I was waiting for the punch line, confident that somebody extremely high up would quickly receive an angry phone call, telling the FBI they'd made a hugely embarrassing mistake. Obviously they didn't know who I was. I tried to keep the mood friendly, no hard feelings when they got the order to release me. I was sure the situation would change momentarily. I could be magnanimous for an hour or so.

Keep dreamin' baby.

My expectations changed radically and abruptly when Special Agent Chmiel sat me down with a copy of my full indictment under the Patriot Act.[3] His finger shook slightly as he pointed to the bottom line: 25 years in prison under Federal Sentencing Guidelines. (Mandatory sentencing got set aside, and reduced to "recommendations" by the U.S. Supreme Court[4] in December, 2004, nine months after my arrest). A powerful surge of horror exploded in my heart. I stared numb and disbelieving at the rundown of the charges, trying to determine who the hell had ordered my arrest. I felt a jolt like a heart attack when I realized that everybody I ever trusted had betrayed me on a massive scale.

Stunned, I demanded to know what exactly I had done wrong? The FBI Agent replied glibly that my attorney would explain my criminal actions later. Need I say, that was hardly satisfactory after suggesting I might spend 25 years in federal prison for violating the Patriot Act—a 7,000 page document that I happened to know nobody on Capitol Hill actually read before voting to approve.

Almost immediately my arrest began to expose the dilemma for defendants on the Patriot Act. If you rob a bank, or smuggle drugs into the U.S., or commit a violent robbery, then the accused person can recognize what actions constitute that particular crime. When a person gets indicted on the Patriot Act, what does that actually mean? What triggers the criminal action which the Patriot Act seeks to punish? I had no idea. The FBI Agent could not explain it either. That struck me as grossly unfair. I mean, if you're going to spend 25 years in prison, you have a reasonable right to know why.

The government's position was not strengthened by the disingenuous nature of the few specific actions detailed by the Justice Department. For example, I was formally accused of "Organizing Resistance to the United States"[5] in Iraq. My mind flashed back to the previous summer, and my brief contact with an under-cover FBI agent, presented as a "Libyan Agent" in the indictment, a false flag to inflame the media. Quite the contrary, I recognized that he was some form of American Intelligence—and teasingly, I called him out the way that spooks do. We have our ways of letting each other know that we know, even if someone's on cover.

And what plot did we hatch that posed such grave threat to the Occupation? I distinctly recall that we discussed the critical importance of promoting free elections and free political parties in Iraq, and how Iraqi detainees should not suffer torture or sexual abuse, and should have access to attorneys to protest their detentions by American soldiers.[6] Here the Republican leadership was bragging about the U.S. liberation of Baghdad, while I faced years in prison for supporting genuine democratic reforms and human rights inside the "New Iraq." It screamed hypocrisy.

Another federal agent interrupted the conversation. They were ready to take me to Court. He warned me that a small group of journalists waited outside the building for my perp walk. I would be photographed in handcuffs on my way to Court.

I saw Paul Hoven's face framed tight in his doorway that last time we said goodbye, forever, though I didn't know it yet. The smiles and warmth had gone. I saw him deadly serious now. And I heard him again:

Scream your head off, Susan!

Federal agents shoved open the door of the FBI Baltimore office. A huddle of local journalists with a couple of TV cameras rushed into position:

Scream!

I took a deep breath, holding it until I got directly in front of them. Then I shouted:

"I am an Anti-War Activist and I am innocent!" I yelled. "I have done more against terrorism than anybody. Everything I have done was always good for the security of the United States and good for security in the Middle East."[7]

The FBI Agents grabbed me from behind, and shoved me faster towards a black sedan. They thrust me in the backseat and slammed the door. I gazed out the window into the horrified eyes of a camera man, who followed us when I cried out.

For one moment, one photo-journalist recognized that something terribly wrong was happening in America. He got a glimpse of the truth, but it was enough. Television footage of my arrest beamed around the world. I know from friends in Canada, France and Taiwan who saw it. He took my story to the White House door, summoning the Washington and international press corps en masse. For one moment, a single camera man showed the White House the force that journalistic freedom can unleash as a check on tyranny.

For one moment, we almost won.

Much later, media pundits would decry the administration's policy of crushing dissent in the intelligence community, attacking the patriotism of individuals who opposed the Republican War policy in Iraq, and their practice of systematically tearing down the CIA to take the blame for "faulty" pre war intelligence. The Intelligence Community would be demoralized for years afterwards. Ironically, the GOP would leave it gutted in ashes.

On the morning of my arrest, I saw with total clarity that I was the first casualty of the Republican War on Truth. With total clarity, I recognized that my indictment was a political smoke-screen to shut me up, because I possessed first-hand knowledge of events that Republican leaders desperately wanted to reinvent. Even so, I had no idea how far afield of our Constitution they would go to protect their grip on power.

What those TV cameras captured in their sound-bite was the head-on collision of my double life as a clandestine, back-channel Asset in counter-terrorism for the CIA and Defense Intelligence Agency, and my public life as an Anti-War activist, as seen by friends, neighbors and family. In truth, I was both women. On that fateful morning, I had no idea that that construct of duality in my life would prove more difficult for the Court to understand than the prospect of my innocence. Explaining that duality would become my hardest battle. On the morning of my arrest, I had no idea how difficult or frightening that fight would become.

My FBI Agents sped off to the Federal Courthouse in Baltimore. Shaken by my outburst, they hardly spoke on the drive. I was dumped unceremoniously in the custody of court bailiffs to wait for a court-appointed attorney to fight for my bail. Meanwhile the Feds skulked off to devise a new strategy for containing the GOP's "Susan Lindauer problem," already backfiring on the White House and Capitol Hill.

In a tiny holding cage, I examined the federal indictment more closely, while I waited for the extradition hearing that would transfer my case to Chief Justice Michael B. Mukasey in the Southern District of New York in Manhattan.

A metal desk was bolted to the floor with a bench seat. The cage door locked directly behind me, allowing perhaps two feet of standing space. A guard shoved a roll of bread with something like turkey and mayonnaise through a slot in the door, along with some potato chips and a can of soda. I took a bite, and couldn't eat.

Locked inside such a claustrophobic space, my breathing got rapid, and I experienced a roller coaster of emotions. I kept thinking to myself how the media would react when they discovered that I had not exaggerated my involvement in anti-terrorism. I'd been active since 1993. And here the Justice Department had locked me up in a jail cell like some criminal! What incompetence that the Justice Department didn't know who I am! Somebody didn't do his homework!

Or maybe they did. A whisper nagged at the back of my brain. They obviously knew my second cousin on my father's side was Andrew Card, Chief of Staff to President George W. Bush. And it struck me as highly improbable, extraordinary even, that the Justice Department would admit no prior knowledge of my extensive work in anti-terrorism, going back to the first World Trade Center attack in 1993.

What did my intelligence handler say, when I complained about heavy surveillance that sometimes got excessive or rough? "Don't get all high and mighty on us, Susan! If they're not tracking you—based on all of your contacts in the Middle East—they're not doing their jobs."

Oh, they understood what they were doing alright. This had to be a political hit. I knew first-hand where all the bodies were buried in a graveyard of national security initiatives that looked nothing at all like what Americans were told.

They had to take me out so they could reinvent the truth. It was that simple.

I looked more closely at the indictment—"Acting as an Unregistered Iraqi Agent" in "conspiracy with the Iraqi Intelligence Service."[8] Not espionage, I determined quickly.

That satisfied me somewhat. The Justice Department wasn't so stupid as to accuse me of trading state secrets, which would be grossly inaccurate.

But $10,000 from the Iraqis?[9] The Feds understood more than they pretended. Locked in that tiny holding cage, I got so angry that I shouted for a bailiff to protest. I wanted to tell the bailiff the indictment was loaded with excrement. There was no other way to describe it. I had yet to learn that filing criminal charges against an individual was relatively simple. Everybody said you could indict a ham sandwich in New York City. Getting charges dismissed proved infinitely more difficult, however. Federal prosecutors typically do not enjoy confessing publicly that they read the evidence wrong.

Oh but I would have a few things to say when we got to Court!

For starters, after 9/11, Israel was the only foreign government trolling to buy national security documents in Washington. Iraq didn't need them. Baghdad already had the best. They had the most devastating access in the Middle East. Powerful stuff. Israel coveted that access hungrily for what their arch enemy in Baghdad could reveal. If Iraq didn't have it already, Saddam's government would know how to get it.

The real treasure hunt after 9/11 was for financial or banking documents that would expose the cash network for key figures tied to Osama bin Laden and Al Qaeda. Iraqi officials boasted that they had financial documents of extraordinary value that would prove a Middle Eastern connection to the Oklahoma City Bombing and the first strike on the World Trade Center in 1993. If so, Baghdad had not overstated the value of its cache.

They wanted to trade that intelligence as part of a comprehensive settlement to lift the sanctions.

By the summer of 2001, back channel talks with Iraqi diplomats in New York were far advanced, under the watchful eye of the CIA. The peace framework developed from November 2000 through March 2002[10] created an option that defined what future U.S.-Iraqi relations might look like in a post-sanctions world— without penalizing the United States for supporting brutal U.N. sanctions for 13 years. It asked critical questions of what Baghdad would give the United States to prove its commitment to behave like a responsible neighbor in the region.

After 9/11, Baghdad brought these papers to the table.[11] Those papers potentially qualified as the most significant contribution to successful global anti-terrorism efforts by any nation in the world. Baghdad's intelligence on terrorism was that good. Really, it was the best.

My U.S. Intelligence handlers had been informed immediately, which sort of explains how Israel would have heard the news.

And so a Mossad contact had phoned repeatedly while I was on a trip to Iraq, telling my housemate, Allison H— that they would deliver a "suitcase full of cash anywhere in the world to get those documents."

"Susan's traveling in Milan," Allison told him.

"No. She's not. She's nowhere in Italy."

"But how do you know that? Who are you? Why did she leave Italy?" Allison was floored.

"Tell her it's Roy. If she calls, tell her we'll meet her anywhere in the world. Any city at all. We will come to her. We'll bring a suitcase full of cash."

The truth of my travel itinerary to Baghdad had been concealed from all but a few of my friends in Washington. My CIA handler, Dr. Richard Fuisz, received approximately 30 to 40 phone calls informing him of the dates of my trip, and nagging for payment for a series of outstanding debts, mostly connected to Lockerbie. Mind you, I was absolutely desperate to receive payment before my departure. I pushed hard to get it.

I also begged Dr. Fuisz to follow through on Congressional promises of payment for my extensive work on Lockerbie, tied to the hand over of the two Libyans. Leaders in Washington and London had made grand speeches at press conferences, promising spectacular rewards for my work. Unhappily for Assets, those promises were forgotten as soon as the TV cameras packed up. It was all an empty publicity stunt, a public fraud.

Only I was real flesh and blood, and I needed to get paid. I needed to buy groceries. It was Dr. Fuisz's job as my handler to make that happen—which accounted for the high volume of phone calls before my trip to Baghdad. My urgency and desperation was so great that even the Israelis heard gossip about it. The Mossad acted to fill the gap, while the notorious Beltway Bandits in Washington poached off Black Budget earmarks for the 9/11 investigation.

And for good cause.

In Baghdad, I expected to meet top ranking Iraqi officials, in part to discuss the acquisition of those documents—which Iraq would only turn over to the FBI or Interpol—in other words, only credible law enforcement, no spooks. Still, I had the papers in my reach. That whet some appetites in the intelligence community. Just not appetites in the Bush Administration, unfortunately, though I did not understand that in March 2002.

And so an Israeli agent urged me to name my price. Any price.

I turned him down after my trip to Baghdad.

A suitcase full of cash... No matter how badly I needed that money—and I was hanging by a thread financially, at this point — I could never sell documents affecting national security to a foreign government. Cash transactions go on more frequently than anybody wants to admit. Not the sale of U.S. documents, which is strictly verboten and punishable by endless years in prison. Trafficking in foreign documents like those from Baghdad goes on all the time, however. To stay so pure requires a certain naiveté that clashes with the ruthless nature of intelligence-gathering. It reflected my own distaste for the Mossad, certainly. With regards to this indictment, however, it might have been my salvation.

In that holding cage I resolved that I would challenge the Court: If I would not accept a suitcase full of cash from a friendly ally like Israel—non traceable income with no taxes that might add up to a couple million dollars, if the Samsonite luggage was large enough – why oh why would I take $10,000 from the Iraqis—who were desperately cash poor under UN sanctions? Obviously I hadn't, and no evidence ever suggested I had. Mercifully, Allison had no ties to the spooks. They could not stop her from testifying.

Oh but pride goeth before the fall, doesn't it? Israel would have taken the financial records on Al Qaeda. They would have paid any price for them. They would have shut down the financial pipeline to Osama's network, and stopped the flow of funds used in other attacks today in Afghanistan, Pakistan, Mombai, the Philippines and the Anbar Province of Iraq. I was just so pure that I could not allow myself to be "corrupted."

I had no idea when I turned down Israel's generosity that America would refuse to accept such critical intelligence. I could not fathom that Washington would reject documents that would pinpoint the inner workings of Osama bin Laden's financial network, and incidentally show a pattern of Middle Eastern involvement in the Oklahoma City bombing in May, 1995 and the first World Trade Center attack in February, 1993. It left me baffled and bewildered, more so because it was never explained.

The White House was more interested in launching war in Iraq than protecting our country from terrorism. They would not accept those papers strictly because they came from Baghdad—even though sources in Baghdad promised to deliver those papers promptly to an FBI Task Force, as good faith for its other commitments in our back-channel talks. The United States left that money in circulation.

Such calculated indifference, despite so much grandstanding after 9/11, broke my heart irrevocably. It qualified as massive public fraud, which endangers our country and the global community to this very day. In the end, that deception destroyed my relationship with the two men I loved and respected most in the world, Paul Hoven and Dr. Richard Fuisz, my "handlers" or "case officers," who supervised my work with Libya and Iraq from 1993 to 2002. I would have done anything for either of those men. In the end, I could not understand why my successful efforts to win Iraq's cooperation with the 9/11 investigation cost me their friendship. And they were prohibited from explaining. In my heart, I have clung to the hope that they were just as perplexed and baffled as I was.

For truly I was the last to know.

Israel had always known.

And so the Mossad tried to acquire the papers directly from me.

How could Washington have acted so irresponsibly to shun Iraq's cooperation, with such high stakes in play? In that tiny holding cage, I wanted to shout at the bailiffs, like I'd shouted to myself many times, stupefied by the loss of it.

How could they do such a terrible thing to all of us? They hurt everybody.

I dared not examine those questions too long. Self pity would not free me from that cage. I would have to hold myself together, and stay focused and calm, if I wanted to wrestle control of the situation. I would have to get over my emotional shock. I could beat the Justice Department, if I kept my wits about me.

I brought my mind back to the terrible document in front of me—the federal indictment that carried a maximum 25 year prison sentence.[12]

"Acting as an Unregistered Iraqi Agent."[13]

Fuck you, motherfuckers!

Straight off the top, I had a worthy and reliable rebuttal to that accusation. For close to a decade, I had performed as a U.S. Asset covering Iraq at the United Nations, with oversight by U.S. Intelligence. I'd been recruited as a back-channel in the early 1990s, because of my anti-sanctions activism. They sent me to the Libya House in May, 1995 and the Iraqi Embassy in August, 1996. They supervised everything I did, debriefed every conversation after my visit to the Embassies.

We specialized in anti-terrorism, and my bona fides were some of the best. Our work in the 1990s set the bar awfully high, as a matter of fact. It would be fairly simple to prove, because I had played a public role in identifying Dr. Fuisz as a crucial source of knowledge in the bombing of Pan Am 103. My efforts had been well documented during the trial of the two Libyans at The Hague. The Scottish attorneys for the Lockerbie Defense could testify to Dr. Fuisz's intelligence background and our long-established working relationship together. My defense would be much easier for it.

Wouldn't it be fun to bust the Justice Department in court! I'd slam prosecutors to the wall for bringing such outrageous charges against me. "Foreign agent," indeed. After all my contributions as an Asset, I would never be so generous as to accept a plea bargain in this case. We'd go to trial. I'd make the Prosecutor apologize to the Court and the media for daring to accuse me of criminal activity. They'd eat crow for this!

The whole thing struck me as foolish—except the holding cage felt awfully real.

And what was this accusation: "Conspiracy with the Iraqi Intelligence Service?"[14]

The indictment listed two co-defendants, Raed Noman Al-Anbuke and Wisam Noman Al-Anbuke. I'd never met either of them, nor heard their names spoken. Only later would I learn that the Anbuke brothers were also Assets covering the Iraqi Embassy at the United Nations in New York. The sons of an Iraqi diplomat, they agreed to help the FBI track visitors to the Iraqi Embassy. Their cooperation had been fairly innocuous, videotaping guests at Embassy events, nothing terribly dramatic.

The Justice Department had exploited them with promises that the brothers could stay in America after the invasion. When the FBI had no more use for the boys, they got arrested as "Iraqi Agents"—along with another brother and sister accused of no crimes at all. The whole family got thrown in prison at the Metropolitan Correctional Center in Manhattan, in attempt to coerce confessions from the brothers. The tactic of arresting innocent family members on the Patriot Act smacked of Saddam Hussein's own brutality. It was fairly disgusting.

I could see now the Justice Department had made a clean sweep, arresting all three of us who covered the Iraqi Embassy at the United Nations before the War. It struck me as awfully convenient that those of us with birds-eye views inside the Embassy should all be gagged and silenced by phony indictments. Meanwhile, Washington officials would be liberated to bombard the air waves with false reports about the mediocrity of our Pre-War Intelligence reporting.

Such rubbish!

For my part, I had been a vocal anti-war activist, campaigning aggressively against the invasion on Capitol Hill and at the United Nations, with a trove of documents and FBI wire taps to prove it. For heaven's sakes, I stood formally accused of telling U.S. officials that war would be disastrous. And yet in this New World Order, my indictment on the Patriot Act effectively gagged me from publicly disclosing any part of my warnings to White House officials and members of Congress. While I faced prosecution, those same leaders on Capitol Hill vigorously complained to the public that I had *not come forward*, and my failure to speak was responsible for the war-time catastrophe facing our nation. A very clever strategy! And totally dishonest.

My eye stuck on the first "overt act" of conspiracy. "On or about October 14, 1999, Susan Lindauer aka "Symbol Susan," met with an officer of the Iraqi Intelligence Service in Manhattan."[15]

"Symbol Susan?" I rolled my eyes. Somebody at the Justice Department had a sense of humor. I was a "symbol" alright. The Justice Department intended to scare the Intelligence Community out of criticizing the Republican leadership about its war policy. They made a bold example of me, flaunting the brutality that could crush anybody who dissented from Republican national security policy. Fine, then. Let them call me "Symbol Susan." I'm made of tougher stuff than that. While they're at it, I thought, let them explain in front of a jury how they scapegoated me for accurately forecasting the horrific consequences of this War. Let them show the world how they mistreated those of us who got it right.

Now that first "overt act of conspiracy" on October 14, 1999 intrigued me very much. It was so long ago, yet so definite and precise. For the first time that morning of my arrest, I actually smiled. Yes, I was still shell-shocked, but I began to see how easily the indictment could be torn apart. Shredded, really.

October 14, 1999. Those bastards got that date from me! I reported it to Paul Hoven, one of my intelligence handlers, when I warned him that Iraqi diplomats in New York had requested my help in locating a top Republican official to receive major financial campaign contributions for the 2000 Presidential election. Those poor bastards in Baghdad wanted to shower George Bush with campaign cash, in the hundreds of thousands of dollars, in the hope that once victorious, he would reciprocate by lifting the sanctions. [16]

The sincerity of Iraq's good will towards the Republican leadership poignantly illustrated the greatest tragedy of the War: Saddam's government urgently desired to reconcile with the United States, and prove its loyalty as an ally to Washington. Baghdad yearned for days past, when Iraq had been strategically positioned as a buttress to Islamic radicalism in Iran. Then, Baghdad's progressive views towards women and moderate Islamic attitudes had been highly prized. Alas, in October, 1999, my U.S. Intelligence contacts demanded that I block them. Hoven threatened to bomb Baghdad himself if Iraqi officials gave money to the Republican Party.[17] I described Iraq's desire to contribute to Republican coffers in two letters to my second cousin, Andrew Card, Chief of Staff to President Bush, on March 1, 2001 and December 2, 2001. That explains how Republican leaders learned of Iraq's attempt.

In my holding cage, I scorned them all. See you in court, Mr. Prosecutor! *(Not likely!)*

I scanned the indictment a little further—"On or about September 19, 2001, Susan Lindauer met with an officer of the Iraqi Intelligence Service in Manhattan."[18]

That would be my part in the 9/11 investigation— and me a first-responder, like the fire fighters at Ground Zero, taking appropriate steps to secure Iraq's cooperation with global anti-terrorism objectives.

So now the Justice Department had declared it a crime to contribute to a terrorist investigation? And they dared to cite the U.S. Patriot Act in order to do it? Tell it to a jury, Mr. Prosecutor! While you're at it, explain that to Congress!

My confidence grew bolder. I read other dates in January and February, 2002, when I met with Iraqi diplomats at a hotel close to the United Nations.[19] These were marathon sessions to finalize Iraq's agreement to resume weapons inspections, according to rigorous standards for maximum transparency demanded by the United States, before the matter got handed over to the United Nations. The U.S. had demanded that Baghdad agree to weapons inspections "with no conditions," the operative phrase for "unconditional surrender."[20] It was entirely legitimate on my part, supervised by my CIA contacts-and designed to guarantee Iraq's performance. Our back channel dialogue from November 2000 to March 2002 made weapons inspections a successful reality.[21]

Gleefully, I noticed that some of the dates in the indictment were flat wrong. I was confident that I could prove I was at my home in Maryland on several of those days.

As an Asset with a long history of close relationships to Iraqi diplomats, I had a serious advantage over the Justice Department. I understood how they'd jumped to the wrong conclusions. My diplomatic contact in New York had a girlfriend named "Susan," a young American who worked at the United Nations. How delicious that the FBI should have gotten us confused! Apparently this Iraqi diplomat had shared some inexpensive lunches with this other Susan, while I was safely tucked 200 miles away in Maryland, out of danger of prosecution. Such poor intelligence! The claws of my Cheshire cat struck back. I would teach the FBI not to mess with Assets cooperating with other Agencies. They would never want to do this again.

And the coup de gras: "On or about January 8, 2003, Susan Lindauer delivered to the home of a United States Government official, a letter in which Lindauer conveyed her established access to, and contacts with, members of the Saddam Hussein regime, in an unsuccessful attempt to influence U.S. foreign policy."

That was actually my 11th letter to Andy Card, Chief of Staff to President Bush. The same letter also got hand delivered to the home of Secretary of State Colin Powell, who lived next door to my CIA handler, Dr. Fuisz.

Interestingly, the indictment made no mention of the previous 10 letters to Andy Card, outlining the progress of our back channel talks on resuming the weapons inspections. Secretary Powell received several of those reports, as well.

But by God, the Justice Department finally got something right in its indictment! I had warned my second cousin, Andy Card—and Secretary Powell and members of Congress in both parties— that war with Iraq would prove disastrous for U.S. and

Middle East security. Invading Iraq would be simple. Occupation would be brutal. There would be no roses in the streets for American soldiers. We would face a bitter and tenacious enemy not afraid to die for God, in order to throw us out of their country. It would raise Iran as a regional power, and fire up an insurgency modeled on Al Qaeda. Here's an excerpt from that letter to Andy Card that the Justice Department judged to contain treasonous ideology:

"Above all, you must realize that if you go ahead with this invasion, Osama bin Laden will triumph, rising from his grave of seclusion. His network will be swollen with fresh recruits, and other charismatic individuals will seek to build upon his model, multiplying those networks. And the United States will have delivered the death blow to itself. Using your own act of war, Osama and his cohort will irrevocably divide the hearts and minds of the Arab Street from moderate governments in Islamic countries that have been holding back the tide. Power to the people, what we call "democracy," will secure the rise of fundamentalists."[22]

Mind you, I wasn't the only one offering up that analysis. Others in the intelligence community, amongst a few experts interviewed all too briefly on the 24 hour news channels, reached the same conclusions. Kudos to all! We might have been the minority, but we foresaw that Occupation would turn Arab opinion sharply against the U.S. The groundswell of popular support that we'd enjoyed after 9/11 would be thrown away. Once the international community witnessed the chaos of U.S. mismanagement and the brutality at Abu Ghreib, we would be finished as the world's favorite. The cycle of destruction and death in Iraq would prompt the Arab community to rank George Bush as a greater danger to Arab peoples than Osama bin Laden. Young jihadis fighting Occupation would emerge as heroes defending their peoples against western tyranny.

My letter to Andy Card would become a reality show on the nightly news, known as "Today in Iraq."

And they wanted to punish me with prison for daring to tell America's leaders the truth? For getting it right? I was "Symbol Susan," indeed.

I could not have been prouder.

I had a broader perspective. I recognized the fear of my enemy. I saw their weakness. And with total clarity, I understood exactly what the Government was trying to hide.

This was no mistake.

What pundits could not know was that thirty days before my arrest, I had contacted the senior staffs of Senator John McCain, future Republican Presidential nominee from Arizona, and former Senate Majority Leader Trent Lott of Mississippi.[23] I had formally requested to testify before the newly appointed Presidential Commission investigating Pre-War Intelligence. In fact, I'd practically demanded the right to testify.

With unbridled enthusiasm, I informed Senate staffers that I was one of the very few Assets "on the ground," covering the Iraqi Embassy for seven years.

If Congress wanted to study Pre-War Intelligence, they had better talk to me.

From my perspective, Pre-War Intelligence looked pretty outstanding— at least the part that wasn't politicized and sold as hamburger meat to the American people. I wanted to testify that real intelligence from the field appeared to have been deleted from Congressional talking points. Factions ruled the intelligence community, like any other politically active body, but the dynamic of internal squabbling and debate had been healthy and vigorous in the run up to War. Dissension and debate come with the territory—if you appreciate vitality in democracy.

Alas, Congress was singing from a different hymn book. Having forced a horribly unpopular war on the American people, they cringed from responsibility for their poor decision making. They vigorously battled to blame Assets for the War. Never mind that from what I sat—behind bars— there was almost no similarity in what Assets told the intelligence community, and what Congress and the White House told the American people that we told the intelligence community.

In February 2004, I was blissfully in the dark about that strategy to reinvent history. Hearing about the new blue ribbon commission on Pre-War Intelligence, I rushed to inform Senate staffers that I had a great deal to say.

FBI wire taps captured my phone calls to Senator Lott's office, including conversations with his Chief of Staff and Legislative Director. What follows is the official FBI transcript for just one of those conversations on the evening of February 2, 2004, this one with Mitch Waldeman, the legislative aide covering Iraq—a few weeks before my arrest.[24]

WALDEMAN: "Senator Lott's office. Mr. Waldeman speaking."
(Followed by niceties of introduction)
LINDAUER: "Well, I have enormous respect for Senator Lott. I know you love this country. I am in possession of information which now is turning out to be maybe painful…, very painful to the Republican Party."
WALDEMAN: "Hmph hmph, hmph hmph."
LINDAUER: "That's why I'm coming to you. Um, I was acting as a back-door between Iraq and the White House…"
WALDEMAN: "Hmph hmph."
LINDAUER: "And I happen to know, for example, that Iraq offered for two years to allow the return of weapons inspectors, and after September 11th, for example, they offered to allow the FBI to come to Baghdad to interview human assets in the war on terrorism."
WALDEMAN: "Hmph hmph"
LINDAUER: "Including al-Anai. And the White House refused to do that, and the White House perhaps misrepresented, ah, you know…"
WALDEMAN: "Hmph."
LINDAUER: "Iraq was behaving like an innocent country that did not possess weapons of mass destruction."
WALDEMAN: "Hmph hmph."
LINDAUER: "And Iraq was very eager, ah, that Iraq believed it had information on Oklahoma City and that it was able to provide break-through information for us that they thought we would reward them for. Now I would not have been doing those interviews. The FBI would have been doing it."
WALDEMAN: "Hmph hmph."
LINDAUER: "So the FBI would have been determining the real quality of the information…"
WALDEMAN: "Yeah."

LINDAUER: "I'm not trying to say I would have been inserting myself into that. I had been involved in the Lockerbie negotiations, and that's how I got involved in this."

WALDEMAN: "Hmph hmph."

LINDAUER: "Now the question is (slight laugh), and maybe this is something you need to think about. Am I overstating the importance of what I know? I don't think I am."

WALDEMAN: "Hmph hmph."

LINDAUER: "Um, I'm not eager to create a crisis for the sake of creating unhappiness."

WALDEMAN: "Hmph hmph."

LINDAUER: "Let's not say crisis. Let's not say unhappiness. At the same time, does Congress need to know this? Where are my obligations?"

WALDEMAN: "Right. Were you working for the Government at the time?"

LINDAUER: "I'm not on the Secrets Act. However I have been an Asset."

WALDEMAN: "Okay. Right. Oh my."

LINDAUER: "On the other hand, I mean, this was not a failure of U.S. Intelligence."

WALDEMAN: "Right."

LINDAUER: "And it's being portrayed that way."

WALDEMAN: "Let me ask you. Who else have you spoken with?"

LINDAUER: "I called Mr. Gotschall first. (another senior staffer in Senator Lott's office). It's because of my enormous and profound respect for you, for your office and your integrity and also that you are concerned about National Security. You know, Presidential politics is…"

WALDEMAN: "Right."

LINDAUER: "You know."

WALDEMAN: "Messy."

LINDAUER: "It's messy."

WALDEMAN: "(Laughs). Right."

LINDAUER: "And I'll tell you something else, Andy Card is the person who received all this information. He is my cousin. So you can be sure he got it."

WALDEMAN: "Oh my."

LINDAUER: "You can be sure he got it."

WALDEMAN: "Okay."

LINDAUER: "So we can't say that the President didn't know because…"

WALDEMAN: "Right. How would you recommend that we approach this dialogue?"

LINDAUER: "I was hoping you could tell me."

LINDAUER: "Um, I will tell you something else, that Iraq, right before the War, was also offering Democratic reform."

WALDEMAN: "Hmph hmph."

LINDAUER: "They were offering to hold elections. The Iranians had made a statement. They were floating an idea that had come from the Iraqis. To allow the United Nations to monitor free elections in Iraq with free opposition parties, free opposition newspapers, ah, free opposition headquarters."

WALDEMAN: "Yeah."

LINDAUER: "You can argue whether this stuff is good or not, but we always were on the right track. I helped negotiate that, and the things we were negotiating were good things."

WALDEMAN: "And you thought that they were substantive, obviously?"

LINDAUER: "They were substantive."

WALDEMAN: "Yeah."

LINDAUER: "And there was also, ah, U.S. oil."

WALDEMAN: "Hmph hmph."

LINDAUER: "Iraq offered to give the United States the LUKoil contract. The United States could have had all the oil that it wanted."

WALDEMAN: "Right."

LINDAUER: "It points to a vendetta."

WALDEMAN: "Hmph hmph."

LINDAUER: "An obsession with going after Saddam Hussein and the problem is, is that all the real criteria for the war fell apart."

WALDEMAN: "Hmph hmph. Hmph hmph. Right. Do you think there's an opportunity now that the President has called for a commission that some of this will come out?"

LINDAUER: "No."

WALDEMAN: "Part of that?"

LINDAUER: *"They'll absolutely never let this out. And see, that's the problem. I feel an obligation to do something. It seems obvious I have to tell. I'm just not somebody who ever reacts on a knee-jerk basis."*

WALDEMAN: *"Well I appreciate you calling. I mean this is (sighs). I guess I would say that just over the course of the past year, I've actually heard bits and pieces of similar–"*

LINDAUER: *"Hmph hmph."*

WALDEMAN: *"Similar things."*

LINDAUER: *"Probably things that I had done (unintelligible)."*

WALDEMAN: *"Ah, maybe."*

LINDAUER: *"Yeah."*

WALDEMAN: *"Maybe. Bits and pieces and ah...Some of it actually. I mean there was some public discussion of on-going negotiations. There was never really any, any public debate or discussion over the substance of what they potentially led to and..."*

LINDAUER: *"Hmph hmph."*

WALDEMAN: *"And so it, I mean, I think there was a general sense that some of that was going on, certainly was going in the past administration, as well."*

LINDAUER: *"Yes."*

WALDEMAN: "Let me talk with Bill and give you a call."

LINDAUER: "Okay, thank you."

Hanging up the phone that evening on February 2, I felt excited. It appeared that Senator Lott's staff probably had received debriefings as our back channel talks progressed on resuming the weapons inspections. Waldeman had some knowledge of the range of Iraq's peace offerings. Critically, he admitted knowing that our talks originated during the Clinton Administration, which betrayed long term awareness of the project.[25]

Quite rightly I believed I had set a chain of events in motion on Capitol Hill. I envisioned Congressional staff rushing to get subpoenas for my testimony. At worst, I expected to be forced to give closed door testimony, which would strategically restrict public access to knowledge about our comprehensive peace framework before the War. That irked me. I had not decided how I would handle that.

I was right about the subpoenas, for sure. Within a couple of days of my conversations with Senator Lott's and Senator McCain's staff, Republican leaders hurriedly convened a grand jury in New York, rushing to subpoena witnesses so they could indict me before I started talking to the media.

It's kind of funny, if you've got a sick sort of humor.

The rest, as they say, is history. On March 11, 2004, I got arrested as an "Iraqi Agent."[26]

FBI Special Agent Chmiel told me the grand jury debated my charges for a full month before handing down my indictment. By the FBI's own admission then, my Asset file got turned over to the grand jury just a few days after my request to testify at Congressional hearings.

For one brief moment in that cage, I sympathized with the Republican predicament. If I had invented such a fabulous lie to justify going into a disastrous War, I would not want anyone to know, either. I especially would not want anyone to know how easily the War could have been avoided altogether. Nor would I want voters to learn about the failures of Republican terrorism policy, thrown up as a bulwark to appease Americans for the cock-up in Iraq.

I would be afraid of me, too.

By this time I was composed. I had my legal strategy mapped out, and a list of witnesses sketched on the back of my legal papers.

I vowed to myself that I would fight to the end.

I almost felt sorry for them.

CHAPTER 2:

ADVANCE WARNINGS
ABOUT 9/11

"The first casualty, when war comes, is Truth."
–US Senator Hiram Warren Johnson, 1918

I was locked in a holding cage, and the truth was locked up with me.

It wasn't just Iraq that frightened them. Our team also gave advance warning about a 9/11 style of attack throughout the summer of 2001. And I carried the message.

That scared them a helluva lot more

I thought back to August, 2001 and the crucial weeks before the September 11 strike.

I was talking by phone to Dr. Richard Fuisz, my CIA handler about Robert Mueller's nomination to head the Federal Bureau of Investigation.[27] Our conversation scorched my heart, as I sat shackled in that tiny cell, waiting for a Judge to throw my bail, like I was a criminal.

Bastards.

"There's never been a terrorist investigation that sonovabitch didn't throw!" It was the day of Mueller's Senate confirmation hearings, and I was smoldering.

"Lockerbie, yeah. Mueller changed directions when Congress wanted to salvage Syria's reputation and shift the blame to Libya,"[28] Dr. Fuisz agreed with me. (Mueller headed the Justice Department's Criminal Division during the Pan Am 103 investigation,

a.k.a Lockerbie.[29] Dr. Fuisz and I believed that Libya was wrongly blamed for the attack).
"What else?"

"The Oklahoma City bombing. Isn't Mueller one of the key figures who decreed that Timothy McVeigh and Terry Nichols acted alone?[30] We all know that's crap. Why would anyone reward McVeigh's megalomania as the sole conspirator? Mueller is the Arlen Specter of anti-terrorism."

"Mueller plays to the politicians. That's why his nomination will sail through Congress."

Admittedly, most Americans would vigorously object to characterizing Mueller as a shrewd political animal. My views are frequently more idiosyncratic than the general public. However, our conversation about Mueller's confirmation hearing accounts for why I recall the timing of events so precisely and with such clarity in the weeks before 9/11. I can pinpoint my actions to the day of the week, because of this hearing.

With regards to the Oklahoma City Bombing, Mueller would reopen the investigation of a possible broader conspiracy in 2005. I could not know that in August, 2001.[31]

"You want me to crash the nomination hearings this afternoon? Lay a little truth on Congress?"

"No. No, it's too late for that."

"Too late for the hearings? Or too late to stop the attack?"

"Both, I think."

"You think it's that soon???"

"I think it could be."

It was the 2nd of August, 2001. I was aghast.

The phone got quiet for a moment.

"We can't do nothing, Richard."

"Of course not."

His snappish reply spoke volumes about the depths of his concern. We'd worked together for seven years by this time, and we could read each other so well, without speaking if need be. It would all be communicated in our eyes, messages between us that nobody else could decipher. My relationship with my other handler, Paul Hoven, was the same, though Paul leaned towards more explosive responses, pummeled with expletives. Paul carried a well of rage in his heart, something old from Viet Nam. And I was a peace activist turned Asset covering the Iraqi and Libyan Embassies at the United Nations in New York.

It could make things harder. But Paul and Richard Fuisz were like older brothers to me. They might growl at me, or treat me like a little sister who gets troublesome. But throughout those many years, they never let me down. They shared the jubilation of my discoveries. They patiently pushed me back if I veered down the wrong track.

But until September 11 broke our hearts, we were all incredibly close.

"I'm going to New York. I'll ask the Iraqis again. I'll push them hard, Richard."

"What? When are you going?" Alarm saturated his words.

"I'm going this weekend."

"No, no, no. This weekend? Don't go to New York, Susan. Don't go."

"It's just the weekend. The day after tomorrow. I'll be up and back."

"God damnit. I don't want you to go— I don't think that's wise."

"I've got to make this trip. I've been pushing the Iraqis all summer, Richard. I've got to find out if they heard anything from Baghdad. Then I won't go back."

"Yeah, don't. I don't want you going back again."

"Just this once. I have to. I have to find out."

"For God's sakes, Susan, don't stay there. This is very dangerous. Get in and get out. Speaking of Mueller's confirmation—what if this happens before he's confirmed? There might not be an FBI Director when this goes down. Jesus, what would that mean?"

"You think this attack might happen before he's confirmed? Oh fuck. That would be like, the end of August? Or September?"

"Yeah, it's definitely possible."

"Richard— Am I to understand that you believe this attack is "imminent?""

"Yes. Yes, I do."

"What are we going to do? We've got to tell somebody."

"I don't know yet."

I could feel that tension again. It meant he was thinking. And frustrated.

"OK. I'll come by Monday, (August 6th) as soon as I get back from New York, ok?"

"Good. OK Listen to me. I've told you before. We're looking for anything at this point. Even something very small. They might drop something on you that appears totally irrelevant from where you're sitting. You might not even understand what it means."

"I got it. I got it."

"No, listen to me. Don't filter this stuff. Don't wait to see if you can confirm it. Give it to me. We'll confirm it. Just get it. Don't try to figure it out yourself."

"I understand."

Our anxiety had been growing since the previous summer. The Lockerbie Trial at a special international court of The Hague in 2000 got us thinking about what the next terrorist scenario would look like. The bombings of Pan Am 103 on December 21, 1988, which killed 270 people, and UTA (French airlines) in September, 1989 had been the last attacks involving airplanes prior to September 11, 2001. Throughout the Trial of the two Libyans, our team worried openly that the pathetic display by Scottish Prosecutors would inspire a sort of "tribute attack" to the success of Lockerbie.

The problem is that while most Americans refuse to accept Libya's innocence, terrorist groups have always known the truth. And they can't figure out why the United States has been protecting the real culprits.

Famed terrorist Abu Nidal freely proclaimed his role in the bombing of Pan Am 103,[32] on behalf of the Fateh Revolutionary Council. He steadfastly disputed that the two Libyans participated in planning or executing the attack. Translated as "father of the struggle," Abu Nidal was the first terrorist to put together a global organization committed to hijacking airplanes and extorting ransoms. Nidal was credited with launching terrorist strikes in 20 countries over two decades.[33] He joined the civil war in Beirut in the 1980s, and afterwards holed up in Libya until 1998. After his death in a shoot out with Iraqi Intelligence in Baghdad in July 2002,[34] there was much talk of Nidal's confession to the Lockerbie conspiracy. His family and friends also acknowledged it, and expressed some regret that an innocent man got convicted for Nidal's crime.

Britain and the U.S. have refused to accept Nidal's confession. The question is why?

The real masterminds of the Lockerbie bombing were professionals, not baggage handlers or airplane ticket agents like Libya's two men, Abdelbaset Al Megraghi and Al Amin Khalifa Fahima. They played high stakes terror games at the master level through a vast and highly dangerous network of accomplices. Blaming Megraghi, because of prejudice towards his Libyan nationality, was absurd and racist. It surprised nobody when his so-called accomplice, Fahima, got acquitted in January, 2001. The only shocker was that Megraghi did not go free with him.

Indeed, Scottish prosecutors made such a poor showing against the two Libyans that the failure of the Scottish Court was gossip throughout the Arab world.

In Dr. Fuisz's opinion, the politicization of Lockerbie and the weakness of the Court's forensic evidence carried much more ominous consequences. In the months before 9/11, Dr. Fuisz opined frequently that the United States had seriously damaged its credibility in anti-terrorism, because of the Lockerbie Trial. Terrorist groups now questioned if, for all the mighty resources of U.S. Intelligence, the United States was too stupid to catch the real terrorists. Or else the U.S. was afraid, because the real terrorists are "too big."

Either of those beliefs would create a powerful and irresistible provocation for the upcoming generation of jihadis, Dr. Fuisz argued. Younger terrorists watching the Lockerbie Trial would be inspired to launch some sort of tribute attack to the heroes who came before, and were too great to take down. Tribute attacks are fairly common in those circles anyway. Dr. Fuisz feared this judicial failure would be the ultimate temptation.

In that basis, during the Lockerbie Trial, our team mapped out an extreme threat scenario that the next major attack would most likely involve airplane hijackings or airplane bombings.

On August 2, 2001, during the Senate confirmation hearings on Robert Mueller's nomination, Dr. Fuisz, Hoven and I suspected that our worst strike scenario was about to hit the mark with devastating accuracy.

None of us wanted to be right. We fervently believed, however, that a major terrorist conspiracy was actively in play—and imminent.

I remember it all so vividly, like a home movie playing before my eyes, winding back and starting again. So painful to watch. So disappointing in its aftermath.

In April, 2001 I received a summons to visit Dr. Fuisz at his office in Great Falls, Virginia. We met almost weekly anyway. On this occasion, he rang my home and asked me to come straight away. He inquired when I planned my next trip to the Libyan and Iraqi Embassies. He wanted to talk before I left, and he wanted me to go soon.

I visited him immediately. Dr. Fuisz instructed me to issue a formal demand that Libya and Iraq must hand over any intelligence regarding terrorist conspiracies involving airplane hijackings or airplane bombings. He demanded that I warn Iraqi diplomats particularly that Baghdad would suffer a major military offensive, worse than anything Iraq had suffered before, if it was discovered that Saddam's government had possessed such intelligence and failed to notify the United States through my back channel.

Admittedly, I was reluctant to deliver such a harsh message. I have always been an anti-war activist. The consistency of my opposition to violence on both sides accounts for my success in dealing with the Arabs. I don't issue threats, only appeals to avoid confrontation and violence. So on my next trip to New York, I soft pedaled Dr. Fuisz's message. I requested that diplomats send cables to Baghdad and Tripoli seeking intelligence on possible airplane attacks. But I made no threats of violent reprisal against either nation.

When I got home to Washington, I met with Dr. Fuisz, who demanded to know how Iraqi diplomats had responded to his threat. I had to admit that I stopped short of threatening military retaliation. But I assured him that I had requested their cooperation.

At that point, Dr. Fuisz became enraged. In all of our years together, I recall no other time that he lost his temper and shouted at me. He stormed up and down the room. He demanded that I must return to New York immediately. I must tell Iraqi diplomats particularly that "the United States would bomb Baghdad into the Stone Age, worse than they've ever been bombed before, if they failed to help us identify terrorist conspiracies involving airplane hijackings or airplane bombings. They would lose everything. We would destroy them."

He was not pacified until I promised to deliver his message with all the force that he communicated. He expressed tremendous satisfaction that I would make sure they understood the warning came from him— not me— backed by military and political forces above him.

Dr. Fuisz was determined that Iraq should know the U.S. threat was deadly serious.

Right then I recognized that Richard was motivated by more than a desire to check our trap lines on the terrorist circuit.

Something was moving.

In late April, 2001, Dr. Fuisz was already onto it. He fired back proactively to discourage Arab governments from supporting the conspiracy. Without knowing more, I wanted to help.

In May, 2001, I returned to New York and delivered that message exactly as he dictated.

Tension built throughout the summer of 2001. Again and again, my talks with Dr. Fuisz turned to airplane hijackings and/or airplane bombings. Only now the threat scenario became more detailed. Our talks turned to a strike on the World Trade Center, in a reprise of the 1993 terrorist attack by Ramzi Youssef.

It sounds uncanny, but our team understood exactly what was going to happen. Our belief in that target was very precise. We believed the attack would finish the cycle started in the 1993 World Trade Center attack. And we expected some form of an aerial strike involving airplanes.

We discussed that scenario many times, though exactly how Dr. Fuisz knew so much, I cannot say. Throughout June and July of 2001, he continued to prod and push hard for any fragment of intelligence from Iraq. He didn't ask about Libya at all.

Over and over again, Dr. Fuisz demanded that I threaten Baghdad—not Libya— if the strike occurred. He emphatically declared that the threat of military retaliation originated far above him, and he wanted me to make that crystal clear to Iraqi diplomats.

That threat was not ambiguous. There's no question in my mind that months before 9/11, some ranking leaders at the top of the government already anticipated this strike scenario, and decided that Iraq would pay the ultimate price if and when this 9/11 style of attack occurred. They were already prepping parts of the Intelligence Community to accept the inevitability of War with Iraq in the aftermath.

At the same time, Dr. Fuisz beseeched me not to filter intelligence or test its accuracy before informing him. During our meetings, he would try to explain how urgently he needed to collect even fragments of intelligence, whether any of it made sense to me or not. He begged me to hold nothing back. He appeared to be frantically searching for anything that would nail down enough specifics of the pending attack to plan an appropriate response. In all fairness, Dr. Fuisz urgently wanted to pre-empt the strike.

Our threat of retaliation against Iraq struck me as a high stakes gambit. I'd cultivated diplomats at the Iraqi Embassy over several years, since 1996. These were professionally productive relationships that I would not have wanted to destroy for any reason. And now I was the messenger delivering threats of war. Memories of it break my heart still.

On August 2nd, I reassured him again.

"I understand what you guys want. I've been pushing Iraqi diplomats all summer for intelligence on this attack, Richard. They know what's up. I told them you guys would bomb them back to the Stone Age if they've got something and don't tell us. Just like you told me. They know that, ok?"

"That's right, we will. Tell those fuckers again. They've never been bombed the way we're going to bomb them. Understand? If they know something, they'd better tell us. Or we will fuck them. They've never been fucked like that before. Make that clear."

I promised. It would be my last trip to the Libya House and the Iraqi Embassy in New York before that fateful September 11 morning.

Afterwards, I would ache wondering if I had misinterpreted a subtle cue. If I had pushed my contacts hard enough. If I could have done something more. Above all, I would regret that I did not go back to New York after the middle of August. For years, I would regard the 9/11 strike as my personal failure. On many black nights I would question if Paul and Richard thought so, too. Those doubts would torment me, as I suspect in my heart it also tormented them.

For you see, stopping that attack was my job. I'd been a back channel for anti-terrorism for years. That was the biggest part of my life.

And this time I could not do it.

To all the families, I am sorry. But all of America is wrong to conclude that our team did not take that threat very, very seriously. Throughout the summer of 2001, ferreting out actionable intelligence to stop that hijacking conspiracy was our greatest priority.

To appreciate the gravity with which I regarded Dr. Fuisz's instructions and paranoia, you must first understand his CIA credentials.

As a matter of policy, the CIA never acknowledges its officers. However I received an extensive debriefing on Dr. Fuisz's background from my other handler, Hoven, at the time of our introduction in September, 1994. If we were going to work together, I had a legitimate "need to know" whom I was dealing with. Over the next eight years, his bona fides got corroborated repeatedly by my Libyan and Arab sources— and by Dr. Fuisz himself.

Much of his actions in the Middle East were shrouded in secrecy. However, his own curriculum vitae provided some tantalizing clues.

His company, Folkon Ltd. claimed to "perform diverse services in the Middle East, including Syria and the U.S.S.R. from 1980-1990."[35]

A second off-shore company based in Bermuda, called Oil Field Services, Ltd. "supplied manpower and technical assistance to the Syrian oil industry from 1989-1990, with offices in Damascus, Syria."[36]

And finally, Medcom Inc. founded by Dr. Fuisz in 1970 "specialized in medical military training throughout the Middle East and North Africa." Medcom "trained thousands of Arab nationals in professional skills," mostly in Saudi Arabia.[37]

Scratch that surface and Dr. Fuisz had been a top CIA operative in Syria and Lebanon in the 1980s, something he admitted proudly. In private conversations, he described how his team in Beirut coordinated the hostage rescue of Terry Anderson et al in Lebanon. It was Dr. Fuisz's team that located the make-shift prison cells in the back alleys of Beirut, and called in the Delta Force for a daring rescue. Outrageously the rescue got postponed for several months in the original "October Surprise—" until weeks before the 1988 Presidential election of George H. Bush, Sr. Dr. Fuisz never forgave the CIA for using the hostages in Lebanon as trump cards for politicians in Washington.

In the course of his desperate search to locate the hostages' whereabouts, Dr. Fuisz had become a first-hand protagonist to the events leading up the bombing of Pan Am 103.[38]

The CIA fought desperately to block his testimony in the Lockerbie Trial. As a compromise, when Dr. Fuisz gave his deposition at the Federal Courthouse in Alexandria, Virginia, U.S. District Judge White sealed his testimony.[39] The Lockerbie Defense Counsel was barred from revealing any part of his deposition inside the United States. It could only be read overseas.[40] Even then, Scottish solicitors were barred from reviewing the entire deposition, because parts of it are double-sealed. As an added obstacle, the Court took the unusual step of prohibiting the U.S. attorneys who conducted the deposition in Virginia from conveying critical information of what the double-seal contains to their Scottish colleagues. Thus, Scottish solicitors have no idea of the value of his testimony. Only a Scottish Judge can unlock it and review the entire document.

And they should. Because the double seal contains the names of 11 men who participated in the Lockerbie conspiracy. Why the cloak and daggers? Because a few weeks after we met in 1994, Dr. Fuisz was declared legally out of reach on national security matters. U.S. District Judge Royce Lamberth issued a definitive court ruling on October 14, 1994 in Washington, DC: "The claims of state secrets privilege asserted by the United States shall be and is hereby UPHELD." [41]

"Information described in the United States' ex parte, in camera classified submission shall not be subject to discovery or disclosure by the parties during all proceedings in this action, and shall be excluded from evidence at trial."

"As the United States deems necessary, U.S. attorneys may attend all depositions and make objections as necessary to protect national security information." [42]

"Ex parte in camera" applies to an extraordinary category of evidence beyond the sight of defense counsel, presented only for the Judge's eyes. The defense attorney is not informed that it exists, and cannot dispute it. In the early 1990s before the Patriot Act, this special classification was rarely invoked.

Judge Lamberth's ruling forever empowered the U.S. government to bar Dr. Fuisz's testimony on any criminal or civil matter, by invoking the Secrets Act. Only the President of the United States could override the Director of the CIA, in a written memorandum, to allow Dr. Fuisz to reveal his knowledge and sources on matters linked to national security, large or small.[43] Neither the Secretary of State nor any member of Congress could override that provision. Even if Dr. Fuisz himself desired to testify, he would be prohibited from doing so.

That would apply to Lockerbie, to any 9/11 inquiry — and to my own criminal case as an accused Iraqi Agent.

Word of Dr. Fuisz's first-hand knowledge of Pan Am 103—and his strange inability to testify— got reported in Scotland's Sunday Herald at the height of the Lockerbie Trial, when Scottish families recognized the Crown's lack of evidence against Libya, and started demanding real answers.

In May, 2000, Scottish journalist, Ian Ferguson asked Dr. Fuisz directly if he worked for the CIA in Syria in the 1980s.[44] His response was less than subtle. "That is not an issue I can confirm or deny. I am not allowed to speak about these issues. In fact, I can't even explain to you why I can't speak about these issues.' Fuisz did, however, say that he would not take any action against a newspaper which named him as a CIA agent."

The verdict was unanimous among my Arab sources: Dr. Fuisz was a master spy. My own interactions with Dr. Fuisz affirmed his superior intelligence background. Therefore, when he demanded that I focus my energies on persuading Iraq to divulge any intelligence that it uncovered of an emerging conspiracy involving airplane hijackings and some sort of aerial strike on the World Trade Center, I took his request very seriously. I had good reason to trust him.

As it happens, there were extraordinary reasons for Dr. Fuisz's concern. The "chatter" between terrorist cells monitored by the National Security Agency reached unprecedented levels by May 2001, which accelerated until September 11, 2001.[45] In mid June, an Al Qaeda video became public, in which Osama bin Laden announced, "Your brothers in Palestine are waiting for you. It's time to penetrate America and Israel, and hit them where it hurts the most." [46]

July turned out to be pivotal for the 9/11 warning.

On July 10, 2001, CIA Director, George Tenet, was so alarmed by a classified debriefing he received on the terrorist threat from Al Qaeda that he marched straight to the White House. A top CIA analyst suggested a major attack was coming in the next few weeks, but cited no specific date. To his credit, Tenet wasted no time providing that information to Condoleezza Rice in writing. He also brought along one of the CIA officers tracking bin Laden, who gave Rice and others an oral debriefing. [47] Richard Clarke strongly endorsed the importance of the report. The CIA officer who gave the briefing said that the nation had to go "on a war footing *now*."

More remarkably, the Foreign Minister of the Taliban provided a direct warning to Washington that Bin Laden was preparing to launch a huge strike on the United States.[48] Prior to 9/11, the Taliban received financial support from the U.S. to destroy Afghanistan's poppy crop, which supplies 90 percent of the world's opium and heroin. Their warning should have been treated with utmost seriousness.

Though short on actionable intelligence, U.S. Intelligence was onto the 9/11 plot. Friendly foreign intelligence agencies relayed serious warnings of a late summer, early autumn attack that would utilize airplanes as weapons to attack targets inside the United States. Israel, Jordan and Egypt, all longtime collaborators with US intelligence, provided similar warnings of an imminent terrorist strike four weeks prior to 9/11.

On September 7, 2001, French intelligence sent an urgent message, warning of an imminent attack using airplanes as weapons inside the United States. [49]

The German press reported that 206 international telephone calls were made from the 9/11 hijackers prior to the attack. The NSA has refused to provide detailed list of the calls, but they were reportedly made to Saudi Arabia and Syria.[50]

Perhaps the most damning indication of prior knowledge about a major al Qaeda attack against U.S. targets came out of the State Department's regular warning system to assist American citizens traveling overseas.

On Friday, Sept. 7, the State Department issued a worldwide alert: *"American citizens may be the target of a terrorist threat from extremist groups with links to [Osama bin*

Laden's] al Qaeda organization." That report cited information gathered *in May, 2001 as* suggesting an attack was imminent. It warned that individuals in al Qaeda have not distinguished between official and civilian targets."[51]

As a senior intelligence operative with a specialty in Middle Eastern terrorism since the 1980s, Dr. Fuisz would have enjoyed privileged access to that sort of raw intelligence data.

What was missing was actionable intelligence to prevent the attack— who were the terrorists, how many, which airport, what airlines, what flight numbers.

Just a name. Just a fragment, Dr. Fuisz exhorted me from May 2001 onwards. He pleaded with me exhaustively to bring him anything at all. He swore to me that the NSA and CIA would bust overtime to flesh it out and stop the attack.

My Arab sources in Iraq just did not have that information. On my last trip to New York, on August 4, 2001, Iraqi diplomats threw up their hands. They had no intelligence to share with us. They understood that they would get blamed if something awful happened. They'd been warned of the consequences for months, since May, in fact. Retribution would be swift and severe. None of that changed the hard truth that Iraq had nothing to give us.

At our next face meeting on August 6, 2001, Dr. Fuisz was grim.

Something would have to be done. We needed help.

Locked in the holding cage of the Baltimore Federal Courthouse as an accused "Iraqi Agent," I recalled explicitly what Dr. Fuisz and I hashed out.

At the instructions of Dr. Fuisz, I telephoned the private office of U. S. Attorney General John Ashcroft to request inter-agency assistance from the Justice Department.

It was the week of August 6 – 10, immediately after my last trip to the Iraqi Embassy. The September 11 strike was a month away. There was still time to pre-empt the attack.

At the urging of Dr. Fuisz, I phoned Mr. Ashcroft's private staff inside the Attorney General's office, consisting of about 20 people. Quickly I identified myself as a U.S. Asset covering the Libya House and Iraqi Embassy at the United Nations on anti-terrorism. That way I could be sure the bureaucrat on the other end of the telephone appreciated my special access to high level intelligence as a primary source, which should be weighed carefully before disregarding my call.

Once I had the staffer's attention, I made a formal request for Attorney General Ashcroft's private office to broadcast an emergency alert throughout all agencies at the Justice Department seeking any fragment of intelligence pertaining to possible airplane hijackings or airplane bombings. I explained that we believed a major attack on the United States was imminent. We believed the target was the World Trade Center, which would suffer some sort of aerial strike. And we urgently requested cooperation across all agencies to pre-empt the attack. I provided as many specific details as I could to help focus the investigation.

Attorney General Ashcroft's staff advised me to contact the Office of Counter-Terrorism at the Justice Department immediately, and repeat what I had just told them.

I did so without delay. I repeated the warning in full detail, and indicated the alert should be marked "top urgency." Any possible relevant information should be submitted immediately as the attack was deemed "imminent."

Clearly our 9/11 warning was not something Republican leaders wanted American voters to hear about— not with the 2004 Presidential Campaign in play—nor the 2008 Campaign, for that matter.

Oh yes, I would be gagged through two presidential elections.

25

With those calls to the Attorney General's private staff and the Office of Counter-Terrorism, the U.S. government lost its cover of deniability. If I testified before the 9/11 Commission or any other congressional inquiry—or any federal court of law—the Justice Department would have been forced to admit that some of its own top staff received formal warning about the attack, along with an urgent request for assistance. In August, the U.S. government had plenty of time to coordinate a response to stop the hijackings and thwart the demolition of the World Trade Center.

I didn't stop there. Most Americans would be stunned to know that in mid-August, 2001, our team was so convinced that a 9/11 style attack was "imminent," that I took further proactive measures, visiting my second cousin, Andy Card, Chief of Staff to President Bush, to request his intervention at the Justice Department.

I parked on the street outside his house in Arlington, Virginia, and waited in my car, chain smoking for almost two hours. Occasionally, I could see neighbors peering out their windows and frowning at me. In my head, I rehearsed what I would tell Virginia police or the Secret Service, if they showed up to investigate this strange car parked outside the home of the Chief of Staff to the President of the United States.

Unhappily, Andy did not return that afternoon. I finally left without sharing our fears.

Driving away, I distinctly recall questioning if I might be making the greatest mistake of my life. Throughout all these years, it is one of my few regrets.

Oh I see. You prefer the official, sanitized story that nobody in U.S. Intelligence had a clue about the 9/11 conspiracy.

Is that really more comforting? Let's see, the greatest intelligence community in the world, with vast technological superiority, was "incompetent" to anticipate 9/11?

That's what you think?

Sorry to disappoint you. It doesn't make sense. And it's not true.

We knew that a conspiracy was in play. The CIA knew. The Justice Department knew. The Office of Counter-Terrorism knew.

I know that for a fact—because I told them. (And they told me.)

I was arrested to stop me from telling you.

Symbol Susan, indeed!

Those were my thoughts as I waited inside the holding cage at the federal court house in Baltimore for a Judge to throw my bail, and a public defender to take my case. I could not afford a fancy, high priced attorney despite a decade of work in counter-terrorism. Members of Congress apparently forgot their obligations to provide resources for Assets and fieldwork, as soon as they walked off the sound studios of CNN and the Fox News Channel. They had shockingly poor memories, in fact. Those who wished to suppress the truth about 9/11 forever might have triumphed, except "unhappily" the U.S. Intelligence Community and the Justice Department were not the only parties aware of my 9/11 warnings. After my arrest, to its great chagrin, the FBI quickly discovered that I had warned some of my civilian friends about the possibility of a 9/11 style of attack in the summer of 2001 as well, particularly friends with family or professional ties to New York City.

That's where the Feds got crossed up.

A Personal Warning to a Friend

Dr. Parke Godfrey was one of my closest friends in Maryland, working on his doctoral dissertation in computer science at the University of Maryland in College Park. He had family living in the Connecticut suburbs of New York City. We spoke frequently, socializing a couple of times a week, and shared much of the same political outlook.[52]

Godfrey has gone on to launch a distinguished career as a tenured Associate Professor of Computer Science and Technology at York University in Toronto, Canada. He presents a calm, studied demeanor. He is a precise and methodical thinker who chooses his words carefully. During difficult courtroom questioning, he would frequently pause and take his time to give an accurate, thoughtful response. He proved a superior witness by any measure.

In shattering testimony a mere 1,000 yards from ground zero of the World Trade Center, Godfrey told the Court how, starting with the Lockerbie Trial in the year 2000, and several times in the spring and summer of 2001, I warned him that we expected a major strike on the southern part of Manhattan, and that the attack would encompass the World Trade Center.

In courtroom testimony, Godfrey said I told him that, "a massive attack would occur in the southern part of Manhattan that would involve airplanes and possibly a nuclear weapon."[53]

He testified that I told him "the attack would complete the cycle of the first bombing of the World Trade Center. It would finish what was started in the 1993 attack."

Godfrey: "I asked her about the nature of it. She said that she thought it would be something very, very big. I asked her, well, what do you mean? She said that what was started in '93, she thought was going to come back."

Shaughnessy: "What started in '93?"

Godfrey: "Well, the attempt on the World Trade Center."

Godfrey: "She said that there would be an attack in late summer, early fall. She thought it was some time imminent."[54]

On cross examination, he was more specific, declaring that I warned him in August, that the attack was "imminent."

Equally devastating, Godfrey testified under oath that he told the FBI about my 9/11 warning during a sit down interview in Toronto in September, 2004, a few months after my arrest—and before the 9/11 Commission issued its report, meaning information about the warning could have been submitted to Congressional investigators.[55] The FBI interview with Godfrey was jointly attended by the Canadian Royal Mounted Police. Asked why a member of the Canadian Police had been present at the FBI interview, he replied with a smile: "They were there to assure my protection."

Unfortunately, nobody was present to assure *mine*.

The fact was I knew too much, and I was starting to talk. That's why I was sitting in that holding cage waiting for my bail arraignment.

My arrest came hard and fast after I approached Senator Lott and Senator McCain's offices,[56] asking to tell the whole saga from start to finish.

U.S. Intelligence understood exactly what that meant. I would blow the whistle and expose the façade. I was their Asset, after all. They'd been supervising my work for many years, and they were intimately familiar with how I operate and what I would reveal. They already knew I warned about a major attack on New York City identical to the 9/11 scenario throughout the summer of 2001. They knew I had a vast wealth of first-hand knowledge about Pre-War Intelligence, including Baghdad's cooperation with the 9/11 investigation. And they knew that my truth would be nothing remotely similar to what Congress and the White House was selling to the American people.

Perhaps most significantly, from their intelligence profiling they understood that once I made up my mind to talk, it would be nearly impossible to shut me up. I would find a way to speak, one way or another. That was my nature.

Only one thing could be guaranteed to stop me. I would have to be "terminated with extreme prejudice—" the operative phrase for destroying an Asset or Intelligence officer, body and soul, usually as an assassination.

In that holding cage at the Baltimore Federal Courthouse, I had no idea yet how "extreme" that act of prejudice would be.

Our little intelligence war was just getting started. And it would be a fight to the death.

CHAPTER 3:

PEACE ASSET

There's a saying in the Intelligence Community: When they want you, they will come and get you.

But sometimes I forget how extraordinary all of this strikes outsiders. I mean, how does an American peace activist get tapped to become a U.S. Asset engaged in counter-terrorism, dealing regularly with the Iraqi Embassy at the United Nations? Or the Libyan Embassy, for that matter?

My clandestine life began quite unexpectedly, with a collision of events tied to the first World Trade Center bombing in February, 1993.

Yes, like some sort of Greek Tragedy, the great moments of my life all turned on the World Trade Center, start to finish.

At a National Press Club lunch for Palestinian women's leader, Hanan Ashrawi in late 1992, I leaned across the crisp linen table cloth and whispered to a diplomat from Tunisia that I had information about somebody who might be engaged in terrorism.

"He's a real terrorist. He was held in an Israeli prison for a year, and his mother thinks he's dead," I recall saying to the diplomat.

My attempt at conversation was interrupted by Ashrawi's excellent speech, but I contacted the Tunisian Embassy in Washington DC several weeks later. I asked the Embassy to help locate the diplomat from the luncheon, explaining that it was imperative that we should finish our conversation at the earliest possible convenience.

On that mysterious note, Tunisian diplomats determined that I had spoken with a member of Ashrawi's travel entourage, and that the diplomat had returned home to Tunis.

Sensing the urgency behind my request, however, Mr. Mounir Adhoum invited me to visit him instead at the Tunisian Embassy in Washington DC.

With much trepidation, we met, and I confided that I believed the World Trade Center was about to get attacked by Islamic fundamentalists from the south of Egypt who sought the overthrow of Egyptian President Hosni Mubarak.

The full scope of our conversation remains extremely sensitive to this day. Let's just say, the people who 'need to know' already have that information. Beyond that circle, it would be considered extremely unfriendly to expose all parts of our discussion. I will only say that my warning was fully accurate in all details. I have never withdrawn any part of the remarks or observations that I made to Mr. Adhoum on February 24, 1993. Eerily enough, it makes my work in anti-terrorism a perfect cycle that started and ended with warnings about the World Trade Center. That stuns some people. Even me.

Mr. Adhoum was polite, but skeptical. His reaction didn't surprise me. I was completely unknown. I appeared out of nowhere to share some extraordinary information, then I retreated to the shadows. For me, it was enough that I fulfilled my obligations to come forward.

Attitudes at the Tunisian Embassy changed quickly, however. Two days after my meeting with Mr. Adhoum, the World Trade Center suffered its first historic attack on February 26, 1993, when a truck loaded with explosives detonated in the Secret Service section of the parking garage.

The explosion ripped through three floors of concrete and steel in the 110 story building, scattering ash and debris, and starting a fire that shot smoke and flames up one of the Twin Towers.[57] It also left a gaping hole in the wall above the Path underground station. Miraculously, only five people died in the crush of concrete. The World Trade Center lost all electricity and lighting, and elevators stopped working. It was a chaotic crisis that put thousands of lives at risk.

That moment changed my future forever. Fast on the ball, the Justice Department announced to an excited throng of journalists that an unnamed woman had warned of the terrorist strike two days before the attack. The Justice Department assured the media that all leads from the woman's warning would be pursued aggressively.

The next day, the warning was retracted as "a hoax."

It was not a hoax. I was that woman. Only the substance of my message, including my description of efforts to overthrow President Hosni Mubarak, remains far too sensitive for public disclosure, even years later.

If the media was totally ignorant of my identity and the substance of my warning, however, U.S. law enforcement and the Intelligence community were intensely aware of me—especially as it became obvious that I had correctly anticipated the threat to President Mubarak's government in Egypt in its full scope. Sheikh Abdul Rahman and Ramzi Yousef, both convicted in the conspiracy, agitated for the violent overthrow of President Mubarak's secular regime, in favor of a radical Islamic government based on the Islamic Shariah.[58]

Very quickly U.S. Intelligence and the FBI turned a harsh spotlight on me. At first, the investigation terrified me. But my paranoia was not irrational, as some have accused.

I was 29 years old. My mother, a source of inspiration for me, had died the previous year of cancer. All of a sudden, having correctly warned about the first major terrorist attack inside the United States since Pearl Harbor, involving the World Trade Center no less, I found my life subjected to extreme scrutiny. That's really an understatement. It was baptism by fire.

All parts of U.S. law enforcement mobilized rapidly to capture the terrorists. Overnight, I became a 'person of interest' in the truest sense. When I shunned publicity, they got very curious as to why I did not rush to claim my 15 minutes of fame. Why not take credit? On the other hand, my silence must have been highly desirable since it created a false sense of security for the terrorists, who had no idea of the depth of information the U.S. government already possessed about their cause. That gave the FBI, the CIA (and several other alphabets) an advantage in their work. At that point, surveillance techniques became intrusive enough to discourage me from changing my mind about coming forward.

On the bright side, the furniture in my apartment got dusted more thoroughly than it's ever been since. I couldn't rub a finger over any surface in my living room and find a speck of dirt anywhere. It was spotless, like a Stepford wife's house.

Small teams of FBI agents and NSA types staked out my apartment in the vibrant immigrant neighborhood of Adams Morgan. When I left for work in the morning, somebody would tail me to the Dupont Circle metro, stopping at the top of the escalator as I went down. On the other end of my commute, the same woman would wait every morning at the top of the escalator at the Capitol South Metro, standing there, going nowhere. When I got off the escalator, the woman would fall in behind, escorting me all the way to the Longworth House Office Building where I had started working as Press Secretary to Congressman Peter DeFazio, an Oregon Democrat, before switching over to the office of his rival, Congressman Ron Wyden, who ultimately defeated DeFazio in a Senate race.

Street surveillance continued every day for 5 or 6 months.

Some of the surveillance struck me as comical. Carrying groceries one afternoon, I was accosted by a genial Arab fellow wearing dirty jeans and a t-shirt about a block from my apartment. According to my journals, this occurred in May or June of 1993. The Arab man greeted me loudly, with a huge smile plastered on his face.[59]

Very quickly he got to the point. And there was nothing subtle about it.

"I am visiting from the south of Egypt. Do you know anybody from the South of Egypt? Do you know any terrorists? Really, I am very serious. Do you know any terrorists? You should tell me."

At that point, he made a clumsy overture to pay me for sex, pulling a large wad of hundred dollar bills out of his tattered jeans pocket. I burst out laughing and slammed the door in his face.

In ordinary circumstances, the idea of subjecting a young American woman to foreign surveillance in Washington DC would raise eyebrows. It would be unthinkable. In truth, such encounters were the tip of the iceberg.

From the perspective of law enforcement, that sort of aggressive surveillance might have qualified as a necessary infringement on my civil liberties. However, as a 29 year old woman living alone in Washington DC, all of that attention felt dreadfully unnerving. It didn't continue very long, fortunately. I'd done the right thing. The more the FBI and the NSA verified the accuracy of my warning, the more they had to respect that I came forward to try to stop the attack. At least I tried to do something, instead of looking away.

I kept a journal after the 1993 World Trade Center attack. Many years later, some of those entries on surveillance gave ammunition to critics, who accused me of "irrational paranoia," during my imbroglio with the Justice Department.[60] However, my writings only seem paranoid because my warning about the first World Trade Center attack had been kept secret from the public. In light of my actions, it's not terribly surprising the government acted aggressively to track my activities. In a sense they had to.

After the 1993 attack, the style of surveillance struck me as overt and deliberately intrusive. As an Asset, I learned that if the government desires to conceal its surveillance, you would never guess you're a target. If you're aware of surveillance, it's because they want you to be conscious of it. Intrusive surveillance is designed to scare you off. It's a method of psychological warfare. And believe me when I say, it can be very effective.

Still, I considered it excessive. For one thing, I am the social opposite of the terrorist network I exposed. I am a life-long peace activist opposed to violence in all its forms.

My mother, Jacqueline Shelly Lindauer, raised me to oppose War and violence from my earliest childhood during the Vietnam War in the 1960s. A college teacher of children's literature at Cal Polytechnic in Pomona, California, Jackie Lindauer testified at numerous draft board hearings to keep her students out of Vietnam as "conscientious objectors." A few of her students fled to Canada, with her encouragement.

Jackie also counseled young American soldiers who returned from Vietnam emotionally damaged, as they tried to adjust to college life.

Years later, when our family moved to Alaska, my mother became a bright light on the small Anchorage social scene. She served as President of the Anchorage Fine Arts Museum Association, and entertained various foreign dignitaries and foreign policy experts, who would speak before the World Affairs Council in Anchorage, while traveling in the wilds of Alaska. To her immense credit, she launched five country radio stations and 10 weekly newspapers throughout rural Alaska.[61]

As publisher and editor-in-chief of her small Alaska media empire, Jackie championed sustainable fisheries management in Alaska, the protection of Alaska Native culture, the restoration of Russian Orthodox churches, rural education and health care, among other local causes. Fiercely pro-development, Jackie nevertheless mobilized Alaska's fishing community to support a ban on drift-nets that wiped out millions of fish and sea life in the open ocean. She also lobbied hard for an international treaty to stop over-fishing in international waters called the "Donut Hole," between the U.S., Japan and Russia. She was much loved and civic minded.

In a switch from her past, Jackie frequently entertained top military brass at our home, including some of the Generals from Elmendorf Air Force Base and Fort Richardson who got their stripes in Vietnam. On occasion, at her parties, these Generals would tease her about military dossiers tallying her protests of the Vietnam War, and her transformation from 1960s radical activist to civic leader. But the Generals and military attaches in Anchorage always made a point of praising the support she gave young soldiers coming home from Vietnam. My mother opposed the War; she never opposed the young men drafted to fight it.

In a real sense, I followed in my mother's footsteps as an Anti-War activist. During Vietnam, my mother had a poster that read: 'War is harmful to children and other living things.' She taught us that all life should be treated as precious and sacred. She revered civil rights activist, Rev. Martin Luther King. While America battled racism in the 1960s, my mother made sure that we played with little black and Hispanic children in our home. In 1968, that was different.

As a result, from my earliest childhood in the 1960s, I learned a profound respect for the cultural rights of other peoples, a lesson that crossed racial and ethnic lines.

It also meant that anti-war activism and social justice formed the deepest core of my political philosophy long before the first Gulf War in 1990.

As a graduate of Smith College (one of the Seven Sisters colleges) and the London School of Economics, I opposed virtually all American foreign policy during the Reagan-Bush era. Most ironically, the focus of my politics bitterly opposed the CIA. I campaigned hard against apartheid in South Africa and opposed U.S. intervention in Latin America throughout the 1980s. Politically, I championed the Sandinistas against the Contras in Nicaragua, and abhorred the death squads in El Salvador and Honduras (many of them trained and financed by the CIA). I argued passionately against war and militarism. I supported liberation theology and nuclear disarmament. Anti-war philosophy profoundly shaped my dogma and religious viewpoints.

My favorite economics professor at Smith College, Dr. Andrew Zimbalist, campaigned for years against the Cuban trade embargo, and ranked as one of the foremost opponents of sanctions policy in his day.[62]

Now a leading expert on American baseball franchising and sports economics,[63] in those days Zimbalist showed me how sanctions reduce entire nations to struggling poverty, with long term consequences that harm the rise of new markets for U.S. goods. In that sense, he showed me how sanctions cripple economic prosperity for trade partners in both directions.

From there I came to see that sanctions break down communications exactly when diplomacy is most urgently required to address conflict. They lay barriers to quid pro quo solutions, which are vital to breaking deadlocks, in favor of "all or nothing" solutions, which are most difficult to attain. Very serious conflicts continue to fester without relief, as a direct result of sanctions policy.

That lesson would affect me deeply. My passion against sanctions that I nurtured at Smith College would catapult me into a most surprising opportunity in my future. Above all, Smith filled me with a sense of empowerment, and inspired my unshakeable belief that women should expect to contribute solutions to difficult issues. That sense of confidence encouraged me to embrace the challenges of performing as an Asset dealing with conservative Arab governments. And it's what saved me when the Justice Department tried to smash apart my sense of identity and achievement, and the pride I felt for my accomplishments. Without Smith College, I could never have survived the harrowing ordeal of my indictment. I could not have fought so hard to defend myself, or had the confidence to hold onto my beliefs, when confronted with such powerful foes.

I owe Andy Zimbalist and Smith College everything.

After Smith, I headed to graduate school at the London School of Economics. There I gained something equally pivotal to my life, though I did not realize how important it would become. L.S.E. gave me close, personal exposure to the sons (and a few daughters) of high ranking government ministers and diplomats around the world, including Pakistan, Egypt, Iraq and Iran. And the School philosophy exposed me to a global diversity of policymaking, including an Islamic philosophy of government that contradicted everything I understood about politics. It challenged me at every level.

At the outset, I admit I was not tolerant. As a young feminist, I was both tantalized by the teachings of Islam, and frightened by its repression of women. Yet Arab culture excited me. As a spiritual person, I discovered that I feel genuine admiration for Islamic teachings. Ultimately I learned to respect them culturally, and I learned how to discuss non-violence in the context of Islamic philosophy, in such a way that they could hear me, and we could understand each other. In that way, my immersion at the London School of Economics made it possible for me to communicate successfully with Arab diplomats years later at the United Nations. Without that early confrontation with diversity in government agendas and policymaking at the London School of Economics, it's doubtful I could have been effective in building bridges to those embassies.

All of those aspects of my early life forged into a passionate support for dialogue and opposition to militarism that proved fairly unique in its application.

There is one more striking aspect that defines my life. I have a life-long and profound interest in spiritualism and metaphysics. Since my earliest childhood, I have possessed psychic abilities, including telepathy and precognition, which I have always embraced.

Ultimately, what I cherish as a beautiful gift would prove to be the most controversial aspect of my life. It painted a bull's eye on my back during my legal battle, though many people around the world share those same types of experiences, and hold them to be quite wonderful. In my case, whatever you choose to call this presence, it is loving and righteous. And it has brought me to some extraordinary moments.

One particular event has stoked controversy over my spiritual beliefs. Though somewhat mysterious, like so much in my life, it happens to be entirely truthful.

It occurred on the morning of April 15, 1986, after U.S. and British fighter jets bombed Colonel Gadhaffi's camps in Tripoli. The story goes that when fighter planes crossed Maltese airspace without permission, Malta's Prime Minister called to warn Gadhaffi, who narrowly escaped death at his family compound.[64]

As fate would have it, that night I was stuck at the Moscow International Airport in the old Soviet Union, returning to London with a school travel group. Unbeknownst to any of us, the United States had issued a special warning to the Kremlin that all Soviet planes must stay grounded during the attack on Libya. Any Soviet planes lifting off any runway would be interpreted as threatening the United States, and would be shot down. This was Ronald Reagan's Administration, already infamous for joking that "the bombing starts in five minutes."

Without our knowledge, our student group from the London School of Economics had just become pawns of the Cold War. After hours of delay, our flight was rushed out of the Moscow airport. Shortly after take off, a U.S. fighter jet appeared on our wing and escorted us out of Soviet airspace. That's something you don't forget.

The next morning, safe on British soil, we discovered why the fuss. Banner headlines in the "Times" of London proclaimed "President Reagan Bombs Tripoli."

During that school year, I lived in the Earls Court neighborhood off Cromwell Road and Kensington High Street, the heart of a thriving Arab community in London. I was excited about my trip to Moscow and Leningrad, and I decided to walk to Holland Park near my home.

Rage on the street was palpable. Fist fights broke out in the neighborhood. Inside Holland Park, police cordoned off the British Commonwealth Institute because of a bomb scare.

I sat down on a park bench.

An old Arab man, very dignified with a black cane, cautiously sat down next to me.

What followed was the most extraordinary conversation I've ever shared with any soul in this life-time. Our meeting fully changed my life and opened my heart to the opportunities that I would confront later on. Almost immediately it became apparent to me that this dignified old man possessed a great gift of precognition. That's stunning to a western audience, but much better understood and accepted in the Middle East. Given my own predilections for spiritualism, I responded encouragingly.

For about an hour, the old Arab man spoke extensively about the future of the Middle East—and the future of my life in highly subtle and precise detail. I was fascinated. He spoke with such patience and confidence and an uncanny sort of ancient wisdom. He was an extremely conservative Arab, who addressed me as a woman, in the old way— from the side of his mouth, with his eyes lifted away from my face.

Mostly he spoke about Libya and Iraq. With striking precision, he described how the United Nations would impose sanctions on Libya for the bombing of an airplane that would go down on the roofs of Scotland. When he raised his hands forward, I could see red clay roofs through the ripped fuselage of an airplane. There was no mistaking it as the Scottish town of Lockerbie.

He also harshly criticized what he called 'the War of the Tigris and Euphrates—' For these purposes, I have updated my vocabulary to call this the "Iraq War."

The old Arab man issued special condemnation against United Nations sanctions on Iraq that he claimed would cause 'horrific suffering and deaths for the people of the Tigris and Euphrates after the War ends and'— quote "before it continues." Without question, he saw the possibility of a second phase in the war and vigorously wished to stop it. We know that, of course, as the Iraq War. He described the situation inside Iraq in tremendous detail, as if he was standing on a street corner in Baghdad, watching the violence unfold.

Most interesting to my Arab and Muslim friends, in advance of the War, the old man declared what's called "a fatwa," that all true Muslims would be required to help Iraq. Very precisely he insisted that "true Muslims would be required to oppose the sanctions and the War."

As for the War itself, he said: "We must all do everything in our power to stop the fighting." Muslim peoples "would be required to compensate the Iraqi people for their suffering and help them rebuild." That's what he demanded, in his own words. His warning was redlined: All violence committed against the Iraqi people was strictly prohibited under Islamic law—and Arabs particularly would suffer punishment if they hurt the Iraqis. No sanctions. No suicide bombings. Interestingly, he stressed his authority under the Shariah to justify his fatwa. Perhaps more controversially, Arab behavior towards the Iraqi people mattered more to him than the Infidels.

Now, it's important to understand that the old Arab man was speaking on April 15, 1986—the morning after the bombing of Tripoli.

Pan Am 103 got bombed and crashed over the roofs of Lockerbie, Scotland on December 21, 1988— two and a half years after our conversation. The United Nations imposed sanctions on Libya in 1992. That's six years later.

The United Nations imposed sanctions on Iraq in August, 1990—four and a half years after the Old Man's fatwa. The United States launched the first Gulf War against Iraq in January, 1991 and the second War in March, 2003.

Nevertheless, the old Arab man described all of those world events in explicit detail on the morning after the bombing of Tripoli, as if all of it was happening in the current day. He foretold it all, years in advance. It's controversial, but no hoax. I refuse to recant it.

One more observation struck me personally as uncanny. Repeatedly the old Arab man told me, "The authorities of the Court are going to ask you questions about me." That's how he described it—'authorities of the Court.' And he urged me not to be afraid of answering those questions. He was so adamant about the "authorities" wanting to interview me, that while we sat on the park bench in Holland Park I began to look for police. I wanted to get that interview over with! And he just smiled, and said, "No, no. That's later on. You will testify in a courtroom."

What he described would indeed occur— 20 years later.

The old Arab man was so emphatic that I would be interrogated by 'authorities of the court" that during the Lockerbie Trial in the summer of 2000, I insisted to Libyan diplomats in New York and my American Intelligence handlers that they must allow me to testify at the Lockerbie Trial, because the old man had foretold it. One Libyan diplomat asked me if I thought perhaps there would be a second trial.

Our conversation over that single hour affected some of the most important decisions of my life. More than 24 years later, the old man's observations continue to have great validity to my experiences—and to events in Iraq and the Middle East.

All of these factors influenced who I am, and how I came to work as an Asset, despite my progressive politics and my frequent propensity to criticize U.S. foreign policy.

From the start, I recognized that Iraq would be the war of our time, which defines our global age. When the Gulf War started in 1990, I attended demonstrations in protest.

As the old Arab man predicted on the morning after the bombing of Tripoli, the brutality of the U.N. sanctions on Iraq grieved me, profoundly. Sanctions closed down the entire Iraqi economy and devastated the people. Iraqi families could not buy food or medicine or school books or basic household commodities. Children starved and died. Literacy was wiped out in a single generation. The future of the country was ravaged in all parts. It was deliberate cruelty and a mockery of the humanitarian principles embodied by the United Nations.

As the cruelty of U.N. sanctions took its toll, I began to search for more effective ways of participating to end the conflict. My education encouraged me to believe that I should participate in tackling social problems. I was young enough not to feel discouraged from trying. Perhaps the natural hubris of the young protected me, since I was unaware that most attempts like mine end in failure and disillusionment.

Primarily I wanted to find a way to help Iraqi women. I wanted to help Iraqi mothers feed their children. I wanted to help teachers so that children could thrive in the classroom. I wanted to help doctors get medicine for the sick. I looked to the history of the Silk Road through Persia hundreds of years ago, and I recognized that trading goods and cultural exchange would give momentum to social and political reforms.

Like any other activist, I recognized how small I am. But I also recognized that hard work and dedication compensate for my small size and lack of financial resources.

All of these factors were known to the U.S. Government after the first World Trade Center bombing, as a result of intensive scrutiny from the terrorist investigation. I was already identified as holding strong anti-war and anti-sanctions beliefs. I was recognized to have a personal interest in spiritual metaphysics and psychic phenomenon. They knew about the Old Arab man from London. Above all, I appeared to have an uncanny capacity for recognizing terrorist scenarios, and correctly configuring all the random parts to anticipate events and trends.

Everything was on the table. My handlers and U.S. Intelligence understood every part of who I am, all my strengths and foibles. They had full comprehension of my capabilities and political biases. I had been fully vetted in every conceivable way.

None of that changes the remarkable choice of tapping a life-long peace activist to serve as a U.S. Intelligence Asset, dealing with Iraq and Libya on counter-terrorism at the United Nations.

Yet that's exactly what happened to me.

In late August, 1993 I received an unexpected phone call from Mrs. Pat Wait, Chief of Staff to Congresswoman Helen Bentley, a Republican from Baltimore, Maryland. Mrs. Wait was briefly acquainted with my father, John Lindauer, who lost a race for Governor of Alaska on the Republican ticket. Ostensibly, she called to express sympathy for the death of my mother, and invited me to lunch in Alexandria, Virginia. Mrs. Wait lived next door to Senator Strom Thurmond of South Carolina. That would be the same Senator Thurmond who famously told my former boss, Senator Carol Moseley-Braun (the only African American in the Senate) that he would sing "Dixie" until she cried. I suspect that communicates the depth of Mrs. Wait's own conservative philosophy.

Privately, for six months since the 1993 World Trade Center attack, I had wept to friends over the phone about how desperately I missed my mother, how I grieved her death. I could not confide to my friends what I had done, warning about the terrorist attack on New York. I might have exposed them to danger. So instead I blamed my grief on my mother's death, which they could understand. For awhile I cried a lot. I was tremendously sad after the first World Trade Center attack. Once we got to know each other, Pat Wait confided that the spooks had known this, and deliberately appealed to my sense of loss of my mother to establish contact with me.

We met at a diner in Alexandria. The two of us could not have been more different. I was a progressive democrat, and she a hard core neoconservative. We were fierce opposites on all matters of importance in my life. We'd been sitting together no more than five minutes when Pat declared that she'd campaigned against the Equal Rights Amendment, and took great delight in seeing it defeated. Well, I'm a life-long feminist. And my mother, whose life we were presumably honoring, had lobbied hard for state governments to support the E.R.A. It struck me that Pat was not remotely repentant for the loss to American women.

About that time, she glanced up from the menu to announce casually that a close friend of hers, Paul Hoven, would be joining us for lunch.

I looked up just as a big mountain of man climbed out of a white pick up truck. Pat peeked above the menu and declared, "Paul works for the Defense Intelligence Agency."

Then she popped her head down, silently giggling over my obviously terrified reaction.

It could only be described as an ambush. All I could think was what would happen if this Pat Wait and Paul Hoven discovered my secret—that I'd warned about the terrorist attack on the World Trade Center a few months earlier. What would happen to me then?

I felt like I'd wandered into a lion's den, and these were real lions. I was a goat. I was going to get eaten.

Much later, Paul and Pat delighted in assuring me they had both known the secret about my World Trade Center warning before we ever met at the diner. They assured me that given our extreme political differences, they would never have made time for me otherwise. But apparently it had been decided that somebody really ought to watch over me in Washington. Somebody needed to keep me out of trouble. That task had been assigned to two hard-right Republicans who would not tolerate any liberal shenanigans.

But I did not understand that yet. I still believed in "coincidences."

I resolved to shake them off. They hated my politics, right? So it should have been simple to make sure we never crossed paths again. Well, they had other ideas. They refused to be shaken off. And I quickly discovered that these two—Pat Wait and Paul Hoven—were real players. For all his blood red conservatism, Hoven had accomplished some truly remarkable things, which I respected. And Pat Wait was a formidable political historian in her own right. For all of the differences in our outlooks, I developed tremendous respect for her analysis, though I always opposed her extreme conservative philosophy.

Hoven was a hero by anybody's standards.[65] In Vietnam, he saw active combat from 1968 to 1970, as a 23 year old helicopter pilot who flew medical evacuations into hostile enemy zones. In Vietnam, his first combat mission was the assault on the Y Bridge in Saigon. But mostly, as a chopper pilot, he would haul out American soldiers trapped under enemy fire. He would fly straight into live mortar fire to save young soldiers desperate to get out of a jungle fight, and frequently injured or dying. He'd land his chopper in the thick of battle. Sometimes soldiers died in his arms, but he never left a man behind. Paul is fierce that way. He got shot down at least twice over hostile territory. In all, he flew 1392 hours.

He also served in Laos. According to Leslie Cockburn in "Out of Control,"[66] Hoven "had an enormous range of contacts in the murky world of special—i.e., clandestine—operations." By some accounts, some of his compatriots included famous spooks like Carl Bernard, Ted Shackley, Tom Clines and Richard Secord.

But there was a surprising philosophical side to Paul Hoven, too.

For all his Soldier of Fortune bluster, Paul had rubbed elbows with some highly respected and credible liberal activists in Washington, including Daniel Sheehan, an attorney who championed the causes of Daniel Ellsberg and Karen Silkwood.[67]

I was definitely intrigued.

Spartacus summed up Sheehan's extraordinary career: "Daniel Sheehan was involved in the prisoners' rights movement at Attica State Prison in New York. During the Attica riots in 1971, he attempted to negotiate a peaceful solution before Governor Nelson Rockefeller ordered authorities to take down the prison by force. He was a member of F. Lee Bailey's law firm, which represented Watergate burglar James McCord. At Harvard Law School, Sheehan co-founded the *Harvard Civil Rights and Civil Liberties Law Review. He* served as general counsel to the Jesuits' social ministry office in Washington."[68]

In 1980 Sheehan became general counsel for the Christic Institute, a small public-interest group "dedicated to uniting Christians, Jews and other religious Americans on a platform for political change." For his part, Hoven was a staunch Catholic.

During this period, Hoven worked for the Project on Military Procurement, exposing fraudulent billing by defense contractors.[69] It was Hoven's group that exposed the

$10,000 screw and the $30,000 toilet at the Pentagon, among other eye popping items on procurement lists.

In Hoven's own words: "Much of our information was supplied by the infamous Pentagon Underground. The underground was made up of a loose confederation of Military Officers and Pentagon civilians who believed two basic points: that weapon systems were not tested fully before purchase, and that the Pentagon was not responsible with its money."[70]

"We supplied documents and assisted reporters with information about things military…Our offices on Capitol Hill were broken into a number of times. My apartment was broken into. Nothing was ever taken, but items on my desk would be rearranged. The front door dead bolt would be unlocked, and the door would be opened a quarter of an inch,"[71] Hoven said.

Working together, Hoven and Sheehan got deeply ensnared in one of the hottest spook conspiracies ever to rock Washington. The two of them played catalyst roles exposing Oliver North and the Iran-Contra scandal, which involved drug and weapons shipments in Latin America and arm sales to Iran, in order to finance illegal U.S. operations in Nicaragua.

Paul used to brag to me that the idea for a special prosecutor on Iran-Contra was hatched in his kitchen.

Hoven's relationship to Iran Contra has been substantiated independently. Political analyst, David Corn, sums up Daniel Sheehan's involvement with Paul Hoven and the history of their exposé of Iran-Contra in his book, ***Blond Ghost: Ted Shackley and the CIA's Crusades* (1994).**[72] It provides critical independent validation of my own interpretations of Paul Hoven's extensive ties in the murky world of intelligence:

As Corn tells it in "Blond Ghost," "Throughout 1985, Paul Hoven, a friend of Sheehan's and a Vietnam veteran, regularly attended parties of ex-Agency men and weekend warriors, some associated with *Soldier of Fortune* magazine.

At a Christmas bash, Carl Jenkins, a former CIA officer who had been assigned to Miami and Laos, introduced Hoven to Gene Wheaton.

Wheaton served as an army detective in Vietnam, and in the mid-1970s a security officer at a top-secret CIA-Rockwell surveillance program in Iran called Project IBEX. In 1979 he returned to the United States, and held a string of security-related jobs. When he met Paul Hoven, Wheaton was scheming with Carl Jenkins and Ed Dearborn, a former CIA pilot in Laos and the Congo, to win federal contracts to transport humanitarian supplies to anticommunist rebels, including the Mujahedeen of Afghanistan and the Contras in Nicaragua. However the trio had failed to collect any contracts. They had complained to a State Department official that Richard Secord and Oliver North improperly controlled who got the Contra-related contracts.

At the *Soldier of Fortune* party, Hoven agreed to assist Wheaton. Hoven set up a meeting with a congressional aide who followed the Afghan program. Hoven did not realize that Wheaton had more on his mind than contracts. Wheaton had spent much of the previous year hobnobbing with arms dealers, ex-CIA officers and mercenaries, and he had collected information on past and present covert operations, including the secret Contra-arms project.

Wheaton was obsessed with the 1976 assassination in Iran of three Americans who worked on Project IBEX. He believed the killings were linked to U.S. intelligence, and that a ring of ex-spooks was running wild in Central America and elsewhere.

So when Wheaton met with the congressional staffer and Hoven, he launched into a speech about political assassinations related to U.S. intelligence. He rattled on about the mysterious IBEX murders. Wheaton made his bottom-line point obvious: a rogue element in the U.S. government had engaged in a host of nefarious activities, including assassinations.

The congressional staffer wanted nothing to do with Wheaton's intrigue. But Hoven was interested. He called Danny Sheehan, thinking he ought to hear Wheaton's tale.

By early 1986, press accounts had revealed that a clandestine Contra support network ran all the way into the White House and that Oliver North was involved, even though Congress had barred the Reagan Administration from militarily aiding the rebels.

Here was the perfect target for Sheehan: a furtive program supporting a covert war against a leftist government. He wondered if he could strike at it in the courts. Then he met Gene Wheaton, who had a helluva tale for Sheehan.

Sheehan and Wheaton sat down in the kitchen of Hoven's house in early February of 1986. Wheaton tossed out wild stories of clandestine operations and dozens of names: A whole crew was running amok, supporting Contras, conducting covert activity elsewhere. Drugs were involved. Some of this gang had engaged in corrupt government business in Iran and Southeast Asia."

According to Spartacus, "Wheaton and Jenkins gave information about political assassinations organized by members of the CIA in Vietnam in 1974 and 1975. Called the Phoenix Project, it carried out a secret mission of assassinating members of the economic and political bureaucracy, in attempt to cripple the nation's functioning after the U.S withdrawal from Vietnam. This Phoenix Project assassinated some 60,000 village mayors, treasurers, school teachers and other non- Viet Cong administrators. Ted Shackley and Thomas Clines financed a highly intensified phase of the Phoenix project in 1974 and 1975, by smuggling opium into Vietnam from Laos." [73]

As Blond Ghost relates: "As Sheehan talked to Wheaton and Jenkins, he had something else on his mind: a two-year-old bombing in Nicaragua. On May 30, 1984, a bomb exploded at a press conference in La Penca, Nicaragua. Afterward, Tony Avirgan, an American journalist who suffered shrapnel wounds, and his wife, Martha Honey, accused a group of Cuban exiles with ties to the CIA and the Contras of planning the murderous assault. Their report noted that some Contra supporters were moonlighting in the drug trade.

Come late spring of 1986, Sheehan was mixing with spooks in Washington DC, collecting information on the Contra operation. Then Sheehan made a pilgrimage to meet the dark angel of the covert crowd: Ed Wilson. The imprisoned rogue CIA officer made Sheehan's head swim. The essence of Wilson's story, Sheehan claimed, was that the Agency in 1976 had created a highly secretive counter terrorist unit apart from the main bureaucracy of the CIA. The mission: conduct "wet operations" (spy talk for assassinations). After the election of Jimmy Carter, this group was erased from the books and hidden in private companies. Shackley was the man in charge, both in and out of government.

At one point after Sheehan met with Wilson, it dawned on him: everything was connected. The La Penca bombing, the North-Contra network, the Wilson gang, all those CIA-trained Cuban exiles, the whole history of Agency dirty tricks, the operations against Castro, the war in Laos, the nasty spook side of the Vietnam War, and clandestine CIA action in Iran. It was an ongoing conspiracy. It did not matter if these guys were in or out of government. It was a villainous government within a government.

Sheehan applied the resources of his small Christic Institute to the case. He knitted together all this spook gossip with a few hard facts, and dropped the load. In a Miami federal court, Sheehan filed a lawsuit against thirty individuals, invoking the RICO antiracketeering law and accusing all of being part of a criminal conspiracy that trained, financed, and armed Cuban-American mercenaries in Nicaragua, smuggled drugs, violated the Neutrality Act by supporting the Contras, traded weapons, and bombed the press conference at La Penca.

Sheehan's plaintiffs were journalists Tony Avirgan and Martha Honey. He demanded over $23 million in damages. With this lawsuit, Sheehan believed, he could break up the Contra support operation, and cast into the light shadowy characters who'd been up to mischief for years.

Hoven and Jenkins were stunned. Neither expected Sheehan to produce such a storm. Sheehan was not about to be a quiet disseminator of information. "I had been left with the assumption," Hoven noted, "that I was set up to pass information to Sheehan. But they—" [whoever set up Hoven to contact Sheehan] "—mucked it up because Sheehan was not playing it close to the script."

In fact, Sheehan advocated the impeachment of President Ronald Reagan and Vice President George Bush for their role in Iran Contra, and demanded that Oliver North face criminal prosecution. Celebrities like Bruce Springsteen, Jackson Browne, Don Henley and Kris Kristofferson helped raise funds for the impeachment campaign led by the Christic Institute.

In the final round, Lawrence Walsh, the special prosecutor, gave prosecutorial immunity to 14 defendants. When President George Bush, Sr. lost his re-election in 1992, one of his last acts in office was to pardon the remaining six individuals indicted by the special prosecutor for Iran Contra. The Christic Institute moved to Los Angeles in 1995.[74]

Seven years had passed since Danny Sheehan and the Christics busted open Iran-Contra, with a little help at the right moments from Paul Hoven.

Now Hoven showed up with Pat Wait to meet me in August, 1993. Politically, we could not have been more opposite. For the first couple of months, we sort of danced around each other. We were not friends. We were not colleagues. To put it bluntly, Paul did not appear to like me. But he would not go away. He told me straight up that it had been decided somebody must watch over me, because of my warning about the World

Trade Center attack. That task had been delegated to him. And he took his assignment very seriously.

As to who recruited Hoven for this assignment, that was always mysterious. But one night Hoven made a point of explaining how Congress prohibits the CIA from conducting operations inside the United States, or otherwise targeting American citizens for domestic surveillance. Those sorts of domestic operations for anti-terrorism purposes— like I was caught up in— fell under the auspices of the Defense Intelligence Agency, Hoven told me. He wanted me to know that no person or agency was breaking the law, or violating any congressional mandate by shadowing me. By chance, this conversation took place a couple of nights before I was going to meet Congressman Ron Wyden to discuss a press secretary opening in his office. That's when Paul told me on a "need to know" basis.

Thus, I believed from our first days together that Hoven performed in some liaison role to Defense Intelligence, whatever technical definition he chose to give it. It was a natural conclusion, based on very precise conversations from the beginnings of our relationship.

Hoven told me that he had been forced to retire as a "contract officer" on permanent disability, because of a cardiac virus he picked up in Panama. He'd been a guest producer with Mike Wallace at "Sixty Minutes," covering the U.S. invasion of Panama, when he suffered a viral infection that destroyed 40 percent of his heart's functioning capacity. In early 2005, Hoven had a heart transplant at the Mayo Clinic.

Though forced to retire on disability, Hoven had no difficulty filling the role of my "case officer" or "handler." Always he told me bluntly that our meeting was not a random event. "They" asked him to watch over me. "They" planned the approach with careful attention to personal details of my life. One of Paul's friends was a Rosicrucian in Minnesota, and I was known to have a keen interest in spiritualism and metaphysics. Paul emphasized that "they" considered the value of his friendship with this Rosicrucian in assigning him as my watcher, because they expected it would help establish a bond between us. He stressed this numerous times.

It was also Hoven who informed me the Defense Intelligence Agency ran a special operation on psychic research parallel to the Soviets during the Cold War. He told me that he knew one of the Directors of the psychic research program, and they'd spoken about me. All of that reinforced my expectations that Paul was deeply connected to the murky world of intelligence.

If you looked up 'spook' in the dictionary, I'm pretty sure you'd find a picture of Paul Hoven. Everything pointed that way. He was definitely enmeshed in those circles.

Even his heart attack brought out the spooks.

At a Spartacus "education forum" on September 13, 2007, Hoven told the story:[75] "At the time of my heart attack, two events were taking placed that I was involved in: 1) the meeting at Marine Headquarters to get Oliver North transferred out of the White House, and 2) the cancellation of the Division Air Defense program 40 mm Bofors Cannon on the old M-48 tank body. This was the first time that an active Pentagon weapons system was cancelled."

"When I started having chest pains after drinking some orange juice, I assumed it was a muscle cramp. Finally, my roommate called 911. I lived in Arlington, Virginia, and

Arlington County ran the only ambulance service. I was given some nitroglycerin, and the stretcher was placed on the ground in front of the ambulance."

"A second ambulance arrived, and the two crews started to argue over who was to take me to the hospital. The second crew mentioned that I was the person involved in canceling DIVAD. [Note: The ambulance crew arrived knowing those highly specialized details about Hoven's current projects, which would have been classified.] "They were both informed that I was to go to George Washington Hospital in Washington. The second ambulance crew won the argument, and proceeded to take me to a Northern Virginia hospital, instead." [Closer to Langley.]

"We pulled into the building, and 16 doctors, nurses and techs were there to greet me. They saved my life. After three days, I was transferred to my HMO hospital in Washington. I was informed by Knut Royce (former interpreter for the Emperor of Ethiopia) that one of my nurses was the daughter of the CIA liaison in the White House."

"Months later, Carl Jenkins [another famous spook who trained Cuban exiles in Mexico for the Bay of Pigs] and I were at O'Toole's Bar in Langley, [a CIA watering hole]. We met an ex-special forces doctor on his way to Afghanistan to provide medical care to rebels fighting the Soviets. My heart attack came up in conversation. He asked if I drank something cold before the attack. I mentioned that I had some orange juice. He said there was a substance that causes heart attacks and is delivered in cold beverages. Danny Sheehan told me there were 9 or 10 of us [involved in Iran-Contra and the Project for Military Procurement] who had heart attacks. I was the only one who did not die."

But was Hoven a spook?

Once I asked Paul how I could identify spooks that might approach me at the United Nations. He just smiled and shook his head.

"Susan," he said. "If it waddles like a duck, and it quacks like a duck, it's a duck."

"But Paul!" I said. "How can I be sure?"

"Susan," he said. "It's a duck."

He wasn't the only one.

Early on, I discovered that Pat Wait had special access to multiple high level intelligence sources. She claimed to have known Richard Fuisz, my second handler, and his intelligence ties to the CIA for 20 years. On numerous occasions, Pat assured me that both Dr. Fuisz and Hoven had deep connections to the shadow world of U.S. intelligence. After my arrest, Pat Wait swore to me that Hoven and Fuisz "could face prosecution for perjury and obstruction of Justice, if they denied" their intelligence ties or supervising me.

But not everybody was so informed. Some people had known Paul and Richard for years, and were totally clueless as to their intelligence activities. That's the nature of intelligence. Nobody volunteers this information. If you don't need to know, you're out of the loop.

If they don't want you to know, they'll keep you guessing. They can hide behind all sorts of technical language to deny it, if they wish. It's nothing to get upset about. That's how the spooks work. It's the nature of the beast. I find it amusing.

From my earliest conversations with Hoven and Mrs. Wait, it was clear some part of the government thought I needed close supervision as I wandered through Washington. I suspect that for awhile, they tried to figure out what to do with me, whether or not I might have any possible use, or if my warning about the 1993 World Trade Center attack had been a fluke.

To his credit, Hoven took a big chance on me. In May 2004, he proposed that my apparently uncanny ability to filter counter-terrorism scenarios, and my steadfast opposition to war and sanctions, might find application in real politics in the Middle East.

Very cautiously, he floated the idea that I might approach Libyan diplomats at the United Nations about starting talks for the Lockerbie Trial.

I would become what's known as an "Asset."

"Assets" are private citizens who have developed some specialized field of expertise or interest that grants them special access to target groups desirable to the Intelligence Community.

In a practical sense, an Asset resembles a pawn in a chess match. It stays on the playing field as long as possible, to be leveraged and exploited for a greater purpose (typically obfuscated from the Asset's view). Except this game is so extraordinary and dynamic, most people wouldn't care that they've been caught or exploited. It's an opportunity to play in a real game. In the case of Libya or Iraq, two nations under sanctions, it would mean access to high ranking Arab officials that very few individuals could talk to, establishing a point for back channel dialogue, for the purpose of encouraging support for counter-terrorism policy. My efforts to win their cooperation would allow me to contribute towards ending the sanctions that I loathed so deeply.

I jumped at the chance. As I'd gotten to know Hoven, I had come to appreciate what his brand of participation might mean. It could be very exciting. I saw it as an opportunity to contribute to an agenda of non violence in the Middle East at a tangible level. I would get direct access to some key decision-makers, at least in Libya. (Iraq was added to my agenda a year later).

As an activist, it was everything I could wish for. I rationalized that I would not be compromising my anti-war principles by supporting counter-terrorism policy. Quite the contrary, I envisioned pursuing anti-terrorism goals using an anti-war, anti-violence platform. In turn, my actions would help create a platform for ending the sanctions.

In my contacts with Arab diplomats, I hoped that the consistency of my support for non-violence in all directions would win respect from Arab governments, and ultimately their cooperation.

I would not work against Arab peoples or Arab culture or the Islamic religion. I would prove that anti-terrorism could succeed on the basis of diplomacy and respect for cultural dignity, without military threats or sanctions, both of which I bitterly opposed.

It would be a One-Woman Experiment with a new and wholly different approach to counter-terrorism. Success would depend on my ability to cultivate difficult relationships with Libyan and Iraqi diplomats in the opposite direction of official U.S. policy. If I succeeded, I hoped to win the grudging respect of U.S. military types like Hoven, who ordinarily equate anti-terrorism with mandatory threats of force. I wanted to prove that engagement would succeed just as well.

I had one iron-clad condition. Under no circumstances could the U.S. government interfere with my activism for any reason. I had opposed the first Gulf War with Iraq, and I fiercely opposed any second war. I demanded full rights to lobby Congress and the United Nations against U.S. militarism and sanctions on Iraq and Libya, and in the Middle East overall. If that seems contradictory to a U.S. Intelligence agenda, in fact the success of my anti-terrorism work would depend on the sincerity of my anti-war and anti-sanctions activism. The two parts would be inextricably linked. That's what the U.S. wanted to leverage. That's what the U.S. would have to tolerate.

My condition was fully accepted and understood. But first there was somebody Hoven wanted me to meet.

Paul teased me by withholding the name of his CIA contact until right before our meeting. It took several months to get approval for a face to face conversation. I was Press Secretary for Congressman Ron Wyden, an Oregon Democrat at the time. So I thought I was hot stuff. But that only got me so far with this crowd.

These people are trouble-shooters in a crisis. They stay in when everybody else gets out. They fix things that others have broken and abandoned as hopeless. They're intensely creative risk-takers—24/7. You're taught that every encounter, every experience provides a weapon or a tool. Every crisis creates new opportunities. You've got to be incredibly tough and tenacious to play in their game. The stakes are high because a good Asset can impact the opportunities on the playing field for everybody else. That's the whole purpose of an Asset.

When I finally met Dr. Richard Fuisz in September, 1994, [76]I got insight to the special diva status the Intelligence Community affords itself. Though I was a congressional staffer for a leading Democrat, Dr. Fuisz would not deign to come to Capitol Hill for our first meeting. I, the Congressional staffer would have to go to him in Virginia. His office was deemed appropriately "secure."

Hoven promised the trip would be worth it. Driving out to Chantilly, Virginia, he took all the back roads and cut through neighborhoods, so I would have difficulty returning. The next day I drove back to the office and found it on my own. Paul was impressed.

On our drive, he gave me the low down on Dr. Fuisz's remarkable career as a top CIA operative in Syria, Lebanon and Saudi Arabia in the 1980s. Hoven described Fuisz in almost legendary terms. His team in Lebanon had coordinated the hostage rescue of Terry Anderson et al., locating their make-shift prisons in Beirut and calling in the Delta Force for a daring raid.

Later, Dr. Fuisz testified before Congress about U.S. Corporations that supplied Iraq with weapons systems before the first Gulf War. He ran a fashion modeling agency with Raisa Gorbachev that incidentally sold computer systems to the Soviet government during Glasnost, when Mikhail Gorbachev was President of the Soviet Union. He had gotten outed as CIA by Damascus, after stealing the blueprints for Syria's brand new telecommunications system from a locked storage vault.

Finally, Dr. Fuisz claimed to know the real story of Lockerbie, including the identities of the terrorist masterminds, whom he insisted were not Libyan at all.[77]

Remarkably, Dr. Fuisz lived up to all the hype.

In those days, Dr. Fuisz looked like a cross between Robert DeNiro and Anthony LaPaglia, a devastatingly handsome man of Hungarian descent, whose playground ran to Monte Carlo and Paris, when he wasn't trouble-shooting in Beirut. He had an apartment in Paris overlooking the Seine, until one of the Saudi princes borrowed it for a weekend with his girlfriend, who refused to leave, invoking Parisian laws of "squatters' rights."

Without question, Richard Fuisz is the most fascinating and complicated individual I've ever met. For him, it's effortless. He's brilliant and unforgettable. As a scientist and inventor, he's got a drawer full of patents on pharmaceutical products. He's like an alchemist. Working with him and Hoven was the best thing I've ever done in my life. I have no regrets at all.

During negotiations for the Lockerbie Trial at the United Nations, I put together a sworn statement about our first meeting in September, 1994:[78]

Dr. Fuisz told me that he had maintained close business ties to Lebanon, Syria and Saudi Arabia during the 1980s. As part of his work, he infiltrated a network of Syrian terrorists tied to Hezbollah, who, at the time of his residence in Beirut, were holding Terry Anderson and a number of Americans hostage. Dr. Fuisz impressed on me that his team had identified the kidnappers behind the hostage crisis, and located the streets and buildings where the Americans were held captive, at tremendous personal risk, in order to orchestrate a rescue. Once he identified their locations, he had called in the Delta Force to execute a synchronized raid. The order for the hostage rescue was rescinded by top officials in Washington, and delayed several months, until right before the 1988 Presidential election of George H. Bush, Sr. Fuisz called it the original "October Surprise."

We talked a great deal about how the sale of heroin/opium from the Bekaa Valley in Lebanon finances terrorist activities on a global scale. In part, Dr. Fuisz explained how the bombing of Pan Am 103 was intended to strike down a team of Defense Intelligence Agents, who were flying back to Washington to protest the CIA's tolerance of heroin smuggling as part of locating the hostages in Beirut. The bombing was an act of terrorist reprisal for their aggressive drug interdiction efforts, he claimed. They wanted to stop the DIA officers from reaching Washington.

To my surprise, Dr. Fuisz swore of his ability to identify who orchestrated and executed the bombing of Pan Am 103. He stated categorically that no Libyan national was involved in the attack, in any technical or advisory capacity. He also complained about suffering harassment after he tried to provide this information to the families of Pan Am 103 and the Justice Department.

Dr. Fuisz asked for my help as a congressional staffer to resolve a problem. After testifying before a congressional committee about a U.S company that supplied Iraq with SCUD mobile missile launchers, he complained that he suffered serious harassment by the Internal Revenue Service. Efforts by his attorneys to stop this harassment had been answered with warnings from the highest levels that he should never have talked about U.S. arms supplies to Iraq, and that he should stop trying to contact the families of Pan Am 103 about the real Lockerbie Conspiracy.

That was how the bombing of Pan Am 103 arose in our conversation. Dr. Fuisz informed me that he could provide a great deal of information about Middle Eastern terrorism, except the U.S. doesn't want anybody talking about Libya's innocence. Then he jumped into the Lockerbie case by way of example of terrorist cases that he has the immediate capability to resolve. He complained that he was getting shafted for trying to assist a cause that American leaders profess to care very much about. In essence, he insisted the messenger was getting shot for delivering an honest message.

Because of his Syrian ties, he told me he "was first on the ground in the investigation," to use his words. At that point, I tried to sound tough. "Oh yeah, *everybody knows Syria did it.* The U.S. repaid them for supporting us during the Iraqi War by shifting the blame to Libya."

Immediately he cut me off.

"Susan, Do you understand the difference between a primary source and a secondary source? Those people in Virginia are analysts. They're reading reports from the field, but they don't have first-hand contact with events as they're happening on the ground. Or first hand knowledge about what's taking place. So they don't actually know it, even if they think they do."

"*I know it, Susan.* I know it. That's the difference. Because of my Syria contacts, I was there. They're reading my reports." (Then he laughed sarcastically.) "In my case, they're reading them and destroying them." (And he threw up his hands.) He continued on:

"Susan, if the government would let me, I could identify the men behind this attack today. I could do it right now. You want a police line up? I could go into any crowded restaurant of 200 people, and pick out these men by sight."

"I can identify them by face, by name." He started gesticulating, and counting off on his fingers. "I can tell you where they work, and what time they arrive at their office in the morning—if they go to an office. I can tell you what time they go to lunch, what kind of restaurants they go to. I can tell you their home addresses, the names of their wives if they're married, the names and ages of all their children. I can tell you about their girl-friends. I can even tell you what type of prostitutes they like."

"And you know what, Susan? You won't find this restaurant anywhere in Libya. No, you will only find this restaurant in Damascus. I didn't get that from any report, Susan." Dr. Fuisz started shaking his head. "I got it because I was investigating on the ground, and I know. Do you understand what I'm saying to you now? I know!"

To which I answered. "For God's sakes tell me, and I'll get my boss to protect you—" a reference to Congressman Ron Wyden.

Then he got really mad. "No, no! It's so crazy. I'm not even allowed to tell you, and you're a congressional staffer."

This was how I learned that Dr. Fuisz is covered by the Secrets Act, which severely restricts his ability to communicate information about Pan Am 103 or any other intelligence matter. Though he states freely that he can identify the true criminals in this case, he requires special permission from the CIA to testify, or a written over-ride by the President of the United States, if the CIA refuses to grant permission.[79]

I believed that was tragic on two accounts. First, the accused Libyans were denied the right to a fair trial where they might bring forth witnesses to launch an effective defense, which could immediately exonerate them of all charges. And secondly, the Lockerbie families were denied the ability to close this terrible wound, and experience the healing that would be gained from discovering the complete truth and facts surrounding this case. On both accounts, I could not stay silent. I recognized that our disclosures might pain the families of Pan Am 103, with the revelation that vital information had been withheld on the case. And yet it's precisely because I abhor all such violence—terrorist and military— that I believed we must pursue the truth.

As it turned out, there was a second purpose to Dr. Fuisz's candor about Lockerbie. Somebody needed to approach Libya about the Lockerbie Trial. Somebody like me—who recognized and accepted the truth of Libya's innocence— and who passionately opposed sanctions and recognized possible terrorist scenarios, would be ideal to initiate contact with Libyan diplomats at the United Nations. I might have a shot at persuading Libya to accept a trial, whereas nobody else could get in the door. Everyone else was stumped how to go about it. Since I would be working outside the limitations of that agenda, perhaps I could move it forward. Perhaps I could get the negotiations unstuck.

I seized the offer to approach Libya. (Iraq was added to my agenda one year later.) From that point on, in our private conversations, Hoven identified himself as my "case officer" or "handler." Many of my private papers from the mid-1990s onwards refer to Hoven as my "Defense Intelligence handler" or "DIA contact."[80] That's not something I invented afterwards. It was always there. I always believed that Hoven filled an important liaison role or technical support to defense intelligence, even though he was officially retired on disability. Both men debriefed and supervised me. They provided instruction and guidance. I trusted them fully to stand behind me.

Dr. Fuisz made no attempt to hide his connection to the CIA. He had a vast network of contacts throughout the Arab world, and penetrating insight to Middle East politics. At my own trial in New York, proving Dr. Fuisz's intelligence credentials would be vastly simplified by documents from the Lockerbie Trial. That would be sufficient for my legal needs.

Hoven was more cagey about his connection to Defense Intelligence. But there was no way to have a conversation with Hoven, and not conclude he had deep spook ties. He talked about the Defense Intelligence Agency all the time. He used to talk about visiting "the Farm," a euphemism for DIA. I would tease him with questions about the animals on this Farm. I called it the "Old McDonald game."

"Are there chickens on your farm?" I'd ask. "No," he'd say. "But surely there are cows?" "No," he'd shake his head with a smile. "Oh, is it a pig farm? Do you have horses?" He'd say "no, it's sort of an under-ground bunker built into the side of a hill, with a wall of technology gadgets when you entered the building."

It's sometimes hard for outsiders to understand. But it's the nature of intelligence to behave that way. Only a handful of people knew what I was doing all those years, either. It's something you hold close. It's how intelligence functions.

The bond that I forged with Hoven in 1993 and Fuisz in 1994 lasted almost a decade. I knew these men intimately. And they knew me. Paul loved teasing that I was a "goofy peace activist." That never offended me.

And extraordinary as it sounds, the instructions I received from the Old Arab Man in London on the morning after the bombing of Tripoli in April, 1986 proved extremely valuable to the success of my outreach to Iraq and Libya. While controversial in the West, the old Arab man called it right on the mark, with frightening precision, in fact. Decades later, I am still discovering that he told me everything about my own life on that morning. It's quite exceptional, and intensely uncanny. To myself, most of all. Yet it's impossible to deny that it happened.

So it went. As an Asset throughout the 1990s, I gained direct, "primary" access to the day by day flow of cooperation from Libya and Iraq on counter-terrorism. Virtually no one else enjoyed such close proximity to either of those U.N. Missions during that period.

All of that explains how, when Republican leaders decided to go to War with Iraq, the depth of my involvement and knowledge created a major obstacle to their revisionist brand of history. If the White House hoped to invent a story about this War that could defeat the actual facts of history, they would have to get rid of me first. Their lie could not exist alongside my truth.

They would have to destroy me.

Oh how they would try.

CHAPTER 4:

A SECRET DAY IN
THE LIFE OF AN ASSET

On my desk sits a bronze statue of a little girl in a frilly dress, riding a rhinoceros. That's my life—feminine but slightly dangerous. OK, more than slightly dangerous. Rhinoceros have horns and armor plates to protect them in rough play through all sorts of adventures.

My adventure as an Asset lasted from 1993 until 2002. My countries were Iraq and Libya. But my efforts encompassed Egypt, Syria/Hezbollah, Yemen and Malaysia. If that doesn't communicate high level security interests, I don't know what could. There were some extraordinary consequences for that level of involvement. But it was all worth the price. I wouldn't change a single moment of my experience.

Those were exciting times. Under the intense supervision of Dr. Fuisz and Hoven, I established contact with the Libya House in May 1995, and the Iraqi Embassy at the United Nations in August, 1996. About every three weeks, I would travel from my home in the suburbs of Washington DC to visit diplomats at the United Nations in New York. In a crisis, or when various projects intensified, I traveled to New York more frequently. By 2002, I estimate that I had met with Iraqi and Libyan diplomats over 150 times each.

Our outreach was not exactly covert. From the outset, diplomats from Libya and Iraq understood that I sought to create a back-channel in support of dialogue that would break the stalemate and help end the sanctions. All of us understood each other.

My first meeting at the Libya House involved a shockingly frank conversation, in fact, of my connection to Dr. Fuisz and his ability to identify the terrorists who plotted the bombing of Pan Am # 103, a.k.a "Lockerbie." Dr. Fuisz was already well established as a major CIA operative in the Middle East, who tangled with Syria and Lebanon during the Terry Anderson hostage crisis during the 1980s. So when I explained that my work involved Dr. Fuisz, Libyan diplomats understood with utmost clarity what that meant: I had high level contacts deep inside the CIA.

I recall that the Libyan diplomat, Mr. Amarra, glanced up from his small white Turkish coffee cup, and smiled with a mischievous sense of irony.

"Why, thank you CIA. On behalf of Gadhaffi, on behalf of Libya, we thank you. Yes, thank you CIA. Thank you, CIA. Thank you for helping us end our sanctions!" He had a good laugh.

Once that genie's out, there's no putting it back in the bottle.

I remember my first introduction to the Libya House with amusement, like a sort of slapstick Laurel and Hardy comedy of intelligence errors.

For security reasons, I dropped by Libya's embassy at the United Nations unannounced and uninvited, with a request to meet the diplomat handling Lockerbie and the Libyan sanctions. Our team wanted to walk away and disappear if the meeting backfired.

But making contact proved more exasperating than Dr. Fuisz and Hoven anticipated.

When I arrived without an appointment, the Libyan concierge demanded that I go back outside to a payphone across the street from the Embassy. In an absurd game, he instructed me to telephone him and request permission to enter the lobby.

"But I'm already here!" I protested.

"No, no! You must go to the phone outside, and ask for permission to come in and speak to me," the concierge tutted. "That's how it must be done."

There was a light rain outside. I had advance warning that a squad of intelligence officers watched the Libya House from a nearby building. By now they were probably curious about this lone visitor to the Libyan embassy, too. But I resolved not to panic. Except that when I phoned the Libya House, the concierge asked for my name, which sent daggers through my heart, since a phone so close to the Libyan Embassy had to be wiretapped. Sure enough, Dr. Fuisz told me that after I left, my fingerprints got lifted off the phone receiver.

So much for Spy Games 101. The concierge gave me permission to enter the lobby. When I returned, he smugly told me that I should come back tomorrow at 10 o'clock.

I groaned.

On my second approach to the Libya House, stony-faced embassy staff descended en masse to the lobby, and bickered in Arabic over whether I should be allowed upstairs. All of us crowded into the elevator. No one spoke. They glowered. Every suspicious eye turned on me. As we got off the elevator, diplomats took my purse and my light rain coat, convinced that I carried recording devices.

"Why have you come here?"

The Libyan diplomat, Mr. Amarra, could have been a bedouin, tall and lean, haggling over spices at the soukh. Except he was sharp eyed, and I learned later that he spoke seven languages fluently.

"Why have you come here?" His fingers twisted on the tiny Turkish coffee cup. In the doorway embassy staff hovered, listening to every word I spoke, ready to fetch more of the exquisite Arab coffee, a thick almost syrupy concoction, which the Libyan diplomat generously offered. I remember that he leaned forward, eyes piercing me and very much suspicious.

"That is a very important question. It requires a very important answer."

A SECRET DAY IN THE LIFE OF AN ASSET

The "very important" explanation is that I was "an Asset"— a private citizen with specialized interests or skills that allowed me to establish contact with otherwise extremely difficult to reach groups and individuals on behalf of the intelligence community. Most ironically, my own value as an Asset derived from the profound sincerity of my activism against sanctions and military aggression—the formal thrust of U.S. policy towards these same countries. My outspoken opposition to the official direction of U.S. sanctions policy, and my deep confidence in the ability of dialogue to resolve conflicts, gave me a critical advantage. Indeed, my work could not have been accomplished otherwise.

Globally, there were just 5,000 Assets before the 9/11 attack, according to George Tenet, CIA Director for both the Clinton and Bush Administrations.[81]

Only three Assets covered the Iraqi Embassy at the United Nations—and the other two started after 9/11.[82] Nobody else covered Libya at the United Nations for most of the 1990s, because of Libya's extreme isolation. Thus, we occupied a fairly unique and privileged group. In my case, I approached Libya to start talks for the Lockerbie Trial, something Washington politicians and U.N. diplomats had given up trying to do, believing it was far too difficult, maybe impossible.

I visited the Libyan Embassy to get things "unstuck." In the course of that effort, I established a friendly channel for dialogue that tackled several other obstacles with Libya, as well. Later I would do the same for the weapons inspections in Iraq.

Often Assets are teasingly called "useful idiots." Far from derogatory, it marks a necessary distinction inside Intelligence circles. Assets exist outside the ordinary boundaries of the community, even while supplying "must have" access and information that make us critical to the total operation. An intelligence officer who oversees an Asset is known as "a handler." The Asset exists as a mark to be exploited, or mined, to determine whatever we know. Many times Assets have no idea whatsoever that they have been tapped by intelligence. They might be deeply offended to realize that the CIA or Defense Intelligence has begun tracking them. Ignorance strengthens their indignation— and deniability — if challenged. That can be highly advantageous.

Intelligence officers routinely use covers for introduction to potential Assets, in order to protect themselves from hostile reactions by unwilling individuals, who might get upset and rebuff the approach if they understood who was really making it. That's universal to intelligence gathering around the world. An Asset only gets a fragment of the truth on a "need to know" basis— if they're trustworthy. However, if you're around long enough—and if the Asset proves strong enough—you can figure out what the handler is really trying to do. A strong Asset strives to create the opportunity that intelligence relies on to move forward.

That's the game for an Asset. That determines our value. It's not a passive role. In effect we agree to play with all of the smoke and mirrors and cul de sacs, applying our most stubborn tenacity and creative risk taking to advance shared goals. That's crucial to understanding why I wanted in, and why Arab diplomats at the United Nations responded so positively towards me.

If you're a Mark, it is critically important to figure out why somebody has approached you. What do they want to accomplish? What's their agenda? What's stuck that the Asset is determined to fix? There might be advantages for both sides if the project succeeds— like getting out from sanctions. Irregardless, it would be disappointing if the Mark doesn't recognize that something's in play. That's part of testing their sophistication and worthiness to join the game.

And it is a game. The first rule is that there are no rules. That gets a little hairy sometimes. You're there to get something done, usually because it's needs a good kick to get unstuck. Whatever gets in the way, gets jettisoned.

By the way, it's usually flattering to be approached. It means you've got something worth having or knowing.

A friendly approach is much better than an unfriendly approach.

On the downside, meetings between handlers and Assets don't usually disclose the full purpose of the Operations, or the activities of other players. Assets don't receive intelligence reports, except on a strictly need to know basis, for example if knowing one part will guide how the asset interacts with another part of a project. We are pawns on a chess board. We are not allowed to see the whole game.

In short, by our very function and purpose, Assets are not "agents," properly called "case officers" of one or another U.S. Intelligence Agencies. As Hoven used to remind me, "agents" are foreigners. Americans are "case officers" by right of birth. That's one way older spooks get around admitting their affiliations, he used to joke. If they're asked to identify themselves using incorrect language— "Are you an agent?" they can deny it without perjury.

So what's the purpose of an Asset? What gives the Asset value?

Assets are specially prized for our access. We are vital and necessary surrogates for intelligence officers who otherwise lack the specialization necessary to penetrate those exclusive groups. In this way, Assets form the core of human intelligence.

We are eyes and ears— primary sources of information—in contrast to secondary sources called "analysts" who review raw data collected from Assets, and try to piece it together in some cubicle at Langley. Assets are "on the ground" with greater breadth and intimacy than a cold report. It's why some experts call human Assets the single best source of raw intelligence, far superior to electronic surveillance. That's particularly true if the Asset is highly perceptive and capable of connecting random facts into a reasonable picture of unfolding events. A corollary is that screwing your Assets undermines the entire foundation of intelligence gathering.

And where did our team fall on this spectrum?

Dr. Fuisz told me that I was "uncanny" in my perceptiveness. Paul Hoven told me that I could deduce trends and scenarios "weeks and months ahead of the analysts."

Most significantly, because of the U.N. sanctions and the resulting isolation of my countries, I was almost unique in having those contacts. The pariah status of Libya and Iraq throughout the 1990s stymied other approaches routinely used to outreach less controversial embassies. U.S. and British intelligence couldn't get to Libyan or Iraqi diplomats—except through me. So we needed each other. It was a symbiotic relationship.

For obvious reasons, therefore, my handlers would not have wanted me, the Asset, to stop functioning in my normal sphere of public activities. Put another way, the pursuit of my specialty work—my activism against war and sanctions— was recognized as necessary to build those difficult relationships.

Incidentally, during the Clinton Administration, a State Department official once observed in private conversation that they had an extra design in using me: They were showing these authoritarian governments, most cleverly, that in a democracy, activists who oppose the government in one topic can be recruited as allies on other issues. Opposition in one area does not render an activist an enemy on all things. That's the greatness of democracy. We respect each other, and we disagree with each other. And still we can work together.

My activism was most genuine, however. I campaigned passionately against sanctions at the United Nations and in the Halls of Congress for years. I considered it morally disgraceful that the United States would inflict such misery on the Iraqi people, particularly. I grieved for Iraqi mothers who struggled to feed their children, and Iraqi teachers who despaired of books and pencils to educate their students; and doctors facing empty medical cupboards when suffering people begged for pain killers or heart medication or oxygen canisters to breathe.

Those peoples were my motivation. Anything that I could contribute to help lift those wretched sanctions, I would gladly do. If my contribution was to act as a back channel to Baghdad, for the purpose of supporting counter-terrorism and non violence, then I would dedicate myself wholeheartedly to the task. At least on that one topic, I would try to make a difference.

And so I was never quiet about my beliefs. On the contrary, I was outspoken in my criticism. I could get "into the room" with Iraqi diplomats. And I could get "into the room" with American Intelligence. And I never stayed silent in the presence of either group. I lobbied Iraq and Libya to support non-violence in all forms, including anti-terrorism and weapons disarmament. By turn, I lobbied Congress and U.S. Intelligence to oppose sanctions and military aggression, even short bombing raids. I beseeched Ambassadors on the United Nations Security Council to wake up to the misery of sanctions destroying Iraqi society. I warned embassies that their actions undermined the integrity of the U.N.'s humanitarian mission on all fronts, which should be to support diplomacy and engagement, supply medical and social services to needy peoples, and build up infrastructure that promotes self sufficiency and economic development.

While my outspoken activism evidently frustrated officials at the Justice Department, U.S. Intelligence expected me to continue opposing U.S. policy while visiting the Iraqi Embassy or the Libya House. The authenticity of my activism was paramount for maintaining the strength of my contacts. Otherwise my whole outreach would have collapsed. Only somebody on the outside, who does not understand how Intelligence works, would question the efficacy of those actions. Those should be called "Intelligence Dummies." Sure as heck, they have no understanding of the difficulties of engagement.

Oh yes, we understood each other very well. If the CIA had demanded that I make a choice, I would have chosen my activism first. We would have said our good byes, for I would never give up my values. And yet the strength of my sincerity and my unshakable devotion to my causes made the rest of my work possible. In turn, I enjoyed an extraordinary opportunity to contribute to the causes I loved most. That was my motivation for participating.

The Justice Department should not have worried. Oversight of my activities was always intense. I had two handlers, Paul Hoven and Dr. Fuisz. So it makes sense that I had twice the number of debriefings. Typically, Dr. Fuisz and I met every 10 days until the Lockerbie Trial in 2000. At that point, our visits increased to weekly meetings. By

2001, during back channel talks with Baghdad on resuming the weapons inspections, Dr. Fuisz and I spoke on the phone every single work day, in addition to our weekly meetings.

My relationship with Paul Hoven was doubly intense. From the start in 1993, Hoven and I met at least once a week, more frequently during a crisis.

The question was, could I prove it? The answer was yes.

Crucial for my future legal defense, a group of heavy-hitter Republican Congressional staffers gathered socially every Thursday evening at the old Hunan Restaurant on the Senate side of Capitol Hill.[83] The Hunan served alcohol, though Hoven and I never drank. The restaurant was pitch black, and the crystal shrimp with walnuts was delicious. That made everybody happy, while this cabal of Congressional staffers talked policy and plotted conspiracies. That's where Hoven and I caught up, whispering in one of the dark corners.

The Chief of Staff for Senator Kit Bond from Missouri used to come. Legislative staff for Senator Chuck Grassley would be seated at the long table in the pitch black room. Pat Wait, Chief of Staff for GOP Rep. Helen Bentley was a regular fixture, as was Kelly O'Meara, Chief of Staff for GOP Rep. Andrew Forbes. Nobody in this crowd could be called a light weight. Mixed in would be top White House journalists like Jerry Seper from the Washington Times. And Hoven and me.

Occasionally other spooky types would show up at the Hunan, as well.

As the token progressive Democrat— on the opposite end of the ideological spectrum on all issues—my presence baffled these hard leaning conservatives. But the dark corners of the restaurant gave Paul and me a safe place to retreat for private conversations about Libya and Iraq. During crises or periods of intensive action on our projects, Hoven and I would meet a second time at our homes, as well.

My witness list would not be boring, for sure. At trial, some of these folks could expect subpoenas. They would be compelled to acknowledge that Paul Hoven and I forged a tightly bonded relationship for almost 9 years that was publicly observed. It's doubtful they understood the full nature of our work. It was clandestine, after all. But they could definitely confirm that Hoven and I had done it together. That would be the crucial admission, which accounts for why Hoven and I chose the Hunan for our meetings in the first place. We wanted high level witnesses to observe our engagements, in case anything should happen to either one of us.

To put that in context, between 1993 and 2002 I met approximately 700 to 800 times with both Hoven and Dr. Fuisz.

That process of debriefings safeguarded me as an Asset. Debriefings guarantee full disclosure, oversight and prompt feedback. For those good reasons, Assets are scrutinized at all times. Nobody has to worry that an American citizen would be wheeling and dealing with Libya or Iraq for a decade without somebody paying attention. That would never happen. In my experience, it would be impossible.

After my indictment, I was confident the candor of my disclosures would save me from prison. Nobody could claim ignorance of my activities. Nothing had been concealed. For example, the Justice Department indicted me for taking a trip to Baghdad in March, 2002. As it turns out, my invitation to Baghdad as a guest of Iraq's Foreign Ministry had been reported to Andy Card (and copied to Dr. Fuisz) in a letter dated March 1, 2001—one year before the trip occurred.[84] I offered to delay the trip or reject the invitation outright, if so instructed. I promised to meet any official to discuss the trip. That letter to Andy Card was one of 11 progress reports to the White House and CIA, describing the success of our back channel talks to resume weapons inspections.[85] My commitment to full disclosure was reliable at all times.

Other individuals—such as Jesse Jackson, Scott Ritter and ex-Chess Champion, Bobby Fischer, did receive warnings not to travel to Iraq or Yugoslavia. By contrast, U.S. Intelligence chose not to warn me off my travel plans. I interpreted that as a deliberate and informed decision on their part. Given the length of my experience as an Asset, I understood the complexity of logic in their response, and the advantage they expected to gain from my covert adventure. At that moment, we were making excellent progress on behalf of the 9/11 investigation and securing Iraq's commitment to maximum transparency in the weapons inspection process.[86] All aspects of our project carried great value to the U.S. and its allies in Europe and the Middle East. At this stage, I don't think the majority of rank and file U.S. intelligence had insight to the secret war agenda of the Bush Administration. For certain, they did not confide in me.

There was another reason. By the nature of the work, an Asset always seeks to maintain and expand that circle of contacts, in order to broaden the scope of access. A handler would be loath to warn off an Asset from expanding those contacts. The Asset gains value precisely because of the ability to interact with difficult sources, and create fresh opportunities for action and dialogue.

That's why Andy Card never discouraged my meetings at the Iraqi Embassy or the Libya House, and why I believe I was never told to cancel my trip to Baghdad. Although secretly the White House intended to pursue a totally different course of action than what I offered, policymakers needed to know what Iraqi officials were thinking and planning. They needed my raw intelligence. My conversations with Iraqi officials gave insight to Iraq's intentions towards the world community. For different reasons perhaps, both sides needed to exploit my back-channel. And I agreed to be exploited.

Whether we liked each others' politics or not, this needed to get done. And it had to get done right. It was really that simple. And I had a strong track record of success.

You need only look at Libya today to know that back-channel dialogue succeeded admirably, in fact.

Today Libya has fully reformed, having renounced its sanctuary for terrorists and development of WMDs—my two favorite causes as an Anti-War Asset. That was not the situation in May 1995, when I first approached Libyan diplomats. My first meetings at the Libya House occurred at a time when Tripoli held pariah status in the international community. The FBI snatched anybody who walked into the Libya House even once, and sat them down for a serious conversation.

They did not try to stop me.

Why? Because Assets can be extremely difficult to replace—especially with regards to countries like Iraq and Libya. Nobody else could step in, particularly in those years.

And yet it was incredibly shrewd of American Intelligence to use me. Because of my anti-war and anti-sanctions activism, I could establish a rapport with individuals that they could not otherwise get close to, inside nations with no official relationship to the United States. Most unusually, Arab diplomats respected the motivations for my engagement—which were absolutely sincere on my part. They welcomed me as a guest to their embassy. I opposed acts of violence, not people or culture or religious teachings. Because of my genuine opposition to violence on all sides, they recognized that I opposed military aggression by the United States with the same passion that I supported anti-terrorism policy. As such, I could engage in discussions that would ordinarily be off limits.

For those who would criticize me for leveraging my anti-war activism towards such efforts, consider this:

I acquired all of my success without wiretaps, water boarding or warrantless searches. I never engaged in rendition, kidnapping men off the streets of one country and transporting them to secret prisons for brutal interrogations. I never seduced young jihadis to plot bombings, so that I could arrest them and build a reputation for myself.

Quite the opposite, I applied myself to old-fashioned dialogue and diplomacy. Long before anti-terrorism was fashionable in Washington, I opened a back-channel with Middle Eastern countries that could contribute something important to counter terrorism policy. I worked to support values of non-violence that were clearly stated upfront to all parties, and fully understood. I worked to get difficult problems unstuck. I never solicited media attention for my successes. My satisfaction came from working to achieve my values, not from a need for personal celebrity.

For all those reasons, it is a ghastly twist of fate that my Asset work achieved notoriety—but not public respect. Because in fact I accomplished a great part of what America's leaders and the American people hail as your highest priorities. The global community's greatest good was served. My efforts protected U.S. security and Middle Eastern security, and laid a foundation for a wider scale of cooperation in multiple sectors.

And you know what? My back channel dialogue worked.

Time would show that the Arabs had much greater respect for my participation, and vastly more incentive to cooperate, because they recognized the sincerity of my opposition to violence in all directions. Arab governments responded enthusiastically to the consistency of my beliefs. For my part, I never betrayed my original values. On the contrary, through this work, I found a practical way of expressing my beliefs and working to achieve them.

Dialogue didn't mean the U.S. had gone soft on Iraq, either. For sure Dr. Fuisz and Hoven did not give a damn about the immorality of sanctions or U.S. militarism. Nobody had to worry that they would go soft on Saddam. They were warriors, not sentimentalists. They wanted to leverage access from my activism to develop high-level contacts inside these embassies, because they understood that Iraq and Libya would always have the best intelligence on terrorist activity in the Middle East. And the U.S. needed to capture that intelligence.

It was simple logic. They could not afford to blind their sight because of hostilities with Baghdad or Tripoli. They needed the Lockerbie Trial and the weapons inspections. I was the one who lobbied for lifting sanctions in order to reward cooperation. But it was really a Catch 22. If Iraq or Libya had refused to cooperate, that would have created another justification for holding sanctions in place. So in a sense, my back channel created a pressure valve.

Strikingly, however, my handlers and I discovered that we shared a value system in support of non-violence, as well. And I was far more desirable as an Asset than weapons traders or international drug lords, who are the most common types of Assets. As one would expect, weapons traders play all sides of a conflict, and typically only reveal intelligence that would harm their competitors. Likewise, drug lords provide high value intelligence or quotas for drug busts, in order to shield their own cartels.

Those sorts of Assets are shady and duplicitous, frequently engaging in the very same illicit activities which Assets strive to expose. Those sorts of Assets limit Intelligence to whatever fits their group agenda. They don't deliver reports straight up. They fudge it. They play with it. They redact what isn't helpful to their cause.

I was infinitely more reliable. Some of the spooks might have strongly disagreed with my politics. But they understood from my platform that I would never incite violence. And I would discourage others from doing so.

I wasn't half bad, after all.

Over time, my successful engagement with Libya and Iraq would prove definitively that my style of approach to Arab diplomats achieved many worthy results.

I recall my visits to the Iraqi Embassy in New York with tragic clarity.

The United Nations Mission of Iraq resided in a gorgeous old brownstone on the Upper East-side of Manhattan, half a block from Central Park and a brief walk to the Metropolitan Museum of Art on Fifth Avenue.

Five video surveillance cameras marked the entry door and inner foyer. During crises with the United States, an American security guard would be posted in front of the building. I would get waived inside.

Many times I dropped everything in my private life to visit the Iraqi Embassy in New York during flare ups in hostilities. I aspired to be a source of calm, a counter-weight to tensions and belligerent threats that would ratchet up the stakes inside Iraq. I did not always succeed, but at least I earned my reputation as a peace activist honestly. I saw for myself that even one small voice urging restraint can make a difference. Kindness and dignity matter.

Ah, but is it "grandiose" to contribute to peace efforts? Perhaps. But nothing can change the fact that I did so. I worked very hard for this. I dedicated almost a decade of my life to it.

Walking into the Iraqi Embassy in Manhattan, one would be struck by a sense of worn elegance, tattered on the edges, but proud and timeless nonetheless. Beautiful plaster crown molding tipped the ceilings over elegant honey wood floors, slightly scuffed. A marble fireplace on the main floor and, for awhile, a large chandelier drenched with crystal prisms remarked on better days, when the Embassy was alive with high profile guests seeking audience with the Ambassador to discuss corporate investments and cultural missions to Baghdad.

Most afternoons, the embassy was quiet. When I would arrive, the diplomat on guard would bring me cups of sweet Iraqi tea, while my diplomatic contact got summoned to the embassy. In those rooms, conversing with diplomats, I saw endurance and fortitude such that nobody who actually spoke with those men would question their integrity. These were honorable and good people. Even those who called Iraq an enemy would have to respect them. They were not war-mongers. They were devoted to easing the suffering of Iraqi children under sanctions. I admired them greatly, because they preserved that integrity in the face of the most grueling ostracism and pariah status inflicted by their host country, the United States.

Admittedly, I have a broader perspective of Saddam Hussein than other Americans. I saw Saddam as a political creature of the Middle East, just like Hafez al Assad, Syria's former President for Life, and Hosni Mubarak, President for Life of Egypt, or any of the Emirs and Princes ruling over Kuwait or Saudi Arabia. The United Nations is loaded with dictatorships in Africa and Asia. It's the people who must be protected. For its part, Iraq was more progressive and secular than most Arab countries. Their people shared western values, making conversation easy.

Just three Assets covered the Iraqi Embassy in New York before the War. I never met the other two until all of us got indicted as "unregistered Iraqi Agents" in "conspiracy with the Iraqi Intelligence Service."[87]

The United States did not need us anymore. We had served our purpose and could be discarded. Worst yet, we were up to our eyeballs in direct contact with "inconvenient truths" that contradicted official U.S. policy. Our voices would have been a major embarrassment to the false story Congress was selling to the public. So they took us out, though they had been lucky to enjoy our service at all. Notoriously, under Saddam Hussein's government, the CIA could "count the number of agents inside Iraq on one hand."[88] Saddam killed them all as traitors as quickly as he identified them. And he tortured the hell out of them first.

It helps explain the saying that "Assets have no future. Only a bullet."

Foolishly, I never thought that axiom applied to me. Never would I have anticipated the insulting rhetoric by Republicans on Capitol Hill, not after all I had done against terrorism. I am fiercely proud to this day of the work that we accomplished.

I considered it a tremendous privilege and challenge.

Above all, Asset work provides a unique opportunity to roll up your sleeves and dig into hard problems in the international community. An Asset participates directly and immediately in changing the dynamics of the conflict. "Think tanks" abound in Washington. They only talk about issues and problems. Asset work gets you into the room where the problems are hammered into solutions. If you really believe in a cause, it's a chance to make some crucial difference—or to beat your head against the wall trying. It's creative and proactive—the enemy of passivity and inertia. It's "doing," not wringing your hands in grief.

You don't like the situation. Change it.

When you're an Asset, you can.

Where then do misperceptions about "Double Agents" come from?

Those misperceptions are surprisingly common: Very simply, when one Agency captures an Asset—almost nobody in other Agencies knows who they are. Or what they're doing. Or that their work is being closely watched. They don't know about the Operation. They can't identify who's running it. And the Asset doesn't know all the facts either, which can exacerbate the confusion. So if confronted, the Asset might give unexpected answers, which makes other Agencies—or factions inside the same agency—very nervous.

Other foreign Intelligence agencies likewise don't know what it's all for. They only observe that some individual has initiated contacts with some awfully extraordinary groups of people. That's all they see. *And they are paying attention.*

In my situation dealing with Iraq and Libya, you'd better believe those other Intelligence factions steadily reported the fact of my meetings to their higher ups—including foreign intelligence services. They would have been negligent not to. Sometimes they might have been told to look the other way. Or they might have received heated instructions to "get me." These groups are so disparate and unconnected to one another that one faction could flag a series of contacts as potentially threatening, while another team or faction was aggressively pushing to maintain those same projects. Because they fight over control of assets and budgets and staffing, one agency—or faction within the agency—might refuse to disclose an operation. Another faction might then attack the asset. It happens all the time. It's the peril of Asset work.

When it came to the Lockerbie negotiations, certain factors aggravated the hardships, because there was outright hostility to the Trial in some quarters. Factions played against each other fiercely. Defense Intelligence championed the Lockerbie Trial. Parts of the CIA feared it. As the Asset who started the talks, I got caught in the cross-fire. Even though the U.S. government categorized the Lockerbie Trial as a formal policy goal, I was bitterly harassed.

I was also heavily protected. Paul Hoven stayed over night at my house with a gun a few times during the Lockerbie talks, when unfriendly folk would come to Washington. (Except I don't think he slept.) By contrast, there were no threats when our team started back channel talks with Iraq on resuming the weapons inspections—just heavy tracking, especially after 9/11. Ironically, as long as they kept showing up, I felt safe. I was reporting, and they were responding.

But I cannot stress enough that it would be anathema to the whole system of intelligence gathering to discourage Assets from maintaining contacts within the target circle. If one agency in the Intelligence Community gets into the habit of burning assets used by other factions or agencies, the entire process of intelligence gathering would be defeated. It would break down irreparably. It would guarantee the destruction of U.S. Intelligence.

There were other drawbacks that I would come to recognize later on. By then I had become so engrossed in this life that it would have been impossible to change my destiny.

Truthfully though, I would never have wanted to.

Iraq's Collision With Fate: Why 9/11 Had to Happen

I get asked all the time why Washington allowed the 9/11 attack to happen. Because that's what they did. They allowed it to happen. 9/11 was the outcome of a shadow policy of "deliberate avoidance." Senior officials got warned over and over what was coming by numerous, highly knowledgeable sources. The government very deftly resisted appeals to coordinate a preemptive response between agencies, which would have made it possible to acquire more "actionable" intelligence to block the attack. (That's "nuts and bolts" intelligence.)

In the aftermath, it's obvious that 9/11 provided the vehicle for War with Iraq. Everyone can see that.

But very little has been offered to explain why.

What obstacles faced Washington before 9/11 that forced the Pro-War Camp to take such drastic measures to topple global opposition to War with Iraq?

Why did the Bush Administration consider a "Pearl Harbor Day" necessary to achieve its secret objectives in Baghdad? That "why" has been a black hole in the debate. And it's much more than a rhetorical question. There's substantial history of parallel events involving Iraq in the twelve to eighteen months leading up to 9/11 that has never been discussed at all in this context.

In my opinion, understanding that parallel history inside Iraq is critical to understanding what happened to the United States on that tragic date.

My Asset work and my activism at the U.N. level made me much more attuned to those undercurrents. Several factors playing out in the international community came very close to swamping the White House agenda altogether. Those events provided the enticement for Republican leaders before the 9/11 strike.

It was all right there below radar. Americans proceeding blissfully in their lives had no idea what was coming: It was peace.

Flagging International Support for Sanctions

When President-Elect George W. Bush swore the oath of office on January 20, 2001 his new Administration faced a serious problem: Peace was breaking out all over the world—much of it focused on Iraq. Emissaries from around the globe traveled to Baghdad, openly expressing sympathy for Iraq's plight under U.N. sanctions and encouraging Baghdad to return to the fold. Trade emissaries looked forward to restoring economic ties with Iraq. They had begun to negotiate reconstruction contracts in all economic sectors, which would be implemented as soon as sanctions could be lifted. The European Union, Russia, China, the Arab League and the Non-Aligned Movement all agitated for a major policy shift on Iraq. Baghdad moved closer to ending the hated U.N. Sanctions every day.

By this time, Iraq had suffered 11 years under brutal sanctions that blocked the free-flow import of food, medicine and equipment necessary for factory production in every sector. The international community could tolerate it no longer. International support for sanctions was rapidly collapsing in the face of Iraq's great misery.

Health and medical services deteriorated the most severely. Most of the international community has forgotten that before sanctions, Iraq performed the second heart transplant in the world, and boasted some of the finest hospitals and medical staffs on par with the United States and Europe.

Under sanctions, Iraq could not purchase chemotherapy drugs or insulin or digitalis for heart conditions outside of the "oil for food" program. Iraqi health officials could not purchase x-ray machines or oxygen canisters for hospitals. A visiting U.S. Congressional delegation reported in 2000 that hospitals lacked incubators for new born babies or air conditioning for seriously ill patients in the desert climate.[89]

On my trip to Baghdad in March 2002, three hospitals threw back their supply doors in random floor inspections to prove that doctors had almost no prescription drugs of any kind on site—nor any pain killers for hospitalized patients, not even aspirin. Oxygen canisters were in such short supply that patients occupying adjoining hospital rooms had to hand them back and forth five to ten minutes at a time. When the canisters would run out of oxygen, hospital patients would receive no breathing assistance at all. Not surprisingly, many hospital patients died for lack of life support.

This policy of cutting off Iraq from all outside trade was implemented by the United Nations, at the demand of the United States and Britain. The U.N. "oil for food" program allowed Baghdad to sell $5.26 billion worth of crude oil every 6 months with which to buy food, medicine and all other supplies necessary to run a country of 22 million people. On a per capita basis, the "oil for food" program averaged $252 in humanitarian assistance for each Iraqi citizen.[90] However, Iraq relied on that allowance to bankroll every other part of its economy as well, including heavy equipment for its oil facilities, clean water treatment and sewage systems, electrical production, housing and food storage.

On the high end, Iraq was restricted to $600 million worth of oil parts and equipment every six months to staunch the rapid deterioration of its oil industry after 11 years of deprivation. Inevitably those monies cut into the allocation available for food and medical supplies. It proved impossible for Iraq to increase its oil output, nonetheless, because the destruction of its pipeline and pump structures was too far advanced.

Worse still, Iraq received substantially less than the $5.26 billion allotment, because both the United States and Britain made a practice of putting holds on relief contracts, and typically froze about $1.5 billion worth of equipment and replacement parts in all sectors.[91] That trend produced dire consequences for long term repairs to Baghdad's electrical grid, water and sanitation systems, and agriculture, something that would prove deeply problematic for all of Iraq's future governance.

Independent of that U.N "oil for food" program, the Iraqi people had no access to their own national wealth and natural resources, most notably oil. The U.N. bureaucracy controlled it all.

Once some of the best educated peoples in the Middle East, under sanctions Iraqis could not purchase pencils or desks or books for school children. Every Iraqi school child was allocated just 6 pencils, 2 erasers, 1 pencil sharpener and 6 exercise books that had to last the entire school year.[92] Humanitarian aid workers opined that sanctions wiped out literacy in a single generation. Except for an elite minority, the "sanctions generation" would enter adulthood with only the minimum educational requirements necessary to participate in rebuilding their country.

In context, by 2003, 18 year old males in Iraq had been living under sanctions deprivation since they were 5 years old. With dangerously few personal resources to recommend the future, or provide a way for them to participate in it, it's not surprising that so many young Iraqi men give their muscle and backbone to the insurgency movement to oust the Occupation. They have nothing else to look forward to.

It's unfathomable for consumer-driven Americans and Europeans to comprehend the society that the United Nations created in Iraq under the trade embargo: Iraq was prohibited from importing any sort of consumer good at all—unless they could afford to buy it on the black market. Translated to daily life, Iraqis could not buy cars to drive. Or computers. Or dishwashers. Or washing machines. Or dishes and silverware. Sanctions prohibited the imports of chairs, couches, tables and light fixtures; television sets and stereos; stoves, refrigerators and microwave ovens, and every other conceivable item for daily use. The United Nations seized all of Iraq's oil wealth, paying six figure salaries to bureaucrats in New York and Geneva, who managed "humanitarian" programs and weapons inspections to verify Iraq's disarmament. Central economic planning by the United Nations created the sort of deprivation expected in the poorest third world countries, not in a nation sitting on the world's second richest oil reserve.

At the start of the Gulf War in August, 1990, three Iraqi dinar bought $1 U.S. dollars. By the time of President Bush's inauguration, the value of the dinar had collapsed to a rate of 2,000 dinar to every $1 U.S. dollar.

To put that in context of family income, a typical Iraqi government pension ran 250 dinars a month[93]—the equivalent of 12 U.S. cents. On that income, a middle class Iraqi family made do with a piece of bread and a cup of tea at the noon meal followed by rice for dinner.[94] Poor families in Iraq fared infinitely worse, forced to choose which child to feed each day, because government rations got exhausted by mid-month, leaving them with nothing to eat at all. Malnutrition reached staggering levels.

By the end of sanctions, in 2003, 1.7 million Iraqis had died from starvation and lack of medicine, counting only children under the age of 5 and adults over the age of 60.[95]

The deaths of children age 6 and over, and adults age 59 and under, were excluded from mortality statistics on sanctions-related deaths. Otherwise the death toll would have climbed dramatically higher.[96]

As it was, the World Health Organization reported that 500,000 children had died by the end of 1996, raising alarms that the U.N. sanctions had become a policy of "mass death." [97] The United Nations Children's Fund (UNICEF) acknowledged that in state-controlled areas of Iraq, the mortality rate of children under the age of 5 had more than doubled in 10 years.[98]

Officially, UNICEF estimated that between 5,000 and 7,000 children under age 5 died each month.[99] However, the Iraqi Health Ministry published statistics averaging 11,000 dead each month in 2000, much higher than the United Nations wanted to acknowledge.[100] The Iraqi Health Ministry documented 8,182 child deaths from diarrhea, pneumonia and malnutrition in January, 2000 alone, compared with just 389 deaths in the same month of 1989, the year before the trade embargo went into effect.[101]

Under the guise of demanding Iraq's disarmament, the United Nations had succeeded in killing more Iraqi people with its sanctions policy than all the nuclear, chemical and biological weapons of mass destruction ever used in history, combined, according to the prestigious Foreign Affairs Journal. [102]

Internationally, the Iraqi sanctions acquired a harsh reputation as a policy of genocide.

On top of that, only 41% of Iraq's population had access to clean water, and 83 % of Iraqi schools required substantial repairs.[103]

The "oil for food" program was such a failure that top bureaucrats at the United Nations were ashamed to run it. A year before President Bush's inauguration, the senior humanitarian coordinator for the U.N., Hans von Sponeck of Germany, tendered his resignation from the "oil for food" program, calling the Iraqi sanctions "a true human tragedy that needs to be ended."[104]

"The very title that I hold as a humanitarian coordinator suggests that I cannot be silent over that which we see here ourselves," Von Sponeck said.

Jutta Burghardt, head of the U.N. World Food Program in Iraq, joined him in resigning so as to protest the depth of human misery created by their own relief programs.

"How long the civilian population, which is totally innocent on all this, should be punished for something they have never done?" Von Sponeck posed a rhetorical question that echoed through embassy chambers at the United Nations.[105]

That criticism displeased the U.S. and Britain. But Von Sponeck's despair echoed Dennis Halliday, the first humanitarian coordinator of the "oil for food" program, who likewise resigned from a 34 year career at the U.N. in September 1998 after reaching the same conclusions.

Halliday called the sanctions "a totally bankrupt concept."[106]

"We are in the process of destroying an entire society. It's as simple and terrifying as that," the former assistant Secretary General to the United Nations warned in his resignation.

"The middle class and the professional classes, the very people who might change governance in Iraq, have been wiped out, and those that remain are struggling to stay alive and keep their families alive."

The severity of damage to the middle class and professional Iraqis qualified as a critical flaw in the sanctions policy design.

On the other side of the debate, some people have wondered how human rights activists, who champion democratic freedoms for all peoples, could oppose a policy tool like sanctions, which on the surface appears to undermine despotic governments. It's because we believe, passionately in fact, in the rights of all people to have input to government policy and to speak freely about government decision making, including the right to criticize the government. The rights of democracy are essential to what we do every day, and we want those rights for all people.

We oppose sanctions out of recognition that ordinary people have almost no power in those societies. It seems unfair to punish them for government activities and policies that they cannot possibly hope to change. Worst still, the extra burden of sanctions has the effect of crushing those people even further. All of their energies must shift to providing basic necessities for their families. There's nothing left to engage in community transformation or political reform movements. By necessity, their daily life must focus entirely on economic survival.

Sanctions defeat any hope of real political reforms.

Alas, the United Nations was caught in a macabre steel trap of its own design. Under its own resolution, sanctions could not be lifted until Iraq proved that it possessed no Weapons of Mass Destruction.

Iraq, in turn, cried that it had no weapons left to destroy—which the U.S./ British invasion verified as tragically accurate. The United Nations had already destroyed every weapon system in the country before its inspection teams pulled out of Iraq in 1998. Post-war assessments show that Iraq's weapons stocks had been eradicated by late 1996.

All those Iraqi people had suffered and died for nothing—1.7 million people died for a lie.

For Iraq's part, after the departure of weapons inspectors in December, 1998 Iraqi officials called the U.N.'s bluff and refused to let them back into the country. Where the U.N. expected contrition, they got scorn. Iraq resolved that any resumption of weapons inspections must stipulate a guarantee that once Baghdad demonstrated compliance with the inspections process, and proved the status of its disarmament, sanctions would be lifted. Inspections could not go on endlessly without producing evidence of weapons production, as before. Iraq would reject any sort of cooperation that would not achieve that goal.

There was some morality in Washington, if only a token for humanity. In the year before President Bush's inauguration, future Democratic presidential candidate Dennis

Kucinich teamed up with Democratic Whip David E. Bonior and Rep. John Conyers, soon to be chair of the House Judiciary Committee, to introduce a bill that would have permitted the export of food and medicine to Iraq. The bill had 70 co-sponsors in the House of Representatives.[107]

Chief sponsor, Rep. Bonior, called the sanctions "infanticide masquerading as policy." He swore that some members of Congress "refuse to close our eyes to the slaughter of innocents."

Alas, by and large, when President Bush swore the oath of office on January 20, 2001, the American people could have cared less about Iraq's suffering.

But the International Community was a different matter. In the months before 9/11, the international community was waking up to the misery it had manufactured through the United Nations' system of central economic planning, and the effect of handicapping political reforms for average Iraqi citizens. Ordinary people around the world had begun to realize that a horrible policy mistake was underway inside Iraq, and the United Nations had caused it. Pressure was rising in Europe, China and Russia to resolve their conflict with Baghdad. The International Community was sick to death of watching Iraq's misery from the sidelines.

After 10 long years of international passivity, in September, 2000 humanitarian groups around the world took bold and courageous action.

In a lesson straight out of the Berlin Air Lift, humanitarian groups from around the world mobilized to organize rescue flights into Baghdad International Airport, transporting activists, medical staff and urgently needed medical supplies to the Iraqi people.

Notably, the Germans and the Russians came first, memorializing that great lesson of breaking the blockade on East Berlin during the Cold War. The French and the Italians seized the example—and finally Jordan sent a plane carrying ministers, doctors and medicines to Baghdad.

It was the first Arab flight to Iraq in 10 years. Yemen and Morocco took heart from Jordan's leadership and flew into Baghdad, too. The flights sparked fierce debate on the U.N. Security Council, with France insisting that planes only needed to notify the UN bureaucracy of their flight plans. France and Russia pointed out that no flight ban was contained in the U.N. sanctions resolutions. The flight ban had been self-imposed, and was thus righteously rejected.

Baghdad International Airport had been designed and built by a French architectural company in 1982 to handle 7.5 million passengers annually. The airport had been closed since the outbreak of the Gulf War on the night of January 16, 1991. It reopened on August 15, 2000. [108]As champions of human dignity mobilized internationally and refused to bow to the crude absurdity of the U.N. sanctions any longer, the emptiness of moral authority of the sanctions exploded into the open.

When I saw the humanitarian airlifts organized by activist groups all over the world, I knew the sanctions would fall.

Far more importantly, my contacts in American Intelligence recognized it too. Truly those courageous pilots flying those medical airlifts changed the whole dynamic of peace. By their actions, they showed that the world could not stomach this cruelty against the Iraqi people any longer. Sanctions would have to go.

Parts of the United Nations Community had started to reach the same conclusions. In August, 2000 the U.N. Sub Commission on Human Rights issued a report by Belgian law professor, Marc Bossuyt declaring that sanctions were "unequivocally illegal."[109]

After 10 years enforcing sanctions, the United Nations woke up to recall that the 1949 Geneva Conventions prohibits the collective punishment of civilians, and "expressly prohibits the starving of civilian populations and the destruction of what is indispensable to their survival." After a decade of denial, the UN Human Rights body finally admitted that "All economic activities are seriously affected (by sanctions in Iraq), particularly in the areas of drinking water supplies, electricity and agriculture."[110]

The UN report concluded "that sanctions have led to a disaster in Iraq comparable to the worst catastrophes of the past decades."

Finally, sanctions had been judged a massive policy failure.

If Europe was a new convert to anti-sanctions philosophy, sentiments among the Arab peoples had always championed Iraq's cause. The Arab Street discovered its collective voice in opposition to U.N. sanctions amid the continuous U.S. bombings of Iraqi cities—20,000 air sorties by the close of the Clinton Administration. Arab fundamentalists had rallied to Iraq's cause for years in a boiling froth of rage over the deaths of innocents in Baghdad. At first Arab governments smirked over the take down of Saddam, glad for America's wrath to point at other leaderships every bit as totalitarian as their own. But the Arab Street was alive with the fires of retribution.

After 10 years, Arab governments finally began to heed the street chants to defend the Iraqi people from the United Nations' cruelty. By the close of the Clinton Administration, Arab governments usually friendly to Washington issued blistering criticism of sanctions policy. Qatar called for Gulf Nations to normalize relations with Iraq and lift the sanctions. Oman, Bahrain and the United Arab Emirates followed Qatar's example, and took steps to reactivate their diplomatic ties with Baghdad.

The United States faced one more problem: A chilling prophecy out in the deserts of Afghanistan was coming to fruition. In late December, 1998, an intrepid journalist for TIME Magazine,[111] Rahmullah Yusufzai had trekked out to the secret encampment hiding a young jihadi named Osama bin Laden. Bin Laden emerged from his caves to wax eloquent praise on the masterminds of the terrorist bombings of the U.S. Embassies in Dar es Salaam and Nairobi, Kenya—and to claim credit for attacking targets inside the United States as early as 1993—encompassing the first attack on the World Trade Center and the Oklahoma City Bombing.

When Yusufzai asked what the U.S. should expect from him now, Bin Laden gave a chilling reply: "Any thief or criminal robber, who enters another country, in order to steal, should expect to be exposed to murder at any time. For the American forces to expect anything from me personally reflects a very narrow perception. Thousands of millions of Muslims are angry. The Americans should expect reactions from the Muslim world that are proportionate to the injustice they inflict."[112]

The Arab Street was ready to unleash its impotent rage. Europe had awakened to the implications for Middle East volatility. The United States and Britain, however, clung to their shared superpower status as a false cloak of protection, convinced that no government, much less a small guerilla entity, could knock them off their pedestal of power and cultural elitism.

It was the final days of the Clinton Administration. The U.S. and Britain had become isolated on the U.N. Security Council. The world of nations collectively opposed any further aggression against the Iraqi people. Coming into power, newly elected President George Bush had no chance to peddle his game plan to oust Saddam Hussein. The mere suggestion of war with Iraq would have sparked outrage and gotten denounced forthwith as a "rogue action" without provocation.

An Era of Peace was breaking out over the world community. U.N. sanctions on Iraq rushed towards the end. Humanitarian activists braced to score a great victory. And a time bomb was ready to explode in the Arab Street.

The CIA was fully conscious of all these factors. It was the political reality that confronted them. They had to deal with it. They had a legitimate purpose, however, which was to guarantee that the United States would control the agenda for resolving the conflict with Iraq at all phases. They did not want to relinquish that power to their allies on the U.N. Security Council or other Arab governments. It was their job to hold power tightly in the hands of the United States.

Like it or not, that motivation was entirely rational from the standpoint of US intelligence. It was such a matter of political necessity that the Pro-War cabal could not ignore it, either.

Unhappily, Republican leaders would have to overcome the obstacle of peace, if they hoped to achieve their secret agenda of leading the international community to War in Iraq. And they would have to turn the whole world topsy turvy to get their chance.

As horrific as it was, 9/11 fit the bill.

CHAPTER 5:

IRAQ'S PEACE OVERTURES TO EUROPE AND THE UNITED STATES

In such a radically changing political climate, the CIA could not stay passive.

International loathing for the U.N. sanctions on Iraq had serious implications for U.S. policy. Simply put, the status quo had to change. With pressure building in the international community to force a change, the CIA recognized that it would have to adapt in order to retain control of the outcome in Iraq, and secure the most favorable benefits for Washington.

Warming relations between Iraq, Europe, Russia and Asia weren't the only "bad news" for Pro-War Republicans watching Iraq in the months before 9/11. Woefully for the War Camp, Iraq was actively campaigning for peace with all of its former allies. Baghdad engaged in a two-prong strategy to undermine whatever international support for sanctions remained. The Iraqi Government aggressively wooed foreign corporations to visit Baghdad, and publicly rewarded trade missions from Europe, Russia and Asia with highly lucrative reconstruction contracts, in any post-sanctions period.

That created a perplexing problem with regards to future oil rights in Iraq. U.S. demand for Iraqi oil contracts, and its desire for future exploration and development concessions had continued unabated throughout the decade of U.N. sanctions. Despite U.S. hostilities to Saddam's government, U.S. refineries proved to be Iraq's best customers from the latter 1990s onward, importing 750,000 barrels per day, or 9 percent of total U.S. imports.[113] Big U.S. oil corporations running the most Iraqi oil through their refineries included Chevron, Exxon-Mobil, Bayoil and Koch Petroleum.

If the U.S. was Iraq's most loyal customer, for obvious reasons it was not Iraq's favorite customer. Iraq made a practice of rewarding friends that opposed sanctions with major concessions for future oil exploration and development in any post-sanctions period. Among those allies, Russia stood out. Baghdad gave favored status to Russian shipping and trading firms, "taking large volumes of crude…. away from previous customers."[114]

Thus, as Russia confronted its own critical period of economic upheaval, it emerged as Iraq's largest trading partner, winning more than 40 percent of all contracts to export Iraqi oil under the "oil-for-food" program. The transfer of contracts to Russian oil traders was widely regarded as payback for Russia's refusal to allow the U.S. and Britain to revise sanctions in the Security Council, as opposed to ending them outright. At the same time, Russia's President Vladimir Putin declared a strong desire for close bilateral relations with Iraq.

Most significantly from the standpoint of U.S. intelligence, Iraq awarded a highly lucrative contract to LUKoil, Russia's premiere oil corporation. The 1997 LUKoil contract to develop the West Qurna field, expected to produce 600,000 barrels per day, was the largest deal signed by any international oil company in Iraq under Saddam's government.[115] Oil rights carried an estimated value of $20 billion for LUKoil, with 3 percent ownership by the Russian government.

Mega U.S. Oil Corporations shuddered in dismay when the LUKoil contract was announced. Even promises that U.S. corporations could compete to share second tier and third tier sub-contracts for development of the West Qurna field could not alter the blow that Russia's priority status was going to cause for their shareholders. It locked into place a structure for oil rights in Iraq that would seriously crimp the long term earning potential of corporations like Halliburton and Chevron Texaco that had been eyeing Iraq's oil potential after sanctions.

Contrary to Iraqi rhetoric in the European media, France, Russia and China weren't the only recipients of bounteous reconstruction contracts, however. A substantial offering was made covertly to the United States, too.

And the CIA was determined to drive a hard bargain.

As early as October 2000, Iraq signaled a desire to negotiate a "comprehensive resolution to its conflict with the United States that would be mutually beneficial to both parties." [116]

Central to those discussions, before back channel talks began, Iraq agreed in principle to accept the return of U.N. weapons inspectors. It was a ground-breaking shift in Baghdad's policy, a major break in the deadlock over Iraq's disarmament, and the CIA accepted the talks with that understanding in place. Notably, the offer occurred 18 months before Iraq's commitment was disclosed to the U.S. and international public.

To be fair, as of November and December 2000, Baghdad hoped to structure the new agreement in such a way as to prevent the belligerent and insulting behavior practiced by Richard Butler's teams before the 1998 pullout of the U.N. inspectors.[117] At the start of talks, Iraq wanted a statement of intent that U.N. inspection teams would behave with a modicum of respect for their host, without racial slurs against Arab culture or mockery of the suffering of Iraq's people, which was endemic to the previous inspections.

IRAQ'S PEACE OVERTURES TO EUROPE AND THE UNITED STATES

There was legitimate basis for Baghdad's concern. I overheard derogatory remarks about the Iraqi people myself in the United Nations cafeteria in New York, of all places. One such conversation between U.S. and British diplomats scorned the deaths of Iraqi children, and ended with laughter. So I know racial insults were fairly common. Iraq demanded that the UN teams should behave like professionals.

Above all, Iraq wanted to establish a mechanism for lifting the sanctions as compliance went forward, so that any new round of weapons inspections could not continue indefinitely, as before, without acknowledging substantial proof of Baghdad's cooperation and verification of disarmament.

Over and over, Iraqi diplomats fretted over how the U.S. would respond when they found no weapons of mass destruction. How could Iraq compel the United Nations to accept the evidence that there was nothing left to destroy? Once the U.N. teams found nothing, what would happen next? How could Iraq make sure the U.N. would follow through to end the sanctions?

There was so much despair over those questions among Iraqi diplomats, and so much distrust, that I knew in my heart no weapons would be found in Iraq. To lighten up the conversation, I would tease diplomats that Baghdad should buy some weapons from Iran (formerly Iraq's mortal enemy), and import them through Syria (another mortal enemy). When the weapons got to the Iraqi border, Iraqi officials could call a press conference and officially unveil them, with the announcement that Baghdad was turning them over to the United Nations, because weapons inspectors refused to go away empty handed. The Iraqis could say to the United Nations, "Now you have your weapons, go away! We have bought them especially for you. Leave us in peace!"

But it was actually a very serious problem in the structuring of sanctions policy. Sanctions presumed that at all times Iraq would have illegal weapons that should be turned over to the United Nations. Once Iraq stopped possessing weapons— and thus stopped turning them over to U.N. inspections teams— Baghdad would fall into a state of Non-Compliance, because it would no longer be providing the U.N. with weapons.

In a perverse twist, Iraq's inability to hand over weapons amounted to a violation of the sanctions. Nothing in sanctions policy established procedures for what to do after Iraqi weapons stocks had been eradicated. Because of the rigidity of the structure of sanctions policy, the U.N. bureaucracy could not adjust to that shift in reality. Suspiciously too, the oversight of Iraqi affairs had become a full scale bureaucracy inside the United Nations, with high profile jobs and six figure salaries in New York and Geneva. The bureaucracy had a competing purpose—to preserve its own existence. U.N. bureaucrats had every incentive to perpetuate sanctions indefinitely.

It's unforgivably obscene, if you consider the humanitarian purpose and ideology of the United Nations. But that's how it was done.

There was a second problem. Like all sanctions regimens, the nature of its rigidity eliminated any possibility of quid pro quo in talks. It forced an all or nothing solution, blocking intermediary steps that ordinarily would have been implemented to move out of deadlock. Thus, unhappily, the goal of resuming weapons inspections struck many diplomats as impossible. Iraq would have to forsake its national pride to comply. Meanwhile, the U.S. demanded exceedingly tough standards for access and transparency, which Iraq considered burdensome beyond the scope dictated by the United Nations. At the end of the day, very few world-class diplomats at the U.N. wanted to stake their reputations to resolve this headache for the international community.

Just like negotiations for the Lockerbie Trial, that meant the field was wide open for a third party back channel to kick start the process— if someone could be found who was not intimidated by impossible constraints and overwhelming obstacles, as the Iraqi weapons inspections issue was considered to be.

As it happened, this was just my cup of tea. All of this was familiar territory to me. I had already gone through it in back-channel negotiations for the Lockerbie Trial, which my team had started with Libya's diplomats. That was considered impossible, too, for all the same reasons. So I understood the expectations—and my limitations and boundaries. We would get this process unstuck with Iraq, and solidify a commitment to resume the weapons inspections. The preliminary agreement would then get handed back to the United Nations. U.N. legal staff would ratify the agreement in technical language and claim victory. Congress would pontificate. And we would watch our success from the sidelines. The key for us was to achieve an agreement that would be comprehensive and satisfactory to the U.S, before the United Nations got involved.

Straight off Lockerbie, I was eager to help, genuinely enthusiastic. I hated sanctions. I grieved for the suffering of the Iraqi people and lobbied hard against sanctions policy on Capitol Hill and at the United Nations. I was willing to assume the political risk. And I was fully committed to seeing it through to the end, with the great hope that the sanctions I despised finally would be lifted, and the brutal suffering of the Iraqi people would end.

And so I grabbed the opportunity with full heart. I never considered that I was selling out my values. I saw this as a unique and precious opportunity to resolve Iraq's humanitarian crisis once and for all. So I rolled up my sleeves and got to work. I swore to my CIA handler, Dr. Fuisz that anything the United States wanted from Iraq, I would make sure it got.

I was well-positioned to carry this project forward. As a long-time Asset, I had fairly unique access to Iraq's senior diplomats at the United Nations in New York. And I had all the right contacts inside the U.N. Security Council to help me, too.

Of all the diplomats at the United Nations whom I was privileged to meet, Dr. Saeed Hasan, Iraq's Ambassador to the U.N. stood out as the most courageous and highly moral individual that I encountered. Dr. Hasan was fully dedicated at all times to decision-making that would protect the future of Iraq's children.

Most importantly, as Iraq's Ambassador to the United Nations, Dr. Hasan recognized the scope of commitments that would be necessary for Baghdad to get out from under the sanctions. He accepted the personal risk of delivering that message to Saddam Hussein, at a time when our proposal to resume inspections was still highly controversial in Baghdad.[118] He understood the greater issue of disarmament for the West. Yet he was fiercely protective of Iraq's sovereignty. This solution to the sanctions quagmire was entirely possible because of Dr. Saeed Hasan. He broke the deadlock.

In October, 2000, when Iraq indicated it was ready to move forward to discuss a "comprehensive settlement on all outstanding issues," that offering was communicated from Dr. Hasan through my back channel to Dr. Fuisz and Hoven, and from them to the upper echelons of the CIA and other concerned parties in the Intelligence Community.

All agreed that after the November, 2000 Presidential Election, I could take up the weapons inspections with Ambassador Hasan at the United Nations. My role would be to persuade Iraq to accept the rigorous demands for compliance and transparency dictated by the United States. According to the CIA's conditions, I would have no part in determining what those technical standards should be. I would push Iraq to accept U.S. demands in all areas. I would not criticize U.S. demands publicly or in private conversation with Iraqi diplomats. My remarks would be limited to demanding that Iraq satisfy the United States before sanctions could be lifted. Most critically, my American contacts made clear that it would be a fixed price. There would be no haggling. The U.S. would define the terms. Iraq would have to agree "with no conditions," on all matters.

The CIA was hot for a public victory of forcing Iraq to accept the return of the weapons inspectors, according to the rigorous standards for transparency dictated by the United States.

Most critically, U.S. Intelligence wanted to show its European allies that it had stolen back control of the situation, at a time when international support for sanctions was rapidly collapsing. That would mark a huge success for the Americans. By usurping control of the agenda in Iraq and controlling covert talks on issues that would precede ending the sanctions, the CIA could play both sides: forcing Iraq to submit to verification of its disarmament, while preventing Baghdad from punishing U.S. corporations for Washington's decade of brutal support for the U.N. sanctions policy. The return of weapons inspectors to Baghdad remained paramount; but Iraq's wooing and sweetheart deals with France, China and Russia created a new imperative that U.S. Intelligence was determined to rebalance. The CIA would move heaven and earth to protect market access for U.S. corporations in any post-sanctions period.

And so, in November, 2000, while votes in Florida were still getting counted, I sat down with Iraq's Ambassador Dr. Hasan at the Ambassador's House to hold preliminary talks on resuming the weapons inspections.

The meetings in November and December, 2000 culminated in a letter to Vice President Elect Richard Cheney, dated December 20, 2000.

At this stage, the Presidential Election continued to be a cliff-hanger. No one had a clue whether the Democrats or Republicans would win the White House. The return of weapons inspectors to Iraq would be gift-wrapped for either of the two Presidential contenders, Vice President Albert Gore or Texas Governor George W. Bush, with no party favoritism in the outcome. By the Inauguration, the CIA expected to hand the new President the first foreign policy victory of his Administration, comparable to the release of the Iranian hostages from the U.S. Embassy in Tehran, as President Ronald Reagan was sworn into office. The new White House could tout a major foreign policy achievement from a problem left over by the outgoing Administration. It was designed to launch the next President onto a platform of muscular leadership on the world stage.[119]

All of my U.S. intelligence contacts expected gratitude from the new President. With those expectations, our back channel laid out a framework for required action by Iraq.

First and foremost, Iraq would have to accept the return of the U.N. weapons inspectors and guarantee maximum transparency to verify disarmament. In a short time, the demand would be amended, requiring Iraq to accept weapons inspections "with no conditions."

Secondly, Baghdad would be required to provide maximum cooperation with U.S. counter-terrorism goals on a number of ongoing projects.

Thirdly, Iraq would have to guarantee reconstruction contracts for U.S Corporations in any post-sanctions period. Our team sought guarantees that all U.S. Corporations engaged in non-military sales to Iraq before the first Gulf War would be authorized to reenter Baghdad and perform at the same level of market share as they had enjoyed prior to 1990. Oil rights were a major concern. Any comprehensive solution would require guarantees for U.S. corporations, including oil contracts, to be publicly declared and ratified to authenticate the understanding.

Does all that seem impossible? In fact, my efforts proved far more successful than currently understood. The CIA had floated these conditions to the Iraqis before agreeing to the talks. Iraq had already issued a general affirmative response before the meetings started.[120] All sides expected to reach a major settlement in a very few weeks.

Notably, Iraq's Ambassador, Dr. Hasan swore that "the conversation would be short, because Baghdad was fully committed to complying with all current U.S. demands." It would take "only a couple of weeks to hammer out the details, and no longer," he assured the U.S. in a letter to Vice President-elect Richard Cheney, dated December 20, 2000.[121] On behalf of the Iraqi government, Ambassador Hasan declared that he was authorized to say that Baghdad would welcome "covert or non-covert talks with any U.S. official in New York or anywhere in the world."

Infamously, newly appointed Secretary of State Colin Powell jumped on the Iraqi promise of quick agreement on "all current U.S. demands," telling Congress that any talks on weapons inspections "would be a short conversation." In doing so, Secretary Powell was paraphrasing the Iraqi Ambassador.

There was one great surprise for all of us. Newly elected President Bush appointed Andrew Card, my second cousin on my father's side, to serve as White House Chief of Staff. Critically, it must be understood that the decision to go forward with covert back channel talks had been reached more than two months before Card's appointment. Planning for the talks and my first two meetings with Dr. Hasan occurred several weeks before Card's appointment was announced. I cannot underscore sufficiently that back channel talks never hinged on my cousin's promotion.

It was sheer fate that all correspondence detailing the progress of talks to resume the weapons inspections got addressed to Andy Card. In a practical sense, he filled the role of a "picture frame" for correspondence intended for the CIA, the White House and national security apparatus. That satisfied one of Iraq's chief concerns that back channel talks should be addressed to policymakers—not the Intelligence Community. However, all correspondence addressed to Card, detailing progress on the talks, was received by both parts of the U.S. government. By the end of 2001, that portfolio totaled 11 letters to Andrew Card, jointly received by the CIA.

The stage was set for victory.

To the surprise of all, President Bush had other plans. Shortly after his Inauguration, on February 16, 2001 he ordered the bombing of Baghdad.

And instead of a "short conversation" and "fast resolution," preliminary talks on resuming the weapons inspections dragged on until February, 2002, when our side was sufficiently satisfied with Iraq's offering to hand over the matter to the United Nations.

At this stage, President Bush's war agenda remained hidden from the American public and significant parts of the Intelligence Community. Assets like me had no comprehension of the depths of President Bush's determination to lead the world into War with Iraq.

And so, despite the February bombing, talks to resume the weapons inspections continued with senior Iraqi diplomats, albeit more slowly than expected. Dr. Hasan ended his tenure as Iraq's Ambassador to the United Nations and returned to Baghdad to take up the post of Deputy Foreign Minister of Iraq. No matter, I was assured that Iraq's new Foreign Minister, Naji Sabri, approved of the dialogue and was receiving communications about all meetings in Baghdad. My talks continued with other senior diplomats, including Salih Mahmoud, Saad Abdul Rahmon and Abdul Rahmon Mudhian, who had been assigned by Baghdad to handle this issue.

At no time did Andy Card suggest that I should shut down my project, or cease functioning as an Asset or back channel to Baghdad. There was definite subterfuge by the Pro War Camp at the White House, with regards to its intentions towards Iraq. They kept me in the dark, while I continued to perform.

One sees now the dilemma faced by the Intelligence Community as it tried to serve this President. Only in retrospect does the world fully grasp how diplomacy posed a significant threat to the vanity of unilateralism in the Bush Administration. One sees too late that George W. Bush was a suspicious and impotent leader, who dissembled to disguise his personal weakness. He did not understand the strategic value of solving problems to maintain U.S. control of a situation. Solving problems was never his strength. So he kept everyone else off balance, in order to maintain control.

But in the opening months of his Administration, the Intelligence Community could be forgiven for the difficulties it faced trying to figure out this new master.

Campaign rhetoric throughout the 2000 Election had emphasized Bush's non-interventionist philosophy of foreign affairs. The Bush family had close relationships with the Arab-American community and received a king's ransom of campaign funds from them. Indeed, the Bush family had longstanding ties to Saudi oil. Throughout the campaign, Bush Jr. had emphasized fiscal moderation. Nobody expected George Bush to be a "buck burning" President.

For its part, the Intelligence Community saw with great clarity that the international community was ready to throw off the U.N. sanctions on Iraq, and seize all those tantalizing reconstruction contracts for itself, worth tens of billions of dollars in revenues and jobs.

The Intelligence Community had a legitimate concern from the standpoint of protecting U.S. interests. And so they took a proactive position to guarantee a major foreign policy victory for the new White House. Over the next 17 months, we built a platform that would guarantee continuing U.S. influence in Iraq in any post-sanctions period. The CIA was determined that the U.S. must retain power to mark out the requirements necessary to satisfy a broad framework for ending the sanctions, including some major objectives that George Bush and his cabal had not considered.

Over a span of time, the Intelligence community would come to recognize President Bush's leadership ineptitude, and would experience real frustration over the burdens posed by his weakness. In the meantime, problems had to be solved. If the United States refused to provide input to decision-making, or otherwise stood down from a leadership role in problem-solving, then other nations and coalitions would assert their own leadership and direction without the United States. That would shut the U.S. out of dialogue and control over the agenda, which the CIA considered folly in any circumstance. Allowing American influence to collapse in a vacuum of White House leadership would have been a radical failure for U.S. policy in the Middle East.

In the first term of the Bush Administration, the CIA still functioned well enough to recognize that paradigm, and act on it. And so U.S. Intelligence made sure that my interaction with Iraq was heavily supervised and controlled. The CIA exercised fierce control over the agenda in all parts, and demanded that I must not question or challenge whatever new or additional demands the U.S. chose to impose on Iraq. In exchange for my unquestioning obedience to the U.S. agenda, I could work towards suspending the U.N. sanctions.

For my part, my motivation was strictly humanitarian. I was horrified by the misery and suffering of Iraqi families and children. I saw the CIA as providing me with a unique and precious opportunity to contribute to the solution. And so I rolled up my sleeves and got to work.

Again and again, Iraq agreed to all U.S. demands.

Very quickly I began to hunt for help-mates among my diplomatic contacts at the United Nations—with some noteworthy success.

During the Lockerbie negotiations, I had struck up friendly relations with senior ranking diplomats from Malaysia, which served as a non-permanent member of the U.N. Security Council, under the leadership of Ambassador Hasmy Agam.[122]

When back-channel talks got underway with Iraq, I approached Mr. Rani Ismail Hadi Ali, my contact at the Malaysian Embassy for help. There's no point in U.S. Intelligence denying it. My relationship with senior diplomats at Malaysia's UN Mission and their input on Iraq are substantiated by phone taps, letters and email communications. Malaysia's support for the peace process, and its advice throughout this back channel process, was quite precious to me.

Malaysia proved an outstanding partner, in fact. Malaysia[123] boasts a vibrant Islamic community and vast wealth as one of Asia's financial capitals, with over 30 major international banks operating in Kuala Lumpur. A major exporter of electronics and telecommunications equipment, Malaysia has a fully diversified economy, and claims literacy of 89% in a population of 24 million. More strikingly, Islam is the official religion of the country, and the government actively promotes relations with other Islamic nations, including those in the Middle East.

In its eagerness to advance its relationship with Washington, Malaysia's Foreign Ministry offered to assume a formal role as intermediary between Iraq and the United States in any covert talks.

It was a valuable strategic offer that promised to yield results, involving a range of Middle East and Islamic issues, including Iraq.

Most graciously of all, Ambassador Hasmy Agam, whose career encompassed 30 years of high profile diplomacy in the Non-Aligned Movement, offered to act as the designated contact between Iraq and the United States. His participation offered a way to jumpstart talks on all matters of the conflict, since it was understood that Iraq and the United States could not sit down together, despite Baghdad's oft expressed desire to do so. The outstanding leadership of Ambassador Agam provided a way forward. He assigned a senior diplomat, Rani Ali, an expert on U.N. sanctions policy who staffed Malaysia on the U.N. Security Council, to liaison with me as discussions moved forward.[124]

Without explanation, Republican leaders took no action on Malaysia's generous offer— and so squandered a powerful alliance, which could have interceded on a number of difficult Middle Eastern matters.

Though disappointing, in fairness, U.S. intelligence had already voiced a strong determination to retain control of any settlement with Iraq. They weren't eager for any international participation. However, clearly the Republican leadership failed to understand how strategic alliances could be leveraged to strengthen U.S. influence in other parts of the world. The Bush White House was so myopic that it could not understand how partnerships with Malaysia and other nations would have been reciprocated by advancing U.S. priorities in those regions, and moving their domestic policies closer to ours.

Diplomacy was too subtle for Republican leaders, even when it was constructed to dictate outcomes controlled by the United States, and favorable to our agenda. In a global age, Republican leaders did not understand that proactive management would create strategic foundations that strengthen America. They do not understand why problems should be solved proactively at all.

Now that critical weakness in Republican foreign policy began to show.

For its part, the CIA faced the unhappy prospect of bucking the Bush Administration, while it experienced what appeared to be a steep learning curve.

We would just have to make do. Malaysia proved to be a valuable resource to my efforts, nonetheless. Throughout the months that followed, the Malaysian Embassy provided a sounding board and technical guidance for my preliminary talks on the weapons inspections. Malaysia's diplomats guaranteed that back-channel talks with Iraqi diplomats would conform to United Nations standards of compliance once it got through U.S. gates.

For his efforts to rebuild peaceful relations with America and Iraq's neighbors in the Middle East, Iraq's Ambassador Dr. Hasan should have won the Nobel Peace Prize, along with Malaysia's Ambassador Agam. Dr Hasan showed true vision of what would be necessary to restore Iraq's infrastructure after sanctions, while Ambassador Agam and his diplomatic staff stood off-stage, quietly contributing to a successful resolution. I have never known any two men who deserved a Nobel Peace Prize more than those two.

Ambassador Agam's prodigious diplomatic talent was fully recognized and rewarded by Malaysia's appointment to chair the Non-Aligned Movement in 2003.

On account of all those contributing factors, by early 2001, a successful peace with Iraq was within grasp.

It looked so hopeful. On all matters, Iraq agreed to U.S. conditions again and again, in total contradiction to what Americans were told before the War. All matters large and small were resolved through back-channel dialogue.[125] Diplomacy proved a great success.

Iraq's enthusiasm to resume inspections quickly was only outdone by the United States' extraordinary reluctance to get started. It began to appear that Washington was dragging its feet out of awareness that Iraq had nothing left to disclose or destroy, and thus recognized the wastefulness of the exercise, and was afraid of it. Meanwhile Baghdad hankered for implementation. Iraqi officials saw the momentum for change in sanctions policy coming from the international community, and pushed forward to greet the new day with verification that its old weapons stocks had been destroyed long ago.

The behavior of Iraqi officials, and especially their eagerness to resolve the impasse on weapons inspections, convinced me totally and without qualm that no weapons of mass destruction or illegal production facilities would be discovered in their territory.

I was convinced that the Intelligence Community could read the tea leafs, too. It did not look good for U.S. propaganda on Saddam's weapons stocks.

My job was not to criticize, however. It was to secure maximum compliance, and wrest as many concessions from Baghdad as possible, as part of a comprehensive resolution. I kept going.

Over the next 18 months of back channel talks, Iraq's offer to the United States came to encompass all of the following: [126]

1. **As of October, 2000, Baghdad agreed to resume U.N. weapons inspections.** That was 18 months before the world community was told of Baghdad's acquiescence.

2. **Likewise as of October, 2000, Iraq promised to grant U.S. Oil Companies access to first tier contracts for oil development and leasing on all new exploration sites. The U.S. could receive second tier and third tier contracts under sites already leased to Russia or France.** Taking first tier contracts away from Russia or European countries would have been controversial at this phase and politically impossible. However, Iraq had ways of cutting U.S. Oil into the mix of existing exploration and development contracts. Future oil development would have included the U.S. on first tier concessions. Iraq also promised to make major purchases of U.S. oil equipment, which it freely declared to be the best in the world.

3. **Baghdad offered to buy 1 million American-made automobiles every year for 10 years** in order to replace its citizens' outdated fleet of automobiles throughout Iraq. Because of purchase restrictions under U.N. sanctions, most automobiles in Iraq predated the mid 1980s. That guaranteed an enthusiastic market for U.S. auto manufacturers in any post-sanctions period. Iraq's commitment to purchase 1 million U.S. automobiles every year would have translated into thousands of high-paying Labor Union jobs in the Rust Belt of the United States—concentrating heavily in Michigan, Ohio, Indiana and Pennsylvania, which have been crippled by the loss of factory investment. It would have guaranteed a foundation of prosperity for America's workers.

4. **Iraq promised to invest heavily in U.S. telecommunications products and services.**

5. **Iraq agreed to lean heavily to the purchase of U.S. health care and hospital equipment and services, in any post-sanctions period.**

6. **Iraq promised to allow all U.S. Corporations to reenter the Iraqi Market in any post-sanctions period at the level that they had operated prior to the first Gulf War.** I was careful to avoid any dual use military industries or factory production at this phase of my talks. Dr. Fuisz had provided critical testimony in a Congressional investigation of U.S. corporations that supplied weapons systems to Iraq before the first Gulf War. There was no danger that he would have tolerated, or mistakenly supported, dual-use weapons contracts in addressing opportunities for American corporations in post-sanctions Iraq.

7. **Iraq agreed to contribute as a major partner in U.S. anti-terrorism efforts.**

Time and again, Baghdad made it quite clear: Any special preference that the United States demanded, the United States could have—anything at all.

Every offering was reported to Dr. Fuisz and Andy Card. We followed the same strategy and reporting process that had worked so successfully for us during the Lockerbie talks.

IRAQ'S PEACE OVERTURES TO EUROPE AND THE UNITED STATES

There were no surprises at CIA when I seized this chance to promote a solution to the sanctions conflict. The CIA understood my way of thinking— that both sides urgently needed to find new ways to address our problems. And for all the insults I suffered from the Justice Department after my indictment, I was very good at what I did. Throughout the 1990s, everybody was pleased on both sides. The Arabs loved me, too.

Because of Iraq and Libya's pariah status, other foreign Intelligence Agencies sometimes had a legitimate security interest in observing my activities, as well. In fact, I suspect that I was a primary source of information for most of the Intelligence networks tracking Iraq and Libya, right up to the War, particularly during the Lockerbie talks and after 9/11. By way of example, throughout the talks on resuming the weapons inspections, British Intelligence would often appear at my lunches with senior diplomatic staff on the Security Council, or Libya's diplomats, or Malaysia's diplomats, when we met at restaurants in Manhattan to discuss the progress of talks with Iraq or other anti-terrorism matters.

It had a comical side for sure. A number of times an upper-crust British couple would arrive at the restaurant, following on the heels of my diplomatic host. They would take a table close by. I would watch as a dollar bill (presumably of high denomination) would slide across the table. In a crowded dining room in New York City, bustling with activity, the British couple would order no food, only tea or coffee and water. They would not be interrupted by waiters for the next two to three hours, while my lunch or dinner conversation proceeded nearby. As my guest and I got up to leave the table, they would call the waiter—presumably to leave another large tip.

With all that surveillance, and scrutiny of my work by Dr. Fuisz and Hoven, could the Justice Department truly have been ignorant of our relationship all those years? Could they have seriously believed I was acting as an "Iraqi Agent?"

It seems impossible to me. I believe their motivation was something very different. Because of my high level access to Iraq's Embassy staff at the United Nations, I had vast knowledge of opportunities for a comprehensive peace with Baghdad, including promises of economic contracts for U.S. corporations and Iraq's cooperation with the 9/11 investigation, that the U.S. and Britain urgently wanted to hide.

Given my passionate activism against war and sanctions, it was a good bet that I would talk.

And I would have a lot to say.

CHAPTER 6:

9/11: A PATTERN OF COMMAND NEGLIGENCE

With Michael Collins

Shortly after September 11, retired General Wesley Clark spoke with Tim Russert of NBC News about a call he'd received after the strike. A member of a foreign think tank had called General Clark on his cell phone. The caller wanted General Clark to claim the 9/11 strike originated from Iraq at the direction of Saddam Hussein. General Clark isn't accustomed to taking orders from strangers. But he was curious about this call to his private cell phone. He asked the caller to provide evidence to support this claim. The call ended quickly, without the evidence, and that was that.

Apparently General Clark gave the motivation for War with Iraq a great deal of thought over the years. At a major speech in Texas in 2006, he said:

"Now why am I going back over ancient history? Because it's not ancient, because *we went to war in Iraq to cover up the command negligence that led to 9/11, and it was a war we didn't have to fight. That's the truth—*"

"I've been in war. I don't believe in it, and you don't do it unless there is absolutely, absolutely, absolutely no alternative." [127]

General Clark's argument that War with Iraq was a diversionary strategy to distract angry Americans from the command failure to stop 9/11, stands out as unique and provocative among the upper echelons of the military establishment. As somebody who gave advance warning about the 9/11 strike, I agree wholeheartedly with his assessment.

Only I take his conclusions one step farther. I believe that when his theory of "command negligence" gets factored in with my team's advance warnings to the Office of Counter-Terrorism in August 2001, there is finally a "coherent" explanation for 9/11—if allowing an attack on the United States could be defined as a "rational" thought process. (Clearly there's nothing rational about it.)

Consider the military lexicon for command responsibility:

Command: (Department of Defense) 1. Command includes the authority and responsibility for effectively using available resources, and for planning the deployment of, organizing, directing, coordinating, and controlling military forces for the health, welfare, morale, and discipline of assigned personnel.[128]

Negligence: Failure to exercise the care that a reasonably prudent person would exercise in like circumstances."

How can we assess whether "command negligence" actually occurred?

Three levels of proof of command negligence

There are three levels of proof to support General Clark's assertion that 9/11 resulted as a consequence of command negligence, which in the opinion of many Americans, facilitated a secret pro-war agenda. Put simply, top leaders ignored simple actions that would have preempted the attack, so they could justify war with Iraq.

The first level of proof examines the Commander in Chief's use of available military resources to interrupt the attack on sovereign U.S. soil, and whether those resources got deployed in an appropriate fashion.

Consider, first of all, that the North American Aerospace Command (NORAD) had practiced military responses to attacks on major buildings, including the World Trade Center, in the two year period before the September 11 attacks.[129] In one exercise, fighter craft performed a mock shoot down over the Atlantic Ocean of a jet supposedly laden with chemical poisons headed toward a target inside the United States. In another scenario, the target was the Pentagon — That drill stopped after Defense officials declared the attack scenario unrealistic.

The point is that NORAD had organized training exercises in preparation for an attack on U.S. soil exactly like this one. Ironically, military exercises were organized after U.S. intelligence exposed a master plot to hijack commercial airplanes, and use them as aerial weapons to strike the World Trade Center.

Called "Project Bojinka," the plot was hatched by the mastermind of the first World Trade Center attack in 1993, Ramzi Yousef, as a way to fulfill his dream of toppling the twin towers. Yousef was captured in the Philippines in 1995 and extradited to the United States. Convicted at trial in 1996, he was sentenced to life without parole. His co-conspirator, Sheikh Abdul Rahman, was a famous Egyptian radical Islamist, who sought the overthrow of President Hosni Mubarak.

Yousef has emerged as a central character in the history of al Qaeda, 9/11 and the Iraq invasion. A tactical mastermind with exceptional gifts for creating chaos and misery, Yousef spoke several languages fluently, and graduated with an electrical engineering degree from Swansea University in Whales, England. He joined al Qaeda in 1988, and became a bomb maker. Born near the Pakistan-Afghanistan border, Yousef's family lived smack in the cultural milieu that produced the radical Muslims, recruited, trained and funded by the United States to fight the Russians in Afghanistan.

It was Yousef who devised the tactical model for September 11 from his hide-out in Manila, capitol of the Philippines, after the 1993 World Trade Center attack.

The "Bojinka" project conspired to attack the United States using commercial airplanes. According to Yousef's plan, eleven commercial jets would be hijacked on the same day, and used as missiles to attack the White House, the CIA headquarters in Langley, Virginia, and other national symbols of U.S. global pre-eminence, including the World Trade Center.

Philippine police struck gold when they broke up a meeting of Muslim terrorists in Manila during 1995. They suspected this visiting bomb maker had been involved in several local terrorist attacks, as well.

They arrested Yousef, confiscated his computer, then enlisted the help of a local computer expert to decode the hard drive. That's how Philipino authorities discovered "Bojinka." The contents of Yousef's computer proved invaluable, helping to convict him for his role in the 1993 World Trade Center bombing.

Yousef's diabolical plot was no secret. The scheme was unveiled at his trial in New York in 1996, at the federal courthouse a few blocks from the World Trade Center.

Vince Cannistraro, former director of the CIA's Counter Terrorism Division called it "extraordinarily ambitious, very complicated to bring off, and probably unparalleled by other terrorist operations that we know of." [130]

For the next few years, "Bojinka" lay dormant.

Then, in the spring of 2001, U.S. Intelligence got wind that terrorists intended to carry out a strike remarkably similar to "Bojinka." Concern reached such a heightened status that starting in April, 2001 and throughout the summer, I was ordered to tackle my Iraqi sources for any fragments of actionable intelligence, regarding its execution.

At the same time, the North American Aerospace Command (NORAD) was planning war games in Canada and Alaska—thousands of miles away from the potential target, already believed to be located inside New York City. On September 9, 2001, the Air Force announced "Operation Northern Vigilance."[131] This major military exercise would be a synchronized response to a Russian military exercise near Alaska. The US Air Force would simulate the protection of North American air space, as though the Russians were attacking the U.S, a common tactical maneuver, whereby the United States and former Soviet Union plan military exercises to coincide with one another. This was such an occasion. [132] (i, ii,iii)

The U.S. Air Command scheduled the War Games in Canada and Alaska to run from September 10 – 14th.

Critically, the U.S. Air Force ordered personnel to operate on a state of heightened security throughout the continental United States, to defend against any intrusion on U.S. airspace on those days.

NORAD had trained for "Bojinka" for two years.

And yet, tragically, the full scope of reasoning for the heightened security alert had not been properly explained to the military.

Indeed, NORAD has acknowledged that U.S. forces were advised to go on alert *only* because of the ongoing Russian military exercises. The U.S. military was not warned that "Bojinka" might be in play, though factions of U.S. intelligence were shouting from the rooftops about a possible attack and requesting multi-agency cooperation at that very moment.

Failure to adequately alert and deploy the Central Command of the U.S. Armed Forces, despite the known heightened security risk of a possible strike on a known target— identified as the World Trade Center— would definitely qualify as "command negligence." Through no fault of its own, despite ongoing exercises in September, 2001, the U.S. military was only half-armed for a massive strike on U.S. sovereignty, when it should have been fully braced to confront a major domestic assault.

Subsequently, Air Force commanders experienced confusion on September 11, 2001. The regional NORAD commander for New York and Washington reported that some commanders at NORAD thought the 9/11 attacks were part of the military exercise.

"In retrospect, the exercise should have proved to be a serendipitous enabler of a rapid military response to terrorist attacks on September 11," [133]Colonel Robert Marr, in charge of NEADS, said. "We had the fighters with a little more gas on board. A few more weapons on board."[134] However, other NORAD officials were initially confused about whether the 9/11 attacks were real or part of the exercise." [135]

As a result, at the exact moment when US and foreign intelligence around the world expected a massive terrorist attack on New York City, citing the World Trade Center as the primary target, the US Air Force was locked and loaded— for war games off the coast of Russia. The U.S. Air Force was on high alert throughout the Continental United States from September 10 onwards, yet received no effective communication regarding a high level threat inside New York City. With better communications, there's no question that the Air Force would have done much better than to dispatch a single fighter pilot to lower Manhattan and another to Washington, DC. They would have launched all available aircraft to bring down the hijackers.[136]

Regardless, it's time to 'fess up to the people. We did know the 9/11 attack was coming.

The government had enough intelligence to anticipate the method and target of the attack, even if we lacked actionable intelligence to stop it—identification of the airport hubs, the airlines, the number of hijackers, a single name or flight number. We could not stop the hijackers from boarding the planes. However, we understood what they intended to do. And regardless of that foreknowledge, pre-emptive actions to warn NORAD, or deploy other military options failed to materialize.

As a result, the most powerful Air Force on the planet was badly misused, despite its formation to practice military exercises the week of September 10, and its previous training to offset a 9/11 strike scenario.

The second level of "command negligence" relates to the failure to coordinate an appropriate and unified response to the threat in communications between U.S. intelligence and federal law enforcement. Heightened cooperation between the CIA and FBI would have required "command leadership" from the White House.

Bottom line: "9/11 was an organizational, not an intelligence, failure,' said John Arquilla, of the Naval Postgraduate School."[137]

According to a Joint House-Senate Congressional inquiry,[138] in March 2001 an intelligence source claimed a group of Bin Ladin operatives were coordinating an unspecified attack on the United States. One of the operatives allegedly resided in the United States.

In April 2001, U.S. Intelligence learned that unspecified terrorist operatives in California and New York were planning a strike in those states.

Between May and July of 2001, the National Security Agency reported at least 33 chatter communications, indicating a possible, imminent terrorist attack. These individuals appeared to possess no actionable intelligence that would have identified who, how many, when or where the attack would start.[139]

In May 2001, the Intelligence Community obtained information that Bin Ladin supporters planned to infiltrate the United States via Canada in order to carry out a terrorist operation using high explosives. Further investigation by the Department of Defense indicated that seven individuals associated with Bin Ladin had departed various locations for Canada, Britain and the United States. [140]

By May, U.S. intelligence had gathered sufficient information to show that some Middle Eastern terrorist group was planning an imminent attack on key landmarks including the World Trade Center. This coincides precisely with the timing of the portentous warning from Dr. Fuisz that I must confront Iraqi diplomats, and aggressively demand any fragment of intelligence regarding airplane hijackings.

In June 2001, the Director of Central Intelligence (DCI) had information that key operatives in Bin Ladin's organization were disappearing, while others were preparing for martyrdom.[141]

In July 2001, the DCI gained access to an individual recently traveling in Afghanistan who reported, "Everyone is talking about an impending attack." The Intelligence Community was also aware that Bin Ladin had stepped up his propaganda efforts to promote Al Qaeda's cause.

Sometime between August 8-10, I telephoned Attorney General John Ashcroft's private staff and the Office of Counter-Terrorism at the Justice Department with a request for an emergency broadcast alert throughout all agencies, seeking any fragment of intelligence regarding possible airplane hijackings and/or airplane bombings. I described the threat as "imminent," with the potential for "mass casualties." And I definitely cited the World Trade Center as the expected target.

On August 16, 2001, U.S. Immigration detained Zacarias Moussaoui in Minneapolis, Minnesota.

On September 4, 2001, the FBI sent urgent cables about the Moussaoui investigation to the Intelligence Community, including the Federal Aviation Administration (FAA), the Secret Service, and several other agencies. Despite urgent warnings from the Minneapolis FBI office about Moussaoui's likely involvement in some terror conspiracy, U.S. Attorney General John Ashcroft declined to get a warrant to search his computer from the secret intelligence court in Washington.[142]

Finally, on September 10, 2001, the National Security Agency (NSA) intercepted two communications between individuals overseas, suggesting imminent terrorist activity. These communications were not translated into English and disseminated until September 12, 2001. These intercepts gave no indication where, when, or what activities might occur. It remains unclear whether they referred to the September 11 attacks.[143]

To a degree then, U.S. intelligence performed in an outstanding capacity, in measuring the threat posed by al Qaeda.

All of which raises serious questions as to how Central Command could have allowed such valuable raw intelligence to go unused between agencies?

Various factions of U.S. intelligence buzzed that an attack was about to occur. There was an outpouring of pleas for aggressive coordination and pre-emptive planning among all agencies. In its frustration, the Intelligence Community made a herculean effort to break through the gridlock and appeal directly to the Justice Department. In August 2001, we requested "cooperation across all agencies" to avert the "imminent attack."

That should have opened a second front for preemptive action. Unhappily, law enforcement agencies under Attorney General Ashcroft received no "command" support from the White House or top echelons of the Justice Department to coordinate resources. That sort of top level mandate would have been necessary for cooperation to occur between these two very different Intelligence and law enforcement communities.

Options for pre-emptive action were definitely available.

When a small aircraft buzzed the White House in the 1980's, missiles got placed on the rooftop to shoot down future aircraft that came too close. A couple of months before 9/11, world leaders gathered for an Economic Summit in Milan, Italy. Intelligence suggested terrorists might strike the gathering of world leaders by crashing an airplane into the conference building. As a result, very quickly Milan became heavily fortified with anti aircraft missiles, along with significant NATO Air Force protection. The Summit progressed unscathed.

Didn't all of this advance intelligence in the United States warrant the deployment of a few missile batteries on top of the World Trade Towers— and the Pentagon, too?

It would have been shockingly simple and cost effective to implement. Throughout the summer of 2001, there was ample opportunity to mobilize a lean but effective anti aircraft battery on top of various landmark buildings, including the World Trade Center. Various factions of the Intelligence Community agitated for just such a unified and proactive approach.

Intelligence sharing functioned properly. Yet nothing happened. The command leadership—outside of the military and intelligence—dropped the ball, pure and simple. Command leaders failed to pull resources across agencies that would implement those most basic precautionary safeguards. That qualifies as a significant "command failure" and "command negligence," as defined by General Clark and the U.S. military establishment.

The third argument for "command negligence" involves the White House failure to assume responsibility for its command position after 9/11. When there's a tragedy or crisis, Americans expect our leaders to stand forward and embrace their responsibility to protect our country.

President Bush's performance as Commander in Chief at the start of the attack was awkward at best. At a town hall meeting in Orlando, Florida on September 12, a young audience member addressed President Bush:

Question: "One thing, Mr. President, you have no idea how much you've done for this country. And another thing is that – how did you feel when you heard about the terrorist attack?"

PRESIDENT BUSH: "Well – Well, Jordan, you're not going to believe where – what state I was in, when I heard about the terrorist attack. I was in Florida. And my chief of staff, Andy Card – well, actually I was in a classroom, talking about a reading program that works. And it – I was sitting outside the – the classroom, waiting to go in, and I saw an airplane hit the tower of a – of a – you know, the TV was obviously on, and I – I used to fly myself, and I said, "Well, there's one terrible pilot." And I said it must have been a horrible accident." [144]

The President's statement was largely incoherent. Somehow he translated the child's question: "How did you feel when you heard about the terrorist attack?" to a more concrete "What state was I in when I heard about the terrorist attack?" "Oh, Florida." He interjects seemingly random comments about Andy Card, and barely makes it through the answer. But this sort of disconnected rhetoric was typical and expected by those who followed President Bush closely.

More than that discredited the White House. After 9/11, Republican leaders pushed very hard, as long as possible, to avoid an investigation, hiding from criticism of their pre-9/11 inertia. When the 9/11 Commission was finally established, the White House granted it a budget nowhere close to sufficient for a serious investigation.

Blue ribbon commissions are a trademark of the federal government. When a topic appears too hot for Congress to handle, a commission of distinguished officials gets formed from the top ranks of both political parties to address it. But President Bush and Vice President Cheney wanted no part of a 9/11 investigation. Cheney called up former Senate Majority Leader Tom Daschle (Dem-South Dakota) and asked him to limit the investigation to communication failures between agencies.[145]

"The Vice President expressed concern that a review of what happened on September 11 would take resources and personnel away from the war on terrorism," Senator Daschle told CNN.

Unable to stop the 9/11 investigation, the White House tried to starve the Commission of funds, refusing a budget request for $11 million, a pittance of what Congress spends on far less important tasks.

Once the commission was finally formed, the White House saw to it that a White House insider was selected for the all important job of staff director. Phillip Zelikow was a close professional colleague of Condeleeza Rice. They wrote a book together on foreign policy, and Rice brought Zelikow onto the Bush 2000 transition team. An academic of some distinction, Zelikow authored two notable position papers for the Bush transition team. The first studied how to manage terrorist threats. The second justified a preemptive invasion of Iraq.

In other words, Zelikow was neck deep in the policies that produced the command negligence for 9/11 and the preemptive invasion of Iraq.

It's hardly surprising, therefore, that so much of this information never got published in the 9/11 Commission report.

General Clark stops short of declaring that President Bush engaged in "deliberate" command negligence, in order to justify going to War with Iraq. He leaves open the possibility that top White House officials showed incompetence in their organizational leadership, and may have used the Iraq War as a distraction from their own mediocrity.

That's where I diverge from General Clark's outstanding arguments. I take a stronger position. I agree that "command negligence" occurred, building up to 9/11. But I believe that key leaders deliberately looked away from multiple advance warnings presented by domestic and foreign intelligence sources, and willfully failed to enact the most basic cautionary measures to defend the World Trade Center—which was already identified as the primary target of the attack.

That raises the most controversial questions that have spun through the 9/11 Truth Community for years: Was 9/11 allowed to occur to build public support for an invasion of Iraq?

Put more succinctly: Did the White House practice "deliberate negligence" in a successful effort to foment public outrage and justify its secret agenda of war with Iraq?

Unequivocally, I believe the answer is yes.

Alternatives to War—the 9/11 Incentive

Given the rallying for peace with Iraq in the international community in 2000-2001, the concept of War was inconceivable without some major provocation. The International Community had reached the end of its tolerance for punishing the Iraqi people for Saddam's leadership. Europe, Russia and Asia loathed the continuation of U.N. sanctions, and sought better relations with Baghdad. Friendship offerings had been proposed by Iraqi officials to all of Baghdad's former allies, as a method of restoring ties. Most surprisingly of all, Iraqi officials had launched a diplomatic offensive to placate all aspects of U.S. demands, necessary to achieve a viable and mutually beneficial relationship with Washington in any post-sanctions period, as well.

For its part, a faction of U.S. Intelligence had analyzed potential flashpoints for future tensions with Iraq, and moved to neutralize them. The peace framework developed through our back channel addressed all of the major U.S. interests in Iraq, including some objectives not previously considered by the Bush Administration. In so doing, the CIA seized control away from the United Nations, ensuring that U.S. priorities would be satisfied before the U.N. Security Council got its hands on Iraq, and tried to negotiate its own settlement that might not recognize the United States' particular interests.

From the standpoint of U.S. interests, the CIA's covert channel to Baghdad was entirely rational and legitimate. U.S. intelligence would have been negligent not to have acted, given the rising bitterness towards U.S. policy on Iraq. The United States had lost the public relations battle on sanctions in the international community. The CIA could not define the future of Iraq without some form of covert interaction. Its purpose was to control the outcome.

The White House was fully apprised of all progress to implement U.S. goals. The corollary to that means the White House was thoroughly debriefed on the international loathing for U.S. hostilities towards Iraq, pre-9/11, and our rapidly sinking sanctions policy.

That illustrates damnably why the Pro-War camp needed 9/11. They had to set up Iraq as a paper-tiger, an external enemy that would incite American hatred, and overcome international resistance to continued hostilities towards Iraq. They had lost all legitimate justifications. So they had to invent one. Osama bin Laden saved the day, when he came along with a conspiracy to hijack airplanes and strike the Twin Towers. Right up to that point, the Bush Administration had lost every other excuse for War. Without 9/11, it was flatly impossible to pursue their secret agenda. Before 9/11, the world community was enflamed with a desire for peace with Baghdad. The world community would have condemned U.S. aggression against Iraq as a "rogue" action.

Was the goal seizing Iraq's oil after all? Vice President Cheney fought for years to keep his pre- invasion meeting with U.S. oil executives confidential. But there have been enough leaks to speculate that the meeting carved up Iraq's oil reserves, and replaced the existing set of contracts held by foreign oil companies— none of which included the United States.

In testimony before Congress, executives of the major U.S. oil companies denied attending any such meeting with Cheney. But in late 2005, a White House document confirmed that a meeting between Cheney and U.S. oil companies took place.[146]

There's also the Caspian Sea Pipeline, which runs from Kazakhstan through Iran. A primary source of Russian oil, it is geographically sensitive to hostilities between Iran and the West. Some top officials might have desired a concentration of U.S. military bases in Iraq as a check on Tehran's ambitions to dominate and manipulate oil supplies.

Unhappily for Republican cronies in the oil industry, instead of securing vast wealth for its stockholders, war and U.N. sanctions accomplished their own worst objectives, by fundamentally annihilating Iraq's oil infrastructure and pipelines for the foreseeable future. That costly damage to Iraq's oil infrastructure, already profound before the War, has been exacerbated by repeated acts of sabotage by the Iraqi insurgency. A substantial percentage of the Iraqi people believe the United States invaded to Iraq to seize its oil resources. Why else would the United States have launched the Invasion? A critical sub-group of that population has chosen to degrade their own oil infrastructure, rather than allow the U.S. to steal Iraq's national wealth.

The absence of a strong and consistent rationale for the invasion lends credibility to General Clark's argument: "We went to war in Iraq to cover up the command negligence that led to 9/11."

Or, as I believe, pro-war Republican leaders allowed command negligence to occur before 9/11, so that they could justify going to war with Iraq, which would otherwise have been impossible to launch, given the powerful forces coalescing into peaceful coexistence in the international community.

Tragically today, the vast majority of citizens have no confidence that we've been told the truth about 9/11. From that despair, the "9/11 Truth Movement" has emerged. All over the country, ordinary citizens have put together a Terror Timeline, culling information that the government would not provide. For me, that's heart breaking to watch. I know from personal experience the ripples of advance warnings that ran like wildfire through the intelligence community before 9/11. I recall my own desperation trying to outreach the Justice Department to urge a unified and proactive front to preempt the attack. And I know the idea of War must have been floated, in some forum, because my handlers demanded that I issued threats against Iraq, if such a bombing occurred.

Clearly some factions of the intelligence community wanted to establish that War with Iraq would inevitably follow any 9/11 style of strike. That indicates to me that War was on the table before the attack occurred. Instead of preempting the attack, some parts of the Intelligence Community got prepped to accept War with Baghdad—not Afghanistan— as a response.

One more thing threatened pro-War Republicans. I had full knowledge of Iraq's extensive efforts to cooperate with the 9/11 investigation, and how that effort had been snubbed. When war started, I smoldered in fury for the dangers that snubbing could manifest for the future.

EXTREME PREJUDICE

I was always one to call a spade, a spade. Citing my direct contact with Iraq, I was ready to turn Washington on its ear, by declaring the War on Terrorism an "abject failure," and the failure of Peace with Iraq an act of public fraud. Those in the intelligence community, who had watched me at work for almost a decade, had no doubt that I would do it.

CHAPTER 7:

SEPTEMBER 11, 2001

Finally you are told some facts.

Surely they make a great deal more sense than the semantic games played in Washington all these years. Yes, the greatest Intelligence Community in the world expected a major terrorist strike according to a 9/11 style scenario. We lacked actionable intelligence to identify airport hubs or flight numbers, which would have been necessary to stop the attack. Yet far more tragically, the command leadership necessary to coordinate a pre-emptive inter-agency effort to gather that intelligence, or deploy anti-aircraft guns on top of the Trade Center, or activate NORAD during its pre-scheduled military exercises, failed to mobilize.

It was not for lack of trying by those of us at the mid-level, below the leadership. We raised the alarms. Alas, Republicans at the command level chose not to act.

Instead, throughout the summer of 2001, the U.S. threatened Iraq with military retaliation "worse than anything they'd experienced before," if a 9/11 style of attack occurred. Yes, U.S. intelligence abhorred the concept of a 9/11 attack, including my own handlers. But a handful of puppeteers controlling the stage at the highest levels of government aggressively prepped some factions of U.S. Intelligence to accept War with Iraq as the inevitable outcome of a 9/11 strike. In which case, they made no effort to block 9/11, so that they could fulfill their quest.

It's critical to understand that Intelligence is not a monolithic mega-entity but a community of factions, broken down into small teams. Once advance warnings about the World Trade Center attack enter into the equation, it becomes entirely conceivable that some different team within a competing faction, called an orphan, might have entered the World Trade Center in the midnight hours, and positioned explosives throughout the buildings, with the intention of maximizing the demolition impact whenever the hijacked airplanes struck the buildings.

That theory has been argued before. However it becomes vastly more credible in light of U.S. threats against Iraq throughout the summer of 2001. An orphan team might have found its motivation upon learning of that advance decision to pursue War with Baghdad following a 9/11 style of strike. That secondary outcome might have persuaded an orphan team to do the unthinkable—plant explosives in sufficient quantity to bring down the towers, so the option of War with Iraq could be guaranteed. Regrettably, everything falls into place in the Terror Timeline once those advance warnings about the attack and threats against Iraq are understood.

Does that truth satisfy you?

It has cost me a great deal to tell you. I have waited a long time and suffered through a frightening and horrific ordeal for my chance, spending a year in prison on a Texas military base without a trial or guilty plea, as you're about to discover.

That ugliness was coming faster than I ever dreamed. However, have some patience, friend. First, some more truth. Because you see, just as I warned about the 9/11 attack, I also functioned as a "first-responder" in the 9/11 investigation, covering Iraq's cooperation with U.S. counter-terrorism objectives.

I told you. I know everything. Those facts have been concealed from you, as well. And they are more devastating than you know.

First though, think back with me. Do you remember what you were doing when you first heard that an airplane had crashed into the World Trade Center? Did you hear it on the radio, driving to work? Were you taking the children to school? Can you recall your split second reaction to the news?

I was at the Post Office in Takoma Park, my little peacenik hamlet in the suburbs of Washington DC. Someone behind me groaned excitedly that a crazed, grief stricken pilot must have committed suicide.

I recall my split second reaction like a punch in the gut: *We knew it! Richard and I told them this was coming. Oh God, why didn't they listen to us?*

I rushed home and got on the phone with Dr. Fuisz. Talking over each other, we shouted at the images of carnage playing on our televisions. From our living rooms, we commanded that office workers must not go back inside the damaged towers. I demanded that Richard stop them. In my grief, I endowed him with super human strength to right all wrongs, fly down amidst the chaos, and issue vital instructions for the preservation of the crowds.

To no avail. On September 11, 2001, 3,017 souls lost their lives, and 6,291 were seriously injured when the Twin Towers of black glass imploded and crashed to the concrete floor in a frightening cloud of dust. Firefighters and rescue workers died with them.

Alas, 9/11 proved that none of us are super human. Not to diminish the irresponsibility of the government's role, but I seriously doubt that the inner circle of U.S officials who allowed the attack to occur comprehended the full extent of the blow, or the scope of repercussions, when they made the fatal decision to keep their hands off an effective, preemptive response. To put that in context, the 1993 World Trade Center attack killed 5 people, while the 2000 U.S.S. Cole strike killed 17 people.

I am quite certain they anticipated only minor damage, in line with the first attack on the World Trade Center in 1993, or the U.S.S. Cole bombing in Yemen in 2000—in other words, an attack according to the scope of what had come before. They never expected such tragedy as this.

I mean, come on. Nobody imagined the Titanic would sink either. Right?

The Titanic did sink, though, didn't it? And more government officials had been debriefed about this "imminent" terrorist scenario, coming in late August or September, than you would allow yourselves to envision. Everybody we could think of had been warned.

Many times I've been questioned about Dr. Fuisz's other sources who fed him intelligence before the attack. Truthfully, he never revealed them to me.

But I have guessed. Immediately after the attack and shortly after the first tower collapsed—but before the second tower collapsed, Dr. Fuisz blurted something to me over the phone. It regarded the videotape of the hijacked airplanes flying over the Manhattan harbor moments before ramming full force into the World Trade Center. The video camera was held by steady hands in a controlled setting, not whipped around by an amateur bystander, responding hysterically to surprising, fast breaking events.

Dr. Fuisz demanded to know if I thought it was "an accident that a man and woman happened to be waiting on the sidewalk with a video camera outside the World Trade Center, ready to record the attack?"

He was highly agitated. He challenged me. "How often does a bystander have a camera cued up to record a car accident on the street? It never happens, Susan. It never happens."

Then Dr. Fuisz said, "Those are Israeli agents. It's not an accident that they were standing there. They knew this attack was coming. They were waiting for it."

In my grief, I was outraged and shocked by the images on the television. I shot back something to the effect of, "You mean to tell me, we've been looking for intelligence on this attack for months! And the Israelis knew about it? And they didn't tell us?"

Immediately the phone line cut dead between us.

I called him right back. Very calmly, he said, "Susan, we must never talk about that again."

We never did. But it prompts some serious questions. Did the Israelis fail to warn us? Or did White House officials ignore the Israelis like they ignored everybody else?

It would be irresponsible to speculate. And Dr. Fuisz gave no hint.

A couple of details are worth noting, however, about this alleged Mossad team. Dr. Fuisz was knowledgeable about their intelligence identities and the existence of the videotape about 24 hours before the media broadcast it on television. He definitely told me about the videotape shortly after the first tower collapsed, while the second was still standing. Yet research suggests the videotape of airplanes crashing into the World Trade Center did not air on television until September 12. Now then, Dr. Fuisz enjoyed absolute superiority in his intelligence sources. But the way I see it, this video must have been distributed to the top echelons of U.S. Intelligence with lightning speed to become available so quickly. That would signify the video came from a friendly Intelligence Agency. Only somebody with top level access could pull that off so rapidly.

Is that significant? I could be wrong. But I don't think so.

One more thing occurred that morning. Dr. Fuisz and I made a crucial decision in the first hours after the attack. Whether it proved correct or not, I leave history to judge.

We agreed to avoid recriminations in the first days after the attack. We did not believe that U.S. Intelligence needed to hear 'we told you so's.' Not from us. It was not a conspiracy of silence. We never agreed to bury the truth. We only agreed to delay confronting it. Everybody recognized that a terrible mistake had been made. They knew our team had warned of the strike. What they needed most urgently was help after the attack. Our help and the help of everyone with special experience and sources in Middle Eastern anti-terrorism, who would have the skills to tackle this enormous challenge. They needed us. Beating up the community would have demoralized the men and women who now had to mobilize all of their energies to launch an effective counter-response to the strike.

We wanted to be part of that effort. And so we decided to wait before pointing out that the 9/11 strike scenario had been predicted in exact detail. I always expected a Congressional inquiry to bring our warning to light. It was a question of a few weeks, I figured, while everyone focused on addressing the investigation.

There would be serious repercussions from our hesitation. I myself would suffer appalling personal consequences. We had no way of knowing how serious or terrible.

As they say, the road to hell is paved with best intentions.

For me, it meant the abyss.

CHAPTER 8:

IRAQ'S COOPERATION WITH 9/11 INVESTIGATION

Everyone wanted to help after 9/11. Very few people actually could. I was one of those. There's nothing grandiose about it. The U.S. required a rapid turn around of high value, actionable intelligence from all possible Arab sources, in order to launch a muscular response to Al Qaeda's ambitions. Iraq and Libya, especially, were known to possess a significantly higher quality of tracking intelligence on terrorist cells in the Middle East. As such, my access to those embassies and my prior experience securing their cooperation with U.S. counter-terrorism objectives carried a premium value in any serious investigation.

To put that in context, by September 11, 2001, Paul Hoven and I had worked together for eight years, going back to the first attack on the World Trade Center in 1993. Dr. Fuisz and I had worked together from September, 1994 onwards. I had established contact with the Libya House in May, 1995 and the Iraqi Embassy in August, 1996. Our work encompassed significant parts of the Middle East, including Egypt, Syria/ Hezbollah, Yemen and Malaysia. However, primarily I focused my energies as a back channel to Libya and Iraq at the United Nations, leveraging my anti-war and anti-sanctions activism to build relationships with diplomats on all matters involving counter-terrorism.

This was a well-oiled machine. Virtually no one else enjoyed such close proximity to either Iraq or Libya's embassies before 9/11. Both countries had been isolated for years, though Libya's relations in Europe and Africa had started to thaw following the Lockerbie Trial.

As for Baghdad, the CIA has declared that before the Invasion, it could "count on one hand the number of agents working inside Iraq,"[147] for the simple fact that Saddam tortured and killed them all as quickly as he uncovered their duplicity. He executed them as traitors. Globally, there were just 5,000 Assets, making us a fairly elite group.

That put me in a prized position in New York at the United Nations. Only three U.S. Assets covered the Iraqi Embassy—My two comrades got drafted by the FBI at the end of 2001. Raed Al-Anbuke and Wisam Al-Anbuke were sons of an Iraqi diplomat, brothers who desired to remain in the U.S. after their visas expired. In exchange for validating their green cards and work visas,[148] the brothers videotaped and photographed guests at Embassy parties.[149] I know that because as co-defendant, I received copies of their legal discovery and saw the paltry evidence.

The Anbuke brothers were very young, in their mid-20s, and worked at a dry cleaners and a video rental store in Manhattan.[150] By contrast, I had graduated from Smith College and the London School of Economics. I had worked as a Congressional Press Secretary and Capitol Hill journalist in Washington DC. Throughout the 1990s, anti-terrorism was my specialty. Most unusually our back-channel was not covert, in that I operated with the full knowledge of Arab diplomats and Ambassadors, who understood my motivation as a desire to help end the UN sanctions. This was an open and direct line.

In short, if the U.S. government was serious about its objectives to accomplish anything substantial with regards to Iraq, they required my help. There was nobody else who could do it.

As such, it would have been irresponsible—and possibly criminal—if I had refused to contribute to the 9/11 investigation. During my nightmarish federal indictment, I frequently pondered the irony of that point. Refusing to participate might have constituted "obstruction of justice," or "hindering the 9/11 investigation." My extensive background and unique contacts in Iraq and Libya created a moral imperative to provide assistance. Many times I pictured that "alternative" court session— how Judge Mukasey might have lectured the Court on my stunning failure to provide for the community's welfare, if I had refused to help. He might have denied my bail, or handed down a heavy sentence to teach everyone a lesson of the obligations that we all bear to our society.

I would have deserved it.

After all, pressure to secure Iraq's cooperation was intense after the 9/11 attack. The Pro-War camp hurled outrageous accusations about Saddam's support for Al Qaeda. On November 28, 2001, Presidential hopeful, Senator John McCain declared— "There was a meeting between Iraqi Intelligence and Mohammed Atta [chief conspirator of the 9/11 attack] in Prague."[151]

Two weeks later on December 9, 2001, Vice President Richard Cheney said on "Meet the Press," "It's been pretty well confirmed that he [Atta] did go to Prague, and he did meet with a senior official of Iraqi Intelligence Service."[152]

Republicans in Congress jumped fast on that bogus bandwagon, trumpets blaring.

I suffered no suspicions. From where I sat, Congressional leaders had zero comprehension of Saddam's philosophy for holding onto power, or his deep paranoia of all Islamic fundamentalists, terrorists or not. He tracked those individuals mercilessly. What's more I had full confidence that Baghdad would have supplied us with any fragment of intelligence on the 9/11 conspiracy, as demanded, if they had come across it. Providing that intelligence would have brought Iraq closer to the U.S. and Europe. I had underscored that advantage many times in conversations over the summer of 2001. Helping to preempt the attack would have emphasized Iraq's secular commitment and moderation. Baghdad understood that. They simply had nothing to give us. Or they would have done so.

In truth, throughout the summer of 2001, Iraqi officials raced full steam to topple the U.N. sanctions, actively wooing trade missions from Europe, Asia and the Persian Gulf to rebuild bridges and overcome that isolation barrier. My back channel focused on the critical importance of resuming the U.N. weapons inspections to verify that all weapons stocks had been eradicated. But tantalizing side conversations promised the U.S. a bonanza of economic reconstruction contracts in various economic sectors.[153] Trying to win over Washington, Baghdad dangled major contracts in telecommunications, transportation, health care equipment and pharmaceuticals, in addition to the oil sector. Whatever the CIA asked for, the U.S. could have. Diplomats swore a thousand times that it would be mine.[154] After 11 years of hellacious misery, the end of sanctions loomed closer every day. Iraqi officials would have done nothing to jeopardize that progress. It was their greatest hope for the future.

In short, there was zero chance that Iraq had any incentive to participate in the 9/11 conspiracy, or withhold information about it. They would have lost everything at exactly the moment they were poised to prevail over all their obstacles.

September 11 was their tragedy, too.

I was never fooled by Republican rhetoric to the contrary. Yet even those of us who correctly recognized that Iraq had nothing to do with 9/11 should have been enthusiastic to receive Iraq's cooperation with the War on Terrorism.[155] Baghdad had some of the best tracking intelligence on the workings of terrorist networks anywhere— Saddam's secular government loathed and reviled Islamic fundamentalists, and presumed that sooner or later they would become "enemies of state." So Iraqi Intelligence monitored them constantly, and tracked them all over the Middle East. They would often appeal to his government for sanctuary, anticipating his hatred of the United States. If so, they failed to understand that Saddam desperately hoped to reconcile with America. Getting access to that superior trove of intelligence would have made a phenomenal impact on U.S. goals— and Saddam understood that.

The U.S. would have difficulty achieving long term results without that input.

On the other hand, you can see the problem for Republican leaders.

Finally, after 9/11, President Bush had a chance to hurdle international antipathy towards U.S military aggression against Iraq. Right up to that moment, world opinion had turned against the U.N. sanctions. Current U.S. policy against Iraq was doomed. Baghdad was poised on the cusp of rehabilitation. Cooperation with the 9/11 investigation would have been one more factor to justify that end. It didn't take Saddam very long to figure that out.

If our back channel achieved significant success and demonstrated Iraq's commitment to cooperate with U.S. anti-terrorism policy, where would that leave the White House? Back at square one without an excuse to launch their war.

But I did not understand that yet.

With the world discombobulated by 9/11, the White House seized its advantage and rushed to rev up its propaganda machine, with Vice President Cheney and Senator John McCain as its mouthpiece. In a calculated push to link Iraq to Al Qaeda, the White House launched one of the most blatant and audacious deceptions in the War on Terrorism.

Not for the first time, my credentials posed a serious problem if the White House and Congress intended to perpetrate this fraud. Our team had monitored Iraq's enormously poor enthusiasm for various jihadi groups since 1996. We received Baghdad's cooperation on matters of anti-terrorism. And finally, we had tracked Iraq's possible relationship to Osama bin Laden back to 1998, immediately after Osama delivered his infamous jihad fatwa against the west.[156] As early as the spring of 1998, before the U.S. Embassy bombings in Dar es Salaam and Nairobi, Kenya, I played a first-hand role in assessing whether Bin Laden would find sanctuary or financial support from Libya or Iraq.[157] In one of the very first investigations of what I call "Pre-Al Qaeda" structure and support, I approached both embassies, and expressed sympathy and appreciation for Bin Laden's cause. Their reaction was stark. Libyan diplomats declared me 'persona non grata' at their Embassy in New York, and commanded that I must go away and never return. They would not meet with me.

As for Baghdad's reaction, Iraqi diplomats voiced great alarm. They quizzed me extensively as to what Islamic cleric had set up shop in Washington DC, who could possibly preach support for Bin Laden's cause. They urged me to explore Islam through a different mosque, and expressed dismay that ordinarily my understanding of Islam was so positive, and now suddenly it had become so dark. Iraqi diplomats argued that Bin Laden does not follow true Islamic beliefs. They warned that in my quest to understand their religion, I had come across unholy teachings, and I should not trust them. They urged me to abandon any new friends teaching these terrible things. And they pushed very hard to discover who those radical Islamic friends were. They wanted names and nationalities.

All of this was reported to Dr. Fuisz, who delightedly instructed me to return to the United Nations and apologize to Libya and Iraq, telling them that I had made a great mistake in my enthusiasm, and that I recanted my support for Bin Laden.

Diplomats from both embassies expressed profound relief.

Our project was important because it established one of the earliest benchmarks for the response that would greet Osama in Middle East nations alienated from the United States. Would his compatriots find sanctuary and welcome in Libya or Iraq? Absolutely not. Baghdad and Tripoli were onto Osama's game years before Al Qaeda hit our radar. They saw him as a serious threat. They demanded that I should stay away from his followers— or stay away from them.

My career as an Asset was itself a history of Iraq's opposition to radical Islamic terrorism.

And so within days of the 9/11 attack, I headed for New York to meet with Libyan and Iraqi diplomats. Both Dr. Fuisz and Hoven urged me to act as rapidly as possible to secure the highest levels of cooperation from both countries. There was no indication that either of my handlers participated in the GOP deception. Quite the opposite, I performed at their demand.

Dr. Fuisz was typically smooth, quoting John F. Kennedy: "Ask not what your country can do for you, ask you what you can do for your country. You don't ask for anything right now."

Paul Hoven would later tell the FBI that he spoke with me 40-50 times after 9/11.[158] That speaks for itself.

It must be understood that I had to do the fieldwork before Dr. Fuisz and Hoven could provide reports to the Intelligence Community as my handlers. At the end of the day, I was the one in direct contact with Iraqi officials. I was the one with the diplomatic sources. My handlers would succeed or fail—and the policy would succeed or fail—based on the aggressiveness of my outreach. After 9/11 nobody was playing. The CIA damn well wanted everything turned over immediately. People like Dr. Fuisz and Hoven took this investigation very seriously. They pushed me to the limit. The attack required it.

For that matter, I had Libya, too. That was easy. In my conversations with Libya's Ambassador Issa Babaa at the United Nations immediately after 9/11, he quickly reminded me that Libya was the first nation in the world to warn Interpol about Osama bin Laden in 1995. (Egypt issued the first warrant for his arrest in 1996.) Given that long-standing animosity between Gadhaffi and bin Laden, it was determined that Libya would have no present day linkages to Al Qaeda that could be exploited for intelligence purposes. However, Libya was praised in media reports for other cooperation that it provided, and its expression of sympathy for victims of the attack, including its recognition of the many international citizens who died. Over 90 nations lost their fellow countrymen in the September 11 strikes. The tragedy that day struck world-wide.

I communicated those messages from Libya's Ambassador to Dr. Fuisz. When the media praised Libya's cooperation after 9/11, I reasonably concluded that my messages had made it up the intelligence chain, and that the success of my efforts was recognized and appreciated.

With regards to Libya, I think it was appreciated.[159] A few weeks later, the New York Times lauded Libya's contribution with the headline: "Three New Allies Help CIA in its Fight against Terror." "Since Sept 11, CIA officials have opened lines with intelligence officials from several nations that Washington has accused of supporting terrorism."

Importantly, those meetings at the Libya House occurred on the same days—the same trips to New York—as my meetings at the Iraqi Embassy. I would visit one after the other.

It is with a mixture of pride and amused disgust, therefore, that I recall one count of my federal indictment: "On or about September 19, 2001, Susan Lindauer a/k/a "Symbol SUSAN," met with an officer of the Iraq Intelligence Service in Manhattan."[160]

The date was actually September 18, one week after the 9/11 attack. The feds got the wrong day. And I certainly hoped my diplomat friend, Salih Mahmoud, had ties to Iraqi Intelligence. It would make my success much easier to achieve. That was the whole point of the trip, after all.

It must be underscored that the Justice Department never disputed that my work occurred. On the contrary, the federal prosecutor, Mr. Edward O'Callaghan, argued that I should serve 10 to 25 years in prison *because it did occur.* He simply argued before the Court that my CIA handler, Dr. Fuisz, was interested in Libya and only Libya—Not Iraq.

That's right! According to the Justice Department, the CIA did not care about Iraq's relationship to Al Qaeda after 9/11. They did not want to know anything about it.

I am not making that up.

The alleged evidence supporting this portion of the indictment is what I call "hinky." And that's putting it politely.

According to the FBI, an Iraqi diplomat named Salih Mahmoud (whom I fully acknowledge working with) treated me to lunch on three afternoons in Manhattan.[161]

On September 8, 2001, the Iraqi diplomat allegedly bought us both lunch for $33.50. My half of that was apparently $16.75 with tax and tip.

On September 13, he bought the two of us lunch for $27.57 at 2:17 pm, according to a time-stamped receipt. My half of that bill would have come to $13.78.

And on September 22, he apparently bought us lunch for $31.85—and my half was $15.92.

The grand total of this misadventure totaled $92.92—By deduction, my half share for three lunches in the most expensive city in the world totaled $46.46. I found that somewhat insulting, though most amusing. All receipts were date and time stamped. So the feds couldn't fudge the meetings, which helped my defense enormously.

Curiously, none of those lunches took place on September 19, 2001—the date cited in my indictment. Yet this was the evidence presented to justify criminal charges against me.

I mean, come on—didn't the FBI have anything better to do? The Justice Department wanted to put me on trial for eating a cheeseburger?!

Ah, but was it American Cheese! Was it a patriotic cheeseburger? Or was it the "French" fries, which irked the Justice Department? That's what a jury had to decide.

Remember now, a defendant is innocent until proven guilty—even under the Patriot Act.

Here's the punch line, which I could not wait to share with a jury: The FBI had the wrong Susan. The diplomat in question, Salih Mahmoud, had a girlfriend named Susan who worked at the United Nations. We joked about her all the time, that he had "another Susan, since he couldn't have me." She was the "other woman." Or maybe I was the "other woman." Whatever—we were two different American women.

Apparently the FBI didn't figure that out in its investigation. That's what happens when the U.S. arrests its Assets! Nobody knows what's really going on. It's pandemonium!

I used to giggle deliriously, anticipating my pleasure as I exposed my "rival" to a jury. Given the gravity of the charge—eating a cheese burger with a friendly Iraqi diplomat, you can only imagine how I savored the imaginary moment.

And how did we know this 'other Susan' was the real cheeseburger fiend? Because September 8 was three days before 9/11. For one thing, witnesses would testify that I stopped visiting New York several weeks before 9/11.[162] They would testify that I warned friends and family to stay out of New York City, too. The CIA had not yet decided they wanted me dead. They were still trying to keep me alive. Thus, on September 8, I was tucked at home in Maryland, safe from terrorists and federal prosecution.

I also had a hard alibi for September 13, 2001. When the FBI broke open the hard drive of my computer, they recorded that somebody created a letter to Andy Card at the White House, at exactly the time I was supposedly sitting in that restaurant with Salih Mahmoud.[163] The date and time stamp on the visa receipt proved it was impossible for me to have traveled to New York for the lunch, except in a time warp. Or perhaps a magic carpet!

Did I mention that New York City lies 214 miles from my home in Takoma Park, Maryland?

Later, staff at the Bureau of Prisons speculated that perhaps a friend snuck into my house and posed as me, creating the letter to Andy Card as an alibi. (And you guys think I'm paranoid!)

It added to the pleasure of my jury fantasy. After all the trouble, I hope it was a good hearty burger! I think New York City owes me one on the house! Hell, they should name a cheeseburger after me on Wall Street after all the trouble they caused me! And by God, it better have American cheese! Or maybe pepper jack! That's spicy enough!

All of which explains why I wear my indictment with a peculiar sort of pride. The indictment proves beyond any doubt that I functioned as a "First-Responder" to the 9/11 tragedy. I confess wholeheartedly that I appeared at the scene of the crime, even if the FBI got all its facts and dates wrong. Without question, I visited my embassy contacts in New York after 9/11.

But if I wasn't that "other Susan" eating cheeseburgers with Salih Mahmoud, then what exactly did I contribute to the 9/11 investigation? And why would the U.S. government want to arrest me so that I would be gagged from disclosing it?

Where do I start—

Brace yourselves.

Iraq's efforts to contribute to the 9/11 investigation were far more substantial than Republican leaders wanted to acknowledge to the American people or the world community.

With tragic irony, I strongly believe that the Republican leadership's refusal to accept Iraq's assistance has resulted in long term damage to the War on Terror, with dire consequences for future security. Without Iraq's help, the War on Terror, which Republicans have declared their legacy, could be construed as a massive leadership failure. In my opinion, the Republican failure has left a back door wide open for another major terrorist strike on the United States.

And let me tell you why.

Iraq's Official Response to 9/11: Frustration and the Oklahoma City Bombing

Immediately after 9/11, Iraq was much more frustrated and reluctant to contribute than Libya.

First of all, Iraqi diplomats in New York and Baghdad numbered among the very few who possessed direct knowledge that U.S. Intelligence unequivocally expected a 9/11 style of attack throughout the summer of 2001, involving airplane hijackings and some sort of strike on the World Trade Center. How did they know? Because I told them. Our team pushed Baghdad hard to supply details of the conspiracy from May, 2001 onwards. And we threatened them with a massive retaliatory attack if they failed.

In Iraq's eyes, that strained our credibility.

In back channel communications from Baghdad, Iraqi diplomats challenged me sternly: "Obviously you knew the attack was coming, because you kept telling us about it. You should have stopped it, Susan —instead of blaming us today. *Why didn't you stop it?*"

"We will tell you why. You didn't stop it, because you've been planning to attack us all along. This is your excuse. That's why the United States let (9/11) happen! *You didn't want to stop it.*"

"Your government allowed this to happen to its own people so that you could declare war on us in Baghdad. And now you complain!"

The Iraqi diplomats nailed it.

They also guessed, probably correctly, that their old enemy, the Israeli Mossad, gave us intelligence about the attack—and the Mossad now sought to lay blame at their door.

To Baghdad's way of thinking, that made perfect sense. That did not make Iraqi diplomats sympathetic, however. Most Americans will not like to hear this. But any sort of debriefing requires candor. Otherwise it's worthless. So I will say it straight up: Iraqi diplomats got incensed by our outrage over the 9/11 strike.

"This bombing, it happens every day all over the world. And Americans don't care! Other families suffer. Other homes are destroyed. Schools are bombed. Commerce is disrupted. This is the way. It is your way. This is what America does to other countries. America drops the bombs! Now you are suffering, too, and you're angry. Well, damn your hypocrisy!"

On my first trip to New York on September 18, those were the sentiments of Iraqi diplomats. What else could we expect after running 20,000 sorties over Iraq's sovereign air space by this time? And that clock would keep running on the sanctions and no fly zones for an additional 18 months, until the U.S. invasion.

The problem was that Baghdad possessed vast amounts of exactly the sort of data and sourcing that the U.S. required to launch a muscular and effective counter-strike on Al Qaeda. Say anything else about Saddam: his government had phenomenal tracking on terrorist cells throughout the Middle East, particularly with regards to Islamic agitators. Baghdad, for example, would have access to bank accounts or financial records. If Saddam didn't have it already, he could get it. And that was exactly the sort premium intelligence the U.S. desired after 9/11.

Iraq had the goods alright. The problem was getting the stuff handed over to us.

Immediately after 9/11, I began badgering my diplomatic contacts by phone. I urged Iraqi officials to express condolences for the 9/11 families. And I pushed hard for cooperation with the 9/11 investigation, especially with regards to identifying Al Qaeda operations and financial mechanisms. Dr. Fuisz and I had very precise conversations about what sort of documents would be worthwhile to lay hold of.

On September 18, 2001—one week after the 9/11 attack—I headed to New York to meet my diplomatic contacts.[164] Libya was generous in its condolences for the 9/11 victims and their families, noting the international scope of suffering. Iraq was scathing. In conversation, Baghdad had caught on with lightning speed that the U.S. government stayed remarkably silent about its advance knowledge of the attack. They were also sharp on point that their great tormentor, the United States, urgently required their help in order to achieve the most substantial results.

Our need galled Iraqi diplomats for sure. They stressed that New York had no authority to grant my request. The decision would have to come from the highest levels of government in Baghdad. From Saddam himself. Or Tariq Aziz. Diplomats in New York would take no action until authorization was received. "Oh no, no," I shook my head. "You must push Baghdad hard. The global community demands a rapid reply."

And that's what we got.

Very late on the night of September 21, 2001, my diplomatic contact, Salih Mahmoud, phoned my home in Maryland with an urgent request that I should return to New York as quickly as possible to receive the official response from Baghdad.[165]

Early the next morning, on September 22, I jumped in my car and hit Interstate 95, heading north to Manhattan through Delaware and New Jersey. At my speeds, it's about 3 ½ hours in each direction, a long day after meetings, but always productive.

When I got to New York, my meeting with Salih Mahmoud took place inside the Embassy. I wanted to gather as much feedback from other diplomats as possible. Also, the spooks could audiotape any meetings that occurred at the embassy, standard practice during a crisis. In this situation, Langley would have the capability to authenticate my reporting, and they could add to the analysis. So it was necessary for the conversation to stay inside the embassy. Unhappily for federal prosecutors, I would have resisted any suggestion to move our meeting to a restaurant.

Salih was late arriving. Apparently he was enjoying lunch with his girlfriend, the "other Susan." That's a lunch I would dearly wish to have shared with them, since I am ultimately the one who paid for it. And it cost a great deal more than $31.85, I can tell you now.[166]

Immediately Salih handed me a written, decoded statement.

What follows is the official verbatim transcript from Baghdad on September 21, 2001 in reply to my request for cooperation after 9/11, including grammar and parenthetical comments.[167] (See Appendix) The brackets are my own insertions:

1. If the request had been made in different circumstances, it would have been possible for us to agree or go along with it.
2. With the continuation of U.S. and U.K. aggression and the tense atmosphere in The United State of America against Iraq, any step to be taken by Iraq might be interpreted in a harmful manner to Iraqi reputation and to the keenness of Iraq to maintain its dignity.
3. Despite of that, all the points proposed by you [meaning me, Susan Lindauer] reflect the real Iraqi position.
4. If U.S. declared that it intends to halt (stop) the air raids against Iraq (or such things like this) in order to concentrate on other Matters, the situation would be different (better).
5. However, we are prepared to meet any American official in a covert or non-covert manner to discuss the common issues.
6. In any case, Iraq has suffered from terrorist and its leaders, including his excellency, Mr. President has been a target to many assassination attempts, in addition to the attempt to assassinate Mr. Tariq Aziz in first of April, 1980. In fact, he was injured, as well as some Iraqi leadership members who suffered from such terrorist acts.
7. Iraq demonstrated a good faith towards U.S.A. in 1993 after Oklahoma trade center previous accident, and informed American government through Iraqi interest section in Washington that it (Iraq) was prepared to provide U.S.A. With Some Information about the perpetrators of 1993 accident, if American side would send a delegate to Baghdad. But the American side dealt with our offer improperly and they said to Us (Iraq) to deliver this information. That means eventually they rejected to meet us.
8. This is the Iraq official position.

Reading over it, I jumped on the references to Oklahoma City and the first World Trade Center "accident" in 1993.[168]

My eyes got big. I was immediately glad that we stayed inside the Embassy for the meeting. I began by asking some disarmingly simple questions. I tried to avoid questions that would arouse excitement or cause Salih to alter his story to please me. I wanted to know exactly how the paper arrived. Who had access to it? Whether the Ambassador or other senior diplomats in New York might possibly have edited it?

Above all, did the document that arrived actually use the word "Oklahoma," or had Salih guessed? It was important that he should not be afraid to correct a mistake, if he'd made one.

Salih replied candidly. The message had arrived in code. He had deciphered the paper himself. Nobody else was authorized to lay hands on it. So the message had originated wholly in Baghdad, without amendment of its political content by diplomatic staff in New York.

Salih assured me that it came from the "top of the government, far above the Foreign Minister. Nobody would be authorized to change it without facing serious troubles."

I suspected that meant Saddam Hussein or Tariq Aziz.

And finally, yes, the coded message from Baghdad included a cipher for "Oklahoma." Salih faithfully swore that he had checked the document carefully. It was not a mistake on his end in New York.

I pressed a little harder. Did he understand the geography of the United States? Did he understand that Oklahoma was not part of Manhattan, but more than 1,000 miles away? Did Baghdad understand that these were two separate locations? It could be an innocent mistake by someone who lacked knowledge of American geography. Both of them had suffered horrific terrorist attacks.

"Yes," he replied. "We know they are two separate cities. I know it, and Baghdad knows it. We know they had two separate 'accidents.'"

"I think the message refers to both of them," Salih leaned back on the sofa, and kicked his feet up on the coffee table, suddenly conspiratorial.

"I understand that it is still possible for you to receive this information. This door is not closed. If we give it to you, Susie, there is no problem. When you give it to America, they're going to say that we have it. With the tensions between us, Baghdad fears taking any action that would expose us to harm. You've been threatening us for months, Susie."

"If you had not threatened us, we would not be so concerned now."

"Why didn't you stop the attack, Susie? You told us about it. We learned about it from you. Obviously you know more than anyone. So how can you blame us? Perhaps you should not look so far away."

"Baghdad has to consider all of these things."

"But this message is very positive," Salih insisted. "Baghdad would be ready to cooperate if our interests are not damaged. Then you can have what you want. I see no problem in giving it to you. I think you will get it."

Here you see the value of an Asset. Iraqi diplomats would give this information to me, because of our longstanding relationship. They would never deliver it to the United States directly. Those were my relationships that prompted a remarkably fast response from Baghdad, with a three day turn around from September 18 to September 21, followed by a meeting on September 22. Iraq trusted me as the point person, though they had no trust for the United States whatsoever. And they would do favors for me, which I would request to serve those greater needs. Expecting that, the CIA would leverage my relationships and network of contacts for its own advantage. That's how our back-channel worked.

That official response from Baghdad was communicated in a letter to Andy Card, Chief of Staff to President Bush, dated September 24, 2001.[169] That letter faithfully records that I visited the Iraqi Embassy in New York on September 18 and September 22, proving that nothing was concealed from the White House and Dr. Fuisz, who also received copies of my reports to Andy Card, and prompt debriefings on top of that.

Despite all of my troubles, I stand by my conclusion in that letter to Andy Card. As I wrote then: "Iraq has remained silent against the accusations playing in the media not out of malice, but because of frozen communications. I believe Iraq does not know how to speak to the United States, so that you can hear what they are saying, and that's because they are so traumatized."[170]

"They are frightened of an irrational U.S. response—because they've seen the previous Administration retaliate with attacks inspired by fuzzy data, or inadequately researched speculations, usually to distract from some media scandal or other. That's why the Iraqis—and some others, frankly—are freezing up, and the common peoples of some Islamic nations have voiced a distrust of the information against Bin Laden. (They see it) as political justification for a witch hunt against an old enemy."

"To regain credibility, in this first situation you are going to be held to a higher standard of scrutiny from the Arab Street. You've got to show this is not the same... old cynical leadership. They respect your strength, there is no question. But they also must respect your judgment, so that you retain all of your moral authority."

"And so I urge the Administration to hit your mark, but keep your focus tight. Don't use excuses to expand the circle of targets. Everyone in Europe and the Middle East will see through you, and your actions will only diminish America's moral justification."

There was no hostility in my assessment, and I was correct on all accounts. Yet this letter would become a focal point of my five year legal battle over whether I performed as an "Iraqi Agent," and whether I deserved to spend 10 to 25 years of my life behind prison bars for delivering such prescient advice to the White House.[171]

Fortunately I did not know that yet. After 9/11, I seized on Iraq's claims about the Oklahoma City Bombing and the 1993 World Trade Center attack. I became determined to wrestle the evidence out of Iraq's hands.

In the next weeks, I would return to New York frequently to investigate what Iraq offered the United States. I was convinced that intelligence cache would possess exceptional value.

Intriguingly, Iraqi diplomats in New York and Baghdad swore their documents proved active Middle Eastern participation in both the Oklahoma City bombing and the first World Trade Center attack in 1993. Senior diplomats, including members of a delegation from Baghdad, claimed the evidence was irrefutable that Timothy McVeigh and Terry Nichols had not acted alone, but in fact received technical guidance and financial assistance from pre-Al Qaeda forces, sometimes called the "Inter-Arab" group, prior to 9/11.

Diplomats repeated their claims to Rita Cosby, former Chief Correspondent for the Fox News Channel, a highly credible, western (non-Arab source). It's my understanding that diplomats promised to show her those papers during any future trip to Baghdad.

As a long-time Asset with ties to the Embassy since 1996, Iraq was mine to chase. Anything from Baghdad would have to come through me. The United States had a total of three Assets covering Iraq at the United Nations —and two of them were brand new after 9/11, and in their mid-20s. They had no experience with this sort of work. By contrast, I had several major projects in play already— including a special project in support of U.S. anti-terrorism policy.

FBI Task Force Invited to Baghdad

Prior to 9/11, there was already a major platform on the table that would have dramatically enhanced the United States' pursuit of terrorists seeking sanctuary inside Iraq. Our team had already been working for a full year to get President Bush's approval for an FBI Task Force to go into Baghdad. We had persuaded Iraq to authorize the FBI to conduct terrorist investigations inside Iraq, with the right to interview witnesses and, most controversially, the right to make arrests. We just needed authorization from the White House to implement the agreement.[172]

The idea for an FBI Task Force emerged in the aftermath of the strike on the U.S.S. Cole in October, 2000.

A year before 9/11, Iraqi diplomats had provided advance warning about a major terrorist attack targeting the port facilities in Aden, Yemen. Iraq's warning came just 10 days before the October, 2000 attack on the U.S.S. Cole by forces linked to Osama bin Laden.

Intelligence about the conspiracy came through my back channel, with an emergency summons to visit the Iraqi Embassy. Diplomats informed me that Baghdad had swiftly deported a Saudi national from its territory after discovering that he was conspiring to attack a port facility elsewhere in the Middle East. Iraqi diplomats protested that they would not dare to arrest a foreign national, a Saudi most of all, for fear of international reprisals. There was too much controversy. Even cracking a major terrorist conspiracy harmful to the Saudi royal family would not be sufficient for Iraq to act, because of repercussions in the international community. It would not be feasible under any circumstances. Diplomats protested that they could only deport the jihadi, and notify us. The Iraqi diplomat was quite emphatic, however, that the Saudi man had traveled on to Yemen after leaving Iraq's territory.

Without delay, I notified Dr. Fuisz and Hoven that the Port of Aden in Yemen might be targeted for attack.

On a rapid turn around trip to New York, I quickly warned Yemen's Deputy Ambassador at the United Nations, Mr. Al Sindi, of the threat. Yemen had served as a non-permanent member of the Security Council during Lockerbie, and we'd become friendly. For awhile Mr. Al Sindi visited me socially in Washington, and took me out for dinners in Georgetown. So when I told him about the possibility of an attack over dinner in New York, he took my warning seriously.

Regrettably the warning came too late to stop a small boat laden with explosives from ramming the U.S.S. Cole while it docked for refueling five days later.

But Iraq gave a chilling explanation for the logic behind the conspiracy. Apparently, the Saudi group hoped to alienate the local population from Yemen's central government and the United States. The terrorist group hoped the Yemeni government would be so disorganized in its response to the terrorist assault that the United States would be provoked to impose some sort of sanctions as punishment. That would cause hardship for the local people, and cost support for the West and the central Yemeni authority. The conspirators' vicious logic infuriated officials in Baghdad.

Alienated populations in rural border communities could then be persuaded to embrace a sort of freedom fighter/terrorist/insurgency amalgamation. That could provide cover for the Saudi group to burrow deep into rural Yemeni communities and launch attacks on Saudi oil fields from Yemen's territory. Yemen is scrabble poor. Many tribal families in the border lands bitterly resent Saudi extravagance, and perceive them to have seized Yemen's historic territory in order to expand their wealth. Some of the rural tribes might welcome raids on Saudi oil fields.

In short, the U.S.S. Cole attack was predatory and opportunistic, pure and simple. The terrorists sought to create hardship for the Yemeni people, so that it could profit strategically from their misery and isolation. The Saudi group in question would soon have a notorious name, and a more infamous reputation: Al Qaeda. The attack on the Port of Aden in Yemen would launch a major effort by this Al Qaeda group to achieve dominance in global terrorist circles.

Knowing all of that, my warning had been two-fold: 1) notifying Deputy Ambassador Al Sindi of Yemen of the possible attack on the Port of Aden, and 2) discussing strategies for cooperation, so Yemen could hit the ground running and satisfy U.S. authorities.

If they couldn't stop the attack, at least Yemen would be braced for U.S. investigation tactics. And so, five days later, when a small boat laden with explosives rammed the USS Cole, Yemeni officials were not caught wholly off guard.

Demands for an FBI Task Force in Baghdad erupted out of the CIA's frustration over Iraq's impotence to thwart foreign terrorists setting up shop inside its borders.

Baghdad complained bitterly that it had no desire to provide sanctuary for Islamic groups, which Saddam's government despised. However, young jihadis arrived at their borders regardless, attracted by perceptions of the lack of central authority in Iraq. Correctly or incorrectly, terrorists perceived that the international community would hinder Iraq's ability to police its territory, and sought to exploit that weakness. But once they got to Iraq, they found no friend in Saddam. They posed a genuine threat to his secularism, and risked stirring up fanaticism among his poverty-weary people. Saddam's government was already weakened; he did not relish any outsider taking advantage of the porous desert to set up camp inside his country.

The bombing of the USS Cole stood out as a frustrating reminder of those complications. Iraq's complaints were legitimate, unfortunately. Iraq could not arrest foreign nationals without provoking an international crisis. Nobody suggested Baghdad should reverse that policy. Yet clearly something had to be done. The U.S.S. Cole created an imperative to demand action from Baghdad.

Immediately after the attack on the USS Cole in October 2000, Dr. Fuisz gave instructions that I should corner Iraqi diplomats with a demand to allow the FBI or Interpol to set up a Task Force inside Iraq. Dr. Fuisz instructed me to demand authority for the FBI or Interpol to conduct investigations, interview sources and make arrests inside Iraq. If Baghdad could not control the entrance and movement of terrorists inside its borders, who might be attracted by the perception of Iraq's flagging security under sanctions, as diplomats insisted, then the international community should be allowed to provide additional safeguards against terrorist conspiracies.

Remarkably, by late February, 2001, Iraqi officials in Baghdad had agreed. The FBI was formally invited to set up shop inside Iraq eight months before the 9/11 attack.

Regrettably, for all the tough talk on terrorism, no action on the security arrangement was undertaken by Republican leaders.

And so another critical opportunity was missed before the World Trade Center attack.

The tragedy of 9/11 gave the U.S. a second chance.[173] I was convinced that an FBI Task Force would provide a major windfall of intelligence for global counter-terrorism efforts, and so renewed my push for Baghdad to allow the FBI (or Interpol or Scotland Yard) to operate inside its borders. It was a logical demand. Given new disclosures about the cache of documents establishing a Middle East link to the Oklahoma City bombing and the 1993 World Trade Center attack, the FBI seemed best positioned to execute a rapid turn around. They could acquire all of the available financial records on pre-Al Qaeda transactions in one throw, as opposed to what I could get piecemeal from Iraqi diplomats. The FBI could act immediately to subpoena bank accounts identified in the papers, and move rapidly to seize suspicious funds. They could deploy teams of law enforcement to chase down terror suspects.

The FBI would get the glory to show up the success of its operations. That accounted for some hostility at CIA towards the project. However, given the dynamics, it seemed appropriate for law enforcement to take a lead role, as the most effective means of putting that intelligence to rapid use.

There was just one foreseeable problem: Dr. Fuisz warned that it might take a directive from Congress to bring the CIA and the FBI together on the project, because of longstanding hostility between the two agencies.

That proved to be the greatest understatement of all.

CHAPTER 9:

IRAQ'S CONTRIBUTION TO 9/11 INVESTIGATION, PART II

After 9/11, everything moved into high gear, making rapid progress on all fronts with Iraq. For the first months after the attack, 9/11 looked like it might become a catalyst for great good.

If War was unavoidable in Afghanistan, a full arsenal of peace options flanked the troops in Iraq.

My projects had been underway for a full year. Now we rallied to the finish line.

Weapons Inspections

Through our back-channel, Iraq's Ambassador to the United Nations, Dr. Saeed Hasan had formally welcomed the return of weapons inspectors to Baghdad as of November, 2000.[174] Still, there was a striking disconnect in the concerns of the two sides, which our back channel sought to address. The CIA trumped all, demanding a hard commitment from Iraq on key points before the agreement got turned over to the U.N. Security Council, a sort of tacit acknowledgement that U.S. demands might exceed the scope of the U.N. resolutions.

Foremost for the U.S., there had been much talk of Iraq's national pride and past insults by Australian Richard Butler's weapons inspection teams. That worried the CIA. Even the slightest risk of confrontation, once inspection teams were deployed on the ground, made U.S. Intelligence wary of accepting Iraq's invitation. The CIA intended to push Iraq hard during inspections. They feared that Baghdad would abruptly refuse to cooperate with "excessive demands" for access to possible weapons sites, and the entire operation would be jeopardized.

The CIA was adamant. Iraq must agree to weapons inspections "with no conditions." That was the operative phrase. It meant no restrictions or qualifying factors. The CIA saw that as unconditional surrender. Iraq would have to brace its people for the most rigorous standards of compliance ever practiced in the history of disarmament verification, with maximum transparency and five minute access—long enough to find a key and open the door. The U.S. also wanted the right to interview scientists outside the presence of Iraqi officials—a demand that intimidated Iraqi scientists, who feared the U.S. would twist their language and manipulate their reporting in the media. There was obviously a deep absence of trust on both sides.

That much was widely reported.

On the Iraqi side, concerns were strikingly different. Unbeknownst to the American people or the international community, Iraqi diplomats welcomed the return of weapons inspectors without hesitation, from November 2000 onwards.[175] But senior diplomats agonized over what would happen next, once the U.S. and Britain discovered no weapons caches or production facilities at any of the inspection sites. How would the process for ending sanctions move forward once U.N. inspectors found nothing? What mechanism would protect Iraq, and require the U.S. to validate the results, once Iraq's disarmament had been thoroughly verified? How would the U.S. and British governments react when their weapons fantasy turned out to be a delusion? We spent a lot of time talking about how to get the trapped giants (the U.S. and Britain) out of their corner.

Iraq understood the concept of pride. They understood that London and Washington had a personal stake in the inspection results. The U.S. had pounded its breast and declared before the world that Iraq was hiding illegal weapons caches. Diplomats recognized that the United States would have to save face somehow, when its theory proved entirely wrong. Iraqi diplomats spent a lot of time debating and fretting over how to handle that final stage.

That's what ultimately convinced me Iraq had no weapons of mass destruction in the country. Iraq actively worried over how the United States and Britain would handle the embarrassment of their defeat. That revealed a lot.

Another thing, from November 2000 onwards, top Iraqi officials swore that U.N. weapons inspections could resume within a few weeks. So while the U.S. and Britain publicly chastised Iraq for withholding access to sites, in back channel negotiations Iraq was throwing the door wide open, urging the U.S. to send the weapons teams right away. Baghdad was eager to act as a friendly host, and insisted that inspectors would be well treated, whereas the United States dug in its heels and balked at sending the inspectors. That appeared to be a sort of admission that the U.S. and Britain recognized the outcome would embarrass the West.

Above all, Iraq made clear that it wanted friends. It was ready to embrace a different future. All of Iraq's future trading partners, who hankered for the end of sanctions to legalize their reconstruction contracts, gave the same ultimatum: Baghdad must accept weapons inspections before everyone could get on with business. All of Iraq's future friends agreed unanimously and unequivocally on that point. They hated the sanctions. They desired a new chapter of friendly relations with Baghdad. But there was no way to surmount the weapons inspections. Iraq would have to acquiesce.

And so, over and over again, Iraq assured the U.S. through our back channel that it accepted the inevitability of the inspections process.

That's a total contradiction of what Americans and the international community were told.

Cooperation with the Global War on Terrorism

Another great contradiction was Iraq's so called "lack of cooperation" with U.S. anti-terrorism policy. Congress had no idea what it was talking about, suggesting Iraq embraced any sort of terrorist philosophy. Throughout the 1990s, Iraq had been one of the United States' best sources on counter-terrorism. Our back-channel existed first and foremost as a back door to receive that intelligence. Baghdad was always enthusiastic to contribute, irregardless of the sanctions. Congress had nothing to fear.

Support for global anti-terrorism had been Baghdad's strongest suit in the 1990s, as a secular Arab government keeping tight rein on radical Islamic fundamentalists inside its borders. Baghdad flatly abhorred the notion that it willingly provided sanctuary to jihadi terrorists. Diplomats protested that image vigorously. Quite the contrary, Saddam would have liked to arrest all young jihadi types, and send them to rot in prison. On that point, Saddam had a lot in common with former Vice President Dick Cheney.

It must be understood that Saddam's government defined "terrorism" as craven acts of unprovoked violence against civilian targets, either to unsettle political or economic interests. Saddam's government did not consider "acts of liberation" to constitute terror-ist assaults—like the Palestinian fight against Israeli Occupation. Baghdad never shared intelligence with the U.S. on those jihadis. Quite the opposite, those "freedom martyrs" received special protection and financial support from Baghdad, which never wavered throughout those years. Leaders in Washington and London should have thought hard about that, before sending U.S. soldiers into Baghdad, since it's considered proper Islamic upbringing to oppose Infidel Occupations.

But Saddam was supremely paranoid about religious zealots ready to commit acts of violence in the name of Islam, for the sake of violence itself. He provided no comfort to those individuals. They would come to Iraq, eager to attack the United States or (mostly) Saudi Arabia, expecting to receive a sympathetic audience in Baghdad. Saddam would throw them right out, howling in protest to the U.S. through my back channel that sanc-tions acted like a magnet for those groups, to the detriment of the Gulf Region. He hated them more than we did.

Diplomats complained bitterly that the international community prohibited Baghdad from arresting these Jihadis on the spot. "You don't want them in your country!" They complained. "Why should we allow them in ours? If we discover jihadis who want to attack Saudi interests, do you think we can arrest them? No! We would like to help protect the Saudis. But the International Community would never allow it! They would never forgive us! So what can we do?"

The problem was that Iraq could not effectively block border access to jihadis attracted by the perception of Baghdad's lack of central authority under sanctions. They recognized Saddam's government had limited options for handling the influx. And they were correct; his only real option was deportation. So they came in as visitors and kept a low profile for a few months until they could resist no longer. At that point, they would come into confrontation with Iraqi authorities, who would ship them off to a new outpost.

Against that backdrop, our push to get an FBI or Interpol Taskforce into Iraq won rapid approval in Baghdad after the October, 2000 bombing of the U.S.S. Cole in Yemen.

Iraq only hesitated long enough to insist that any terrorists discovered by the FBI would hail from Syria, Jordan or Lebanon. Baghdad swore they would not be home-grown in Najaf or Mosul. Iraqi officials insisted their country was a transit point only. Saddam feared what their fanaticism could inspire among his people, so he squashed them. Saddam wanted them gone.

And so *eight months before 9/11*, Iraq consented to the presence of an FBI or Interpol Task Force inside its borders. The FBI could have been operating inside Baghdad from the spring of 2001 on.

After 9/11, the agreement had to be revalidated. Baghdad correctly feared that any intelligence sharing might be portrayed in the West as an admission of guilt by Baghdad, as opposed to a cooperative effort in the global war on terrorism, like Pakistan, Jordan or Egypt.[176] Iraq desired to be treated like any other nation contributing responsibly towards a solution to this problem. Their fear was not so unreasonable.

But given Iraq's history of cooperation with anti-terrorism efforts, it was a fairly simple matter to persuade Baghdad. Once we had the task force on the table in February 2001, I just had to keep it on the table, until we could get it implemented after 9/11.[177] But without question, it was a serious and meaningful effort. All of us presumed the FBI would send its best and brightest agents, who would act aggressively to implement the agreement. They would have the right to interview witnesses and conduct investigations. Most controversially, they would have the right to arrest terror suspects. This was the motherlode.

Revelations that Iraq possessed documents proving a Middle Eastern link to the Oklahoma City bombing hit me totally by surprise, however. The Oklahoma bombing in April, 1995 preceded my approach to the Iraqi Embassy by 16 months.

But wait a minute, I can hear you thinking. That was Timothy McVeigh's gig, right? Didn't he go to his execution by lethal injection, swearing that he'd acted alone?

Yes, he did. And a lot of smart people think McVeigh lied, including R. James Woolsey,[178] former Director of the CIA and McVeigh's own attorney, Steven Jones. And yours truly.

My old handler, Paul Hoven had made himself an expert on the Oklahoma City bombing. He studied the detonation pattern and architectural designs of the building. He found it most peculiar that employees of the Bureau of Alcohol, Tobacco and Firearms (ATF) had not shown up for work the day of the bombing, as if they'd got advance wind of a possible attack. Hoven studied the "skin-head" angle and the Aryan Nation connection, the possible revenge for Ruby Ridge and the tragic conflagration at Waco, Texas. He understood all the different angles and contributing factors. But Hoven gave strict instructions that I should grab anything at all that hinted of Middle Eastern involvement in the bombing, which killed 168 people, including 19 toddlers and infants[179] at a nursery school on the ground floor of the Alfred P. Murrah Federal Building.

It strained logic to think that Timothy McVeigh and Terry Nichols acted alone.

Think about it from a practical level. Building a bomb of that detonation force requires massive sophistication and expertise in storing and mixing dangerous chemicals, maximizing detonation capability, storage of the completed bomb, and technical planning for delivery—all without triggering a premature detonation.[180] Timothy McVeigh and Terry Nichols were ambitious, yes. But in all probability, inexperienced bomb-makers would blow themselves sky high before they got so "lucky" as to create a bomb of that magnitude, and protect its separate components until delivery and detonation. This was a bomb capable of destroying a nine story building, and laying it to waste in concrete rubble, after all. There's some difficult chemistry here.

Some of us strongly believe that somebody must have provided McVeigh and Nichols with technical guidance for handling it. Travel and supplies required financial assistance, as well.

There's a remarkable documentary film that lays out this argument called "Conspiracy? The Oklahoma City Bombing." I strongly recommend it. For a more in depth and devastating analysis, I also recommend "Third Terrorist: The Middle Eastern Connection to the Oklahoma City Bombing" by Jayna Davis and "Oklahoma City Bombing Revelations," by Patrick B. Briley.

"Conspiracy?" does a beautiful job reexamining the facts about the Oklahoma City bombing, including recaps of the eye witness observations by 10 men and women, who claim to have spotted Timothy McVeigh with a young, Middle Eastern man at the Alfred P. Murrah building on April 19, 1995—minutes before the explosion.

Three employees of the Ryder shop, where McVeigh rented the truck, swore independently under oath that two men entered the store together, identified as Timothy McVeigh and an unknown Arabic man in his mid-20s. The truck was rented from a small store in a small town, with a limited number of daily transactions. It was not a busy operation. There was no confusion two days later when the FBI showed up after the blast. All three employees agreed. Two men rented that truck. One of them appeared Middle Eastern.[181]

Likewise, two Middle-Eastern looking males were spotted sprinting at break neck speeds away from the Murrah building, and jumping into a dark truck just a couple of minutes before the explosion. They sped away and almost ran over a woman four blocks away.

As former CIA Director Mr. James Woolsey told film makers, "The number of witnesses puts the burden of proof on those who say there was no foreign involvement of any kind."[182]

And here's the bomb shell: Terry Nichols' passport showed that he traveled to the Philippines five times from 1990 through 1995, ostensibly to collect his "mail order" bride. But afterwards, Nichols mostly traveled to the Philippines unaccompanied by his wife.

Strikingly, Terry Nichols and Ramzi Yousef both visited Southwestern College in the Philippines, a notorious recruiting ground for the Islamic Abu Sayef group, during the same months from November, 1994 to January, 1995. That would be Ramzi Yousef, mastermind of the 1993 World Trade Center attack, who went into hiding in the Philippines from 1993 to 1995.[183]

More curiously, a police informant visually identified Nichols as having attended a meeting with Ramzi Yousef, at which bomb building and detonation strategies were discussed—the missing technical assistance for the Oklahoma City Bombing. Nichols apparently introduced himself as "the farmer." (Back home in Kansas, Nichols was a farmer.)

By the by, the 1993 World Trade Center attack relied on the same M.O. as the Oklahoma City Bombing– a Ryder truck loaded with fertilizer explosives and ammonium nitrate.

And the shoe drops.

That's an awful lot of coincidence, folks. That two notorious terrorists would inhabit the same small Philippino community for several months, meet together to talk shop in late 1994 and early 1995, then apply the same technical strategy for bomb building— without conspiring on the attack that occurred four months later in April 1995— strains credulity.

My handler, Paul Hoven studied the inner workings of the Oklahoma City investigation exhaustively, and he thought it was a cover up, a la Arlen Specter and the theory of the single bullet that killed President John F. Kennedy. In his megalomania, Timothy McVeigh even loathed sharing credit with Terry Nichols. As such, he might not be reliable, as far as identifying other participants in the conspiracy.

And now top officials in the Iraqi Government claimed to possess documents in Baghdad proving a Middle Eastern connection to the Oklahoma City bombing and the 1993 attack on the World Trade Center, (which involved the same Ramzi Yousef who met Nichols in the Philippines in 1994 and 1995).[184]

Well, I wanted to see what Iraq had. Anybody else doing credible anti-terrorism work would want to see it too. *In my opinion, it would be irresponsible not to examine it closely!*

And so I returned to New York frequently to investigate what Iraq was offering. Iraqi diplomats responded enthusiastically to my questions. They made additional inquiries to Baghdad, and received confirmations that the documents definitely pertained to both the Oklahoma City bombing and the first World Trade Center attack in 1993.

And what's the one (known) connection between those two attacks? Ramzi Yousef. He's the primary known link, at this time. *Could it be that Iraq possessed financial documents tied to him*?

As one Iraqi diplomat traveling with a delegation from Baghdad put it, "We don't *think* this will be valuable to the United States, we *know* this will be valuable to your efforts."

If it related to Ramzi Yousef, that would be a phenomenal understatement!

Iraq's contribution would be priceless. It might outline the whole Al Qaeda spider web of illicit financing from its earliest days!

A picture of these documents began to emerge, which excited me very much. Reports from Baghdad clarified that in its treasure cache, Iraq was holding copies of financial transactions and/or banking records from the early to mid 1990s, linked to both of those two attacks. There had to be a tie into Ramzi Yousef. It's exactly what Dr. Fuisz and I hoped for. Such a cache would have incalculable value from the standpoint of tracking the financial pipeline of Al Qaeda finances. Identifying even a single bank account would allow a back trace on all funds moving in and out from other accounts. Some monies would have involved legitimate transactions. Others would not, and would yield information on even more accounts. Gaining that information could have resulted in the seizure of tens of millions of dollars that otherwise continue to circulate internationally, financing Al Qaeda and other Inter-Arab terrorist networks in Europe, Afghanistan, Pakistan, the Philippines and Asia, and Iraq to this day.

IRAQ'S CONTRIBUTION TO 9/11 INVESTIGATION, PART II

Tracing this spider network of cash from New York to European banks to Middle Eastern banks to the Philippines would have disrupted a whole river of finances keeping this global terrorism network afloat in "happy cash." I call it happy cash, because most of it comes from heroin trafficking. That's the real source of financing for terrorist activities— not donations to Islamic charities, whereby loyal Muslims tithe their income during Ramadan to finance schools and hospitals and assistance for widows and orphans. It infuriates me when the U.S. seizes bank accounts of Islamic charities engaged in community building, which offset the hopelessness and despair that feeds into alienation and violence. It's a publicity stunt for politicians.

Seizing those charity funds does not—I repeat, does not— interrupt the flow of finances circulating through the terrorist pipelines. Any politician in Washington who goes on CNN or FOX News Channel to claim otherwise has just proved he's a fool.

An astounding 90 percent of the world's heroin supply comes from the opium produced in the poppy fields of Afghanistan. All global drug cartels draw from those fields. The Islamic religion has nothing to do with it. These are drug profits.

That's what the world community has to identify and stop.

Iraq offered a way to do that, effectively.

And we refused to accept it.

That Iraq would possess such documents was totally believable to me, given the superiority of its tracking and proximity to actual terror cells. The difficulty would be transferring that intelligence to us.

Iraq had just one stipulation: They would only hand over those documents to the FBI or other international law enforcement agency— not the CIA. They insisted on supporting legitimate terrorist investigations, as opposed to getting swallowed in the miasma of intelligence. I sympathized enormously. (The Intelligence Community might easily identify something unpopular in a document, and classify it and lose it forever.)

From my perspective, Iraq's concern demonstrated the integrity of the documents. They were "results oriented only," not for show.

That should not have been a problem. It fit perfectly with our first objective of getting an FBI Task Force into Baghdad. The FBI would certainly find a lot to keep them busy.

I took one more precaution: I told Iraqi officials that if the documents truly pertained to Oklahoma City, then the Chief of Police of Oklahoma City would very likely travel to Baghdad with the FBI to receive the documents. I explained that the Police Chief was like a tribal leader, who would know the families of the Oklahoma City bombing personally. He would probably go to church with them—just like Iraqi tribal leaders attended mosque with families in their own community. He would be personally offended—and Iraq's reputation for cooperating with anti-terrorism goals would be smashed for all of the future— if this Police Chief arrived in Baghdad and found the documents were worthless. He would be ashamed to go home to face the families. The United States would never forgive Baghdad. (And nobody would ever forgive me!)

Many times I urged diplomats that it would be better to abandon their claim about Oklahoma City than to create false hope for those families. I gave them plenty of opportunities to back out.

Nothing scared off Iraqi diplomats in New York. Several vouched for the Oklahoma City connection and insisted on the superior value of their documents. Reflecting their

113

confidence, they repeated their claims to Rita Cosby, Chief Correspondent for the Fox News Channel.

By November, 2001 our teams' efforts were shaping up to a brilliant success on several fronts.

Oh yes, our team was riding high to victory. That's when I made an extraordinary discovery.

Saddam Hussein was a romantic.

There was a man at the Iraqi Embassy. *Oh yes, there had to be one.*

It started back in 1997, one of those teasing romances. Only like everything else in my life, my affairs proved slightly more colorful in the end.

Mr. A——was dark, tall and dashing, in his mid-30s. He had a muscular build. And he was incredibly sexy, with a mustache and a great wide mischievous smile, quite playful.

For all those years, it was fairly predictable that whenever the U.S. bombed Baghdad, I would visit the Iraqi Embassy in New York. Any number of times, I dropped by while the United States engaged in military action against Iraq. I would be inside the embassy, while Secret Service Agents would be posted outside the embassy, depending on the severity of the confrontation.

Late one of those nights, during a major bombing raid on Baghdad, Mr. A——swept me up in his arms. We slow danced for the better part of an hour, in the front greeting room of the Embassy. I kicked off my high heels, and danced with him in my stocking feet. There was no music. So he sang Iraqi love songs to me, which occasionally he would stop to translate.

Outside the embassy, Secret Service agents were posted on the street to prevent any confrontation with American citizens that might escalate hostilities between the two countries. Through the window, I could observe their reactions. Clearly they saw us. It was a cold and rainy night. They looked slightly shocked, as they stared back through the glass.

Our affair was incredibly romantic. And ever so slightly dangerous.

Now four years had passed since my friend got ordered back to Baghdad. It was November 28, 2001, and I was visiting the embassy for a meeting with other diplomats.

When I looked up, I saw my old lover, larger than life, standing in the doorway watching me, a haunted smile on his face.

My heart stopped for a moment. Then I jumped up from the couch in mid-conversation with another diplomat.

I grabbed him and kissed him without any thought for the reaction. There was a gasp around us, I recall, and a few shocked expressions. And some embarrassed laughter.

As it turned out, Mr. A——was traveling as part of an Iraqi Delegation to New York after 9/11. And he was carrying a message from Iraq's top Leadership. A message for me.

A decision to resolve all outstanding matters had been reached in Baghdad. The haggling was over. My friend was authorized to communicate Iraq's acceptance of all parts of my previous requests at this meeting on November 28, 2001.[185]

Strikingly, Saddam chose my old friend to courier the message.

The substance of the agreement was relayed through my back channel to Andy Card and Dr. Fuisz, in a letter dated December 2, 2001.[186] It made our final Framework for Peace comprehensive and complete:

Most notably, as of the November 28, 2001 in New York, Iraq agreed to resume weapons inspections "with no conditions—" the operative phrase sought by the CIA.[187] That committed Baghdad to the most rigorous standards of compliance demanded by the United States, with maximum transparency and swift access to all sites, including the rights to interview scientists outside the presence of Iraqi authorities.

When I heard this, I cheered out loud and threw up my arms in a "V" for victory. We had worked so hard for those three little words—"with no conditions." It appeared so simple. Yet it meant so much. It required that Iraq would not equivocate in its commitment to the inspections. Iraq would accept what had to be done, without complaint.

That meant everything.

Secondly, once more Iraq authorized an FBI or Interpol Task Force to operate inside Baghdad, with full rights to conduct investigations, interview witnesses and make arrests. The FBI would have authority to review all documents and financial records, proving a Middle Eastern link to the 1993 World Trade Center attack and the Oklahoma City bombing in 1995.[188]

In a further show of good faith, Iraq granted the FBI immediate authorization to interview Mr. Al-Anai, the Iraqi diplomat from Prague who allegedly met with Mohammad Atta, the mastermind of Al Qaeda in April or May, 2001.

My Iraqi friend, Mr. A— assured me that he had personally interviewed Al Anai, who denied that such a meeting ever occurred. Mr. A— extrapolated that Al Anai was a secular leaning Muslim, who would not have sympathized with Islamic radicalism in any regard. He drank. He smoked. He chased women. However, the Iraqi Embassy agreed that FBI agents would have permission to speak with Al Anai one on one, and hear it for themselves.[189]

That was significant. That very day, November 28, 2001, future Republican Presidential hopeful John McCain had demanded that Iraq come clean on this alleged meeting in Prague between Mr. Al Anai and Mohammad Atta. On ABC's Nightline, McCain issued a fierce demand for Iraq's cooperation with the 9/11 investigation, with special rights for law enforcement to interview Mr. Al Anai.[190] Two weeks later, on December 9, 2001, Vice President Cheney repeated the accusation on "Meet the Press."[191]

It was a done deal before Vice President Cheney opened his mouth. Baghdad agreed to the FBI interview on the very same day that Senator McCain issued the demand.

White House Chief of Staff Andy Card was notified of Iraq's agreement to that effect by December 2, 2001—one week before Vice President Cheney added his voice to the outcry.[192] From the sidelines, in my opinion, it appeared that Cheney was grand-standing, in order to maximize the impact when the White House informed America that Iraq had capitulated to the Republican leadership. Republican leaders knew they'd already got what they wanted.

And yet, stunningly, despite all that posturing by top Republican brass that this interview should be one of the highest priorities of the 9/11 investigation, no action was taken on Iraq's offer. The demand to interview Al Anai proved to be a false flag—part of the cynicism with which politicians in Washington began to manipulate the emotional tragedy of 9/11 for their own political advantage.

As the Asset responsible for securing Iraq's cooperation, I was appalled—and not for the last time, unfortunately. So much of 9/11 was a circus performance of political grandstanding. But it was all showmanship and spectacle. I just didn't know it yet.

Third on our agenda, and a particularly great victory for the United States, Iraq promised that U.S. Oil Corporations would be guaranteed Oil Exploration and Development contracts on equal par with Russia and France. The United States would not be penalized for supporting U.N. sanctions, or its many acts of military aggression. Some first tier concessions for oil development had been granted already to LUKoil of Russia and other French oil conglomerates. Iraq would not violate its previous commitments by rescinding them. However, effective immediately, the U.S. could bid for 2nd tier and 3rd tier concessions on those projects. In the future, the United would receive lucrative first tier contracts for major oil development projects, as well.[193]

U.S. companies would also receive special preference for major purchases of equipment for oil production and pipeline construction.

Fourth, another huge win for the CIA—Baghdad agreed that U.S. Corporations could return to Iraq in all economic sectors, and function at the same market share as they enjoyed prior to the first Gulf War in 1990. U.S. corporations would suffer no penalties for the years that the U.S. government inflicted the cruelty of U.N. sanctions on Baghdad. "Dual use" production would still be controlled. (Dr. Fuisz had testified before Congress about U.S. corporations that supplied weapons to Iraq before the first Gulf War. He would never have neglected that concern.) [194]

As an additional show of friendship, U.S corporations would receive priority contracts for the reconstruction of Iraq's hospitals and health care system, including pharmaceutical supplies and medical equipment. U.S. telecommunications corporations would also receive special priority contracts. Those contracts amounted to billions of dollars in corporate revenues—and major profits for shareholders. [195]

During my trip to Baghdad, Iraq added another tempting carrot to this bundle: Iraq would guarantee the purchase and import of one million American automobiles every year for 10 years. That would have a secondary benefit of creating market density for U.S. automotive spare parts. That would create thousands of high-paying union jobs, on a long term basis, in the economically distressed Rust Belt of the American Heartland—Ohio, Michigan and Indiana.

That deal would have saved the U.S. automobile industry. In turn, the domino effect would have saved the Detroit and greater Michigan economies and housing market, or at least cushioned the other blows.

It would be a lot to gain. And a lot to lose.

Last and finally, Iraq agreed to cease firing on U.S. and British fighter planes patrolling the no-fly zone over northern and southern Iraq for 30 days before any direct talks occurred, or before a comprehensive settlement got implemented. If the U.S. would consent to resolve the outstanding issues, Iraq would demonstrate its good faith with this ceasefire, effective immediately.[196]

In short, as of November 28 2001, at the close of the first year of the Bush Administration, and fully 16 months before the invasion of Baghdad, Iraq had agreed to the full framework of demands put forth by the CIA in November and December 2000. The CIA had succeeded in controlling the agenda on Iraq, and secured all major U.S. interests in any post-sanctions period.

I was elated. We had accomplished something momentous for the 9/11 investigation and for peace in the Middle East. We'd secured economic benefits for U.S. corporations, post-sanctions, and maximum transparency in the weapons inspection process. I expected our team's efforts to be supremely praised by the White House, bipartisan members of Congress and the Intelligence Community. America's leaders had defined the objectives, after all. Our team had met the challenge to fulfill them. It was a stunning victory.

Our success contrasted mightily with Republican complaints that Baghdad was refusing to cooperate in a number of areas—or that Assets failed to develop an effective platform of options for peace prior to military engagement. Quite the contrary, our success proves that White House and Congressional leaders actively engaged in fraud, selling War to the American people. It was more than a mistake in interpreting intelligence.

Our success was reported to Andy Card in a letter dated December 2, 2001. A copy of the letter was delivered to Dr. Fuisz. So the White House and the CIA were informed immediately of our tremendous success, in addition to the verbal debriefing that I delivered to Dr. Fuisz after my return from New York.

Given the ramifications of the Peace Framework, it would have been extraordinary *not* to tell them. Indeed, why would I have done all of that work if I did not intend to report it? What would be the point? My actions depended on communication to the CIA, in order to validate our progress. And as my handlers assured me numerous times over the years, it would have been irresponsible if the agencies had not paid attention to my interactions with Iraq. That's their job. To deny it now would be the ultimate dishonesty on their part. If any party had gone into Court and sworn against it under oath, they would be guilty of perjury and obstruction of justice. It would be hugely embarrassing, not to mention, criminal. They could face prosecution. And I would demand sentencing.

It seemed a grand gesture that Saddam chose my old friend to courier the message. There was an element of potential danger given our past. I could not afford any mistakes. Special precautions would be required to protect him. Indeed, his safety would become a serious priority.

In the paranoia of the intelligence world, there's no such thing as "coincidence." If this particular diplomat showed up in New York, given our past together, it signified that Saddam was using him for some purpose. The question was what purpose. For sure, nobody trusted Saddam.

There was no actual danger yet. I would have to watch for it.

The end was in sight. But I wasn't quite finished.

The Christmas Holidays were fast upon us. That would put a hold on action. Still, I expected the White House and CIA to evaluate the peace framework, and act shortly after the New Year.

Come spring-time, various Congressional offices, Democrats and Republicans alike, would confirm in private audiences with me that they had received intelligence debriefings about the advanced status of our talks.

Leaving nothing to chance, in January and February, 2002, I met again with Iraqi diplomats in marathon sessions in New York.[197] The purpose of our discussions now shifted to the examination of conflicts that had emerged during the previous weapons inspections regimen.

The U.S. claimed that certain behaviors by Iraqi officials had aggravated perceptions of non-compliance in previous inspections. For the sake of future success, every problem situation from the past was studied and picked apart exhaustively in private meetings with diplomats.

Iraq had to agree to do everything differently. Diplomats had to clarify specific changes that would be made, point by point. Nothing was left to chance.

Once again, I can prove the meetings occurred, because the Justice Department indicted me for conducting them, though some of the dates in the indictment are not accurate.

Surveillance photographs support my claims that U.S. (and possibly British) intelligence shadowed my meetings in New York in January and February, 2002.[198]

We met at a small hotel close to the United Nations. Our meetings could not be conducted in an open setting, like a restaurant or bar. Our conversations ran so late into the night that it was impossible for me to return home to Maryland. Within half an hour of checking in, like clock-work I would hear the noisy elevator stop at my floor, and a man and woman would get out and enter the room directly next to ours. It happened every time. That reassured me the Intelligence Community was fully alert. Though I could not know which alphabet agency was surveilling us, I was confident somebody was tracking our meetings closely.

More comically, at the very start, I suspect the American side hoped to limit us to a single room at the hotel. Diplomats and I returned after a few weeks hiatus to find an astonishing sight: The bed was unmade, the blanket tousled exactly as I left it *three weeks earlier*. A half empty liter of Diet Coke sat on the table, and the trash still contained the leftovers from our take-out chicken dinner. Maid service had not cleaned the room *in three weeks, and nobody else had stayed there.*

Iraqi diplomats and I took one look at that hotel room and rapidly leapt to the same conclusion. The room had to be loaded with bugs. The spooks must have showed up an hour after I left, because they'd interrupted the hotel cleaning services. They'd quarantined the room and reserved it exclusively for us. (The Iraqis demanded another room immediately).

Was I paranoid? Perhaps. Candidly, this was the hottest spook party in town. If you wanted to know what Iraq was up to after 9/11, you had to get inside this room, with us, to find out.

The CIA required this to get done right. No matter what political agenda dominated the White House, the CIA had a legitimate responsibility to secure the integrity of the weapons inspections process, and everything else. The opportunity for U.S. corporations to participate in economic reconstruction after sanctions mattered enormously. Cooperation with global counter-terrorism efforts after 9/11 demanded critical attention. There was a critical need for all of these projects to succeed. Nothing could be left to chance. If it was going to happen, it had to be done right.

Weapons inspections didn't just "happen to work." They were made to succeed because of rigorous planning and 17 months of upfront effort that made the difference. Whatever else you think of the CIA, on Iraq, they fulfilled their obligations to the highest possible degree. These men are warriors who built a strong and reliable framework for peace. It was comprehensive and proactive, covering all possible areas of U.S. interests. It was not flimsy; it was not idealistic. It was constructed to be demanding and solid.

Time would show that all camps—peace activists, conservatives skittish on the War, and all members of the international community— depended on the success of our team's advance work as the best chance to prevent this dreadful War.

I categorically deny that I engaged in criminal activity. The obvious proof of surveillance, in the photographs,[199] proves that the U.S. government was fully informed *by me* when and where those meetings would take place. Nobody suggested I should break off engagement.

And my results were outstanding. So much good was accomplished that I was quite delighted to share the good news. I always stressed my openness to feedback. If the CIA wanted me to take a different approach, or push for additional demands, they only had to ask. I would have accommodated any request immediately. That had been emphasized in private reports to Dr. Fuisz. I was anxious to comply and secure maximum results, for the sake of ending the sanctions.

After those marathon sessions with Iraqi diplomats in New York in January and February, 2002, identifying conflict scenarios in the previous weapons inspections, there was nothing more for the United States to demand from Baghdad.

It was time to hand over Iraq's agreement on the weapons inspections to the United Nations.

In early February, 2002, I grabbed up the agreement and delivered it myself to members of the United Nations Security Council, and a wider circle of Embassies known to deplore the crippling impact of sanctions on Iraq. My actions are substantiated by faxed documents to the various Ambassadors at the United Nations.[200] I am deeply proud to have done it. It's pointless for my detractors to deny, since the U.S. Justice Department collected evidence to prove it in court.

Most perplexing, the United Nations would only act once ambassadors and senior diplomats saw that Iraq was already committed to the agreement. Until preliminary talks guaranteed success, they would take no action at all, nor participate in negotiations to solve the problem. Except for the courageous leadership of Ambassador Hasmy Agam of Malaysia[201]—willing to guide and mentor the next generation of rising diplomats in the Malaysian Embassy, who he assigned to liaison with me—they would risk none of their political capital towards a solution. They would not lift a tea finger to make it happen. It had been the same with Lockerbie.

In follow up phone calls to various Ambassadors offices, I urged members of the U.N. Security Council that Iraq's agreement should be ratified immediately. I urged the Security Council to seize the opening and move forward on implementation without delay.

Within 48 hours of receiving my faxes of Iraq's agreement to resume weapons inspections "with no conditions," all members of the Security Council declared that it was time for direct dialogue with Baghdad to hammer out the technical language of the agreement. The United States and Britain stayed silent. It was a great victory after all my work—even if I had to celebrate it anonymously.

Immediately, the Security Council invited Iraq to send a delegation to attend meetings in New York starting March 8, 2002.[202] As long as Iraq had already agreed to the rigorous U.S. conditions, the United Nations would draft up the technical language of compliance pronto.

My work was almost done.

There was just one thing left. Then my 18 month project to resume the U.N. weapons inspections, which started in October 2000, would be finished.

Prior to the Iraqi delegation's arrival in New York, I scheduled a one week trip to Baghdad for the first week of March, 2002.[203] My visit would end on the first day of talks in New York.

A great deal was at stake, and I had a large personal investment in the success of the U.N. talks on March 8-9. It would have been disastrous if Baghdad backed off its commitments in New York. Every conceivable precaution was necessary to ensure the U.S. had not been deceived by false promises or mis-communications between New York and Baghdad. That was critical to a successful outcome.

In any event, the CIA understood my travel plans. I categorically deny that I would have traveled anywhere in the Middle East, without making sure somebody could find me if I got into trouble. Some particularly dangerous people did not appreciate my efforts. That's one time complaints about my paranoia hit the mark dead on.

Confirming my belief, the spooks had surveillance photos of my meetings in New York, while we planned the trip in February. Revealingly, the FBI posted no wire taps on my phones or internet communications until five months after the trip, at the end of July, when I started making the rounds on Capitol Hill to discuss the comprehensive peace framework. At trial, my attorney, Brian Shaughnessy would have argued that the absence of FBI wire taps indicated nobody thought I was doing anything illegal by going to Baghdad.

Oh but I have such bitter memories of begging Dr. Fuisz for payment of the debts that I accrued from Lockerbie—30 to 40 phone calls in the two weeks prior to my trip. I beseeched him to arrange payment for my substantial contributions to anti-terrorism work, overall. In those days, Assets received compensation after the completion of a project, so that it would really get finished. All of these projects were considered extraordinarily difficult, requiring an extensive personal investment upfront. Most people would give up, which explains the justification for withholding rewards until after the project's completion.

Oh yes, I remember it all so vividly, trying to collect on that U.S. promise sworn Live on CNN and FOX News by Faithful and Determined Congressional Leaders, who swore that my work mattered so much to them. Black budgets were loaded up with gadgetry for surveillance and voice recognition. Government bureaucracy swelled. But Assets? Field work? That was our pleasure to serve, right? (We didn't have cameras watching us.) It doesn't mean there wasn't money. Dr. Fuisz received approximately $13 million from the emergency "black budget" appropriations for the 9/11 investigation, a few weeks after the attack. I was in his office when he shared the wonderful news.

As my handler, Dr. Fuisz controlled the flow of funds, though notably, his contribution to anti-terrorism involved supervising my work. He had no direct contact with Iraq or Libya himself. And so immediately I asked for part of that money, what I consider a legitimate request. Payment was not only for my sake, but for my Iraqi friend in Baghdad, whom I hoped could be convinced to help us. At that point, I still had to explore the relationship. He would be risking his life, if Saddam decided that he had become overly friendly to the FBI Task Force on Terrorism. Before my trip to Baghdad, I wanted us to provide the strongest possible incentive to inspire his cooperation. And he would be worth everything, if I could persuade him to help us.

Knowing about that pot of money—$13 million, folks— I leaned hard on Dr. Fuisz for cash. That's what Congress intended it for, right?

Later on, the FBI and the Prosecutor would float the extraordinary suggestion that I had not contacted Dr. Fuisz at all. I just ran off to Baghdad! Yeah, sure I did!

Blissfully ignorant of my twisted future, in Baghdad I received full assurances from the Foreign Ministry that Iraq was fully committed to the success of the weapons inspec-tions. [204]By the time I finished a sit down meeting with Deputy Foreign Minister Saeed Hasan, Iraq's former Ambassador to the United Nations and a personal friend, I was satisfied that all of our back-channel efforts had succeeded magnificently. It was exciting and personally gratifying.

My trip to Baghdad had a second purpose, obviously, to explore how far my relation-ship with my old diplomatic friend, Mr. A— could be developed, if at all. That's where that $13 million off the "black budget" would have been profoundly beneficial. We could have invested a third of that money, and achieved all of our goals, with ample funding for the whole field project, including payment to Dr. Fuisz, Hoven and myself. The sum of $13 million was excessive by any standard, and yet Dr. Fuisz would not share any part of that money with us. He was building a massive house in Virginia, a stone's throw from CIA headquarters. He kept it all.

Now it got very interesting in Baghdad. My friend had authorization from Iraqi Intelligence to act as a sort of liaison in Baghdad to the new FBI Taskforce. However, Saddam's professed desire for cooperation with U.S. anti-terrorism policy could not alter the reality that the FBI and CIA would probably demand more than his government might be inclined to give. Any real progress might become hazardous to this man's life, if Saddam perceived that he was getting too close to the Americans. Or some jihadi might take him out.

From the outside, it looked so easy. Yet it was fraught with danger.

Suffice it to say that my special appeal for his help was immediately rewarded. My friend agreed to accept great personal risk, in order to help the FBI (or Interpol or Scotland Yard) identify terrorist targets moving inside Iraq. He promised to advise us when they arrived; where they stayed; their activities; and whom they met. Some of those people would be despised by Saddam. But a few might be receiving special protection from Baghdad, which my friend would have to thwart.

Once I got home, I expected to receive heaps of praise for my clever resourcefulness in developing this contact inside Iraq's Intelligence Service, no less. That's a pretty big deal—if you "count on one hand the number of agents inside Iraq,"[205] as CIA Director Tenet told Congress.

As proof of his ability to perform, my friend's first offer of assistance involved hand-ing over a group of jihadis from Jordan, who had fled into Iraq for medical treatment the first week of March, 2002. Possibly they had joined the fighting in Afghanistan, and trekked through Iraq on the way back. After suffering war injuries, they could not go home to Jordan, on threat of arrest.

One jihadi in particular was a monster, my friend claimed. The timing and his descrip-tion matches that of the young Abu Musab al Zarqawi, later famed for orchestrating a massive bombing campaign against the U.S. Occupation that murdered hundreds of Iraqi citizens and U.S. soldiers.[206] Hundreds of bombings, kidnappings and beheadings would be carried out against the U.S. Occupation under his banner.

Indeed, it's factually known that Zarqawi arrived in Baghdad seeking medical care for a war injury in the first week of March, the same time as I did. More recently, some sources have pushed back Zarqawi's arrival to May, 2002. In my opinion, that's revision-ist, typical of the ignorance spewed about Iraq in Washington over the years.

My friend told me the jihadi was a young man of craven violence urgently sought by Jordanian authorities. As my friend put it, "some men are animals. This man is the worst I have ever seen. He belongs in a cage, and he should stay there." (sic)

My friend offered to deliver him to the FBI Task Force. Iraqi Intelligence expected him to create serious problems wherever he went. But the U.S. would not take him.

I also gave my friend a list of terrorists involved in the Lockerbie bombing, including famed terrorist, Abu Nidal. I asked him to exert his power to arrest Nidal if he showed up in Baghdad.

In July 2002, Iraqi police stormed a building where Nidal lived, and the world learned that the fabled terrorist died in a hail of gunfire fighting off arrest, or perhaps committed suicide. Immediately after his death, friends in Lebanon and members of the Iraqi government talked openly about Nidal's involvement in the Lockerbie bombing, and his regret that an innocent Libyan had been sentenced to life in prison for Nidal's crime.[207]

I'm convinced my Iraqi friend played an instrumental role in arranging Nidal's capture.

If the U.S. ambitions in Iraq had any sincerity at all, acquiring the help of this strategically placed Iraqi Intelligence Officer would have had phenomenal value. My actions had been enormously successful. Not only had I secured access for the FBI to operate inside Baghdad, with authorization to conduct investigations and make arrests, I had persuaded an Iraqi source to aid their pursuit. In my opinion, when the U.S. played games about handling my Iraqi friend, it showed bad faith in the War on Terrorism— and bad judgment by policy makers in Washington.

During my indictment, I would face bitter attacks for the actions I took to win over this Iraqi man, and protect him in Baghdad. Those attacks would show how the U.S. holds cheap the lives of foreign helpmates. Congressional leaders and the upper echelons of U.S. Intelligence ought to think hard about endorsing such a message. It certainly makes us look very bad.

I feel that I deserve an apology.

Democracy Initiative

By far, the most fascinating development on my trip to Baghdad emerged quite unexpectedly at a lunch with a member of Saddam's Revolutionary Counsel at the "Iraq Hunting Club."

Throughout the lunch, the Senior Iraqi official was identified only as "His Excellency." Asked a couple of times for his name, his entourage replied with a smile– "We have told you. You may call him "Excellency."

"That is his name?"

"Yes."

Through photos and videos broadcast of Saddam's cabinet meetings, I have visually identified him, I believe, as an attendant to Saddam at Revolutionary Council meetings, carrying papers and leaning over the Iraqi Leader for his signature.

That adds a tantalizing quality to "His Excellency's" surprise query at this luncheon.

"What value would the United States place on Democratic Reforms in Iraq, as far as lessening tensions between our two countries?"

According to "His Excellency," "maybe Saddam would not be there. He might be gone." The mere suggestion was so shocking to me that I pondered if possibly Saddam was dying. Otherwise, speculation about his future would be treasonous. Dictators don't like underlings talking about the succession to their regimes. People get killed for conversations like this.

Registering my astonishment, His Excellency assured me that Saddam was preparing to assume a more distant role in government, and that he would support the development of democratic institutions that would promote power sharing.

An activist for democracy myself, I responded enthusiastically, and cited the European Union's push for democratic reforms in Turkey, as a pre-condition for EU membership. Still, I expected only a symbolic or token proposal of Iraq's commitment to reform. I was astonished, therefore, by the depth of thoughtfulness and the creativity of problem solving contained in Iraq's proposal. Their package of democratic reforms was obviously well considered.

Critically, it must be stressed that this proposal was floated a year before the Invasion—and months before the U.S. publicly threatened a military assault on Baghdad.

It laid a path for regime change without resorting to violent warfare and Occupation.

Safeguarding the Exiles

According to His Excellency, Iraqi officials had conceived a highly original plan to safeguard Exiles returning from London, Tehran and Detroit, so that they could join the political process.[208]

Iraq would invite the international community to reopen embassies in Baghdad, which His Excellency observed are "sovereign territory" of those countries. He stressed that Baghdad could not attack or arrest anyone associated with those embassies, as violence against embassies constitutes an act of war, or near to it.

His Excellency suggested Iraqi Exiles could return home to Baghdad, and take up housing in those protected domiciles. Iraq would allow the embassies to beef up security for their protection, and would allow the embassies to take over neighboring houses to expand their compounds sizably. This was still Iraq; eminent domain prevailed over individual rights to property.

The Exiles would be granted safe passage from those embassies to their Party headquarters around Baghdad, and to other meeting points. Security provided by those embassies would guarantee their safety inside the country.

Establishing Political Parties and Party Headquarters

Upon returning to Iraq, the Exiles would have the right to establish political parties, including opening party headquarters around the country.[209] They would have the right to operate newspapers, and possibly a television or radio station. His Excellency stressed that the latter would depend on the United Nations' willingness to amend U.N. Sanctions, which tightly controlled and restricted media development inside Iraq. However, Saddam was prepared to allow some revenues from oil sales to be shared with Iraqi exiles to promote their activities, so long as the level of funding did not negatively impact food and medicine for the Iraqi people.

Iraq's own plan for repatriation covered security protection and housing for the returning exiles. It covered access to media, the creation of party apparatus, and the right to receive funding to start up their party organizations, which would allow them to participate in Free Elections.

In conclusion, His Excellency suggested that former U.S. President Jimmy Carter might head a delegation to monitor the fairness of future elections in Baghdad.

Jimmy Carter leads election monitoring teams all over the world. He would not tolerate any voter fraud in Baghdad. The international community could have confidence that such an eminent observer, of such renowned integrity, would safeguard this "new democracy" in Iraq, in a substantial and effective way.

The flow of conversation at the Iraqi Hunting Club that afternoon astonished me. The man was talking treason. Merely to suggest Saddam might not control every facet of the government in the future could be construed as an executable offense. After consideration, I questioned if Saddam might be terminally ill and stepping back from the daily regulation of government, and thus more accepting of the inevitable public grasping for power.

After the invasion proved that Saddam was not terminally ill, I concluded that he had behaved in the fashion of a survivor. He recognized what must be done, and he set about developing a strategy for implementing the inevitable, so that he would not be destroyed by it, but would find a proper balance and sanctuary for himself and his family.

Whatever motivated this conversation, it was definitely a brilliant and creative opening for Democracy, the likes of which Iraqis never got from George Bush or the U.S. Occupation. This plan laid the foundations for major reforms and the creation of political institutions necessary for pluralism, without requiring the deployment of military forces or aggravating sectarian strife. It's a blueprint worthy of attention in other conflict zones.

Back at the Al Rasheed Hotel, I checked the internet and discovered that the Lockerbie Appeal had just ended, too. The legal appeal for Megraghi, the one Libyan convicted of bombing Pan Am 103, had failed in the Scottish Courts. There was nothing more that Dr. Fuisz or I could contribute to the Lockerbie case. That meant my work with Libya was over, as well. Libya's future appeared bright and dynamic, according to what I saw, with a cadre of (mostly British) Intelligence jumping in to carry forward.

I felt satisfied and content. I considered that my work as an Asset was essentially over, with mostly good results all around.

It was March, 2002—one year before the invasion. Winter was ending in Takoma Park, Maryland, where I live in the suburbs of Washington DC, a few miles from Capitol Hill. When I returned home from my adventures in Baghdad, the world looked ahead to peace and prosperity in the Middle East. I watched on CNN and MSNBC, much amused, as pundits and senior statesmen strutted before the television cameras to prattle about my baby—the return of U.N. weapons inspection teams to Iraq.

After such a long labor, I was at peace to watch them.

CHAPTER 10:

BLESSED ARE THE PEACEMAKERS

You'd never guess from all our success securing Iraq's cooperation with anti-terrorism policy that I suffered from chronic exhaustion. My double-life was becoming more difficult to sustain.

While the whole country grieved over 9/11, I had to swallow my pain. My part in the 9/11 investigation allowed no time for grief. But that didn't mean I wasn't suffering like everyone else.

By early October, 2001, I began to experience panic attacks whenever I had to cross the street. My heart would start pounding; I would feel faint and dizzy. My legs would teeter, as if I might collapse on the pavement in the middle of oncoming traffic. I'd have to stop myself from grabbing the arms of strangers to get across the road. Lunchtime on Connecticut Avenue in the heart of downtown Washington about killed me.

I suffered terrible insomnia. I would wake up at three in the morning, and sit on my back porch, chain smoking cigarettes until I could fall asleep. A couple of times I saw flashes of camera lights, and wondered if one of my early rising neighbors in artsy Takoma Park had photographed my self-abasement—or if the spooks were checking up on the lady who warned about 9/11. My paranoia skyrocketed. However, someone definitely photographed me several times late at night, in November and December, 2001. That's also true. I saw them do it.

I beat myself up with recriminations over our failure to prevent 9/11. I tortured myself wondering what more we could have done. (Honestly, nothing). That didn't stop me from long nights imagining the possibilities. What if I had not left Andy Card's house that day in mid-August? What if I'd waited another hour in my car? (I waited two hours.) Why didn't I go back to drop off a written warning about our suspicions?

I considered 9/11 my personal responsibility. I would report to Dr. Fuisz's office, and I would physically shake. My legs couldn't stop bouncing—tapping my feet on the floor. I was totally wired, so much that it hurt. But I couldn't come down off it, either.

I'd always been addicted to danger. I thrived in harsh situations. I'd contributed to previous terrorist investigations. So to a degree, this was my element. I visited the Iraqi embassy whenever Baghdad suffered bomb attacks by the United States. Diplomats raved that I was unnaturally calm in a crisis. Throughout the 1990s, I was notoriously not afraid in situations that would overwhelm most people. I never flinched from those encounters.

"Paranoia" was another matter. Paranoia was a necessary part of my job and my life. And the surveillance targeting me during any terrorism investigation could get intense. These agencies needed to know what the hell was going on. And I would be the first to find out, because of my direct contacts with these Arab governments. So I would get tracked quite heavily.

By example, at the close of the Lockerbie negotiations, on the night that Tripoli handed over the two Libyans for trial, I went down to the basement of my house and found ten to twelve audio cables dangling from my ceiling. The ceiling tiles had been torn out. I could see how the cables winded through every room in my house. Ceremoniously, I got a chair and cut the heads off the listening devices. I felt quite satisfied. My landlord, however, was highly perplexed.

That intensity of surveillance, while perfectly legitimate in this context, aggravated my stress levels all the more. It was not "irrational" paranoia, as some have questioned. But it was stress provoking, nonetheless, because that degree of surveillance gets highly aggressive. Sometimes there'd be whole teams following my movements in New York. Over the years I learned to identify them. That didn't make them the enemy. It was just part of the culture. A stressful surveillance culture.

After 9/11, they followed me into restaurants and hotels, when I visited Arab diplomats in New York. They checked into hotel rooms next to mine in New York to monitor my meetings with Iraqi diplomats on resuming the weapons inspections— totally legitimate. They tried to wire hotel rooms that we might use again. They always tapped my phones. They'd jump out like paparazzi with cameras at restaurants, if I was dining with diplomats. It happened twice in Washington, dining with Rani Ali of Malaysia, and also with Libya's Ambassador Issa Babaa in New York—and others. I'd be sitting in a chair, and somebody would pop up close to my face, whisper a code and disappear like a ghost. *We're in place. We're ready.* Face gone.

In late November or early December, 2001, I saw Richard— for the last time, it turns out—though I had no inkling that afternoon. I was debriefing him jubilantly about my successful visit with the Iraqi delegation in New York, and the comprehensive peace offering from Baghdad that achieved all of our objectives. I voiced concern over how detailed my letter to Andy Card, dated December 2, 2001, should be, as far as detailing the peace framework. Richard replied: "You don't have to worry. We always know exactly where you are, and everything you're doing. We know it as soon as it happens. If you give us the Andy Card letters or not, we're going to know anyway."

Then he said something that I regarded as strange: *"Even if I could not communicate with you directly, Susan, for any reason, you can trust that at all times, I have full knowledge of the status of this project. And I expect you to complete it. Do you understand?"*

In retrospect, I suspect that around this time, Dr. Fuisz got debriefed on the early war planning against Iraq—which he could not discuss with me, under any circumstances. It got confusing on my end, for sure. But I don't blame Dr. Fuisz for that. After 9/11, the spooks played at the top of their game. As long as they showed up in New York, I felt safe. Their appearance meant that my messages to Dr. Fuisz as to meeting times and locations made it up the chain. This was Iraq's cooperation with U.S. anti-terrorism policy, after all, and resuming the weapons inspections. This was the hottest party in town. It's incomprehensible that anybody would argue that the Intelligence Community should have had no interest in tracking this. That's absurd. And wrong. They tracked it very heavily.

My pain was altogether different and private.

After 9/11, I was overwhelmed by "what ifs." I recycled non-stop through my conversations with Dr. Fuisz in the summer of 2001. I thought back to the day of FBI Director Robert Mueller's nomination hearings, when Dr. Fuisz urged me not to go back to New York.

That's why I remember everything so clearly to this day. I wanted to be ready to testify before Congress about our actions before the attack. I could never have believed that Congress, as leaders of the American people, would not want to know precisely and accurately what our warnings entailed. So I replayed my conversation with Attorney General John Ashcroft's staff in mid-August over and over in my mind. I replayed every detail of hanging up the phone to Ashcroft's office, and immediately dialing the Office of Counter-Terrorism at his staff's insistence—right down to the last irrelevant details. I wanted to be ready. I made a decision to read no reports by other sources –not even the 9/11 Commission Report— so that external sourcing would not influence my first-hand recounting of our warning.

By November, there was a new thread in my midnight meanderings: How extraordinary that nobody appeared willing to acknowledge our warnings before the attack?

Now that stumped me. I suffered no delusions that I gave the only warning. You'd be wrong to think that. *There were others. Trust me.*

Exhaustion was starting to wear me down. Something didn't sit right. It struck me that somebody was cooking the intelligence books. I was just too exhausted to figure out why. I was so damn tired! And that proved my undoing.

All of my energies had to stay focused on Baghdad—and fulfilling the mandate from all those politicians and pundits who railed against Iraq on CNN and the Fox News Channel after 9/11.

Dr. Fuisz and Hoven pushed me hard for results. They watched "Meet the Press," too. They listened to the speechifying on Capitol Hill, and all of us recognized that Iraq was the second hottest front in counter-terrorism after Afghanistan and Pakistan. And Iraq was our baby. If the White House was guided by a secret agenda of leading our nation to War with Iraq, they dropped no hints to an anti-war Asset who campaigned aggressively against sanctions. Truly I don't believe that Dr. Fuisz or Hoven understood that agenda for awhile to come, either.

You see the obstacle that I had no idea I was confronting?

Let me underscore this point: Every time White House officials or Congress opened their mouths to issue public demands for Iraq's cooperation with U.S. anti-terrorism policy, they were speaking to me. I was the Asset designated to carry out that particular mission. My back-channel had filled that purpose since August, 1996.

For those reasons, Dr. Fuisz urged me not to get distracted by our advance warnings about 9/11. We'd confront them later, he said, after our work got finished. He didn't say when it would be safe to discuss. I don't think he knew. He only said that he couldn't use me if I fell apart.

I definitely exhibited signs that I might. I suffered night sweats. I'd wake up from nightmares where I'd spin like a twister out of my body. Then I'd crash into my bed drenched in a cold sweat, my sheets and nightclothes soaking wet. Those are clear signs of Post Traumatic Stress Disorder.

Does that disappoint you? It shouldn't.

Everyone can help in good times when things are easy. Everybody's your pal. Everybody wants to contribute. What separates the "men from the boys"—or the "women from the ladies" is who stays in when situations get really tough. Who doesn't give up? Who doesn't quit?

After 9/11, you needed me. I considered my actions on your behalf to be the proudest thing I've ever done in my life. Because I did this work when it got hardest for me. Because I pulled myself through my own pain and grief after 9/11, and I gave everything I had in myself. I tore myself apart for this. I did not break. I did not give up.

Regrettably America, *you* did not help *me*.

When I begged for a budget to support my work, Dr. Fuisz said, and I quote: "Ask not what your country can do for you. Ask what you can do for your country. You don't ask for anything."

Paul Hoven echoed those sentiments, with a few anti-feminist expletives thrown in. "Susan: President Bush said you're either with us or against us. You'd better get to work and stop asking my friend for money." And so I kept going.

By November, Dr. Fuisz accessed a large pot of money totaling $13 million from the "black budget" for the 9/11 investigation. While I remain convinced that money existed to support our field operations, Dr. Fuisz handled it as his own private financial compensation. When I pleaded desperately to receive "something" from those revenues to support my efforts to secure Iraq's cooperation with the 9/11 investigation, he vigorously refused. He had started building a house in Virginia earlier that year. An architect had stolen $3 million dollars off the $8 million project, Dr. Fuisz claimed. As a result, construction on his house had stalled throughout the summer. Having listened to phone calls at his office, many times on my visits, I could see for myself that he could raise no more cash to finish his mansion.

All of a sudden after 9/11, Dr. Fuisz was flush again. When I expressed heart-felt relief for the availability of funds, Dr. Fuisz told me straight out this $13 million (definitely from the feds) gave his family the opportunity to start construction on their house from scratch. He talked about buying new land, and starting from the foundation up. And this house would be spectacular, because now he had $13 million to build with! I have wondered if he used some of that money to buy houses for his college-age children, as well. Either way, he gave me nothing.

BLESSED ARE THE PEACEMAKERS

My request for funds to secure Iraq's cooperation with the 9/11 investigation: **_Denied_**.

Did Richard make that decision? Or did the Pro-War faction at the White House issue a clandestine order to Dr. Fuisz to stall our Iraqi project? Or did Richard augur the future War policy, and conclude on his own that the White House would be supremely pleased if that pot of money got invested anywhere except to secure Iraq's cooperation with the 9/11 investigation? In which case, nobody at the White House or CIA would mind if he used those funds for construction of his mansion in Virginia.

Whatever that answer, Dr. Fuisz definitely received a sizable chunk of cash from emergency government funding intended for the 9/11 investigation. And he spent every dollar of it on the construction of his house in McLean.

Possibly, senior officials at the White House speculated that if they provided no budget resources for my work, I would get fed up and quit. If so, they had a poor understanding about our team. We accepted the challenge under any conditions that we had to face. Dr. Fuisz gave me a personal check for $2,500 in October, and I kept going. This had to get done. We would make sure that it got done right. These men aren't quitters. Neither am I. If members of Congress aren't who they pretend to be, that had nothing to do with us.

Not surprisingly though, the lack of funds made it vastly more difficult for me on a personal level. I had to push forward with no safety net at all. My furnace broke that winter, and I had no heat for almost 10 days from Christmas Eve until after New Year's. I cranked up my kitchen stove, so I could stay warm throughout the Holidays. Dr. Fuisz sent me a honey baked ham for Christmas dinner. But life got awfully grim in my household, while Homeland Security beefed up its bureaucracy, and the National Security Agency splurged on high tech gadgetry.

I shudder to recall it, even today. Honestly, I felt heart-broken and I suffered for it. Yes I did. For months I pushed Richard to intercede on my behalf to secure payment for the work that I had performed on Lockerbie, the U.S.S. Cole, 9/11—you name it. I was fully entitled to receive payment for each of these projects, usually set up as an annuity. Failure to honor that obligation amounted to public fraud.

Meanwhile, the "Black Budgets" exploded to $75 billion a year—all of it taxpayer dollars off the books to federal auditors—paid from the salaries of hard working teachers, doctors, construction workers, farmers, and every day Americans across the country, who sweat, like me, from paycheck to paycheck. There's no accountability for the handling of those "black budget" appropriations. Nobody overseeing the black budgets has any idea whether appropriations reach the field, or if the monies get used up by bureaucrats "managing" the projects.

Failing to provide resources to me as I continued this work with Iraq, which Congress declared its highest priority, amounted to gross command negligence. There's a time honored tradition in military style structures that leadership entails a responsibility to provide for the welfare and supplies for the people under the command. Underlings give obedience, and commanders act in good faith to care for their honest needs, not extravagantly, but at a basic threshold. It's known in the military as "Jus in Bello," and it's critical for the success of the total wellbeing of the unit. It's fundamental to a command structure.

This time they failed badly, and I suffered intensely as a result.

And all because of the total absence of oversight from any watch dog over black budget monies. Black budget monies are equivalent to 100 percent, interest free appropriations to Beltway Bandits in Washington, who grab for that cash with open fists. They have no obligations to provide any services in return, or to repay the money, if they sell their business for a profit down the road. Small business owners across America would be so lucky. They'd be thrilled.

As a result, it is impossible for me to hear leaders on Capitol Hill brag about their outstanding leadership support for Assets and anti-terrorism without becoming very, very angry. Congress should keep its mouths shut, until whatever time the black budget system gets reform. Indeed, an overhaul of intelligence appropriation is long overdue.

Unhappily after 9/11, I needed to buy groceries and pay my mortgage and utility bills just like other Americans. I tightened my belt and kept going. After 9/11, I got to New York twice a month on average for meetings with Iraqi and Libyan diplomats. I went after Iraq's cooperation pretty hard. And the spooks kept track of it all.

Later on, when I got accused of acting as an "Iraqi Agent," I dreamed of going into Court wearing a shirt that read: I Warned About 9/11 And All I Got was This Lousy T-Shirt & a Federal Indictment.

Pretty scandalous, eh?

Bottom line: Republicans on Capitol Hill got a free ride on the publicity train after 9/11. They never paid the fares. That deception carried a horrific cost for me, the Asset.

After my indictment, my emotional stress after 9/11 would become a matter of fierce conjecture and debate. The spooks would grab for any excuse to stop my trial, and thereby prevent the exposure of Iraqi Pre-War Intelligence and our 9/11 warnings. My panic attacks and chronic fatigue would provide the vehicle for their reprieve. They would not let it go.

Ominously, the Justice Department attack would spiral beyond their grasp. And Congress would hold no inquiry to check the facts of my story as an Asset. They would not want the truth about Iraq coming out either. My indictment helped a lot of people tell a lot of lies.

And so it's important to know what really occurred during this six month period after 9/11. My "emotional state" turns out to be nothing remotely similar to what it was portrayed to be.

Chronic fatigue should not be confused with depression. It has quite the opposite effect. I experienced stress and anxiety, which I associated with my disappointment over our team's failure to thwart the 9/11 attack. However, I continued to feel motivated to pursue my work. I worried for my future, but I also expected that any private setback would be short term. Throughout those months I never stopped appealing to Dr. Fuisz for funding.

I suspect chronic fatigue is something that I have shared with Heath Ledger and Michael Jackson. It's a condition where your body becomes so tired that you can't sleep at all, because you're throbbing with energy of what has to be done. You know that you must sleep, and it hurts physically that you can't. You're just too wired and hyped. It's a bad cycle to fall into. It's more likely to occur, I think, if you're forced onto a sustained level of high energy, when your body does not get a chance to recuperate or slow down as part of its normal cycle.

In fact, my chronic fatigue was the brunt of hard work. I was accustomed to the quirks of my trade, and perfectly content. I lived my life the way that I chose. I pursued projects that I loved. Dr. Fuisz and Hoven never coerced me for help. Our team was incredibly close, and I wanted to do this, despite the lack of funding, which I considered grossly unfair and selfish. Up to this point, in every respect I lived the best life that I could have chosen, given who I am. I made sacrifices, but I considered those worthwhile. I was a good sprinter. I was at the top of my game, no matter how exhausted I felt.

What I needed was a serious vacation on a tropical island for six months, with snorkeling and horseback riding and a private masseuse. Or a hike through the Australian Outback. I certainly deserved it! I had earned those rewards promised on Capitol Hill.

Alas my daily life had to be far more practical. After my trip to Baghdad, I started a job as Press Secretary to Congresswoman Zoe Lofgren, a Democrat from San Jose, California. That proved to be a horrible mistake.

There's an honorary code of silence among former Hill staffers. Suffice it to say that Washington PACs keep Lofgren in office, no matter what happens to San Jose, California. She's a safe Democratic seat. She's not going anywhere.

In fact, she got promoted. Today Rep. Lofgren chairs the House Ethics Committee.

I had no tolerance for that sort of behavior on Capitol Hill. As it was, I lost eight weeks sitting at a desk in Lofgren's Capitol Hill office, doing absolutely nothing. Sure I needed the rest quite desperately. But every day I chomped at the tether, longing to get back to work.

It all came to a head when my old friend, Rita Cosby at the FOX News Channel breathlessly informed me that Iraqi diplomats told her about the documents proving a Middle Eastern connection to the Oklahoma City Bombing and the 1993 World Trade Center attack. I was convinced those papers tracked Ramzi Youseff's financial accounts, at the birth of Al Qaeda. That made the decision for me. I had to get those papers. When a situation came up inside Lofgren's office, I managed to extricate myself from her ego trip within the hour. I was not alone in the flight out of her office. She'd hired four press secretaries in the previous 12 months before me. That says everything.

I was glad to get out of there. I had real work to do. Working made me feel better.

PART TWO:
THE TROUBLE WITH TRUTH

Truth will come to light;
Murder cannot be hid long;
but at the length, truth will out
— Shakespeare

CHAPTER 11:

THE OLD POTOMAC
TWO-STEP

It's not the size of the dog in the fight.
It's the size of the fight in the dog.
–Mark Twain

Arguably, I just might be the most slandered woman in America. In which case, I am also the subject of the greatest farce.

Think I'm exaggerating?

You've all heard the rap: Bad Intelligence before the war. No options for peace. Lousy Assets got our facts wrong. Incompetent! Poor risk taking and creative problem solving.

Oh yes, it's my fault the U.S. invaded Iraq! I'm the fool who ruined us!

That's right. Assets are supposed to be proactive and creative fighters, aren't you? You guys are supposed to stick your fingers in the dyke to hold back catastrophe.

You're supposed to find a way when the situation's hopeless. You're supposed to create opportunities for action where there are none. That's what an Asset does. It's what an Asset's for.

So where the hell did you disappear to before the War? Did you get lost in the Gobi Desert, and couldn't get an internet connection to find out what lunacy was seizing Washington? Were you stuck in a Siberian gulag? Lost in the Australian Outback? Hiking in the Himalayas on a quest to find the true Dalai Lama? Did you find Amelia Earhart in Tonga?

Where did you go? Why didn't you do something, when all of us needed you so badly?

You dealt with Libya and Saddam Hussein for years. Couldn't you handle Andy Card and Colin Powell? Was Nancy Pelosi really so difficult?

Oh, I see. If only I'd gone to Capitol Hill, and confronted congressional staffers about the gross mistakes in their assumptions about Iraq's weapons stocks! Maybe Congress would have allowed U.N. weapons inspectors to finish their jobs, instead of racing to spout war propaganda, loaded with salacious intelligence "facts" that were totally wrong! Surely they would have listened to me, because obviously I had better access to higher quality intelligence than they did! I was a primary source for intelligence on Iraq, after all.

If only I had debriefed Congress about the comprehensive peace framework, constructed by the CIA, which advanced all components of U.S. interests in Iraq—

Oil contracts? Got it.

Lucrative reconstruction contracts for U.S. corporations in telecommunications, transportation and health care? Bulls eye.

Anti-terrorism? Done.

Weapons inspections? Not a problem.

Democracy? Some very creative ideas on the table.

Surely if I informed them, Congress would have recognized that the problems identified by the United States could be resolved without firing a single missile. No American soldier had to die or lose his arm or leg in five tours of duty in Mosul and Fallujah. No Iraqi civilian had to lose their home or watch their future destroyed.

Picture the streets of Baghdad with no IEDs. No suicide bombings. No fragmentation of Iraq.

There would be no quagmires. No Trillion Dollar deficits. No financial meltdown on Wall Street. Just peace and prosperity for all of our days! A future of contentment and envy around the world, while the Greatest Super Power of All Time enjoyed bountiful blessings and continued to dominate the global agenda.

The world could have been spared so much pain…

Why didn't I think of that!

My apologies to Nancy Pelosi, but my actions totally demolish the rants on Capitol Hill, complaining about Assets and Pre-War Intelligence.

I might have been the "last to know" on the Intelligence food chain of what the Bushie Boys were up to in Iraq. But I certainly got the message that something was wrong before the rest of the American people or the world community.

I am a life-long peace activist, after all. I live six miles from Capitol Hill. It's a 12 minute metro ride. Door to door, it's a half hour trip. I worked as a congressional press secretary myself back in the 1990s. I know how Congress works. I know how to schedule meetings with staff.

When I hear this nonsense in TV sound bites about how poorly Assets performed before the War, I have learned to roar with laughter. Am I a punch line? Or a punching bag? Or both?

I can only say that the truth feels much more tragic, because it so intimately relates to my own lost hopes for the Iraqi people.

Before my trip to Baghdad in March 2002, the finish line looked so close. By April and May of 2002, it appeared more distant. None of our successful arm-twisting in

Baghdad was sinking into the Washington mindset. "Think tanks" spewed endless mis-informed conference papers. Congress appeared to grasp none of the facts about Iraq's current status. It was not difficult to conclude that information about Baghdad's coopera-tion was not reaching Capitol Hill.

OK. I could fix that. How hard could it be?

By mid-May, 2002—almost a year before the Invasion— I began a round of meet-ings on Capitol Hill to bring top Republican and Democrat staffers up to speed on the substantial gains from Iraq's cooperation with the 9/11 investigation. This was good stuff after all.

Throughout May, June and July of 2002, a lot of Democrats and Republicans on Capitol Hill got the good news that Andy Card had already received: We had built a sub-stantial framework for peace with Iraq that covered all major concerns, protecting U.S. interests in Iraq in any post-sanctions period. *Hallelujah!*

As part of the debriefing, senior staffers in those House and Senate offices got cop-ies of the most important Andy Card letters detailing Iraq's response to 9/11, and its efforts to cooperate with U.S. demands. By the spring of 2002, a healthy smattering of Congressional staff on key committees had been debriefed in sit down meetings about efforts to safeguard U.S. interests at multiple levels in any post-sanctions period.

My first stop was Senator Carl Levin's office, days after I returned from Baghdad. I was confident the Michigan Democrat and Chair of the Senate Armed Services Committee would be thrilled to hear of Iraq's promise to purchase one million American automobiles every year for 10 years, post-sanctions. U.S. corporations would also enjoy preferential awarding of telecommunications and health care contracts. That would mean thousands of high paying union jobs and equipment purchases for Michigan, Indiana and Ohio. The Rust-Belt of America, so aptly named for its faded industrial glory, would receive some of the most substantial economic benefits from this agreement. Iraq's com-mitment would have to be publicly ratified before the international community, giving American workers a measure of protection. Senator Levin's constituents would benefit enormously from long term economic development multipliers.

There would also be substantial progress targeting genuine terrorist cells, as opposed to frightened taxi drivers and plumbers in the general Arab population, who have nothing to do with terrorism. The vast majority, in fact.

Neither rendition, nor water-boarding nor the Patriot Act would have been neces-sary instruments of this success, something that should have appealed to all Americans and world citizens. Nobody had to worry that funds would be seized from legitimate Islamic charities engaged in community building, financing schools and health clinics for the poor, providing food for widows and children—all those good things that encour-age hopefulness in the community. There would be no worry of deploying the National Guard to Buffalo, New York, a shocking prospect that White House officials actually debated during this same time period.

And since "real" terrorism financing comes from global heroin trafficking, we would tackle that other monster, the global profits of illegal narcotics, at the same time. We could cripple heroin profits for those cartels on a global scale. (Except apparently Congress does not understand how one pays for the other.)

My conversation with Senator Levin's staff was dynamic and far reaching—with great implications for the U.S. Notably, his staffer indicated the office had been debriefed about the comprehensive peace framework already. He was already familiar with the different parts of it.

That gave me hope, as I continued my rounds.

Senior staff for Senator Debbie Stabenow's office, also serving Michigan, got the same private debriefing. Ultimately, both Senator Levin and Senator Stabenow opposed the Iraq War Resolution in October, 2002. However neither Senator informed Michigan voters about these substantial opportunities that would have addressed so many economic concerns for the local community, in addition to making significant headway against terrorism.

I carried the good news to Senator Wellstone's office—that much beloved and unabashed liberal Democrat from Minnesota. Senator Wellstone provided a strong voice for peace until his tragic death in an airplane crash.

I visited leaders of the Black Caucus, including Rep. Elijah Cummings, and several other key representatives from Maryland, including former Rep. Connie Morella (GOP) and Rep. Chris Van Hollen, who represents my tiny hamlet of Takoma Park. In fairness, Rep. Van Hollen was newly sworn into office, weeks before the Iraq invasion. He faced a steep learning curve before the War, and our particular meeting included a group of 20 local anti-war activists. There was not an appropriate moment to debrief his staff about the peace framework, however Rep. Van Hollen hit the ground running, as one of the good guys in his attitudes towards the peace community.

Rep. Van Hollen's predecessor, Rep. Connie Morella, got the Andy Card papers in May of 2002. Rep. Morella stood out as one of only six Republicans in the House of Representatives to vote against the War Authorization bill. Courageously, she bucked the party machine and voted with her constituents, something that Marylanders like me greatly appreciated. It took guts to go against Karl Rove and my dearest cousin, Andy Card. She deserves real praise for that, too.

Outrageously, some of the most aggressive attacks on Assets involved in Pre-War Intelligence came from a handful of the House and Senate offices that received my debriefings—and lied about it afterwards. The chief of staff and legislative director for Rep. Jane Harman, a California Democrat on the House Intelligence Committee, received copies of the Andy Card letters, including the peace framework, with a request to share them with Rep. Harman.

As it happens, Rep. Harman and I are both alumnae of Smith College, one of the Seven Sisters women's colleges in Northampton, Massachusetts. The college prides itself on building women's leadership. If not for Smith College, I would not have carried the confidence in myself to fight so hard against the Justice Department in the battle that waited ahead.

Imagine my astonishment, therefore, to open the Smith Alumnae Quarterly, and read criticism from Rep. Harman as to how Intelligence Assets failed to develop a Peace Option to the War—in essence trapping Congress into War, by failing to provide alternative solutions to the conflict. That's exactly what I had done. And senior staff in her office knew it.

She was not alone in repackaging the truth.

Ah but to my face, the staff in these Congressional offices smiled, all peachy and nice. They might have shared a desire to shut me up—like Senator Lott and Senator McCain in February, 2004, leading to my arrest on the Patriot Act. But for the most part, staffers were not so uncouth as to threaten me to my face.

Quite the opposite, staff for Senator Don Nickles of Oklahoma, Majority Whip for the Republican Party and Rep. JC Watts of Oklahoma thanked me graciously for gathering new leads on the Oklahoma City Bombing, including efforts to acquire financial records on Al Qaeda. I felt deeply gratified by their praise—which doesn't mean they did not complain to the FBI afterwards.

Senator Lott's and Senator McCain's staff were very polite, too—And they got me indicted.

That was mid-June, 2002.[210] And so the question of who carried out the threat, and sicked the FBI on me—the Democrats or the Republicans— becomes quite intriguing.

By July 2002, somebody in those Congressional offices contacted the FBI about my debriefings on Capitol Hill.

Shockingly, instead of turning its focus onto terrorist finances, as I expected, the FBI turned its sights on me, and launched a major investigation of my anti-war activities.

We know the timing, because the FBI was forced to turn over wire taps[211] for 28,000 phone calls, over 8,000 emails and hundreds of faxes after my arrest. FBI phone taps started in mid-July, 2002—five months after my trip to Baghdad in March, 2002, but just a few weeks after I started making the rounds on Capitol Hill in mid-May.

Surveillance photos prove the FBI or National Security Agency captured my meetings with Iraqi diplomats in New York, while the trip to Baghdad was planned. If the Feds believed I was breaking the law—instead of organizing my trip the way I thought I was supposed to—the FBI would have registered a phone tap and email capture immediately, as part of a criminal investigation. Nobody did so, for another five months. That screams volumes that my trip to Baghdad was no big deal.

It's crucial to understand that ordinarily the FBI applies for a wiretap separately from the National Security Agency. The NSA had tapped my phones for years, going back to the 1993 World Trade Center attack. But those wire taps would not automatically get shared with the FBI, unless the Intelligence Community referred my activities for a criminal investigation.

The FBI took no such action until five months after my trip to Baghdad.

Instead—by coincidence I'm sure, the FBI started its phone taps—within weeks of my first meetings on Capitol Hill, and exactly when the Senate Foreign Relations Committee planned a series of hearings on Iraq in late July, 2002.[212]

That timing suggests the FBI wanted to monitor what Congress would learn about the realities of Pre-War Intelligence, which contradicted so dramatically from what the White House was preaching on Capitol Hill.

In which case, the Justice Department discovered that I told Congress a lot—and Congress rewarded the White House by pretending that I had not said a word.

But phone taps don't lie. Numerous phone conversations with various Congressional offices indicate that I identified myself as one of the few Assets covering Iraq.[213] Some of my calls described the peace framework, assuring Congressional staffers that diplomacy could achieve the full scope of results sought by U.S policymakers. Other conversations warned how Imams in Baghdad threatened to tear American soldiers apart, limb from limb, if the U.S invaded Iraq. On my trip to Baghdad in March, 2002, Iraqi Imams threatened to use suicide bombs, and swore that even Iraqi women would launch a powerful resistance to any U.S Occupation. Over and over, I warned Congressional staffers that Iraqi Imams promised it wouldn't matter if the people hated Saddam. They hated the United States much more, because of the sanctions. There would be hell to pay if the United States tried to occupy Baghdad.

FBI phone taps captured it all, making a lie of complaints that Assets failed to warn U.S. leaders off this catastrophe. My phone calls were loaded with pleas to turn back from disaster.[214]

Ironically, a large part of my debriefing focused on the need for leadership support on Capitol Hill to bring the CIA and the FBI together to launch a Task Force on Terrorism inside Iraq. Most Congressional staffers could spout flaming rhetoric with regards to anti-terrorism policy. But they could not grasp necessary strategies for achieving results on the ground. Their eyes took on a blank glaze when I described how the FBI and the CIA would have to engage in inter-agency cooperation, in order to secure those financial records from Iraq. And of course, I explained the value of identifying the cash pipeline and shutting down those financial accounts.

Closing down the financial pipeline for terrorist activities should have been a top priority for Republicans and Democrats alike. And let nobody forget, those monies come from heroin trafficking, a network that runs from Afghanistan and the Bekaa Valley in Lebanon to Colombia. Genuine terrorist organizations are heavily interconnected with those smuggling cartels; that's where their operating dollars come from.

I expected Congressional staffers to seize the opening to cut off those cash reserves. I expected them to rally to the opportunity.

Indeed, it remains a mystery as to why any responsible government official would resist an opportunity to investigate those accounts, and trace the flow of cash in and out of them.

Unconscionably, Republicans preferred to deprive Baghdad of an opportunity to cooperate with global anti-terrorism, instead of shutting down that pipeline. Failure to act allowed those drug monies to continue circulation. As a result, that cash flow remains accessible for use in other conflicts in Iraq, Pakistan and Afghanistan to this day. It probably financed attacks on Mombai, savaging Pakistan's peace with India. Indonesia is experiencing a low-grade insurgency against Islamic rebels. The list goes on.

Without question, the failure to grab those financial records from Iraq would prove to be the most dangerous failure of the Republican leadership, with potentially devastating consequences for the Wars in Iraq and Afghanistan, and the future security of the United States.

There's a significant probability that the next major terrorist attack on America will receive financing through those same international accounts. It was grossly negligent not to seize that money—and suspicious.

Instead, the United States made a great show of seizing donations to legitimate Islamic charities engaged in community building. There's a tragic sort of irony in that, because the health, education and food programs funded by those donations provide the best deterrents against violence in the community. Those programs create hopefulness and a sense of future, in addition to providing for basic survival. Seizing that money is not only morally wrong, it's desperately short-sighted. It's the worst sort of grandstanding in Washington. It demonstrates that U.S. leaders have no understanding how terrorism originates, or what keeps it alive. U.S. leaders are cutting down the community infrastructure that might make it possible to stop the violence.

On top of all that, the FBI wanted to eat the CIA's lunch. They tried to swallow up the CIA's mission overseas. That did not sit well in Washington, and complicated possible joint ventures like this one. Instead of cooperating like Sister Agencies, the FBI sought to push the CIA out of the picture altogether, and took advantage of the CIA's perceived failure to stop 9/11 in order to savage the competence of the agency.

Leadership from Congress would have put those relations back on track. But it never emerged. As an Asset, I was greatly frustrated. I could see that Congress lacked the skill to carry its agenda into the real world. Cut past the rhetoric, and Congress was not the high flying, results-driven leadership it was selling to the American Heartland.

Within six months of the 9/11 attack, terrorism had become a media spectacle, a Big Top Circus of hype and drama on Capitol Hill to hold people's attention. But all of that emotional regalia after 9/11 did not translate into action that would have made a difference to terrorism controls in the field. It was purely a publicity stunt.

Most aggravating of all, Congress appeared to be afraid of losing the public's attention. CNN was calling for guest interviews. Voters held their leadership in great esteem. Beneath the veneer of patriotism, Congress was reviving the art of demagoguery. Pushed to deliver substance by somebody like myself, who understands the dynamics of anti-terrorism at the field level, Congress proved useless to provide oversight, or resources, or any sort of leadership assistance to support my efforts, or bring the FBI and CIA together for cooperative projects.

Unfortunately, they quickly saw that nobody would know the difference. So the rhetoric on Capitol Hill became more aggressive after 9/11, while their performance flagged far behind.

Then, in July, the Senate Foreign Relations Committee decided to hold hearings that would examine U.S. policy in Iraq. The Senate Chamber was packed to overflow, but I got a seat in the audience. There I listened, dumb-struck, while Senate leaders bandied about ridiculous allegations about Iraq's illegal weapons stocks and refusal to accept U.N. weapons inspections, in contradiction to all current facts on the ground.

I couldn't believe the stupidity of what I was hearing. It was all political grandstanding. I was absolutely furious.

CHAPTER 12:

THE BATTLE FOR PEACE

I was furious, and I was not alone.

Americans were awake after 9/11. And now, in record time, the forces of Democracy mobilized for one helluva fight to protect peace in the Middle East.

At the first trumpeting for War on Capitol Hill, Americans of all political stripes, every ethnicity and socio-economic background, young and old, rallied together in opposition. People who had never participated in demonstrations before raised their voices against War with Iraq.

Leaders in the anti-war movement—MOVE on, International ANSWER, and United for Peace and Justice unleashed the fury of the internet as a critical tool for mobilizing public opposition on a massive scale. Through rapid-fire email alerts and online petitions, they organized signature campaigns and ambitious phone blitzes to the White House and Congressional offices, identifying Congressional reps for activists and providing phone numbers and a 30 minute time block for every caller. With such aggressive behind the scenes' organization, protests to Congress rolled throughout the days, and the anti-war movement swelled across the country at warp speed. Hundreds of thousands of letters arrived on Capitol Hill every week, running 10 to 1 against the War. Thanks to the internet, the strength of the anti-war movement rivaled the momentum achieved at the end of the Vietnam War.

And so the blueprint for internet activism was born.

If the leaders of the United States ever cared about democracy, this was a moment to be fiercely proud of our country and our people.

Instead, on October 10 and October 11, 2002 the U.S. Congress approved a Joint Resolution Authorizing War with Iraq by a vote of 77 to 23 in the Senate, and 296 to 133 in the House.[215]

Senator Robert Byrd of West Virginia has dubbed the Senators who opposed the War resolution "the Immortal 23."[216] But of those, really just a handful of Congressional leaders actively took up the anti-war cause and fought with urgency and passion to head off the disaster.

The podium for peace was a lonely place. The most formidable leadership came from Senator Byrd himself, and Senator Edward Kennedy of Massachusetts, who worked tirelessly to interject a modicum of rational thinking into the debate. Senator Byrd took to the floor every day during the debate on the war resolution. After that fight was lost, he battled for peace right up to the invasion, and for disengagement from Iraq thereafter.

Senator Kennedy likewise entreated America's leaders to think ahead to the consequences for America's moral leadership in the world community:

"We can deal with Iraq without resorting to this extreme. It is impossible to justify any double standard under international law. America cannot write its own rules for the modern world. To do so would be unilateralism run amuck. It would antagonize our closest allies whose support we need to fight terrorism, prevent global warming, (and) deal with many other dangers that affect all nations. It would deprive America of the moral legitimacy necessary to promote our values abroad. And it would give other nations, from Russia, to India, to Pakistan an excuse to violate fundamental principles of civilized international behavior."[217]

Wiser words have rarely been spoken on Capitol Hill.

A rising leader in the Democrat Party, Barak Obama did not get elected to the U.S. Senate until November, 2004, after the War started. However, he "got it," too. In remarks declaring his anti-war philosophy in October, 2002, a week before the Senate vote, Obama demonstrated more foresight and courage than most of his fellow Democrats.[218]

"I suffer no illusions about Saddam Hussein. The Iraqi people would be better off without him," Obama said. "But I also know Saddam poses no imminent and direct threat to the United States, or to his neighbors; that the Iraqi economy is in shambles; that the Iraqi military is a fraction of its former strength. In concert with the international community, he can be contained until, in the way of all petty dictators, he falls away into the dustbin of history."

"I know that even a successful war against Iraq will require a US occupation of undetermined length, at undetermined cost, with undetermined consequences," Obama said. "I know that an invasion of Iraq without a clear rationale, and without strong international support will only fan the flames of the Middle East, and encourage the worst, rather than best impulses of the Arab world, and strengthen the recruitment arm of Al Qaeda."

"I am not opposed to all wars. I'm opposed to dumb wars," Obama said. "You want a fight, President Bush? Let's finish the fight with Bin Laden and Al Qaeda *through effective, coordinated intelligence, and a shutting down of the financial networks that support terrorism, and a homeland security program that involves more than color-coded warnings.*"

I could not have said it better myself.

Alas, in direct contrast to the overwhelming directives of the American people, as of October 2002, Obama, Byrd and Kennedy constituted the minority on Capitol Hill.

Only 23 Senators and 133 House members—including just one Republican in the Senate, Lincoln Chafee of Rhode Island, and six Republicans in the House, had the courage and vision to oppose the War Authorization bill. Support from the Democrats proved just as obstinate. Less than one-third of the House opposed the War bill.

In the days before the big vote, I was appalled by the irrational propaganda on Capitol Hill. The rhetoric was totally divorced from the reality that I was connected to on a first-hand basis as a primary intelligence source at the United Nations. It was pure political invention, real political theater. Members of Congress spoke of Iraq in language devoid of any understanding of the substantial developments over the previous two years.

By that time, I had talked with many Congressional staffers in different offices.[219] My meetings with Republicans and Democrats to explain the Peace Framework continued right up to the Invasion. Several high-ranking sources told me they'd already received debriefings. As such, all that disinformation could not have been random mistakes caused by ignorance. It struck me that Congress was deliberately trying to eradicate the truth about opportunities for a peaceful resolution with Iraq, so they could sell a non-truth to American voters that required a military option. It was all patently false.

After the October vote on the War authorization, there were some notable conversions to the peace camp. Senator Joseph Biden (D-Delaware), Senator Richard Lugar (R-Indiana) and Senator Chuck Hagel (R-Nebraska) emerged as outspoken advocates for using diplomacy and coalition building to its greatest possible good, before engaging in military confrontation.

They played a critical role, arguing that dialogue had already achieved results by securing the return of the weapons inspectors to Iraq. And they urged the White House to give weapons inspections a chance to succeed. Notably, all three served on the Senate Foreign Relations Committee, which I had made a special effort to debrief on the success of back channel dialogue.[220] That gave me hope that more leaders could be swayed.

On the House side, meanwhile, Rep. Ron Kind (Wisconsin) and Rep. Sherrod Brown (Ohio) led a coalition of 123 Congress members, urging the White House to give U.N. weapons inspectors ample time to complete their jobs. Fully one-quarter of Congress signed a letter to President Bush supporting the U.N.'s process for verifying Iraq's disarmament. All were Democrats.[221]

Unhappily, disinformation continued to be more plentiful than courage.

Even the most rudimentary knowledge of the Middle East should have frightened Congress away from any sort of military conflict with Iraq. Yet despite all the debriefings by the intelligence community, and appeals to desist by foreign policy gurus and military experts alike, Congress failed to grasp the magnitude of consequences of its actions. Leaders on both sides of the aisle demonstrated the poorest conceptualization of issues framing the Middle East. They refused to hear the message pounding from all sides.

Phrases like "quagmire," "dead end," "sand trap," all of it was a foreign language on Capitol Hill. Their need for attention and TV time swamped their better judgment. They did not want to hear any doubts or criticism. Congress was caught up in the theatrics of their war propaganda. As a group, they exercised a significant failure in leadership judgment.

If members of Congress thought they could steamroll the American people, however, they were grossly mistaken. The American people roared back in opposition.

On October 26, 2002, two weeks after Congress approved the War Resolution, the American people launched massive demonstrations in Washington and San Francisco, with bus-loads of protesters arriving from the heartland of Nebraska and Iowa, Ohio and New Hampshire, North Carolina and Florida. Internationally, on the same day, hundreds of thousands of demonstrators gathered in Rome, Berlin, Copenhagen, Tokyo and Mexico City to protest the War, as well.[222]

Globally, opposition to the Iraq War was the most powerful act of democracy the world has ever witnessed.

In Washington DC, more than 200,000 Americans attended a three hour rally, followed by a march that circled the White House. The size of the crowds rivaled the largest peace demonstrations at the end of the Vietnam War. Shoulder to shoulder crowds marched for blocks at a time, singing and chanting anti-war slogans. When the front of the procession returned to Constitution Avenue at the starting point of the march, thousands of demonstrators were still heading out on the parade route, still shoulder to shoulder strong.[223]

Every activist who participated in the Anti- War Movement demonstrated heroic foresight that year. Every one of us should be proud that we battled so hard to preserve the peace.

Democracy showed amazing strength across all economic lines and regional boundaries. Without a single classified intelligence debriefing, the American people and the world community saw with great clarity the nightmare that would be unleashed by this war. Together all of us aggressively pushed forward to express our viewpoints, with the full expectation that government officials who championed democracy overseas would first have to respect those principles here at home.

It's a great irony, isn't it?

If our leaders had respected the will of the people, the triumph of the Anti-War movement would have done more to champion democracy in difficult regions of the world than all of the slogans and speechifying by the White House and State Department. We would have won the hearts and minds of the Middle East, Asia, on and on. Through War with Iraq, that possibility has been squandered. In my opinion, it's lost forever.

For myself as an Asset, it was not difficult to decide what I must do. I knew that I could not sit idly on the sidelines, while Congress stampeded the country into War.

Throughout the autumn and winter, I hooked into the burgeoning anti-war network, attending mass demonstrations in Washington and smaller protests by CodePink and other local Washington peace groups, like the D.C. Anti-War Network and Education for Peace in Iraq. Like others, I turned to the internet, which swelled and multiplied the ranks of the anti-war movement in record time.

I got angrier every day. I experienced a great surge of outrage every time White House officials or Congressional leaders swallowed up the airwaves of CNN to reinvent Pre-War Intelligence with false reports on Iraq's links to terrorism or hostility to the weapons inspections. The speakers were ignorant of the facts. They hardly qualified as "Middle East experts" at all.

I was appalled by how recklessly think tanks and media pundits attacked peace. Our framework had been constructed so carefully and thoroughly, in order to advance all components of U.S. interests. Even the slightest amount of direct knowledge of the actual events smashed their rhetoric into tiny fragments for ridicule. Yet instead of testing the White House claims, media pundits fed the hysteria. These were the days of promos on CNN, Fox News and MSNBC like "Showdown with Saddam" and "Countdown to Iraq."

Fuming over the breadth of deception by Congress and the White House, I made a decision to break the cardinal rule of intelligence gathering.

I would not swallow the truth for them.

I would not stand down.

I would not protect elected leaders from their responsibility to the people for their decision-making.

I would not shield them with deniability.

It was a decision that ultimately would cost me everything I had. But to this day I have never regretted what actions I took next.

As an Asset, I had learned how to work a problem and create whatever tools I needed on my own—rapidly and out of nothing. Otherwise I could never have become so effective at what I do.

The situation on Capitol Hill indicated a massive communications breakdown. The solution struck me as fairly simple. It required message confrontation at the broadest possible level, inclusive of every conceivable party to the debate. That would build a critical mass of audience and knowledge at a rapid and exponential degree. And it would preclude "deniability." They couldn't say that they didn't know the facts. They couldn't pretend not to have been shown the mistakes in their assumptions. If they could be forced to confront truth at every turn, they would be more likely to bow to it.

It was an excellent strategy, if I say so myself.

On September 11, 2002, the first anniversary of the terrorist strike that I labored so hard to prevent, I launched a message system that I called "Citizens for Public Integrity." so named to condemn the dishonesty of Congressional manipulation of 9/11 in order to enflame public support for War.

To get the message across, I formed a blast fax and comprehensive email data base for all 435 members of the House of Representatives and 100 Senators. My targets encompassed Democrats and Republicans alike, guaranteeing that both parties would have equal access to message warnings, without partisan favoritism.[224]

The list included the personal emails for every Chief of Staff; every Legislative Director; every Press Secretary and every Foreign Policy Assistant in the House and Senate.[225]

In short, the email data base covered every top legislative staffer in every Congressional office on Capitol Hill, Democrat and Republican alike.

It was a huge undertaking. I had to call every office to get those names. Phone records provided by my good friends at the FBI prove that I really did so. Then I had to tabulate all of the names into a massive data base to run the emails.

In addition, I created a blast fax for every House and Senate office in Congress— all 435 offices in the House and 100 in the Senate. I also created a blast fax for every Ambassador's office at the United Nations, 185 in all. [226]

Once Citizens for Public Integrity was established, I used those fax and email data bases to launch a massive blitz exposing the dangers of War and Occupation in a series of short papers, which would prove to be incredibly prescient in forecasting the future of the U.S. Occupation and the consequences for the Iraqi people, the Middle East and the financial future of America. About 20 papers in all were distributed to all top level Congressional staffers by email, and faxed to all Congressional offices in Washington and Ambassadors at the United Nations. A number of noteworthy articles by foreign policy experts and leading activists were redistributed as well.

So much for the phony accusation that Assets stayed silent, as Congress raced off the cliff. I shouted from the rooftops. I refused to stay quiet.

And I must say that all of us together hit the mark with a remarkable degree of accuracy.

For example, Citizens for Public Integrity and another anti-war group, Focus on Arab American Issues and Relations (FAAIR), projected a 10 year cost of War and Occupation at $1.6 Trillion Dollars. That turns out to be pretty close to the mark. All in all, a good forecast.[227]

Citizens for Public Integrity researched the history of Iraq's resistance to the former British Occupation in the 1920s, and accurately described the negative consequences for British soldiers in graphic depictions—and their costly defeat, as anti-British rebellions and coups against British puppet rulers spilled blood throughout the 1940s and 1950s, culminating in the bloody anti-Western and pro-Communist revolution of 1958.[228]

Citizens for Public Integrity warned that the costs of War would overwhelm the U.S. ability to provide for essential domestic government services. "The (initial) $100 billion price tag for the War risks forcing a tax increase on personal income and meager corporate profits, at a time when Americans are struggling to resist a backslide into a double-dip recession, and filing a record number of bankruptcies." [229]

Citizens for Public Integrity argued that War would threaten the stability of Wall Street. It would push America's financial institutions to the brink.

In another paper, we wrote: "It is inconceivable that after September 11, Congress would take such rash, poorly evaluated actions to aggressively taunt terrorist retaliations against our country. Evidently, some incumbents think they can distract Americans from the stock market and the dangers of a double-dip recession with all this talk about Iraq."[230]

"Citizens for Public Integrity want to put Congress on notice. We will hunt Congressional representatives whose actions trigger terrorism, just like we hunted Al Qaeda. Only members of Congress won't be able to hide like Osama bin Laden."

I was hardly passive, after all. In fact, I would argue that my efforts exemplify Asset work at its best, when there's a crisis and somebody goes in to reshape the construct of the problem, and create a vehicle for a solution. My actions make a mockery of claims that we Assets demonstrated "gross incompetence," by failing to confront Capitol Hill to spell out the disastrous consequences of this War, and mistakes in Congressional assumptions about Pre-War Intelligence.

Thanks to the FBI, which captured 28,000 phone calls, 8,000 emails and hundreds of faxes, all of my efforts to warn Congress away from the War are fully substantiated.[231]

Yes, I was one more voice in a humongous crowd. I'm fiercely proud of all of us.

And yes, my anti-war perspective was a minority viewpoint inside the Intelligence Community. Nevertheless, my actions prove that thinking opponents of the War shrieked from the rooftops to pull Congress back from disaster. Our numbers might have been small, but we were extremely well organized and resourceful in communicating our message. We were anything but passive or ambivalent towards the impending catastrophe. We saw the mistakes in political assumptions, and we urgently tried to introduce more accurate information to policymakers. That's exactly what I should have done.

Our leaders refused to listen to us—though they are supposed to act as our representatives.

And yes, I faced a backlash from the pro-war camp inside the intelligence community. By example, I relied entirely on the internet and fax lines to distribute my anti-war messages to the U.S. House and Senate, and the United Nations in New York. My blast fax transmitted non-stop, 24 hours a day, for weeks on end, while I slept or went to work. Mysteriously, my phone lines would go down, cutting off my faxes. I would march to a pay phone on the corner, in the freezing cold, only to be told that some unidentified technical glitches had interrupted my service, and a technician would have to be scheduled. It never happened before, and there was no explanation for why it happened now—except for my activism. They'd come out, and trouble-shoot repairs. Low and behold, 10 days later the phone would cut off again. It happened repeatedly.

It wouldn't stop me. I would get everything ready. When the phone would come up, I would rush to get my papers out before the lines shut off again.

So yes, it's true that pro-war and anti-war factions fought each other. But that's part of the intelligence game. It takes a lot more than that to discourage any of us.

Any good Asset is supposed to know how to run a blockade. That's the role we play. By this time, I had done the Lockerbie negotiations with Libya, and preliminary talks with Iraq's Ambassador and senior diplomats to resume the weapons inspections. Any of that would be much more difficult than a tricky phone line.

And yes, I believe the attack was a failed attempt at sabotage by Pro-War factions, trying to interrupt my message distribution.

Hey, I can take it. They would play rough and throw up obstacles. I would rebuff them. That's how it's done. That's the game we play.

It's not really a complaint. It is important, however, for Americans and the international community to understand what I actually did, because my actions prove complaints about pre-war intelligence were false flags to distract angry voters. Washington politicians scapegoated Intelligence Assets, including myself, because they don't have the integrity and character of good leadership to take responsibility for their own decisions. At the end of the day, they're the ones who did this to us. A good number of us desperately tried to stop them.

On the other hand, let's give credit where it's due: Everybody on earth opposed this War. *Way to go, people!*

As the months rolled on, the Anti-War community mounted an increasingly frenetic lobbying effort to oppose the War. Tens of millions of activists took to the streets around the globe.

Entire populations raised their voices to beseech America's leaders not to do this terrible and stupid thing. Here in the U.S, a majority of Republicans and Democrats favored giving U.N. weapons inspectors an opportunity to finish their jobs.

Come January 19, 2003, the force of the Anti-War movement in America had trebled in numbers. The Washington Post acknowledged that more than 500,000 people braved the frigid cold on that January day, and marched 40 deep in crowds that stretched two miles through the streets of Washington DC to protest a U.S. invasion of Iraq.[232]

The Anti-War movement struck ever more forcefully in February. On the weekend of February 14-16, 2003, Anti-War demonstrators rallied in more than 60 countries and 700 cities on every continent, including the McMurdo base in Antarctica. Over 12 million people participated world-wide, by conservative estimates. It was the largest coordinated demonstrations ever in history. [233]

The most staggering crowds turned out in Italy and Spain, where right-wing governments backed the US-British invasion of Iraq, despite polls showing 70% of their peoples opposed the War.

At least 2 million Italians gathered for a massive protest in Rome. The historic center of Rome "between the Coliseum and piazza San Giovanni was packed for hours in a slow-moving carnival of banners, dancing and music."[234]

In Germany, 500,000 protested in Berlin. Another 100,000 marched in Brussels, the largest demonstration ever in the home of the European Parliament and NATO.[235]

In New York City, 500,000 protesters filled the streets for 20 blocks as part of a rally at the United Nations Headquarters. Hit by freezing cold winds, New Yorkers refused to be deterred, despite a decision by New York Mayor Michael Bloomberg to ban the planned march. The people persevered.[236]

Spain outshone us all. Millions joined protests throughout the country, demonstrating against the War: 1.5 million in Barcelona; 2 million in Madrid; 500,000 in Valencia; 250,000 in Seville; 100,000 in Los Palmas and 100,000 in Cadiz.[237] By some estimates, one of every 8 Spanish citizens protested that day against Prime Minister Jose Aznar's stubborn support for War. A year later, Aznar would be thrown out of office by angry Spanish voters.

That weekend marked a fabulous and momentous celebration of democracy and support for peace and diplomacy throughout the world. The tragedy is that such a fantastic and extraordinary groundswell of global democracy did not sway America's leaders to honor the will of the people.

After all, the decision to go to war was undertaken in all of our names—against all of our wishes. And we, the people of the world, continue to pay the price for the mistakes made on March 19, 2003—a day that should live in infamy, a day that global democracy was defeated by a small shadow group of tyrants in Washington DC.

I was just one voice of millions that opposed this War, amidst a whole planet united for peace. Who would have guessed that out of all those demonstrators, one in particular— little me— would pose such a grave threat to White House officials trying to invent a series of false justifications for this debacle, once the gross mistake was recognized.

Bottom line: the men who pushed our world into War with Iraq could not handle the responsibility of their own decision-making. They were cowards.

One of them just happened to be my second cousin, Andrew Card, Chief of Staff to President George W. Bush. When the War started to go wrong, which was almost immediately, Andy and his friends needed a scapegoat. And they decided to pick on the Assets.

In short, they decided to pick on me.

Andy Card

Andy Card. There's a lot of speculation and gossip about who he is to me, most of it not very flattering or polite. *Inquiring minds want to know, right?*

Well, Andy Card is my second cousin on my father's side from Holbrook Massachusetts.

He was the Chief of Staff to President George W. Bush, Jr. and former Deputy Chief of Staff and Secretary of Transportation to President George H. Bush, Sr.[238]

In short, he's a professional hit man for the Republican Party.

While I was growing up in Anchorage, Alaska, my mother owned a string of 10 weekly newspapers and four country music radio stations. Political lines get awfully blurry on the tundra. Alaska's a small town almost three times the size of Texas. Everybody takes care of everybody else. They cut fire wood for their neighbors. They go hunting and fly-in fishing together. And when I was growing up, they all voted for Senator Ted Stevens, because he defended the gun laws and always brought money home for Alaska's villages. People in Alaska love their guns. And they love their federal dollars. They're pretty sure that both are manna from God, and they give thanks accordingly. Which (sort of) explains Sarah Palin.

I first met Andy Card when I was a freshman at Smith College, one of the Seven Sister women's colleges in Northampton, Massachusetts. Traveling home to Alaska for mid-term holidays was impossible. So for Thanksgiving and Spring Break, I would visit my 80 + year old Aunt Mimi, Miss Mildred Platt of Holbrook, Massachusetts. Think of Jessica Tandy, and you've nailed her. Aunt Mimi was the picture of Yankee independence, sharp as a tack and our family historian. She wanted me to learn everything possible about our family genealogy. She was a gem, a good lady who graciously welcomed her "cousin from Alaska" into her home.

It was on visits to Aunt Mimi's grand old house in Holbrook that I met my east-coast cousins, including Andy Card, his brother, Bradford and their sister, Sarah. Andy was much older than all of us. Sarah had recently graduated from Wheaton College. But Brad was a college freshman like me at St. Anselm's College in Manchester, New Hampshire. For a couple of years, Brad used to road trip down to Northampton for weekend visits to Smith. He'd bring his friends to campus parties. He was outgoing and handsome, and I enjoyed our visits very much.

So I want to be clear: Andy Card and I have known each other since the 1980s, though age separated us, and most of my time was spent with his younger brother.

What's more, Andy's a good political player. Come election time, what with my mother's growing media empire in the wilds of Alaska—and her ties to the good and honorable Senator Stevens—it just made sense that Andy Card would make a special nod to our family in Alaska.

Perceptions to the contrary would be grossly inaccurate.

After I warned about the 1993 World Trade Center attack, and started working as an Asset, I had to establish distance from Andy, who had national political aspirations after all.

Our need for distance changed radically overnight when President-elect George Bush, Jr. named Andy to serve as White House Chief of Staff. At that point, my background was fully revealed, all cards on the table, when I approached him in December, 2000 about our back channel talks to resume the weapons inspections in Iraq.

I expected Andy to be surprised. But I was at the top of my game. I had accomplished many good things involving Libya and Iraq, with special regards to anti-terrorism, through a decade of perseverance and creative strategizing.

I expected a man like Andy Card to be proud of my actions. A man who brags to his friends about his outstanding devotion to my field of work in anti-terrorism should be proud that one of his own family members has been on the cutting edge of it.

When you do the work that I have done, you don't apologize for communicating with the Chief of Staff to the President of the United States of America.

At the end of the conversation, you expect him to say thank you.

Think about it. I was a primary source of raw intelligence on Iraq and Middle Eastern anti-terrorism overall. I enjoyed high level access to officials in Baghdad and Libya. It was extremely valuable for the White House Chief of Staff to have first-hand access to major new developments inside Iraq. Given my status as an Asset, and his, it was entirely appropriate for him to receive these debriefings. That was part of his job.

No doubt that explains why Andy Card never suggested that I should break off communications with Iraq—or that I should stop providing him with my insider's assessment of breaking developments in Baghdad.

All of which makes our end so galling.

CHAPTER 13:

THE LAST DAYS

To suffer woes, which hope thinks infinite,
To forgive wrongs darker than death or night,
To defy power, which seems omnipotent
To hope til hope creates the thing it contemplates
Neither to change, nor falter, nor repent
Percy Shelly

Diplomatic activity moved at whirlwind speeds at the Iraqi Embassy in New York, once weapons inspections got underway. Always courteous diplomats clipped with brisk efficiency, hurrying to meetings, making the most of every opportunity to assure anxious observers of Baghdad's compliance with the most rigorous standards for disarmament verification the world had ever seen.

Most nations at the U.N. would have flunked the performance standards demanded of Iraq. They could never have passed their own tests. Ironically, Iraq's performance excelled at the target so much that the United States and Britain were forced to raise the bar ever higher. But in all ways, the U.S. was outdone. Iraq's diplomats craved an end to the misery of U.N. sanctions for their people. They saw the finish line, and they were determined to earn that suspension with fast-paced responses to any U.N. inquiry for data or performance reviews. They were tireless in chasing that goal.

Iraq had been cosmopolitan and secular before sanctions, which meant that diplomats were highly acclimated towards the West— very different than Kuwait or Saudi Arabia or Iran. For all of those years, Iraqi diplomats always made a point of declaring their desire for friendship with the West. Now they had a chance to prove it. They would not miss this opportunity.

Nor did France, Russia or other Security Council members like Syria, which championed a non-military solution to the conflict, let Iraqi diplomats off easily. Quite the opposite, those countries sought to prove the worthiness of peace by demanding that Iraqi diplomats jump through hoops of fire, as well. They were determined to show that conditions for peace would not be lax or ineffectual, as Washington and London argued.

Over 800 inspections uncovered only a few rusted relics of old armaments. Iraqis tolerated the most intrusive searches of factories, employees' cars, purses and briefcases, and home visits to scientists. Every time the U.S. and Britain ramped up their propaganda machine, U.N. inspectors would come up empty-handed. The most aggressive weapons hunt in history risked shaming the U.N., which had inflicted horrific suffering on the Iraqi people, in its self righteous pursuit of weapons owned by every nation on earth— except Iraq.

By this time U.N. sanctions had killed 1.7 million Iraqis, including one million children.[239] That's no exaggeration, unfortunately. The World Health Organization and UNICEF calculated that 500,000 Iraqi children died from sanctions by the end of 1996.[240] It was now 2003, and death had continued its relentless march through the valley of the Tigris and Euphrates. UNICEF estimated that 5,000 children under the age of 5 died every month from sanctions.[241] Iraqi health officials put that figure closer to 8,000 dead children and 3,000 adults.[242] On either end, the death toll was hideous.

Now it appeared the children of Iraq had died for nothing.

Remarkably, the lack of weapons uncovered during the inspections did nothing to dampen dire predictions about what Iraq might still be hiding.

Journalists tracked the progress of weapons inspections, amidst wild and inventive leaks from White House officials about secret weapons caches. Media "experts" fed the hype with speculation as to where Iraq might be hiding those pesky weapons that U.N. inspectors could not seem to find. But around the world, in neighborhoods and restaurants, in universities, corporate offices and family rooms, rational citizens everywhere prayed for weapons inspections to succeed. The whole world held its breath watching for signs that Iraq would crack under duress.

Inside the Embassy, a different scene played out. Iraqi diplomats smiled with hope, serenity etched on their faces. Their acceptance of the demands on their country posed no burden for them. For the first time in thirteen years under sanctions, they could see a better future ahead, one of reconciliation and post-sanctions prosperity and welfare for their people. And so they worked constantly through days and nights to acquire documentation and prepare for meetings with various Embassy staffs in New York. They did not sleep so they could coordinate with Baghdad, which was already approaching night-time when the day was half done in New York.

Perched on a sofa, drinking sweet Iraqi tea and watching the action in the embassy lobby, I remember saying a pray for those diplomats—for all of us really. And yes, I asked God to stay with them. Perhaps that makes you uncomfortable, but if there was ever a time for prayer, it was in those last days. Iraq was not the problem, though. If the world could have looked down from a corner of the ceiling, there would have been no doubt of the sincerity of their actions.

That change was not accidental. We had done so much advance work to get to this day. All of us had made a huge up-front investment to guarantee this success. With Saad Abdul Rahmon and Salih Mahmoud and Dr. Saeed Hasan, and Abdul Rahmon Mudhian, we had planned exhaustively how Iraqi officials would respond differently to every problem situation that tripped up previous inspections.

Objectives had been carefully defined and communicated for 18 months in our talks. Previous problems got picked apart in painstaking detail. How would past failures get handled differently this time? What advance instructions would be necessary to help building supervisors, so they could cooperate effectively? Who at the lower levels would require special hand-holding, so that when approached, they would understand how to respond more effectively? We worked methodically and intensively to make this a different experience.

Watching the inspections unfold, I could see that our dialogue had achieved strong results.

I felt deeply satisfied. I believed the world was starting to become persuaded. Most important of all, the brutality of U.N. sanctions might end for the Iraqi people.

On December 21, 2002 I lunched with my senior diplomatic contact at the Malaysian Embassy, Mr. Rani Ismail Hadi Ali.[243] Rani Ali was an expert on U.N. sanctions policy who staffed Ambassador Hasmy Agam on the Security Council. On behalf of Ambassador Agam and Malaysia's foreign ministry, Rani Ali provided vital and necessary technical guidance, regarding U.N. criteria for disarmament verification.[244]

To my greatest chagrin, Rani Ali was homeward bound to Kuala Lumpur, having finished his diplomatic tour at the United Nations.

Equally disappointing, Ambassador Agam was also returning to Malaysia. His distinguished career in diplomacy had been rewarded by a much deserved invitation for Malaysia to head the Non-Aligned Movement (N.A.M.), with Ambassador Agam holding a top Secretarial post. Malaysia was scheduled to host a meeting of the N.A.M. in Kuala Lumpur in February.

Rani Ali would be leaving New York in just days. He had some critical parting advice,[245] which I took seriously to heart. He knew all about my heavy campaigning against the war on Capitol Hill. Congress was getting bombarded with anti-war messages from all sides.

The most urgent question now, Rani Ali argued, was how to get the United States out of its corner, so that it could embrace the world position for peace and still come out declaring victory. The U.S. had to appear triumphant. In this phase, Rani Ali urged me to go back to the Iraqis, and look for anything more that I could get for the United States to close that deal.

I agreed wholeheartedly. On my walk up Third Avenue to the Iraqi Embassy on E. 79th Street, I thought about different possibilities.

There was talk that Iraq had cancelled the LUKoil contract with Russia for the development of the West Qurna Oil fields, containing 8 billion to 10 billion barrels of oil. [246]

With profound apologies to Russia, I recognized that if I could persuade Iraq to offer such a major first-tier oil concession to the United States, it might push us over the top to lock in a peace agreement. What can I say? I had to examine every possible opportunity. Frankly I cringed to hear that Iraq had pulled LUKoil's rights to develop that field. It hurt my efforts that Iraq should renege on its contractual commitments to Russia or any other country for post-sanctions reconstruction or oil development. It was important that U.S. corporations should trust Iraqi promises, as part of lifting sanctions. If Baghdad would break its agreements with Russia or France, both long-time and outspoken opponents of sanctions policy, what would they do to the U.S., which had tormented them for 13 years?

See the problem? Still, LUKoil gave me an edge. I wasted no time raising the possibility with Iraqi diplomats later that afternoon on December 21, 2002.

It's important to clarify that I'm the one who made the decision to get the LUKoil contract for the U.S. Rani Ali did not suggest that I take it. It was my own idea.

Iraqi diplomats seized on my suggestion immediately.

On January 8, 2003, I made a final appeal for peace to my dear second cousin, White House Chief of Staff Andy Card.[247]

Reminding him about my special contacts with Iraqi diplomats, I offered to secure the LUKoil contract for the United States. I made sure Andy understood the U.S. could definitely have the West Qurna field. However, if the White House did not want it, I hoped the Iraqis could restore Russia's contractual rights.

The purpose of my letter, however, was greater than the LUKoil contract. I made clear that I would use my back-channel access to get anything the United States wanted, so that the Bush Administration could be satisfied in accepting a non-military solution to this (non) conflict.[248]

My letter on January 8, 2003 provided a devastating forecast of the dangers of invading and occupying Iraq.[249]

"My dearest cousin, this War with Iraq will hurt us, too. In six weeks or six months, it won't matter. Because when it hits, it will hit so hard it will not matter that there was ever a delay. The Iraqi people hate Americans, no matter what they think of Saddam. When I was in Baghdad last March, more than one Imam swore to me their people would tear off the arms and legs of American soldiers, and decapitate them, and drag their bodies through the streets. They swore their women would fight, too."

"Once the U.S. bombing starts, the Iraqi exiles will have no credibility as leaders. None whatsoever. They will be hated as pawns of the United States, and my God, let me tell you, Arabs can hate. A U.S. victory will never be sweet for long."

"Above all, you must realize that if you go ahead with this invasion, Osama bin Laden will triumph, rising from his grave of seclusion. His network will be swollen with fresh recruits, and other charismatic individuals will seek to build on his model, multiplying those networks. And the United States will have delivered the death blow to itself. Using your own act of war, Osama and his cohorts will irrevocably divide the hearts and minds of the Arab Street from moderate governments in Islamic countries that have been holding back that tide. Power to the people, what we call "democracy," will secure the rise of the fundamentalists."
"And before the next Presidential election, Andy, it will become a disaster."
"You are in my prayers. Let me help you. Please."

Warning Secretary Powell before his U.N. Speech

Andy Card was not the only White House official that I approached to outline opportunities for peace in January, 2003.

By happy chance, Secretary of State Colin Powell lived next door to my CIA handler, Dr. Richard Fuisz in McLean, Virginia.[250]

For years I'd been told that soldiers appreciate peace more than anybody else, because they understand what battle actually costs. They understand what it means to ask men to die, and to send men to kill. They understand the sacrifice for soldier families, and the price of destruction unleashed on the community by their weapons. As General Wesley Clark said, you don't go to War unless there's "absolutely, absolutely, absolutely no other way."[251]

War should be a last resort when all other options fail.

With that understanding, many of us in the anti-war community pinned our hopes on Secretary Powell. A retired four-star General and Chair of the Joint Chiefs of Staff, from the outside it appeared that Secretary Powell had serious doubts about the necessity and consequences of a War with Iraq. We all hoped the wisdom of his extraordinary military experience might persuade civilians running the Pentagon to slow down and give peace a chance.

Concerned that Secretary Powell might not have access to the full range of peace options before the War, I decided to approach Powell at his home on January 8, 2003— the same day that I delivered my 11th letter to Andy Card. In the package for Secretary Powell, I included several of my earlier progress reports to Andy Card on our talks to resume the weapons inspections, including Iraq's response to the 9/11 attack dated September 24, 2001—and the comprehensive framework for peace outlined in a letter to Andy Card dated December 2, 2001.[252]

I advised Secretary Powell that the peace framework continued to be viable and productive.

On January 27, 2003, I returned a second time— just a few days prior Secretary Powell's speech at the United Nations on February 5, 2003. In greater detail than before, I advised him that Iraq's enthusiasm for the inspections was so strong during the preliminary talks from November 2000 to March 2002 that it was unlikely Iraq might be hiding Weapons of Mass Destruction.[253]

This message was not ambiguous.

On January 27, 2003, I told Secretary Powell:

"If what you claim is really what you want, this is a viable framework that would allow President Bush to declare a moral victory for his leadership. Working from a formidable position of power, having soldiers ready in the Gulf, the White House could achieve a victory without going to War."

"What I have to say next will be more aggravating, but I have an obligation to advise you."

"Given that Iraq has tried for two years to hold covert talks with the United States, with the promise of immediately resuming weapons inspections, there's a very high probability that Iraq has no weapons of mass destruction. Forget what the Iraqi Opposition has told you. They're famous liars, and most desperate to engage the United States in their protection. You can't kill 1.7 million people and return home after a vicious bombing campaign to a great parade."

"No, Iraq emphasized for more than a year before Kofi Annan got involved, that Baghdad would jump at the chance to prove to the world they had no weapons.

At any moment Iraq was ready for those inspections to begin, and that says to me that they felt always they had nothing to hide. They simply insisted that without U.S. support for the plan, it would have no benefits or meaning for resolving tensions. Current events have proved that they were right."

"Don't deceive yourself, Mr. Secretary that War would have no costs. Believing your own rhetoric at this moment would be the most rash and incendiary mistake. Fighting street battles searching for Saddam would entail deadly risks for U.S. soldiers. No matter what Iraqis think of Saddam, the common people hate the U.S. for sanctions and bombings, and they would consider it traitorous to help you. Under these circumstances, the brutality necessary to win this war would be consumption for the entire Arab world. It would produce a disastrous period of occupation. The Iraqis have fought occupations before, and they would strike back wherever possible."

"Outside Iraq, Islamists would point to the failure of west-leaning leaderships to protect the Iraqi people. Fundamentalists would seize on that failure to force concessions for their strict cause. There would be a shift to the will of the people alright. *No wonder Iran has been chuckling to itself. Iran and Osama—not the United States—would be the greatest victors in this war. The Arab Street would rush to their side.* "

(Yes, I called the rise of Iran, here and in other papers.)

"Please let me help you. You can still achieve a greater victory, Mr. Secretary, and maintain the force of America's moral authority in the world's eye. The objectives of the Bush Administration can be achieved without igniting terrorist revenge and international boycotts. Or destroying political alliances in the War on Terrorism. Or forcing massive deficit spending that will prolong the U.S. recession and scare the hell out of Wall Street and the Middle Class. Or starting a Holy War—which this would become."

Well, OK jury. What do you think? Were those the words of a "foreign agent provocateur?"

Does that qualify as "treason?"

Actually, I offered a rational argument worthy of Secretary Powell's consideration. As a long-time U.S. Asset covering Iraq, I had primary access to special information that could benefit his decision-making, and I took appropriate action to make sure that he was formally advised of it. A military commander entrusted with the welfare of hundreds of thousands of U.S. soldiers needs as much input as possible to define his options. In this situation, the United States could have demanded anything from Iraq, and gotten it all, without engaging in battle. The U.S. could have demonstrated victory without the hell of War and Occupation—a sort of "unconditional surrender," without sacrificing U.S. soldiers or destroying the lives of Iraqi civilians.

And so I think my action was legitimate, so long as my approach demonstrated respect for Secretary Powell's seniority and stature, which I certainly tried to do.

Notably, in 2007, the Senate Intelligence Committee singled out the "outstanding quality" of intelligence reporting in January, 2003, calling it "one of the few bright spots" in Pre-War Intelligence.[254] The Senate Committee cited the sorts of warnings that I detailed in my January letters to Andy Card and Secretary Powell.

Senator John Warner (R-Virginia) called it "chilling and prophetic."

As for Secretary Powell's ability to identify me as an Asset, my CIA handler, Dr. Fuisz was Secretary Powell's next door neighbor—and a well recognized member of the intelligence community. My relationship with Dr. Fuisz was easily discovered. Either a quick background check or a google search on the internet would have turned up our link together on Lockerbie. My knowledge of his home address surely had to come from next door. It's not rocket science.

All of that makes it difficult to understand why Secretary Powell should have turned his copies of the Andy Card letters over to the FBI.—something he surely forgot when he gave his famous exclusive interview to Barbara Walters in September, 2005.[255]

In that extraordinary sit-down interview that aired on "20/20", Secretary Powell excoriated mid-level bureaucrats at the CIA—not the top dogs, but the mid-level bureaucrats— for not coming to warn him in late January 2003, before his notorious speech at the U.N.— that his claims about Iraq's weapons capacity and development were not realistic or substantiated. Richard Armitage likewise complained bitterly that no one had the courage or foresight to warn Secretary Powell off the bad intelligence that laid the foundation for his remarks.

Nobody except me.

And I got arrested for it.

As they say, no good deed goes unpunished in Washington.

But I was stupefied when I heard Colin Powell's complaint to Barbara Walters. It was an appalling lie. There's serious question as to whether General Powell violated his oath of military service to the detriment of the welfare of U.S. soldiers, when he made this false declaration. I think he should face a court-martial to answer for it. By then, I was gagged by the indictment. I could say nothing.

Ah, but I'm getting ahead of myself.

I was blessedly ignorant of the dark outlook for my future. I carried on my anti-war outreach to Capitol Hill and the United Nations in New York as passionately as ever.

Syria and Malaysia—The World's Best Hope for Peace

The departures of Rani Ali and Ambassador Agam from the Malaysia Embassy did not handicap my efforts in New York. Over the years I had cultivated widespread contacts at the United Nations. With the storm of War darkening the horizon, I made every effort to use all of them. With the help of Rani Ali, I tracked down phone and fax numbers for every Ambassador's office[256] in the U.N. General Assembly.

By January, I was bombarding senior diplomats at the U.N. with appeals to support peace. FBI wire taps prove that I lit up phone lines all over the Security Council and key embassies.

In January and February, 2003, I floated an idea that the United Nations should draft Ambassador Agam—who had 30 + years of senior diplomacy under his belt— to lead a "working group" into Iraq that would hammer out the technical language for all parts of Iraq's previous offerings to the United States. I argued that the existing framework addressed all parts of the conflict, and thus rendered War with Iraq fully avoidable and unnecessary.[257]

What we needed was the technical language to ratify Baghdad's commitments, just like we had done with the weapons inspections.

Recently, Syria had taken a non-permanent seat on the U.N. Security Council. In a letter to Syria's Ambassador Wehbe on February 3, 2003, I wrote:[258]

"Many more opportunities for diplomacy exist even now. I urge Syria and other peace-seeking nations on the Security Council to support the formation of a Working Group that could go to Baghdad, and build a framework as an alternative to War. After talks in Baghdad, the Working Group could present its findings to the United Nations for debate. If accepted, the framework would remove any necessity for a military occupation."

"This framework would create a parallel track to War preparations. Its purpose would be to define the Iraqi Government's own commitments on a full range of social and political rights that have been stymied by Baghdad's necessary preoccupation with grinding sanctions. With that understanding, the United Nations could better decide whether War is necessary at all."

In Washington style, I circulated the Wehbe letter all over the Security Council and the General Assembly.

I also suggested the "Working Group" should be charged with implementing the collection of democratic reforms proposed by senior Iraqi officials in Baghdad a year earlier. Iraq's proposal included some highly creative suggestions, such as housing Iraqi exiles in various embassy compounds, and granting Iraqi exiles the rights to establish political parties, party headquarters and opposition newspapers. They would have had the right to announce their candidacy for office, and actively campaign for election around the country.

Each part of this framework would be ground-breaking. And it could be guaranteed. The hardest part had been accomplished already. Baghdad had accepted the demands, some as far back as November 2000. All that was missing was a technical agreement to begin implementation of the various components, which the "Working Group" could handle.

To his great credit, Ambassador Agam had declared months before that he would come out of retirement, if necessary, to lead comprehensive peace talks with Iraq. He was fully committed to the project and totally capable of delivering it.

At the February, 2003 meeting of the Non-Aligned Movement in Kuala Lumpur, Ambassador Agam and my old friend Dr. Saeed Hasan, now Iraq's Deputy Foreign Minister, discussed the possibility. Traveling to Baghdad for talks would have been out of the question, because of loud whispers that War was imminent.[259] Nonetheless, talks could have been held in Geneva or Paris.

The situation was not hopeless. War was not inevitable. There was not a lack of viable options. That's flat wrong.

It was only a question of who had the courage to pursue peace. Some of those answers are surprising. Malaysia's contribution behind the scenes certainly deserves recognition, praise and appreciation from the international community.

As it turns out, Malaysia was not the only farsighted leader on the world stage.

In New York, Syria had just taken a non-permanent seat on the U.N. Security Council, representing the Middle East region.

On the evening of February 4, 2003, wire taps by my good friends at the FBI prove that I contacted the Syrian embassy at the United Nations in New York, and spoke directly with Syria's Ambassador Wehbe.[260] I urged him to promote the original framework for peace that had been developed in 2001-2002, as the basis for conflict resolution between the U.S. and Iraq.

It helps to know that Ambassador Wehbe and I had been briefly introduced by Rani Ali at a Lebanese Taverna popular among U.N. diplomats. On other occasions, he observed me lunching with diplomats from Libya and Iraq. That would have stood out, since Western contacts with either of those countries was highly unusual in those years. My role in talks for the Lockerbie Trial would have been known to Syrian diplomats, as well.

All of that helps explain why Ambassador Wehbe probably recognized who I was, during this phone call.

> Ambassador Wehbe: "The Ambassador is speaking."
> Lindauer: (Laughs) "I did not expect you to answer your own phone."
> Ambassador: "Indeed!"
> Lindauer: (Laughs) Ah, my name is Susan Lindauer...
> Ambassador: "Yes."
> Lindauer: "And I ah, sent something to you by fax yesterday."
> Ambassador: "Yes."
> Lindauer: "It is pertaining to the Iraqi issue. This is ah, a peace framework."
> Ambassador: "Right."
> Lindauer: "I have been involved– I live in Washington."
> Ambassador: "Yes."
> Lindauer: "I have been a back door…"
> Ambassador: "Hmph hmph."
> Lindauer: "between Iraq and the White House."
> Ambassador: "Yeah."
> Ambassador: "I know."
> Lindauer: "Okay."
> Ambassador: "I know."
> Lindauer: "Okay, good. I have sent that to your, ah, consular."
> Ambassador: "Did you ask for a meeting?"
> Lindauer: "I was going to be in New York and I was going to have some meetings with a couple of other embassies."
> Ambassador: "Do you like to come ah, this evening?"
> Lindauer: "I am in Washington."
> Ambassador: "Oh I thought you are here."
> Lindauer: "I realize you are incredibly busy, but I would like to share this. Let me put it this way. I do ask you please. I know you're very busy, but it is very important that you see what I have sent."
> Ambassador: "Okay, I will ask for it."
> Lindauer: "Thank you so much."
> Ambassador: "I will ask for it, and I will see it."

Ambassador Wehbe showed a remarkable degree of civility and respect for the contributions of an ordinary woman from outside his own country, I think. If my experience has taught me nothing else, it's that a government willing to discuss ideas from ordinary people— and listen— is doing some things right. One might argue that listening to common people marks the foundation of all genuine democracy. I find it intriguing, therefore, to compare Syria's handling of the situation to Colin Powell's reaction to the very same information.

Syria's Ambassador Wehbe did more than listen and read my proposal. To his great credit, Ambassador Wehbe's diplomatic staff checked out the framework with Iraqi diplomats, and verified that the platform was accurately portrayed and entirely valid.

Then Syria followed through, and took action to carry it forward.

Kudos to Damascus!

Several weeks after the Obama Inauguration, in February 2009, I confronted the Senate Intelligence Committee in Washington[261] over the abuse that I suffered as an Asset, and the gross dishonesty of defaming Pre-War Intelligence, with such a strong peace framework ready for implementation.

At that point, the CIA reluctantly acknowledged that Syria had approached them with an identical proposal in early 2003, in the 11th hour before the invasion.[262]

According to Joseph Farah, who publishes the G2 Bulletin, CIA sources have confirmed that Ambassador Wehbe and Syria's senior diplomatic staff approached the United States covertly, possibly through a third party, seeking to open a back channel to the Secretary of Defense, in order to implement that comprehensive framework, which Iraq was offering.[263]

According to the G2 Bulletin, Iraq offered six unconditional terms to Defense Department policymakers. The terms were:

- Full support of America's Arab-Israeli peace process
- Support for U.S. strategic interests in the region.
- Priority to the United States for Iraqi oil
- Elections within two years, under U.N. auspices.
- Disarmament—direct U.S. involvement in disarming Iraq. The U.S. could send 5,000 troops into Iraqi to search for weapons of mass destruction.
- Full cooperation in the war terror—including the hand over of Abdul Rahman Yasin, who was involved in the 1993 bombing of the World Trade Center. To this day, he is still at large.

The CIA implied that it arrived too late to act upon. The G2 Bulletin reported that the Republican leadership laughed in Syria's face saying, *"See you in Baghdad."*

Why solve a problem, when you can have a war instead?

In which case, they acted like fools.

And yet, like Malaysia, Syria deserves the most profound gratitude and praise from the international community, for the simple fact that its leadership had the courage to support peace to the very end. Both Syria and Malaysia's foreign ministries handled this crisis extremely well. They could not have done better.

Their diplomats had the courage to recognize the frightening consequences of this tragic and stupid war. Instead of getting paralyzed, their leaders used their position on the Security Council to support dialogue, offering themselves as intermediaries. That's the U.N. at its best.

THE LAST DAYS

As someone who watches trends in the Middle East, I must say that Syria's proactive spirit greatly impressed me. Syria's diplomats saw the possibility of common ground, and put the good of the world community before any possible differences. I admire that tremendously. It's extremely hopeful for the future, and it speaks to Syria's leadership potential in other Middle East conflicts, for the good of conflict resolution.

Critically, when the CIA acknowledged all parts of Syria's proposal, they acknowledged mine—since the two are almost 100% identical, and FBI wire taps prove that I shared it with Syria's Embassy at the start of February, 2003.

That is valuable for corroborating the legitimacy of the peace framework itself. Clearly the peace option passed the vetting process for authenticity with Baghdad, since Syria's government required verification from Iraqi sources before submitting it to the Bush Administration.

That means I was spot on. My claims about the substance of the framework are meticulously correct in all detail.

Unhappily, problem solving was not what Pro-War Republicans wanted. It was not in the best interests of Big Oil and the War Profiteers, the only winners of this catastrophic War.

But Peace was always possible.

That's critical for all of us to know. Although this conflict appeared overwhelming and intractable, dialogue and diplomacy could have achieved results right to the last moment—thanks to the courageous leadership and vision of nations like Malaysia and Syria.

An opportunity for a substantial peace with Iraq existed to the very last days, which would have gotten the United States and Britain everything they wanted. It would have been a prosperous peace, with oil and reconstruction contracts for the United States, Europe and Asia; weapons disarmament; cooperation with anti-terrorism efforts; even democratic reforms. All of it could have been won without firing a missile, or killing a single Iraqi child. Every one of these objectives was attainable to the end.

By corollary, every sacrifice made to support this War effort has wasted our financial resources and the talent of future generations. And it never had to happen.

For me, it's a bitter disappointment to know what could have been accomplished so painlessly. Yet it should give us hope for our future that we don't have to go down this path again.

Resolving conflict is always a question of leadership, courage and vision. No matter how bad a situation looks, there's a path towards conflict resolution. It might appear difficult. But it can be done.

It's always about dialogue, dialogue and more dialogue. When you go looking for allies, you will find them in the most unusual places.

To Syria and Malaysia, many thanks!

CHAPTER 14:

SAY GOODNIGHT, SAIGON...

And Jesus wept
–Gospel of John 11: 35

March 19, 2003. It was a cold and wet night in Washington, like heaven was storming tears of anguish. Or maybe they were mine.

All of the peace community was grief-stricken.

For that was the night the United States and Britain launched what the military bragged would be the most ferocious "shock and awe" bombing campaign in the history of the world. CNN brought the whole nightmare right into our homes and living rooms. Watching that pounding horror of explosions and fires that streaked Iraq's skies, the brutality of that bombing horrified many of us as well.

Around the world America would never be regarded in the same light of humanity and moral righteousness again.

With every bomb that crashed down, the tradition of America's virtue got smashed and broken in the flames.

When Baghdad fell, so did we.

Granted, most of us didn't know it yet. We could not have envisioned how America's destiny of influence and prestige could be so interlinked to the perceptions of other nations and peoples. Without that recognition of America's inherent goodness, other nations would no longer trust our moral leadership, and they would start to question us on a wide range of issues. I think history has already shown that America lost its Super Power throne on that dreadful night.

There are so many 'what ifs' that we face together as a people. If peace had triumphed instead of War, what would our nation look like today? What would we have achieved? Would we have a better health care reform policy? Would we have a stronger military? Would there be any major terrorist scenarios on our horizon? Would we have better odds for overcoming the financial adversity on Wall Street? Better job prospects? Would our government face mountains of debt as mighty and treacherous as the Colorado Rockies? We can only speculate.

That's a lot to lose. I can't really blame Americans who are still in denial about what the Iraq War has cost this country. They haven't come to grips with it yet.

The rest of us, with our eyes open in dismay, have discovered that our Great America, protector of the weak and downtrodden, vanished from the world's eye that night.

In its place stood a tyrant.

Well, that just doesn't work for me. I don't feel like handing my country over to a few stupid men, so they can ruin us. That makes no sense to me. America might have tyrannical leaders, but with all my heart, I believe we're not a tyrannical people. And I bitterly resent any White House official hijacking what's precious about Our Country to promote get-rich quick schemes for his Beltway Bandit friends in the oil and defense establishments.

But what could ordinary people do about it? That was a much tougher question.

I spent that bitter night driving along the neighborhood back streets in Maryland, poking at that question, and listening to the radio for news breaks on the war. I couldn't go home. I couldn't stand to watch the explosions and fiery skies of Baghdad on CNN or FOX News. And I couldn't turn it off in my mind.

I was heartbroken and seething with rage.

And folks, let's be honest. I had a lot to be angry about. Where do I start?

I could never forgive or forget that months before 9/11, the U.S. threatened Baghdad with massive military retaliation, citing a 9/11 scenario throughout the spring and summer of 2001. I was sick to my heart that I had delivered those warnings myself, describing the 9/11 attack with precision detail. Obviously, the upper ranks of U.S. intelligence had known all about the threat. We lacked actionable intelligence to block the hijackings. That's absolutely true. However, it seemed to me that top U.S. leaders—not my handlers— deliberately avoided easy opportunities to thwart the attack, for example by alerting NORAD or deploying anti-craft guns on top of the Twin Towers. By taking no action, the Pro-War Camp let those Americans die, so they could create a pretext to declare War on Iraq, a decision I now believed was reached months before 9/11.

Wouldn't that send you into orbit?

After that, it was a toss up for me whether the lies about our advance 9/11 warning were worse than the performance failure during the 9/11 investigation. Despite all the pomposity on Capitol Hill, the Justice Department failed to seize critical opportunities to cut off the cash flow to terrorists. They didn't want to acknowledge financial documents regarding early Al Qaeda figures like Ramzi Youseff, because acquisition of that intelligence would have demonstrated Baghdad's commitment to the global war on terrorism. Monstrously, the FBI left that financing in circulation. Instead of sending a Task Force to Baghdad, the FBI harassed taxi drivers and plumbers on their way to Mosque. They seized donations to Islamic charities intended for community building— schools and hospitals that would create hopefulness and thwart the path to violence. And the U.S. bombed Baghdad, in a foolish attempt to link Iraq with 9/11.

On the night of March 19, 2003, that sent me through the roof. In my mind, there's serious question as to whether the "War on Terror" turned out to be a hideous fraud.

That struck me as unforgivable, after such a grievous national tragedy.

In my opinion, our leaders have endangered the United States and the world community for the long haul, because of their calculated incompetence.

To put that in context, before 9/11 and the Iraqi War, I estimate that only 200 to 300 men in the entire world focused their lives on trying to destroy symbols of the United States. Many more had fixated on Israel, surely. But only the real die-hard terrorists dreamed of glory for attacking the United States. That would be half the size of a small high school auditorium.

Today, thanks to the Iraq War, Guantanamo and Abu Ghraib, I would put those figures between 3,000 to 5,000 individuals—whose entire lives now focus on attacking the United States any way possible. This War on Terror has multiplied the number of terrorists two hundred fold. Now that strikes me as a cock-up situation. If there are more terrorists now than when we started, our strategy has backfired.

Wouldn't that make you angry, too?

Driving alone that dreadful, rainy night, my thoughts raced with images of the massive explosions in Baghdad and the brutality that our leaders inflicted on innocent Iraqi people, in our name as Americans. The lies from the White House appalled me. I could not believe our leaders would launch such destruction so casually and cynically.

If you had told me on that dreadful night that within a year, I would get blamed for providing the poor quality of intelligence that led to this War, I would have beat you senseless. I would have stomped you. You could not have crawled away like a dog on your belly.

That's got to be one of the most outrageous and despicable lies ever told in Washington, which let's be honest, tells a lot of them.

Instead that night, one of those really great DJs on the radio seemed to understand the massive shock and disbelief breaking over our community, which teams with devoted anti-war activists. Some wonderful DJ played the old Richard Harris version of "MacArthur Park" that's so maudlin and sad[264]—*MacArthur Park is melting in the dark, all the sweet green icing flowing down....*

Just like Baghdad. I had to pull my car to the side of the road to cry.

Pain scorched my heart. We had tried so hard to build a reliable framework for peace that would resolve the U.S. conflict without war. I'd worked on this project for two years with Iraqi officials and U.N. diplomats, overseen by muckymucks at CIA issuing sometimes outrageous demands to protect U.S. interests. We had started before the threat of War appeared on the horizon. We'd worked proactively and energetically to achieve every imaginable U.S. objective. And we had succeeded on every single issue.

Someone left the cake out in the rain...I don't think that I can take it, 'cause it took so long to bake it. And I'll never have that recipe again.

I put my head on the steering wheel and sobbed as it played on.

We did everything right. Our peace framework was tremendously positive for the United States, first and foremost. But it was also very good for our allies in Europe and the Middle East. And I think it was excellent for the Iraqi people, too.

None of that mattered. We could not overcome the insanity of our leaders.

I will win the worship in their eyes and I will lose it. And after all the loves of my life, I'll be thinking of you. And wondering why?

I've asked myself a thousand times why they did it. Others have begged me to explain it, too. Honestly, I see no answer. War with Iraq was wholly avoidable and unnecessary. Such an incredible waste of human talent and life's ambitions and dreams. For nothing. For no purpose at all. No reason justified this sacrifice.

I thought of Richard Fuisz and Paul Hoven, and all of our years together, almost a decade that ended so abruptly without explanation or goodbyes.

And I thought about what we'd lost that night as a nation. America, what have we done to you? I wept with my head on the steering wheel.

I kept asking myself what could be done? How could we, the people resurrect what I consider the most beautiful values of our country, when our leaders are ready to smash us to hell? And damn the consequences!

I drove all night until I ran out of gas. By the end, I thought I had an answer. It was admittedly very simple. But it sounded pretty good at two o'clock in the morning. It was this.

America does not belong to the politicians. It's not theirs to take. It's not theirs to destroy.

America belongs to the people.

And by God, we are going to take it back!

CHAPTER 15:

WARNING. THIS MESSAGE CONTAINS DEMOCRACY

"The pen is mightier than the sword."
Edward Bulwer-Lytton, "Richelieu; Or the Conspiracy," 1839.

I suppose you could call this my year in the wilderness. In which case, it helps to remember that I'm from Alaska. If anybody can survive in the wilderness, it's me.

I was now on the outside. We were long past "burn notices" from the CIA, when the intelligence community declares an Asset trespassing or "persona non grata'. Otherwise, they'd be flapping all over my doors and windows, shooting down the chimney.

Oh, but I was not alone. Trust me when I say the spooks stayed close, and circled hard.

Oh, I see. You think I'm "paranoid."

Let me prove you wrong.

The peace camp in Washington folded up its tents shortly after the invasion. Nonetheless, some die-hard friends and I wanted to make a difference to the Occupation.

What else could we do? Our activities evolved continuously. Some of my wonderful activist friends, like Muthanna al Hanooti and Mohammad "Mo" Alomari, headed for Baghdad and tried to help the Sunni community integrate into the "New Iraq." They tried to show Sunnis how to participate in elections, and protect their political rights without resorting to violence. Both Muthanna and Mo had provided humanitarian assistance to Iraqi citizens during the U.N. sanctions, through a relief organization called "LIFE for

Relief and Development," one of the NGOs licensed by the U.S. State Department to transport medicines and supplies to Iraq under the sanctions. So my friends had long-standing ties throughout Iraqi society.

Unlike al Hanooti and Alomari, U.S. and British forces discovered that their own Iraqi allies, like Ahmed Chalabi, while exuberant in victory, had no friends or followers inside Iraq. Nobody supported them. The only Exiles who boasted small camps of followers were Ayatollah Mohammad Baqir al-Hakim, who founded the Supreme Council for the Islamic Revolution in Iraq (SCIRI), and members of the Islamic fundamentalist Dawa Party, both of which had sought refuge in Iran during Saddam's reign. Most secular Iraqis bitterly despised their Iranian connections. And though the western media tried to downplay it, most Iraqis regarded the Exiles' support for the miserable U.N. sanctions policy as unforgivable War Crimes against the Iraqi people. Except for their protection by U.S. and British soldiers, the Exiles would have been butchered on arrival, and orphaned by history.

Al-Hakim was assassinated shortly after his return to Baghdad by rival factions promoting Moqtada al-Sadr, whose family had stayed with the Iraqi people during sanctions and Saddam.

Returning Iraqi Exiles appear to have grasped what a fragile position they occupied in the "New Iraq." From the first weeks of Occupation, Iraqi Exiles executed one fundamental strategy for coming to power. Immediately after the fall of Baghdad, they started using American soldiers to burst into the homes of ordinary Iraqi citizens in the midnight hours, in order to arrest former Baathist officials, teachers, Judges, civil servants, young and old, who might challenge their power base and authority.

That first wave of arrests by U.S. soldiers began months before the Iraqi insurgency kicked off. There was no Iraqi Resistance at that point. Al Qaeda had not emerged as a force of reckoning. But in some villages, any Iraqi male over 5 feet tall was taken into custody.

Right from the start, Iraqi Exiles hunted out political challengers. They sought to remove any group of individuals who might create a leadership alternative in the community. Today it's an open secret that Iraqis outside of the Exile Community, which nurtured its ambitions in London, Tehran and Detroit, are largely prohibited from participating in leadership of the country. In the 2010 parliamentary elections, 511 candidates were barred from the ballot, mostly domestic Iraqis.

When I saw this activity, I found my own purpose in the Occupation. I thought the Iraqi people should have real democracy and human rights—not what I call "gun democracy." Banning candidates from the ballot negates all claims of a fair and free election, as far as I'm concerned. In a real democracy, anybody who wants to run for office can throw their hat in the ring. The opposition doesn't get to choose candidates, or strike off the winners.

So I took on the role of watch dog from Washington. And I stayed busy.

Tragically, the Occupation was already going horribly wrong. At the beginning of June, 2003, an explosive story hit the British press. British soldiers had photographed naked Iraqi prisoners graphically positioned to emulate acts of sodomy and oral sex. British soldiers stood by laughing. Another Iraqi hung naked from a rope tied to a forklift truck, bound hand and foot.[265]

A very brave young woman named Kelly Tilford spotted the pornographic pictures taken on the battlefield in Iraq at her photo shop in London, and called the police immediately.

"I saw the look on his face. He was petrified," Tilford told the British Sun. "I will never forget that terrible stare."

Another photo showed a close up shot of the naked backsides of two Iraqis, as if they were simulating anal sex.

This story broke almost a year before the exposé of identical torture and sexual abuse of Iraqi prisoners at Abu Ghraib prison, under control of the U.S. Close similarities in the graphic sexual abuses practiced by British and American soldiers suggest that the policy was deliberate and coordinated between the two groups, in order to emasculate Iraqi males.

Indeed, sexual degradation was applied across the country, from north to south, since Britain and the United States subjugated different parts of Iraq.

British and American soldiers who got arrested for these gross human rights violations, like Gary Bartlam of the 1st Battalion Royal Regiment of Fusiliers,[266] and Lynndie England of West Virginia in the United States,[267] have no one to blame for their shameful abuses. Each was convicted of taking photographs of naked Iraqis forced to perform or simulate sexual acts for the amusement of other soldiers. However, it's also evident that U.S. and British officers winked at this sort of behavior. Clearly senior officers failed to motivate soldiers under their command to act honorably towards Iraqi citizens. That command failure produced incalculable damage to subjugation efforts from the start of the Occupation.

On those grounds, I make no apologies for a letter that I submitted to British Ambassador Jeremy Greenstock at the United Nations on June 4, 2003,[268] threatening legal action on behalf of abused Iraqis.

A year before the horror Abu Ghraib broke in the media, I wrote to Ambassador Greenstock:

"The British government should consider itself hereby warned of (our) intention to file criminal charges against Prime Minister Tony Blair and the United Kingdom for violations of the International Geneva Conventions of War. It is our fullest intention to seek maximum financial compensation for all Iraqi victims of British and American war crimes, in equal measure to what Britain and the U.S. have demanded in the past for their own citizens. You will find the price of degrading human life is not cheap, Mr. Ambassador."

"To protect the British treasury—if not for human decency— we urge Britain and the U.S. to immediately allow the International Red Cross to gain access to all warehouses and camps where Iraqi Prisoners of War continue to be held. You should be warned, sir, that reports abound of prisoners being chained and hooded 24 hours of the day, and abused in circumstances worse than Guantanamo Bay."

"It would be in Britain's greatest national interest to guarantee a reversal in this horrific trend, for you should never doubt, sir, that Britain's criminal actions will carry an enormous price… We are ready to protect and defend that law, with the knowledge and certainty that we are in fact defending the best moral values of humanity."

And by God, I meant every word!

Amnesty International carried the day, forcing the British military to put several soldiers on trial for war crimes, and conduct a lengthy investigation of other prisoner abuses that bear uncanny similarities to the U.S. atrocities at Abu Ghraib.[269] Amnesty kept Tony Blair's government on the hot seat, and forced attention at the command level.

As for myself, I explored avenues to raise money for a two part legal project, both inside Iraq and at the International Court of The Hague. My goal was to hire a legal team inside Iraq to provide a measure of protection for Iraqi detainees captured in those midnight raids across the Sunni Heartland. Our team of Iraqi attorneys would have established a legal clinic, on behalf of impoverished families who could not afford legal representation to secure the release of their captive sons and fathers.[270]

Investigators would also document the rampant thefts of cash and property like satellite phones or small art treasures taken from Iraqi homes by American soldiers, and the many rapes of Iraqi women and random shootings by American and Coalition soldiers, reported to U.S. authorities and routinely ignored. These abuses quickly embittered the largely impoverished Iraqi population. We wanted to document offenses by Coalition soldiers, so that habitual offenders could be court-martialed and abuse practices could be outlawed at the command level.[271], [272]

Sadly, without that reporting mechanism, abuses of Iraqi citizens have continued and worsened over the years. As of 2009, the U.S. military acknowledged that between 70 percent and 90 percent of Iraqi detainees never committed any crime, but suffered wrongful accusations for revenge or profit, since the Americans paid cash rewards of up to $2,500 to informants for each arrest. Many of those Iraqis continue to be detained without trial, sometimes for years.[273]

The second part of my project focused on The Hague. I envisioned a team of international attorneys, backed by Iraqis, who could establish a legal precedent for mandatory human rights protections for citizens under Occupation, with financial penalties for violations.[274] That would have provided an enforcement mechanism for the International Geneva Conventions of War, a potentially valuable legal tool, which remains largely voluntary. The U.S. has mostly ignored it.

For this part of the project, I identified a highly respected human rights attorney named Stanley Cohen of New York City, who has pioneered the use of international law to assert the rights of Palestinians living in the West Bank and Gaza. With courageous forward vision, Cohen's team has sought to hold Israel accountable to international law, in order to shield the Palestinians. If the International Courts could succeed in staunching human rights abuses, the thinking goes, we might persuade minority groups in these countries to trust the Courts, instead of resorting to violence to remedy their injustice.

Was our vision too idealistic? Perhaps, but that was my plan. I needed financing to the tune of about $500,000 to pull it off. Half of the money would have paid for Stanley Cohen's team at The Hague.[275] The other half would have financed the team of Iraqi attorneys and investigators for the legal clinic inside Baghdad. It would have been a paltry sum compared to what great good our project might have accomplished.

Needless to say, the CIA did not appreciate in any way, whatsoever that one of their former Assets was aggressively harassing the British Ambassador to the United Nations, and threatening legal action against the "Coalition of the Willing," in order to protect Iraqi citizens from human rights abuses by undisciplined soldiers. Oh no, they didn't like that at all.

FBI wire taps captured my faxed letter to Ambassador Greenstock on June 4, 2003, along with dozens of faxes sent to Congress and the United Nations before and after the invasion, protesting the War and Occupation policies.[276]

On June 12, I received a single warning from my old compatriots at the CIA to shut my god damn mouth on all matters tied to Iraq.

The threat was not ambiguous. It arrived as an email marked "life insurance policy" under the name of the former Iraqi diplomat, Mr. A——who, prior to the war, had agreed to help the U.S. identify foreign terrorists playing hide and seek with Saddam's Intelligence Service inside Iraq. The use of his name in that email proved that U.S. intelligence understood our special relationship very well.

There was nothing subtle about the message. They weren't going to limit their attacks to me. They were going to hunt down my old contacts in Baghdad, as well. The email said that if I wanted to keep them alive, I should go to ground and stay silent on all matters dealing with Iraq.

That just pissed me off.

Hey, they were pissed off, too.

We were both at each other's throats at this point. I recognized that email would not be the end of it. Spooks become dangerous animals when threatened. No doubt they decided that somebody better investigate what I was up to, and how far I had progressed. It didn't take them long to mobilize. *As I have said before, when they want you, they will come and get you.*

That's exactly what they did.

Very early on the morning of June 23, 2003, I got a phone call at about 7 a.m.[277]

A man with an Arab accent asked to speak with me before I headed off to work that morning. He asked if I could meet him in the parking lot of a local restaurant called Savory in Takoma Park, where I live. He was already here. And clearly he had scoped out my little peace-nik town. I'd walked my dachshunds that beautiful summer morning, and it appeared very likely that he knew I was dressed for work when he requested the meeting.

Now truly, most people would run like the devil in the opposite direction if they got a call like that. Assets are different creatures. We're supposed to handle this kind of stuff. Though I was officially retired, once you're in that game—and it is a game—then you are expected to play whenever called upon. The game's never over. You're never really out of it.

On that expectation, I agreed to show up in 30 minutes, as requested.

We walked around the streets of my neighborhood and talked for no more than 10 minutes. On our short morning walk, I learned that "Adam" claimed to have traveled from Michigan. He told me a small group of investors wanted to put together a peace project inside Iraq to try to influence the Occupation. Of critical importance, in that first conversation, "Adam" claimed to know my friend, Muthanna, who's also from Dearborn, Michigan. The conversation was necessarily brief, because I had to go to work. However, I agreed to meet him at a hotel in the Baltimore Marina later that night on June 23, 2003.[278]

Given who I am, I don't take things on faith just because I'm told. The timing struck me as awfully suspicious. I'd sent my letter to British Ambassador Greenstock on June 4. I'd received the "life insurance" email on about June 15-16. And it was now June 23.

So of course I made a connection. According to the schematics of the intelligence world, I recognized this approach as a rational action on their part. At the same time, something was in play, and as part of the game, I had to figure out what it was.

A lifetime of expectations influenced how I viewed this man. From the opening, I considered that I was dealing with his "cover," and only a small part of it had been revealed on our morning walk.

Right off the bat, I saw that it was possible, but not likely, that his cover was authentic. Perhaps he knew Muthanna. Perhaps he did not. Right then Muthanna was traveling in Iraq. So I could not inquire. That did not matter though. It would be remarkable, truly perplexing, if after my decade as an Asset, I failed to grasp that some kind of game was in play. I'd have to erase every experience that I ever had not to be confident handling this.

I saw three options.

One, he was a jihadi. That struck me as extremely unlikely, since all my Arab friends and contacts understood that I famously oppose war and violence in the Middle East in all directions. It would have been awfully risky to approach me. He could expect to get rebuffed. He would gain nothing from the attempt.

Two, he was a spook. That was always the most probable scenario, given my activities since the invasion, and the threat that I received a week earlier.

Here's where it got interesting. If he was a spook, I saw two possibilities. Most likely, he was unfriendly and wanted to keep tabs on the progress of my projects. In which case, I had nothing to hide. My actions supporting democratic reforms and human rights in Iraq are legal in any courtroom in the world, outside of North Korea, Mynamar. There was no danger that he might distract me. Nothing could persuade me to abandon my work for democracy and human rights under any circumstances. If they wanted to know what I was up to, I would jolly well tell them. They could hear from it my own mouth.

There was a second possibility that intrigued me very much. Just maybe, he was a friendly spook, looking to build a team to go into Iraq, for the purpose of countering bad actions by Occupation forces and major mistakes in Washington. Maybe he was part of a faction that wanted to push things onto the right track.

What quickened my pulse was that the U.S. State Department had just been evicted from Iraq by the Pentagon. Right then, pro-Arabist cliques were regrouping in Washington, still hoping to influence the Occupation. If one of those groups was feeling me out, it might present a worthwhile opportunity to exert pressure in a totally different direction. That possibility tantalized me. It would mean a choice between fighting the Occupation from the outside, or trying to make things better from the inside. It would be a hard decision. Either way, I intended to challenge the Occupation.

Third, his "cover" story might be authentic. He might have told the truth that a group of Arab-Americans in Michigan wanted to finance some kind of peace project inside Iraq. Given my strong reputation opposing military aggression and terrorism, I would be a safe American to approach. My involvement would give the others some protection. Nobody could accuse them of supporting violence with me in the group.

Which of those possibilities would prove correct, I could not say.

But as an Asset, you're expected to play. Paul Hoven, my old handler, always encouraged me to think of it like a dance. When a man asks a woman to dance, she's supposed to say yes, because that's what she's gone to the Club to do. Then, over the evening, she's supposed to identify her partner, and get to know him. She doesn't have to go home with him. Maybe she goes on another date, because there's something particular they'd like to try out together. Maybe the relationship goes nowhere after three or four dates. That's just like an Asset.

An Asset has to figure out who has approached you, and why. It's sort of a courtesy to agree to the first meeting, because somebody has gone to a good deal of trouble to learn who you are, and understand your projects. And he's gone to the trouble to come find you. It's far more difficult than it looks, because everything's done on the Q.T. There are many obstacles that a third party would have to overcome to collect that information. So it's important to find out why that person made the effort.

All of that explains how I met Bassem Youssef, aka "Adam" on the night of June 23, 2003, in a gorgeous five star hotel suite overlooking Baltimore Harbor.[279]

The choice of location had some historical significance, I noted gleefully to myself that night. Baltimore Harbor happens to be where Francis Scott Key wrote the "Star Spangled Banner," while imprisoned on a British flagship during the Battle of Fort McHenry in the War of 1812. Watching the guns blaze off British war ships throughout the night of battle, Key wrote a beautiful poem anxiously awaiting the morning light, which would show whether our young nation had prevailed against British forces. That evening I found the coincidence rather poetic, since my conversation with Youssef focused on how to guarantee the rights of fledgling democracy in Iraq, and whether a true democracy could be established at all.

Little did I imagine that night I was conversing with a British agent-provocateur! And one sent on behalf of British Ambassador Jeremy Greenstock himself to stop American citizens from championing the rights of democracy and self determination in Baghdad!

I want an apology from the Queen!

For indeed, our conversation that night revolved around how to create a pathway for achieving genuine and meaningful democratic reforms and protecting human rights in Iraq. Thanks to FBI body wires worn by Youssef, there's no question that's exactly what we discussed.[280]

Lindauer: "We would have a legal challenge in international court—
Youssef: "Hmph hmph."
Lindauer: "that the Iraqi people have a God-given right— we call it an inalienable right—to choose their own Government and... that it would be a violation of International law for anything to impose a Government on the Iraqi people from outside. We would go to the International Court and file an appeal demanding that the Court guarantee the right, and enforce the rights of the Iraqi people to form political parties of their own choice and to hold elections, so that the United States and Britain cannot, under international law, interfere with the domestic process of the Iraqi Government. That's the point."
Youseff: "Now—"
Lindauer: "I don't understand where—I don't know where you're coming from. And just think about it. Even if you don't agree with it entirely, just think about it. Because the next part of it is also very important. We would sue. We would say one, we demand that the Court enforce the natural rights of the Iraqi people to choose their own Government and to form political parties, and do whatever

the hell they want. No outside force can choose a Government for the Iraqi people. There can be no 'puppet government' of Iraq."

Youseff: "Hmph hmph."

Lindauer: "And secondly, that only a Government chosen by the Iraqi people can spend Iraqi oil money. Only a Government chosen…"

Youseff: "That sounds reasonable."

Lindauer: "—by the Iraqi people. Okay."

Youseff: "Now where are you and Muthanna and the lawyer in this process right now?"

Lindauer: "Muthanna is in Baghdad or somewhere in Iraq. He's supposed to be identifying an attorney, or a team. Because it has to have an Iraqi face. It has to be the Iraqi people asserting their own integrity."

Youseff: "Yes."

Lindauer: "We have to help them, but we have to get out of the way, too. You know what I mean? We can't do this for them. We need to empower them, and provide financial resources. In order to succeed, there has to be something. Now it doesn't have to be a lot of money. I mean probably a tragically small amount of money is going to help them enormously."

Youseff: "Well, for a good cause, I don't think that there will be a problem."

Lindauer: "And then there would be an international component that the Iraqis will organize from the inside, and they would receive technical assistance in presenting their case, getting things to The Hague, filing the briefs, doing the international attorney law work."

Youseff: "Are there guarantees this would work?"

Lindauer: "There are no guarantees in international law."

Youseff: "Of course."

Lindauer: "But you know, the thing is, you have to try… You can't just let the United States get away with this. We need to, as much as possible, we need to use the precedents that the United States has used for itself."

Youseff: "Sounds reasonable."

Youseff: "It seems from what you're telling me that nothing is really finalized. This is something in the works."

Lindauer: "It can only be finalized if the Iraqi people want it to be finalized."

Youseff: "Well, of course."

Several months later I would get arrested for what I told Youseff that night, charged with "Organizing Resistance to the United States."[281] And so, vigorously I dispute the notion that Pro-War Republicans supported democracy at the start of the Occupation. Ultimately, activists in Iraq and around the world pushed leaders in Washington and London to accept true democratic reforms, but only because we dragged them to it. In truth, they bitterly resented us for forcing it on them.

There would only be two meetings between Youseff and I, the first on June 23, almost three weeks after I contacted British Ambassador Greenstock, and the second on July 17. My birthday. I thought that was a nice touch.[282]

Close to the end of our first meeting, Youseff began to drop hints of his knowledge about my intelligence work. However it was really only at the start of our second (and final) meeting, that Youseff revealed he'd been thoroughly debriefed on my intelligence background.

The whole tone of the conversation changed immediately as to whether I might help his team in some way in Iraq.[283]

Youseff: "I must tell you they like you so far very much."

Lindauer: "Oh good."

Youseff: "I have to ask you very seriously…"

Lindauer: "Okay."

Youseff: "Are you ready to work with us?"

Lindauer: "Oh yes! Yes. That's why I brought all of this. So you could see my commitment is real."

Youseff: "Excellent, excellent. And so far, we are very happy that you are ah, you are coming over to our side and that's why I've asked you a very straight, very honest question."

[A note to readers: as you're about to see, there was nothing "straight" or "honest" about it. This was an inside spook approach. Honest and straightforward is not how I would describe it. Quite the opposite, our conversation was loaded with double-entendres. It helps to remember that this is a game. A perverse little game with lots of diagonal cuts. However, this was my playground. I knew my way around the yard.]

Yousseff and I had exchanged pleasantries for about five minutes in our second meeting, when he laid a crucial card on the table:

Youseff: "We must know when you began your relationship with the ah, the Arab Intelligence agencies. It's very important, because like I said, the people who are now over there, the Americans are talking to them. We don't know who's who."

Real people don't talk like that! Right there, he outed himself as a spook. He could never go back on that. Everything changed in that moment. Youssef continued to ask for the names of my Iraqi contacts. And immediately I began to look for a chance to call him out as American Intelligence. It was important to put him on notice that I had broke through his cover. Only then could we start to have a real conversation.

So how would I do that? For one thing, from our first bright eyed morning walk in Takoma Park, Youseff told me that he knows Muthanna. That gave me a wedge. Our conversation was rolling fast now. For all the sweet talk at the beginning, it looked to me like a hostile approach. Until proven otherwise, this was not an intelligence faction that I would ever support. Later, my friend, Parke Godfrey, would testify in Court that I told him about the meeting, and laid 50-50 odds that Youseff was an FBI agent.[284]

And yet—what if "Adam," as he called himself was part of a State Department faction that recognized mistakes in the Occupation, and hoped to accomplish something to undo that damage? What if they turned out to be hopeful, instead?

Though it seems unlikely to outsiders, frequently that's what Intelligence factions have to do. Policymakers make a mess. The spooks go in to clean it up. I'd done that myself on several occasions, involving Libya and Iraq. If that was the case, I might want in. So as this conversation rolled on, I kept juggling. How hard did I want to slam the door? How could I keep that door open a crack? And yet I had to be clear that I was drawing a line. I could not support the Occupation as it existed. If my commentary appears harsh, it should be understood that Youseff's group needed an honest and straightforward declaration, whoever they were, before they could put me on the ground in a war zone, in Iraq. They needed to know my politics. And I needed to tell them. Neither one of us could compromise in such a situation. Brutal honesty mattered.

So how could I finesse it? All of that pulled at my brain during this conversation.

Lindauer: "What if we, uh, put a good list and a bad list? (Laughs)"

Youseff: "Okay."

Lindauer: "Muthanna has done something that I'm very upset about."

Youseff: "Hmph hmph."

Lindauer: "Ah, Muthanna does not know about you."

Youseff: (Unintelligible mumbling).

Lindauer: "Categorically." [In other words, Youseff lied about how he learned of my work.]

Youseff: "You have not told anybody, anything about…" [Read that, yeah, I lied, but you haven't exposed us for approaching you? That would be death to the whole effort, if we tried to do something later in Iraq.]

Lindauer: "Categorically, categorically." [Youseff lied, but I hadn't told Muthanna, who had just returned from Baghdad, that a U.S. agent had used his name to approach me.]

Lindauer: "Ah, but it, it shocked me, ah, that Muthanna was over in Iraq, and he was having daily meetings—Daily meetings! with the Occupation forces. He was trying to set up a consulting job with the Occupation forces."

[That's essentially what I thought Youseff wanted to explore with me. That appeared the direction our own conversation was heading.]

Youseff: "Hmph."

Lindauer: "He thinks he's helping the Iraqis."

Youseff: "This is what he told you?"

Lindauer: "This is what he told me."

We began to discuss more of the Iraqis whom I had worked with in the past, and whether I could work with them again. The question remained whether I would want to.

Youseff: "And when you went to the Embassy, did you feel comfortable?"

Lindauer: "Oh, I have always had very, very, very good relations with Iraq."

Youseff: "Always, from the beginning?"

Lindauer: "Very good relations."

Lindauer: "Um, there is another man who is absolutely reliable, who it would shock me if he was not reliable. [meaning reliable for Youseff] I would be shocked."

Youseff: "You said that list, who's on that list?"

Lindauer: "Ah, Muthanna."

Youseff: "Okay."

Lindauer: "I, I'm sorry to say that. I'm, I'm very sorry to say that."

Youseff: (unintelligible mumbling)

Lindauer: "I'm very sorry to say that. He can't even. I mean, Muthanna's struggling. But the fact that he's struggling… To me, it's very clear cut."

Youseff: "Hmph hmph."

Lindauer: "There's no way that I could go over to Iraq, unless I was working, doing it literally at your request."

Youseff: "Absolutely."

Lindauer: "I could not."

Youseff: "And we will talk about that. Okay."

Lindauer: "Yeah, I mean I could never go to Iraq and pretend that it was acceptable. I, I couldn't do it."

Youseff: "Hmph hmph."

Lindauer: "I mean, you'd have to be—you'd really have to, I mean, if you asked me to do I undercover…I would do it for you."

Youseff: "Right."

Lindauer: "But I would never just…"

Youseff: "Yeah."

Lindauer: "I couldn't. I couldn't rationalize it. I couldn't justify it."

Youseff: "So we can be comfortable to say that you would not go unless we asked you to do that?"

Lindauer: "Absolutely, absolutely."

Poor Muthanna would be horrified to hear himself described as a collaborator. He's a loyal peace-maker and community builder. He dedicated his life to opposing sanctions and bringing humanitarian relief to the Iraqi people. But I had to get my point across. It was strictly a matter of necessity. I had to make my position crystal clear.

From that point on, our conversation turned to spook talk, and it would be ludicrous to pretend anything else. Until the end of the meeting, Youseff gave mixed signals as to whether his group wanted to improve the Occupation, or not. The only thing positively certain was that Youseff represented some faction of U.S. intelligence. It frustrated me enormously that I could not tell whether they wanted to reverse the damage of bad decisions by Occupation leaders. By contrast, I underscored my opposition to Occupation policies with every breath.

One more event involving Youseff illustrates the more sinister aspects of the Patriot Act. In our second conversation, Youssef and I discussed my knowledge of Lockerbie at some length. I mentioned some papers that he might like to see.

Imagine my surprise, therefore, to return home from work about a week later to find those same papers laid out on my desk, and one of the drawers of my filing cabinet broken and hanging crooked. It took me seconds to know that somebody had rifled through my home office.

Now, it would have taken me several hours to locate those papers, amidst everything I've got, for the simple fact that those are older documents and buried deep. And I have a good idea where they would be. I suspect it would have taken Youseff several hours to find them, too.

Yet there was my Lockerbie collection, nicely compiled, and neatly laid out on my desk, next to my open computer screen. And behind it, a broken filing cabinet.

Welcome to the Patriot Act, friends. It's a brave new world.

I'm convinced that Bassem Youseff exercised what's called "a warrantless search" on my house, possibly in league with another FBI agent, what formerly qualified as a serious violation of my Constitutional rights as a citizen of the United States. There was no cause for a warrant, since I had engaged in no criminal activities. All of my actions supported democratic reforms and the protection of human rights in Iraq.

But under the Patriot Act, the government no longer requires cause to enter a private home, and conduct a search without the knowledge of the occupant. They have no obligation to inform the individual that they've entered your home at all. Federal agents have power to come and go at will. I suspect that I must have interrupted them when I came home from work, because the papers got left behind in the rush to get out my back door. Obviously Youseff understood he had no business in my home, and fled.

Ah, the plot thickens fast. When the break in occurred, I did not know that Bassem Youseff was an under-cover FBI agent, or that he had just executed a "warrantless search" on the Patriot Act. I concluded he was an unstable young man, perhaps pushed to the limits of his reason by the War. I was frazzled, too. But I'm an unmarried woman. I don't need unstable men breaking into my house uninvited, and tearing apart my private office. Can you imagine it?

A few days later I got even more upset when Youseff phoned to ask for the papers left behind in his rush to get out of my house![285] I was floored! He made no apology for entering my house without permission, mind you. He just wanted the papers. With some consternation, I agreed to hand them over. I considered it the wisest course of action. Seriously, if he wanted them so badly, he could have them.

That wasn't all. He asked me to leave the papers in a manila envelope in a children's park close to my house.[286] Now I had to wonder if he'd been stalking me, perhaps while I walked my dachshunds past the park, since he had obviously studied the lay out of my neighborhood. Oh joy!

Without question, I believed that if I refused to deliver the papers, he would break into my house a second time, and take them. I had no idea what else he might do, given his apparently agitated state. I had no desire to find out.

So I did what he asked. I left a manila envelope in the park.

That illustrates in graphic detail what abuses the Patriot Act has inspired.

First of all, it's offensive that anyone who campaigns for democracy and human rights in any country of the world should be treated as a criminal. My activism should not be judged by federal authorities as a waiver of my civil liberties under the Constitution.

When the Patriot Act was passed, Congress insisted that "only criminals" had to fear the new, highly invasive surveillance rules. My situation makes a lie of that. The Feds are using that law to come after activists as well, even those of us who support non-violence and democracy.

I have to wonder what's going to happen when the Feds come up against a law abiding American who defends his rights to bear arms under the 2nd Amendment. Somebody's going to get shot. And speaking from personal experience, I will feel no sympathy on that day when somebody like Bassem Youseff gets caught red-handed, stealing papers from a home without a search warrant, and gets a bullet from somebody who has no idea why he's there. It's a vulgarity. It's a gross violation of everything our country stands for. And it's guaranteed to cause a lot more problems, because the law was so badly written in the first place.

As for me, Youseff was darn lucky that I got home before my former housemate, Alyce— an honest, law abiding woman who happens to have a concealed weapons permit.

Alyce carries a gun in her purse at all times to protect herself from muggers— and home invasion. She would have shot Youseff "a.k.a" Adam point blank. If he fired back, as a more expert marksman—and killed her inside her own home, who would be to blame?

I'll tell you: It would be the members of Congress who approved this wretched law. As far as I'm concerned, the Patriot Act was a declaration of war against the American people. Members of Congress who voted for the Patriot Act acted as traitors to our country.

But I'm getting ahead of myself.

About three weeks later, I got an agitated phone call from Youseff, saying that some federal agents had interrogated him, and he was scared.[287] I gave him the name of a good attorney, but I couldn't tell if Youseff was using that ploy to drop me, or if he was really in trouble. He still claimed to have "investors" who might finance my democracy project in Iraq. I had no idea if they would turn out to be as explosive and unstable as he was.

How could I possibly get in trouble for giving somebody the name of a good attorney? We haven't reached a point where that would be illegal. Have we?

Against this backdrop, the situation in Iraq was deteriorating rapidly. Somebody urgently needed to reverse the disastrous policies of the Occupation. Iraq was getting ready to blow. And I had a very good understanding of what that would mean.

If Youseff hoped to distract me from my projects, he failed miserably. I took my threat of legal action to the United Nations. In a letter faxed to French Ambassador Jean Marc de la Sabliere on July 23, 2003 (also captured by FBI wire tap), I praised the "courageous foresight (of) President Chirac in rejecting" this war.[288]

I wrote: "We intend to prove that the International Courts can achieve justice for less powerful nations against the tyranny of unlawful usurpers.... forcefully and effectively, without necessitating violence."

"Thwarting the Courts of Law would be the greatest mistake in a military conflict already fraught with bad decisions. If the U.N. tries to prevent the Courts from guaranteeing the protections of international law to all peoples, uniformly and without prejudice, then it would become difficult to argue that violence is not the only avenue to justice. In which case, nations that send soldiers and weapons to Iraq would become primary targets."

I would get arrested for this, friends. My actions supporting free elections and human rights in Iraq would be called "Organizing Resistance to the U.S. Occupation." [289]

In the indictment, dear Youseff would pretend to have posed as a Libyan Intelligence Agent.[290] Which astonished me. If one thing was clear, it's that I believed he was American Intelligence. And there was no third meeting.

The Justice Department might have hoped to hang me in the court of public opinion, but they couldn't possibly sell that to a Judge and jury. And they knew it.

Shocking, isn't it? I got arrested for supporting democracy in Iraq.

If you ask now, was it worth it? I would say absolutely yes. If supporting genuine democracy anywhere in the world qualifies as "Organizing Resistance to the United

States," then by God, sign me up! Something has gone terribly wrong in America. It's time to make a stand right now, and take our country back!

What's extraordinary is not why I chose to devote my activism to supporting a platform of democracy and human rights in the "New Iraq," but why the U.S. and British governments attacked me for it. My arrest makes a lie of liberation, doesn't it?

I can sense you're puzzled. Surely the U.S. and Britain supported democracy in Iraq, without need for watchdogs like me? Wasn't that a primary justification for the invasion?

Not originally. Not when you read the fine print. Free elections were not part of the original blueprint for Iraq's future. Working together, activists inside Iraq and around the world brought the U.S. government to it. We won a critical victory in the end. But it was a people's victory over politicians and bureaucrats. For all of the media hype afterwards, Washington and London did not appreciate our interference at all.

No, the original U.S. policy announced by Paul Bremer, former Tsar of Iraq, on November 15, 2003, declared that Iraqis would have no direct vote in choosing their new government.[291]

In the original transition plan, Bremer's staff at the Coalition Provisional Authority intended to hand pick the new leaders, who would form a transitional government.

Each of Iraq's 18 provinces would hold a political caucus run by "professionals, experts and tribal leaders." Participants in the Caucus would be screened by a 15 person "organizing committee," which would also be hand-picked by the Americans.

The Caucus would choose representatives from its own group to attend a National Convention. The Convention would write a Permanent Constitution and choose candidates for a 250 member transitional assembly.

The assembly would elect a President and cabinet from within its ranks. Direct elections by and for the people would be held several years down the road.

You could have heard a pin drop in the room when Bremer announced this thinly disguised plan for U.S. autocracy in Iraq. Then there was shouting from all quarters. No! No! No!

So many bad decisions had been foisted on Iraq by this point. Efforts to deny Iraqis a direct vote for the new government was the last straw. There was open rebellion to the plan.

Ayatollah Sistani emerged from seclusion in Najaf **to** declare a fatwa—that's a religious edict—opposing Bremer's proposal.

"There is no guarantee that the council would create a constitution conforming with the greater interests of the Iraqi people and expressing the national identity, whose basis is Islam, and its noble social values," Sistani decreed.[292]

That's what saved democracy in Iraq. A religious edict. An Ayatollah's fatwa! Democracy resulted from an uprising of the people so powerful that it overturned the autocracy of Washington.

Oh yes, and whatever happened to my good friend, Muthanna al Hanooti?

While other Iraqi Exiles floundered trying to establish a base of political support inside Iraq, Muthanna flourished—always a peace maker, never a collaborator. Unlike most of the Exiles from London and Iran and Detroit, who supported the notorious U.N. sanctions that inflicted such misery on ordinary Iraqis, Muthanna had brought humanitarian relief to the people during the hated sanctions. Now they honored him for it. He emerged as a respected bridge builder, enjoying a remarkable level of support among the common people.

If Muthanna al Hanooti emerged in the leadership of the "New Iraq," we would have a shot at real peace in the region. He's that good.

So what did the unpopular Iraqi Exiles do to knock down this outstanding man?

Jealous of his extensive contacts throughout Iraq, former Iraqi Exiles campaigned vigorously for Muthanna al Hanooti's arrest in the United States. They finally got their wish. Five years after the fall of Saddam, in March, 2008 Muthanna got indicted as an "unregistered Iraqi Agent," on the ridiculous allegation that he received 2 million barrels of oil from Saddam's government.[293]

Two million barrels of oil?

I was dumb-founded when I heard this. First I was speechless. Then I laughed uproariously, because it's so incredibly stupid. I first met Muthanna in 2002, while we both campaigned as activists against war and sanctions.[294] Because of my past, I made it my business to know a great deal about Muthanna's private life. Chalk it up to occupational hazard. Anyway, those accusations against Muthanna were the kind of baffling nonsense only the Iraqi Exiles could invent. They're highly imaginative in their scheming. In all my years covering Iraq, I never got over my sense of amazement for every new fantasy they concocted, with such embellishes and bellicose lies. I was sure they should win prizes for literary fiction.

They say you should judge a man by the strength of his enemies.

Hey, if the Iraqi exiles don't like somebody, you know that person's got integrity, like Muthanna al Hanooti.

The corollary to that is if the pro-war factions in Washington led by Vice President Cheney and Senator John McCain oppose your activities, you must be doing something right.

I was about to discover that for myself.

CHAPTER 16:

THE CRYING GAME

The few rose petals died quickly in the Iraq summer sun.

Simple things in the modern world, like shortages of electricity and food, turned Iraqi frustrations to hatred and rage. U.N. inspectors on the hunt for WMDs bagged nothing, disgracing a key justification for the war. And Americans soon realized the only Al Qaeda forces in Iraq arrived shortly after the fall of Saddam, mocking another rationalization for our misadventure. In no time at all, American soldiers hunkered down behind razor wire and concrete barricades, without adequate body armor, while the War of Ramadan launched a full scale insurgency using suicide bombers and improvised explosive devices made of absolutely anything. Violent resistance swept from the mosques to Sunni strongholds in Fallujah and Mosul, and Shi'ite dominated Najaf and Nasiriyah.

The stagecraft of victory collapsed within months. Liberation doctrine lay battered beneath the rubble, smashed beyond recognition alongside charred claims of triumph.

It happened so fast.

Americans woke up one morning to find themselves a losing army, a conquered Occupier.

"Vietnam" was on everyone's lips. Soldiers who expected to serve one tour in Iraq got sent back five times, more badly scarred by post traumatic stress with every deployment.

The country demanded to know why. Americans resent getting tagged as "bad guys" in any conflict. Our soldiers want to be the "good guys."

In Washington, Congressional leaders got scared. They had shut their ears to hundreds of thousands of voter pleas, in letters and faxes and phone calls and demonstrations that begged Congress to stay out of Iraq, and let U.N. weapons inspectors finish their job. Americans never wanted to sacrifice for this war. Now we had to mortgage our future to sustain the failure of it.

Congress faced bitter recriminations and vicious election fights against a backdrop of the most passionate anti-incumbent sentiments in years.

Iraq and 9/11 were ubiquitous killjoys in the debate. Were Republicans really more qualified to lead the War on Terror? Had they accomplished what they promised? People started to ask some important questions: When did the CIA get its first itch that a terrorist attack could be imminent? There started to be low rumblings that we expected the 9/11 strike. It would take more time, but whisperings of truth would break out, as ever it does.

The Presidential sweepstakes towered frightfully large. If the Democrats could beat the GOP machine, they would take down a lot of Republicans on Capitol Hill.

Congress fretted. They whined. And they looked for a scapegoat—anything to avoid taking responsibility for their own mistakes in rushing to War. Iraq cost America all of her prestige abroad, and the critical ability to foist a U.S. agenda on trusting international allies. Not to mention boatloads of cash needed for schools and public works projects and police departments.

It was a great deal to lose, exactly as the Intelligence community warned it would be.

Their own congressional seats would be a great deal to lose, too.

Now that would be truly disastrous! If they had to take responsibility for this war, their political careers would be finished! They'd be ruined!

But what if someone else could take responsibility for them?

Intelligence Assets, perhaps. *Someone like me.*

Come again?

That's right. Assets who put together Pre-War Intelligence reports for the CIA and Defense Intelligence Agency. *We could take the blame–*

There were very few of us—maybe a dozen, at most.[295] If we could take the blame for faulty intelligence that guided decision-making before the War, *they would be saved*.

Say now, that was a plan. Congress and the White House could channel public fury onto the Intelligence community, arguing for the failure of Assets and our handlers. Over and over Congress could rip us apart for lacking aggressive risk-taking and strategic thinking skills—"imaginative risk taking," a Presidential Commission would accuse later on.[296]

Officially, the White House and Republican attack machine would declare that Assets had performed "incompetently." That would have frightening and ominous implications for my future.

It took a Washington heartbeat—which is slow, like a snake— for Republicans and Democrats alike to see that Assets would be the perfect fall guys.

The stakes were so high. I'm sure they expected us to understand.

There's a time honored tradition on Capitol Hill. When Congress makes a mistake, blame always falls on congressional staff. As a former staffer myself, I was expected to know this.

It's never a Senator's or Congress member's fault that an important speech or constituent meeting got missed. It's the scheduler or press secretary who screwed up. Republicans are every bit as guilty as the Democrats in this regard. There's nothing partisan about this trend. It's the unhappy norm on Capitol Hill.

Unfortunately, playing hooky from responsibility becomes habitual, without consequence.

THE CRYING GAME

Cowardice ruled over Capitol Hill.

That selfishness, and to a degree cowardice, explains a lot about why Republicans and Democrats united so quickly to heap scornful epithets on the so-called "incompetence" of Assets and intelligence gathering at the CIA and Defense Intelligence Agency before the war.

It was the ultimate Crying Game. Democrats and Republicans both played the role of victims to what they called a massive "intelligence failure."

In the months ahead, Rep. Jane Harman, a top ranking democrat on the House Intelligence Committee, swore that Assets bore the blame for failing to develop options to War, or speak up to Congress if our work got misrepresented in the public debate. Why didn't any of us try to set the record straight?[297]

Rep. Harman concluded that the failure of Assets to take a proactive role in correcting "misinformation" compelled Congress to acquiesce to the White House instead of resisting the debacle of this war policy. Congress had no options, because Assets created no options.[298]

There was just one serious flaw in that strategy of denial: I had done all of those things. I had even debriefed Congresswoman Harman's own Chief of Staff about the CIA's alternative framework for ending the conflict with Iraq, built over a two year period before the invasion. Her senior legislative staff got copies of the Andy Card letters, too.

Therein lay the problem for Congress.

I wasn't "feeling" their pain quite the way they hoped.

When I established "Citizens for Public Integrity" after 9/11, I chose the relatively conservative moniker because I despised this lack of accountability. I wanted truth with teeth, not a whitewash. I wanted to take this fight to their door, and I would not stop until I knocked it down. Frankly, I was sick to death of Washington doing business this way.

After the Invasion of Iraq, in my watch dog role, I continued to distribute papers on Capitol Hill, decrying human rights abuses in the "New Iraq," and championing genuine democratic reforms. I championed the rights of detainees to have legal counsel to protest their arrests, and the right not to be attacked by dogs or sexually degraded.[299] I'd already heard horrors about Abu Ghraib by August or September, 2003—months before the scandal broke. It was right below the surface. Finally, I campaigned hard for Iraq's right to form political parties and map a political future without relying on Iraqi exiles, who sought to squash political opposition.[300] The "New Iraq" had to be borne from inside, not imposed from outside.

At home, I made no secret that I despised Republicans particularly for lying about our advance knowledge of 9/11, and boasting of their "outstanding leadership performance" on matters of counter-terrorism and national security. That was political fraud.

I scorned suggestions that 9/11 resulted from a lack of mid-level intra-agency cooperation. I whispered through the Washington mill that Republican appointees at the top of the Justice Department, responsible for oversight, had refused requests for multi-agency planning to block the 9/11 attack. Cabinet level authorization was necessary for cooperation to occur. Lower level people—read that, non political appointees, like me— recognized that intra-agency cooperation was vital. Unhappily, we lacked authority to require it to happen. But we certainly tried to raise the alarms. That's why my CIA handler, Dr. Fuisz, urged me to approach Andy Card at his home in Arlington, Virginia in mid-August, 2001. We wanted to bypass that political constipation at the Justice Department, and set up a pre-emptive strategy for blocking or deflecting the attack.

Based on threats I delivered to Iraqi diplomats myself from May, 2001 onwards, it surely appeared that top-ranking U.S. government officials had seized on the impending attack as a rationalization for war with Baghdad. The intelligence community correctly anticipated the attack in all specific details. My handlers urgently tried to stop it. But that secret agenda to create a war with Iraq was already in motion. Instead of heeding our urgent and proactive warnings, the top of the government ignored simple counter-measures that would have blocked the terrorists, like alerting NORAD or hoisting a single anti-aircraft gun on top of just one of the World Trade Center towers. That would have protected both buildings. Knowing what was coming, top leaders stood down from obligations to protect the sovereign territory of the United States, an act of deliberate command negligence. And that's unforgivable.

There were also serious questions of what happened to all that "black budget" money designated for field-work after 9/11. Almost $75 billion got appropriated by Congress— Yet somehow it got siphoned off from active projects "on the ground" like mine, and diverted to Washington bureaucracy and high-tech gadgetry. There are strong indications from my own experience that substantial sums of Black Budget money vanished into the private bank accounts and fancy houses of the Beltway Bandits in McLean, Virginia, the CIA's own back yard.

Where federal dollars for anti-terrorism did not get invested was on Assets like me— who perform the work of anti-terrorism itself— or the recruitment of Agents in the Middle East, like my Iraqi friend. That infuriated me.

If anti-terrorism policy mattered to the leadership beyond the level of propaganda, those problems would fire off alarms all over Capitol Hill. Such a major debacle should demand a Congressional investigation, and an immediate overhaul of the "black budget" rules for dispersement of funds. It would demand very serious scrutiny.

And yet Congress has steadfastly refused to examine the "black budgets," or hold federal agencies responsible for the mis-management of funds. Beltway Bandits are faithful campaign contributors—which sort of implies the money off the "black budgets" is getting funneled back to Congress at election time. Those are American tax dollars, friends. That tax money comes from a teacher in North Carolina, a plumber in Ohio, a realtor in Scottsdale, Arizona and a techie geek in Silicon Valley. American taxpayers work hard for that money. There should be accountability.

Who was to blame for all of this?

Indisputably, the Republican Party controlled these federal agencies, for the simple fact that whoever controls the White House controls executive policy and top appoint-ments throughout the executive branch.

This happened on the Republican's watch. If the Democrats had done such a poor job after 9/11, Americans would scream bloody murder against them, too, because these are seriously flawed decisions. These decisions undercut our national security, and continue to threaten us now.

Instead, Republican leaders demagogued 9/11, whipping up the emotional pain of Americans for their own vainglory.

Senator John McCain and Vice President Cheney—not the Democrats— played the 9/11 card to incite irrational fears about Saddam Hussein's alleged ties to terrorists. Again and again, top-shelf republicans like Senator John McCain issued demands in the media for Iraq's cooperation, trying to ignite public hysteria and ramp up support for War.

On Capitol Hill, I hit back hard, with facts about our success securing Iraq's cooperation with the 9/11 investigation. Our team achieved significant results that would have substantially crippled the ability of terrorists to play hide and seek with Iraqi Intelligence, taking advantage of weakened civil authority under sanctions.

If Republicans truly believed that terrorists were using Iraq as a sanctuary, or playing hide and seek with Iraqi Intelligence, as they swore on the FOX News Channel, then an FBI Taskforce on the ground would have provided a strong force of deterrence. Iraq authorized the FBI to conduct investigations, interview witnesses and make arrests inside the country. That would have provided phenomenal value at the field level. In fact, the FBI could have been operating inside Iraq from February, 2001 onwards—nine months before 9/11. Baghdad agreed to this proposal after the attack on the U.S.S. Cole in October, 2000.

Yet after inventing a phony problem, Senator McCain rejected such a valuable tool— an FBI Taskforce authorized to operate in Baghdad.

That Republican leaders refused to act, after stoking the public's imagination about Saddam's ties to 9/11, exposes a gross lack of sincerity on this issue.

Likewise, Senator McCain demanded that the FBI must have access to Mr. Al Anai, the Iraqi diplomat who allegedly met with 9/11 mastermind, Mohammad Atta in Prague. Once more, officials in Baghdad consented to the interview hours after McCain first issued his demand.

Ignoring the facts, Senator McCain refused to acknowledge Iraq's immediate consent. Instead, he continued to posture for the media, repeating the demand, as if Iraq had not already responded in the affirmative. First McCain claimed the interview was of tremendous importance to the 9/11 investigation. Then he failed to exert his leadership to guarantee that the interview would be conducted, as agreed. That's more hard proof that Republicans used Iraq as a prop for grandstanding on such an important matter as the 9/11 investigation. That's unforgivable.

Worst by far, the Republican Leadership took no action, indeed refused, to close down the financial pipeline feeding Al Qaeda, which I consider the most offensive, dangerous and idiotic government decision of this century. They refused to accept documentation of banking and financial transactions, because it came from Iraq—which probably possessed the best and most valuable intelligence cache on early Al Qaeda terrorist cells in the whole world. Saddam tracked these people obsessively. Nobody in the world tracked jihadi groups as aggressively as Saddam Hussein. He made it his business to know all of their secrets and hiding places.

Those finances continue to fund terrorist activities all over the world today, including Iraq and Afghanistan, Pakistan, Indonesia and the Philippines. And I fear the next attack on the United States, which is probably moving to advanced planning stages today.

That next attack on U.S. soil will be bigger and badder than anything that's come before, probably a dirty nuclear device targeting the financial district of New York City. On that day, these former White House leaders should be "court-martialed," and stripped of any honoraria and pensions in retirement. They have endangered our national security in the worst imaginable way, and they should be forced to bear responsibility for the harm that their negligence causes.

No matter what politicians in Washington promise, it's too late to change that outcome.

And let me tell you why.

Saddam's Curse

Iraqi diplomats warned that Washington would be gravely disappointed, if they expected to invade Baghdad and capture those financial documents through warfare and occupation. Baghdad had no intention of allowing the United States to profit from both wars.

Iraqi diplomats stressed the trade off that Washington faced. If the United States embraced Iraq as a global partner against terrorism, we could achieve all of our greatest objectives in the fight against Al Qaeda. In a War with Iraq, America would lose everything that Baghdad could give us in the War on Terror. All of those financial documents on Al Qaeda would be destroyed, the intelligence lost forever.

That was the choice: We could score a victory against Terrorism. Or a victory in Baghdad.

The United States could never have both.

That posed a serious problem when Republican politicians raced to claim triumph in the War on Terrorism, clinging to the mantle of national security to placate voters enraged about Iraq. It was flat wrong. Republicans projected their own wishful fantasy that they had succeeded in anti-terrorism onto an unquestioning media. In fact, they had failed.

The one thing that could have made a substantial difference to the success of the War on Terrorism— the chance to cut off the financial pipeline used by Al Qaeda —no longer existed.

Saddam made a bonfire of those documents once bombs started falling on Baghdad. As of February, 2003, diplomats in New York assured me the documents still existed, but not for much longer. At the very end, the Iraqi Ministries worked over time shredding documents. Financial records that could have made substantial progress crippling terrorist efforts, for the benefit of the global community, were destroyed at the last possible moment, an irrevocable setback to anti-terrorism efforts. It would be impossible to amass such a historical record ever again. Those financial documents had been collected covetously over a decade of U.S. embargo, held as a valuable chit for ending the sanctions. They could not be duplicated.

Oh yes, Saddam played that card strategically, urgently enticing the U.S. to embrace peace. He swore that America could not get that intelligence outside of a comprehensive resolution of the overall tensions. And I have no doubt that Saddam kept his word. When the Pro-War camp rejected peace, they sacrificed the War on Terrorism—Saddam's papers were destroyed forever.

And so miraculously, that cash pipeline linking global terrorists from the Middle East to the Philippines and Indonesia and Afghanistan and Egypt survived the 9/11 attack, which should have obliterated it. Documents that would have identified those early hiding places, so that supply lines could be cut off—and all those hundreds of millions of dollars seized— all were sacrificed for the vanity of taking down Saddam Hussein.

That could only be described as a supreme loss for global security in the international community.

Any politician in Washington who claims otherwise would be a liar. He would be committing fraud against the people.

For those reasons, I believe that effective immediately the House and Senate Intelligence Committees should be purged of all members, Republicans and Democrats alike, on the grounds that Congress failed abysmally to provide effective oversight of White House activities, in defense of critical national security objectives. Failed oversight enabled Republican officials to make claims about their performance that went unfulfilled, to the severe detriment of U.S. and global security. Inattention from Congress allowed them to shirk responsibilities to the people.

Ironically, oversight is about the only contribution that Congress makes to anti-terrorism activities. They don't really do anything else. They give money, and they watch. For all the grand speeches, they could not exert what little authority they have to protect the U.S. It was a fiasco, very disappointing.

Finally, I am dismayed that Congressional leaders, mostly Republicans, so callously refused to investigate Iraq's claims about a Middle Eastern connection to the Oklahoma City Bombing, which destroyed a nursery school, among others in the Alfred P. Murrah building. I guess toddlers don't vote. But until their parents assure me that it's OK to stop hunting Timothy McVeigh's co-conspirators, I don't think the Justice Department has a right to ignore this sort of intelligence. It would have spotlighted the Inter-Arab origins of Al Qaeda, which coalesced from several different groups, about whom we know very little. Inaction was stupid and wasteful. It cost us something precious.

Frankly though, it surprises me. On June 17, 2002, I met with senior staff for Senator Nickles of Oklahoma and Rep. JC Watts of Oklahoma to debrief them on Iraq's claims.[301] Both Nickles and Watts served on the Republican Senate and House Majority Leadership, respectively. Their offices could have launched this investigation on behalf of their own Oklahoma constituents with a single phone call. My efforts received much praise from their staff. I left both offices convinced that appropriate actions would be taken. After all, this effort impacted their own Oklahoma constituents.

Low and behold, there was no follow through.

That hurts me, on behalf of those Oklahoma families. Their own elected leaders gave them lip service, and took no action to advance their cause. That's offensive.

It wasn't my failure as an Asset that anybody in America had to worry about. It was theirs, as failed leaders. And I made it loudly known that I regarded that failure as very serious, indeed.[302]

In all of this, Republicans carried most of the guilt, by an order of magnitude. They demagogued 9/11 and created political theater from the War on Terror, strictly for publicity purposes. They played to the emotions of the people, and turned 9/11 into a spectacle for election campaigning. Unhappily, there was nothing substantial backing it up. Once you got past the front gates of Guantanamo and the opening title of the Patriot Act, Republican terrorism policy was awfully empty on performance.

It was all trash talk and campaign propaganda, a lot of noise, a lot of bells and whistles. But the actions that would actually matter, that would accomplish something real to shut down terrorism on the ground, much of that was never done.

After dedicating almost a decade of my life to this work, I saw it as a con job to attract voters, and I was bitterly astounded by the waste of it..

Unfortunately, as a consequence of those decisions, our strength has been depleted. The next attack could hurt us in a way that no other attack ever has.

I'm still angry about that.

Therein lay the problem for Congress.

I was not going along with the program. As a long-time Asset, I wanted the American people to have the facts. I wanted to talk. Any truth telling at all would have made it impossible for Congress to sell its deceptions to the voting public.

Two actions I took finally tipped the balance against me.

In February, 2004, to appease public unhappiness, President Bush was forced to announce the appointment of a blue ribbon Presidential Commission to examine failures in Iraqi Pre-War Intelligence.

Within days, I approached the senior staff of Senators Trent Lott and John McCain, and formally requested to testify in front of the Commission.[303]

FBI phone taps recorded several conversations with Senator Lott's staff showing that I identified myself as a U.S Intelligence Asset. In several phone calls, I told Senator Lott's staff that I possessed by far the most extensive knowledge of Pre-War Intelligence anywhere, as a primary source. And I wanted the new Presidential Commission to hear my story for the public record. One of those conversations with Senator's Lott's staff is documented in chapter one of this book.

From a work phone, I also called the office of Senator John McCain of Arizona on my lunch hour. I had my address book, loaded with family addresses in Arizona. On my mother's side, my great grandmother pioneered Arizona at the turn of the century. I assured McCain's staff that I've got ties across Arizona—from Tucson to Tempe and Chandler and Scottsdale and Phoenix and Glendale, all the way up to Flagstaff and Payson and Pinetop in the White Mountain Apache Reservation. My grandfather taught me to fish on Lake Roosevelt.

I read through every zip code in my address book to prove that my father, cousins, grandparents, aunts and uncles are McCain constituents to this day. Above all, I insisted that my own flesh and blood had a right to hear the facts about my activities as an Asset before the War.

Just to make sure I got my point across, I took a second critical action, as well. I sent a fax to every Congressional office in the House and Senate, Democrats and Republicans alike. I admit this was like waving a red flag in front of an unhappy bull. But frankly, they deserved it.

In this message captured by my friends at the FBI, gratis of the Patriot Act, I warned the following:[304]

"There's a lot of bad information circulating in government circles about Iraq's pre-war activities. For the sake of historical clarity, I am releasing the following letters that were signed and delivered to Andy Card, Secretary Colin Powell and the U.N. Security Council. The letters detail Iraq's efforts to resume weapons inspections, beginning the month before President Bush's inauguration and Iraq's attempts to cooperate with the International War on Terrorism after September 11."

THE CRYING GAME

"Contrary to reports coming out of the White House, they knew very well that Iraq tried for two years to prove it had no Weapons of Mass Destruction. Iraq always behaved like a nation anxious to prove its compliance."

"The White House also knew that Iraq had invited the FBI to interview human assets in Baghdad for the War on Terrorism, including Mr. Al-Anai and others holding information about Al Qaeda, as well as the Oklahoma City Bombing. Baghdad was convinced this information would be prized by the Intelligence Community. Yet the U.S. refused to conduct those interviews."

"Unhappily, the Leadership of the United States was more excited by the grandiose disinformation circulated by the Iraqi Exiles than by warnings of the Intelligence Community or Anti-War Protests by American voters."

"Many of us are gravely concerned that those Iraqi Exiles have so easily manipulated America's Leadership."

"But this is NOT, repeat NOT the failure of U.S. Intelligence. It is most definitely the failure of a Leadership that refused to consider any information that did not fit into its agenda—an agenda created wholly to benefit an Exile Community famous for its lies and deceptions. Most tragically, this policy is igniting more attacks on the U.S. and thus damaging U.S. security."

Now Congress had a serious problem.

The report by the new blue ribbon commission was supposed to spotlight the failure of the intelligence community. If my information got in front of the public, Americans would discover that at least some parts of the intelligence community had done a pretty damn good job. We aggressively sought to warn Congress off this War.[305] Not only that, a substantial peace option had been available throughout the congressional debate, which would have resolved the U.S. conflict without firing a shot, or costing one young American his arm or leg.[306]

Any way you cut the cards, though only a small handful of us qualified as active Assets engaged with Iraq, my team's actions would have deflected from mistakes by any other source—if politicians in Washington had been willing to consider peaceful diplomacy as an alternative to military conflict. We'd laid a path out of their troubles.

That truth especially scared Capitol Hill. The existence of a credible peace option couldn't be allowed into the public arena. Not with the Presidential and Congressional elections running neck and neck, amidst skyrocketing anti-incumbent sentiments. I would have to be stopped.

Both Democrats and Republicans hoped to double-talk their way out of trouble with voters.

But only one party was dirty enough to point the cross-hairs of its attack guns at Assets involved in anti-terrorism and Pre-War Intelligence.

When I made my phone calls to the offices of Senator John McCain and Senator Trent Lott, Republican leaders recognized something would have to be done to shut me up.

My own second cousin, Andy Card, Chief of Staff to President George W. Bush gave Republicans the green light to do their worst.

No question about it. This decision came from the very top.

CHAPTER 17:

THE PATRIOT ACT

"I am bound to say what seems right to me,"
responded the Senator.
"But if you say it, I will kill you," the Emperor warned."
–Senator Robert Byrd
Floor Statement Opposing Homeland Security Act of 2002
Congressional Record, 11/19/2002

In the parlance of the intelligence community, it's known as "termination with extreme prejudice."

"Extreme prejudice" involves the assassination of an intelligence operative, or such physical destruction to body and soul that speech would be rendered impossible or meaningless. It goes far beyond the destruction of an Asset's credibility or reputation. That's secondary, a side dish for sadists. The central purpose of "extreme prejudice" is annihilation, purposefully killing an Asset's physical and spiritual being.

It's the most severe degree of punishment that gets meted out to those who irrevocably damage the reputation of the intelligence community, or otherwise threaten to expose its dirty laundry. Ah, and what qualifies as national security, if not something the government does not want its people to know? Like our advance warning about 9/11. Or Iraq's cooperation with anti-terrorism policy. And so, finally, "extreme prejudice" gets invoked as a policy of last resort, when Assets pose a significant threat to crooked politicians desperate to escape exposure and blowback for their own schemes gone awry. When truth becomes treason, when something's so dirty that somebody powerful will stop at nothing to hide it, that's when "extreme prejudice" comes into play.

It explains why there's a sort of urban legend in the intelligence community— that an Asset has no future. Only a gunshot to the head when what you know becomes too inconvenient.

Foreign assets captured by the other side typically got tortured before dying, so as to squeeze out every bit of intelligence they've handed over to the Americans. Or so I've been told. The bullet at the end becomes almost a symbolic act of mercy. For old times' sake. In remembrance of whatever comradeship existed before the betrayal. Until that moment, the Asset faces maximum pain for payback.

Surely they couldn't do that to me? I "had people" watching my back all those years. They could vouch for my past, even if my anti-war activities infuriated them in the present. Otherwise they would be guilty of perjury. I was always a peace activist, and I'd done exactly what I told Hoven and Dr. Fuisz I would. I opposed any second War with Iraq. I never imagined my faith in my handlers was naïve, though I'd been warned that you can't trust your friends in the intelligence community, any more than you can trust your friends' enemies. My CIA handler, Dr. Fuisz, used to say it's nothing personal. Assets are simply expendable. One side will trade you to the other in a heartbeat.

And what code of honor had I violated?

I wanted to proudly represent the voice of dissension on War policy, which got a lot of things right. I would explain that I'd done exactly what Assets should, building a message platform to sound the alarms about mistakes in assumptions on Capitol Hill. We practiced healthy and vigorous dissension from the pro-war camp, in the best tradition of our democracy, which embraces a wrangling over ideas. Oh yes, and I wanted to testify that back-channel diplomacy produced substantial opportunities for conflict resolution with Iraq. The foresight of this faction had guaranteed that the U.S. controlled the agenda for resolving the conflict with Iraq. Our comprehensive framework maximized advantages for the U.S. in any post-sanctions period. Only pro-war Republicans in Congress and the White House had opted for different policy scenarios.

Those would be the same pro-war Republicans who now sat on the blue ribbon commission, and desperately sought to shift blame for their own judgment failures onto my shoulders. They looked at us as easy scapegoats. If there were fewer of us in number, so much the better. There would be fewer of our voices to shout down.

I was a paradox certainly, on a number of levels. If they hoped to shout me down, however, I had no intention of obliging. I believe the people have a right to accountability from our leaders. We have the right to confront them over decisions they make as our representatives. So there might be fewer voices, but mine would be loud.

Mine would roar.

For sure I would see them in Hell before I, a life-long peace activist, would take the blame for this catastrophic war that I worked so hard to prevent. Can you imagine the absurdity of blaming an Asset like me for faulty pre-war intelligence? After all of my innovative efforts to educate Congress and White House officials about peace options that made war avoidable and unnecessary? All of my urgent warnings? My correct forecasting about the horrific consequences of this mistake? All those issue papers sent by blast fax and staff emails throughout Capitol Hill and the U.N? Distributed to every Chief of Staff, every Legislative Director, every Press Secretary and Foreign policy assistant in the House and Senate? Democrat and Republican alike?

I shouted from the rooftops, warning everybody of the catastrophe that would engulf us!

And now they imagined that I would take the blame?

I'd see them damned first.

Hell and damnation were exactly what Dick Cheney and John McCain had in mind.

As an Asset for many years, I counted as an investment. However, by this time, I'd paid all my dividends. Now I was a distinct liability.

I had kicked up a hornet's nest with my request to testify.

While I waited, Congressional staff were busy getting subpoenas alright. They were racing to issue subpoenas before a grand jury in New York City, seeking my indictment as an "unregistered Iraqi agent."

It's almost funny.

The White House and Justice Department frantically crafted a plan to knock me out of the loop, and silence me forever.

Whatever it took, they would stop at nothing to bury the truth.

Later, Andy Card would receive high marks for his cooperation with the grand jury in Manhattan, preparing my indictment.[307] There's just a small problem that somehow he forgot to explain in his testimony that I was a long-time Asset supervised by handlers from U.S. Intelligence. He could hardly plead ignorance. My special history was explained in my progress reports on our talks to resume the weapons inspections. Andy Card was fully knowledgeable that my work in anti-terrorism lasted nine years, starting with my advance warning about the first attack on the World Trade Center, and encompassing Libya, Iraq, Egypt, Syria/Hezbollah, Yemen and Malaysia. Apparently he forgot all of that when he addressed the grand jury.[308]

Perhaps it was "stage fright." The indictment was political theater, after all.

There had been 11 progress reports on Iraq before the War.[309] Andy Card forgot to mention any of those papers to the grand jury, either. He deliberately concealed his knowledge of my identity, and the purpose of our long-term communications, which was entirely legitimate and based on securing Iraq's agreement with U.S. demands in multiple areas, as articulated by the CIA.

In which case, it appears that Andy Card might be guilty of perjury before the grand jury, and definitely obstruction of justice.

Ordinary Americans would face prosecution for such a thing. By contrast, Andy Card's grand jury statement got sealed from view. Despite numerous challenges over the next five years, my attorneys and I were never allowed to examine it. At the same time, my federal prosecutor Edward O'Callaghan repeatedly denied in Court before Judge Michael B. Mukasey, and then Judge Loretta Preska, that grand jury testimony had authenticated my role as a U.S. Intelligence Asset.[310] The prosecution claimed total ignorance throughout the proceedings.

If that's true, it can only mean Andy Card lied.

It was a breathtaking lie, of course. But FBI Special Agent Chmiel, in charge of the investigation, sat silently in court next to O'Callaghan, when he said it.

If O'Callaghan was telling the truth—and there's a big question mark next to his reliability— then his own statements validate my grievance that Andy Card and other officials misled the grand jury. Knowing that they lied, the US Attorneys Office sought to protect them by blocking access to evidence of the crime, and denying our requests to review the statements.

In which case, the Justice Department knowingly shielded a White House official in the commission of criminal acts— making false statements to a grand jury and obstruction of a federal investigation.

It wasn't just Iraq, either.

Notoriously, senior officials at the Justice Department benefited directly from the deception by the U.S. Attorney's Office, as well. At that moment, the 9/11 Commission was finishing its report,[311] which would bewail the incompetence of the intelligence community for failing to anticipate the attack. The 9/11 Commission would strongly condemn the lack of cooperation at the mid-levels between law enforcement and the intelligence community to stop it.

Imagine, if at that moment, I went to trial and highly reputable witnesses testified under oath in a federal court of law—1,000 yards from Ground Zero—about my 9/11 warnings. The entire premise of that 9/11 Commission report would have collapsed in embarrassment,[312] with our plea for inter-agency cooperation to preempt the strike. My warnings smashed 'plausible deniability' for Attorney General Ashcroft's private staff and the Office of Counter-Terrorism at the Justice Department. It would have been a train wreck for Republican leaders. The Commission would have been forced to acknowledge that its findings were politically constructed to deflect responsibility from the top levels of government.

In all probability, revelations of that nature would have impacted the outcome of the elections, as well. Voters might have started asking hard questions about GOP performance on national security, overall. Surely Attorney General Ashcroft would have been accused of misleading Congress and the people about the command failure before 9/11, feeding the popular frenzy to oust the GOP already flourishing across the country.

And so a Cover Up was born.

Oh yes, a lot of important Republicans and lobbyists benefited from keeping me silent. Their strategy for damage control was so Machiavellian, however, that it would have done the old Soviet Union proud in the grand old days of Joseph Stalin and the Gulags.

In my wildest imaginings, I could not have conceived what the Feds were cooking up.

I guess I wasn't paranoid enough.

It started early on the morning of March 11, 2004, about a month after my phone calls to Senator McCain's and Senator Lott's offices. I awoke to the shock of FBI agents banging on the front door of my house in Takoma Park, Maryland.[313]

I was more astounded to discover that the FBI had come with handcuffs and a warrant for my arrest. They'd come to take me!

Low and behold, I had a new distinction in my career as an Asset. And it was every bit as dramatic as my advance warnings about the first attack on the World Trade Center, the bombing of the U.S.S. Cole, the 9/11 attack; starting negotiations for the Lockerbie Trial with Libyan diplomats; and holding preliminary, back-channel talks to resume weapons inspections with Iraq's Ambassador to the United Nations.

Along with Jose Padilla, I was now distinguished as one of the very first non-Arab Americans to discover the slippery and treacherous legal terrain of the U.S. Patriot Act.

With supreme irony, the indictment categorized me as an "unregistered agent of Iraq," in "conspiracy with the Iraq Intelligence Service" for purposes undisclosed.[314] That gave me a status very close to an Enemy Non-Combatant. You've got to admit, that's pretty amazing for a life-long peace activist! And so the Patriot Act, which Congress approved after 9/11 to smash terrorism, was first used to punish an American citizen who spent a life-time opposing all violence in terrorism or war, and who gave advance warning about the 9/11 attack in precise detail, and sought Arab cooperation with the 9/11 investigation.

At first blush, invoking the Patriot Act appeared to contradict its stated objective. However, prosecuting political defendants like me leverages the law to its most logical purpose, in fact. The act was written to create a legal framework to interrupt individual questioning of the government in power. The Patriot Act equates terrorism with any civil disobedience that challenges government policy. Both are cast in the category of sedition. Using that line of reasoning, the Patriot Act authorizes the Justice Department to apply the same tools to smash political dissention that Congress intended to interrupt the workings of terrorist cells.

That's the logical end, though, isn't it?

Free thinking leads to criticism of government policy. Criticism must be treated as a threat to the functioning of the State, and crushed when possible.

In short, the Patriot Act lays a road to the Gulags. Most Americans don't understand yet that it creates a legal framework for fascism, and the beginning of all dictatorship in America.

My case demonstrates how "benevolent" such dictatorship can be.

Like Alice falling through the Looking Glass, I had stumbled into a "Brave New World" at the Justice Department, with frightening similarity to the visions of Aldous Huxley and Franz Kafka.

Before it ended, I would face a horrific legal nightmare that would spotlight a number of critical reasons why the Patriot Act should be repealed immediately to safeguard our country and our freedom.

Unhappily, I would discover the Patriot Act has been crafted as the ideal tool to silence whistleblowers. My own case would establish the law as the premiere tool for government cover ups. On the morning of my arrest, I did not know that yet.

Inside a tiny holding cage at the federal courthouse in Baltimore, I studied the indictment against me. The cage was approximately 3 ½ X 3 1/2 feet, big enough for a bolted metal desk and stool.

The indictment formally accused me of "acting as an unregistered Iraqi Agent," on the grounds that I delivered a letter opposing the war to my own cousin, Andy Card, practicing freedom of speech in my family circle. What was in that letter that made Andy's blood boil? A prescient warning, it turns out. I gave Andy Card a simple history lesson. For thirteen years the U.S. had dropped bombs on Iraq at a constant pace. That bloodshed, plus the immense suffering caused by U.N. sanctions, had stirred a deep abiding hatred for America in total. In war-time, ordinary Iraqis could lay hands on the source of their misery. Their vengeance would be overwhelming. Thousands upon thousands of jihadis would rise up in Iraq to fight U.S. troops.[315]

My crimes against the State would turn out to be simple accuracy: Forecasting the failure of the Occupation to the Chief of Staff for President George W. Bush. There was nothing hostile or threatening in the letter. I closed with the promise that I "would pray for Andy" to support peace. And my warnings proved tragically accurate.

That did not matter under the Patriot Act.

Opposition to Republican war policy qualified as treason to the end degree. It rendered me an "Enemy of the State." End of discussion.

Machiavelli would have been proud. My indictment allowed Republicans to play it both ways. In grand Washington style, I got indicted for telling Republicans the truth about Iraq. Then, with me safely removed and "legally indisposed," members of Congress marched out to complain that Assets like me never came forward to correct mistakes in intelligence reporting on Capitol Hill. Assets were "incompetent." Our silence duped Congress into racing off the cliff.

Pretty clever, huh?

Something more sinister was omitted from the indictment. The treasonous letter in question was actually delivered to two individuals—Andy Card, and also to Secretary of State Colin Powell.[316]

In the shadowy world of the Patriot Act, I was never allowed to know which man— Andy Card or Colin Powell— filed the original complaint against me. Under the Patriot Act, the superior power and social standing of those men afforded them additional rights over mine, such as protection from being exposed as my accusers. That sort of consideration, based on the greater political access of one's accusers, rings ominously similar to the legal system of the former Soviet Union or Eastern Bloc countries. It's the prerogative of dictators and their collaborators. It is decidedly prohibited by the Constitution of the United States.

One critical safeguard in our judicial system proves that Secretary Powell did give his copies of the Andy Card letters to the FBI. In legal discovery, my attorneys received photocopies from the FBI of the manila envelope with Powell's address and my handwritten notes to him.[317] So we know that Secretary Powell participated in the FBI investigation leading up to the indictment, even though my Defense team was never allowed to view his statements to the FBI or grand jury.

Shockingly enough, in five years of indictment, my legal team was never allowed to read the FBI interviews *of any witnesses* in my case, gratis of the Patriot Act. Grand jury testimony was also strictly off limits, under the banner of "national security."

Under the Patriot Act, we had to take the Justice Department's word for everything. That turned out to be the greatest obscenity of all.

The grand jury essentially functioned as a "Star Chamber."

Access to legal discovery supporting my Defense was limited to documents pulled off my computer by the FBI; transcripts of phone taps; and captured faxes. That provided a bonanza of documentation, however, since the FBI captured 28,000 phone calls; about 8,000 emails, and hundreds of faxes.[318] We had plenty of evidence to substantiate my story—but not a single statement from the grand jury or FBI interviews of potential witnesses.

Ironically, my defense was hardly a burden, despite these handicaps. My identity was remarkably easy to verify, thanks to my work on the Lockerbie Trial with Dr. Fuisz. That was the caveat to Andy Card's alleged perjury before the grand jury. Even *if* the Prosecutor was correct that Andy Card gave false testimony and created temporary confusion over my role as an Asset—and *if* the FBI failed to grasp the scope of my relationships to the intelligence community before my arrest— they would have figured it out rapidly afterwards. Once the FBI interviewed Dr. Fuisz and Hoven, they would have quickly recognized their mistake. Within the first two weeks after my arrest, the facts surrounding my identity as an Asset should have emerged with crystal clarity.

If either Dr. Fuisz or Hoven made false statements to the FBI, I would demand that they face prosecution today for obstruction of justice. I would demand that the Justice Department indict them at once. Ordinary Americans have the right to enjoy protections from false indictment and false imprisonment, just like more powerful and elite Americans.

Interestingly, Dr. Fuisz and Hoven denied participating in the strike against me, or knowing about it in advance. I'm told they learned about my arrest on CNN and the Fox News Channel. Both were allegedly floored that anybody would come after me like this. I'm told they considered it a stupid thing to have done.

For one particular reason, I believe them.

It's sort of "inside baseball," within the intelligence community. It's considered a stupid idea to go after an Asset without consulting that individual's handlers first to discover the scope of an Asset's projects. In my case, it appears the White House and the Justice Department wanted so desperately to silence me on 9/11 and Iraq that they failed to perform the most elementary due diligence within the agencies, a sort of internal background check.

The FBI did not learn before arresting me, therefore, that Dr. Fuisz and Hoven had made a critical decision at the beginning of our relationship, designed to protect me in any legal setting.

Since I would be working on terrorism issues, in direct contact with Libya and Iraq, they decided that I should not be required to sign a non-disclosure agreement. And I never did. Not once in nine years. In any court setting, I could disclose everything.

By the time I approached Libya in 1995, there was already a tradition at the Justice Department of indicting or legally harassing anyone who disputed the official version of Libya's guilt in the Lockerbie bombing, as our team intended to do. They'd gone after Les Coleman,[319] imprisoned as pay back for his book, "Trail of the Octopus," which exposed the role of heroin trafficking in the Lockerbie conspiracy. Dr Jim Swire, spokesman for British families of the Lockerbie victims, declared: "The gross maltreatment of Coleman by the American authorities appears to fit a pattern of victimization of the people who challenge the official version that Libya was solely to blame for Lockerbie."[320]

Vince Cannistraro, the CIA's former Chief of Operations and Director of Intelligence Programs for the National Security Council[321] likewise got indicted— and acquitted—as punishment for questioning the official version of Lockerbie.

Clearly this fight carried serious risks. Since our team was part of the faction that opposed the cover up of Lockerbie, too, Dr. Fuisz determined that for my own legal protection, I would retain my rights to total disclosure for all times. It meant that I would have the full capability to mount a proper legal defense for myself, if attacked. I would have the legal right to tell everything in a court of law, as necessary to protect my liberty. That decision probably saved my life.

That should have stopped the Feds cold from coming after me. If they had known.

Their obvious ignorance suggests that, in all likelihood Dr. Fuisz and Hoven are telling the truth that nobody spoke to them prior to my arrest.

They would have thrown cold water on this thing in a jiffy. Because in fact, if somebody wanted to silence me, the worst thing you could do would be to put me in a courtroom with an attorney and subpoena power. I could conduct my very own oversight investigation live on Court TV. I could whomp everybody. If the White House wanted to silence me, going to Trial would be a very bad way to do it.

That explains why, after the shock of my arrest wore off, I had a great big smile on my face for the rest of that day, waiting for my bail hearing. They'd handed me a golden opportunity to wallop them all.

By the end of the day, I have no doubt that Andy Card realized it, too. The White House had made a monstrously stupid mistake. They had gotten blinded by visions of thrashing me for criticizing their war policy. They never thought to the next step—my trial, where I would give them a thrashing. It was typical of the Republican Party in general.

Ironically, it means that while Andy Card possibly lied to the grand jury—so the Prosecutor, Edward O'Callaghan insisted throughout my indictment[322]—O'Callaghan himself also lied in Court months later, when he told Judge Michael B. Mukasey that nobody could verify my story. O'Callaghan repeatedly scorned my defense arguments, filed pro se at one point, that grand jury testimony and FBI interviews supported my claims.[323]

By that time, the FBI had already spoken to a number of my witnesses. Those same witnesses freely repeated their statements to my attorneys—Brian Shaughnessy and Ted Lindauer, in our own interviews for the Defense. So we know what they told the FBI. We know they fully corroborated my story. And we know that O'Callaghan was guilty of gross prosecutorial misconduct and withholding exculpatory evidence from the court, when he repeatedly denied those confirmations to the Court.[324] [325] In a real sense, O'Callaghan perjured himself in front of Judge Mukasey, who replaced Alberto Gonzales as U.S. Attorney General.

To get away with it, the Justice Department gambled on its ability to restrict our access to "secret evidence" under the Patriot Act. That should frighten all law abiding citizens who trust and rely on the Courts to guarantee fair proceedings at trial.

Appallingly, the Patriot Act sanctions and facilitates this sort of behavior in the courtroom. My case would show that it's a perfectly crafted license to commit judicial fraud.

Medieval despots would have adored this law. Friends of Joseph Stalin in the old Soviet Union and Eastern bloc governments would have quavered in rapture for it. Anti-democracy forces in China and Mynamar must chortle in delight over U.S. hypocrisy, with the Patriot Act on the books. Tyrants love this stuff. It's ideally constructed to smash anti-government activities, and crush whistleblowers who threaten to expose government corruption.

Think about it. With me silenced, Congress and the White House had free rein to pretend to have accomplished vastly more good for anti-terrorism than they actually did. With me gagged by indictment, they could invent any story they desired about Iraq and 9/11, in order to seduce American voters and hold onto power.

And that's exactly what they did.

In the holding cage at the Baltimore courthouse, I saw at once the indictment was loaded with payback, if not criminal actions.

THE PATRIOT ACT

My work supporting democratic reforms and human rights in Iraq was characterized as "Organizing Resistance to American forces." Gratis of the Patriot Act, the Justice Department argued that advocating the use of international law to protest human rights violations constitutes a criminal offense, if it seeks to hold the United States responsible for abuses. Efforts to apply the International Geneva Conventions of War to the conduct of the United States constituted a crime, as well.

I could not be prouder of my activism. However the accusation exemplifies the cynicism of the Republican age, launching media campaigns to promote democracy throughout the Middle East and Asia, while criminalizing activities that support democracy at home.

And yes, with "extreme prejudice" in play, clearly some factions of the intelligence community (but not all) seized the chance to punish me for not going along with the official story of Libya's guilt on Lockerbie.

Like children squabbling on a playground, it sent a zinger to me.

We finally got you, bitch.

Oh yeah? Tell it to the Judge! (I didn't think so.)

My witnesses don't have to lie. Yours have to lie. And I will prosecute them when they do.

And I wasn't kidding.

So actually I felt safe. If the indictment was loaded with payback, it was also packed with desperation.

Surprisingly enough, reading the indictment calmed my nerves. I stopped being afraid. Politically motivated or not, no Prosecutor could risk taking such a case to trial. I saw at once the Justice Department could not hope to get a conviction. Nothing in the indictment rose to the level of a misdemeanor, much less a serious crime worth exposing the enormity of fraud on Capitol Hill, all the political huffing and puffing about the greatness of Republican national security policy. Indeed, a trial would have defeated the purpose of silencing me.

My reaction strikes me as entirely reasonable.

Alas, we were wrestling in the mud and the muck of the Patriot Act. This would be the starting point of the legal nonsense.

Nothing would be logical. Nothing would be rational.

Nothing would be Constitutional.

Four years into this drama, my legal debacle would prompt a marvelous headline on an incisive political blog, WelcomebacktoPottersville.com:[326]

"Susan Lindauer, Meet Franz Kafka."

Hey, you gotta love the feds.

Secret Charges and Secret Evidence

My case would shine a klieg light on how the Patriot Act damages essential protections in a courtroom, otherwise guaranteed by the U.S. Constitution.

Courtroom proceedings against me would be scattered with "secret evidence" and "secret testimony." I would lose the right to face my accusers. Or the right to hear the substance of their accusations described by another source.

Most offensive of all, the indictment contained two "secret charges" that illustrate the real dangers and abuses of the Patriot Act. My attorney and I were given the dates that the two offenses allegedly occurred, one on October 14, 1999, a very specific date almost five years before my indictment, the other "approximately" October, 2001.[327]

Beyond those dates, my attorney and I were not allowed to know what my actions allegedly consisted of, or what offenses they might constitute. The Justice Department had no obligation to describe, even generically, what type of law might have been violated. (For example, on October 14, the defendant entered a liquor store. The defendant robbed the liquor store using a gun. That action constitutes armed robbery.)

I got none of that. The Justice Department invoked the Patriot Act to declare that some unidentified action occurred on October 14, 1999, which violated some unidentified law. That's all we got to know.

I was told, however, that conviction of either of the "secret charges" would get me five years in federal prison.

If that was not Kafkaesque enough, the Patriot Act relied on "secret evidence" which could be applied to those "secret charges." Quite literally, the Prosecution had the right to ask a jury to convict me of the "secret charges," without revealing any evidence whatsoever to prove that the alleged criminal actions even occurred. The Prosecutor had no obligation to provide any evidence that I participated in the actions, let alone demonstrate why those actions rose to a level of criminal behavior that deserved prison time. The Patriot Act authorized the Prosecutor to ask a jury to "take it on faith" that some unspecified law had been broken. If a Judge so instructed before deliberations, the jury could be required to ignore the lack of presentation of evidence, in weighing whether to convict me. The Judge could simply instruct a jury that the Justice Department regarded the evidence as "sufficient" to constitute a crime, and that would be "sufficient knowledge" for their deliberations.[328]

The fundamental question of "guilt beyond reasonable doubt" got shattered under the Patriot Act. The jury system in the United States got bludgeoned, as well.

Most ominous of all, evidence that might exonerate me of the charges could be ruled "secret and classified," and therefore inadmissible, as well. My attorney and I would be prohibited from knowing of its existence. It remained to be seen if the Court would allow us to present sensitive information to a jury, if we located it on our own. Even evidence seized from my home, which belonged to me, including private papers or phone taps that helped dispute the allegations against me, got blacked out and redacted, sometimes absurdly.

One lengthy phone call to United for Peace and Justice in San Francisco was marked "classified" by the Justice Department[329]—though it's one of America's largest anti-war groups.

The serious question is why?

Grand jury testimony fell under the same category, because it involved public officials. The Justice Department barred it from my sight or use in pre-trial proceedings, even though it should have authenticated my claims that I functioned as an Asset, and resulted in dismissal of the charges. I would have been saved. Yet as a defendant, I was prohibited from receiving it or using it. For that matter, under the Patriot Act, the Prosecutor can submit papers "in camera," to the Court, for the Judge's eyes only. My attorney would not be allowed to receive copies of the Prosecutor's submissions to dispute it. The Justice

Department does not have to acknowledge that an "in camera" submission has been made.[330]

Along those lines, *if* big shot Washington officials like Andy Card or Colin Powell lied to a grand jury to advance a government cover up, the Patriot Act could be invoked to protect them from exposure. They faced no risks in making false statements, since their grand jury testimony could be concealed from the defense.[331]

Those in power win. Those out of power go to prison.

That's the Patriot Act. It's the new American way.

This point must be underscored. No matter if evidence or witness statements tossed out the whole case against me, and might save me from years in prison, under the Patriot Act, my attorney and I would not be entitled to know of its existence, or receive copies of it. My own attorney could not argue its merits in front of a jury.

That's exactly what happened to me.[332]

Oh yes, the proceedings would get very, very scary before the end.

How secrecy rules work

Within the category of "secret evidence," the law pretends to establish a safeguard by allowing two levels of secrecy.[333]

Under the main category of secrecy, both the attorney and defendant are prohibited from laying eyes on evidence.

In the second sub-section, the defense attorney may petition the government for a security clearance, in order to review some parts of the "secret evidence," but only what the Prosecutor chooses to reveal. The process of getting the security clearance drags out, while most defendants languish in prison waiting for trial. (In most national security cases, there's no bail. And because the case involves the Patriot Act, most male defendants get held in solitary confinement, in the pre-trial phase. I learned that the hard way. I would have to fight tooth and nail to stop from getting stuck in "the hole" myself.)

Getting that security clearance for an attorney can take six months to a year, at a minimum, costing the Defense valuable time to review the evidence and plan a rebuttal.

That's not all. Depending on their backgrounds, different attorneys qualify for different levels of clearances. An activist attorney with a history of pro bono cases, working on behalf of the American Civil Liberties Union, or say the Center for Constitutional Rights, might qualify for a very low security clearance. Previous case-loads might pose a "threat to the State," if an attorney has a history of supporting socially motivated causes that conflict with current government agendas. As a result, one attorney might have more or less access to secret evidence than another.[334] But a Defendant choosing an attorney would not know the difference until the security review is complete.

By then, you're close to Trial. It's too late.

Mostly it's irrelevant, unfortunately. To put that in context, in five years under indictment, I had two separate attorneys with vastly different levels of security clearances. My first was a public attorney, Sam Talkin, with no experience on cases of this sort. My second attorney was Brian Shaughnessy, a former federal prosecutor assigned to Judge John Sirica's court in Washington. In his elite law practice, Shaughnessy regularly handles the highest level domestic and international cases, including others involving security issues and U.S. intelligence. Yet neither Shaughnessy, who is extremely clever and blessed with a top security clearance for much of his career, nor my first public attorney, who was not, could ever determine what those two secret charges contained. Neither attorney ever got to review the "secret evidence" behind those "secret charges."

And so, lest hope floats and expectations rise, the safeguard for attorney clearance turns out to be largely meaningless anyway. That safeguard turns out to be mostly procedural. It's window dressing.

Even if a security clearance is granted, the attorney does not get to examine all of the "secret evidence." It's the prerogative of the Justice Department to decide what merits secrecy versus disclosure.[335] The Defense attorney has no ability to challenge the security classification, because he or she has no idea what other evidence is still hanging out there in the legal ether.

And regardless, the attorney is strictly prohibited from revealing to the Defendant whatever "secret evidence" gets released. It's for the attorney's eyes and knowledge only. The Defendant cannot see it or know about it, and therefore cannot provide an effective response to it.[336]

An attorney who violates the Patriot Act, by confiding to the Defendant the nature of the "secret charges" or the "secret evidence," could face court sanctions under the law, or possible disbarment from the legal profession, even criminal prosecution.

That's right, under the Patriot Act, an attorney would risk going to jail or losing the right to practice law entirely, if he or she informed the defendant about the nature of secret evidence, even in non-specific terms, for the purpose of building a rebuttal to the charges.

It's grotesque and flagrantly unfair. Not surprisingly, most attorneys are afraid to challenge that rule, because the cost of testing the law would be too high, even for the most skillful practitioners in the law. They'd be risking everything.

Thus, the Patriot Act cripples a defendant's capability to assist in preparing a rebuttal strategy to an unreasonable degree that surely impacts the outcome of the proceedings.

In the strictest interpretation, invoking the Patriot Act renders any defendant "incompetent to assist in his own defense." It's an interesting point, because it has nothing to do with competence to function in daily life or understand courtroom procedures. Legal competence pertains exclusively to a defendant's capacity to assist an attorney in preparing a defense, which is frankly impossible without knowing the charges against him, or seeing the evidence that would make or break the case.

Ah, the plot thickens.

Speculation on Secret Charges

Ah, but I can hear some of you sputtering now! Surely, the American people can trust the Justice Department to properly limit "secret evidence" and "secret charges" to that which involves only the highest matters of national security. Indeed, such legal matters must be so sensitive as to require the most delicate touch.

Are you ready to stake your freedom on that?

Let me enlighten you.

In five years, my attorneys and I could only speculate about the alleged offenses contained in the "secret charges." But on our end, we certainly could identify my activities during those time frames. We surmised that with regards to October 14, 1999, I got indicted for *blocking* the Iraqi Government in Baghdad from making financial contributions to the Republican Presidential Campaign in 2000. That's right. With immediate assistance from my U.S. Intelligence contacts, I stopped Iraq from making illegal campaign contributions to the election of George W. Bush— at least through my channels.

Ironic, isn't it? My old handler, Paul Hoven, had been apoplectic over Iraq's attempts, threatening to go nuclear on Baghdad himself, if I failed to stop them from making campaign contributions to the Republican Party. Iraq's attempts would have been highly embarrassing for Republicans at all levels of the government. For that reason alone, I had been commanded to do everything in my power to stop Baghdad.

Notably, my actions were reported to Andy Card in two letters, dated March 1, 2001 and December 2, 2001.[337] So Republicans in the White House got alerted to the conundrum by me. It has been speculated that, perhaps, GOP leaders feared Saddam gave money to the Campaign through some other channel. And they didn't want anybody snooping around. Perhaps I got indicted to stop the Democrats from using subpoena power to go after campaign organization records to determine which fundraisers might have drawn the illegal money.

If we're correct about the nature of the charge, it illustrates how the Patriot Act was abused to protect political ambitions. There's nothing remotely related to national security in the events themselves. It's not clear how I allegedly broke any laws, because I stopped the Iraqis from making the campaign donations. I stopped a crime from occurring.

Nevertheless, I got arrested! And secrecy got invoked strictly to protect Republican leaders, with no other beneficiary. The welfare of the American people had nothing to do with it. I was threatened with five years in prison, gagged by indictment to stop me from alerting voters—who have a right to keep track of who's buying access in Washington.

When the indictment was finally dismissed, five years later, my attorney and I were still in the dark on the second charge, listed as occurring "sometime in October, 2001."[338]

We're fairly certain the second "secret charge" involved my efforts to collect health statistics from Baghdad regarding depleted uranium left behind from the first Gulf War. Depleted uranium has resulted in a spike in Iraqi birth defects and cancer rates from long-term exposure. In Baghdad, health officials say cancer in children runs as rampantly as the flu. It's an epidemic.

A trial would have raised the profile of those health problems and potential birth defects, causing discomfort for the Pentagon. Especially with American soldiers serving two or more tours of duty in Iraq, prolonged exposure to depleted uranium definitely poses serious long term health risks for them—and their unborn children. There's the rub. Birth defects rise in male soldiers as well as female soldiers. That would raise expectations about the military's financial liability for long term health costs, as from Agent Orange or Gulf War Syndrome.

It appears that's all it took to justify categorizing "depleted uranium" as a "secret charge," supported by "secret evidence." The deception was essentially designed to shield soldiers and their families from vital health information and to deny them future health care benefits.

Only by invoking the Patriot Act could the Justice Department claim authority to arrest an American citizen for engaging in public health education. Only by invoking "secret charges" and "secret evidence" could the Justice Department pretend that such innocuous activities qualified as something more sinister and criminal that should be prosecuted.

Look, it's so terrible, we can't tell you what it is.

It turns out that it's only terrible for Pro-War Republicans who want to hold back health benefits for hardworking American soldiers.

And that's a real crime!

The X-Factor.

The wild card or x-factor in any criminal case on the Patriot Act would be the Judge. How my case unfolded would depend on how Judge Michael B. Mukasey, later named U.S. Attorney General, decided to enforce this new law, with all its constitutional restrictions.

At the start, his predilections were unknown to all of us. Over time I came to believe that Judge Mukasey had a razor sharp eye on the bigger picture of my case. I'm convinced he could see that once the hype was stripped away, my actions scarcely rose to the level of criminality that would justify prosecution.[339] If the Justice Department acknowledged my work as an Asset, and if my handlers cleared up a few minor points, the case would have collapsed immediately.

Worst by far, my case would make bad law. It would set dangerous precedents that could be cited in other cases affecting other defendants. I believe that Judge Mukasey questioned if the mediocrity of the evidence against me justified the potential damage to due process. For the sake of courtroom integrity and the protection of established legal principles of due process, one could not blame Judge Mukasey if he wanted to get the case out of his courtroom.

I believe that's critical to understanding Judge Mukasey's actions in my case.

It was clear that I, the defendant, could never plead guilty to any of these charges. Organizing resistance to the United States? Forget about it. Performing as an Iraqi Agent? Conspiracy with Iraqi Intelligence? God no! Absolutely not!

A plea agreement was impossible.

I had to demand a Trial. In which case, Judge Mukasey would have to find another way to kill the case, and clear it out of the federal court system.

The question was how? That's not so easy to do.

And so I forgive him.

The Patriot Act is so dysfunctional when applied to courtroom procedure that it took one of this nation's truly preeminent Judges to outmaneuver it.

A lesser Judge could not have done it.

That's truly frightening to consider, given how it was ultimately done. The actions against me provide the most damning evidence of all why this horrific law should be repealed at once. Our path would be monstrously evil. And yet, from the Judge's perspective, it would be the lesser of two evils, compared to applying this atrocious law to court procedure.

Unhappily, I had a junior public attorney, who lacked the sophistication to handle such a complex legal case. A more senior attorney would have been capable of fighting on the merits of the issues, and would have created more options for Judge Mukasey's consideration, possibly knocking out parts of the Patriot Act.

My ordeal would provide a terrifying lesson why our Constitutional rights of due process must be regarded as sacred for all defendants, and protected at all costs. The Patriot Act would aggressively bludgeon those rights in the most unthinkable ways. With every blow, I would discover most painfully why those rights are vital to the integrity of the judicial process.

And so I will give thanks until the day I die for Judge Mukasey's perspicacity in using the tools available to his office to kill this case. He saved my life and my freedom.

Because what the Justice Department tried to do next was pretty close to attempted murder. This was "extreme prejudice," after all.

The Justice Department and the Intelligence Community could not allow me to survive. Once the attack swept into play, they had to carry it all the way to its most vicious conclusion. Anything that stopped short of total destruction would leave ground to take down the Republicans on national security, overall.

On the morning of my arrest, I did not understand that yet. I vowed that I would go all the way to Trial, come what may.

In an awful sort of way, I regarded this attack as the highest honor Republicans could pay me. I am intensely proud that I stood out like a thorn for warning Congress of the catastrophe of War, and trying to tell Americans the truth about 9/11. I have never for one day regretted the consequences that I would have to pay.

Still, I had no idea that my nightmare under the Patriot Act was just beginning. I was ignorant that all of our most sacred constitutional rights, enshrined by our founding fathers to protect Americans against political prosecutions, would be lost to me.

I had no idea that the Patriot Act would devour the next five years of my life.

I would never get my day in court. There would be no trial by jury, according to the Constitutional rights guaranteed to all Americans for over 200 years. By the end, I would come very close to getting destroyed utterly—body, mind and soul.

The powers that control the government had every expectation that the abuses in the judicial process would lead to a lifeless Susan Lindauer, physically and spiritually damaged and discredited beyond repair.

Frighteningly enough, but for one honest Judge, they would have succeeded.

Come into my nightmare now, and let me show you why.

CHAPTER 18:

THE CASE OF THE MISSING TRIAL

If you can keep your head when all about you are losing theirs and blaming it on you;
If you can trust yourself when all men doubt you, but make allowance for their doubting
too; If you can wait, and not be tired by waiting or, being lied about, don't deal in lies;
Yet don't look too good, nor talk too wise
"If" by Rudyard Kipling

The Justice Department had mounted a high stakes bluff by indicting me. But I had no intention of backing down. The Republican leadership would need its "big guns" because I intended to put up one helluva fight. And I intended to win.

I was never afraid of going to Trial. And I never considered pleading guilty. Not for a moment. I had my entire legal strategy mapped out within the first couple of hours after my arrest. I could see lots of mistakes in the indictment, and I quickly identified which witnesses and evidence would be necessary to repudiate the whole lot.

I viewed it as legal harassment. But I also recognized that once a trial exposed the ridiculous nature of the charges, I would win. And the public would win, too, because they'd learn some important truths about Iraq and 9/11 and lost opportunities to advance counter-terrorism policy at a substantial level—like collecting financial records on Al Qaeda from Baghdad, in order to close down the cash pipeline for terrorist activities.

The public just didn't know who I was— yet. That would change with witness testimony. It would not be boring, that's for sure. I could swiftly prove my anti-terrorism credentials. Once a jury in New York City understood the scope of my work on the 9/11 investigation, I was convinced they'd be appalled by the proceedings and vote for acquittal.

I had a stellar cast of witnesses, including former Congressional staff and international journalists, like Ian Ferguson, who interviewed Dr. Fuisz for the Glasgow Sunday Herald during the Lockerbie Trial.[340] One of Scotland's finest Solicitors, Edward MacKechnie, who won acquittal for his Libyan client in the Lockerbie Trial, immediately promised to travel at his own expense to testify to the credentials of Dr. Fuisz, my CIA handler.[341] [342] That would validate my claim to have worked as an Asset supervised by U.S. intelligence. MacKechnie's generous offer of assistance, backed up by emails, was beyond dispute.

I had no worries on that score. Speculation to the contrary would be erroneous, strictly disinformation by the U.S. government.

Another stroke of luck, I could present Dr. Fuisz's deposition from the Lockerbie Trial, taken in the U.S. District Court of Alexandria, Virginia in January, 2001.[343] The deposition established Dr. Fuisz's role in Middle East anti-terrorism from the 1980s onwards, focusing on his direct knowledge of events building up to the bombing of Pan Am #103. The deposition included a list of 11 names of terrorists who participated in the attack, under double seal, and mapped out the conspiracy showing how all the tentacles combined together, in a sort of paramilitary defense of heroin trafficking out of the Bekaa Valley in Lebanon.

Sealed by the original Court inside the United States, it could only be opened by another federal Judge—like Judge Mukasey—or any Judge in Scotland. It's so devastating the CIA only allowed the deposition to go forward on condition that nobody inside the United States could read it. In all likelihood, a jury could not examine it. However, it would have been highly valuable for advancing Judge Mukasey's understanding of my activities with Dr. Fuisz. Without question, it simplified my legal strategy enormously.

At Trial, Mr. MacKechnie's testimony combined with Dr. Fuisz's deposition threatened to blow open the Lockerbie case again.[344] That meant serious headaches for the Justice Department, which has tried to clamp down discussion of Mr. Megrahi's innocence, arguments well known in Europe and the Middle East, but poorly understood in the United States.

As for proving Dr. Fuisz's ties to Iraq-related issues, that was remarkably simple as well. Dr. Fuisz had testified before Congress in 1992,[345] identifying an American corporation that supplied Iraq with the SCUD mobile missile launchers before the first Gulf War. He was an expert on Iraqi military purchases. Armed with a slew of Congressional documents from Rep. Charlie Rose's inquiry, I had more than sufficient proof of Dr. Fuisz' involvement in Iraq.[346] It would be an easy matter to establish the legitimacy of his role supervising my back-channel efforts to get the U.N. weapons inspectors into Baghdad.

I was in great shape. Very few defendants could hope for so much. Without question, I felt strong enough to shoulder that load.

I just had to practice patience for a few months—until after the November elections, unfortunately. But hey, I was free on $500,000 bond. Notoriety did not frighten me, or I could never have dealt with Libya and Iraq in the first place. I considered it disgraceful that top Republican officials had orchestrated the false arrest of an Asset, so they could deceive voters about key election issues—9/11, Iraqi Pre-War Intelligence, and above all, the Republicans' performance in the War on Terrorism.

What a fiasco! Anti-terrorism was not the "outstanding success" that Republicans pretended. The truth was flagrantly opposite. But voters would be denied the facts until after the Presidential and Congressional elections.

And now the Grand Old Republican Party had distinguished itself by arresting the woman who provided advance warning about 9/11 and secured Iraq's cooperation with the 9/11 investigation.

Did that qualify as "outstanding leadership support for anti-terrorism?"

I would say not!

It smacked of cowardice! Republicans couldn't face voters with the truth about their performance failures. So they resorted to the tactics of tyrants, throwing Assets in jail, so they could hold onto power. With knowledgeable sources connected to real events out of the way, they could invent achievements and falsify reports on their "devotion" to those of us who actually engage in that work.

In flights of fantasy, I envisioned Republicans wearing dunces' hats on CNN, and placards that proclaimed: "I Will Not Lie to Voters About Terrorism Again."

In the aftermath of Bush's surprise upset in 2004, and the emergence of Senator John McCain as a powerhouse in the Republican Party in 2008, the question must be asked: Would Bush have won a second term as President if Americans had known the truth about our 9/11 warning and Peace Options before the War? Would voters have been disturbed by failures in the 9/11 investigation?

In March 2004, getting through the Pre-Trial phase after my arrest struck me as far more obnoxious and frustrating.

From the opening hours of my arrest, the international media began hammering on my family relationship to Andy Card, Chief of Staff to President Bush. The White House faced serious blowback. It wasn't going to bite the Democrats that a former Congressional press secretary in a couple of Democrat offices got jumped as an accused "Iraqi Agent." It was going to bite the Good Old Boys in the GOP, that I delivered 11 progress reports to my cousin, the White House Chief of Staff, detailing Iraq's agreement to resume the weapons inspections.

Worse for the White House, on the morning of my arrest, I'm convinced that my old handlers, Dr. Fuisz and possibly Hoven, frantically contacted U.S. Intelligence, reminding everybody that no non-disclosure agreement existed to stop me from talking.[347]

I could tell everything. And I would.

Andy Card's day had to be going from bad to worse.

All of the world's media crushed into my tiny hamlet of Takoma Park, in the suburbs of Maryland, just a few miles from Capitol Hill. Russian television interviewed shopkeepers and neighbors. Friends caught the story in Taiwan, Malaysia, France, Canada and Great Britain. The global media gleefully proclaimed the same story: *Andy Card's cousin got arrested as an Iraqi Agent. Oh joy!*

Even more salacious, some media wrongly reported that I was accused of spying for Iraq. Though untrue, it added to the damage.

Now then, I'm notoriously tenacious and stubborn in the face of controversy, or I could never have dealt with Libya and Iraq. The same could not be said for my cousin, Andy.

While I was locked in the holding cage at the Baltimore Courthouse, with the global media pounding the White House for sound bite explanations, Andy Card's "Susan Lindauer problem" mushroomed by the hour. Andy's cabal must have raced frantically to find a solution. They needed something to knock me off the pedestal of media martyrdom. From those first hours, I'm convinced the White House recognized the mistake of going forward with prosecution. And they could see I would not submit quietly to a guilty plea, as they must have hoped (foolishly). That message was spattered in blood on the wall. A trial would be loud and ugly. And they would lose, because I could easily prove that I'm telling the truth. And it's a good truth.

I was like a tornado that threatened to rip open the Grand Old Party's circus tents, giving voters everywhere a clear view of the stage props and parlor tricks in the Greatest Show on Earth, known as the "War on Terrorism."

Andy's cabal at the White House needed a strategy that would shut me down. And they needed it fast.

At the start, their assault looked so innocuous. It was deceptively simple, in fact.

At the end of a long and tiring day locked in my holding cage, my case finally got in front of federal magistrate Susan Gauvey at about 4pm. She had the honor of deciding my bail in Baltimore, and approving my extradition to New York City.

The Prosecutor ran forward to huddle in front of the judge. Apparently he had "information." Breathlessly, he told Judge Gauvey that a family member had told Pre-Trial Services that I threatened suicide several weeks before my arrest. On those grounds, the Justice Department was demanding that I submit to a psychiatric evaluation, as part of my bail conditions. Otherwise, the Justice Department had no objections to my release, since I was not a flight risk and maintained strong ties to the local community, including owning a home. [348]

They just wanted me to undergo a simple psychological evaluation. That's how it started.

A wonderful public defender was handling the bail release for me in Baltimore. He scurried back to me and dropped this bombshell!

I was astonished. I had no idea that I was suicidal. I imagined Andy Card slapping some White House colleague on the back! *Good job, man! All those democrats are crazy!*

Hey, if you're opposed to George Bush and the War in Iraq, you've got to have a screw loose, right? It wasn't Dick Cheney and Donald Rumsfeld who made a mistake in Iraq. It was me, the Asset. My incompetence. My lack of risk taking and problem solving.

"Suicidal?" I laughed in his face. "You are kidding, right? Are you sure they've got the right case? There must be two Susan Lindauers in court today, because I can assure you they've got the wrong lady. I've never been suicidal in my life."

I was so "not suicidal," that I had told friends many times that if anything should happen to me, they should confidently scorn any suggestion of suicide. I was admittedly paranoid that somebody might try to stage my death so it would look like suicide, given my recent unpopularity in the intelligence community. But my friends understood that I would never do such a thing. I consider life a great adventure, even in the worst of times. Even today.

Hearing this preposterous suggestion, I demanded that my public attorney march back to the Judge, and deny the Prosecution's report as ridiculous nonsense that was politically motivated.

"Your story's running all over the media," the attorney told me. "The White House is in serious trouble over your arrest. They're looking for a way out. We'll deny that you're suicidal, but really you don't have a choice. You'll have to agree. They're willing to accept bail if you accept the evaluation. The Judge will see that as very reasonable. Then you can go home."

I looked at the clock. It was 4 pm. I looked at the rows of journalists crowded into the judge's hearing room, waiting for the next play. The White House wanted to make the evening news.

Well, okay. Getting out of that tiny holding cage and sleeping in a proper bed that night sounded like a fair trade to me. Doesn't that argue for my sanity? The evaluation would take an hour. They promised that it would be completed that evening. Afterwards, I would be transferred to a half-way house for the night, until my father arrived from Phoenix, Arizona. Then I would be released into his custody. I'd wait at my home in Maryland until the Trial.

I could go along with that. I had no emotional issues to chat about to a psychologist. I'm not the kind of personality that finds psychology attractive. Quite the opposite, I consider it whining and malingering, a waste of time and energy. As for this preposterous suggestion that I'd been suicidal a few weeks earlier, that showed desperation. The Justice Department was playing dirty. Surely it would get repudiated by any honest psychologist performing the evaluation. It was just one meeting, and I'd tell the guy I had no interest in counseling.

How much trouble could one psych evaluation cause?

In retrospect, I should never have agreed. Because right then, I made a fatal concession that irrevocably damaged my credibility on all matters and injured the rest of my case.

On that evening after my arrest, I just wanted to go home. Having no prior experience in the courts on any civil or criminal matter, a psych evaluation appeared trivial and meaningless to me. I had no difficulty cooperating with requests from the Court. I thought it best to show the Judge that I was cooperative to get bail, and set a positive precedent for my future case.

What harm could it cause? A great deal apparently.

If only somebody had warned me, I would have protected myself from some outrageous slander and character assassination that flagrantly contradicts the facts of my life. Over time, I developed a strategy for beating back the corrupt practices of court psychology, but only after some hard lessons, unfortunately.

I remember that night keenly, in living color. I was so exhausted and hungry that I kept falling asleep. The jerk psychiatrist kept banging on the table to wake me up. My eyes kept closing and my head bounced up and down, when he smacked the table. I dug my fingernails into my hands trying to stay awake. He complained to the Court that my "responses wandered."

Fortunately, my first public defender in Baltimore was terrific. My attorney demanded that the evaluation be postponed until the following day, so I could get some food in my stomach and a good night sleep. The day had wiped me out. Did the wise and perceptive psychiatrist pick up on that? No, the rational attorney did. The shrink doing the evaluation tried to inflict maximum damage, dismissing my adamant denials that I had been suicidal, and that I had no idea where such a ridiculous allegation came from. He concluded that I was "not aware" of my suicidal impulses, but they must be there somewhere. (Oh that makes a lot of sense! I don't know that I wish to kill myself. It's a secret! I mean, give me a break. I was appalled.)

Somebody also told the feds that my brother has bipolar disorder—which is not exactly true. My brother, John Lindauer, experiences symptoms of 'seasonal affective disorder," a.k.a the winter blues. I lacked the heart to tell my brother that he's worse than bipolar. He's confident, creative and intellectual, the most virulent threat to psychology out there.

Demonstrating a profound lack of logic, the shrink declared that if my brother suffered bipolar swings, than obviously I must, too. (My brother and I are surely identical beings.) In fact, there was no sign of bipolar disorder in our interview, since I was practically asleep. My attorney and I expected some measure of honesty in that regard. We expected the shrink to report my exhaustion to the Court. He omitted any mention of it. That was my first lesson into the gross dishonesty of court psychology, which invents, falsifies and ignores for its own purposes.

But I couldn't prove it. It was my word against his. I would learn that lesson again, with more devastating results, until I discovered a solution, which I will gladly share. There are ways to protect yourself from this kind of fraud that make all the difference to the outcome.

By sheer dumb luck, I had done one thing right. I refused to meet the psychiatrist unless my attorney could be present. So my attorney stopped the loony shrink from doing even worst damage. My attorney put the Baltimore psychiatrist on notice that we intended to get a second evaluation from a different source closer to my home in Takoma Park, over the weekend if necessary, before I faced Judge Mukasey on Monday morning in New York. We intended to argue that the second evaluation had more validity, given the extreme circumstances of the first evaluation (falling asleep and lack of food that day). Any referral for counseling would be performed by the second evaluator. So the first shrink could not grab a federal contract for himself—which it became obvious he wanted to do. He wanted the business.

I had never been arrested before. So I learned the hard way that psychology has become the new ambulance chasers in the Courts, defaming defendants as a source of income.

Providing a community service for stressed defendants is no longer the motivation of court-ordered counseling. It has nothing to do with "helping people." It's a power trip, and psychologists approach these evaluations as trolling for long-term accounts. They're out to nab defendants as a business contract, so they can pay the mortgage and make the car payment. Defendants are cash cows, an ATM card to make withdrawals off the state and county budgets. The Feds pay beautifully. The shrink gets a fee and their practice gets a fee. Everybody makes out. Cherry picking defendants has become supremely popular at every possible opportunity. It's all about money.

It's also highly subjective—not scientific at all. That sort of explains how the second evaluation two days later by Dr. John S. Kennedy, a psychiatrist at Family Health Services in Hyattsville, Maryland, reached a wholly different set of conclusions.[349]

Notably, Dr. Kennedy told me that he had never faced such intense political pressure to deliver a negative evaluation on any defendant in his whole career. He told me that he'd received several phone calls from Pre-Trial Services in Baltimore and Greenbelt anxious to impress him about my need for a psychiatric intervention. He told me that he was shocked by it, that he regarded it as "unprofessional and unethical" to slant an evaluation for what he deemed political purposes. And he would not do it. He assured me that he would report only what he saw.

Here's what Dr. Kennedy submitted to Judge Mukasey:[350]

"Two days ago, the patient was indicted on four counts of being an Unregistered Agent of a Foreign Government. There was considerable media interest in the case. The patient's father told authorities that his daughter had recently spoken of suicide. Thus, within hours of the indictment, the patient was evaluated by Dr. Roskes, a forensic psychiatrist. Dr. Roskes felt she was "hypomanic or manic," and prescribed olanzapine 5 mg."

"The patient describes herself as a very energetic and creative person. She is outgoing and intense. She becomes engaged in projects and may work late into the night. However, she denies longer periods of sleeplessness or loss of reality testing. She denies depressed mood or suicidality. She denies the use of alcohol or illicit drugs."

"Mental Status Exam: Eye contact was fair. Kinetics were activated. Speech was rapid and somewhat pressured. Affect was congruent and full in range. Thought processes were logical, linear and goal directed. Thought content was free of hallucinations, delusions, homicidality, or suicidality. She expressed confidence in an acquittal. Judgment and insight were fair. Cognition was grossly intact."

Dr. Kennedy discontinued the olanzapine, and prescribed Depakote instead, for use if I should become panicked or excessively frightened during my indictment. It was not for daily use, only to calm myself down if my indictment started to overwhelm me. I had no prior arrests or experience in court proceedings. No person knows in advance how they're going to respond to such a threat, and I could not anticipate whether I would use the drug or not. You can experience some bad days, that's for sure. A defendant must stay relatively calm, in order to focus on preparing a legal strategy. I agreed to have the Depakote with me, in case I needed it. There were some days that I took it. I got one prescription refill (30 tablets) over the next 18 months.

Once they snagged me for the evaluation, however, the psychology crowd would not let go. Dr. Kennedy recommended weekly counseling for 4 to 12 weeks,[351] while I sorted out my emotional reaction to the indictment. I considered it tedious, but I could endure it for 12 weeks.

By the time I got in front of Judge Mukasey on Monday morning. Pre-Trial Services and the Prosecutor demanded that I undergo court-ordered counseling right up to trial, as a condition for bail. The phony suicide threat had done its worst.

I was very curious as to how Pre-Trial Services had concocted this bizarre suicide threat. I discovered that apparently somebody had asked my father, who lives in Scottsdale, Arizona, what he knows about my life in Washington, DC. The truthful answer was "not much." My father volunteered that several weeks prior to my arrest, he mailed me a newspaper advertisement seeking healthy women to participate in gynecological experimentation of a new drug for ovarian cancer. Since my mother died of ovarian cancer, he thought I might want to participate in medical testing of the new drug.

I was not so altruistic, with regards to loaning my female anatomy to the National Institutes of Health for use by teams of medical researchers. So I tossed the paper in the trash can.

Pre-Trial Services seized on that action: Tossing the crumpled newspaper advertisement into the trash, they decided, constituted a suicide threat, because my mother had died of that form of cancer.

Outrageously enough, that's how the court-order on forced psychology was imposed.

Given what I would suffer because of the order to attend psych meetings, I have come to regard the phony suicide threat as defamatory sexual harassment and a degradation of women prisoners. I consider it grossly unprofessional and sexist. Friends have compared my situation to "The Handmaid's Tale" by Margaret Atwood. Indeed, it resonates.

It's particularly amusing, in a dark and Kafkaesque sort of way, because people ask me all the time "why I'm still alive" after dealing with the government in my case.

I told everybody it's because I refused to die until I got my trial. So I was probably going to live forever. *I mean, suicide? Me? It would never happen. Seriously, you need drugs!*

In any event, that explains the twisted path that led from the White House to a court-order forcing me to attend psychology meetings in Maryland after my arrest. Psychology was a political tool to discredit me.

There's no question but that I plainly hated the order to attend weekly meetings. Still I obeyed for a year, until the following March, becoming progressively annoyed as no trial date emerged.

Dr. Taddesseh, the Maryland psychologist who saw me at Family Health Services, agreed with me that the court order was instigated to combat international media attention on my family relationship with White House Chief of Staff, Andrew Card.

Ominously, Dr. Taddesseh warned that Pre-Trial Services in Greenbelt phoned repeatedly asking him to put me on drugs. When he refused, Pre-Trial Services requested that he refer my case back to them, so that I could be designated to another psychology practice. Dr. Taddesseh told me that in his opinion, the government was shopping for somebody to drug me. He considered it grossly unprofessional and corrupt for Pre-Trial Services to interfere with our psychology meetings. He regarded it as more evidence of politics trying to guide the application of psychology against me. Thankfully, he resisted.

After the stunt pulled by the first psychiatrist on the night of my arrest, I had no doubt that somebody with less integrity would go along with Pre-Trial Services, in order to keep their business. Court psychology is rife with corruption and fraud. There appears to be an attitude running through psychology that any defendant is lucky to attend meetings with them. There's a sense that if they're lying and making up stories, it's to the benefit of the defendant who somehow will escape punishment, because of a psychologist's opinion. Aren't we lucky that they're willing to manipulate the Court on our behalf! That's become a bizarre justification for poaching off the courts. And it seems to rationalize their system of dishonesty and corruption.

Even Dr. Taddesseh, who had vastly more integrity than most in the psychology business, was shocked that I was wholly disinterested in anything he had to say. I told him that I had no intention of changing anything about my life. In one year I intended to be exactly the same person as when I first walked into his office.

I took a cook-book to the first meeting, and forced him to listen to recitations of recipes, sans commentary. When he asked if I intended to cook any of the recipes, I assured him I would never do such a thing. I said I considered his insights as useless as a recipe that I would never bake.

Dr. Taddesseh had the good sense to feel embarrassed. At subsequent meetings, he'd bring a copy of the Washington Post, and we'd discuss news articles and current affairs. That's all I remember about our meetings. In fact, I don't recall that we discussed anything except the Washington Post and my complaints about how court-ordered psych meetings interfered with my employment, since the bail order stopped me from working full time. I had to take a part-time job, which killed me financially. It was a huge waste of tax dollars.

It was also incredibly tedious. I called it my "babysitting job." I joked with friends that I had to go "check on Taddesseh once a week to make sure he was okay." For awhile, to create conversation, I counted how many traffic lights flashed red versus green on the short drive to his office. This gave us something to chat about. He asked once what traffic lights "symbolized" for me. I said that obviously it symbolized him, and the stop-and-go boredom of these road blocks thrown up by the Justice Department to delay us from going to trial.

Another morning, I stared off into space experiencing serious brain death. Apparently I sighed deeply. "What is it, Ms. Lindauer? What are you thinking?" He leaned forward intensely. "I'm thinking about what kind of ice cream to buy for lunch. I'm thinking if I should stop at Baskin Robbins or if I should go to A & W for a root beer float."

Dr. Taddesseh sighed. "I can't help you with that."

"Of course, not," I snapped back at him. "Do you honestly think I would consult you on something so important as ice cream!"

After a year of this nonsense, I point blank refused to continue. If the Court wanted to revoke my bail, so be it. I told Taddesseh that he contributed nothing to my life. I accused him of selfishly interfering with my employment, so he could make money off the court. He was happy to see me go.

As fate would have it, our meetings had some unexpected value, however. The 12 months of observation notes on my mental status, submitted by Dr. Taddesseh to Pre-Trial Services, would provide a critical reference in my terrible court fight to come.[352]

Here's what Dr. Taddesseh documented in his monthly reports to Pre-Trial Services: [353] (See Appendix.)

In May, 2004: "Ms. Lindauer appears to maintain psychological stability."

In June, 2004: "Ms. Lindauer appears to maintain stability and reports no major psychiatric symptom that may require additional or special attention."

In July, 2004: "Ms. Lindauer reports no mood swing or other psychological problem. She points out that she is not taking any medication. She considers that she is stabilized."

In August, 2004: "Ms. Lindauer expressed concern about her future due to the legal problem. She appears stable and reports no symptom of mood or other psychological problems."

In September, 2004: "Ms. Lindauer reports for therapy as scheduled. She expressed concern and frustration about her legal problems. She shows no unusual sign of mood or anxiety, and she feels comfortable and capable of managing her psychological and emotional challenges without aid of medication."

In October, 2004: "Ms. Lindauer reports for therapy on a regular basis. She reports no symptom of mania or psychosis. She seems stable and focused on her legal problem. At times she gets anxious and worried of fear of going to jail."

In November, 2004: "Ms. Lindauer's mental exams show no sign or symptom of psychosis or delusion. However, at times she gets tense and excited when talking about her legal ordeal. Yet she seems goal directed, and her judgment is within normal range."

In December, 2004: "Ms. Lindauer reports for scheduled sessions as arranged. She shares her feelings and thoughts in an open manner. She expresses concern about her freedom and her future. She shows no sign of mood disturbances or psychosis and delusions. She seems focused and goal directed."

In January, 2005: "Ms. Lindauer reports for therapy as required. She appears to maintain psychological stability and shows no sign or symptom of mania or psychosis. However, she appears concerned about the outcome of her legal problem."

At the conclusion of one full year, in March, 2005:

"Ms. Lindauer remained concerned about her legal problem. So far she has shown no sign of mania or depression and symptom of any psychosis that may require additional intervention."

All session notes were filed with Pre-Trial Services in Greenbelt, Maryland and the Southern District of New York in Manhattan.

They provide critical observation of the consistency of my mental health and emotional stability for a full year after my indictment.

According to Family Health Services, there was nothing wrong with my mental status at all.

I was just fine— mentally, psychologically and emotionally. What's more, all those observations had been handed over to Pre-Trial Services. So the Justice Department was fully aware that I demonstrated no history of mental problems, or any emotional upset of any kind. None of the observations in those session notes justified further psychiatric action against me.

Interestingly, despite my requests for copies of the session notes, Pre-Trial Services in Greenbelt and New York argued for months against releasing them to me. They flat out refused to hand them over. So I had to get sneaky. I pretended that a wonderful lady in the peace movement was actually a psychologist who might start meeting me privately. I requested that copies of the session notes from Dr. Taddesseh should be sent to her,[354] explaining that she needed to know the current status of my "mental health," Otherwise I could never have laid my hands on these documents at all.

Thank God I did! Those session notes proved most precious indeed.

Dr. Taddesseh and I could not know that in the future, those session reports would provide critical documentation that would save me from the most horrific abuse ever attempted against a U.S. Asset since the Cold War. It would be my only protection from the vicious brutality conceived by the Justice Department. But it would be enough.

For that, I thank Dr. Taddesseh forever. He had ethics and integrity in a court psychology business short on both. He never tried to hold onto my case for profit, and he faithfully documented my mental stability so the Court order could be lifted. It's not his fault that Pre-Trial Services in Greenbelt and New York had become so corrupt in protecting Republican leaders that they continued to abuse the court order on forced psych counseling, which should have only existed for my benefit, not for any politicians'. There was no justification for forcing me to attend these meetings, but it was Dr. Taddesseh who helped end it, over a lot of resistance from Pre-Trial Services, which he called "unprofessional and unethical."

At the time, I could not see past my fury at the court's intrusion into my private life, however. I considered it a Soviet-style abuse of psychiatry, like what Moscow had done to intellectuals and dissidents under the Communists. It was Stalinist, for sure. I regarded forced attendance at psychology meetings as slanderous to my reputation, for the purpose of diminishing my credibility before trial. I resigned myself to suffer through it. In fact, I had no choice.

But I resolved that when the Justice Department was forced to play its hand, all of those puffed up, empty accusations would crash back down on them. The worst they behaved, the worse it would fall for them.

Never did I contemplate that the Justice Department had just discovered a powerful weapon to stop me from going to Trial.

I understood my rights under the Constitution.

I did not understand my lack of rights under the Patriot Act.

And I had no idea that in New York, my public attorney, Sam Talkin, had just been invited to a classified debriefing at the Justice Department to discuss my case.

I was about to get blind-sided in the most horrifying and unimaginable way possible in a modern court of law. This was "extreme prejudice," after all.

CHAPTER 19:

SECRET DEBRIEFINGS AND THE "NEW PSYCHIATRY" (A LITTLE INTELLIGENCE WAR)

"Treason is a matter of dates."
–Cardinal Richelieu

I was gunning for trial.

Unbeknownst to me, my public attorney, Sanford Talkin of Manhattan, had been invited to a "classified debriefing" to discuss my case.

The "secret attorney debriefing" was held at the Justice Department on February 10, 2005.[355] There's no record of who attended, or what intelligence agencies were represented. I was completely in the dark that the meeting occurred, though it would have grave consequences for my legal rights and my freedom. Only four years later, when Talkin finally turned over copies of his legal discovery to the private attorney who replaced him, the esteemed and honorable Mr. Brian Shaughnessy, did we learn about it. In typical style, Talkin forwarded the legal discovery one week after the case got dismissed[356]—and 16 months after Shaughnessy officially took over. That speaks volumes in itself. It was grossly unethical, but par for my case. Talkin refused to cooperate on any matter of my defense.

Amidst thousands of pages of legal documents and wire taps, Shaughnessy and I discovered a "Non-Disclosure Agreement for a Classified Debriefing," signed by Talkin.[357] The agreement acknowledged that information contained in the briefing justified a security clearance. It expressly prohibited Talkin from disclosing whatever transpired during the debriefing to anyone, including me, or any subsequent attorney, without written consent from the Justice Department.

Welcome to the New America.

I'd just been stung by the Patriot Act, with its rules of "secret evidence," and its extraordinary authority to force attorneys to withhold that "secret evidence" from defendants or other attorneys involved in the case.

The non-disclosure agreement for the "secret attorney debriefing" was handled by the Department of Justice, Compliance Review and Litigation Security Group, Security and Emergency Planning Staff.

The two page document reads in part:

"I hereby accept the obligations contained in this Agreement in consideration of my being granted access to classified information…. marked or unmarked….including oral communications."

"I hereby acknowledge that I have received a security indoctrination concerning the nature and protection of classified information, including the procedures to be followed in ascertaining whether other persons to whom I contemplate disclosing this information have been approved for access to it."

"I will never divulge classified information to anyone unless… (b) I have prior written notice of authorization from the United States Government Department or agency responsible for the classification of the information."

It was signed by Sam Talkin on February 10, 2005. (See Appendix.)

The pages are in black and white. So the fact that a "classified debriefing" occurred in Washington or New York cannot be disputed. Since I was never told the meeting occurred, though I had an urgent right to know, it appears the fact of the meeting itself was regarded as "classified," too.

Predictably, the secret meeting had nefarious ambitions. Up to that point, Talkin had promised to file a "government defense," arguing that I had authorization to deal with Iraq because of my Asset status. As of early February, Talkin promised to travel to Scotland to interview Scottish solicitor, Edward MacKechnie from the Lockerbie Trial, who could verify the CIA credentials of Dr. Fuisz. His Lockerbie deposition would be enlightening, as well.

However that "secret attorney meeting" on February 10, 2005 proved pivotal. The non-disclosure agreement coincided with a remarkable sea-change in Talkin's defense strategy.

Abruptly, external forces determined that I was not going to use a "government defense," after all.

In fact, I was not going to have a trial.

In flagrant contradiction to the most fundamental protections in the Constitution, which I cherish, my right to a trial would be denied over my own most bitter objections.

SECRET DEBRIEFINGS AND THE "NEW PSYCHIATRY"

I had no idea it was happening. I was kept in total ignorance of that development.

After replacing Talkin, my new attorney, Shaughneessy and I still had no idea what he'd done. Talkin never told us how he came to throw my case—though his actions convinced us he had, no matter what he swore in court. We could see it. When he adjusted my defense to suit the Justice Department, Talkin broke the cardinal rule of warfare: Never let your enemy choose the battleground. You do so at your own peril. Voila! My winning defense was gone.

Shaughnessy and I are not helpless by our natures, mind you. As defendant, I had copies of the original legal papers from the FBI after of my arrest. That totaled 28,000 phone taps, 8,000 emails, hundreds of captured faxes and every computer document that I ever created. However, through subpoenas, we'd picked up crucial supporting evidence, including bank records of Dr. Fuisz's payments to me[358] in May and October 2001, which strengthened my arguments of our relationship during the period of the indictment.

Likewise, friendly witnesses like Eddie MacKechnic, the Scottish Solicitor for Lockerbie, had supplied supremely useful documents to Talkin, relating to Dr. Fuisz's intelligence credentials and his connection to Iraqi matters. The documents showed Dr. Fuisz's central role in the 1992 Congressional investigation of a U.S. corporation that supplied SCUD mobile missile launchers to Iraq before the first Gulf War.[359] That would have been extremely valuable at trial.

Talkin withheld all of that documentation, until after dismissal.

The Patriot Act injected an extra burden to this dynamic. Under the rules of "secret evidence," Talkin was barred from telling me the substance of his conversation with the Justice Department that resulted in their collusion. I'm sure Talkin did not relish my response if he had.

I would have blown a gasket. I was fully conscious of my rights to due process, and I emphatically refused to surrender my right to a trial, so that I could face my accusers and challenge the evidence in open court. It's not pleasant to go to trial. However my position was simple but logical. The Justice Department has no business filing criminal charges against any American citizen, if they're not prepared to back it up in a court of law. Political prosecutions to attack opponents of government policy need to be exposed and fiercely condemned.

Indicting a U.S. Asset for allegedly eating a cheeseburger with a diplomatic source, during a terrorism investigation, smacks of foolishness to begin with. Indicting an American citizen for supporting democratic reforms and human rights in Iraq screams of hypocrisy. The charges against me should have been dismissed immediately, with an apology. However once the Justice Department made those accusations, as the defendant, I had a Constitutional right to prove that my actions did not rise to the level of criminal activity. I'm not even the woman who ate the cheeseburger. Supporting international democracy and opposing torture constitutes protected political speech. That's something I will fight for.

Unhappily for Republican leaders at the White House, a defendant's right to plead "not guilty" is sacrosanct anywhere in the world. The right to a trial has been recognized by tyrant monarchs since the feudal age. A defendant could get a trial in China, North Korea or Iran.

225

A trial would never be denied because of a "secret classified debriefing." (Well, maybe in Mynamar!)

Yet that's exactly what happened to me.

A Soviet Brand of Psychiatry

Once the deal was cut in the "secret debriefing," the Justice Department required a vehicle, or pathway, for implementing the "secret decision" to deprive my rights to a trial.

About two weeks prior to the classified debriefing, on January 18, 2005 Talkin had asked me to attend a psychiatric evaluation by Dr. Sanford Drob, former Director of Psychological Assessment at Bellevue Hospital in New York City.[360]

In April, 2005, Dr. Drob joined the faculty of Fielding Graduate University in Santa Barbara, California, where he teaches how to perform psychiatric evaluations for the Courts. At Bellevue Hospital in New York, he had been responsible for setting standards for psych assessments and training staff how to conduct evaluations.[361]

My evaluation by Dr. Drob was presented as routine and benign, a method of exploring possible strategies to help our case. At this point, Talkin and Dr. Drob did not advise me that they intended to challenge my competence to stand trial. I would have been appalled if they had. It's legally absurd, given my background. Instead the interview was portrayed as a non-specific assessment to determine what, if any, psychology angle could be used in my defense. I thought about my chronic fatigue and anxiety after the 9/11 attack. At least that would be honest, though whether it mattered to these court proceedings, I could not say.

The interview with Dr. Drob took place in New York on January 18, and lasted approximately 2 ½ hours before I drove home to Maryland.

To put that in context, psychiatric evaluations typically require 8 to 10 hours of interview time. Our meeting time was far below acceptable standards, except in hospital triage.

There was a follow up meeting in New York for a Rorschach Ink Blot Test, a couple of weeks later.[362] Dr. Drob arrived late, and that second interview lasted no more than 35 minutes.

There was no other psychological testing, including no MMPI. That's a personality test from the 1970s, which consists of 500 multiple choice questions, with yes or no answers. It poses such incisive queries as, are you afraid of mice? Are you afraid of thunder or lightning? Did you play with dolls as a child? Do you like to climb trees? Do you like to talk to people? Do you like to read books? It's loaded with 500 questions that are equally inane.

In the religion of psychiatry, the MMPI is considered "the Bible" for evaluations. That's important, because I never took it until after the Defense and Prosecution psychiatrists both issued their findings.

No, I drove 214 miles from Maryland to Manhattan, and home again, to take a Rorschach Ink Blot Test for 35 minutes. Gracious!

By now I could see that Dr. Drob lacked an understanding of the stress of intelligence operations, which would be necessary to explain my anxiety and performance pressures after 9/11. That was more than Dr. Drob could handle in this pre-trial phase. To show I grieved for it, I would first have to prove it occurred. So this evaluation was premature.

Ironically, any sign of post traumatic stress (PTS) had vanished from my life by the time of these evaluations. Therefore, PTS never registered as a "diagnosis," though I continued to be highly susceptible to it. Fresh traumas or anxiety would provoke it later on, like flare ups. However at this point, it was non-observable. Interestingly then, the one condition that might have been legitimate never got flagged.

And so at the second meeting for the Rorschach test, I pointedly informed Talkin and Dr. Drob that I had no intention of using psychology in my defense. I intended to stick with a straight "government defense," proving that I had worked as a U.S. Asset. I was polite but frank. I had no interest in the evaluation, and honestly, I find psychology itself to be pretty worthless.

Most critically, in advance of our meetings, I signed a waiver for Dr. Taddesseh and Family Health Services to submit the 12 months of session notes to Dr. Drob and my attorney.[363] Those papers documented that in 12 months of observation, I exhibited no symptoms of mental defect. On a constant basis, I suffered "no delusions," "no mood disturbances," "no psychosis," "no emotional or mood instability." Dr. Taddesseh declared that I "required no further or additional psychiatric intervention." (See Appendix.)

If the session notes had revealed any sort of emotional disturbances or "mental instability," Dr. Drob would have been entitled to use it. Instead, he was fully apprised that a year's worth of psych observations emphasized the absence of "symptoms."

What's more, Dr. Drob was aware that Dr. Taddesseh and I were taking action to end the psych meetings, which I considered a huge waste of time and taxpayer dollars.[364] From Dr. Taddesseh's perspective, the psych order only existed to protect the Court, if I got overwhelmed by the indictment and harmed myself, something I showed no inclination to do. Both of us agreed there was no point prolonging the agony of boredom in our sessions.

It's probably of great importance that I complained to Dr. Drob that Pre-Trial Services had refused to give me copies of those session notes. Very likely he believed I would never lay eyes on those records. He did not know that I had resorted to a sneaky end run to overcome Pre-Trial Service's objections. I had arranged for the records to be sent to a fellow anti-war activist in Washington, whom I pretended was a private psychologist, needing to understand my "mental health history," for possible future meetings.

Within the next few weeks, through this ruse, I got hold of Dr. Taddesseh's notes. I was quickly reassured that Dr. Drob could gain no ammunition of any kind from them. I felt greatly protected. I mean, how could any ethical and credible psychiatrist dispute reality? We had a year's worth of observation of my sterling mental health. It would be fraud and malpractice to pretend anything else. Wouldn't you say?

Finally, Dr. Drob could see for himself that no "symptoms" manifested in our conversation. Hence, the 2 ½ hour meeting that would ordinarily last 8 to 10 hours.

Our interview on January 18 was blasé at best. There were no emotional issues to chat about. Dr. Drob scrounged for conversation, and I had no inclination to provide it. Psychology flat out bores me. I consider such whining and malingering to have no place in the courts, except under the most striking circumstances. A defendant had better suffer serious schizophrenia to earn my sympathy. A seriously battered wife or child who strikes back against an abuser would merit my compassion. Otherwise I'd vote to convict. Low IQ doesn't cut it for me. I don't want to hear that somebody suffers bi-polar disorder, and therefore won't accept responsibility for embezzling money, bank robbery, identity theft, or what not. Psychology provides no excuse for criminal behavior, in my opinion.

I think Judges are terribly victimized by the confusion created by psychiatry in the courtroom, for the sake of its own grandiosity and glorified self-importance. Psychiatrists falsify and embellish their testimony. Then they spout nonsense of how their interpretations are "scientific" and "medical," and must not be questioned. That's not helpful to individuals, either. It's much better to take responsibility for good and bad decisions in our lives. Then we have the capacity to make new choices, and develop new habits. Ironically, psychiatry takes away that empowerment, because it pretends that behavior constitutes a disease, or mental defect. Calling bad decision making a "disease" indicates these people can't repair their lives. They're designated as throw-aways, as opposed to people who've made some bad choices that could change in the future. Change is a hopeful thing. Rejecting victimization is the first step to self-improvement.

I did not sugar coat my opinions for Dr. Drob. I spoke candidly in opposition to using him as a witness in my case. I told him that I objected to distracting my attorney from vital work to prepare for trial. He was fully conscious of my beliefs and my strong desire to clear my name.

A perceptive psychiatrist would have anticipated that such deeply held beliefs would stay constant and unchanging throughout the proceedings. I'm a strong personality. I'm not a Defendant who would appreciate efforts to manipulate a Judge. That offends me enormously.

As for post traumatic stress, psychiatric testimony might have clarified the impact of chronic fatigue in my life after 9/11, and how my exhaustion delayed my understanding of the nuances of White House policy on Iraq. On the other hand, it might not have mattered. After 9/11, Republicans deliberately concealed their intention to go to War. They had a secret agenda that they chose not to share with anyone, certainly not a Peace Asset opposed to sanctions and killing. Psychiatry could contribute no real understanding to that dynamic— except to explain that I was too exhausted to figure it out for myself, without somebody telling me directly. And nobody did.

Once I met Dr. Drob for our first and only interview on January 18 in New York, I recognized that he could not provide that sort of affirmation about my stress after 9/11.

I'm convinced that Dr. Drob recognized it, too, which explains why the evaluation was so perfunctory. He made no effort to extend the second meeting beyond the Rorschach test, which lasted all of 35 minutes, including greetings and good byes. After the ink blot test, he left my attorney's office, and I headed home to Maryland, a huge waste of driving time.

Psychiatry appeared to be a dead issue in my case.

Then, on February 10, 2005, the Justice Department hosted that "secret attorney debriefing," as evidenced by the non-disclosure agreement.[365]

Low and behold, psychiatry hurled its ugly weight onto my case.

Three weeks later, on February 28, 2005, Dr. Drob issued an extraordinary report declaring me "incompetent to stand trial."[366]

Welcome to the New Psychiatry!

A declaration of insanity would have required evidence to substantiate the "diagnosis," and there was none. But incompetence?

Dr. Drob offered the most sparse and perverse logic to justify his findings:[367]

"Ms. Lindauer insists that she does not want to proceed with an insanity defense, and insists that her lawyer follow up leads and witnesses that will demonstrate (1) that she did not receive the alleged moneys, (2) that she was an extremely important intelligence asset working for the DIA [Defense Intelligence Agency] and CIA. *It is Ms. Lindauer's insistence upon her relationship to CIA handler, Dr. Fuisz that is apparently frustrating counsel's efforts to provide her with a viable defense."*

"It is not simply Ms. Lindauer's refusal to go along with counsel's suggestion of pursuing a psychological defense in this case that renders her incompetent."

"It is rather Ms. Lindauer's insistence that counsel pursue witnesses and leads that may make her, by reason of mental illness, incapable of effectively cooperating with counsel in her own defense, and which is apparently actually impeding counsel in preparing a viable defense."[368]

That's right: My desire to validate the authenticity of my story through witness testimony and available evidence, in Drob's opinion, demonstrated a major psychological impairment that rendered me "incompetent to stand trial."

Put another way, my desire for a trial qualified as a mental defect.

Now I would say that's crazy.

It's also bloody well unconstitutional. You can't deny somebody a trial on the grounds that she has asked for a trial. That's legally absurd. Yet that's how psychiatry attacked me.

Months later, when I finally received a copy of Dr. Drob's report, I would be struck by the astonishing lack of "reality contact" and the undertones of sexism, ignoring the substantial history of women's contributions to intelligence work dating back to World War II.

Otherwise, Dr. Drob offered no explanation for the disparity in the session notes from Family Health Services, which documented that I suffered "no symptoms of mental defects" in the previous twelve months—"no depression," "no mood disturbances," "no symptoms of psychosis," and "no other types of symptoms that would require additional psychiatric intervention."

Dr. Drob had copies of those monthly reports. He ignored it all.

A year later, Judge Mukasey would call a special court meeting, in outrage, to demand an explanation for the discrepancy.[369] Unhappily, by then, our "learned professor" from Fielding Graduate University had done his worst damage. And it would be savage.

Dr. Drob's degree in psychiatry was supposed to suffice for the Judge to accept his opinion as "scientific fact." And so, in contradiction to multiple witness statements, on the basis of the most mediocre evaluation, a Rorschach ink blot test, and a short conversation that manifested no emotional upset of any sort, Dr. Drob concluded that I was "unable to assist in my Defense," and "not competent to stand trial."

Strikingly, I was not allowed to know that Dr. Drob's evaluation was finished, or what it contained. I was not allowed to review it, or comment on it with corrections and clarifications. For months and months, I had no idea that he had already declared me "unfit for trial." My attorney continued to assure me that we would go to Trial, as I urgently requested.

Truly I believe that "secret attorney debriefing" at the Justice Department marked the change.

Interestingly enough, the "diagnosis" of incompetence matched up precisely to what Senator John McCain and the Republican leadership (and a lot of Democrats) were complaining in floor speeches about Pre-War Intelligence at that very moment. Congress was hard at work on the 24 hour talk shows, bashing Assets for failing to build options to war, and failing to correct faulty assumptions before the War —all the things I was indicted for doing. According to Congress, Assets provided wrongful assessments throughout the intelligence process. The "incompetence of Assets" had thrust our nation into the abyss. The Presidential Commission on Iraqi Pre-War Intelligence cited the "lack of creative risk taking," the "lack of development of Assets," and the "Incompetence of Assets," specifically.

Dr. Drob's evaluation lined up perfectly with that Republican message, though surely, my actions rebutted all of those complaints.

All of my bona fides, my hard-won achievements, got cast aside in preference for Dr. Drob's fanciful inventions about my personality and private life—which were suspiciously non-specific. He swept aside all sources of confirmation from supremely high caliber witnesses—Scottish attorneys involved in the Lockerbie Trial, former Congressional staff, journalists—private papers, phone records, emails and everything else that substantiated my activities.

Dr. Drob constructed a whole new reality contradicting all facts.

And it happened within three weeks of that "classified debriefing" at the Justice Department.

"It was a game play straight out of the Cold War, a strategy that paralleled the abuse of writers and intellectual dissidents in the old Soviet Union," says Shaughnessy, my brilliant, top-drawer Washington attorney who replaced Talkin. "That's what struck me the first time I heard about Susan's situation, and that's why I took her case."

The similarities are disturbing. Not so long ago, Soviet intellectuals got locked up in mental institutions and gulags for "anti-social behavior," while corrupt psychiatrists took the government line. If a Soviet dissident opposed government policy, psychiatry declared something must be defective in his mental workings. It required correction, preferably involving shock treatment and psycho-tropic drugs. After a couple of years locked up on a psych ward, the Soviet intellectual would be persuaded to reconsider his or her anti-social behavior that criticized government policy. Once the Soviet intellectual learned to agree with the government, he or she would be judged "mentally healthy" again.

Of course, a psychiatric record diminishing the intellectual's credibility would now exist. If that person ever made the mistake of "relapsing" into anti-social behavior that criticized the government, he would be picked up by "concerned" authorities once more.

That's what the Justice Department planned for me.

It's shocking for the novice who expects psychiatry to employ some rational methodology and integrity. However, according to the constructs of psychiatry as defined by Dr. Drob and others like him, reality does not depend on external factors and measures. It depends on the interpretation of a psychiatrist.

Factual evidence does not have to be considered at all.

But that would not end the debate. Unhappily for Dr. Drob's brand of psychiatry, factual evidence and witness testimony would surface non-stop to repudiate his outrageous allegations.

The horrors of my case would demonstrate beyond any doubt that psychiatry is neither medical, nor scientific. It cannot survive the most basic scrutiny or "reality testing." On the contrary, it requires the suspension of reality in order to gain credence. It is wide open for corruption.

Once reality comes into play, psychiatry falls apart.

So it happened to Dr. Drob.

My Achilles Heel

Imagine the absurdity of my situation.

A year after my indictment, I was gunning for trial, totally ignorant of my attorney's collusion with the Justice Department, or the strategy to deny me a trial. Worst of all, I was fully innocent of the various methods of corrupting a psychiatric evaluation, or that the easiest way apparently involves declaring a defendant "unfit to stand trial."

That could mean anything.

Most ironically of all, since I had no idea what my attorney was up to, I proceeded full steam to help prepare my defense. I was too poor to hire a paralegal. So I rolled up my sleeves, and applied my best efforts where I could. Mostly I concentrated on writing background papers on witnesses. I also culled computer and phone records to establish alibis for dates that I was not in New York eating cheese burgers with Salih Mahmoud. I persevered in ignorance, while Talkin promised that he was still preparing for trial.

And I found the alibis!

Alas, according to psychiatry, the very fact that I pushed Talkin to "interview witnesses and follow leads" demonstrated a "mental defect" that rendered me "incompetent to stand trial."

The only way they could advance this crazy scheme was to keep me ignorant of their actions—which they did for several more months.

I trudged on in the dark. Yet something didn't feel right. Friends started asking questions about my rights to a speedy trial.

And I began to worry that not one of my key witnesses had been interviewed. That gnawed at my gut. You see, I had just one Achilles heel, but I recognized that it was a critical flaw in my defense. I had a public attorney. Talkin was over-worked and underpaid for such a complex case. Most worrisome, he lacked any basic understanding of the intelligence community, or the inclination to develop an understanding. My legal battle demanded a more senior attorney like Brian Shaughnessy, who took over the second half of my defense—and argued vociferously for my capacity to assist him.

Later I helped Shaughnessy submit a legal brief to the United States Supreme Court, on behalf of another client. If my skills are good enough to handle the filing protocols for the Supreme Court, I imagine they're good enough for the Southern District of New York any day.

In short, my capabilities did not jeopardize my defense. Unhappily, my attorney's did.

Aggravating his ignorance of intelligence work, Talkin had bad instincts. Briefly, Talkin hired a criminal investigator in New York who traveled to Washington exactly once— on the night of the 2004 election.[370] A lot of my witnesses are connected to national politics, and probably stayed up all night watching election results. They took the next day off. Talkin's investigator got frustrated and left town that afternoon, and he refused to come back to Washington. Talkin shrugged it off. That hurt us.

Very simple things got messed up. For example, the wrong phone company got subpoenaed for calling records.[371] Restaurant receipts in New York were date and time stamped. If phone records could prove I was at home in Maryland —not eating cheeseburgers with Salih Mahmoud in New York— we could argue for dismissal of the minor charges.

Makes sense, right?

We'd struck out four of the days already. We had five more to go. Phone records were logical for that purpose.

In Talkin's mind, it didn't matter which phone company got the subpoena, because all phone companies would possess the same records for all customers in the Washington Metropolitan area. Nine months passed, while he haggled with the wrong phone company,[372] despite my pleas to go back to Judge Mukasey for the correct subpoena. Unhappily, by the time he acknowledged the mistake, Starpower had merged with another company, and older calling records had got erased. It was a great loss for my defense.

Some of the mistakes were more outrageous.

Talkin subpoenaed the Defense Intelligence Agency for all records in my file. Yet he made no challenge when the agency limited its search to "unclassified" documents, and "a two hour search window."[373] (See Appendix.)

Like that would do any good!

We know this, because the Defense Intelligence Agency was required to outline the scope of its research in answering the subpoena. So we have hard documentation of their actions.

According to their communications with Talkin, all "Top Secret," "Secret" and "Confidential" documents had been excluded from the search.

A "two hour search" of "unclassified documents" was deemed sufficient to pull out all relevant information pertaining to my work in anti-terrorism from 1993 until 2002, covering Iraq, Libya, Egypt, Syria/Hezbollah, Yemen and Malaysia.

That two hour window covered my warning about the first attack on the World Trade Center; the Lockerbie negotiations with Libya ; the Lockerbie Trial; the bombing of the USS Cole; the Oklahoma City Bombing; my team's early investigations of Al Qaeda; right on through our team's efforts to secure Iraq's cooperation with the 9/11 investigation.

I'm not the slightest bit surprised that the Agency located nothing for us in the "unclassified" section of their records. All of my work would have been "Sensitive" or above. "Unclassified" was probably the only category that would yield nothing! It would be worthless.

And what about this two hour search? Did Defense Intelligence seriously expect to perform a thorough review of all those issues, going back all of those years?

That was a joke. Realistically, it should have taken a whole legal team several days to pull everything for our subpoena, even a couple of weeks.

Yet Talkin registered no protest when Defense Intelligence demurred from conducting a more thorough inspection of its files. He agreed to accept whatever they could locate in the "unclassified" areas only, in that "two hour search window."

There was another ugly twist. The Defense Intelligence search was conducted on February 4, 2005—one week prior to the classified debriefing at the Justice Department on February 10. That's the "secret meeting" that culminated in the "secret agreement" to deny me a trial.

And the dagger drops.

A Few Good Men

Ah, but you see, they forgot one critical factor in any Intelligence War: They have power over their actions. They don't have power over mine.

I would not play their game. I would run their blockade. That's what any good Asset does.

Right at that moment, Providence smiled with a true gift for my case. My own beloved uncle, Ted Lindauer.

Ted has a deep care for family. He's got four children of his own, and six step-children. And he would go through any sort of hell to protect all of them. Actually, they're upstanding and educated professionals. I got into more trouble than all of them combined. Yet Ted made a special effort to protect me, too.

Blessedly, Thayer "Ted" Lindauer also practices commercial and civil law at a senior level. As a graduate of the University of Chicago Law School years ago, he's got the depth of legal knowledge to work his way through any crisis situation, which mine was fast becoming.

I would rely on Ted's tenacity and dedication many times before this nightmare ended. At critical moments, he would appear and take action that would save me. He would go to a great deal of trouble to act on my behalf, when Talkin could think of nothing to help me.

It's almost eerie how Ted Lindauer arrived on the scene exactly as my court-appointed attorney cut a deal with the Justice Department. My prosecutor, Edward O'Callaghan, had just demanded that I meet his psychiatrist, Dr. Stuart Kleinman. And I was pushing Talkin to get on the ball interviewing my witnesses—which had not occurred a year after my arrest.

Regarding psychiatry, Ted told me not to worry. No matter what psychiatry hoped to accomplish, I had the right to a hearing. I would have the right to call rebuttal witnesses, and submit evidence of my mental status to the court. That year's worth of session notes from Dr. Taddesseh in Maryland started to look awfully appealing.

More worrisome, several witnesses had voiced alarm that Talkin had snubbed their efforts to set up interviews.[374] More than once, Talkin looked me straight in the eye, and swore those individuals never contacted him. He pretended that star witnesses like Edward MacKechnie, the Scottish Solicitor from the Lockerbie Trial, were not responsive to our approach. Unhappily for him, MacKechnie had copied me on every email.[375] So the bald faced lie got smashed at once. Nevertheless, Talkin insulted a top international attorney willing to travel at his own expense to New York City to testify for me, possibly waiting several days to appear on my behalf. It was an act of extraordinary generosity, and Sam Talkin threw it back at him.

As of early February, Talkin promised to visit Scotland to meet MacKechnie, and read Dr. Fuisz's deposition for the Lockerbie Trial, which is sealed in the United States.

After the "secret attorney meeting," those sorts of important projects abruptly stopped. I could sense the inertia, even if I did not understand what triggered it.

What could be done about this?

Ted Lindauer jumped on it. He agreed to conduct the most important interviews himself.[376] (See Affidavit in Appendix). He made a special effort to contact Eddie MacKechnie, and quickly verified the most important elements of my story, that MacKechnie could validate the CIA credentials of Dr. Fuisz and our work together on the Lockerbie Trial. This was critical to establishing my involvement in anti-terrorism matters, under Dr. Fuisz's supervision. We could prove Dr. Fuisz's involvement in Iraq through his Congressional testimony in 1992 identifying U.S. corporations that supplied Iraq with weapons systems before the first Gulf War. Once we established his CIA connections, my defense would be secure. That was the key point.

MacKechnie's testimony would be profoundly valuable. A senior international attorney of the most upstanding reputation in Europe, he would be a gem of a witness, priceless for any defendant. As Scottish solicitor, he'd won the acquittal for one of the two Libyans accused of the Lockerbie bombing, an extraordinary victory. It helped that Faihma was innocent, but MacKechnie had an uphill fight to overcome Scottish prejudice. He won a landmark terrorism trial at a special court of The Hague. And Sam Talkin would not reply to his emails.

Uncle Ted was far more gracious.

After that conversation with MacKechnie, Ted called me, thrilled. "You are totally safe," he said. "You're going to win this thing. You can prove everything that you've told me."

Eddie MacKechnie was a powerhouse witness, alright. Ted freely confessed that he felt greatly relieved by the excellence of my legal strategy and the superiority of my witness line up.[377] Ted also spoke with Parke Godfrey, who confirmed the authenticity of my 9/11 warning [378] and Paul Hoven, who doubly validated the CIA identity of Dr. Fuisz and our long working relationship. To this point, we know that Hoven was telling the truth about our work together, though the intelligence community urgently wanted my case to go away.[379]

Needless to say, I was very pleased.

That should have been the undoing of psychiatry in my case. Indeed, on the basis of Ted's interviews, we could have argued for dismissal.

Meeting Dr. Kleinman for the first time, I felt remarkably at peace with myself. I could handle a trial, I assured him, if the Prosecutor refused to drop the charges. I had no intention of pleading guilty. Ted had finished his interviews the week before, and I enjoyed the supreme calm of knowing that witnesses supported me 100 percent. I could rise to the standard of proof required by Judge Mukasey. And that's what I told Dr. Kleinman.

Our first interview struck me as quite pleasant. Alas, I had not read Dr. Drob's evaluation for the Defense. I had no idea how Dr. Drob had sabotaged me, attacking the integrity and quality of my witnesses. I presumed his evaluation was still in planning stages. So after my conversation with Dr. Kleinman, I made a special effort to alert Dr. Drob to my uncle's involvement in the case, and his success on my behalf.

By the time I hung up the phone, Dr. Drob was fully aware of the supreme caliber of my witnesses, like Eddie MacKechnie from the Lockerbie Trial. And he heard my sharp criticism of psychiatry for distracting my attorney from important tasks, such that family members felt compelled to assist me. I concluded that I was very lucky that my uncle had practiced law for 40 years at such a senior level.

Alas, one crucial mistake would cost me everything: I trusted the integrity of these men.

I imagined that once psychiatry was informed that highly credible sources had confirmed my story, their evaluations would have to acknowledge that truth. If Dr. Drob had questions, he could speak with Ted directly, who would vouch for it. If his evaluation was complete, wouldn't he have an ethical obligation to update his report, and correct mistakes in his conclusions?

Alas, I did not understand the practices of psychiatry in the courtroom.

Combating Psychiatry in the Courtroom

Learn from my mistakes, people, and remember these few tips. These suggestions might save your freedom and your reputation some day. If only somebody had warned me, I could have protected myself. These simple rules apply to everything from criminal cases to custody battles.

You have a right to protect yourself. There are ways that you can.

Rule Number 1: Never do a psych evaluation on an empty stomach, or if you're tired. If you're already at court, your attorney should get you a sandwich before starting. On the night of my arrest, I was so exhausted and hungry that I kept falling asleep. The jerk psychologist kept banging on the table to wake me up. Wisely, my attorney demanded that the evaluation get postponed until the following day, so I could get some food and a good night sleep. Still the psychiatrist tried to smear me, and that cost me.

Rule Number 2: Always take a tape recorder. Never attend any psych evaluation for any reason without a recording device. My case is littered with examples of psychotic shrinks inventing things. They'll tell you straight up– "It's my word against yours. Who do you think they're going to believe, you or me? I am a doctor."

You won't believe it, until it happens. Then it's too late to save yourself.

Get a tape recorder. I would pay a terrible price for not recording the first two psych interviews with Dr. Drob and Dr. Kleinman. Once I stopped relying on the professional ethics of psychiatry, my second attorney, Brian Shaughnessy would pound them again and again. They would shift from one falsification to another. We'd expose the nonsense, and they'd move right on to the next lie. And we'd blow them apart again. Because it was All On Tape, they couldn't lie so easily any more. Once I got it recorded, their appetite for lies dropped substantially.

Stick to your guns on this one. Any psychiatrist who fears tape recording a conversation is going to burn you in court. If they say no recording, you say no meeting. No Judge is going to stop you from protecting yourself by keeping a record of what you've said in a conversation.

It's okay if they want a copy of the tape. But you should not agree to hand over that tape to the Prosecution or spousal attorney in a custody case. You have protections under the 5th Amendment. Specify at the time of the interview that you object to handing it over to the Prosecution, and if necessary, you would argue that you have granted this interview under duress of a court order, not willfully. And you'll file an appeal to the higher courts to stop it.

Rule Number 3: In the interview, demand to see all documents used in the evaluation. Advise the Psychiatrist that you are prepared to challenge their conclusions. Be warned: Some of my private papers *got rewritten* by psychiatrists to sound more outlandish. Always double check. If you have supporting documents, like my 12 months of session notes from Family Health Services in Maryland, explain that in the recorded interview, and why you think it's important.

Rule Number 4: Never meet a Prosecution psychiatrist outside the presence of your attorney. Their job is to screw you. That's what they've been hired to do. Everything you say could end up with the Prosecution. If there are topics you want to avoid, you have every right to refuse to discuss them. Do not present your defense. By showing the

Prosecutor how you intend to rebut the charges, you are giving them leads for how to attack your defense in Court. Invoke your 5th Amendment rights under the Constitution, if necessary. Unless you're pleading guilty, refuse to answer questions regarding the events tied to your alleged crime. They will try desperately to compel or manipulate you to do so. You've got to be firm, but you must refuse.

If your attorney attends the interview, he can stop a psychotic shrink from asking the same questions twenty times, which they do. It means they don't like your answer, and they want you to say something different, so they can twist it.

Stay alert. The first answer is the right answer. After you've replied to the same question twice, you have a right to politely decline to answer it a third time.

The proper way to handle this is to say, "We've already discussed this issue. Do you have any other questions or issues to raise? Or shall we end the interview?"

Rule Number 5: If something's off topic, don't discuss it. The simple response is, "this matter has no relevance to the current legal situation. I'm not going to discuss it. If you're going to pursue that line of questions, then we're finished with the interview. Are there any other topics, or are you done?"

They're fishing. Don't give them anything. Later, they would try to attack my faith in God and my spirituality. Because we never discussed this in our interviews, they had nothing to work with. Mums the word of the day! Don't offer up anything. Keep your comments to the barest minimum. And remember that you don't have to answer their questions.

Rule Number 6: Never presume that a psychologist who appears reasonable and benevolent in discussing your life is actually rational in their own thinking. Psychology can attract individuals who are seriously disturbed in their own lives. A court-ordered psych evaluation is a power trip. They think they look important if they're screwing people.

It sounds unbelievable until it happens to you.

That's why you must get it on tape. Going into an evaluation without some form of recording device could be the greatest mistake that you ever make in your life.

It could destroy you.

Think I'm paranoid?

What happened next was the most frightening nightmare of my life. It would scare the hell out of anyone.

Clearly I was not paranoid enough.

CHAPTER 20:

INCOMPETENT
TO STAND TRIAL

Franz Kafka, Meet Susan Lindauer
—WelcomebacktoPottersville.com

There was no warning. Just a message from my attorney that Judge Mukasey wanted us in court the following week. Talkin claimed he had no idea what the meeting was for.

I was not stupid. I had not been called to court in 17 months, since shortly after my arrest as an "Iraqi Agent." Something was up. My uncle, Ted Lindauer, was concerned too, and immediately promised to fly out from California to attend court with me.[380] It was inconvenient, for sure. Ted was in the midst of relocating to Illinois to become Chief General Counsel for a corporate client. But both of us sensed something was not right. Not for the last time, Ted dropped everything to help me. I might have Andy Card and the White House against me, but I was not without loyal family support.

I'd been pestering Talkin for months about when we could see the psych evaluations. I'd met Dr. Sanford Drob in January for the defense. And I'd met Dr. Stuart Kleinman for the prosecution in April.

It was now September. According to Talkin, Dr. Kleinman had not submitted his evaluation. As for the court meeting, maybe Judge Mukasey was getting anxious about the psych reports, too, he suggested. Maybe he wanted to put the Prosecution's feet to the fire, and get things moving.

I still had no idea if Dr. Drob updated his evaluation after learning of my uncle's active participation in my case, and his success on my behalf. Dr. Drob could have asked to speak with Ted, if he liked. I had explained my uncle's law credentials. I did not offer Ted to Dr. Kleinman, representing the Prosecution. Still, I trusted that both men would have the integrity to acknowledge that high powered witnesses supported my defense. The FBI and the Prosecutor had verified it, too.

Pretending my story lacked independent validation would be perjury, at this stage. Certainly it would qualify as gross prosecutorial misconduct by the U.S. Attorney's office, and an ugly breach of ethics by psychiatrists, equivalent to professional malpractice.

As for Talkin's own incompetence, I'd have to rely on Dr. Drob's perceptiveness to read between the lines. Surely, an insightful psychiatrist would recognize that calling on family help for something as significant as witness interviews suggested my court-appointed lawyer was doing a less than stellar job. At the very least, Talkin required extra help. From the standpoint of my own competence, I had recognized my attorney's need, and answered it effectively. Score ten points for the defendant!

Unhappily, I was used to Talkin mumbling alibis for why something important had not got done. So when he demurred that he had no idea why Judge Mukasey was calling us to Court, I figured he really had no clue. I imagined the Judge could see that nothing was moving. I thought it was a good bet that Judge Mukasey wanted to force the question. So did I.

I fully expected Judge Mukasey to haul us into court and apply some arm-twisting for a plea bargain. In which case, Ted's appearance could be critical. If the Prosecutor, Edward O'Callaghan believed Talkin was the extent of my legal defense, I could get royally screwed. O'Callaghan had to know Talkin was dickering around. It was much better to have a tough attorney like Ted Lindauer on the scene to challenge the merits of the indictment, based on hard facts of alibis and witness corroboration for my story.

That's what should have happened.

Tragically, I had no concept of how psychiatry has become highly skilled at manipulating the courts. Or how defense attorneys, not functioning to the best of their abilities, are eager to help them do it.

Still, neither Uncle Ted nor I was prepared for what awaited us that September afternoon in the Southern District of New York.[381]

When Ted Lindauer and I arrived together at Talkin's office in the Wall Street District, Talkin swore a thousand times that Dr. Kleinman's evaluation was not yet available to the defense. He flat out denied having read it. Talkin told us that he expected it would be ready in time for our meeting with Judge Mukasey.[382]

Ted's appearance unnerved Talkin. He expected me to appear alone, without family guidance and support. By contrast, Ted projected legal muscle, aggressively filling the role that Talkin should have performed himself. Ted's companion, Ashala, was traveling with him in New York, so there was a third party witness to all of what occurred that afternoon.

Almost immediately, Talkin started whining. While insisting that he had absolutely no idea what Dr. Kleinman's report said, he admitted that if it was a negative finding, the prosecution would probably ask for some sort of psychiatric intervention to explore my competence further. But he claimed no advance knowledge of what action would be taken.

Ted Lindauer jumped on point: "That's bullshit! Susan's not incompetent. There's no way that's going to fly in court. We will fight it. She's not going anywhere until that happens."

Ted continued: "I've been reading the laws on psychiatry and incompetence. She's entitled to a hearing before the government takes action against her. She's entitled to call rebuttal witnesses, and show evidence that she's been wrongfully attacked. We intend to exercise her full rights under the law. Her family will not allow this to go unchallenged."[383]

Sam Talkin started to sweat. And whine.

"I don't have a single piece of evidence that proves her story's true."

Ted Lindauer turned to me: "Fire this man. Right now."

He turned back to Talkin. "I have spoken to her witnesses—something you should have done yourself. I had no trouble locating any of them.[384] They were all eager to help. She's got a great case, Sam. If you'd interviewed them yourself, you would know that. You could have pushed for dismissal months ago."

Then Talkin got scared. "I don't know really what the Prosecutor's going to do, because we don't have the report yet. I just think maybe, it could be, that the Prosecution would want her to go to some facility for a few months, just to see if she's okay. If something can be done to make her competent, we can go ahead with a trial like she wants."[385]

Ted jumped in again: "Are you fucking nuts? Do you understand what you're dealing with here! Andy Card and his cronies at the White House will never let her go, once she's locked up in some prison psych ward."

"Andy's my own flesh and blood. But I will tell you frankly, he's a hatchet man for the Bush family, going back decades. He worked for Daddy Bush years ago in Massachusetts. He was Deputy Chief of Staff at the White House and Secretary of Transportation to the first President Bush. That's before he went to work for George, Jr."

"And he didn't get those jobs by being a nice guy, Sam. Andy Card is vicious. And his friends are vicious. That's the only life in politics they know. Somebody like Susan would get screwed to the wall, if these people get a chance at her. They wouldn't give a damn that they have stomped somebody so small. Have you read the indictment?" Ted glared at Talkin. "Susan's in their way, because of what she knows about Iraq. If she goes into some psych prison, they are never going to let her out. She's going to be fucked!"

"I tell you, they are never going to release her! Never! She's going to get trapped there!"

Ted's words would prove prophetic. Mercifully, on that awful day I had no idea how accurate his prediction would be.

Talkin started whining: "I don't know what's going to happen yet. We don't have the report. We have to wait and see."

Ted stayed on point: "No matter what that report says, Mr. Talkin, I am telling you right now. We, her family, are demanding a hearing. We are going to challenge the reliability of those reports. We're not going to lay down, and let the Prosecution screw her."

I turned to Ted, grabbing for that hearing. "Ted, we've got a year's worth of session notes from Dr. Taddesseh at Family Health Services saying there's nothing wrong with me. No depression, no mood disturbances, no psychosis, no delusions. Nothing! Those are current records, which show that I've exhibited no psychiatric symptoms throughout my indictment. We'll get those papers to the Judge. And we'll get Dr. Taddesseh to testify at the hearing."

"There's nothing wrong with me. It's all political. And we can prove it!"

Ted was fierce and unwavering: "Mr. Talkin, you are going to tell the Judge that we demand a hearing."

"If you don't tell him, then I will."

"Susan, you must tell the Court that as of right now, I am acting as co-counsel in your case.[386] Then I can address the Court on your behalf. I want to make a short statement, Mr. Talkin. If you can't handle this case, then we're going to replace you. We'll do that today if we have to, as well."

Talkin sputtered some more about how it was too early to get excited.

It was a short walk to the Federal Courthouse on Pearl Street, but I felt like I was on death row walking to my execution. This was far worse than anything Uncle Ted and I had imagined. It was surreal that my public attorney would lay down the fight, so the Feds could trample us. Uncle Ted looked numb. He told me again that I must inform Judge Mukasey that Ted was acting as co-counsel, so he could address the court. He didn't trust my attorney, either.

Not for the last time, I thanked God for Uncle Ted. I tried to breathe, and stay calm in the face of this shocking turn of events.

A funny thing happened on the way to the courthouse. Talkin vanished. He told us he had to make a couple of phone calls to check on the status of the Kleinman report. I'm sure he wanted to warn the Prosecutor that I brought the cavalry with me, ready for battle. I was not traveling alone in New York, as they'd expected. Whatever worst scenario they'd plotted, they had a strong challenger in my Uncle Ted. He's more of a powerhouse in the courtroom than either of those two lightweights put together.

They would need some dirty tricks to pull off this judicial fiasco.

Once again, as fate would have it, Uncle Ted and I were not paranoid enough.

When Ted, Ashala and I entered the courthouse, we were ushered into the jury room. Talkin met us, and immediately tossed a copy of the missing evaluation by Dr. Kleinman on the table. It was open to the conclusions.[387]

My jaw dropped, as I read the following:

1. "(Ms. Lindauer) grossly overestimates the likelihood of her prevailing at trial. Criminal defendants commonly (grandiosely) overestimate their chances of winning at trial—and associatedly act self-defeatingly. Making poor choices and being (legally) incompetent are not synonymous."

"Ms. Lindauer's erroneous judgment, however, emanates from a reality distorting mental illness—which primarily determines how she assesses and approaches her legal case. She irrationally applies her superior intellectual ability and believes she very likely will win at trial—and that even if she does not, she will be heroically regarded for her purported "anti-terrorism" efforts, and consequently, not be sentenced according to the federal sentencing guidelines."

"She understands the concept of the (federal sentencing) guidelines, but because of her mental illness misjudges the reasoning that would likely be employed in applying them **to her.**" (sic)

2. "She distortedly evaluates the utility, including existence—or at least availability, of evidence she reports she intends to use in her defense."

"The evaluator does not offer an opinion regarding the far ranging covert Government relationships and authorizations she asserts."

"It is, however, reasonable to conclude that it is not reality-based for her to believe she will be able to present convincing evidence she was one of the—if not the Government's primary "anti-terrorism asset(s)", and that once jurors learn of all she declares she has done to safeguard the welfare of the United States, they will 1) indignantly regard her being prosecuted, 2) overlook evidence against her, and 3) probably acquit her. She largely contemplates a psychotically-based defense of justification, in which she projects onto jurors how she views herself and her role in the world."

3. "She irrationally rejects a potentially viable defense, i.e., the "insanity defense."

"The evaluator does not offer an opinion whether her mental state satisfies the criteria (for an insanity defense)—only that it is reasonable to consider employing it."

Thus concluded the psychiatric evaluation by Dr. Stuart Kleinman, Associate Clinical Professor of Psychiatry at the Columbia University College of Physicians and Surgeons.

Well, looking this over, it struck me that a burst of insanity had suddenly seized the Court proceedings. I was appalled.

Ted Lindauer couldn't believe what he was reading, either. He was aghast. In 40 years as an attorney, he told me that he'd never witnessed anything like this before.

In the jury room, he turned to me abruptly.

"Susan, you must fire Mr. Talkin immediately. Fire him, Susan! Or your defense is ruined!"[388]

"Tell the Judge that you're naming me co-Counsel, while you bring a new attorney on the case. Then I will stand forward and address the Court. I will tell the Judge that I have personally interviewed witnesses myself, and your story checks out. And we want a competency hearing to challenge the wrongful assumptions in these evaluations."[389]

"We'll have a list of witnesses to his clerk by close of business tomorrow. You got that, kid? You'll have to work fast to get it ready. I want that list tomorrow, do you understand?"

(I nodded, gratefully.)

"But you must fire Sam this moment," Uncle Ted pleaded with me, fiercely. "You cannot delay. You cannot hesitate. You've got to act right now."

I was in a state of shock. My whole life was flashing before my eyes. I'd worked in anti-terrorism for nine years covering Iraq and Libya.

Yet I was not competent to stand trial?

In my brain, I automatically did a reality check.

In August, 2001, I warned the Office of Counter-Terrorism about a 9/11 style of attack, involving airplane hijackings and a strike on the World Trade Center. As of 2004—before the 9/11 Commission reported its findings— the FBI had confirmed my 9/11 warning in its interview with Parke Godfrey.[390] I suspect that Dr. Fuisz and Paul Hoven also verified it.

But I was not competent to stand trial?

I gave advance warning about the bombing of the USS Cole, and the first attack on the World Trade Center in 1993. But I was not competent to stand trial?

I started negotiations for the Lockerbie Trial with Libyan diplomats in New York. But I was not competent to stand trial?

I held preliminary talks with Iraqi Ambassador Saeed Hasan and senior Iraqi diplomats for the return of weapons inspectors. But I was not competent to stand trial?

It had to be a joke. A sick and twisted joke.

Give me a subpoena, and I could prove my bona fides in any court in the land, with lightning speed. I would humiliate these idiots!

Psychiatry had tossed all external factors of reality out the window. These people were crazy! I mean, seriously disturbed!

Had Dr. Kleinman actually read the charges against me?

I was accused of acting as an "Iraqi Agent." Obviously I came into contact with Iraqi officials over several years. That's one thing the Justice Department and I agreed on. Given the nature of the charges, my rebuttal was wholly relevant, that I worked as a U.S. Asset recruited by American Intelligence, heavily supervised on various anti-terrorism projects.

As for my so-called "grandiosity," thinking I was one of a very few Assets covering Iraq, well golly! It was common knowledge that only a very limited number of Assets did cover Iraq before the War. Banner headlines in the "Washington Post" bemoaned CIA Director George Tenet's grief that he could "count on one hand the number of Agents inside Iraq."[391] Only three of us covered the Iraqi Embassy at the United Nations, and my co-defendants got recruited after 9/11. Before 9/11, in all likelihood, I was the *only* Asset covering the Embassy![392]

So if I was an Asset, I was one of the very few. That's a statistical fact.

And my work heavily engaged in anti-terrorism. That was no joke, either.

Would a New York Jury appreciate that I'd been up to my eyeballs securing Iraq's cooperation with the 9/11 investigation?[393] Would they be impressed that I got the FBI an invitation to send a Task Force into Baghdad? Or that I got Iraqi officials to agree to hand over financial records on Al Qaeda leaders? Or that I worked to secure evidence of a Middle Eastern link to the Oklahoma City bombing and the first World Trade Center attack in 1993? Given the fruits of my labor, might New Yorkers express disgust that the Justice Department sought to punish me for allegedly eating a couple of cheese burgers?[394]

Would a New York jury understand that work was done on their behalf? I'd say it was a good bet. They'd probably ask some hard questions about the 9/11 investigation, too!

Ah, but could I prove my claims through independent witness testimony? That was the clincher. The answer was absolutely yes!

Flipping through Dr. Drob's evaluation on the table next to Dr. Kleinman's, I saw quickly that it had *not* been updated after my exuberant phone call, crowing with victory about Uncle Ted's success on my behalf. My heart dropped.

Dr. Drob's evaluation scorned my confidence in the quality of my witnesses, as evidence of my "mental impairment." My focus on witnesses and leads "impeded the preparation of a viable defense," and had the effect of making me "incompetent to stand trial."[395]

His attack astonished me. This was like the Twilight Zone.

My witness list included former Congressional staffers, journalists, and university faculty.

My star witness would be Scottish solicitor Eddie MacKechnie, who won acquittal for his Libyan client at the Lockerbie Trial. That was a world class terrorism case at The Hague, and MacKechnie won! He excelled in the Scottish Courts on par with Vincent Bugliosi in America, for the sheer power of his legal genius. MacKechnie would impress the Court alright. I had no doubts on that score. His generous support for my cause, and his willingness to travel to New York at his own expense, documented in emails, stood as remarkable testament to my credibility within my own circle of Middle East and international contacts.[396]

It was a challenging case, but I could win. Certainly I had no reason to throw it.

I was dumb-struck. Dr. Drob knew all of this. Certainly Talkin's investigator had fallen down on the job. But my uncle jumped into the breach and saved the day. My witnesses were eager to help, and my story had been amply corroborated months before[397]— just not by Talkin, as I explained to Dr. Drob.

Knowing all of that, Dr. Drob rendered conclusions in his evaluation that could only mislead the Court in its understanding of the strength of my authenticity. That struck me as grossly unethical and dishonest.

I had a strong defense alright. Nobody at CIA or the Justice Department had to worry for little old me.

Really, their concern touched my heart!

The Prosecutor, O'Callaghan, might have some difficulties, however. He'd have to explain why I was indicted for eating cheeseburgers in New York City during the 9/11 investigation. He'd have to explain why supporting democracy in Iraq constituted a major felony. Or why an Asset should face indictment for recruiting a senior Iraqi official to help the FBI identify foreign terrorists playing hide and seek with Iraqi Intelligence. That was phenomenally valuable to any serious anti-terrorism effort in Iraq. It was platinum value. And the Justice Department indicted me for it! Did the FBI understand anything at all about intelligence work? (Maybe not.)

As for this nonsense about Sentencing Guidelines, the Supreme Court had struck down the compulsory nature of the federal guidelines in December 2004, making them advisory only. If a jury did manage to convict me of eating a cheeseburger, the nature of the action was so innocuous— sharing a lunch that cost $15 in New York City— it would be reasonable to expect a Judge to adjust his sentencing, accordingly. Even if they got a conviction, my actions would doubtfully send me up the river for 10 years.

Under the circumstances, my choice of legal strategy and my expectation of the consequences of a conviction—if it occurred at all— struck me as entirely "rational" and "reasonable."

On such a black day, I had to smirk that after 10 hours with me, Dr. Kleinman admitted he "could not offer an opinion if (my) mental state would qualify for an insanity defense."

I rolled my eyes. Obviously there was no grounds for an insanity defense. The Justice Department wanted me to use some sort of psych defense, regardless of better options. It would be like falling on my sword to spare the White House and Congress, who had invented a wild story about the failure of my Pre-War Intelligence activities and 9/11. The whole world could see that Republicans were very fond of that story.

That's a bloody stupid argument for making bad legal decisions, however. My prosecutor, O'Callaghan, was a fool indeed, if he thought I would allow him to choose my defense.

My problem was not poor legal strategy, but a mediocre court-appointed attorney not playing straight with the Judge. Talkin did not have 40 years in the law, like Ted Lindauer. He was over-worked and under-paid. A trial required a lot more effort than he could put into the case. This was an easy way out.

Psychiatry was corrupt enough to oblige him.

I was horrified. This was like a John Grisham novel.

"Fire him, Susan!" Ted Lindauer pulled me out of my shock, back to the moment. We had to act right away. I could not afford a moment of hesitation. We had to stay focused.

"Fire Talkin this moment, and I will request a hearing. That's the law. We're going to hold the Feds to it."[398]

From my shocked consciousness, I heard Talkin start to speak, kind of apologetic, kind of whining.

"Well, see, there's going to be kind of a problem about having a competency hearing. You know? See O'Callaghan (the federal prosecutor) wants her to go for a psych evaluation at this place called Carswell. It's not really a hospital. It's not a prison. Yeah, I guess it's a prison. No, not really."

"She just has to go there for four months. They'll decide whether she's competent to stand trial. Or what's going on. Then we can decide what to do next. If she's not competent, they'll probably just drop the charges. It's just for four months—" Talkin whined. [399]

Clearly, he'd known all along what the Justice Department was going to hit us with.

My jaw was suspended open.

We had just gone from John Grisham straight to Franz Kafka.

"Four months?" Ted was appalled. "Are you serious? We don't agree to that! We don't care what the Prosecutor wants. That's not a deal that Susan wants to accept. Do you, Susan!?"

I shook my head, aghast.

"I have researched this law, Mr. Talkin. There's a fail safe that protects her from incarceration until there's a hearing. We intend to use it. We don't agree to any incarceration until we have a chance to challenge these reports."[400]

Uncle Ted was ferocious. Even in an ambush, he stayed on point.

"I can see holes all the way through these evaluations. I can straighten out some of this when I speak to the Judge this afternoon. I'm going to tell Mukasey I verified her story myself, Sam. We can address the rest of it at the hearing."

I learned that day that Ted Lindauer is a damn fine attorney, who does not crack under pressure. Throw him a poisoned brief, if you will. He will fight for his clients to the death. He is immediately ready, and repositioning himself to thwart any unexpected challenge. It was very impressive that afternoon, trust me.

Ted turned back to me, fierce.

"Fire him, Susan!" He pleaded with me, in deadly earnest. "Fire him now!"

I could only nod. I couldn't even speak. I felt numb and disoriented, in a state of horror.

My emotional shock was about to take a deep turn for the worst.

Bowing out of the room, Sam Talkin returned moments later with Judge Mukasey's senior law clerk. She had a message for us.[401]

She spoke crisp and staccato, as if addressing a full court room, instead of speaking to us privately in the jury room.

"We understand that you're thinking of replacing Mr. Talkin, so that Ms. Lindauer can demand a hearing on this matter. Judge Mukasey is aware of this. We want to make clear that if Ms. Lindauer moves to do that today, she will be seized immediately and taken to prison. As of today, she will forfeit her bail permanently— until the end of the case."

"If she agrees to forego the hearing until after completing a four month psychiatric evaluation in prison, she will be allowed THREE days to get her affairs in order before surrendering to prison on MONDAY MORNING."

It was now Thursday at about 4 pm.

On the jury room wall, "**EXTREME PREJUDICE**" was scrawled in blood graffiti behind Judge Mukasey's clerk.

Can anyone imagine such a nightmare! There I was, falsely condemned in the Drob evaluation, which impugned the strength and integrity of my witnesses. The Kleinman report proclaimed me incompetent, on the basis of declaring my innocence. And now I was denied my fundamental rights to challenge such wild inaccuracies in a simple pre-trial evidentiary hearing, just in case, maybe, I was telling the truth.

Instead, I would go straight to prison without a guilty plea or any sort of hearing. Andy Card and Colin Powell would be spared the embarrassment of facing me at trial. The stage would be cleared for Republican leaders to continue inventing outrageous stories about 9/11 and Pre-War Intelligence, without challenge. They could boast of their "outstanding leadership in anti-terrorism!" Oh yes, I especially loved their oaths of loyalty and devotion to Assets like me, hands on heart—sworn on CNN and the Fox News Channel. Campaign season made me feel so good! The Presidential Debates were especially fun, listening to John McCain!

My story shattered those myths irrevocably! The Democrats were just as bad about reinventing the truth about Pre-War Intelligence. But only the Republicans arrested Assets to stop us from exposing their deceptions. My co-defendants, both Assets like me, spent 18 months in prison before getting deported. And now I was declared "incompetent" and thrown in prison without a trial, too!

Psychiatry sold out its ethics to help them, but this incompetence finding was a farce. Seriously, if I'm incompetent, it's time to shut down the entire United States Court system. We probably need to shut down the Intelligence Community as well!

It was a game plan straight out of the Cold War, a Soviet-style of attack on a political dissident, marshaling corrupt services of psychiatry to succeed. Politicians hated the reality of Iraq. They couldn't admit it was "delusional" to pretend their War policy was successful. I must be "delusional" for calling it a disaster. Obviously my thinking had to be corrected— not theirs.

If you ask me, they exhibited a true "group psychosis."

Stunned and now fully disoriented, Uncle Ted and I shuffled into Court to face Judge Mukasey. The room was packed with U.S. Marshals. Ted whispered that he'd never seen so many marshals in one courtroom at a time, not for the most violent criminal offenders.[402]

We were slightly reassured when Judge Mukasey appeared somewhat dubious of the evaluations himself. He assured us that he did not automatically give credence to what psychiatrists said about any defendant. (I tell you, my Judge was incredibly smart!)

Judge Mukasey said something to the effect of, "just because they've said these things about Ms. Lindauer, doesn't make it true. But I am willing to allow you to pursue it, Mr. Talkin."

In exchange for my acquiescence, he relented slightly on the timing of my incarceration. If I would agree to a voluntary surrender, he would give me 10 days to get my affairs in order – not three days, as the Clerk originally told us. Ten days.[403]

Ted Lindauer gave me the nod that I should stay on the Judge's positive side as long as possible. It might not last very long.

Really though, I had little choice. I had a home mortgage and pets. It would be a lot to lose if I couldn't work out a support strategy for coping while I was gone. Having received no advance warning of the Justice Department's attack, my household was not prepared for a prison surrender, of all things. This way I would have only 10 days to make arrangements. I joked with friends that it's a good thing I'm competent to run my own affairs, otherwise I could never have pulled everything together on such short notice.

It could hardly be termed "consensual," however. I adamantly refused to forfeit my rights to a trial or a competence hearing. Judge Mukasey was very much aware of that.

Still I gasped, more deeply shocked than moments before, when O'Callaghan stood up to announce where the Bureau of Prisons was sending me.

My prison psych evaluation would be handled at Carswell Prison, located inside Carswell Air Force Base outside Fort Worth, Texas.

Not only would I be denied a trial— to punish me for believing in my innocence—I would go straight to a women's prison inside a Texas military base, as an accused "Iraqi Agent" to determine "if I could become competent in the future."

Talkin put up no objections to this de facto plea bargain—which he cut on my behalf, without my knowledge and over my strongest objections.

As for my statutory rights to a competency hearing, I could still have it—after I served my prison sentence.[404]

To be fair, a Judge who regularly sentences defendants to five, ten, twenty years in federal prison looks on a four month sentence as a slap on the wrist. And honestly, it is. It's the best sentence any defendant could hope for in the federal system. The women I met at Carswell used to shake their heads, longingly, at my promise of a four month discharge. From the Judge's perspective, this might have been very sensible. Afterwards, the case could go away. If unpleasant for me, it would be short-lived. And it would get us all out of his courtroom.

Still, prison's prison. No defendant should ever get shipped off to a prison cell without a trial or a guilty plea. Nobody. Ever.

My heart sighs to recall it, even today.

All of that explains how on September 23, 2005, Judge Mukasey ruled that I would be detained at Carswell Prison for a maximum of 120 days— four months and no longer, according to restrictions laid out in federal law.[405]

I would self-surrender to Carswell Prison by twelve noon, on October 3, 2005.

On February 3, 2006, Carswell would have to release me.

After the court meeting, Judge Mukasey's law clerk assured Uncle Ted that the Court expected the prison evaluation to finish more rapidly. Most likely, I would be home within 60 days, the normal timeframe for these sorts of evaluations. That would be after Thanksgiving, but in plenty of time for the Christmas holidays. That gave us reason for hope.[406]

INCOMPETENT TO STAND TRIAL

Those crazy psychiatrists hadn't won a real victory yet. Carswell had to uphold a finding of incompetence to get it ratified. Prisons don't like doing that without a very good reason. Judge Mukasey expected Carswell to throw it back.

Now, it's a risky thing for defendants to second guess their judges' thinking— though nobody can resist. In my gut, I believe the Patriot Act had a strong influence on what happened that day.

I'm convinced a straight arrow like Judge Mukasey hated the components of that law, which strips away so many constitutional protections, and mucks up the U.S. court system and due process. Of course I could be wrong. But for months before that dreadful September day, Judge Mukasey had options to keep my case on the fast track, which he chose not to enforce. He could have rejected the finding of incompetence outright, or granted my request for a hearing immediately. He could have hauled us into court months earlier to set a trial date.

Instead, he gave my Defense every chance to figure a way out of this mine field. He gave the Defense latitude to work out an end-game, which was extremely generous of him, in the larger scheme of things. With a more senior, ferociously dedicated attorney like Ted Lindauer representing me, my Defense would have had more options. With Brian Shaughnessy, my outstanding attorney after Carswell, who regularly swims with the sharks in the most complicated international cases, we would have enjoyed vastly more options still. Shaughnessy had a shot at overturning the Patriot Act, and getting it invalidated. He's that good.

It would have been a different ball game, for sure. But like Judge Mukasey, both Shaughnessy and Ted Lindauer had 40 years in the law.

On September 23, 2005, I had a public attorney running scared from his own mistakes, and his inability to address the complexities of my case.

And I had no money to replace him. I was fucked.

Those crazy shrinks saw nothing about my nature, however. All of us face tragedy of some kind. A survivor knows that there's a moment of clarity, when you see what's coming at you, and you make a conscious decision—You will face this storm without breaking. You will survive this situation. You will bend far. You might stoop low. But you will get through it—whole— on the other side. Because there is no other possibility for you. That is your spiritual truth. And that becomes your reality.

I admit that I had a good cry on my way home to Maryland that night. A State Trooper stopped me for a speeding violation on I-95, and let me go without a ticket.

By the time I hit Takoma Park, I was resolved to endure. I had 10 short days to get my affairs in order. I was thunder struck, but my grief would have to wait.

I had to pack up all of my personal possessions in my house.

I had to arrange for the payment of my mortgage and utilities.

I had to break the news to friends, who shared my disappointment that I'd lost my chance for a trial.

And I had to arrange for the care of my two dachshunds and two cats. My beloved friend, Karin Anderson, the angel of animal protection in Takoma Park, promptly agreed to board my precious dachsies, Raqi Bear and Mahji Bear at her home. She promised to take them to play in our yard once in awhile. My cats would stay at my house, including 19 year old Midnight, who waited faithfully by the front gate every afternoon for my return, as the months passed.

Karin would find renters to live in the house and cover the bills, while I was gone. My dear friend and companion, JB Fields would stay in the house, too, and watch over Midnight and Lou Lou cat. As necessity required, Karin would cough up a fair amount of her own cash to hold my household together.

Several small miracles would occur in Takoma Park in my absence, thanks to this dear lady.

Activists understand the concept of duct tape to fix everything from broken pipes to an empty wallet. We persevere. Whatever comes, we take. We go on whistling in the dark.

We don't fall apart.

Oh yes, they found a fighter when they confronted me.

Oh, but you still think I'm paranoid?

Not nearly enough, friend. Not nearly enough.

On September 23, 2005, my nightmare of "extreme prejudice" was just beginning.

CHAPTER 21:

THE BRIGHT SECRET

There are more things in heaven and earth, Horatio,
Than are dreamt of in your philosophy
–Shakespeare, Hamlet"

On the drive back to Maryland that unhappy September night, I thought about the two things that psychiatry hated about me. I confess I was surprised by the depth of that hatred, and the smoldering bitterness of it. Until this point, I'd never been hated like that in my life.

It was illuminating, to say the least.

Looking over their evaluations, it appeared that Dr. Drob and Dr. Kleinman hated my spirituality. And they hated my strength and motivation as a woman. They wanted me to grovel with apologies for it, and I showed no inclination to do so. That angered them. Perhaps it hurt their pride. I'm not sure I was worthy of their attack, but I'm content that I never recanted.

Because you see, I have a deep spiritual life, which is constant for me and private. I'm not evangelical, needing to convert others to my way of thinking. I'm not discouraged by anyone else's lack of faith. I'm not even terribly religious, perhaps the greatest irony of all.

However faith and spirituality happen to run deep in my soul.

So as long I'm confessing everything else, I confess this freely, too:

I believe in God.

I believe in angels.

I believe in grace.

I believe in prophecy that comes from ancient times, and comes still to those who open our hearts to listen.

Almost nothing astonished me so much as the insults I suffered for the private expression of my faith during my legal ordeal. Interestingly, the men who attacked me had strong connections to the Republican Party, which formally espouses support for religious viewpoints.

My own prosecutor, Edward O'Callaghan left the Justice Department in July, 2008 to work for the Presidential Campaign of John McCain and Sarah Palin. He was assigned to Sarah Palin's top campaign staff in Alaska, handling "Troopergate."[407]

Yet in the hypocrisy of the moment, I was subjected to the most bitter and vicious attacks for quietly practicing my faith more moderately than Sarah Palin herself.

O'Callaghan lampooned the focus on spirituality in my life, in federal court of all places, where citizens should be protected from such attacks. That kind of hypocrisy by a Republican operative should disturb all Americans, regardless of political stripe or personal religious beliefs. It provides damning evidence that the GOP manipulates religious faith for the sake of political advancement, while privately holding spirituality in the greatest contempt. I have nicknamed it "Campaign Christianity." It's a false front to get votes and money. There's no spirituality backing it up. It exploits religion, and it should be offensive to anybody who really believes in God.

That said, I freely declare that as part of my work in anti-terrorism, I invoked my spirituality in establishing contacts with Arab diplomats, in keeping with my anti-war philosophy.

For me, it was important for proving society doesn't have to rely on threats of violence to accomplish these goals. And the Arabs responded graciously to my communications.

They recognized that my opposition to violence had a spiritual motivation, and our relationships evolved more closely as a result.

I hold strong beliefs that terrorism manifests from intense spiritual pain that gives rise to violence. And I strongly believe that you can not oppose violence without love. You can not fight evil with evil. You need love to diffuse hatred, and mercy to diffuse intolerance. And yes, for me, that includes a mindfulness of God.

Throughout the 1990s, those beliefs guided my actions in all of my contacts with Libya and Iraq. And I have never recanted. Surely I have a right to invoke a spiritual dynamic in my own life to protect myself from absorbing the violence around me.

My spiritual viewpoints are uniquely my own. Still, it explains why I faced open hostility in pro-war circles, which resented acknowledging what I accomplished through tactics of non-violence. I wanted to prove that military aggression could be avoided. I wanted to show that my anti-war approach to the Arabs could achieve cooperation in multiple areas, while reducing the stress and tensions that spill over into violence.

It doesn't take a rocket scientist to see that my approach has fallen out of favor. I have faced severe criticism, even scorn, by those who don't understand what I was doing.

Nevertheless, I would argue that my approach accomplished a lot of good. I'm content to know that, even if I'm alone in thinking it today, because of the change in politics.

In my defense, I was always guided by these principles, throughout my engagement with Libya and Iraq. And my handlers, Hoven and Dr. Fuisz were fully knowledgeable of that influence. After my advance warning about the 1993 attack on the World Trade Center, Dr. Fuisz and Hoven supervised me closely. We met weekly for debriefings until

2002. All together, I met approximately 700 to 800 times with both men. In addition, from May, 1995 onwards I met 150 times with diplomats from Libya. And from August, 1996 onwards, I met 150 times with Iraq. I also covered Egypt, Syria/Hezbollah, Yemen and Malaysia.

That speaks for itself. My approach was highly successful, or neither the Americans nor the Arabs would have engaged with me for so many years. Either side could have shut off contact.

Bottom line—my approach succeeded.

Libya's former Ambassador to the United Nations, Issa Babaa once paid me a supreme compliment, saying that "if everyone approached anti-terrorism like you, Susan, all of the Arab countries would want to help America."

Most people aren't in the mood to respect Islam after 9/11. However, as somebody who has done this work successfully for many years, I would argue that respect for all faith creates a bridge between cultures, and establishes a common system of values, which transcend our cultural differences. By relying on those common values, Islamic governments can become allies and partners for the greater good, in solving problems through non-violence.

That's not popular today. But as our governments search for new ways to address conflict, it's worthwhile to understand what kind of strategies achieved so much good in the past. I believe that's hopeful for the future. I believe this approach could work effectively again. At least it's worth trying.

I am not alone in believing that a spiritual life heals more injuries to the soul than focusing on negative experiences and pain.

Nevertheless, psychiatry openly despised me for trusting God to stay with me through my ordeal. They wanted me to doubt. They scorned my faith that God cares what happens to someone so tiny and insignificant as me. The evaluations by Dr. Drob and Dr. Kleinman dripped with sarcasm, using ridicule to discourage me from vocalizing my faith.

Did I think I was big enough for God to love? (No, I thought I was small enough for God to love.) I thought that I too could be worthy of receiving the bountiful love of the universe, the force of God, the Unnamable. And I was grateful for that love.

And no, never on my worst days of my ordeal did I believe that God stood apart from me, or somehow betrayed me.

I never recanted my faith. I was never tempted to abandon my beliefs to escape the criticism that psychiatry tried to beat me with. I never allowed their attacks to trick me into believing that God had abandoned me, or that God had somehow failed to save me from their abuse. Throughout this ordeal, I felt deeply that God never left my side. I believed God was my witness.

There's a true story that you can choose to believe, or not.

The weekend before my arrest, I had no idea that my life was about to capsize irrevocably, almost immediately. I awoke one morning and experienced a genuine state of grace. It lasted for hours. It's the kind of thing that you hope for if you have any kind of spiritual life. It's sort of a nirvana thing, if you're Buddhist. It's an epiphany, if you're Christian. The Arabs call it "seeing with an open heart." It's a mystery, if you appreciate mysticism, as I do. When it came upon me, I felt a deep sense of connectedness to that greater force of creation and beauty in the world, a synchronicity that comes from active mindfulness. It was remarkable and distinctive. I would describe it as a gentle and pervasive force that washed over me, with the purest cleansing love.

Before my troubles started, it gave me redemption. And wholeness. And love.

In short, it blessed me with grace.

I had no idea that a grand jury was closing its debate over my indictment in New York City. I had no idea that I was days from getting arrested for treason on the Patriot Act.

I was only mindful that something so beautiful, a force that I call God, was leaning to embrace me, and lift me up. And it was pure beauty and love—whether anyone believes in God or not. I remember thinking that people suffer through all sorts of ordeals and indignities. (I had no idea what was coming at me!) And all of us wait for just one moment like this. A moment of pure mercy and abiding love. And it puts perspective on everything else, including what's bad. It washes all of your pain away. And it cleanses your soul with unconditional love.

This deep feeling of love—and grace, that's what it was—came out of nowhere. There was no external explanation that I could see. Nothing special happened that morning to invite it to me. It was suddenly there. And it washed over me for hours. I remember thanking God, or the universe, whatever you want to call that greater essence that we belong to, for all my blessings, though my life had been incredibly difficult recently. I thanked God for staying with me.

I wanted to celebrate that moment of grace. So I went out to a nursery, and bought a tree to plant in my front yard. A beautiful Japanese weeping cherry tree with tiny white blossoms that peak in the spring-time. I call it my "peace tree."

Five days later, I got arrested for treason on the Patriot Act.

And yes, I think there's a force of God or something phenomenal out there. And I think it knew. I believe it saw the forces converging on me, and it reached down to comfort me. And it came to me before my troubles. And it gave me love. And it told me that everything was going to be alright. It saw my confusion before I ever experienced it, and it eased my sense of betrayal. And it took away my shame.

I believe that. In my heart, I am sure of it.

CHAPTER 22:

CARSWELL PRISON

With what iron, what blood, what fire are we made
Though we seem pure mist and they stone us,
and say that we walk with our heads in the clouds.
How we pass our days and nights, God only knows
–Odysseus Elytis, Nobel Poet Laureate,
on the Greek Resistance to Fascism

I will always remember Carswell as my own private Guantanamo.

As an accused "Iraqi agent," I was as close to an enemy-non combatant as you could get. Locked up in prison on a Texas military base had to be the last place on earth I wanted to be, while U.S. soldiers were losing a War that I had loudly criticized.

Yet there I was, handcuffed to enter the prison gates at Carswell Air Force Base, north of Fort Worth, Texas.

There would be a reckoning for this. Some things are unforgivable in a democracy, and this would be right at the top of that list.

A Franciscan friend urged me to brace for prison as a sort of "monastic experience." He urged me to stay calm and reflective. I could choose my own thoughts, even if I could not choose my surroundings. It was excellent advice, and that's how I resolved to live. His idea worked well for the first few months of my incarceration, until events turned ugly.

Even so, I was plenty shocked when the full tide of prison life crashed over me.

The prison is located inside Carswell Air Force Base. The main buildings are the site of the former hospital where President John F. Kennedy died after the shooting in Dallas.

It's not without irony that some of the more sophisticated inmates observed that we walked in the footsteps of Jackie Kennedy.

My first vision of Carswell was gray concrete blocs towering over a flat, barren landscape, protected by two walls of 20 foot razor wire fence. There was no shade, just vast concrete buildings, and a brief covered walkway to the Administrative headquarters and visitor center.

The land was grassy green inside the perimeter fence, and the sky, a vivid blue. Beyond the double razor wire fences, a few oak trees created a lush green buffer to the military base beyond. But otherwise the land had no distinction.

If that's all you ever saw of Texas, you would never want to go back.

Why the rush, I asked myself, as I waited through the indignity of strip searches and inmate processing.

It was October 3, 2005. I'd been under indictment since March 2004, without a single court appearance—not one. All of a sudden, after 19 months on bail the Justice Department urgently required that I surrender to prison within 10 days.

What was going on that made it so critical to get me out of the way? There had to be some reason. I was removed because something was happening. What was it? I would have many days to ponder that question, for sure.

"Why do you think they've declared you incompetent?" One of the prison psychologists demanded skeptically, during my in-take interview. "Inmates who have been declared incompetent are generally so mentally crippled that they can't control their functioning. They suffer non-stop hallucinations or schizophrenia, for example. You're nothing like that. We can see already that what they wrote in these evaluations bears no resemblance to you."

"Maybe it's because of post-traumatic stress from my work in anti-terrorism?" I suggested, not sure what to say in this first conversation, without going into all the politics of my case.

"Post traumatic stress would rarely qualify for incompetence." The prison psychologist shook his head. "Otherwise most prisoners in the system would be exempt from prosecution."

He looked at me hard. "How would you describe your attorney's handling of this case?"

He nailed it, but I hesitated over how much to admit about my attorney's failings. If I told the prison psychologist, he would tell the Prosecutor. That could not be good.

"Sir, you raise an excellent point," I replied, distinctly and slowly.

"That's what I thought," he nodded. "Sometimes attorneys get overwhelmed by complicated cases like yours. Especially public attorneys who tend to be overworked in their case loads. They see this as an easy way out." He said, reading my reticence with a high degree of perceptiveness. "That doesn't mean we're going to accept it, you understand."

I nodded. Inwardly, I groaned. Thanks to my idiot attorney, I was going to serve a prison sentence, without a plea bargain. Then I'd have to start back at square one and go to trial, probably with a new attorney, who'd require private financing. The only thing to recommend this strategy was if the case could go away after Carswell, and I could go on with my life without a conviction on my record. That was the trade off for four months in prison. It looked doubtful.

"Judge Mukasey said the evaluation must be completed by February 3rd, but it might finish sooner." I pressed him. At least I had an exit date.

"Oh it won't take that long." He shook his head. "I just don't understand why you're here. I'll have to make some calls about this."

I understood. Anybody could see it was obscene to pretend I'm "incompetent," though I understood the desire to bastardize me. Unforgivably, this psychiatric "diagnosis" lined up beautifully with false claims on Capitol Hill about intelligence failures before the War. It communicated what Congress wanted Americans to think about pre-war intelligence— that "incompetent Assets" shouldered the blame for bad decision making. Assets failed to perform— not elected leaders. Since I was an Asset, I must be incompetent, too. Psychiatry accommodated Washington's agenda with unforgivably corrupt and unethical evaluations.

You had to hand it to Republican leaders at the Justice Department, however. This brute force attack was a masterful strategy to hide the truth about Iraq and our advance warning about 9/11. First, the false indictment gagged me from discussing what I had done before the War, which contradicted everything Americans had been told about 9/11 and Pre-War Intelligence. Then the finding of incompetence killed my reputation as an Asset. Denying me a trial stopped me from gaining a forum in a court of law to expose the corruption on Capitol Hill.

Finally, burying me in prison on Carswell Air Force Base outside of Fort Worth, Texas gave the White House free reign to rewrite the history books without challenge. Even if I was stoic enough to speak out afterwards, in the eyes of many, my reputation and credibility would be destroyed. Nobody would listen. I would be alone.

Oh yeah, I understood alright.

Why the rush, though? That nagged at me. Why, indeed?

When I arrived at Carswell, the prison was so over-crowded that a batch of us new arrivals, about eight of us, had to go to the punishment block, called the SHU, or solitary housing unit.

That's where I got locked up for my first two weeks at Carswell. They had no other beds.

Actually solitary confinement would have significantly improved my living conditions. The cell was a standard eight by ten feet. Crammed into that tiny space, four of us inmates slept on two metal bunk beds. Our few possessions, including a change of prison clothes, got stored in small bins tucked under the bottom bunks. There was an open toilet in the corner, without a lid or proper seat. Toilet paper got rationed between the four of us.

Whoever got the idea that federal prisons are country club havens for pampered inmates has obviously spent no time in either facility.

Sitting on the cold concrete floor, leaning against one bunk, I could stretch my legs and hit the other bunk with my feet. I got a top bunk, and most of the day I had to stay there—crouched on the bed 22 + hours daily.

Twice a week, each of us got to leave the cell for showers. Since it was the punishment block, we had to be handcuffed through a slot in the door any time we left our cell. Even in a medical emergency, inmates on the SHU had to get handcuffed before staff could enter a cell, such as when a cellmate went into diabetic shock early one morning at 4 a.m.

We looked forward to showers all week, so that we could stand up for 45 minutes at a time, getting the cramps out of our legs. Inside the shower room, we had to strip for a visual inspection before we climbed into the shower. After the shower, we had to stay stripped for a visual inspection before dressing to return to our cell.

Often on shower days, guards allowed us to wait our turn inside a small exercise room, with a big bright mural painted on the wall. That mural probably saved the sanity of more inmates in the SHU than all the psychological counseling at Carswell combined.

Outside prison, there's a presumption that inmates have a basic right to one hour of exercise every day, even in a maximum security setting, like the SHU. In fact, all of us on the SHU got one hour outside every week or 10 days, locked inside a fenced yard with a basketball hoop, surrounded by a sky high fence. What passed for that one hour of recreation included the time necessary to shackle us all, and stand us in line. And the time to march us out to the prison yard. Just as we relaxed enough to enjoy the sunshine, it would be time to get handcuffed and marched back to the SHU. When all that time got accounted for, we probably spent 30 minutes outside about every 10 days.

Some of these women got locked up on the SHU for months at a time. Nobody at Carswell started off crazy. But I did meet several women at Carswell, who had been punished on the SHU for such long periods that I questioned if they might be broken. The pattern of their detention was sadistic, their offenses so minor as to warrant a more measured response. Clearly the guards wanted to damage their souls. I saw women whimpering and shattered. Trust me when I say the SHU could be a form of torture, especially without access to recreation or daylight.

The cell was extremely uncomfortable. The bunks stood away from the walls, far enough that inmates could not enjoy such small comfort as resting our backs against a hard wall surface.

We had thin foam rubber pads for a mattress and one thin blanket. Most of the women slept all day, so mostly the lights stayed off during the daytime. To stay occupied, I would read trashy books from the library cart, or write letters home to friends. During the daylight, I would hunker under the one narrow window of our cell to catch the sunlight.

I confess that in those first days I felt too intimidated to lobby for keeping the lights on. My bunk mates had spent a few more nights at Carswell than me. I'd never spent a night in county lock-up, let alone federal prison.

My first week at Carswell even small talk with these women scared the hell out of me.

One pretty Latina inmate looked so young and innocent in our tiny SHU cell. What crime could she possibly have committed, I wondered? Ah, but appearances can be deceiving in prison. At 18 years old, she got hit with a 20 year sentence, which sounded dreadful. In late night conversations, she admitted hanging out with a Los Angeles street gang back home, driving around with guns and drugs in a car. And oh yeah, one of the guys got high on crack and started firing a gun. (Sounded like a drive-by shooting to me, but I didn't push it.) Hey, that happens, right? Somebody smokes a little cocaine and starts acting crazy, shooting out of the backseat. Next thing you've all got 20 years in prison! What a bummer!

Another inmate I liked very much had tattoos of two tears by one eye. Prison staff kept stopping by our cell to ask her about those tattoos. One of the wardens visited the SHU specially to see her. It appeared the guards really appreciated the artwork!

Very sweetly she explained that in prison, tattooed tears usually indicate how many persons an inmate has killed. And she had two tears! She winked at me with a big smile. Most prisoners only have one! Registering my immediate shock, my cellmate swore that she hadn't murdered anybody! Girlfriend just liked the look!

Yeah, so did I.

And what are you in for? They leaned close to hear.

Oh, I'm in for treason! Because I opposed the Iraqi war. But really they think I ate a cheeseburger.

I wasn't about to ask these women to keep the lights on, if they wanted to sleep. I would read in darkness rather than poke an argument in that cell. I imagined I was totally at their mercy. Once I got my bearings, I discovered that I had nothing to fear from (most of) these ladies. Most of us wanted to "do our time" as quietly as possibly, and avoid the stress of unnecessary confrontations. Prison staff at Carswell would be more dangerous to my future. My fellow inmates would help me through it, despite their own traumatic pain.

One man occupied a lot of my thoughts, locked up in that dark SHU cell, where prisoners mostly couldn't tell if it was day or night outside.

That man was former Secretary of State Colin Powell, retired head of the Joint Chiefs of Staff of the U.S. military. Three weeks before my prison surrender, Secretary Powell broadcast a major television interview with Barbara Walters on "20/20" on September 8, 2005.[408] It aired at the exact moment the Justice Department was mobilizing to ship me off to Carswell without a trial or so much as a hearing.[409]

It was a most enlightening interview. Colin Powell complained vehemently to America's First Lady of investigative journalism, Barbara Walters that nobody tried to warn him that claims about Iraq's illegal weapons stocks and weapons manufacturing capability appeared to have been grossly exaggerated by Iraqi exiles. Powell angrily denounced the intelligence community for failing to speak up before his big speech at the United Nations before the War. He particularly criticized "lower-level personnel."[410]

Powell said, and I quote: "There are some people in the intelligence community who knew at that time that some of these sources were not good, and shouldn't be relied upon."

"And they didn't speak up. That devastated me."[411]

There was just one problem. It was all a lie.

Colin Powell had been warned explicitly, by me, identified as a primary Asset covering the Iraqi Embassy in New York, that he should question dubious claims about Iraq's weapons capacity. Twice that January, 2003, I left papers at Powell's home for his review. I pleaded for him to support peace, and one week before his speech at the United Nations, on January 27, 2003, I respectfully urged him to consider the following:[412]

"What I have to say next will be more aggravating, but I have an obligation to advise you."

"Given that Iraq has tried for two years to hold covert talks with the United States, with the promise of immediately resuming weapons inspections, there's a very high probability that Iraq has no weapons of mass destruction. Forget what the Iraqi Opposition has told you. They're famous liars, and most desperate to engage the United States in their protection. You can't kill 1.7 million people and return home after a vicious bombing campaign to a great parade."

"No, Iraq emphasized for more than a year before Kofi Annan got involved, that Baghdad would jump at the chance to prove to the world they had no weapons. At any moment Iraq was ready for those inspections to begin, and that says to me that they felt always they had nothing to hide. They simply insisted that without U.S. support for the plan, it would have no benefits or meaning for resolving tensions. Current events have proved that they were right."

"Don't deceive yourself, Mr. Secretary that War would have no costs. Believing your own rhetoric at this moment would be the most rash and incendiary mistake. Fighting street battles searching for Saddam would entail deadly risks for U.S. soldiers. No matter what Iraqis think of Saddam, the common people hate the U.S. for sanctions and bombings, and they would consider it traitorous to help you. Under these circumstances, the brutality necessary to win this war would be consumption for the entire Arab world. It would produce a disastrous period of occupation. The Iraqis have fought occupations before, and they would strike back wherever possible."

"Outside Iraq, Islamists would point to the failure of west-leaning leaderships to protect the Iraqi people. Fundamentalists would seize on that failure to force concessions for their strict cause. There would be a shift to the will of the people alright. *No wonder Iran has been chuckling to itself. Iran and Osama—not the United States—would be the greatest victors in this war. The Arab Street would rush to their side. "*

(Yes, I called the rise of Iran, here and in other papers.)

"Please let me help you. You can still achieve a greater victory, Mr. Secretary, and maintain the force of America's moral authority in the world's eye. The objectives of the Bush Administration can be achieved without igniting terrorist revenge and international boycotts. Or destroying political alliances in the War on Terrorism. Or forcing massive deficit spending that will prolong the U.S. recession and scare the hell out of Wall Street and the Middle Class. Or starting a Holy War—which this would become."

I knocked it out of the ballpark. My advice addressed every one of the complaints raised by Powell. What's more, he received my second warning on January 27, one week before his speech to the U.N. General Assembly on February 5.

Far from valuing my efforts to provide quality intelligence feedback in the run up to War, Secretary Powell complained to the FBI that somebody as junior as myself dared to contact him.

He turned over those papers to the Justice Department, and I got indicted for approaching him.[413]

He forgot to mention that to Barbara Walters.

His fireworks of fury were a stage act, a spectacle of political theater. Whether you agree with the war or not, that was sheer fraud.

Everybody presumed that my beloved cousin, Andy Card lodged the original complaint to the Feds. Actually it appeared that Colin Powell had done the dirty work, though Andy certainly cooperated with the FBI investigation. Powell began it, and John McCain seized on it as a vehicle for the indictment, so that I would be silenced while Senator McCain's Commission issued some very silly findings about Pre-War Intelligence. But

CARSWELL PRISON

Powell had definitely played a role as instigator. The FBI had copies of my handwritten notes to Powell and the manila envelope delivering the papers to his home.

At Carswell I dreamed of showing those papers to Barbara Walters! In fond moments, I imagined her reprimanding General Powell for lying to his fellow officers and American soldiers, and stripping away some of his medals! If it was up to me, the man would face a court-martial.

As if that wasn't awful enough, within days of that "20/20" broadcast, the Justice Department rubberstamped its declaration that I was "incompetent to stand trial."[414] That guaranteed Powell's lie about Iraq would not face public challenge. I could never confront him or Andy Card as my accusers in a court of law, per my rights under the Constitution.

While Powell launched his "press junket" to rehabilitate his reputation, the feds booked me a bed at Carswell prison on a Texas military base, courtesy of the Patriot Act. While he whitewashed his place in history, I faced punishment without trial, for daring to approach the former Chair of the Joint Chiefs with my analysis of the unlikelihood that Iraq possessed WMDs.

That made Colin Powell "crook of the year" in my book. Truly it was Kafkaesque. My first two weeks in the SHU, I reeled from the shock of it. Every time I got strip searched and handcuffed in the SHU, I smoldered in fury as I thought about Colin Powell, and that mockery of an interview with Barbara Walters." That "20/20" interview rammed home that I was suffering so powerful men in Washington could rewrite their place in history, and sanitize their reputations.

Still, I had to adjust. In the SHU, I learned how Carswell fit into the schematics of the federal prison system. It's worth remembering that on any day, U.S. prisons house one of every 100 Americans.[415] Indeed, the United States boasts the highest rate of incarceration in the world.

Officially called Carswell Federal Medical Center, it's distinguished as the only federal women's prison in the United States that provides hospital and chronic medical care for inmates suffering from cancer, HIV/AIDS, heart disease, post-surgery rehabilitation, hepatitis and liver disease, and other chronic medical conditions. Out of 1,400 prisoners, about half require medical care.[416] The other inmates are completely healthy.

That sounded reassuring, and I was hopeful. At first.

Unfortunately, Carswell has a scandalous reputation for providing horribly poor medical care to prisoners. While I was at Carswell, the Board of Hospital Certification kept threatening to revoke Carswell's board approval, unless they cleaned up their act.

And let me tell you why:

A woman I met with diabetes got sent off for surgery, and had the wrong leg amputated.

Another older woman, locked up with me on the SHU, had heart surgery shortly before surrendering to Carswell.

Prison staff denied her access to heart medications prescribed by her cardiologist for post-surgical recovery. Almost immediately, she suffered another heart attack, and lay on the floor for several hours unconscious. Prison staff stepped over her body, while inmates had the respect to walk around her. But nobody tried to get her into a bed until she regained consciousness three to four hours later. At that point, she crawled up off the floor, and hobbled to her bunk by herself, with no staff assistance.

Another woman had a bulging hernia in her belly. She had to carry her intestines with both hands and arms, lifting her belly at all times. Carswell swore it wasn't a malignant cancer, though no medical tests were run to check the diagnosis. Her requests for surgery got rejected, though her condition surely qualified as a medical emergency. Carswell provided no medical treatment of any kind for her. We'd sit in the prison yard, while she'd groan in pain. Prison staff appeared totally indifferent to her physical agony.

As we watched, the hernia got larger and larger, as if all her intestines had spilled into her gut. They probably had.

I rather expect she's dead now.

Notably, Carswell takes out a life insurance policy on every inmate, and collects financial benefits for every woman who dies. That practice has become embroiled in controversy over whether Carswell has a financial incentive to withhold care until sick prisoners die. It's not a question of mercy. It's a question of profit versus basic human dignity.

Dying at Carswell is a nasty way to go.

The scent of urine wafted through the vents of the hospital wing, making a permanent stench that suggested inmates upstairs were left soaking in their own excrement. At the very least, bed pans could not have been cleaned frequently enough.

An ant infestation got so bad in the hospital wing, a few months after I shipped out, Betty Brink, a journalist for the Fort Worth Weekly reported that "tiny biters were found crawling on comatose and dying patients in their beds, and covering the body of at least one paralyzed inmate."[417]

Before prison inspections, there'd always be a rush to paint the hallways bright white. Miraculously the air quality would improve, a blessed reprieve for our olfactory senses. We prisoners would joke that the feds must be coming. Still, it raised our spirits, because conditions would get better for a few weeks.

Within this prison that warehouses every sort of chronic medical condition—and hundreds of healthy prisoners to boot— there's also a small unit on the third floor called M-1.

Here, I came to believe, was every prisoner's worst nightmare in the flesh, and Carswell's greatest shame.

M-1 houses 40 to 50 women at a time. About half of the inmates on M-1 get shipped to Carswell for psychiatric evaluations before sentencing. The rest are long term inmates with special mental health or physical needs that require close observation. No inmate could be judged criminally insane, but some had suicidal impulses that required special monitoring. Detox was common for chronic heroin users coming into prison. Some had epilepsy. One suffered Alzheimers dementia. Women with Alzheimers got no special care on M-1. It just mitigated the prison's liability until their release.

Regrettably, closer staff observation on M-1 did not translate to a higher standard of health care. A 27 year old woman died of sleep apnea on M-1 several weeks before my arrival, because Carswell denied her access to a special breathing machine at night. Her right to use the machine in prison had been mandated by her Judge. But such court orders meant nothing to prison staff for any inmate. Judges' orders got flouted all the time, even when defendants headed back to court, asking their judges to enforce the original medical orders. It never happened.

That time, a very young woman died. Carswell covered its liability in her death because she'd been housed on M-1. And the prison collected the insurance. That's how the system works.

And yet M-1 looked so good to me after two weeks locked in the SHU. By now I felt like I was starring in my own spy thriller movie: I imagined my acceptance speech at the Oscars. "I would like to thank the Academy for getting me off the SHU. God bless you all!"

At the start, I had no idea that in a few short months, I would fall down on my knees and beg God, truly, to let me off M-1, as well.

But at the start, I was so innocent. I had no idea of Carswell's full reputation.

As for why the rush to get me into prison, the answer fell into my lap quite unexpectedly.

I got a big clue on CNN late one night, a few weeks after my arrival at Carswell—and just days after my release from the SHU.

On Capitol Hill, Democrats were trying to launch a separate congressional inquiry into Pre-War Intelligence in the House and the Senate, led by Rep. John Murtha (D-Pennsylvania) and Senator Carl Levin (D-Michigan).[418] Democrats weren't taking the Republicans' word on anything. Who could blame them? Democrats wanted to explore whether Republicans in Congress had smoothed things over for the Bush Administration—which of course, they had.

In part, the Democrats also wanted to explore if and how pro-war Republicans had punished individuals who dissented from their war policy.

Oh ho! That would shine a nasty spotlight on my case, front and center!

I would have made trouble alright! They were correct about that. I would have some things to say that would open up Iraq, 9/11 and the questionable success of GOP anti-terrorism and national security policy, overall. As long as Republicans controlled the podium, they could block my testimony. If the Democrats controlled the inquiry, the truth would come out. And it was an ugly truth. Understanding that, Republicans turned villainous, removing sources like me, so the Democrats would be starved for bloody meat, and the inquiry would go nowhere.

That in itself shatters Republican boasts of their outstanding leadership support for Assets.

I could speak for myself and the other two young Iraqi Assets, who were my co-defendants. I would describe in graphic living color how all three of us Assets got arrested on trumped up charges, as "Iraqi Agents," while Republican leaders lied to America and the world community about our work.[419]

I would wax eloquent on how my co-defendants helped the FBI, because they wanted to stay in America, and the FBI promised to fix their visas. They betrayed their own father, an Iraqi diplomat, to do it. The Justice Department repaid them most cold heartedly, by arresting their brothers and sisters, and throwing the whole family into prison in New York. The Justice Department demanded that the boys sign false confessions that they deliberately provided bad intelligence to the U.S. before the War, and that they informed Iraqi Intelligence about exiles living in the U.S. who opposed Saddam.[420]

These two boys worked at a dry cleaners and a video store in Manhattan.[421] They didn't know any Iraqi exiles. None of the evidence supported the accusations. But the whole family got locked up for months in prison, while the Justice Department extorted those boys to confess to non-existent crimes.[422] One of the boys demanded a trial, and got locked up for 18 months. Then they all got deported.

That's something Saddam Hussein would do. It's against everything our country stands for.

Transcripts from prison phone calls told their whole nightmare.

And the GOP did all of that so that White House and Republican leaders could invent a fictitious reality of 9/11 and Pre-War Intelligence, and feed it to the American people and the international community

It was truly despicable and cowardly.

Oh yes, I would have a few things to tell a Congressional Inquiry.

I watched on prison television as Rep. John Murtha (Democrat- Pennsylvania) and Senator Carl Levin (Democrat- Michigan) held forth for the Democratic leadership.[423]

I remember Rep. Murtha saying "Assets are slowly coming forward to tell us what really happened."

It was late at night before lights out. There was a night guard. I pulled him into the TV room.

"Murtha's talking about me," I told the guard, practically in tears. "And I can't testify because the Justice Department has locked me up here, pretending I'm incompetent to get me out of Washington."

"I should be testifying on Capitol Hill right now. Not locked up in prison without a trial. Murtha wants Assets to come forward to find out what really happened before the War. Members of Congress want to hear what we have to say."

The guard looked at me sadly, truly sympathetic. "They don't want you talking, Lindauer." And he shook his head, prophetically. "They're not ever going to let you talk. If you want to get out of here, you're going to have to go along with them."

The Democrats' inquiry explained a lot. Yes it did.

If Republicans got lucky, Americans would never discover the existence of the comprehensive peace framework, or learn that everything the U.S. demanded from Saddam could have been accomplished without sacrificing the life of a single American soldier, or bombing a single Iraqi home. There would be no fragmentation of Iraq. No sectarian struggle polarizing the Sunnis and Shi'ites. The whole catastrophe was avoidable.

Oh yes, I would have a lot to contribute to any honest inquiry. Only now my credibility had been destroyed by false allegations of my so-called "mental incompetence."

Who would listen now?

Watching CNN that night, I steamed with fury. Locked in prison, I vowed to myself that I would hold the truth inside me until it was safe. I would not let this go for the convenience of lying politicians. That truth was too important.

I resolved to tough it out. They had power over their actions. They did not have power over mine. Really though, what else could I do?

I stayed focused on my release date. February 3rd burned onto my brain. I kept my cool and waited. It was four months. Ok, I could do that. I'm a pretty tough lady. I've got my wits, and I'm mostly calm under pressure. I could do that time "standing on my head," as the saying goes.

Just four months. Then it would be over. Or so my attorney, Sam Talkin, swore to me in prison phone calls from Carswell. The White House had its pound of flesh for my opposition to Andy Card's war. Colin Powell's reputation had got redeemed. The Justice Department would drop the charges, Talkin promised. And the case would go away. I would have no prison record. No conviction. For the first months, I had no choice but to trust him. He'd cut the deal. I was stuck with it. But he had to know what was going on. I tell you, he sounded awfully convincing. Uncle Ted and I wanted so much to believe him.[424] And could you blame us?

Uncle Ted and I had a back up plan if anything went wrong. Ted would demand a hearing on my behalf immediately. But surely this would be the end of it? That's why they'd done it. To have an end game. That's what Talkin kept promising us.

I got tons of letters of encouragement from friends. I stayed active. I walked four to six miles a day on the out door track. That's anywhere from 80 to 120 laps every day. I'd walk half of it in the morning and half in the evening. I read lots of books. An old college friend sent me the complete Harry Potter Series, which delighted me and calmed my nerves. I read lots of spy thrillers and mysteries. I also entertained myself with New York Times Crossword puzzles. I got pretty good at identifying four letter words for "betrayal."

But mostly I settled into the "monastic" experience of prison life, and tried not to get eaten by bitterness. I tried to be pleasant to other inmates, and I made some friends whom I will cherish forever. These women provided a strong support network. We cheered for each other victories, and ached for each other's private battles. We prayed for each other constantly. Though it sounds unlikely, I am a better person because I have known these women.

M-1 had its quirks. It's a locked unit, which restricts prisoner entry and exits. The doors open every 30 minutes to an hour, depending on the mood of the guards. Why it's locked, nobody could explain, since it's a punishable offense for prisoners to wander beyond their designated areas anyway. We spent a lot of time waiting for guards to bring the keys so we could go outside, or come in. The guards griped about it constantly.

A second unit, called M-2, houses another 70 to 80 inmates after sentencing, whose health conditions range from chronic heart disease to depression and moderate suicide risks, to bulimia and old age, which require separation from the more rowdy and boisterous prison population. That's not a locked unit. It's also not highly medical in function— That's where my older friend collapsed from her heart attack—in full view of a "nurse's station." Yeah, it's kind of a joke. That's the point.

The hospital wing takes up the top floors for inmates that require bed care. A lot of these women suffer AIDS and cancer. Dying and comatose prisoners are kept out of sight there. Tragically, I saw lots of wheel chairs at Carswell, mostly transporting young women. It's a distressing sight. They sank faster, because even though Carswell supposedly functions as a hospital, the nursing staff had a suspicious lack of medical supplies.

By way of example, a friend on M-1 suffered a double fracture in her hand, when she punched a concrete wall. Prison staff wrapped her hand in a removable gauze bandage, but she had no splint or sling to hold the hand steady. In constant pain, she had to cradle her broken hand with her other arm for weeks until it healed. A few basic medical steps would have helped, but Carswell had no medical supplies to care for something as mundane as broken bones.

Poor medical care was not the only hazard faced by women inmates.

Coercive sex and outright rape are not uncommon at Carswell, either. Since 1997, eight professional staff members of Carswell have been convicted of rape, averaging about one a year. They include two prison chaplains, a gynecologist, a psychologist, a supervisor of food services and three guards.[425] Some of those offenses involve sex for bribes, like special access to contraband cigarettes, or staying out of trouble if prisoners got caught breaking rules. However, some of it qualifies as violent rape. Women prisoners are helpless to fight back, without getting accused of assaulting a prison officer—which adds extra years on her sentence. That makes it difficult not to yield, and difficult to prove afterwards that the rape was forced, not consensual.

It's shocking to think of the sorts of high level staff who have sexually abused prisoners.

In 2008, Vincent Inametti, Carswell's Catholic Chaplain for the previous seven years, got sentenced to four years in prison for what his judge called "surprisingly heinous sexual crimes" against two women prisoners.[426] It's possible there might have been more victims who got released, or transferred, or feared to come forward. Inametti had a terrible reputation when I was at Carswell in 2005-2006. Other women whispered that we should never accept favors from Inametti, and should avoid getting caught alone in his office. We always stayed in pairs, dealing with that man. He was the prison's Catholic Chaplain, and women inmates couldn't trust him alone, even for spiritual counseling.

In addition to rape, abuse of the legal rights of women inmates would prove to be a serious problem at Carswell, too. But I didn't know that at first.

I was determined to stay good-natured as long as possible.

I settled into prison life, helped by the generous and devoted support of my friend and companion, JB Fields, waiting at home for me in Takoma Park.

JB Fields was a computer techie, who worked in Naval Intelligence on submarines before going to the Peace Corps and the U.S. State Department. He used to joke that he spent six years of his life under water. He was a free thinking intellectual, with a blue collar streak a mile wide. He argued passionately in defense of civil liberties, and never hesitated to tackle tough issues, like the rights of gays to work openly in the military. Most famously, he rode a BMW motorcycle! Every weekend he took off on a road trip or a scavenger hunt. He had an "Iron Butt" badge to prove he rode 1,000 miles in 24 hours. He loved diners and pubs. He was gregarious and generous and opinionated. And he loved to blog.

JB was my companion and lover, though some of his friends were told about our relationship, and JB kept others in the dark. Some of his friends urged him to leave me to protect his career. But he never took the easy way. After my arrest, we applied our own peculiar brand of "don't ask, don't tell," for the sake of his work. And he stayed with me through prison. In fact, JB got a Top Secret Security clearance after he moved in with me. So much for the Feds' belief that I was a secret "Iraqi agent!" Before Carswell, we talked about getting married. His support was phenomenal to my spirit. He was my white knight of chivalry. I could never have survived without him.

I had 300 minutes of phone time for all calls out of the prison every month. That's five hours of phone time, in maximum 15 minute blocks. At Christmas, prisoners got an extra 100 minutes. JB and I would count them down together. When I'd run out, there'd be such regret in his voice as he begged me to hold on until I got my next batch of minutes on the 1st of the month. He'd be waiting for my call that morning.

To this day, I have a phobia against cell phones, because it reminds me of counting minutes from prison.

JB came out of military intelligence. So he made a special effort in our conversations to insist that neither of us disrespected the military, though we both hated this Iraq war.

All phone calls were monitored by prison staff, and Lord love him, JB tried so earnestly to communicate that it's patriotic to defend the First Amendment. He would say that old military guys like him signed up to protect the best parts of our liberties and our Constitution, including the right to dissent from the government. Disagreeing on political issues didn't imply that we loved our country any less. Throughout history, American soldiers have died to protect this very cause. So JB swore, with his hand on his heart!

In my first months at Carswell, the large outdoor track in the prison yard was the focal point for my recreation and social life. For the sake of exercise and burning off stress, I walked four to six miles a day, half in the morning, and half in the evening, when the harsh Texas sun cooled off. As the nightmarish months trudged on, my release date becoming a distant fantasy like an impossible dream, I used to imagine that by the end of my ordeal, I would have walked enough miles on that track to take me all the way home to Maryland.

Twice a week, M-1 got "treated" to in-door recreation. A micro-gym occupied a small recreation center at the prison, with four tread mills, four exercise bikes and four Stairmasters. It was somewhat inadequate for a population of 1,400 women prisoners, but very much appreciated. Carswell would be a sorry excuse for a country club. Some surprisingly child-like activities qualified as in-door recreation, such as bowling with gargantuan plastic pins that got knocked down with huge plastic balls, twice the size of basketballs. Board games like Monopoly, Sorry, LIFE and Chutes & Ladders entertained us for hours in the TV room, just to fill the time. We played card games constantly.

Sometimes we got very silly, like the night we played "Monopoly," and I pulled a "Get out of Jail" card. I took it to the guard, and asked to go home.

There was also a very small prison library, which amused us enormously by special-izing in True Crime dramas, stuffing every book shelf. We joked that the prison's choice of reading would enrich our fellow inmates with insights of how to make up better alibis the next time out.

To put that in perspective, when a college friend shipped me a set of Harry Potter books, other inmates tried to buy it off me for commissary (prison currency, legal or otherwise).

Otherwise, for recreation, women crocheted endless dolls and blankets for children and boyfriends back home. There was always a buzz over new yarns, colors and designs and patterns, and who wanted to trade a bed spread for commissary.

For the most part, Carswell inmates are not violent or destructive. In fairness, ten years ago a good number of these women would not have got arrested at all. Today there's a mentality that favors sweeping out households, particularly in drug cases. Nowadays, grandmothers get locked up for refusing to testify against their adult children caught dealing drugs, while grandma cares for their babies. Most people forget that these grand-mothers are holding their little worlds together, keeping children out of foster care. And the Courts punish them terribly as a result. One woman at Carswell was a quadriplegic who got locked up in a drug sting. She could not possibly have walked out on dope deal-ing family members, since she was paralyzed from the neck down.

Another woman got 15 years for refusing to testify against a corrupt cop in Los Angeles who threatened to kill her younger brothers every time her case went before the Judge. He'd show up at her brothers' jobs, force one or the other into a squad car, then drive up and down the California highways pointing out isolated spots where he could dump their bodies. Or he would describe how he could plant drugs on them, and send them to prison. Or how he could fake an attack on himself, so that it looked like the kid assaulted a police officer. This woman was eight years into her sentence for "obstruction of justice" when I met her. And she'd never broke the law in her life. Not a speeding ticket. Her attorney begged the Judge for mercy, since the cop threatened to kill her family. Nobody cared.

That's the new prison system. Some inmates have committed major offenses, like drive by shootings. Others opened the front door for druggie friends of their adult son or daughter, living at home and dealing meth or heroin in the basement. Under federal sentencing guidelines, they all get sentenced as if they actively participated in the drug conspiracy. It's a cautionary tale.

And it's a legitimate reason why some Judges allow psychology to mitigate sentencing.

Some of these women have stories the Courts need to hear.

One young woman at Carswell had been living on the street as a prostitute since she was 16. She'd run away from home because her brother raped her. A serial killer picked her off the street at 19, and confined her to a torture chamber for several days, chained from the ceiling. She got cut up and raped. When the guy went to work, she jumped out a window, naked, and flagged down help. She was a lucky survivor. The police found bodies of other prostitutes buried in the back yard.

Her attorney asked for mercy in sentencing on a drug charge a few years later, citing post traumatic stress from hellacious abuse throughout her young life. She was only 23 when I met her, and this was probably the only break that she got in her sad life. Should we as a society begrudge her that small compassion? A proper psych evaluation (unlike mine) would allow her to share that horrific experience with the Judge, and appeal for mercy. I hope she got it.

One of my most beloved friends at Carswell was a grandmotherly inmate, who cared for the Alzheimers woman on M-1, and brought hugs and comfort to the whole unit. Her brother, a "fire bug" put a pipe bomb in her attorney's car, which exploded when the ignition turned on. She was indicted for conspiracy in that attack, which happened while she was at Carswell for a psych study on another charge, possibly linked to abusing prescription drugs, like Valium. She was self-medicating to stay calm, after intense trauma throughout her life.

It turns out her brother, who's criminally insane—and free— burned her home to the ground twice before, with her children inside the house. While she was in prison, he burned down her teenage children's house a third time. Alas, he was out of control—and untouchable in the Courts.

Apparently, she and her siblings grew up in the most tragic circumstances. There were hints of incest and severe beatings and alcoholism. Her own father shot her with a gun in her foot. I saw the scars. She showed up with a bloody gun shot wound at school the next day, and her teachers took her to the emergency room.

Now this darling woman was maternal and non-violent, except that she had survived a childhood of sheer hell. It broke her brother completely. But she has not committed violent crimes herself that I know of. It's doubtful she ever would. She does animal rescue work, and she's studied for the ministry. I loved her because when I first got to M-1, she helped me make my first prison bed, which has a trick to it. And she was God-sent for the

Alzheimer woman on the unit, who had no idea that she was in prison, and was terribly frightened and confused by other inmates. This grandmotherly inmate kept her safe.

I believe her Judge acted wisely and compassionately in considering the full picture of her history before sentencing her with leniency. Her attorney survived the car bombing, and supported the sentencing!

The case of the Alzheimer woman illustrates the exact opposite of compassion in sentencing, what happens when the Courts don't weigh mitigating factors of a defendant's personal story.

Obviously this woman suffered dementia and couldn't be left alone. So her daughter—an incorrigible drug runner in and out of Mexico—took her elderly mother to pick up drug supplies with her. And they got arrested together coming back across the border. Her daughter should be strung up for this. But the Judge in their case made no allowance for the Alzheimer mother's state of incompetence, and sentenced her to seven or eight years in prison. The poor old lady would wander the hallways, lost and confused, looking for her small children, who have now grown up. She'd think somebody had stolen her children. She also thought some inmates were family members. She'd get frightened at night, and wander into different rooms. She needed a care facility. But with a drug conviction, it's doubtful that any nursing home will take her.

All of this explains how, after my initial fury at getting labeled incompetent myself, I recognized there's a time when this sort of sentencing has merit, and should be applied.

With regards to my case, I have come to think that, apart from psychiatry, which was garbage to me, there's a special angle to incompetence that applies to the Patriot Act, uniquely.

Incompetence applies strictly to one's capability to assist in preparing a defense. Under the Patriot Act, there's serious questions as to how any defendant could possibly assist an attorney, facing "secret charges," "secret evidence," and "secret grand jury testimony." Evidence corroborating my story that I'd worked as an Asset for 9 years in counter-terrorism, and warned about 9/11, got suppressed, too, though it would have freed me of the most serious charges and some of the minor counts. Without question, my attorney received classified information in a secret debriefing, which he was prohibited from sharing with me. Thus, I could not participate in my defense at a serious and meaningful level.

By its very structure and nature, therefore, it could be argued that the Patriot Act has the effect of rendering the most capable defendant "incompetent to stand trial."

During these months at Carswell, I came to question if, maybe, Judge Mukasey had used such a line of logic in my case, different than the official psychiatry—but a logic, nonetheless, that weighs whether a defendant has become incapacitated by circumstances beyond the defendant's control. During those months at Carswell, I spent many afternoons walking the track, wondering if his decision to kill the case was more inspired by repugnance for the Patriot Act.

There's no question but that my case created a different kind of precedent for incompetence, and Judge Mukasey was fully aware of these factors when he chose to accept the finding.

I would argue that the precedent in my case is uniquely this:

No matter how strongly a defendant functions in private life, and regardless of past professional credentials –former Congressional Press Secretary, journalist and U.S.

Asset in anti-terrorism—any individual becomes uniquely handicapped under the Patriot Act, such that he or she becomes incapable of adequately contributing to a legal defense, under the specific and unique burden and circumstances imposed by the government for the handling of classified evidence. My case was loaded up with "secret charges" and "secret evidence," which handicapped my functioning as a defendant and could not be surmounted, given the regulations.

And so, while avoiding the mess of psychiatry— which I despise— I would argue that defense attorneys confronting the Patriot Act should cite my case as a precedent to argue that the law itself creates an artificial state of incompetence to assist in defense strategy. My Judge had a very good understanding of the depth of my background by the time I left Carswell. It could be argued that he would concur, within a range of non-violent activities. Non-violence would be key, also the likelihood of steering clear of criminal behavior in the future.

Yet even such a calculated defense strategy carries inherent dangers, as my situation would illustrate soon enough.

Until Christmas, I was not afraid. In a Christmas card to JB Fields, I posed for a photograph in front of a life size mural of a motorcycle, which I thought he would enjoy.

Soon I'd be home. Or so everybody believed.

Storm clouds had churned above my case when I arrived. But I had not been passive, allowing them to build unchecked.

Carswell's psychology department had two tasks. First, prison psychologists had to deliver an opinion whether the incompetence finding should be ratified or thrown out by the Court. Secondly, they got to recommend whether a defendant might become competent in the future, and what might be done to restore competence. Judge Mukasey would have the final say, regardless.

From my first days in the SHU, Carswell established that I was obviously not suffering hallucinations, or depression, or hysterics, or threatening violence towards myself or others. The only thing left was for Carswell to examine at a basic level whether my story had validity.

It's critical to understand the predicament that brought us to this point. I got locked up because the Patriot Act apparently allowed the Prosecutor to withhold knowledge from the Court of my identity as an Asset, which the Justice Department deemed "classified evidence."

The FBI verified my story early on. We know that because we interviewed the same witnesses. And we know what they told the FBI. In ordinary circumstances, the Courts require Prosecutors to supply that "exculpatory information," as soon as it's available. Unhappily, in my case, the U.S. Attorney refused. The Justice Department wanted to see if my Defense could validate my story by ourselves, without their automatic cooperation.

The false and irresponsible allegations by Dr. Sanford Drob, casting aspersions on my ability to authenticate my story through independent, high caliber sources, had caused tremendous damage and deprived me of my freedom.[427] Of course it was flatly untrue. We had outstanding witnesses from the Lockerbie Trial. To dispute their reputations would be offensive and ignorant. Dr. Drob acted recklessly and dishonestly, by failing to update his report after learning of Ted Lindauer's success.[428] That was not "last minute" corroboration. That was six months before Carswell. Dr. Drob had plenty of time to amend his findings. He could have spoken with Ted himself, if he doubted me. He chose not to.

But reality has very little to do with psychiatry. It's about ego.

I understood that I would have to be proactive to undo Dr. Drob's damage. And I moved swiftly to set the record straight.

I refused to play their game. If the Justice Department wouldn't step up and do the right thing, by admitting the truth freely, I would confront them with it head on. If they expected to rely on the farce of Dr. Drob's report, they would be unhappily disappointed.

So, immediately upon surrendering to Carswell, I gave the chief psychologist, James Shadduck, the phone numbers and email addresses of two high-powered witnesses eager to vouch for my credibility.[429]

The first witness, Ian Ferguson, was a former Scottish journalist and co-author of "Cover Up of Convenience: the Hidden Scandal of Lockerbie,"[430] a revealing expose of the bombing of Pan Am 103.

After the conviction of Abdelbaset Megraghi, Ferguson served as Chief Criminal Investigator for the Lockerbie Appeals, spearheaded by Eddie MacKechnie. He also produced a documentary film that examined evidence in the case. His background qualifies him as one of the foremost experts on the bombing of Pan Am 103.

Ferguson is loyal to truth wherever he finds it. His integrity as an old school investigative journalist requires that he speak up when he sees injustice. I had confidence that Ian would not stand idly by, while the Justice Department locked me away on a Texas military base without any sort of hearing. And he would not wait for Carswell to seek him out, either. True enough, within a few weeks of my surrender, Ferguson began bombarding the psychology staff with phone calls, while they desperately tried to ignore him. He would not go away for their comfort.

His input was critical.[431] Most significantly, because of his long involvement with Lockerbie, Ferguson could vouch for the Intelligence background of my two handlers, Dr. Fuisz and Hoven, and our close working relationships. Ferguson had direct confirmation of Dr. Fuisz's CIA identity from the Lockerbie Trial. As for Hoven, at the point of our introduction to Ferguson, several years earlier, his own sources told Ferguson that Paul filled the role of liaison to Defense Intelligence on Lockerbie for our team. That's why Ferguson wanted to talk with us. If I was wrong, then Ferguson would testify other members of U.S. Intelligence were also mistaken. And that didn't matter, because Dr. Fuisz was unabashedly CIA.

That's all my Defense had to prove— unless the Justice Department contested the legality of a CIA operation inside the U.S. Then Paul Hoven's technical role as liaison to Defense Intelligence would become important. Otherwise, Dr. Fuisz's ties to the CIA would be enough.

Ferguson would make sure Carswell understood that other outstanding witnesses tied to Lockerbie actively supported me, and promised to testify, too. I was not alone.

Although Ferguson's knowledge related to Lockerbie and Libya, once the intelligence connection was established, it would be absurd to suggest that a long-time CIA operative like Dr. Fuisz could not be interested in Libya and Iraq at the same time. It would be particularly hard to dispute, since Dr. Fuisz testified before a Congressional subcommittee in 1992 about a U.S. corporation that supplied SCUD Mobile Missile Launchers to Iraq before the first Gulf War.

Ferguson provided the construct of my defense in one knock-out punch. After that, the authenticity of my identity as an Asset, supervised by members of U.S. Intelligence, should have been indisputable from Carswell's standpoint.

Parke Godfrey was the second witness waiting to speak with Dr. Shadduck. An associate professor of computer science at York University in Toronto, and a close friend of mine since 1990, Godfrey earned his PhD at College Park, Maryland. Until 2000, he visited my home and spoke with me several times a week. He would swear that he observed no signs of mental illness or instability in all of our years together.[432]

More critically, Godfrey would provide valuable confirmation about my 9/11 warning, and how in August 2001 I told him "the attack was imminent," and he should "stay out of New York City, because we expected mass casualties."[433]

There was nothing delusional about any of it.

Godfrey promised us that he would make sure Dr. Shadduck understood he debriefed the FBI about my 9/11 warning in Toronto in September 2004, a year before Carswell.[434]

Above all, Carswell needed to understand that denying my 9/11 warning would be incredibly dishonest at this stage. Given the range of confirmations to the FBI, the Bureau of Prisons, and the U.S. Attorney's Office, deceiving the Court would smack of a major government cover up.

That might explain why prison documents show I had to push Dr. Shadduck for almost two months to interview Ferguson and Godfrey. [435] Obviously, Carswell was reluctant to confront the truth that I was pushing so hard to verify. The psych staff had a knuckle-tight grip on "plausible deniability," and they were reluctant to let go.

Thankfully, Ferguson and Godfrey were both gravely frightened for my safety, and worked tenaciously to get through to prison psychologists. Ferguson was especially vigilant, calling Carswell repeatedly from his home in France for several weeks. Prison staff told Ferguson that Dr. Shadduck was on vacation throughout November—a flagrant lie. Ferguson would not give up. And neither would Godfrey. Everyone recognized the grave risks that I faced, and the intensely political nature of the Justice Department's attack against me. They were determined that it should go no farther.

I was at the prison gym, running on a treadmill, when Dr. Shadduck rushed to find me. Wide eyed, hands shaking, he asked for Ian Ferguson's phone number.

They'd been talking on the phone to France, where Ferguson lived, when the phone cut off. Shadduck had a lot more questions, but "yes," he stuttered, "your story checks out. It's all factually true."

Shadduck told me that he spoke with Godfrey later that day. Godfrey testified in court that it was a short conversation.

Short enough to learn that I had definitely warned abut a 9/11 style of attack involving airplane hijackings and a strike on the World Trade Center in the summer of 2001.

I gloated. The deception by the Justice Department had been confronted and thwarted. Witnesses had prevailed.

Needless to say, I felt greatly relieved, knowing that Ferguson and Godfrey had provided such high level confirmation on my behalf. Few defendants could hope for so much.

Think what that meant—

Staff for the Bureau of Prisons had received confirmation that an "Iraqi Agent" locked in their prison was really a U.S. Asset involved in Pre-War Intelligence, who gave advance warning about the 9/11 attack.

From that point on, any action to harm me would qualify as a government cover up by the Justice Department, impeding accountability to the people of New York, where I was supposed to stand trial before the community, which would assess my actions and render judgment.

Of critical importance, Carswell received all the verification it required for my competence review within my first 60 days at the prison. Staff could have authenticated my story earlier in November, if they'd returned Ferguson's phone calls from France.

In any non-political situation, the competence question would have been debunked. My Asset work and the 9/11 warning stood up to scrutiny. Long time friends in Maryland reported no signs of mental instability in my behavior. After these interviews, it should have been time to discuss getting me home to resume trial proceedings, or dismissing the case, if the Justice Department wanted it to go away quietly.

But my case was off the charts, politically speaking. The competence question was a legal farce. In which case, both Ferguson and Godfrey's testimony had tremendous value for a different reason: If O'Callaghan reneged on his promise to kill the case, it was critical for the Justice Department to understand that I wasn't operating from a weak position, as Dr. Drob labored to imply. It was imperative that they recognize it would be wise to honor their promise to drop the charges.

No matter. For the rest of December, I experienced as much peace as prison allows.

Yes, I was stuck in prison for the Christmas holidays.

But surely the Justice Department had done its worst already.

Carswell had its witness reports. Prison staff could no longer deny that I was telling the truth. Just a few more weeks and Judge Mukasey would either the drop the charges entirely— or the Court would move for trial, and hear the truth, too.[436]

I could wait them out.

Everything moved my way in December, as I counted the days to my release. Down in Texas, locked behind a razor fence, I thought about the weeping cherry tree, my "peace tree" waiting to flower in my front yard in Maryland. At home, caring for my beloved dachshunds, Raqi Bear and Mahji Bear, my good friend Karin Anderson reminded me the tree would start blossoming shortly after I got home. My life and my little family would be waiting for me. JB Fields was tremendously excited, too.

For Christmas dinner, Carswell feasted us with Cornish game hens, corn bread stuffing, green beans and macaroni and cheese, with pecan pie for desert. The dinner was a real treat from our daily fare. I was so delighted that I wrote down the menu, and sent it home to JB, since I'd run out of phone minutes.

My phone calls to JB ended exuberantly with a promise that I'd be home by Valentines Day. And then we'd be together. We talked about getting married. JB promised to pick me up from Carswell on his BMW motorcycle. He swore that he'd ride all the way to Texas to get me. We giggled how I would hop on the back of his bike at the prison gates, and we'd zoom off to glory. Our future looked so hopeful.

Christmas at Carswell was one of those times in my life that I stopped to be mindful of my blessings. I was filled with excitement. In a few weeks I would be home. In the meantime, I had met some strong and fascinating women—Sharon, Nancy, Toie, Jessica, Renee, Karin— some very special ladies who for whatever reason got caught in a bad spot. We laughed and joked together, and talked about our families. We cried together.

We played silly games to entertain ourselves. We poured over law books at the prison library, studying our cases together. I hope we came to respect each other.

I was counting those last days. I had watched other women come in for psych studies, and leave after six or seven weeks. I should have gone home myself, but the Bureau of Prisons wanted to hold me until the 120th day allowed by federal law for these sorts of competency evaluations. There was no purpose to it, except maximizing the sentence.

Alright then, I could wait until February 3rd. This, too, would pass. The government had made its play. There was nowhere to go but dismissal or trial.

Or so we fervently believed.

That all changed on December 23, 2005, two days before Christmas.

Carswell had already authenticated my story. Infamously, they now started looking for ways to eradicate it.

My nightmare of "extreme prejudice" was about to begin in earnest.

CHAPTER 23:

IF AT FIRST YOU DON'T SUCCEED, SHOOT THE HOSTAGE

"I'll be judge, I'll be jury," said cunning old Fury;
I'll try the whole cause, and condemn you to death."
—Alice's Adventures in Wonderland,
Lewis Carroll

The warning shot fired at my head two days before Christmas.

On M-1, one of the prison staff, Dr. Collin Vas, hustled up and thrust a paper in my hand.

"Notice of a medication hearing?"[437] My hands started to shake. "What the fuck is this?"

Drugs? But I knew at first glance. This was "extreme prejudice" for sure. If I understood the intelligence community at all, a serious attack was coming.

And with sudden clarity, I understood why. I had to grimace.

My upcoming release posed new threats to the so far successful cover up of 9/11 and Iraqi Pre-War Intelligence. So long as the Justice Department locked me up tight in prison on a Texas military base, the truth got locked up with me. But once I got released and the indictment got dismissed, that truth about Iraq and 9/11 would crash down like an avalanche on the political comforts of Washington. Republicans—and a few big name Democrats, too—had staked their reputations on a massive public fraud about the "effectiveness" of anti-terrorism policy and Iraq's phony lack of cooperation in the 9/11 investigation. They had adjusted to that lie most comfortably. I took that comfort away.

My threat level had multiplied in prison. The abuse that I suffered in their cover up—false arrest and false imprisonment on the Patriot Act— showed deliberate and calculated malevolence towards our system of political accountability. It suggested premeditated deception, involving top ranking Republican officials. The federal prosecutor in my case, Edward O'Callaghan would later become senior campaign staff for John McCain and Sarah Palin in the 2008 election, for example. The man who covered up our 9/11 warning would brag of advising McCain's Presidential campaign on anti-terrorism policy, according to his internet C.V.[438] If the corporate media woke up from its coma, this could become a hellacious scandal.

Psychiatry had already whored itself once to the White House and the Justice Department by pretending I was incompetent. As behaviorists, I'm sure they recognized that once they sold out their professional ethics, the second act of corruption came much easier—floating the idea that I should be drugged, until I stopped claiming that I worked as an Asset in Pre-War Intelligence, who raised the alarms before 9/11. I doubt very much that they stopped to consider how obscene that proposal really was.

If they hadn't considered it, I was ready to connect the dots for them.

The internal "medication hearing" was scheduled for December 28, 2005[439]— five days away. The hearing notice advised that I was entitled to present witnesses and evidence from outside the prison. I could also call prison staff. But with such short notice from Carswell, the week between Christmas Eve and New Years would be impossible to accommodate my rights, since my witnesses would be traveling for the holidays. Adding to my difficulties, I had used up my prison phone time. So I could not possibly contact witnesses prior to January, when I would get a new batch of minutes. Oftentimes, an inmate's attorney flies in to attend prison hearings, as well.

Without delay, I ran to Dr. Shadduck for an explanation, along with an urgent request for a one week postponement, so I could get everything together.

Shadduck explained that this "medication hearing" was the first of its kind anywhere.

As luck would have it, the 2nd Circuit Court of Appeals, which covers defendants from New York and New Jersey, had just handed down an important decision regarding the rights of federal inmates to reject drugs in prison. The 2nd Circuit had ruled that inmates must have the right to an internal hearing before drug recommendations are presented to the Court. Through this hearing, inmates would receive notification of what prison staff wanted to do, and they would have an opportunity to proffer a rebuttal. The Appeals Court stipulated that defendants had a right to call witnesses at these internal hearings, and show any evidence that supported their cause.

It was a critical tool for prisoner rights, and an outstanding appellate decision. I cannot express sufficient gratitude for the inmate who fought for all of us. It must have been a bitter fight. I was profoundly grateful for it, and I wanted to make full use of it. Indeed, I would be the first inmate anywhere in the federal prisons to invoke my rights under this decision.

Most significantly, it afforded me the capability to prove my authenticity to the wider staff at Carswell through independent sources, which psychiatry had tried to denounce, foolishly and dishonestly. On those grounds, I explained to Shadduck that I wanted Ian Ferguson and Parke Godfrey to testify by speaker phone. I reminded Shadduck that he had already spoken with both men, and they had confirmed the salient points of my work with Dr. Fuisz and my 9/11 warning.

There was nothing delusional about any of it. I wanted his colleagues to know that.

Whatever crooked scheme Carswell hoped to achieve with this "medication hearing," I intended to counter by ensuring that Ferguson and Godfrey's testimony got entered into the prison record. Other prison staff would hear what Shadduck already knew. They would be forced to confront the authenticity of my story. And they would know that Carswell was up to its neck in a vicious cover up scheme. High-caliber witnesses of impeccable character would always be my best protection, in court or in prison.

I just had to cross my t's and dot all my i's, to show that I met the highest standards of proof. They were playing games, obviously. I could not afford to. I had no intention of relying on the integrity of the psychology business, after what I'd suffered at their hands already.

As for my mental status per se, Parke Godfrey had been a close friend in Maryland since 1990, visiting my home every week and speaking with me by phone two or three times a week. By December, 2005, he'd known me 15 years. Godfrey was ready to testify that he saw no evidence of mental illness or instability in my behavior of any kind.[440] That would certainly make it more difficult to justify "involuntary drugging" over my strenuous objections. And I had no intention of going along with such a thing. I abhor drugs of any kind. I would take this fight all the way to the Supreme Court if I had to, and even then I would never agree.

This testimony mattered enormously.

My request for a one week delay was justified to ensure fairness in the proceedings. After the 1st of January, when I got my new batch of phone minutes, I could reach JB Fields, and between the two of us, we could track down Ferguson and Godfrey rapidly. I was positive they would cooperate. I would also send for the Andy Card letters, so that Carswell could see how my communications to the White House had been professional and respectful at all times, never threatening or hostile. Finally, I would submit the 12 months of observation notes from Family Health Services in Maryland,[441] which documented that Dr. Taddesseh saw nothing wrong with me—"no psychosis," "no depression," "no mood disturbances," "no reason for further or additional psychiatric intervention," before I got ordered to Carswell. That was pretty definitive.

I was pretty confident that Shadduck already had copies of Taddesseh's notes from Maryland. But I wasn't taking any chances that he might try to keep them out of the record.

I had to go into this "medication hearing" with all my ducks in a row.

It meant a one week delay, and no longer.

Shadduck refused the postponement.

I was shocked, frankly— and worried. This new "medication hearing" had been carefully crafted to protect prisoner rights in circumstances exactly like mine. By refusing to accommodate a legitimate request to present relevant evidence and witness testimony, Shadduck was deliberately thwarting the 2nd Circuit Court's intentions. A one week delay would hardly cause a drag on the system—not after three months in prison with no action at all.

For his part, Shadduck recognized the critical importance of what Ferguson and Godfrey would say. He understood that his colleagues would hear validation about my 9/11 warning and my longtime relationship with Dr. Fuisz, covering Libya and Iraq. He wanted that exculpatory testimony kept out of the prison record for the same reasons that I wanted it in. And he understood full well that rejecting my request for a brief delay would violate my rights under the new 2nd Circuit decision.

He did so anyway.

Not for the first time I was reminded how reality terrifies psychiatrists, and how fiercely they fight against it, desperate to protect their authority in the courts. Reality goes right out the window, while psychiatry labors hard—and violently— to deny it's there.

At Carswell, I coined a phrase for this phenomena. I call it "delusional psychiatry." It's the elephant in any courtroom.

I was right to be paranoid.

On the morning of the "medication hearing," I was ready to rumble. Even so I was aghast to discover the full macabre horror that Carswell had schemed up for me.

Waiting for me was Dr. Collin Vas and Dr. William Pederson. Shadduck was not present.[442]

Immediately I was handed an internal document titled "Notice of Medication Hearing and Advisement of Rights," and instructed to sign it. The paper left large blanks under the names of witnesses that I desired to speak on my behalf.[443] Carswell wanted to pretend that I had not requested testimony by Ferguson and Godfrey. Dr. Vas grabbed the paper out of my hands when I declared my intention to insert their names under the blank witness list.

On the paper, Dr. Vas wrote for me, "Ms. Lindauer refuses to sign," with an X on the signature line.[444]

There was no time to express outrage over such critical dishonesty.

My attention quickly shifted to the section of the paper marked "Reason for Treatment: Restoration of Competency, Treatment of Delusions."[445]

And above that: "Proposed Treatment: Anti psychotics, Benzodiazepeines, Antidepressants and Mood Stabilizers."[446]

My jaw hit the floor.

Seizing on the most important aspects, the list of drugs for "treatment," I launched my defense with a strong offensive, pounding on the irrational nature of proposing treatment for non-existent conditions.

"I want the record to show that I have requested a delay to get witness testimony, and that has been refused." I started off.

"Let's take a look at this. I see here that some of these drugs are for treatment of delusions? Are we here to talk about drugs for me? Or drugs for you? I ask, because you're the ones who seem to be denying reality in my case." My voice dripped with sarcasm.

"What's this drug for delusions?" I demanded.

"Haldol." Pederson was tight lipped.[447]

"Haldol? To treat delusions, I see. A rhinoceros tranquilizer, I've been told." I forced a smile.

"If you're really so worried, Dr. Pederson, I suggest that you delay this meeting for a week, so we can get these folks on the phone. You can ask them yourself. Nobody has to take my word for anything. I'm quite confident that you'll find there's nothing delusional about any of it."

Indeed, testimony by Parke Godfrey and Ian Ferguson, via speaker phone, would have shot down this "diagnosis" in seconds flat. Session reports by Dr. Taddesseh at Family Health Services in Maryland would have provided another knock out punch.

"Perhaps you're not aware that your colleague, Dr. Shadduck, has already interviewed these witnesses. He's already verified my story.[448] Dr. Vas, here, knows that very well. So I cannot imagine why you think I'd go along with this."

"Here's some reality for you. The Justice Department is pretending that I'm incompetent because Republican politicians in Washington don't want to take responsibility for their mistakes in Iraq. They want to blame the Assets, as if it's our fault that the U.S. marched soldiers into Baghdad. You got to love Washington, though. First they arrest me for telling them the war would be a disaster. Now they're up on Capitol Hill giving press conferences, complaining that I never came forward to warn them off the invasion. They're nothing but god damn cowards."

"I think that's the "real" reality, Dr. Pederson."

"Well let me set you straight: I would never agree to put psychotropic drugs in my body to help out a Republican politician who got himself in trouble in Washington. I'm not going to put poison in MY body to help out George Bush or John McCain. No fucking way."

I started lecturing them at that point:

"Whether you talk to my witnesses today or not, your staff has already verified my story."

"If you go into court, and submit a falsified report saying that my story was not authenticated while I was at Carswell, you would be committing major perjury in a federal court of law."

"You would be lying to a senior federal judge. And I swear before God, I would make sure that you pay for that. Perjury is a federal crime. You could go to prison. And I would not hesitate to prosecute." Then I laughed. "A lot of women are at Carswell today, because THEY LIED to a federal judge or to the FBI, too. So you better stop and think about what you're doing."

"If you want my witnesses to repeat what they've already told Shadduck, we can make that happen. I have no problem with that. I'd love to do it, in fact. I wanted to delay this meeting until next week, so that you could hear what they have to say."

"But I've already made them available to your staff, Dr. Pederson. It's too late for you to deny my authenticity. At this point, if you falsify claims to the contrary—if you lie—you could face prosecution. Do I make myself clear?"

They looked at me, stone-faced and silent.

"Now that we understand each other, let's see this list of drugs you've got. Oh my, anti-depressants!" I started reading the list of proposed drugs.

"Prozac." Dr. Pederson shot back.

"Prozac! My, my! That's a serious anti-depressant alright! How extraordinary that you think I should take a very powerful drug like Prozac when I don't suffer from depression at all!"

Dr. Vas spoke up. "Maybe someday, in the future, you might suffer depression. So this way you won't suffer it. You could be looking forward."

I reamed him: "Wait a minute. I don't suffer depression in prison, which has to be the most stressful and awful experience. Here, I'm active and motivated. I work on my case. I walk 4-6 miles a day on the track. I suffer no symptoms of depression of any kind. But maybe, someday, in the future, years from now, we don't know when, I might suffer depression. Someday I might. So I should start taking anti-depressant drugs now?? Am I understanding you correctly?"

Dr. Vas got all puffed up: "You admit that you suffered a period of depression 20 years ago, when you lived in Seattle. So you admit that it happened before."

I had forgotten all about that, but I didn't let up: "Twenty years ago!?! You're not serious? Twenty years ago I was a kid, right out of college, trying to figure out my life. I lived in Seattle, where it rains non-stop. All the time! Yes, I did get depressed. So I left Seattle. And I grew up. And guess what? I stopped feeling depressed."

I turned to Dr. Pederson: "You cannot seriously think that I would agree to take Prozac today because 20 years ago, I got gloomy when it rained in Seattle? That's not going to happen. No. You can forget about it."

Dr. Pederson pouted: "So you are opposed to drugs. We call it medication, by the way. And you're telling us that you don't believe that you need that, and you're not going to take it."

"That's right," I replied. "I'm not going to put drugs in my body for non-existent conditions. I don't suffer from depression. I have no intention of taking any sort of anti-depressants. Not Prozac, or anything else! I consider it irresponsible for anyone to suggest it, and I won't do it."

"Let me repeat: I will not put drugs in my body for non-existent conditions. Now what's this other stuff?"

"Ativan. That's a mood stabilizer," Dr. Pederson replied. "It's for stress."

"Well, considering that my only stress comes from prison, I'm sure that I'll be just fine once I'm released on February 3rd. So the answer is no. I don't intend to stick around long enough to need Ativan. I haven't needed it in the three months that I've been here. And I certainly won't need it when I go home. I repeat. I am not going to take drugs for non-existent conditions. It's not going to happen."

"What else? We've already established that I'm not suffering delusions, since witnesses have already verified my story for Shadduck. And they could easily verify it for you, if you care to talk with them. It's only because of the Christmas holidays that I can't get hold of them today. But after the first of January, I'd be quite happy to hook you up. That's not a problem at all."

I don't remember what else was said, but I'd swear on the Holy Bible itself this accurately recounts our conversation at this "medication hearing." I was tough all the way through it.

Friends, this was as bad as it gets. I went back to my cell shaking in fear, as I crawled into my bunk.

Haldol? Prozac? Ativan?

I finally understood what three months locked up in prison on a Texas military base had not persuaded me. The Justice Department, the CIA and the White House seriously wanted to destroy me. They had no intention of letting me go. I didn't know how they could work it to hold me. But this was seriously scary stuff. I remember that I gave thanks that I'm a tough street fighter and fast thinking on my feet.

But that day I was blinded by the light.

I confess there's something about "extreme prejudice" that doesn't really sink in until you face the brutality of it full force. "Extreme prejudice" shoots for absolute physical destruction and spiritual annihilation of the Intelligence Asset, the death of body, mind and soul.

Trying to chemically lobotomize an Asset certainly qualifies as "extreme termination."

When they come at you like this, they pull every dirty trick in the book. You have to take every dirty punch. And you have to fight. And fight. And fight.

Because if you stop for anything, to cry or complain that it's not fair, they will take you out.

That's the whole point. And they are bigger, better financed, more powerful and absolutely fucking corrupt. More than anything, they are unashamedly corrupt.

It's a dirty fight until you're down.

But you have advantages, too. You are small. You can pivot in your strategy. And the old intelligence rule still holds: Everything that comes at you is either a weapon or a tool.

To fight back, you have to keep hold of your wits, and you have to build a counter-strategy and take them on, proactively. You cannot afford to be reactive or passive.

One thing more, not everybody opposes you. In an intelligence war, there are always factions. In "extreme prejudice," one faction holds superior force— for the moment— like the pro-War camp in the Republican Party, which supported the Iraqi Exiles on Capitol Hill. And they take no prisoners. However, they are most likely to shoot the hostage in "extreme prejudice" <u>when they are going down or about to fall</u>. That's when they fight dirtiest. That's when they're most sensitive about their vulnerabilities. They're still at peak. So they can attract weak allies, like corrupt prison psychiatrists willing to prostitute their credentials for a few bucks, and get their hands dirty.

For a moment those psychiatrists got to play in a real intelligence game. But that's not their world. They are pawns. They don't recognize how the pendulum swings back the other way—or as I would put it—the sword of Damocles. When it comes back, they're out in the open, and the forces that gave the kill order have left them high and dry.

Other factions hone in on that. So you're out there, fighting alone, and somebody behind the scenes recognizes that tides are turning, and they throw you a wrench, so that you can wage a stronger battle.

You keep fighting alone. But now you're fighting with a wrench. Even so, you can't flinch. You have no choice but to take every dirty blow.

Once extreme prejudice came into play, I was fighting for my life and to protect myself from a chemical lobotomy, which this cocktail of super potent psycho-tropic drugs (Haldol, Ativan and Prozac) definitely intended to inflict. Secondarily, I was fighting for my freedom, to get out of prison. Protecting myself from drugs came first, however, without question.

Calling me "incompetent," ironically, meant nothing to me. Sticks and stones, baby. Smear tactics don't work on me. Notoriety doesn't frighten me, or I could never have dealt with Libya and Iraq, or the CIA in the first place. No insult by a psychology freak ever mattered to me. Reputations are for sissies in games like this.

What terrified me was the threat of forcible drugging. I abhor drugs. I despise drugs. I consider that my brain and my consciousness are precious gifts, and I would not destroy or alter my thinking and the magnificent working of my identity or my soul for anything in the world.

That was unacceptable to me.

I would come out of this fight standing or dead. There was no middle ground.

That first morning, I made a critical decision. I would not allow them to kill me. I would not accommodate them on any level in this terrible game. As the fight continued, my strength would ebb and flow, but my knowledge and confidence of who I am would grow stronger, because to wage this battle, I had to know who I was. I had to believe in who I was. And from that moment on, the illusion of their power to decide who I was, was lost. They couldn't take away my identity, because so long as I stayed alive, I was my identity.

Deep in my gut, at my worst moments, I understood that if I could survive this brutality, once the pendulum swung back, I would be resurrected. The truth that I carry from my past would stay constant and unchanging, no matter who controlled the White House. Many times at Carswell I used to murmur a prayer to the great Rev. Martin Luther King. "The arc of the universe bends towards justice." Over and over again.

A chemical lobotomy, however, would be living death for me. It was too grotesque to contemplate.

And so, while I waited, tense and terrified, to receive the decision by Carswell staff on "involuntary drugging," as they were now calling it, I could not help but consider the powerful forces that had arrayed against me. My adversaries were immensely powerful, indeed.

My own cousin, Andy Card served as Chief of Staff to President Bush all the time I was locked up at Carswell. I often thought of Secretary Colin Powell stumping on CNN to wash the blood and dirt off his reputation.

The only thing more dangerous for me than "delusional psychiatry" turned out to be "delusional" White House officials and Congressional leaders so desperate to hold onto power that they denied any responsibility for their own hellacious stupidity. They lacked courage and integrity to take responsibility for their own decisions. They had to destroy me to obliterate the evidence of their weakness.

Shortly after my release, John McLaughlin, a powerhouse Washington journalist and host of the McLaughlin Group, lamented how the White House and Congress had created "a virtual reality about Iraq," and fought desperately to attack anybody who threatened to expose the cracks in their reality. I was not alone in recognizing the "group psychosis" of the GOP war camp.

Unhappily for me, my case tossed together "delusional psychiatry" with "delusional War policy—" And the crazies in Congress held the balance of power so long as I remained in prison and under indictment..

I was Dorothy lost in a Land of Oz created by White House Wizards and Republican leaders. The fact that I was right meant nothing. They could not allow Dorothy to pull back that curtain, and show that all of their spectacle and glitz was a bunch of circus tricks. They were so vulnerable and weak that they could not tolerate the smallest person poking at them.

Once little Dorothy entered the stage with Toto, the Wizard of Oz was finished. Republicans in Congress recognized that little Dorothy might metamorphis into Susan Lindauer.

I thought about all of these factors as I waited anxiously for Carswell's internal decision on involuntary drugging. Thinking proactively, I began mapping a strategy for appeals if they attempted to carry out this terrifying threat.

My heart was pounding when prison staff thrust the internal staff decision under the door of my prison cell.

I ran to grab it, and flipped anxiously through the pages to the end of the report, my heart thumping fast and hard.

"Involuntary medication not approved."[449]

I gasped. I had won this round! I laughed deliriously and hugged my cellmates. I danced around our cell, jumping up and down like a kid. I was elated.

When I calmed down, I examined the internal report more carefully. [See Appendix] On page 4, the hand-written "Summary of Evidence" stated the following:[450]

"Lindauer reported she was against medication of any kind, including psycho-tropic medication."

"She denied the possibility of mental illness, once again reporting in detail her belief that the government is having her detained because she represents a threat to the administration due to her differing beliefs about their policies on Iraq. She states she has been a government agent for 9 years working in "anti terrorism.""

"Lindauer denied any wish to hurt herself or others, and denied any history of aggressive behavior."

"The document is signed by William M. Pederson, MD and Collin Vas, MD."

There was no ambiguity in that hand-written memo.

The original hand written document provided shocking and irrefutable evidence of the Bureau of Prison's logic and rationale for recommending drugs. Proposed treatment with heavy psychotropic drugs had one purpose: to "cure" my beliefs that I worked as an Asset.

No other evidence from Carswell was offered to justify drug treatment. They described no symptoms of depression, weeping or hysteria, no behavioral problems dealing with guards or other inmates. There was no mention of hallucinations or hearing voices, or suggestions that I suffered disjointed thoughts, and showed poor cognition skills.

No. The rationale for psychotropic drugs was strictly to "correct" my claims of work-ing as a "government agent for 9 years in anti- terrorism." Carswell suggested that drugs would be necessary to "cure" my "detailed belief" that the government was prosecuting me for dissenting from the Republican policy on Iraq.

Nothing else got cited as justification for "treatment."

There was just that small pesky problem. My story happened to be true. And they all knew it.

Even the corporate media had acknowledged from its coma that the White House had a fondness for punishing dissension to protect its War policy. And now Carswell had made a play straight out of the Cold War and the Soviet Union.

My strong offensive at the internal "medication hearing" stopped them. When I saw that document, however, and I saw the desperation and illogic behind it, I knew that prison staff would not stop trying. They hadn't figured out how to do it yet. But it seemed doubtful that they could resist looking for another way.

Under a second page of the report, there were boxes:

Had the inmate requested witnesses? Dr. Pederson marked "no."[451452]

Liar!

Under the second box marked "Evidence Presented," there was a category for "Statement of witnesses." He checked off "not applicable."[453]

Bastard liar!

That told me a lot. Carswell would not acknowledge my witnesses, even if falsifying a report amounted to perjury in federal court—which would be a punishable felony.

Well, they'd been warned.

I took a deep breath. I'd won this round!

If it was only up to the prison, the question of involuntary drugging had been decided. I had won the argument. They couldn't pull it off. But I was sure that if the White House or the Justice Department intervened from outside the prison, this attack would not stop.

I was willing to bet it would get really ugly.

On January 1st, I called JB Fields and told him that it looked doubtful that I would be coming home on February 3rd.

Sometimes it helps to be paranoid.

CHAPTER 24:

CORRUPTION AT CARSWELL

"All that is necessary for the triumph of evil is that good men do nothing."
—Edmund Burke

Something more sinister was happening at Carswell than prison rapes and withholding health care from very sick inmates— as if that wasn't bad enough.

Much worse, the prison had a history of refusing to release women inmates after the completion of their sentences, on the most flimsy grounds.

It happened more often than anyone would like to think.

The first time I witnessed it, I could not believe it myself.

A woman prisoner from Chicago had won a tremendous victory in the United States Supreme Court. She'd filed what's called a "pro se" appeal, meaning that she prepared a legal brief by herself without an attorney's assistance. She challenged her conviction and sentencing alone.

That the United States Supreme Court took up her appeal was quite impressive in itself. No matter the merits of a case, there are umpteen thousands of appeals that never get heard at all, most filed by experienced attorneys, let alone those submitted "pro se" by defendants. From out of that multitude, the Supreme Court chose her case for review.

More impressively still, the Supreme Court granted her appeal, striking down all or part of her conviction and sentencing, with a declarative order that she should be released from Carswell immediately.

That's a tremendous victory for any defendant, manna from on high! It's what we prisoners dream of, getting our day in the Supreme Court—and winning! It almost never happens. Even if a Supreme Court Justice agrees to review a petition, at best you hope they accept parts of it. In her situation, the Supreme Court accepted her argument in its entirety. And they didn't send her back for re-sentencing. They expressly ordered her to be freed with time served! Hallelujah! I read it with my own eyes.

So what do you think happened to this woman who'd just triumphed at the Supreme Court of the United States, getting her conviction and sentencing overturned?

Given Carswell's history of dealing with other appellate court rulings and federal judges, do you think prison staff gave a damn what a Supreme Court Justice had to say?

They didn't care what the 2nd Circuit Appellate Court had to say about inmates' rights at "medication hearings." They didn't care what federal judges had to say about the rights of prisoners to have sleep apnea machines, or access to heart medication for post-surgical recovery. Prisoners have died, because Carswell flouted federal court orders.

And so, horribly enough, Carswell Prison refused to let this woman go home.

She had filed her appeal "pro se," so she had no attorney on the outside to enforce the Supreme Court order on her behalf. Instead, Carswell sent a message to all those other women inmates who might think about filing appeals, too. It wouldn't do any good. Carswell prison staff would mete out punishments. No outside court authority, no Federal Judge was going to contradict them.

If a defendant had a court order from the United States Supreme Court itself, Carswell staff would not be compelled to obey it.

And so, while the Supreme Court ruled in her favor sometime in November, Carswell poohed and pouted about filing the paperwork for her release, dillydallying with the central Bureau of Prisons until mid-April.

She suffered an extra five and a half months of prison detention.

With a Supreme Court decision in her hand, carried from staff office to office, never leaving her person 24 hours a day, that freed woman could not leave the prison.

One prison staffer snidely told her that "when she got to Washington, she could complain."

Unconstitutional? Without question.

On all counts, it was despicable and corrupt. That's Carswell, in a nutshell.

Flouting a direct Supreme Court order wasn't the only example of Carswell manipulating procedures in order to deny prisoners their freedom at the end of a sentence.

The case of Kathleen Rumpf, a Ploughshares activist and Catholic lay worker, exposes another way that Carswell routinely skirts the courts, in order to hold prisoners after their release dates. Rumpf spent 8 months at Carswell for "rewriting the welcome sign for the School of the Americas at Fort Benning, Georgia, to read "School of Shame."[454] The School of Americas is also called the "School of Torture" by peace activists, because its graduates include members of the violent juntas of Latin America, famous for murdering intellectuals and political dissidents.

For messing up the sign, Rumpf and four fellow Ploughshares activists each got sentenced to one year in prison and fined $2,000.

On the day of her release, other peace activists gathered at the prison gates to celebrate. "West Wing" actor, Martin Sheen, a Ploughshares activist with 58 arrests in his own right, flew in from Los Angeles to welcome Rumpf home.[455]

Carswell Prison Warden, J.B. Brogan, didn't like those rabble-rousers outside his gates. He decided that Rumpf would be ordered to sign a promissory note for the $2,000 fine—or else she would be held "indefinitely" at Carswell. As part of the promissory note, she had to agree that if she was unable to pay the fine, she would be subject to re-arrest and sent back to prison.[456]

Rumpf, who lives on Social Security disability, refused on the grounds of poverty.

Very well, Brogan refused to grant her release. She would stay at Carswell, until she worked out her finances.

Maureen Tolbert, Rumpf's attorney, called it "unconstitutional," pointing out that the obscure statute "basically allows prison officials to re-sentence someone who has already served his or her time."[457]

Carswell is one of the very few prisons that enforce this mostly unknown federal statute. When women prisoners can not pay court fines, at times Carswell continues their detentions, until family or friends agree to post the money on their behalf. If they can't pay, because they're alone in the world, they don't go home. If they promise to meet a payment schedule and break it, they are subject to re-arrest. They have to agree to this, in order to get released from prison.

No Judge oversees the prison's decision to continue detention. There's no provision for a hearing, no right to an attorney, nor any time restraint on how long the Bureau of Prisons can hold prisoners who can't pay or else refuse to sign the agreement—even if they are desperately honest that they can't be sure how they would honor it. Most are incredibly poor, with limited job prospects after prison. This poses a serious burden as they try to reintegrate with society.

As Rumpf discovered the hard way, that's a matter of habit at Carswell. In her case, friends paid the fine on her behalf. She stayed in prison an extra two days. Others are not so lucky, and their release gets delayed much longer, sometimes for months. It's prison gossip, when it happens. And it happens at Carswell more frequently than anyone wants to think.

The Story of Neeran "Nancy" Zaia

Politics guides so many decisions at Carswell. But the fates often have a tragic sense of humor, as well.

As it turns out, I was not the only prisoner with a case tied to Iraqi War politics who arrived from Washington the week of October 3rd, 2005. An Iraqi émigré named Neeran "Nancy" Zaia got shipped to Carswell for an extensive psychiatric evaluation, too.

Our friendship was more extraordinary because our cases proved antithetical in all ways. While I got accused of acting as an "Iraqi agent," on behalf of Saddam Hussein's government, Nancy Zaia got indicted for trying to help other Iraqis escape Saddam's religious and political persecution before the War.

She denied helping anyone enter the United States illegally. What she'd done was help families of Iraqi Chaldean Christians secure proper visas from Jordan to the nation of

Ecuador, about 200 in all. The visas were legally acquired from the Ecuadorian Embassy in Amman, as part of a policy to encourage wealthy Iraqis to establish residency in that Latin American country.[458]

The Justice Department claimed some of those Iraqi refugees kept moving northward after arriving in Ecuador. About 40-50 of those Iraqis ended up in the United States, including infants and children. Nancy swore that she had nothing to do with that. She swore she had no contact with the Chaldean families after they left Jordan. However the Justice Department insisted that she should be responsible for their final destination. Nancy's attorney argued the U.S. was running interference in Ecuador's visa policy. Her defense claimed the arrest was extra-territorial, in attempt to strong arm Ecuadorean officials into reconsidering their friendly immigration policy towards Iraqi refugees. It reflected American paranoia after 9/11. But it had nothing to do with her actions.

The hypocrisy in Zaia's case was that the Bush Administration cited Saddam's torture practices as justification for the War.

If that moral outrage had been authentic, Nancy Zaia should have been praised as a hero, not imprisoned as a criminal.

Nancy had been sent to Carswell for a psychiatric evaluation because of evidence that Saddam's security forces had tortured her in Baghdad. She claimed that Iraqi Intelligence hanged her 3 year old son by his throat with a rope from a ceiling fan, and turned it on, so that the fan blades started rotating.

Then one of the men took a butcher knife and started slashing the blade at the screaming, choking child. Nancy kept grabbing for the toddler. Trying to shield her little boy from the knife, she got slashed herself.

She had a 10 inch jagged scar on the inside of her arm to prove it.

Nancy Zaia had also been forced into an arranged marriage at age 13, with a much older Kurdish man involved in the Northern Resistance movement. He had raped her repeatedly throughout her teenage years. When she fled Iraq with her young children, she was fleeing an abusive (mostly absent) husband, and the political troubles that his resistance work caused for her family. When Saddam's security forces could not lay hands on him, they were not above inflicting pain on her.

Her attorney argued that those facts of her life in Iraq should be given substantial weight in the proceedings.

And so it was that Nancy Zaia and I arrived together at Carswell the first week of October, both of us arrested for political reasons that exposed the illogic of the government's position on Iraq, and both of us subjected to the shenanigans of prison psychology at Carswell.

Unfairly, both of our psych evaluations at Carswell had strong political overtones—in opposite directions. While I believe that I showed myself fully capable of assisting my defense, it would be difficult to make the same arguments about Nancy. At the first mention of Iraq, she would become so emotional, paranoid and overstressed that she could scarcely participate in a rational conversation to discuss her defense strategy.

Twice her attorney flew in from Washington to meet with her. Nancy hid from him on both visits, because she couldn't handle a simple attorney conversation about the charges against her. Guards searched for her everywhere. Our circle of inmates found her curled up on the floor of a bathroom stall in a fetal position. She was lost in memories of Saddam Hussein and her old life in Iraq. She couldn't get past that pain. It's doubtful that Nancy could have sat through a trial without an outburst, screaming in Arabic at the Judge and jury. Seriously, I could imagine her suffering a heart attack during trial.

Even dealing with me as a friend, she was subject to bursts of paranoia about my arrest as an "Iraqi Agent," that would stop her from speaking with me for days at a time.

Nevertheless, in the highly politicized world of psychiatry at Carswell, Nancy's evaluation flatly refused to acknowledge her incapacity to contribute to her defense. Carswell decreed that Nancy Zaia's refugee status, and her personal comprehension of the suffering of Chaldean Christians in Iraq and the brutality of Saddam Hussein's government, had no impact whatsoever on her actions. Carswell declared that the personal oppression that she'd suffered, as a 13 year old victim of spousal rape by a 35 + year old man, was completely irrelevant. The attack on her children by Iraqi Intelligence merited no consideration by the Court. According to Carswell, she experienced no irrational outbursts or paranoia that impacted her ability to contribute to her defense.

It's questionable how much Nancy understood of the court proceedings, given her emotional state. She was deeply paranoid and prone to outbursts of hysteria. She saw all events through that prism. During our months together on M-1, we walked hundreds of laps on the outdoor track, talking about our families, our dreams for the future, and our legal cases. Notably, she told me that Carswell had offered her a finding of "competence" in exchange for a guilty plea, with time served. Carswell promised she would go home to her family. They pushed Nancy hard, knowing she could not handle a trial, because of her explosive emotions on the subject of Iraq.

Complicating the matter, the fear of abuse on M-1 hung over all of us. All of us were terrified that Carswell would inflict on us what we saw psych staff do to others. Not surprisingly, Nancy was afraid to press for incompetence, though she's one of the very few inmates who I thought qualified for it. Almost nobody else had justification that I saw.

Apparently after I left, Carswell stamped her competent, in exchange for that guilty plea.

Only somewhere along the way, it appears they pulled a double-cross on her. It's unclear how it happened—Nancy could not explain it when my brilliant attorney, post-Carswell, Brian Shaughnessy contacted her in prison, at my request. Somehow, after dangling time served in front of her while I was at Carswell, her choices changed starkly after the finding of competence. The Justice Department recommended a 15 year sentence, which Nancy felt compelled to accept.[459] I was horrified when I heard. They told her she could have a 10 year sentence, if she agreed to deportation back to Iraq. By now she'd lived in the United States 25 years. All of her children and grand children are here. She accepted five extra years in prison, so that she wouldn't have to relive her trauma in Iraq. That says everything.

By any measure, 15 years was excessive. She got much tougher sentencing than "coyotes," who run hundreds of illegal immigrants from Mexico to Texas and California. Only about 50 Iraqis entered the United States illegally, including children and infants, and her guilty plea declares that she only arranged for their passage to South America—which was handled legally.[460] I can only say that I watched Carswell play head-games with Nancy, manipulating her past emotional traumas to get the guilty plea. Then they nailed her after she agreed.

But was she competent to accept the deal? I seriously question it.

All of the arguments to defame my competence absolutely applied to her. Nancy was so paranoid and explosive that she could not sit in a room with her attorney for an hour to discuss her legal strategy. She'd crawl into a fetal position and hide in the bathroom. Yet the same prison staff who declared me "unfit for trial," swore that Nancy was competent to accept a guilty plea, though she would get hysterical whenever the subject of her life in Iraq arose in conversation.

Go figure. That's the nature of psychiatry at Carswell —inconsistent, political and corrupt.

The Question of My Competence

Then, of course, there was me.

Brass tacks— Was I actually incompetent?

Given my bona fides, it begs the question: Are those the actions of an incompetent Asset? Is it fair to suggest that an Asset who warned about 9/11 and the bombing of the U.S.S. Cole, and the 1993 attack on the World Trade Center; who started negotiations for the Lockerbie Trial with Libya, and the return of the weapons inspectors to Iraq, had performed poorly in this role?

Would the CIA tolerate an Asset to function as a back-channel to Libya and Iraq for years, if that individual was untrustworthy analyzing trends and interpreting events? Given the advanced proactive and analytical requirements for even the most basic intelligence work, does that make sense? Much less that my contacts involved the most volatile region of the world? And my work targeted nations considered potentially hostile to U.S. interests?

I think that's very doubtful. Crazy like a fox, maybe, and non-conformist in my political viewpoints, definitely.

I've always believed that you're judged by the strength of your enemies. Mine included Dick Cheney, Colin Powell, Senator John McCain, Senator Trent Lott, Andy Card and Alberto Gonzales.

How flattering.

But was I really "incompetent—" as Republican leaders in Washington claimed, when I put together a message data base for all House and Senate offices—including every Chief of Staff, Legislative Director, Press Secretary and Foreign Policy assistant, Democrat and Republican alike?[461] Was I "incompetent" when I used that email data base to warn all of those top legislative staffers of the catastrophic consequences of the Iraqi War?

Was I "incompetent" when I warned about a $1.6 trillion dollar price tag for the War and Occupation that would financially stress Wall Street and America's national debt?[462]

Or when I foretold the rise of Iran as a regional powerhouse?

Or when I predicted the rise of charismatic Al Qaeda leaders inside Iraq and the flourishing of terrorist cells, in a violent backlash against the Occupation?

Or when I forecast that forces of democracy would transfer power to Islamic fundamentalists, away from moderate Arab governments?

Those rose petals died awfully fast in the desert sun, just as I forecast, so unhappily.

Was that incompetence on my part? Or was I scapegoated for somebody else's mistakes?

In 2007, the Senate Intelligence Committee cited specific warnings like mine, in declaring that reports from January, 2003 qualified as one of the "few bright spots" in Pre-War Intelligence.[463] They called it "outstanding." I campaigned on every single one of those arguments. I was so aggressive, in fact, that the Justice Department cited my warnings to Andy Card and Colin Powell in January, 2003, which contained those ideas,[464] to justify my indictment.

In 2007, Senator John Warner of Virginia called the substance of it "chilling and prophetic."

In 2004-2006, it was called "treason."

And I got accused of "incompetence."

Could psychiatry really be so corrupt? To put it bluntly, yes.

I had watched other women come in for psych studies, and leave after six or seven weeks. That's all it took for these evaluations. There wasn't much to it. Prison staff would interview us two or three times, typically. Then they'd speak with a couple of outside sources, like Ian Ferguson and Parke Godfrey.

If there was a previous psychiatric history, Carswell would review it. In my case, that would be Dr. Taddesseh in Maryland, who documented that he observed "no psychosis," "no depression," "no mood disturbances," and "no reason for additional psychiatric intervention." His year's worth of observations finished six months before I got sent to Carswell, so it was quite recent. I had a clean bill of "mental health" before I got to prison.[465]

Prison conversations with loved ones at home, and a generous outpouring of letters from loyal friends showed that I had good relationships throughout my life. Prison conversations with JB Fields demonstrated that I was involved in a healthy and mutually supportive relationship. I am not drawn to abusive or violent men. Likewise in prison, I was not socially isolated from the other women. Quite the opposite, I quickly made friends on M-1, though inevitably, some got transferred back to court for sentencing, or sent home after psych studies. I got left behind. That's how prison works.

I required a subpoena to get my hands on the observation notes by social workers and activity coordinators, who saw me daily on M-1. But when I succeeded, I found it highly informative.

Without exception, all staff notes were brief and positive. Every monthly report declared that I "socialized well," showed "good intellectual functioning," and had "good physical health."[466]

Shadduck and Vas and Pederson could hardly complain about that, could they?

The initial evaluation upon my arrival at Carswell on October 3, 2005 cited a goal of "decreasing the intensity and frequency of auditory and visual hallucinations in 120 days."

In the first report on October 26, 2005—three weeks after my arrival—prison staff struck that objective off the page, and wrote in the margins: "not applicable."[467]

I had to smile when I saw that. I have never suffered auditory or visual hallucinations in my life. Another point of harassment was lost.

Instead, staff notes said, "Ms. Lindauer is functioning well on the unit."

Other handwritten notes [468]said, "Functional and not a behavioral problem." That was underlined by M-1 staff.

Another staffer wrote, "Not a problem when confronted about anything."

Another guard wrote, "She is low key and cooperative. Cares for self, good hygiene. Zero behavioral problems. She is focused on getting a trial."

Another wrote, "Pleasant, appropriate appearance, clear speech, good eye contact."

Another wrote, "Cheerful and cooperative."

And another, "Calm, pleasant, appropriate grooming. Good eye contact."

And another, "Pleasant, smiling, appears to be happy, cooperative."

By December, Carswell's goal for "restoring competency" was that I should "A: Explain clearly the pros and cons of legal options within 90 days."[469]

And "B: Demonstrate the ability to work with (my) attorney in a rational manner within 90 days."

Nothing in those staff notes described any behavioral problems that warranted forcible drugging. Or voluntary drugging for that matter. It was medically absurd.

As a precaution, I signed every monthly report with a written declaration that Carswell should interview my witnesses to check out my story.[470] My written requests affirmed my understanding that I would have to prove the truthfulness of my story through independent sources. Clearly I was ready, willing and able to do so. With my signature, nobody could say that I hadn't lobbied hard to get it done – hardly the act of a defendant who expected the Courts to take my word for everything.[471]

Sure enough, when Shadduck finally got around to questioning Ferguson and Godfrey, my story checked out. There was no question of a "delusional disorder." And staff knew it. By Carswell's own admission, I showed no other types of "symptoms." Even Carswell was compelled to rule against "involuntary medication," following its internal hearing.[472]

There was no medical basis for it. Any other inmate would have gone home after that, or back to court, whereas I faced a hard reality that the Feds intended to hold me to the 120th day allowed by federal statute. This would be my only prison time. The Justice Department wanted to squeeze every possible day out of me. I resolved to cope with that.

One more thing protected me. Or so I believed.

Most critically of all, I had a fail safe option, a statutory right to a hearing before the decision on competence got finalized. Federal law guarantees the right to call witnesses and show evidence opposing psychiatric evaluations.[473] Courts are not supposed to rule on competence without due process. That's a flagrant violation of an individual's rights. My rights should have been sacrosanct.

To protect myself, I buckled down at the prison law library, and read up on the law. I also filed a "pro se" request for a hearing with a list of witnesses, according to all the requirements of the law. My request was registered in an appropriate and timely manner.

I clung to the promise of that hearing like a sacrament. Truly I believed that I was covered on all fronts, whatever followed.

Ineptitude of the Court-Appointed Attorney

So what tripped me up?

As part of a competency review, it's standard practice to assess whether a defendant's attorney might be trying to shrug off a complex case by pursuing an incompetence defense. From the first in-take interview, Carswell staff zoomed on my concerns that my public attorney, Sam Talkin, could not maneuver the morass of my legal situation.

From my first days on the SHU at Carswell, staff was informed that my uncle, Ted Lindauer felt compelled to interview strategic witnesses, because of Talkin's bumbling. And Ted himself forcefully assured prison staff that he had personally investigated my story, and I checked out.[474]

Everyone could see that Ted was fiercely devoted to watching over me. In prison phone calls, Ted emphasized that he was reading up case law on psychiatry. By all objective measures, he was on top of my situation.

The need for legal intervention by a family member should have set off alarms over whose competence should be examined—mine or my public attorney's. Even Judge Mukasey was aware that it had been necessary to seek a family member's help in my case.

Under normal circumstances, questions about an attorney's performance would disqualify use of an "incompetence defense," automatically. In my situation, however, my attorney's fumbling was carefully overlooked. No external factors appeared to matter.

Ominously for my legal rights, by 2006, the United States and Britain were officially losing the War in Iraq. Insurgents had seized control of the chaos, and threatened to fragment the country in a violent bloodbath that polarized Shi'ite- Sunni relations from north to south. As battlefield casualties mounted, frothing on Capitol Hill reached a fevered pitch over the "incompetence" of Assets involved with Pre-War Intelligence.

Politicians liked that story. They liked it very much.

From a psychiatric standpoint, Capitol Hill was suffering a major "psychotic breakdown." Furiously Congress labored to reinvent themselves as the victims of deceptive intelligence practices. Not surprisingly, the facts about Pre-War Intelligence turned out to be vastly different than what politicians in Washington told American voters and the international community. And so the Justice Department got its marching orders: Nothing and nobody would be allowed to challenge the story that Republican leaders were selling to the American people.

That was the "reality" that mattered at Carswell.

And so Carswell psychiatrists set about constructing a whole new reality of my identity that protected political interests in Washington—a game that pretended I suffered a "psychotic disorder not otherwise specified."[475].

It's doubtful that I was ever incompetent or psychotic. All those months, I showed no "symptoms of mental illness"—except post traumatic stress from the Justice Department's refusal to end my imprisonment on my release date.[476] That's a fairly sane response to the events, I'd say.

My judicial abuse does, however, provide evidence of a major leadership breakdown in Washington. For all the falderol at campaign time, Congressional oversight failed badly to provide adequate supports and protections for me as an Asset.

Where was the Senate Intelligence Committee when an Asset needed them? Or the House Judiciary Committee? What about my old boss, Senator Ron Wyden? Or Maryland's Senator Barbara Mikulski Both serve on the Senate Intelligence Committee.

Why didn't any of those powerful Senators take action to protect a woman Asset who had come under attack for claiming to be a woman Asset? As if it was laughable that women could do such work. All of Congress bragged about its "outstanding leadership support" for the anti-terrorism work that I devoted 9 years of my life to performing. This was the time to prove it.

An inquiry checking my status as an Asset would not have interfered with court proceedings. It would have spotlighted less than honest practices by factions of the Justice Department seeking to punish dissension from the War policy.

So why did nobody help me?

Infamously, one afternoon I challenged one of the psych staff that Carswell should expect a Congressional investigation, in the wake of the abuse that I suffered as an Asset in their prison.

The man laughed in my face: "They don't care what happens to you. Nobody's going to help you. They're quite pleased with the way we've handled this."

If so, it was a terrible judgment call. My imprisonment set a dangerous precedent in the intelligence community. It borrowed the old Soviet game plan from the Cold War, punishing Assets for knowing "inconvenient truths," and viciously trying to "correct" my thinking, in order to cover up their own political mistakes.

The question was, how low would they sink?

The answer was, as low as possible. They would inflict as much damage as they could get away with. Everything depended on Judge Mukasey, and how much they could fool him. Ted Lindauer swore to me that Judge Mukasey was nobody's fool. He wanted a vehicle to end the case, Ted speculated. But he'd see what they were up to. This incompetence strategy was what Talkin handed him. That's what the Court had to work with.

Really I had no idea what to think.

According to federal law, the maximum detention for a psychological study to determine competence is 120 days, and no longer.[477] After that maximum 120 days, if a person shows no signs of violence towards himself or others, he or she must be released back to the community. That's plenty of time, by the way. Most psych studies can be completed within 60 days, unless it involves a drug detox.

That should have put me out the Carswell prison gates on February 3, 2006—and not one day later, according to federal law.

Grimly, I waited.

As the day got closer, other women prisoners began to notice that basic steps for my release were not taken. There started to be whispers on M-1 that something wasn't right. That kind of prison gossip travels fast.

And so the day of my release approached.

February 3rd started like any other day. There were no goodbyes the night before, a prison ritual with prayers and hugs for those left behind. No staff woke me before dawn to usher me quietly out of the prison before other inmates woke to see me go.

With quiet stealth, the Bureau of Prisons website reported that my release had been postponed "indefinitely."[478]

Back home in Maryland, friends and family panicked at last. They could not believe what had just happened.

Locked inside prison on a Texas military base as an accused "Iraqi Agent," I was terrified.

CHAPTER 25:

PRISON DIARY

Courage is resistance to fear, and the mastery of fear—
Not the absence of fear.
–Mark Twain

I used to think the day would never come
That my life would depend on the morning sun
–New Order, "True Faith"

"What are you saying? They lied? What do you mean? They fucking lied?"

"They can't lie to a federal judge! That's perjury! That's a federal crime. They know it's a crime. Half the prisoners here got arrested for making false statements to the FBI. The other half got sentenced for obstruction of justice. They know they can't do that."

"That's right," Ted Lindauer told me. "People lie in court all the time."

"Yeah, criminals lie. Not staff for the Bureau of Prisons! They're supposed to be the ones telling the truth."

It was February 3rd. My 120 days were up. I was supposed to board an airplane in Dallas to fly home to Maryland. I was practically hysterical as Uncle Ted gave me the low down on my release, which Carswell had delayed "indefinitely."[479]

That wasn't the agreement. Granted, they cut the deal without my knowledge or consent. However, it looked pretty good that morning. In exchange for overlooking the violations of my rights to a hearing before detention, and my cooperation in the interests of "national security," the Prosecutor was supposed to dismiss the charges and send me home—not lock me up indefinitely. That's what they told Judge Mukasey to persuade him to go along with this endgame.

Worst yet, Carswell was now arguing that I should be strapped to a gurney, so that I could be forcibly drugged with needle injections of Haldol,[480] until I stopped claiming that I worked as a "U.S. Intelligence Asset in anti-terrorism for Nine Years,"[481] and that I warned about a major attack involving airplane hijackings and a strike on the World Trade Center throughout the spring and summer of 2001. Carswell decreed it a "psychotic disorder, not otherwise specified."

This attack came out of nowhere.

Or did it come straight from Republican headquarters?

At that point, I had not seen Carswell's report prepared by Dr. James Shadduck, but Ted had. Apparently, it carefully overlooked the unhappy truth that my story checked out in total. The report faithfully omitted critical acknowledgements that Shadduck himself had spoken with two witnesses, and fully authenticated the key structure of my history.[482] Shadduck and Dr. Collin Vas had confirmed my long-standing work relationship with Dr. Fuisz and his CIA credentials, and our coverage of Libya. They knew that I had worked under his supervision. We had documents in Maryland from Dr. Fuisz's congressional testimony proving his expertise on U.S. corporations that supplied Iraq with SCUD Mobile Missile Launchers before the first Gulf War.[483], [484],[485] I checked out alright, not a problem.

Dr. Shadduck had also spoken with Parke Godfrey, who provided critical corroboration that I had warned about a 9/11 style of attack in the spring and summer of 2001.[486]

Godfrey had promised to make sure Carswell understood that he was repeating to Shadduck what he'd already told the FBI in Toronto in September, 2004. So the FBI and my prosecutor, Edward O'Callaghan, already knew it, too—a year before I got sent to Carswell.

My insistence on pre-trial validation had strategically removed "plausible deniability" in my case, whereby one party shields another from responsibility for their actions by withholding vital information, so they can pretend not to have known. I had taken proactive steps to block their "deniability." They couldn't hide behind the pretense of ignorance.

Everybody understood that I was telling the truth, from the FBI to the U.S. Attorneys Office in New York, to Uncle Ted, to the hack psychologists of Carswell. They'd all verified it.

Distinctly, the only individual who had not verified my authenticity was Judge Mukasey. And he was forced to rely on the integrity of the Justice Department, which had a sworn obligation to the Courts not to lie about such things.

Dr. Shadduck was on the inside of the cover up. He had confirmed all the salient points of my defense. At trial, there would be more high-powered witnesses, who would expose more truth. In this pre-trial phase, however, Dr. Shadduck had more than sufficient validation for his purposes. He could see that Ferguson and Godfrey were eager to bring clarity to the legal confusion, and fully cooperative in responding to his questions.

Knowing all that, Shadduck deliberately structured the report so the Judge would conclude there was no independent confirmation. In that way, Carswell effectively falsified the findings of its psychiatric report to Judge Mukasey, Chief Justice of the Southern

District of New York, and one of this nation's most respected and preeminent judges.[487] And the psychology staff sought to forcibly drug a known Asset to stop me from saying that I was an Asset.[488]

With a high enough dosage of psychotropic Haldol, Carswell argued I could be "cured" of claiming that our team gave advance warning about a 9/11 style of attack and participated in Pre-War Intelligence. I could be made to forget the details of my activities at the Iraqi Embassy, which contradicted the new truth invented by Republican leaders, including Andy Card.

As for "indefinite detention," Carswell wanted to hold me in prison until whatever time the psych staff could assure the cure was effective.[489] They told the Court they had no idea how long that would take. The psych evaluations speculated that it would probably require a long detention, however, because my beliefs in my Asset work are so deeply entrenched. (It ain't easy to eradicate reality, even for psychiatry!)

If that's not Soviet style revisionism, I don't know what is. It's something Stalin would have done in the Cold War to punish dissension and enforce political conformity. For sure, when O'Callaghan and Shadduck falsified that report to the federal court, they engaged in gross misconduct. Vital exculpatory knowledge was withheld that Judge Mukasey urgently "needed to know" that the FBI and the Bureau of Prisons had both authenticated, independently.

For those outside the intelligence community, "need to know" status gets conferred when any individual, federal judge or not, risks making a decision that would impact the functioning of intelligence operations, or otherwise cause negative blowback. The person "needs to know" to guide their actions, so they don't do something stupid or interfere with something else underway.

Threatening to forcibly drug an Asset to "cure" the Asset of knowing real intelligence facts would certainly qualify as a most obscene sort of mistake.

Their actions put Judge Mukasey in the position of judicially endorsing a cover up of the 9/11 warning and Iraqi Pre-War Intelligence—something he would never do of his own volition.

O'Callaghan and Carswell didn't stop to consider the consequences for Judge Mukasey's integrity. They only imagined that if they could forcibly administer enough psychotropic drugs, we could all lie about 9/11 and Pre-War Intelligence together.

They wanted to chemically lobotomize me. And they sought to compromise the integrity of a senior federal Judge to get authorization to do it.

Drugging was a political weapon, alright. And my prosecutor, O'Callaghan was a political animal. He left the U.S. Attorney's office in New York to work as a top adviser for John McCain and Sarah Palin's Presidential race in 2008.[490] I could never forget—or forgive— that I got arrested 30 days after contacting McCain's Senate office in Washington, asking to testify before the blue ribbon Presidential Commission on Pre-War Intelligence. The next thing I know, I'm under arrest. What a coincidence that my Prosecutor worked for McCain at election time.

O'Callaghan now works at the Law Firm of Peabody Nixon, the haunts of former President Richard Nixon. His bio claims that he advised the McCain Campaign on anti-terrorism and national security policy.

You can only imagine the horror that I experienced receiving this news about Carswell's intentions. I was beside myself with outrage and fear. "Indefinite detention" could imply the full prison sentence of 10 years. Typically, that's how the Courts handled violent offenders who get declared incompetent. They automatically serve the maximum sentence. It appeared the Bureau of Prisons wanted to test whether the Patriot Act could be applied to that same category of major crimes, pushing me into a permanent legal abyss.

On February 3rd, in a moment of blinding panic, I wasn't sure what part of my situation was the worst: getting stuck in prison indefinitely without due process, because of a bogus psychiatric evaluation. Or getting threatened with forcible injections of Haldol throughout my incarceration.

I would have to say drugs tipped the balance.

Haldol was a rhinoceros tranquilizer. It's a zombie drug that imitates the stone-like symptoms of Parkinson's Disease. And they wanted to shoot me up like some street junkie.

Honestly, I would rather get water boarded.

There was never any question of compromising on the drugs, in exchange for freedom. I would stay in prison as long as it took, but I would never put drugs in my body. Not to please some hack politician in Washington. Not in this lifetime. This would go to the Supreme Court, if necessary. Ted Lindauer and I were confident that there'd been enough irregularities, however, that we could probably overturn any decision on forcible drugging in the 2nd Circuit Appellate Court, before it ever reached the Supremes. "Indefinite detention" could still be in force in that equation, but we did not know.

The greater difficulty would be dealing with the craziness of Carswell itself.

Uncle Ted demanded that I must not panic. He promised to drive from southern Illinois to visit me in Texas, about 700 miles each way, so we could work out a counter strategy together.[491] Obviously, Sam Talkin was out of his depth, and unable to cope with this shocking twist in events. He took no action to fight for my release. He appeared to be stumped as how to proceed.

My beloved Uncle Ted swore that I was not alone. Ted has such a forceful presence as an attorney that he's practically in the cell with you, talking side by side, hammering out strategies. Ted promised to exert his best energies to broker a solution with the Judge that would get me out of the "hoosiegow," as he called it. Ted kept my courage strong in moments of absolute terror and despair, like this. I could never have survived—and won—without him.

But inside those prison walls after February 3, 2006, a surreal drama began to play out. Carswell had verified my story. Now reality was thrown out the window. Staff rigidly declared that my work in Pre-War Intelligence and Counter-Terrorism from 1993 to 2002 was manifestly delusional, and must be corrected. They began to impose their own psychosis on me, brutally reinventing that truth of my life. All external factors stopped mattering at this point. A life-time's work against war and violence, the support of senior Congressional staffers, journalists, attorneys from the Lockerbie case, U.N. diplomats who'd watch my work for years—none of that external reality mattered at Carswell.

They had already tried aggressively to force me to recant, voluntarily. And they had failed. Now they proposed to physically cripple me so that I would be too destroyed to speak. Or think.

The threat of forcible drugging hung over me like a dark hurricane cloud. In one terrifying episode, one of Carswell's prison staff said to me, "Don't worry. I'm going to give you so many drugs, you won't be troubled by those memories any longer."

On several occasions, I protested to one of the senior psychiatrist's that his colleague Dr. Shadduck had already spoken to my witnesses and verified my story. To which he replied: "That doesn't matter. I'm going to tell the Judge you made it all up. Who do you think they're going to believe? You or me?"

"I am a doctor."

Who cared about reality at Carswell? Who cared about the law? Who cared about ethical behavior and truthful testimony?

Nobody that I could see.

One of the psychology staff said to me: "Reality is whatever I say it is."

I remember that I looked him hard in the face. I wanted to stare him straight in the eyes, inmate to prison officer, and when I shook my head and answered: "You Are Wrong."

For these reasons, I am firmly convinced that Carswell should be closed to all psychiatric evaluations immediately. Some women prisoners should be entitled to new evaluations, and a reconsideration of their sentencing and any court-ordered drugging. This corruption of psychiatry did not start with my case. And it did not end with my case either. It's endemic to Carswell's approach to psychiatry and the Courts. A lot of other women inmates have suffered from it, and a lot of other Judges have been fooled by it. Those sentences should be reconsidered at once.

As for me, my nightmare of "extreme prejudice" was beginning in earnest.

It comes down to the old cliché that courage is not the absence of fear, but fighting through fear. Thinking back on it, I was terrified beyond words— and the odds of my victory were stunningly low, at least in the first round, without an appeal to the higher court. The prison staff on the Texas military base had no doubts they would prevail against me. I'm quite sure they did not expect me to win.

I began to have a recurring nightmare.

In my dream, I was living in a room filled with water up to the ceiling. I could only breathe through a small air tube that snaked up to a vent above me.

In my dream, the tube was thin, and breathing was difficult. I had so little oxygen.

I was chained to the floor. Looking up through the water towards the ceiling, I could see the vent. But I could not see behind the vent to know if my oxygen would be cut off by some unseen hand. In my dream, I feared that hand intensely.

I remember distinctly knowing that I must concentrate on breathing and stay focused. If I panicked, I would lose what small source of oxygen I had, and the effect would be terrible.

I could not lose control. Yet I had no control. You see?

Imagine a place where prisoners can be punished indefinitely, and crippled and maimed without any due process at all, and you've got an inkling of what I'm talking about.

My daily life was controlled by an extraordinary confluence of fairly decent prison guards, and a group of sadistic psychology staff. Unhappily, the psych staff appeared to relish their power to inflict tremendous suffering on inmates through crippling dosages of drugs. The women on M-1 had no legal right to protect ourselves from their abuse.

The experience haunts me to this day.

Prisoner Abuse

Lots of bad things happened to women at Carswell. But nobody suffered like the women inmates on M-1. Black, white, Hispanic, everybody got hurt. But black women especially got victimized by the all Caucasian psychology staff, maybe because they are poor and less educated and possibly less familiar with their legal rights. The torture of those women would astonish and devastate most Americans. It would break your heart if you saw them. They had no legal counsel that cared for them.

The outcome was hideous. During my 7 month detention at Carswell, I saw these women at the time of their arrival at the prison. Mostly they were in good health, confident and friendly, not violent, not threatening. Just nice people. That was the most striking thing about their behavior. They smiled. They joked with other inmates. They were the girls next door who'd got into trouble. Mostly, their boyfriends or husbands had done something criminal, and they got picked up together. A large number of these women wouldn't talk to the FBI about their boyfriends' crimes, called "obstruction of justice," or else they got hit with making "false statements" to protect their men. (Ladies, that's a bad idea!)

Loyalty to their boyfriends got them several years in prison, and shot up with Haldol as a double punishment, or drugged with some other psychotropic cocktail that destroyed them, physically and spiritually.

Over the weeks, I would watch their transformation from happy and confident to something terrified and confused. Then zombie-like. It was the most God awful transformation that you could imagine only in your worst nightmares. They would become physically and emotionally debilitated, after the prison psych staff got hold of them. You would be heartless to wish this sort of degradation and violence on an enemy.

None of these prisoners showed signs of schizophrenia or hallucinations. Only one or two prisoners showed signs of true "mental illness" at Carswell. That turned out to be another joke about court psychiatry. Almost none of these prisoners qualify as mentally ill, not until the prison got hold of them. Most of us suffered "post traumatic stress" in the aftermath, in response to the abusive prison structure itself, but nothing else.

In the schism of prison society, we were actually the Most Normal. We were not the murderers or thugs. We were not predatory towards other inmates. We were the "guests" who shouldn't be in prison at all. We were strikingly out of place in prison culture. All of that makes the abuse by prison staff far more ugly in that, in all rational assessment, it should have been totally unnecessary.

Instead of getting abused by hard-core inmates, we got preyed on by abusive and self righteous psychiatrists, who sought to double punish us through crippling dosages of drugs. It's a great tribute to all of these women that despite our lowly legal status, the brutality of the psych department prompted all of us to discover extraordinary inner strength and personal resources to survive the damage that Carswell tried to inflict on us. Some of these women are truly admirable in how they persevere every day with graciousness and stamina, through years of prison trauma.

PRISON DIARY

One of my cellmates kept a haunting poem by Maya Angelou taped to her locker. "And still I rise."

She stood in front of it every day to read it— like a prayer.

A lot of inmates on M-1 got drugged so badly that they slept 15 to 18 hours at a time. Throughout the unit, beds would be full by 1 o'clock in the afternoon every single day.

We ate lunch at 10:30 in the morning, and dinner at 3:30pm. Then everybody on M-1 would take their afternoon drugs and go back to sleep until about 6:30 pm. They'd get up to microwave a snack to eat before the evening count. After the count, most of the women would stay in their rooms, and sleep until the next morning, when the activity staff required us to report for in-door recreation. A striking number of inmates would collapse asleep on the floor of the recreation rooms, as well. Drugs knocked them out cold.

Black women always got drugged the worst.

They could not walk. They could not speak in sentences or answer questions. Typically, a response would be "what?" "dunno," "huh?" Like that.

Eating took tremendous concentration for a lot of the women on M-1, white and black. They could not lift a cup to drink without shaking hands. They would spill juice all over their clothes. They could not lift a fork to put food into their mouths, without intense concentration.

They wet their beds, because they could not coordinate their body movements to climb out of bed at night to use the restrooms. There was such sympathy inside M-1 that inevitably one of the other cellmates would get up in the middle of the night, and wash their sheets, if they got diarrhea, and couldn't make it to the toilet.

Urine could wait until the next morning, except for the stink.

Nobody complained about washing their sheets. We grieved for these ladies.

Most hideous of all, they could not bathe themselves. Staff and fellow inmates had to take these women to the showers, strip them naked, and wash them. Every time they bathed, they required help. It was not an occasional thing.

I can still hear those voices in the shower room now. They are the stuff of nightmares:

"Raise your arms. Lift your titties, so I can wash you. Let me see your back side. Spread your cheeks for me. Good girl. Can you stand up? No? Let's get the chair. Sit on that chair now. I'm going to wash your hair. Lean your head back. Don't get soap in your eyes. Let me towel you off. Let's dry you off, so I can get your clothes back on you. Do you want me to pull up your underwear? Let me pull up your pants. Can you do that? No? OK, I'll do that for you."

Showering in a nearby stall, I would sob for these women. I would turn on the water in the showers, and weep as I listened to the humiliation of these adult women, who'd become infantile, like very small children, totally incapacitated. I mean it, I would cry for them.

It was grotesque and humiliating.

These were mostly young women, in their 20s and 30s. They weren't old or handicapped. They'd been normal, until Carswell got hold of them. I cannot emphasize sufficiently that nothing in their outward behavior would justify such heavy drugging. But Carswell used psychotropic drugs as a form of punishment. Drugs offered another way to inflict suffering, and degrade the dignity of women who'd already lost their families and their freedom anyway. It was sadistic and abusive.

These women understood how badly they had deteriorated, even if they couldn't do anything about it. They understood what was happening to them.

One black woman in her 30s had been tortured like this for years. She suffered all the worst side effects of Haldol, and whatever drug cocktail Carswell kept feeding her. She was docile like a baby. She could no longer speak in sentences, or eat, or dress, or bathe. She slept 18 to 20 hours a day, and wet the bed frequently. All family ties had been lost, since she could not talk on the prison phones. She was so over drugged, it was awful.

But I swear she could sing gospel like an angel. Her name was Priscilla, and she could sing beautifully. She couldn't do it often. We'd have to ask her, and start the lyrics for her. Then something in her memory would kick in, and she'd start singing. The whole room of inmates would immediately go silent to listen to her. Her voice was so melodic and pure, and it accentuated our grief for her daily suffering.

Her prison life was the stuff of nightmares.

Another black woman, about 32 years old, could no longer speak properly. She had trouble eating. Very slowly she would raise a fork, and stare at it for a long time, before putting the food in her mouth. But she made a special promise to the other inmates on M-1 that she would go to the showers by herself every night. She did not want any help undressing or washing herself. She would persevere to clean herself, no matter how bad it got.

Her ability to shower by herself was the only dignity left in her pride. In all other ways, Carswell had utterly destroyed her. To help her out, other inmates kept a chair in the shower room at all times, so she could sit down. By this stage, it had become an arduous task to look for the chair, or carry it any distance. Those simple actions were beyond her skill level.

And this would continue for years, throughout their sentences. It was a thousand times worse than prison itself. You can survive in prison. It's not pleasant. But this stuff qualifies as actual torture. It's cruel and unusual—and grossly unnecessary.

The greatest irony was how Carswell quickly screened and separated prisoners in the pre-trial phase, whom prosecutors wanted to take to trial, and those who had already pleaded guilty.

If a defendant pleaded guilty, and came for a psych evaluation, Carswell would recommend massive drugs as part of the sentencing. Haldol and Prozac were favorite choices for all of those defendants. Almost everybody got the same drug cocktail. It didn't matter what law they violated, or what style of personality or behavior these women demonstrated before the drugging started. Carswell automatically recommended heavy drugging to the court.

But if an attorney sent a pre-trial defendant like me to Carswell, without a guilty plea, toying with an incompetence defense or some sort of psychology angle at trial, Carswell took an entirely different approach. Let's just say a defendant entered Carswell trying to prove "diminished capacity" on the basis of a long-time bipolar disorder, seeking leniency from the Courts before trial.

The first thing Carswell would ask is whether the new inmate used any drugs for depression or mood stabilizers? Almost nobody arrived at Carswell on harsher drugs than that.

If the answer was yes, Carswell would pull back the drugs to test whether the condition was authentic.

Taking defendants off their prescription drugs was the number one method at Carswell for restoring competence to stand trial, or proving that the defendant experienced no true diminished capacity. (Mostly Carswell rejected claims of incompetence.)

Without the drugs, after a few weeks of detox, most of these prisoners would be fine. They'd show their true personality, and low and behold there would be nothing wrong with them. Carswell would then argue in Court—and I would have to agree, based on the evidence of their behavior— that they'd been taking these drugs for years without reason. Somewhere along the way these women had got "mis-diagnosed," encouraged to confuse personal problems with mental defects. They'd gotten comfortable taking prescription drugs. Drugs provided a crutch for their lives. But they functioned just fine, after a medically supervised detox. That surprised some of these women, who'd limited their expectations to fit the constraints of their so called "mental diseases." Some of these women thanked Carswell after the detox! They felt empowered getting off the psych drugs!

That says a lot about how psych drugs affect personal performance and self expectations—and not for the better.

Once they got cleaned up, Carswell shipped these women right back to federal court. They were judged competent to stand trial or plead guilty for sentencing, without much leniency.

That says a lot about the phony medical credentials of psychiatry.

But heaven protect the women inmates who arrived at Carswell with a guilty plea, for a psych evaluation as part of sentencing, or declared incompetent like me.

Those women suffered the most. Carswell would file requests to the Court that those women should be required to take massive quantities of drugs, usually Haldol, Ativan and Prozac, as part of their "rehabilitation." That was standard practice. Everyone got the same drug recommendations. Even prisoners outside of M-1 and M-2 got heavy doses of psych drugs.

I was at Carswell long enough that I observed the new prisoners upon their arrival— healthy, in good spirits, full of good conversation. None of these women struck me as violent or threatening. To the best of my knowledge, I never saw woman prisoners on M-1 threaten other inmates or guards. Most of the women were guilty as charged, and a very few got convicted of serious crimes like bank robbery or child killing. Some might have benefited from counseling, which was only mediocre at the prison. But 9 times out of 10, they committed crimes of stupidity, drug crimes, tax fraud, or crimes associated with a husband or boyfriend. They're not instigators. They're not diabolical and scheming. They are followers. They would not be repeat offenders, if they got jobs after prison. Employment after prison would be the decisive factor.

All of a sudden, they could not speak anymore. They could no longer read a book or write letters home to their families, because though literate, they could no longer hold a pen or process ideas from the written word. Ominously, I'd hear prison staff talking about how a certain woman liked to read the newspaper—particularly black women.

A black woman wouldn't read newspapers at Carswell for long. Drugs would take care of that literacy problem.

Other prisoners had to write letters home for them, though most of these women could hardly put together a sentence to tell us what to write. We would suggest family greetings, and they'd sit next to us while we wrote. Sometimes tears would stream down their cheeks, nodding or mostly grunting, as we proposed messages to their families. It would take some considerable effort to express a simple thought.

Since they could no longer read a book or process ideas in any form, most definitely they could not work at the prison law library on their cases. So they could not appeal their sentencing or assist their attorneys– who let's be honest, did not want their help anyway.

One woman could not remember her husband's phone number, though they'd been married twenty years with an adult son. We took her to the Chaplain's office, so she could try to phone home, and she stumbled several times trying to dial. Dialing was so difficult for this lady that we questioned if she really had a husband or if he was part of a delusional condition. She was a former Carswell prisoner who had stopped taking court-ordered drugs after her release. So the U.S. Marshals picked her up, and doped her to the levels required by Carswell, then shipped her back to prison. She was so over-drugged when she arrived, that she'd lost the ability to perform such a simple task as using a telephone. Her husband had no idea what happened to her. She could not speak to anybody. She had trouble washing herself. All of the ugly things.

As it happened, prior to her imprisonment at Carswell, this woman worked in a bank, possibly in a supervisory position, with no history of mental illness. She got picked up by the Feds in their sweep of an embezzlement scam by other bank staff.

Ignoring the reality of her life, Carswell declared her incompetent over her desperate objections. Like me, she wanted to stand trial. Carswell overruled her rights, and requested a court order to forcibly drug her with Haldol. She was detained 11 months, then released. When she got out, after about a year, she stopped using the drug. Now she was back in prison, but with a different attorney who challenged the original indictment, and questioned why the first attorney argued against her competence in the first place. Critically, her co-defendants filed affidavits saying that she had nothing to do with their crime.

It turned out that this poor woman wasn't guilty after all. With the help of a kick ass attorney, Carswell pulled back the amount of drugs that she was forced to take. And guess what? This poor abused woman showed no signs of any mental illness or instability whatsoever. There was nothing wrong with this woman. It was another case of Carswell viciously brutalizing a woman prisoner for no external reason, just because they could.

Her story proves something of critical importance to the debate on prison psychiatry:

If you change the attorney, you change the prisoner "diagnosis." You change the defense strategy, and all the psycho-babble goes away—It rushes away. That's because most of the time, psychological evaluations are scripted to support the attorney's legal strategy, not a reflection of the defendant's true state of mental health. So when you start poking, there's almost nothing left of a psychological profile, except in the most extreme situations of genuine schizophrenia, or severe bipolar disorder, or long term domestic violence or child abuse.

To put that in context, in 7 ½ months at Carswell, I saw exactly one prisoner with genuine schizophrenia, two prisoners suffering bipolar disorder to a crippling degree, and two prisoners who heard voices—which might have been caused by the heavy psychotropic drugs they were forced to take. The rest of the inmates were normal, but they broke the law. For whatever reason, they engaged in criminal activity. Mostly it meant they wouldn't testify against their boyfriends, or they smuggled drugs from Mexico, and they got sent to prison for it.

Psychology in the courts is all about legal strategy in handling a case, or mostly disposing of the case, so an attorney can get out of it. Like mine.

Unhappily, this poor lady, once a bank supervisor, had to go through Two Tours of Carswell to prove it. The first time she served 11 months, and the second time she served four months. Plus, she had time at home between Carswell, suffering the crippling effects of Haldol, which had been wrongly administered at high dosages for punitive reasons. Last I heard, she intended to file a lawsuit.

It was sheer hell from start to finish, and all because Carswell abuses its authority in the courts, and advocates excessive, unnecessary drugging for all prisoners.

That's what Carswell wanted to do to me. And remember, this was happening in Texas. Think of every worst stereotype of corrupt Texas prison staff, and you're beginning to get the idea.

Without the "inconvenience" of due process of law, Carswell can get away with anything. And they know it. When the Hospital Accreditation Review Board shows up to survey the prison facilities and inmate security, the most chemically lobotomized women get transferred to the SHU, until the performance review has been completed. That way nobody on the outside is troubled to see them. And Carswell doesn't have to answer questions about the crippling impact of drugs on their functioning.

It's a serious problem. I am not the exceptional inmate who was abused at Carswell. I am the exceptional prisoner who escaped abuse. I escaped, because I fought back.

For the good of all prisoners, Carswell should lose the right to conduct psych evaluations for the federal courts. That service needs to be transferred to another facility. Cruelty should not be part of that evaluation and sentencing process. And corruption should never be tolerated when drug recommendations are imposed on prisoners in a court of law.

My Own Private Guantanamo

My nightmare was double-force.

When I describe Carswell as my own "private Guantanamo," and my status as pretty close to an "enemy non-combatant," there are good reasons why.

Along with Jose Padilla, I was one of the very first non-Arab Americans ever indicted on the Patriot Act. There's great irony to that. Congress approved the 7000 pages of law that eviscerated our Constitutional rights in a midnight vote, without reading it first, in frenzied hysteria after 9/11. The Patriot Act supposedly exists to empower law enforcement to break up terrorist cells.

Yet one of the very first American citizens to get clobbered by the Patriot Act provided advance warning about the 9/11 attack. Not only did I warn about 9/11, I covered Iraq's cooperation with the 9/11 investigation. I'm an anti-war activist and a whistleblower to boot—not exactly what comes to mind when Congress argued for the Patriot Act.

Unforgivably, the first use of the Patriot Act was to keep Americans ignorant of national security issues that really mattered. Those of us who know the truth got ravaged by the Patriot Act, so that we could be silenced, while Congress glorified its performance record and invented false truths about 9/11 and Iraq. That's what the Patriot Act accomplished. It has been crafted as an ideal tool for any government cover up. The government arrests the whistleblower, and politicians are safe to make up any story they choose to protect their access to power.

Soldiers at Carswell Air Force Base had no idea that I was a U.S. Asset who got in trouble for trying to provide accurate forecasting about the War to Congress and the White House. They had no idea I warned about 9/11, and contributed extensively to the 9/11 investigation.

If you read the mainstream media, I was caught spying for the Iraqis. That's what a lot of soldiers at Carswell Air Force Base concluded. The indictment was dirty smoke and propaganda. But soldiers believed what they were told. An accused Iraqi agent had got locked up in prison on their military base. Having lost my rights to due process, I lost my ability to challenge their perceptions of my actions.

At that moment, American soldiers were losing the War in Baghdad. U.S. forces sustained heavy casualties in 2006, including thousands of serious injuries, like amputations, paralysis and head injuries from suicide bombings and improvised explosive devices (IEDs). While I was locked up at Carswell, Sunni factions attacked the golden dome of the famous Al-Askariya Mosque in Samarra, launching bloody sectarian strife against the Shi'ites. U.S. soldiers had lost control of the situation, and were heading back for third tours of duty away from their families and children. Returning U.S. Soldiers showed deep emotional scars and post traumatic stress. The U.S. military faced daunting pressure of two battle fronts, with angry Mujahedin in Afghanistan on the sidelines of Baghdad.

Locking up an accused "Iraqi Agent" inside a Texas military base was like waving a suicide bomb vest in front of a battalion. They couldn't stop Al Qaeda in Iraq. But they could sure as hell punish me, an accused Iraqi agent (read that, Iraqi spy).

They tried their damnedest to screw me every chance they got.

My uncle, Ted Lindauer, kept his promise to drive 700 miles from southern Illinois to visit me at Carswell Air Force Base, northwest of Fort Worth, Texas. It's an 11 hour road trip, driving straight through—in each direction.

When he arrived, Ted identified himself as part of my legal defense team, a fully accurate description by this point. He carried documentation to verify his attorney's license. And he explained that our visit was intended to discuss legal strategy. Critically, the soldiers understood that he was coming to see the "accused Iraqi Agent." Constitutional rights required that they grant him access to me as my attorney.

Nevertheless, soldiers refused to let Ted Lindauer enter that military base.

The first time it happened, soldiers swore there was no prison inside Carswell Air Force Base. Quite perplexed, Ted assured the soldiers at the entry gate that they were mistaken. He asked to speak with a commanding officer. The commanding officer on duty came out to meet him, but refused to acknowledge the existence of a prison inside the base, either.[492]

Ted explained that he had traveled 700 miles, and he was quite positive the prison was there. They didn't care. He wasn't coming in. Ted doesn't give up easily on anything, and he doesn't play. So they spent a good couple of hours arguing over whether there was a prison inside Carswell Air Force Base. Above all, Ted argued aggressively for my Constitutional rights as a defendant to have access to my legal representative. *Oh yes, the Iraqi agent wanted an attorney.*

Ted warned that he would go to the Judge, and file a complaint. And that's exactly what he did. He notified Judge Mukasey's clerk that he had been denied access to the prison on a weekend— when it was open for family members, attorneys or not.. He registered a complaint that my rights to an attorney had been violated. That was Ted's first attempt to visit me at Carswell Prison. The second time Ted drove 700 miles and 11 hours from southern Illinois, soldiers at the entry gate had a new excuse for denying him access to the base.

Yeah, soldiers at the entry gate acknowledged. Carswell prison existed. But they swore up and down that the prison had no visiting hours on the weekends. Again Ted argued with soldiers at the entry post that it was ridiculous, and they should phone the prison and ask. Again they contacted a ranking officer. Again, the ranking officer on duty refused Ted's entrance to the base, with the flagrant lie that the prison had no visiting hours on the weekend.[493]

Meanwhile, other families visiting the prison got ushered through the gates around Ted. He watched them go in. Inside Carswell, other inmates had visitors all day.

Ted Lindauer had his attorney papers. He had contact names inside the prison. We'd filed all the necessary paperwork to get him on my visitor's list. Soldiers on the base swore none of that mattered. There was no visiting hours at Carswell prison on the weekends. They told him not to come back the next day, because they would not let him onto the military base then, either. *The Iraqi agent was not getting an attorney visit.* End of discussion.

All this time, my attorney in New York had done nothing to secure my freedom. If any solution could be brokered with the Courts, it would have to come from Ted. There was nobody else to do it. This visit was critically important to ending our stand off.

Knowing that, Ted had done everything properly. He had notified the Court of his involvement in the case. Judge Mukasey had observed Ted's presence in Court on the day that I got ordered to Carswell, so the Court recognized the importance of our relationship. Ted contacted Carswell ahead of his visits. The prison staff on M-1 was fully aware of his close involvement. He gladly flashed his attorney credentials at the front gates of the military base.

He's also 70 years old, and a very dignified gentleman, with 40 years practicing law at a senior level. He doesn't suffer fools. It's sort of a Lindauer thing.

And still soldiers at Carswell Air Force Base refused to grant him access to me.

Now Ted was furious. This was his second trip to Carswell in several weeks, and he'd been refused entry to the base on both occasions, for the flimsiest of excuses.[494]

He warned soldiers guarding the base that he would return in a few days. And by God, he would bring the U.S. marshals with him. And those U.S. marshals would escort him onto that military base, into that prison, if soldiers tried to deny him access to me a third time.[495]

While he was at it, he would see that they all got court-martialed for failing in their sworn duty to uphold the Constitution. (We know a few Generals, too.)

Unhappily, soldiers guarding Carswell Air Force Base appeared to have a very limited understanding of the United States Constitution, which is not particularly hopeful, since they're sworn to protect it. In its most simple maxim, "We, the people of the United States of America" have fundamental protections that define our whole system of government and laws. Those rights exist to protect us from exactly this sort of arbitrary and tyrannical government behavior. For a start, Americans are innocent until proven guilty, with full rights to due process and attorney access. Holding a defendant in prison on a Texas military base does not negate those rights under the Constitution. And by the way, political prosecutions to punish dissenting viewpoints are strictly prohibited under the Bill of Rights, as well.

Alas, none of America's legal traditions mattered on Carswell Air Force Base. Soldiers understood that Ted Lindauer was visiting the accused "Iraqi Agent," and nothing else mattered. He was not entering that military establishment, no matter what the Constitution required.

That illustrates poignantly why prisons should be separate from military establishments. It's disastrous to confuse those institutions, or to allow them to function co-dependently. The military itself does not know how to handle those situations.

Well, Ted Lindauer is a marvelously persevering man. Each round trip to Fort Worth he traveled 1,400 miles, there and back from his home. And still he came all that way to protect me.

When challenged, Ted refused to back down.

First thing Monday morning, he called Judge Mukasey and raised all kinds of hell about my Constitutional rights, and how Sam Talkin's failure to perform had compelled him to intercede, in order to guarantee that I had real, interested legal counsel. He filed a formal protest with the Court, and demanded that U.S. Marshals escort him onto that base.[496]

Judge Mukasey could see the situation was spiraling out of control. The whole agreement sending me to Carswell for 120 days, in exchange for ending the case, had collapsed. Clearly the original deal had been hammered out in the black of night, without my knowledge or consent as the defendant, by a public attorney who now appeared impotent to protect my interests, and took no action to gain my freedom. Now I was trapped in prison.

This violation of my rights to meet with legal counsel was occurring at a critical moment. As a defendant, I desperately required the services of a more senior and experienced legal adviser. Judge Mukasey's hands were tied by the thinly disguised collaboration between the prosecutor and my public attorney. And here was the answer to our prayers— a senior, savvy attorney ready to play a very helpful role brokering a workable solution.

With great perspicacity and fury over the denial of my legal rights, Judge Mukasey agreed to have U.S. Marshals standing by to escort Ted Lindauer onto that military base, when he returned to see me a few days later. Judge Mukasey ordered that this legal visit would be protected by the Court. Judge Mukasey ordered Carswell Prison to open the visitor center just for me.[497]

Ted Lindauer had Judge Mukasey's private cell phone number to call out the U.S. Marshals, at the first sign of trouble or delay.

Judge Mukasey kicked some Texas ass that week. Junior staff at Carswell told me he boxed the ears of top prison officers, who sent the message down the ranks that guards had better find me when Ted Lindauer arrived. There would be no possibility of missing that third visit. There would be hell to pay if Ted traveled 700 miles a third time, and didn't get to see me.

As they say, third time's the charm. It took the threat of U.S. marshals standing by, but Ted and I finally got to talk.[498]

Mercifully, Ted Lindauer possessed the legal insight to craft a workable compromise to our problem. He arrived carrying a pledge for my signature to submit to Judge Mukasey. Very simply, I would have to agree to attend psychology meetings in Maryland. I would have to agree to use any drugs prescribed locally— Experience convinced us that once politics got removed from the equation, there would be no drugs. Nevertheless, I had to consent.[499]

This agreement gave the court a vehicle for addressing the prosecutor's demands for drugs, while sidestepping my refusal to use drugs prescribed by Carswell for non-existent conditions.

It was simple, but it accomplished what my Uncle Ted understood the Judge needed. He'd done his homework, and he got the agreement in precise language that would be acceptable to the Court, in order for me to go home. He forbade me from changing a single word of it. Truly, Ted Lindauer was a blessing, given this massive headache for the Court.

As I've said before, it's always risky to extrapolate a Judge's thinking. However since no defendant can resist doing it, I confess that we believed Judge Mukasey was alarmed and frustrated by these surprise developments.

We did not believe Judge Mukasey expected O'Callaghan to pull this stunt, demanding forcible drugging after the Court accepted the finding of incompetence. It put the Judge in a bad position, having ordered me to Carswell for 120 days, without a hearing that would have answered questions about my story. I had begged for that hearing.

Arguably, it gave the Court something else to chew over. It proved that the strongest defendant could not overcome the hazards of the Patriot Act, whether guided by the most senior counsel like Ted Lindauer, or junior counsel, like Sam Talkin. My attorney relationship was already burdened by "secret evidence," "secret charges." Now I was locked up inside a military base without attorney access facing "indefinite detention." All of these factors crippled my capacity to prepare for trial. As a defendant, I was totally helpless to overcome these external obstacles, which were flagrantly unconstitutional anyway.

Judge Mukasey possesses an extremely sophisticated legal mind, and a profound sense of fairness. His court had a reputation for upholding integrity in the law. Refusing to allow Ted Lindauer onto Carswell Air Force Base for a crucial attorney visit sent a sobering message.

Ted Lindauer particularly believed that Judge Mukasey saw the legal structure impeding my defense. He trusted Judge Mukasey throughout this whole nightmare.

For myself, as a defendant threatened with forcible drugging and indefinite detention, I didn't know what to think. It terrified me not to know how the Court would rule. Judge Mukasey appeared inscrutable, exhibiting a fierce and uncanny depth of insight to the law.

Honestly, I was scared to death.

Saved by the Blogs

This was the most evil thing that I've ever confronted in my life. And I've seen evil before.

People ask me all the time how I survived.

I escaped the fate of other inmates, because I fought back.

I fought back as hard as I've ever fought anything in my life.

The prospect of my success in blocking Carswell's request for forcible drugging appeared stunningly low. Usually the courts rubber stamp prison requests for drugs, almost automatically. There's no doubt that Carswell expected the same for me.

Carswell didn't count on my two secret weapons.

The first, of course, was my very special uncle, Ted Lindauer, who fought forcefully and effectively behind the legal scenes to broker an agreement that would get me out of Carswell.

The second surprised me too—my own beloved companion, JB Fields, who desperately appealed for help in the blog community.

JB refused to stand by passively, and let the attack on my rights go unchallenged.

"JB" stood for J Burford of all things. That's just the initial "J" without any other name attached to it. Born in Kansas, raised in Wyoming, JB was a proud Navy guy who spent six years of his life underwater, trawling the ocean floors on submarines. In 11 years of active Navy service, he toured on the "Grayback," the "Barb," and the "Thomas A. Edison."

He bragged about surviving a submarine accident, with ocean water spilling into the hold up to his chest. For years on Hawaii, he ran marathons and swim races, alongside friends in the Navy Seals. Afterwards, he worked at the State Department in Washington in computer technology. While living with me, he got his "Top Secret" security clearance, and returned to the State Department as a computer contractor. So much for my threat to national security.

JB was a generous, warm hearted man, whose greatest passion in life was his motorcycle, nicknamed "Drifty." Every weekend he blasted off on "Drifty," exploring the back roads of Pennsylvania and West Virginia. Friends joked that JB knew every ice cream stand, every barbecue pit and every diner from Maryland to North Carolina. JB would just smile, and tell you those things are what mattered most in life.

One Christmas, JB gave me some fancy motorcycle gear for winter riding. With a big grin, he said, "Isn't this better than an engagement ring?"

Every moment counted with JB. He had the social flair to enjoy a black tie affair with State Department colleagues, ensconced in policy talk. And the next night, he'd eat crab legs and drink beer at the American Legion in Silver Spring, or at some motorcycle bar. He looked sexy as hell in a Tux, and even sexier in blue jeans and a leather jacket.

Different opinions always excited him. That was key to understanding his nature. He was a fierce civil libertarian, and a strong believer that ideas must be respected. Though he was fiercely opinionated himself, and would argue for hours over the most arcane points, he would faithfully defend the rights of others to hold a different philosophy on life and politics, and he believed those differences made conversation interesting.

Above all, he strongly believed the greatest privilege of the U.S. military is to defend the freedoms of our country, which he adored, and to protect the Constitution, which he held sacred.

And woe to the wicked of Carswell!

From my first days at Carswell, JB championed my cause. He was horrified that I got locked up without any sort of trial or guilty plea. He was appalled that the media didn't care. My case had intense political overtones, involving Iraq and anti-terrorism policy, and a strong human interest angle. Yet corporate media gave short shrift to my nightmare. There was no outcry. My home town newspaper, the Washington Post, showed no curiosity that a U.S. Asset involved with Pre-War Intelligence had got locked up in prison on a Texas military base for doing exactly what Congress swore on CNN that I should have done: Shout from the rooftops against the War.

Journalists wouldn't touch my story, though JB pleaded for attention. Corporate media watched from the sidelines, abandoning its role of community watchdog.

Carswell watched this dynamic, too— closely. Once they saw the media's indifference, prison staff taunted me that nobody cared. Nobody would help me. They could do anything to me, and nobody would stop them.

Sadly, if not for JB Fields, they would have been right.

Terrified by Carswell's refusal to release me, JB Fields hit the airwaves of alternative radio, with some very cool talk show hosts like Michael Herzog, Greg Szymanski, Derek Gilbert, and Cosmic Penguin — to name a few of the alert and awake alternative radio hosts that broadcast my story from the very beginning. Republic Broadcasting, Oracle and Liberty Radio carried my story to their listeners before anybody else would! And their support made the difference!

JB was so frightened that he started posting my story on blogs all over the internet, with a cry for help to defend my rights to a hearing, so I'd have a chance to prove my story in court.

The hand of Providence moved for me again, and JB was soon joined by a passionate and highly articulate activist named Janet Phelan, who's got a long tradition defending America's liberties in her own right. Janet hosted a radio talk show of her own, "One if by Land." An incredibly talented lady, Janet brought a deeper perspective on the abuse of women by psychology, and the Soviet style abuse of creative thinkers and activists under the guise of "mental health." She also fiercely condemned the Patriot Act.

Janet Phelan was phenomenal. Together, she and JB smoked the blogs with outrage over the irregularities of my imprisonment on the Patriot Act, and the outrageous threat to forcibly drug me, until I could be cured of claiming to know inconvenient truths that the government wished to obliterate.

Corporate media might have been sleeping, but the blogging community woke up, and gave JB and Janet a forum to fight. What I call "awake blogs," like "Scoop" Independent News, Smirking Chimp, IntelDaily, OpEd News, American Politics Journal, Atlantic Free Press, and The Agonist joined the battle over time, appalled by what was happening to me. Cutting edge bloggers like WelcomebacktoPottersville.com and Cosmic Penguin, watching the road beyond the mainstream, championed my cause from day one.

As my legal drama continued, one of the truly outstanding blog journalists today, Michael Collins, would pick up my story. Then we'd be off to the races for real.

At Carswell, JB Fields fought like a banshee to free me—what he described as the most lonely and frightening experience of his life. JB declared that he could not say if I was innocent or not—and he did not always agree with my politics, which made for some lively conversations. But he insisted that I had the right to face my accusers in open court. He urged folks to support my right to an evidentiary hearing, so I could have my day in court to prove the authenticity of my story. I deserved a fair chance to call my witnesses!

This was about America, and the bad things happening to ordinary people under the Patriot Act. JB and Janet argued that the legal traditions of this country must be defended. They kicked up one helluva fight. And they refused to back down.

Blowback from the blogs started to shoot shock waves through Washington. Seriously, you'd be amazed who told me they read JB's blog on my case, after I got out.

As long as the corporate media stayed silent, Capitol Hill could pretend this judicial abuse of a U.S. Intelligence Asset was not occurring. Safely guarded behind their ivory tower walls, the Powers that Be in Washington imagined they were untouchable, their fortress impenetrable.

Only now, thanks to JB Fields and Janet Phelan, Capitol Hill confronted the force of the blogs and alternative radio. Today that power is understood. But my case was one of the first, when the blogging community proved it's got the muscle to shatter the media silence.

Without the outcry from the blog community, my fate would have been very different. JB's blog – and all the other bloggers who picked up my story— saved my life and my freedom.

That's what separated my victory from the tragedy of so many others. Other women don't have those resources. Sadly, their stories suffocate and die from lack of exposure, while my ordeal was redeemed by the extraordinary perseverance of JB Fields and Janet Phelan to get my story out to the public.

Finally, JB and I got a break.

On April 24, 2006, the Court made a surprise announcement.

CHAPTER 26:

THE FRIENDLY SKIES OF CON AIR

JB and I used to joke that I was starring in my own Robert Ludlum spy thriller. Every action seemed to invoke a sinister plot twist that got more dangerous as I went along.

Like the lovely April morning I got the news that I was finally transferring out of Carswell.

With a mischievous grin, the guard on duty stuck his head in the doorway to my cell.

"Hey Lindauer, pack up! You're outta here. You're leaving tomorrow night."

I think I screamed with joy, because other inmates in the hallway came running to hear my news. I know I started to grab the guard for a hug before I caught myself.

It was April 24, 2006. After seven months in prison, I was leaving Carswell! I crowed in jubilation, ecstatically thrilled. Elated with joy!

In all, I had been detained 7 months for a psych evaluation that ordinarily takes six to eight weeks, and only because so many prisoners are getting processed simultaneously. Federal guidelines set a maximum of 120 days for prison evaluations.[500] My detention had lasted 210 days— in strict violation of federal law. Not to mention that the evaluation lacked purpose. I'd proven myself over and over again. The whole thing amounted to a convoluted scheme so the Justice Department could escape a trial.

But that morning, I felt overjoyed.

"I'm going home! I'm going home!" I started dancing around my cell.

"Um, Lindauer. Uh, no. I'm driving a bus-load of prisoners to the prisoner transfer center in Oklahoma City tomorrow night. You're, uh, flying to New York. On Con Air."

"To New York? On Con-Air? There must be a mistake. I live in Maryland."

"You're not going home, Lindauer. They're sending you to M.C.C." That's the Metropolitan Correctional Center for Pre-Trial detention in Manhattan."

The wheel of "extreme prejudice" was turning alright. They were coming in for the kill.

At that moment, I wasn't nearly paranoid enough to conceive the depth of their malevolence.

"I'm staying in prison? Seriously? I don't understand. I'm supposed to go home after the evaluation." (Carswell filed its report on December 22, 2005—four months earlier).

"I talked to my attorney yesterday. Why didn't he tell me that I'm going to Court? How could my attorney not know I'm getting transferred?"

"I don't know." The guard shook his head. "Hey, you're out of here, Lindauer."

He leaned closer. "That's a good thing, right? Your Judge has something he wants to say before he lets you go. That's all. Be cool." This guy was a good guard.

"Yeah, yeah. That's got to be it. We just submitted a settlement offer to the Court. My uncle had to do it, because my stupid ass attorney couldn't figure it out."

"That's probably what the meetings for. Hey, Lindauer, it's all good! You're packin' up. You're leaving Carswell. Stay happy."

As for divining my future in New York, my fellow prisoners jumped straight into the tea leaves. Their verdict was unanimous.

"If they're sending you out of here, Susan, you're not coming back. Why else would they go to the trouble? You're done! It's over! Your uncle's taken care of you."

I could not count how many of my fellow inmates wished they had an Uncle Ted Lindauer.

"You're going home. You've just got a stop over in New York first."

JB was ecstatic. He saw it as proof that the blog community had forced Carswell's abuse and threats into the open. The game was becoming untenable to continue.

I was deliriously happy. There are few moments in life that I have experienced such joy. My attorney was less enthusiastic.

"The Judge has called a hearing, Susan. You wanted a hearing, right? Well, you're going to get one," Talkin told me, glumly. "That's why they're sending you to M.C.C."

I gave a deep sigh, and shook my head.

It was everything Ted and I feared when Judge Mukasey ordered me to surrender to Carswell without a hearing in September. It put us back to square one, right where we started. I'd suffered seven months in prison for nothing!

Ted had warned that anger would be a waste of energy. I had to focus on getting home.

I growled to myself, but Ted was right. At least I could prove my story to Judge Mukasey. There would be no more question marks. He could hear it for himself straight from my witnesses— just like the FBI, the U.S Attorney's Office, the prison staff at Carswell, and Uncle Ted. We'd all be on the same page, and nobody could pretend I invented this story.

I imagined that after the hearing, the Court would restore my bail until trial. I'd already surrendered to prison, on the court's whim. I was hardly a flight risk.

But what a waste of 7 months. We could have gone to trial already. I could have been acquitted without spending a single night in a prison cell. I grit my jaw. That made me so angry.

I could see Ted's face, and hear his words: "Stay focused. How you got here is less important than what you do next. We've got to get you out of the Hoosiegow, kid." At least I had an excellent source of legal advice, even if it wasn't my own attorney.

I turned my attention back to Sam Talkin.

"Very well. We'll call witnesses to prove my story's true. That'll put an end to this phony garbage of psychology. Judge Mukasey will get enough to know that it's all baloney."

Now I could see Richard Fuisz before me again, solemnly raising his finger, counting like a metronome. "Every situation, every encounter gives you a weapon or a tool. Anything that comes at you, you can use."

Okay then. A hearing it would be. I would have been overjoyed if the Prosecutor had kept his word about dropping the charges. After 7 months in prison, who could blame me for that? But a hearing gave me other options. If witnesses verified enough of my story, we could argue for dismissing the indictment ourselves. It would be up to the Judge. But this gave us a fresh chance to undo the damage of Dr. Drob's report, which misrepresented the quality of my witnesses. The Justice Department had its pound of flesh. A pre-trial hearing that confirmed the essential facts might be the best thing for everybody. It might satisfy the Court to make the case go away.

Not to mention the great satisfaction I would get, proving the FBI and the U.S. Attorney's Office had always known I was telling the truth. They'd been playing games with Judge Mukasey, gratis of the Patriot Act.

I heard another whisper from my mother, Jacqueline Shelly Lindauer. "Save your emotions for revenge."

Alright then. A hearing it would be!

"I don't know if we want those witnesses—" Sam Talkin began to whine.

"What are you saying? Of course we want those witnesses!"

Idiot! I was thinking, exasperated! As soon as I got home, I intended to replace Sam Talkin. In the meantime, any hearing before Judge Mukasey would be precious for my defense.

"We can talk about it when you get here," Talkin demurred. How do you break the news to a prisoner that she's getting fucked again? (As gently as possible.)

"See, the hearing isn't about your competence," Talkin started whining. "It's a hearing on forcible drugging."

"WHAT THE FUCK are you saying? A hearing on forcible drugging? Are they Insane!??!"

My heart thudded to the floor at this bad news. Now I saw with clarity why Talkin had dreaded telling me before. The mere suggestion staggered with obscenity.

I mean, reality is not a disease. (Psychology might be, however.)

"No, Sam. No f—G—damn way," I'd buffed up my prison vocabulary at the law library, too.

"The law guarantees my right to a competence hearing, and I refuse to give up that right. I'm entitled to call witnesses and show evidence to address all of the issues raised in these idiotic psych evaluations.[501] That's exactly what I'm going to do."

"Yeah well, I told them we didn't need to do that," Talkin mumbled into the phone. "I didn't know the Prosecutor was going to ask for this." He whined, pitifully.

"You did WHAT?!"

This was "extreme prejudice" alright, to the hundredth degree. And my public attorney walked straight into their trap, time and again. He would refuse to listen to me or Ted. He would miscalculate their sincerity, and he would be wrong every time. Except he was playing with another person's freedom. I also suspect that Talkin did not want the Court to hear how Uncle Ted had been forced to interview my witnesses, and how effortlessly he succeeded in validating my story.[502] His success contradicted the image of difficulty that Talkin was projecting, and exposed his own mediocrity in the case.

"YOU agreed to give up MY rights? Oh no. That's not going to happen. I'm going to send Judge Mukasey a letter today. I will demand the Court uphold my rights to a hearing. JB Fields will get in touch with everybody, so they know they have to come. We'll be ready."

"I'm not playing, Sam." I swore adamantly. "I demand the Court uphold my rights under the statute."

"That's one good thing about prison. I've had lots of time to Read the Law." I was ferocious.

"We're having the God damn hearing. I don't give a f—what you told Judge Mukasey. You are not entitled to violate my rights. I'm going to make sure that Judge Mukasey registers my demand, as the Defendant. Parke Godfrey will be in Court on that day, ready to testify that I warned him about 9/11."

"And he's going to tell Judge Mukasey that he told the FBI all about my 9/11 warning a FULL YEAR before I came to Carswell. He talked to Shadduck here, too. So the FBI, the US Attorneys Office and the Bureau of Prisons all know that it's true, and they've all been playing games with Judge Mukasey."

"There's a name for that in prison. It's called perjury."

"If I were the Judge, I would be madder than hell about it."

I always saw Judge Mukasey as the second victim of psychiatry in my case.

Again I saw the face of Richard Fuisz, stern and quiet: "Every situation gives you a weapon or a tool."

That was the best advice I'd heard all day.

Alright then, I was getting out of Carswell. I was going to face my Judge. There'd be no distance between us. I would look him straight in the eye, and I'd bloody well lay out the whole thing. A weapon or a tool was right.

After 7 months cut off from access to my attorney, we'd finally be in the same time zone, the same city! Glory hallelujah!

How could any defendant expect to prepare a legal strategy separated by a distance of 1,600 miles from her attorney? I was stuck in Texas, and my attorney was half way across the country in New York. That's a killer for any defense. It struck me as legally absurd to complain about my ability to assist my defense, then deny me physical access to my attorney.

OK, so a prison transfer to New York would be like paradise. I swore to God on a stack of Bibles that I would never go back to Texas again! I know lots of proud and wonderful Texans. They can visit me in Maryland.

Driving out of Carswell on the prison bus that night felt surreal. We stayed up all night waiting to leave. As I recall, we left at four in the morning, while it was still dark, for the 200 mile drive to Oklahoma City. It felt like a party, a heart-felt celebration.

Some of my fellow inmates had been trapped inside that razor wire for years. Getting on that bus to leave, you wanted to grab that free earth, and give thanks to God!

The prison transit center is located at the Oklahoma City Airport. The detention center commands an island outpost a good distance from the main terminal. It occupies a separate building with its own runway in sight of the main community, which kind of intrigued me. It appeared to house 300 women at a time, with a separate shed for male prisoners.

Inside, the detention center felt like a huge hangar for airplanes. There were no windows that I recall, just extra large holding cells big enough for 40 to 50 people, used for inmate processing. Each holding cell had two open toilets with no seat rim or toilet paper. The toilets were mostly broken and couldn't flush. That's prison for you. They don't want anybody coming back.

After processing, we got escorted into a vast open room behind locked doors, with cafeteria tables and a prison laundry, where some of the women inmates worked to stay busy, bordered by tiny cells.

First though, we had to go through inmate screening. One by one, guards called us out of the holding cell, lined us up and ran through our records. When they called me up, I discovered that Carswell had played dirty. Again.

Carswell had singled me out of all the transfer prisoners, with an urgent recommendation that I should be separated from other prisoners and locked up in the SHU, or solitary confinement during transit, citing the Patriot Act.

To their credit, the Oklahoma City authorities stopped to ask some questions. The men told me that only the most violent and dangerous prisoners go to the SHU in transit. They assured me it would be terribly unpleasant for a woman. Besides that, Carswell's request made no sense. Looking at my prison record, they could see no disciplinary problems. Some of the other women had serious behavior problems at Carswell, and none of them was going to the SHU. The guards finally struck down Carswell's recommendation.

Oh but I understood Carswell's motivation immediately. And it had nothing to do with behavioral problems or confrontations with prison guards.

Just as I contributed to the 9/11 investigation, it should not be forgotten that I also contributed to the Oklahoma City bombing investigation. And I had complained that the Justice Department was suppressing intelligence proving a broader conspiracy in the Oklahoma attack. Iraq claimed to possess irrefutable documents proving Middle East involvement in Oklahoma. There was also circumstantial evidence that Terry Nichols, the lead co-conspirator of the bombing, had meetings with Ramzi Yousef, ringleader of the 1993 World Trade Center attack, while both men visited the same university campus in the Philippines, known for Islamic radicalism. Both attacks relied on truck bombs loaded with fertilizer.

Now I was heading to New York, where I hoped to tell some of that to my Judge.

Carswell didn't want me talking to prisoners or guards in Oklahoma City. They didn't want those folks listening to what I had to say. Odds are those detention officers might know some of the Oklahoma families, and the word would get out. Still, the SHU is a bad place for anybody. It's for punishment. I could only imagine what Carswell would concoct once I got to New York.

Try to imagine this brutal irony from where I was standing—in shackles and prison uniform.

EXTREME PREJUDICE

I would be transported by Con-Air from Oklahoma City, where I contributed to the Oklahoma City bombing investigation. My final destination was New York City, where I gave advance warning about both the 9/11 attack and the first attack on the World Trade Center in 1993. New York had been a primary beneficiary of my efforts for almost a decade.

If that's not ironic enough, the federal courthouse in New York, where I would face Judge Mukasey, sat approximately 1,000 yards from where the World Trade Center used to stand.

Pending the outcome of my hearing, I would be locked up at the Metropolitan Correctional Center (MCC) just a couple of city blocks from Ground Zero. I would be detained in the same prison where Ramzi Yousef and other defendants waited for trial in the 1993 bombing of the World Trade Center—the attack that launched my career as an Asset.

Like the cycle of a Greek tragedy, the most profound experiences of my life turned on the World Trade Center, from beginning to end.

I gave my whole life to this work. A decade of my life, in fact. It defined me. I sacrificed all of my personal life for it. For all of the excitement of it, I enjoyed no public fame. Very quietly I celebrated my triumphs with a small number of people who understood what I had done. If most of my work was publicly anonymous, however, my role as a back channel was no less critical, for the simple reason that almost nobody else engaged in direct conversations with Libya or Iraq in the 1990s. And so I quietly provided an opening for covert dialogue.

If I must say, I think we did a damn fine job.

And this was how America paid me back.

I was not traveling by limousine to a red carpet reception, where the Mayors of New York and Oklahoma City waited to greet me with roses and champagne, or a special plaque with the Keys to the City.

There would be no "first class" seating with a wine bar and cocktails on a 747 jumbo jetliner. No five star hotel accommodations in Manhattan. No private reception at Trump Plaza.

I traveled in shackles and chains.

I would be flying the friendly skies of "Con Air," with hard core criminals and broken-hearted souls and stripped down creature comforts. I would be gawked at by male prisoners who hadn't seen a woman in years. Some of the women prisoners flirted mercilessly, teasing them. Odds are they'd be remembered for years.

Since I was handcuffed, when I had to go to the bathroom, a U.S. Marshal would have to pull down my pants, and raise 'em up again when I was finished.

Oh yeah, it would be a great flight.

And what for? I stood accused of engaging in anti-terrorism efforts that politicians declared their highest priority for national security. Now those same politicians wanted to hide my actions from voters in Oklahoma City and New York.

Is that ironic enough for you? Feeling a little bit ashamed?

I suffered ridicule in Court proceedings,[503][504] for declaring that New Yorkers would be proud of my efforts on their behalf, and they would recognize and appreciate what I had done.

They say New York has a cold, cold heart. Maybe they would care in Oklahoma City, where a nursery school filled with toddlers and infants got destroyed in the bombing of the Alfred P. Murrah building.[505] Do you think those 19 babies died quickly crushed under all that concrete? Did they scream for their mommies, as they suffocated with broken bones?

Do you care?

Well I care. If those parents told me to stop, I would consent, out of respect for their grief. But I would be damned to hell before I ever stop hunting men who kill anybody's children—and certainly not because some creepy politician in Washington winked that it's okay.

It's not okay. But hey, that's just me.

And now I was on my way to Court to argue before Judge Michael B. Mukasey why I should not spend 10 years in prison— without a trial— for contributing to the 9/11 investigation and warning the White House about the catastrophe of invading Iraq.

Or was that 25 years in prison?

That's just too much irony for me.

It was a miserable flight.

Yeah, you bet it was. Some things really are unforgivable in a democracy.

CHAPTER 27:

EXTREME PREJUDICE

"Everyone strives to reach the Law," says the man. "So how does it happen that for all these many years no one but myself has ever begged for admittance?"

The doorkeeper recognizes that the man has reached his end, and, to let his failing senses catch the words, roars in his ear: "No one else could ever be admitted here, since this gate was made only for you. I am now going to shut it."
—The Trial by Franz Kafka

This was the stuff of nightmares. And the worst was coming fast.

I had known since February that Carswell wanted to force a "cure" on me. Assistant U.S. Attorney Edward O'Callaghan proposed that I should be forcibly drugged with Haldol, a heavy anti-psychotic that imitates the stone-like effects of Parkinson's Disease, so that I could be "cured" of claiming to have worked as an Asset in anti-terrorism, involved in Pre-War Intelligence and the 9/11 investigation.

My capability to think and function would be utterly ruined. I would be so doped up that I wouldn't be capable of exchanging ideas through conversation or the written word pretty much ever again.

That was the whole point.

I would become like those other broken women on the notorious M-1 unit at Carswell, who couldn't hold a fork to eat, or raise a cup to drink without spilling on themselves. Women who couldn't shower or dress themselves. Women who slept 15 to 18 hours every day, and sometimes wet their beds at night. Because I was pre-trial, Carswell had requested that I get locked up "indefinitely," which could imply the maximum 10 year sentence in my case. It appeared Carswell was testing the waters to see if the Patriot Act

319

could be categorized with violent crimes, which typically holds "incompetent" inmates for the maximum sentence. Regardless, if the Court accepted "indefinite detention," it would be up to Carswell to recommend when to free me, at whatever time the Justice Department declared that I was "cured." My detention would probably last several years, and my life would become a living torture until that end.

This was "extreme prejudice," alright. The purpose was not only to discredit my reputation as an Asset, but to destroy me as a human being, physically and spiritually.

Only extreme prejudice could protect Republicans on Capitol Hill, who had staked their reputations on a totally false and revisionist myth about their performance on national security, which isn't exactly honest, if you know what actions the government failed to take—like shutting down the financial pipeline to Al Qaeda. They had to go nuclear on me. Nothing less would shield them.

And now we had gathered in New York for a hearing to debate this god awful proposal.

They had not counted on one problem, however. Just because somebody wants to kill you doesn't mean that you have to surrender without a fight.

In which case the FBI should have listened to Paul Hoven more carefully. He used to chuckle, "Susan, if I was taking gun fire in a back alley at midnight, I would want you by my side. Because you would fight to the death."

I understood that psychiatry had nothing to do with reality in my case. This was all politically motivated. Having studied the competency law at Carswell's prison library, I also understood exactly how to tackle it and stop it. The competency law itself gave me all the opportunity I needed to bring clarity to the situation. Satisfying the Court was a simple matter of presenting a couple of participatory witnesses, who could assure Judge Mukasey of the authentic details of my life. I was also entitled to supply evidence to prove my functionality. Any hearing would do, so long as I could exercise my right to challenge the questions raised in the psych evaluations.

Once reality came into play, this bogus psychiatry would get thrown out the window. Oh yes, give me due process, and this phony psych debate would be over. It would be squashed.

At my first meeting with Talkin after Carswell, I made perfectly clear that's the strategy I wanted to pursue. I was furious that I was suffering because he had misread my case so badly. Talkin had gambled with my freedom and lost. Since O'Callaghan was reneging, I wanted to take a hammer to these ridiculous psych evaluations, and go back to my original defense.

Talkin wasted no time disabusing my expectations.

Only the psychiatrists who'd invented this nonsense story in the first place would be allowed to testify. Indeed, the Defense intended to call just one witness, somebody named Dr. Robert L. Goldstein, a psychiatrist on the faculty of Columbia University. I had never spoken with this man, or laid eyes on him until he showed up in Court to testify. But Dr. Goldstein was ready to assure Judge Mukasey that he had greater insight to my life and character than anyone outside of psychiatry who'd known me 15 years or longer.

It was a flagrant violation of my rights under the competence law. I knew that, because I had read the law, and I understood what it meant. Yet here again I confronted psychiatry's unscrupulous finagling of court procedure.

Now I was truly terrified.

Prison guards woke me before dawn on the morning of May 4 for the first of two hearing dates. I showered and ate a small breakfast before getting hustled through the ancient concrete tombs of M.C.C. to the federal courthouse next door.

There I was strip searched, garbed in a special prison uniform for court, and dumped in a holding cage to wait for the Judge. I waited for hours, it seemed, before I got called.

There I stood —the woman who tried to stop the 9/11 attack— just 1000 yards from the rubble of "ground zero," where the World Trade Center once graced the New York skyline.

The whole thing struck me as preposterous, a grotesque obscenity.

I was frantic to speak to my Judge. I had prepared a brief written statement, so I could stay on point, though my emotions burgeoned on hysteria. To my dismay, Judge Mukasey refused to allow me to address the court.[506]

JUDGE MUKASEY: "No. She's got a lawyer. Anything that she has to tell me, she should tell you. You can tell me or not, depending on whether you think it's in her legal interest to do it."

TALKIN: "Ms. Lindauer... wishes the Court to know that she is competent to stand trial, and wishes to stand trial, and she denies all of the reports. It's her position that all of the reports are false and inaccurate."

JUDGE MUKASEY: "I understand that, and there's now a record that that's her position. I think there was a record of it before, and so any effect that might have on subsequent proceedings, the legitimacy or lack of it, in any subsequent proceedings is now clear."

If that sounds harsh, it was. In fairness, Judge Mukasey was stuck between a rock and a hard place, confronting two wretched options. It must have infuriated him. He could accept an incompetence defense for a U.S. Asset who successfully engaged with isolated Arab countries like Libya and Iraq for almost a decade. He had to know that was legally absurd. Or he could reject the incompetence strategy, and force the Defense to go to trial. In that case, he would be forced to implement the Patriot Act in his courtroom, a law crammed with every imaginable weapon for assaulting the Constitutional rights of due process for all defendants in the country. And my case had all the bells and whistles to create terrible precedents for all of the U.S. Courts.

My case made a lot of bad law. A great Judge like Mukasey thinks about that.

A sophisticated attorney, like Brian Shaughnessy after Carswell, had a shot at striking down key planks of the Patriot Act. Shaughnessy had the knowledge and confidence to attack its constitutionality. Alas, he was not leading my defense at this point of time. My public attorney, Sam Talkin was over his head. The result could have been disastrous for everybody else.

"Warrantless searches" on the Patriot Act posed the least of my worries, though I suspect I endured at least two! By far the scariest part of the law pertained to "secret evidence."

"Secret evidence" worked against a defendant in two critical ways, I was finding out.[507] Under the Patriot Act, the Justice Department could deny access to any evidence of its choosing. Neither the defendant, or the attorney, or the Jury would be allowed to see it. As a token gesture, some classified evidence could be revealed to the attorney—depending on his level of security clearance (which took months to acquire, eating up valuable time for trial preparation).[508] Even so, whatever limited access the attorney enjoyed, he would have no authorization to discuss with me, the defendant, or the jury. That carried enormous consequences that American could never imagine— like the "secret attorney debriefing" on February 10,[509] which preceded Dr. Drob's psych evaluation on February 28 that declared me incompetent[510] and denied my rights to a trial.

The Patriot Act made that possible.

"Secret evidence" laid the ground for two "secret charges" in the indictment.[511] If I had a possible explanation, it would be meaningless to share with my attorney. In all likelihood, he would not know the nature of those "secret charges" either. To put that in context, in five years under indictment, I had two attorneys. My second attorney, Brian Shaughnessy had served as a senior federal prosecutor in the Court of Chief Justice John Sirica. He had a top secret security clearance for much of his career, and regularly handles tough international security cases. It didn't matter. The Justice Department never divulged those "secret charges" to him, either.

That creates unexpected logistical difficulties at Trial. Any possible alibi would have to be based on pure speculation. You're shooting in the dark. The Judge might not allow a Defense to argue hypothetical alibis in front of a jury. But what else could you do? Judge Mukasey would have been forced to decide.

For all that, it was dawning on me that "secret evidence" on the Patriot Act carried an even more frightening and onerous burden for my defense that I had not previously understood.

"Secret evidence" that established my innocence and might save me from years in prison, called "exculpatory knowledge," got withheld from my defense, as well, including all important confirmations that I worked as a U.S. Asset for nine years, supervised by U.S. Intelligence! That meant everything to us. And the Justice Department greedily withheld validation of that truth. They simply declared it "classified evidence," and refused to acknowledge it.[512]

The whole premise of the Prosecution's arguments depended on that denial.

That's how we ended up in Court on a fine day in May, fighting over whether I should be forcibly drugged with Haldol to "cure me" of believing what the FBI, the Bureau of Prisons, the U.S. Attorneys Office and the Justice Department all knew to be fully truthful. Ted Lindauer and later Brian Shaughnessy would know it, too—but when confronted, the Feds refused to admit it.

For all of those reasons, I compare the Patriot Act to the old medieval battering rams used to smash castle fortresses centuries ago. Battering rams cracked the castle's stone walls into rubble. Once invaders breached the fortress, they would run amuck in chaos, pillaging and plundering. And the castle, symbolizing social order, would be wrecked for everyone seeking the protection of the State. A trial like mine, invoking the Patriot Act, could tear down Constitutional protections of due process that have existed since the birth of our nation. It's a wrecking ball for democracy and the rights of citizens.

I'm convinced that Judge Mukasey could see that, too.

And so I have tremendous sympathy— and respect— for Judge Mukasey, because I believe he perceived that bigger picture of casualties for the U.S. Court system.

If he could not kill my case, Judge Mukasey might be compelled to instruct a jury that the absence of evidence to substantiate "secret charges" could not be weighed in deciding whether to convict me.[513] Under the Patriot Act, a jury could be instructed that the Justice Department considered that "secret evidence" sufficient to prove wrongdoing in some unspecified criminal action, performed on some non-specific day, violating some non-specific law. And that's all the Jury needed to know.[514] I could get five years in prison, without knowing why.

A straight arrow Judge and preeminent legal scholar like Mukasey doesn't like that. He would enforce it, because that's the law. But a great Judge thinks about the consequence of his decisions for due process and liberties. And at the highest level of Chief Justice, he considers the precedents throughout the Court system. From the first days of my indictment, I could see that Judge Mukasey regarded "secret evidence" with strong distaste. He didn't like what it meant, or where it led. He didn't like enforcing those sorts of rules in his courtroom, creating bad legal precedents in the Courts that he loves.

There was one more problem facing both of us that morning. Judge Mukasey could only work from whatever defense strategy my attorney gave him. Judge Mukasey could not craft that strategy himself, or apply his greater skill to improve upon it.

This incompetence defense was the only option Talkin presented for ending my case. Talkin made no effort to strike any of the charges, even the most innocuous accusations that I ate cheeseburgers on days that I was not in New York, or that I supported free elections in Iraq. This was all Mukasey had to work with. On the face of it, incompetence was grossly insulting. However, under the original agreement, I would have served the most minimal prison sentence possible under federal law, just four months. It would have killed the case without a trial, sidestepping the Patriot Act with its treacherous legal precedents for the whole U.S Court system. And I would walk away with no conviction on my record. Under the circumstances, a Judge might consider this a very reasonable solution. Many inmates would agree with him.

Forcible drugging was a different beast, however. It made a great big mess out of our legal solution. Face it, I'd been a damn good sport about going to Carswell, and this was a blatant double cross. The mere suggestion of Haldol terrified me no end.

Judge Mukasey could see that. He was fiercely attentive to my courtroom demeanor that morning, studying me intensely, fully alert, while I sat quaking in obvious fear.

But his choice—and mine—was whether to throw out the whole incompetence finding, and go back to square one. Or go forward into this storm.

For myself, there was no question. I abhor drugs. There's no way I would consent to ruin my thinking and my consciousness with mind-altering psychotropic drugs.

I would fight forcible drugging all the way to the Supreme Court, though I was convinced it would get struck down in the 2nd Circuit Court of Appeals. I considered it medically unethical and politically motivated. And I would not submit for any reason. Honestly, I've dealt with terrorists who didn't frighten me as much as these crazy fools who call themselves "psychiatrists."

That was the backdrop when Judge Mukasey struck his gavel to call the Court to order, as sunshine burst through the tall windows of his chamber.

The first witness that May afternoon was Dr. Collin Vas, testifying on behalf of Carswell.[515]

Introducing himself, Dr. Vas told the Court that he had worked as a staff psychiatrist at Carswell for a year. He attended medical school in Banglo, India. He earned a postgraduate diploma in psychiatry at the Christian Medical College in Vellore, India, and finished his psychiatric residency at the Mayo Clinic in Rochester, Minnesota.[516]

On behalf of Carswell, Dr. Vas was throwing down the gauntlet, requesting the Court's permission to forcibly strap me to a gurney and inject me with Haldol,[517] until I could be "cured" of claiming that I worked as an Asset.[518] According to Dr. Vas, my "cure" required the harshest drugs available to the prisons, a drug known to imitate Parkinson's Disease, causing heavy loss of motor functioning, especially at the high dosages prescribed by Carswell staff. I had seen for myself how its crippling side effects destroyed the functioning of many women trapped on the notorious psych unit of the prison.

That's what they wanted to shoot me up with.

I confess that I quaked in fear, shackled in that courtroom. I understood exactly how Carswell's dosages of Haldol would rob me of my life.

And why exactly? What desperate symptoms of "mental illness" had I exhibited?

By this time, I had been observed at Carswell for seven (7) months on the M-1 unit, 24 hours a day, 7 days a week. Surely there must have been some serious behavioral issue to justify forcibly drugging an inmate with the harshest drugs available to prison staff. Medical ethics would surely demand that symptoms of a "disease" show itself before recommending treatment to a willing participant. Let alone forcing it upon an unwilling prisoner.

You can judge for yourself whether Carswell met that medical criteria:

That afternoon, the Court cut to the chase.

Had I been observed to suffer hallucinations?[519]

O'CALLAGHAN: "If you could turn to page nine, please. Do you see that?"

VAS: "Yes."

O'CALLAGHAN: "Do you see the cross-outs in that area?"

[The Prosecutor was referencing an observation report from Carswell. On October 3, 2005, the day of my prison surrender, psych staff cited a goal of "decreasing the intensity and frequency of auditory and visual hallucinations in 120 days."

On October 26, 2005—three weeks after my arrival at Carswell—Dr. Vas himself struck that objective from the observation report.

Scrawled across the page was the wording: "Not Applicable."]

VAS: "Yes. That's all my handwriting. The reason why it was crossed out is that during the time that Ms. Lindauer was present at FMC Carswell, she denied that she was ever experiencing hallucinations, and we did not see any external evidence of that."

On cross examination, the question of hallucinations got raised again:

TALKIN: And you said that you never observed any hallucination behavior, you personally never observed it?"

VAS: "No external evidence, yes."

TALKIN: "And basically everyone at Carswell that you spoke to, no one else observed any external evidence?"

VAS: "Nobody observed any external evidence, yes."

TALKIN: "And you say that she denied that she had any hallucinations while she was there?"

VAS: "That is true."

What? No hallucinations! No hearing voices! Nothing at all?

That's correct. What's a poor psychiatrist to do? Why, look for something else, of course!

What about delusions? Any evidence that I suffered those? That would be very helpful!

The "internal medication hearing"[520] on December 28, 2005 cited "treatment of delusions" as necessary for the "restoration of (my) competence." The "summary of evidence" was not ambiguous. It described the nature of my alleged delusions as follows:

"She denied the possibility of mental illness, once again reporting in detail her belief that the government is having her detained because she represents a threat to the administration due to her differing beliefs about their policies on Iraq. She states she has been a government agent for 9 years working in "anti-terrorism."

"Lindauer denied any wish to hurt herself or others, and denied any history of aggressive behavior."

The handwritten document was signed by Dr. Pederson and Dr. Collin Vas. That would be the same Dr. Vas testifying before Judge Mukascy.

There was no concern about excessive weeping, hysteria, depression—which happens in prison. But not to me. I was active, motivated and reasonably friendly to other inmates. I showed no behavior problems. The only thing Carswell could cite to justify drugs was my deep-seated confidence that I worked as an Asset alongside Richard Fuisz and Paul Hoven. Carswell had nothing else to hit me with.

There was just one pesky problem. Carswell's chief psychologist, Dr. Shadduck had confirmed it himself, quite easily, in early December.

O'CALLAGHAN: "Can you please turn to page 11 of Government Exhibit 1. Does it have hand writing on that page?"

VAS: "This is Ms. Lindauer's handwriting. At the top of the working diagnosis section, she writes in "None. Witness proves it's all true."

O'CALLAGHAN: "I direct your attention to page 14 of Government Exhibit 1. Is there handwriting on that page?

VAS: It states: "Susan Lindauer reports no episodes of hallucinations and demands that Shadduck interview witnesses. Disagrees entirely. [signed] Susan Lindauer, January 16, 06."

O'CALLAGHAN: "And directing your attention to page 17 of that exhibit, is there handwriting on that page?"

VAS: "It's got Ms. Lindauer's signature dated March 28, 2006, and "Refused to agree with diagnosis. No symptoms."

O'CALLAGHAN: "What is your understanding of whose handwriting that is?"

VAS: "That's Ms. Lindauer's handwriting."

O'CALLAGHAN: "Turn to page 18. Is there handwriting on that page?"

VAS: "It says "Never suffered those symptoms." That's relating to psychotic symptoms."

O'CALLAGHAN: "And whose handwriting is that?"

VAS: "That's hers. Ms. Lindauer's."

You can not imagine how my hands shook as I clutched the pen to write those words. I looked around M-1 at the damaged lives of other women inmates. I could see what awaited me if I did not fight back hard. And win.

Low and behold, here was the clincher:

O'CALLAGHAN: "And what is the working diagnosis that is recorded on page 11?"

VAS: "Well, it is: "Ruled out delusional disorder." And that's entered in the computer."

O'CALLAGHAN: "And did you rule out "delusional disorder" during the course of Ms. Lindauer's evaluation at FMC Carswell?"

VAS: **<u>"At the end of the diagnostic phase which was completed in December of 2005, delusional disorder had been ruled out, <i>after the behavioral observations, diagnostic interviews and psychological testing</i>.</u>"**

O'CALLAGHAN: "If you could just turn to page three, what should the correct date be?"

VAS: "December 21, 2005."

Wait a minute! What was that?

No delusional disorder?

That's right. No delusional disorder!

Not what you expected, huh?

The Justice Department was out of luck. As hard as they tried, Carswell could find no evidence to justify such a politically tantalizing diagnosis. They could provide no examples of delusional episodes to the Court that I couldn't disprove as medical fraud. That made it awfully difficult to declare that I suffer a "delusional disorder."

My story was fully truthful and authentic! Inconvenient, yes. Disappointing, no doubt. Unhappily for Carswell's psychology department, it all checked out.

What's a psychiatrist to do?

After that, I took the battle to Carswell. I warned that if Dr. Shadduck appeared in Court and denied authenticating my story, I would demand that he face prosecution for perjury. He could expect to spend some quality time in prison himself, if he lied under oath to Judge Mukasey—like a lot of the women at Carswell. I suspect that's why Carswell sent Dr. Vas to testify instead.

Did any of these psychiatrists have the integrity to elucidate in Court why they had to abandon such a prized diagnosis?

Why had Carswell been forced to rule out "delusional disorder?"

Nobody asked those pertinent questions.

And Dr. Vas offered no explanation. There was no mention of my two outstanding witnesses, who bombarded Shadduck with phone calls until the Chief of Psychology finally broke down and verified my story. Dr. Vas gave no reason why there was no way to make a diagnosis of "delusional disorder" stick.

The truth was so glaring they could not risk it. They did not dare.

Dr. Vas gave the date that the diagnosis got ruled out, December 21. And he said no more.

I was astounded by the timing. The internal medication hearing occurred on December 28, one week after the "diagnosis" had been struck. (See Appendix). That was the meeting when Dr. Vas and Dr. Pederson suggested that I should take Haldol, Ativan and Prozac as treatment for my "delusional disorder," for the "restoration of competence."

We had it in Dr. Pederson's own handwriting. Now in Court Vas admitted that "delusional disorder" had been thrown out one week before the "internal medication hearing" took place.

For me, that epitomizes the irrational nature of psychiatry. Would any reputable medical doctor prescribe insulin for a patient *not suffering from diabetes*? Would a medical doctor recommend chemotherapy after *ruling out cancer*? The question answers itself. Any respectable physician would consider it grossly unethical to prescribe treatment for non-existent conditions—much less to impose harsh drugs on unwilling participants, without cause.

Low and behold, when Judge Mukasey issued his ruling, he made a straight declaration that he perceived my Defense lacked satisfactory corroboration of my assertions, according to the evaluation by Dr. Drob, Dr. Goldstein, Dr. Kleinman and Dr. Shadduck. He observed that Carswell and psychiatry in general disputed the authenticity of my story.[521]

Clearly Judge Mukasey had no idea, relying on courtroom testimony and psychiatric reports, that my story had been fully validated by highly reputable independent sources, who spoke with the FBI, Ted Lindauer, and Carswell's own Dr. Shadduck, on behalf of the Bureau of Prisons.[522] They could have corrected those misrepresentations, but that would have defeated their objective—to force a finding of incompetence over my objections.

Wait—This was a court hearing on whether to strap me to a gurney, in order to forcibly inject me with massive doses of Haldol.

What could justify forcibly administering such heavy drugs, if there was no evidence of hallucinations, depression or a "delusional disorder?"

Was I aggressive towards guards or other inmates?[523]

VAS: "She was initially very cooperative and pleasant with us. She wanted to tell us her story, and we listened, and we actually did not have many problems until we gave her feedback."

"At the end of the diagnostic phase, we met with Ms. Lindauer and informed her of her psychiatric diagnosis, and recommendations for treatment with psychotropic medications. She became very angry and enraged and has been hostile towards many members of the treatment team since."

"Until she left Carswell, she was quite hostile and oppositional."

But was that actually true? Was my behavior hostile towards prison staff, guards or other inmates, as Dr. Vas insinuated?

Observation notes from prison staff on M-1 paint a different picture.[524]

On February 22, 2006, M-1 staff wrote: "Ms. Lindauer is functioning well on the unit."

Other handwritten notes said, "Functional and not a behavior problem," underlined by staff.

Another staffer wrote, "Not a problem when confronted about anything."

Another guard wrote, "She is low key and cooperative. Cares for self, good hygiene. Zero behavioral problems. She is focused on getting a trial."

On March 29, 2006, interaction with staff was called "appropriate."

On April 3, 2006, interaction with staff. "Appropriate."

On April 9, 2006, interaction with staff. "Appropriate."

My attorney raised this point on cross examination.[525]

TALKIN: "Throughout the reports, pretty much the interaction with staff on M-1 was appropriate?"

VAS: "For the large part, yes."

TALKIN: "And for the large part, her interaction with everyone, except the psychiatrists and psychologists, was appropriate?"

VAS: "Appropriate is kind of a complex word."

Actually, it's not. No matter how badly Carswell abused my rights, I kept my cool. I tried to stay pleasant and cooperative with M-1 nursing and recreation staff, and the guards. I never created problems on the unit. That's pretty remarkable, if you think about what I was facing.

That explains why in every monthly report, M-1 staff declared that I "socialized well," showed "good intellectual functioning," and had "good physical health."[526]

Throughout those frightening months, staff frequently described me as: "Smiling, pleasant and cooperative. With good eye contact."[527]

What's a "medical doctor" to do about a woman prisoner like me?

As for my hostility towards the psych department, try to imagine the shock for an inmate in prison! What would be the normal reaction of a prisoner denied release on the day promised by the Court? And remember, you've been ordered to surrender to prison over your strongest objections, without a trial or a hearing to challenge the evidence against you. Witnesses are standing by ready to confront the Court with assurances that you've been telling the truth about everything.

Wouldn't that upset you to wake up on the morning of your release, and discover that your prison detention was prolonged "indefinitely"? Up to 10 years without a trial or guilty plea!

Carswell indicated I would be detained until whatever time the Justice Department decided that I was "cured." They speculated my "cure" might take several years because my belief in my Asset work was deeply embedded in my spirit. They warned the Court that it would take much hard work on their part to break me.

All signs pointed to a long period of imprisonment.

Would you be frightened? Would it be irrational to feel scared?

I suspect that would be upsetting for most people.

It's a heart-stopping moment, for sure.

Most "indefinite" detentions are limited to incompetent inmates who are violent or destructive, and pose a lasting threat to the community. Typically, they get detained for the maximum sentence as part of the incompetence decision. It appeared to me that Carswell was testing the waters to see if the Patriot Act could be classified in the same category as violent offenses. That would translate to 10 years in my case, with forcible drugging to boot. Even if maximum sentencing didn't apply, under "indefinite detention," it would be up to Carswell to recommend the timing of my release, when they decided that I was "cured" of my "mental defects." That would stay open-ended for years.

So yes, I freely admit that I was horrified. From that moment on, I feared greatly for my future. That strikes me as perfectly sane.

The question was why?

How does a psychiatrist justify forcibly drugging a prisoner with Haldol, if that individual shows no symptoms of any kind? No hallucinations, no delusions, no depression, no aggressive behavior. If they're cooperative and functional, without any behavioral problems?

Dr. Vas and Dr. Shadduck kicked around until they found a solution—a diagnosis of "psychotic disorder not otherwise specified."[528] No wonder it took 7 months.

O'CALLAGHAN: "And why was that diagnosis determined to be the most accurate diagnosis?"

VAS: "Well, primarily because she does not clearly meet the criteria for the diagnosis I have just stated. When somebody does not meet a specific diagnosis, and if there is inadequate or conflicting data, we come to a diagnosis of "psychotic disorder not otherwise specified.""

O'CALLAGHAN: "Does psychotic disorder "not otherwise specified" contain a delusional disorder component?"

VAS: "It certainly contains a component of delusion."

On cross examination, Talkin questioned what that diagnosis actually means?

TALKIN: "Now that's kind of a catch-all diagnosis. In other words, if someone doesn't fit in to, say, for example a delusional order– and you can't find another psychotic disorder, then you put them in "psychotic order not otherwise specified.""

VAS: "Yes."

TALKIN: "So basically that's a diagnosis that you're not able to completely diagnose the individual?"

VAS: "In some situations, yes."

TALKIN: "As far as you can tell from Susan Lindauer, other than her interactions with you when she became hostile or angry, when you told her she had a disease, *as the reports indicated, she basically functioned normally among the other individuals in the facility, correct?"*

VAS: *"Yes."*

TALKIN: "And Dr. Pederson concluded that Ms. Lindauer wasn't suicidal?"

VAS: "That's right."

TALKIN: "He concluded she wasn't a risk of injury to herself?"

VAS: "Yes."

TALKIN: "Or to anybody else?"

VAS: "Yes."

TALKIN: "Or to property, I believe?"

VAS: "Yes."

TALKIN: "So that's the position of the people at Carswell?"

VAS: "Yes."

TALKIN: "Carswell is a federal medical center, but it's a jail, correct?"

VAS: "Yes."

TALKIN: "It's a prison?"

VAS: "Yes."

TALKIN: "No one's free to leave?"

VAS: "That's correct."

TALKIN: "The interaction among individuals in that jail is different than it would be on the street, correct?"

VAS: "Quite true."

TALKIN: "People are guarded in their behavior with others?"

VAS: "Often times."

TALKIN: "Selective in who they speak to?"

VAS: "That's right."

TALKIN: "Everybody in the jail is like that for the most part—withdrawn. For the most part, people are like that?"

VAS: "Many people are like that."

TALKIN: "That's normal behavior in that type of a setting, correct?"

VAS: "Agreed."

TALKIN: "And throughout the government exhibit that describes her behavior, that's exactly how Ms. Lindauer's behavior is described among her peers, correct?"

VAS: "That she was guarded, yes."

TALKIN: "And selective?"

VAS: "Yes."

TALKIN: "And there was also times that she was smiling, correct?"

VAS: "Yes."

TALKIN: "And there was times that she was happy, correct?"

VAS: "Yes."

TALKIN: "And there was times she was having a good time with other individuals, correct?"

VAS: "Yes."

TALKIN: "And there was times that she wasn't having a good time with individuals?"

VAS: "True."

TALKIN: "Sometimes she had a bad day, correct?"

VAS: "Yes."

I would have expected Carswell to give me a clean bill of "mental health," with that kind of reporting. After all, I suffered no depression. I stayed active. I showed good hygiene. I treated the guards and my fellow inmates with respect. What more can you expect from a prisoner?

And yet, no matter the absence of "symptoms,'" Carswell and the US Attorneys Office argued that I should be strapped to a gurney and forcibly injected with Haldol.

They didn't bat an eye when they asked for permission to shoot me up like a street junkie.

At least Dr. Kleinman and Vas interviewed me. The witness for the Defense, Dr. Robert L. Goldstein, a Professor of Clinical Psychiatry at Columbia University,[529] never bothered to do that.

I laid eyes on him for the first time when he appeared in Court on the second morning of testimony.

On the bright side, at least Dr. Goldstein opposed drugging me. He assured the Court that drugs would not cure my "condition."

Dr. Goldstein also scoffed that I might suffer schizophrenia, though nobody had suggested it to that point. It's still worth noting:[530]

GOLDSTEIN: "The criterion for schizophrenia has never been met in this case, because the patient does not have those enumerated criteria, which do include prominent hallucinations; disorganization of thought and delusions, but delusions of a bizarre quality."

"When I say bizarre, I mean it's a term of art in psychiatry, which means that such things could never happen in the real world. For example, believing that martians have implanted electrodes in your brain to control your behavior or something like that. Whereas in delusional disorder, you have non-bizarre delusions, things that possibly could happen, like somebody could be following you, somebody could want to kill you, somebody could have special talents and relationships as I enumerated before."

That would have been well and good, if he had stopped there.

Instead, Dr. Goldstein put forth a hypothesis that I suffered "delusional disorder, mixed type," that encompassed two areas. Paranoia. And grandiosity.[531]

"Paranoid delusions," according to Goldstein, encompassed "individual beliefs that they're being persecuted, followed, spied on, individuals want to harm them, even kill them, or otherwise cause mischief in their lives. And they spend lots of time trying to protect themselves against these various imaginary enemies."

Right there, Goldstein exposed his own "grandiosity" by trying to invent a reality to support the diagnosis he wanted to make.

Had I experienced paranoia at all in my life? I confess that I've been known to joke with friends that we have our own satellite tracking devices, so the feds can watch over us. That doesn't mean we believe it, however.

I would call paranoia an occupational hazard. For almost a decade, I was part of a community that relies on surveillance for its livelihood. Intelligence. Surveillance. I think I see a connection.

So was I paranoid? Probably.

Was that irrational paranoia? Was that surveillance false?

It would be regarded as de rigueur for any Asset engaged in frequent contact with diplomats from Libya and Iraq. In the context of my lifestyle, it was quite ordinary. Once, when I protested some heavy surveillance during the Lockerbie negotiations, my handlers laughed derisively that they wouldn't be doing their jobs if they didn't track me. If you're dealing with Libya and Iraq, you'd be foolish not to expect it. It would be pitiably naïve.

Court evidence supported my "beliefs": FBI wiretaps captured 28,000 phone calls, 8,000 emails and hundreds of faxes in a two year period before my arrest.[532]

There was surveillance video of me walking my dachshunds in my neighborhood park.

Evidence suggests that I'd been subjected to two warrantless searches on the Patriot Act. And I was subsequently indicted as an "Iraqi Agent."

Maybe I thought I was under surveillance, because I was under surveillance!

Admittedly, my beliefs about surveillance might seem irrational to colleagues who had no idea that I functioned as an Asset in frequent contact with diplomats from all over the Middle East. However, I would never discuss surveillance with friends or family not tied to my projects, anyway. Except in the most extreme circumstances, they would rarely hear complaints from me.

So much for theories that I'm overly paranoid. Most of my life I'd have to say I wasn't paranoid enough.

Was I frightened about this surveillance? Did I "spend lots of time trying to protect myself from imaginary enemies" who might by spying on me, as Goldstein implied?

Notoriously not. My brilliant attorney after Carswell, Brian Shaughnessy, used to chuckle that somebody dealing with Iraq and Libya is doubtfully afraid of anything. The psychiatry crowd failed to grasp that if surveillance truly frightened me, I would have cut off my dealings with the CIA, and stopped meeting diplomats at the United Nations. I would never have contributed to anti-terrorism work. I would have become a librarian. Given the facts of my life, nobody could seriously pretend that I was crippled by occupational paranoia. I was so "not paranoid" that the Justice Department accused me of acting as an "Iraqi Agent—" which has to require some fairly bold actions.

Dr. Goldstein's second "diagnosis" that I suffered delusions of "grandiosity" struck me as equally ludicrous and uninformed, for different reasons.

"Grandiose delusions," according to Goldstein, "involve situations where individuals believe they have special talents or outstanding abilities, relationships with successful or prominent people, or that they have special gifts—being clairvoyant or other special gifts."[533]

That could describe half the populations of Washington, Chicago, New York and Los Angeles. The civic leaders of small town America. And practically all of the guests on CNN, MSNBC and the Fox News Channel.

The better half, I would add.

If I was grandiose, I "suffered" substantially less from it than others I know. And since when has ambition, hard work, self motivation and pride for one's achievement become a personal liability? Is that not the refuge of mediocrity to scorn personal striving for excellence?

If Goldstein had spoken with me, he'd recognize that actually I'm a fairly down to earth woman. I perform like a work-horse, not a show horse. I'm not a celebrity seeker. I'm an activist, motivated by love of my causes, not a desire for publicity.

I understood how difficult it is to create change. I found it amazingly hard. And also worthwhile. I have made the commitment and sacrifices. I have learned to appreciate the smaller moments when a project advances slowly. I have learned not to feel daunted by what's left to be done. I give thanks for my small role.

Grandiose, huh? You don't like motivation and achievement?

Fine. If I'm grandiose, do you think I care what you think? Just spell my name right. Because I did this work— or I wouldn't have been under surveillance for 10 years!

To his credit, Judge Mukasey posed an astute question that swooped right over the heads of these psychiatrists.

He asked Dr. Goldstein, "What is your understanding of the charges against Ms. Lindauer? Do you understand that she has been accused *by the Justice Department* of engaging in these activities?"

Right there Judge Mukasey pointed to a serious flaw in the logic of psychiatry in my case. The indictment depended on my relationships with Iraqi diplomats at the United Nations. The arguments for prosecution hinged on my participation in these activities.

Now these crazy psychiatrists paraded into court, arguing that these events never happened. But if the actions did not transpire, how could the US Attorneys Office continue indicting me?

My wonderful Judge, brilliant and canny, had found his way out of our box. (I just didn't know it yet.) People, I love Judge Mukasey. Thank God for his legal savvy!

The question from the Court's outlook was whether my activities rose to the level of a crime. Was I legitimately acting under the assumption that I was performing as an Asset, under the long-time supervision of members of U.S. Intelligence? The Justice Department was not conceding that those actions never took place. Nor did I deny participating in them. Only the crazy psychiatrists got twisted in their thinking, and wanted to cure me of believing in the occurrence of those events—which was fairly bizarre, given the backdrop for our Court drama.

If the actions never occurred, it would be impossible to justify the indictment!.

The implication flew right over their heads. Instead, Dr. Vas and Dr. Stuart Kleinman swore to Judge Mukasey that with enough Haldol, and enough prison time, I could be cured of believing that those events took place—actions stipulated in the indictment itself.

And how long would this "cure" take?

Psychiatrists frowned. That was a harder question.

How many years of Haldol would be required to eradicate an individual's sense of identity and life's purpose? Would five years be enough? Would it require the maximum sentence?

How many years would it take to destroy my belief that two men named Paul Hoven and Dr. Richard Fuisz had been guiding forces in my life for almost a decade?

How long would it take to destroy my recollections of the terrorism investigations and policy that our team contributed to?

How long would it take to destroy my memories of diplomats at the United Nations? Ambassadors that I'd known socially? To forget conversations from our back channel dialogue?

How much Haldol would it take to destroy my natural sense of privilege and joy that I felt for participating in this work? Four years? Five years?

Could they destroy my dignity any faster than that?

They could certainly try.

For that matter, how much drugs would it take to stop me from claiming I warned about the 9/11 attack? Or insisting that one faction of the Intelligence Community urged Attorney General John Ashcroft's private staff to coordinate an intra-agency response and preempt the attack?

What would it take to stop me from knowing the truth about Pre-War Intelligence and the comprehensive peace framework negotiated with Iraqi diplomats that would have solved America's conflict without War?

How much time? How much drugs?

Psychiatrists told Judge Mukasey that they could not know the answers to those questions. They needed the Court's permission to detain me *"indefinitely."* It might take a couple of years. Or it might take the maximum 10 year sentence to make sure that I was really and truly "cured."

Carswell would be sure to let the Judge know when I was ready for release.

With enough Haldol, eventually, I could be persuaded to forget the whole thing.

My life could be "corrected."

Erased.

Terminated. With Extreme Prejudice.

CHAPTER 28:

METROPOLITAN CORRECTIONAL CENTER

There's a great Robert Redford movie that hits a nerve for me —"Three Days of the Condor." In it, an intelligence operative stumbles on a "black operation" at the height of the Cold War. His entire team gets snuffed while he's at lunch, all of his associates terminated "extreme prejudice" style. He goes on the run, hunted by an assassin, while he tries to figure out what the hell he's uncovered that's got everybody so afraid.

The movie ends with Robert Redford standing proudly in front of the New York Times.

His intelligence chief from CIA warns him to go to ground. "Otherwise someday a car will pull up on the side of the road, and the door will open. They might send a friend."

Oh no, Robert Redford assures his Washington bureau chief. "Look where we're standing—" under the sign of the New York Times. If the spooks harass him, the New York Times will publish everything. The CIA's black operations will be exposed. The murder of his associates will be in the open.

"You don't know that," the bureau chief shakes his head. "You can't be sure."

"I can be sure. They'll do it," Redford retorts, with confident naivety. "They'll publish it."[534]

My nightmare paralleled "Three Days of the Condor" in so many ways—right down to the fact that the New York Times Magazine had the dirt to blow the whole thing wide open. One of the Magazine's writers told me that Richard Fuisz and Paul Hoven vouched for me weeks after my arrest —my 9/11 warning, my role in the Lockerbie negotiations, and how our work together started in 1993, after I warned about the first attack on the World Trade Center. If Dr. Fuisz and Hoven volunteered my bona fides and the focus of our relationship to the New York Times, they probably also told the FBI. Don't you think?

As a former journalist myself, I recognized what a huge story the Times was sitting on. It would rock Washington. Not only that, most of my anti-terrorism work involved New York City, the paper's home town.

Human decency—and journalistic integrity—demanded coverage.

And so I waited, hopeful and desperate, after the May hearings on forcible drugging. Except Robert Redford was wrong.

The loud silence of the corporate media answered my prayers.

If your life depended on the New York Times, you'd be in a helluva lot of trouble.

Now I was frightened out of my wits. Scared like a scalded cat, as the saying goes. My hair turned from dirty blonde to white in a couple of short months after Carswell refused to release me. I had so much white in my hair, before I transferred out of Carswell that the prison hair salon refused to dye it for me. Prison rules prohibit changing an inmate's appearance.

Locked up at the Metropolitan Correctional Center in Manhattan, I existed in a state of constant anxiety and extreme tension over this horrific chain of events that got worse with every throw.

M.C.C. is maximum security detention for pre-trial inmates. It houses every sort of crime—from murder to bank robbery and securities fraud, to drug crimes, terrorism and me.

Ms. Eldridge ran the women's floor of the prison like a sergeant matron of a military boot camp. She could hunt out contraband nail polish like a bloodhound. She kept discipline tight among the 100 women inmates crammed into 10 by 12 foot cells, often sleeping four to a room on double bunks, with an open toilet in the corner.

My heightened state of fear might have added to my vulnerability, except that Ms. Eldridge would not tolerate inmates harassing one another. Discipline was for our own protection, and the guards kept a close watch over me. Other inmates might not have understood my status as a political prisoner, but the guards recognized that something more was going on. One guard would call out "Peace!" when I walked by. They made a special effort to keep me safe, while I waited for the Court. I will always be grateful for that.

At M.C.C. my sleep was black, and my waking hours stormed with suppressed anxiety. In prison, all of your emotions have to be swallowed down, or blocked out. There's no privacy for grieving. Everything's exposed. My status in the law was so degraded at this point, that I had to fight doubly hard to overcome my despair. I lived in sheer terror for the day the Judge would issue his ruling. I had no idea if I would win. Carswell definitely expected me to lose.

The consequences of the Judge's decision could have been monstrous. I would not only lose my freedom, but the best parts of my life— my creativity and my intellect.

By my way of thinking, forcible drugging qualified as a threat of torture. It would mutilate the most precious memories of my life and my happiness for those memories. I happen to enjoy the human condition, with its joys and pain and small kindnesses. I was proud to go to prison for opposing the violence and suffering of the Iraq War. I considered my actions deeply righteous on behalf of the anti-war movement. If I had to pay for that, then I had no regrets or remorse. These are my life-long values, which I cherish with all my heart. I would make any sacrifice for them, because I believe they are important values. And I'm willing to defend them.

Only drugging was abhorrent to me in this experience. Prison life could be harsh. It's terribly unpleasant. But you can survive it. In contrast, this threat of forcible drugging terrorized me, because it aimed to destroy the best parts of what I am. I regarded it as manifestly evil.

I could not believe that strangers would dare to deny my identity and my life's work as an Asset, and somehow they should have more authority, and more rights to speak in a court of law than participatory witnesses—friends and colleagues who engaged in these activities with me, during the period of events covered in the indictment.

If the Court had questions about the authenticity of my story, it struck me that discovering the truth should be a simple matter of calling those participatory witnesses to testify, so the Judge could hear it for himself. Judge Mukasey could confront them with questions. And they would provide insight from our firsthand contacts. Primary sources are always superior and more trustworthy. Who else could possess such authority?

By now, I was desperate to provide that comfort to the Court.

My attorney commanded that I should not write my Judge—and I never did until Carswell refused to release me. By the time I got to M.C.C. I regretted that I had not spoken up for myself sooner.

Now I appealed to the Court in long, desperate letters, begging for a proper hearing.

On four occasions, I sent witness lists with phone numbers and addresses to the Court, urging Judge Mukasey to hear what they had to say before deciding the petition to forcibly drug me.[535] I pleaded to give priority to witnesses connected to the events of my life, above those looney tunes with psychiatry degrees parading before his Court. My arguments for the natural priority of participatory witnesses over "speculative psychiatry," as I called it, would have formed the basis of any appeal to the higher courts, if Judge Mukasey ruled against me.

The problem, as I understood it, was that Judge Mukasey could not over rule my attorney's legal strategy. Even if a Judge saw that changes would benefit me as the defendant, or that my attorney's performance was sub-par, he could not impose a correction. Along those lines, if a Defendant requested a hearing over the attorney's objections, the Judge could not supercede the decision to forego it. That's how they got me.

It was a legal spy thriller worthy of John Grisham or Robert Ludlum. Talkin, meanwhile, did not want witnesses appearing in Court who would reveal how easily my story could be verified, or how my Uncle Ted had felt compelled to interview witnesses for my defense. Hence, my attorney's nickname, "No Talkin.'" He was protecting himself from questions of his own competence.

That didn't stop me from writing letters to Mukasey at 2 a.m in the dark of my cell, listening to Anna Nalick's beautiful song, "Breathe" on the hand radios we carried with ear plugs. When I finished my letters to Mukasey, I would play Free Cell solitaire on my top bunk early into the morning. I hardly slept at all. By this time, I was so desperate that I proposed my old intelligence handler, Paul Hoven, should testify in closed court.[536] I suggested that he could provide more forthcoming answers to the Court without the fear of media exposure.

I promised that Hoven could vouch for:

1. My warning to the Tunisian Embassy two days before the first attack on the World Trade Center in February, 1993, and how that act triggered our relationship.

2. Our close relationship from 1993 to 2002, and how Hoven introduced me to Dr. Fuisz in September, 1994 for the purpose of starting talks with Libyan diplomats for the Lockerbie Trial. The evaluation by the prosecution's psychiatrist, Dr. Stuart Kleinman, acknowledged that Hoven told the FBI he spoke with me 40 to 50 times after 9/11.[537] Ergo, by his own admission, we were in close contact during the 9/11 investigation.

It was a critical acknowledgement, and I seized on those implications.

3. Hoven's heavy supervision of my contacts with Libya and Iraq included weekly meetings. During a crisis or times of intense activity, we met twice weekly. Our relationship could easily be corroborated by a crowd of Republican Congressional staffers who got together for drinks and policy talk every Thursday night at a Capitol Hill watering hole known as "the Hunan," where Hoven and I met near the Senate.

At trial, some of those individuals could expect subpoenas, whether their former Republican bosses on Capitol Hill liked it or not.

4. How Dr. Fuisz's CIA credentials and his bona fides covered Syria and Lebanon in the 1980s, including:

- The hostage rescue of Terry Anderson et al. in Beirut. It was Dr. Fuisz's team that infiltrated the terrorist network hiding the hostages, and located the coven of cells in the back alleys of Beirut, where they were chained. Dr. Fuisz called out the Delta Force to make the rescue only to be stopped by top officials in Washington, who postponed the rescue until right before the 1988 election of President George H. Bush, what Dr. Fuisz called the original "October Surprise." He never forgave them.

- Dr. Fuisz and Raisa Gorbachev, wife of Soviet President Mikhail Gorbachev, launched one of the first Russian modeling agencies in the West—that incidentally imported computers to the Soviet Union at the height of Glasnost.

- His first-hand knowledge of Lockerbie, including his ability to map out the conspiracy and identify who masterminded the bombing of Pan Am 103, and why.[538]

- His Congressional testimony about a U.S. company that supplied Iraq with SCUD Mobile Missile Launchers before the first Gulf War.[539]

- How Dr. Fuisz got outed as CIA by Syria after he stole the blueprints for Syria's brand new telecommunications network from a locked crypt. Syrian agents tried to congratulate him on his success by kidnapping him in London for a private interrogation, a case that involved a decoy and Scotland Yard.

5. Under oath, we would compel Hoven to acknowledge that it was he who recruited me; he who suggested contacting Libya's diplomats to start talks for the Lockerbie Trial; and he who introduced me to Dr. Fuisz. There's no blame attached to that. These were all extraordinary events in my life, and I'm deeply proud of our work together. But I was very young when I met Paul. Approaching the Libya House at the United Nations would never have occurred to me, if Paul had not coached me.

6. How our team started back-channel talks with Iraq's Ambassador to the United Nations, Dr. Saeed Hasan, in November 2000, on resuming the weapons inspections.[540] Our preliminary talks with senior diplomats, Saad Abdul Rahmon, Abdul Rahmon Mudhian

and Salih Mahmoud continued through February, 2002, seeking Iraq's promise to accept the rigorous standards for maximum transparency demanded by the United States.

Once that criteria had been satisfied, I delivered Iraq's agreement to the U.N. Security Council myself. Thanks to the FBI, my Defense had copies of the papers that I faxed to the Security Council to prove it.[541] At that point, the United Nations jumped in, and hammered out the technical language for implementing the inspections program.

7. Finally, Hoven could confirm our team's advance warning of a precise 9/11 scenario of attack, involving airplane hijackings and a strike on the World Trade Center, throughout the summer of 2001.[542]

The key was to ask Hoven direct questions: Did Susan and Richard do this? Does this accurately portray Dr. Fuisz? Yes or no?

Give me a chance and I could prove everything.

My witness list was growing stronger by the day. Reading about my travesty on the blogs, some of the Congressional staffers from our Thursday nights at the Hunan came forward. They abhorred the judicial abuse that I was suffering under the Patriot Act. Despite any inconvenience to their own reputations, they had the integrity to want to make things right—for which I am eternally grateful.

If Hoven committed perjury under oath, he would be exposed. Harsh as it sounds, after what I suffered, I would not hesitate to demand the prosecution of Hoven or Dr. Fuisz today, if it appeared that either of them lied about supervising my work. That's a serious betrayal. It's also obstruction of justice. And I would demand they face maximum penalties in sentencing.

In which case, they'd get front row seats to life at M.C.C.

As maximum security pre-trial detention, M.C.C. is subject to lock downs that confine inmates to our cells a good 15 hours a day. Typically, we'd get locked down for every inmate count. Morning lockdowns lasted until 10 am. After lunch, we'd get locked down again from about 3 pm until 5 pm. Then after dinner from 8 pm to 9 pm—or in that ballpark. At times, I was the only English speaker in my cell, which made conversation an interesting challenge. Mostly we tried to be kind to each other, with lots of pantomimes and smiles. But whenever four people get crammed into a tiny space, there's inevitable tension.

During lock downs on the women's floor, I stayed busy. I worked on my case around the clock, preparing a possible emergency appeal to the 2nd Circuit Appellate Court, in case Judge Mukasey ruled against me. Whatever happened, I would be ready to continue my fight.

Lock downs give prisoners lots of time to think. Indeed, prison life swamps inmates with old memories, floods of them. Dr. Fuisz and Hoven certainly occupied a lot of mine.

I remember sitting in Hoven's truck in 1993, and Paul chuckling to himself, in his dark way.

Hoven: "Do you think it's an accident that I found you, and I just happen to know that you warned about the World Trade Center bombing (in 1993)? I know things your closest friends and family don't know about you."

"What do we have in common? Nothing at all. We're exact opposites. I'm a conservative Republican, and you're a goofy liberal Democrat. I'm a soldier, and you're a peace activist. There's no way that we would have any social contact if it wasn't for your warning about

the World Trade Center attack. They sent me to find you. They think someone needs to keep an eye on you. They don't want you wandering around Washington getting into any more trouble."

Or before my job interview with former Rep. Ron Wyden, now the U.S. Senator for Oregon:

Hoven: "Don't go complaining to Wyden about surveillance. Nobody's violating your rights by watching you. The CIA's not allowed to target American citizens, or conduct operations inside the United States. That responsibility falls to the Defense Intelligence Agency. And they've got a legitimate reason to keep track of you. Nobody's doing anything wrong here."

One conversation particularly echoed back, striking me as particularly tragic. As I recall, this was during the Lockerbie Trial in 2000.

Hoven: "I've been thinking about what I'd say if I ever have to testify about you in Court. You'd better know something. If anybody asks if I'm a Defense Intelligence Agent, I'm going to tell them "no."

"Agents are foreigners. And I could never be a foreigner, since I was born in the United States. Americans who work at the Defense Intelligence Agency are called "officers." To be correct, I'm your "case officer."

"You'd better remember that. Because spooks can be very particular about the use of language. That's how we can deny things without actually lying. If you ever get in trouble, you'd better tell your attorney to ask if I'm your "case officer." Or your "handler." If anybody asks if I'm a Defense Intelligence Agent, I'm going to say no. And that would be the truth."

And how could I forget my first lunch with Pat Wait, Chief of Staff to Rep. Helen Bentley, and that mischievous smile on her face, as she popped up over the menu at the diner in Alexandria, Virginia, and pointed to a mountain of man climbing out of a white pick up truck:

"That's Paul Hoven. He's with the Defense Intelligence Agency."

Pat Wait had known Hoven 20 years, and she believed he was with DIA, too. We had many conversations about Hoven's deep relationships to the Intelligence Community.

Any way you cut it, it would be crazy to deny that Hoven was deeply entrenched in the murky world of intelligence, whatever technical capacity he chose to admit. It's a shadow world of double blinds, certainly. But this was the guy who bragged about exposing Oliver North and Iran-Contra, for heavens sakes. His circle of spook friends included legendary CIA figures like Bill Weisenberger, closely tied to Edwin Wilson, that dark angel of the covert crowd, who served 27 years in prison for a black operation involving Libya. Hoven presented himself as a dedicated intelligence-passer, a straight line to the Intelligence community. He called himself my "handler" and my "case officer." And he gave me protection when some of the less friendly Arabs stuck their heads up to say hello. Heck, his sources would tell us when they were coming.

As Hoven used to tease me, about identifying spooks who might approach me at the United Nations: *"Susan, if it walks like a duck. And it quacks like a duck. It's a duck!"*

Hunkered on my top bunk on lock down at M.C.C, I used to ask myself: After all of our work together for so many years, how could these men stay silent while this happened to me? Knowing that I faced "indefinite detention" for up to 10 years and forced injections of Haldol to erase my knowledge of our work together, how could they take no action to help me?

I had never expected such cowardice. How could they live with themselves?

We know they told the truth at first. They told the truth to the New York Times Magazine, which botched the story. Hoven spoke with Ted Lindauer, and acknowledged everything. Yet throughout my indictment, Dr. Fuisz refused to speak with any of my attorneys. He would hang up immediately when they called. Sometimes he'd shout obscenities at them.

It was a striking betrayal.

I think I got a glimpse into his fear one afternoon, locked up at M.C.C. As a court meeting with Judge Mukasey finished, FBI Agent Chmiel leaned back and whispered that Dr. Fuisz denied knowing of my trip to Baghdad.

That astonished me. I recalled, with pain, those 30 to 40 phone calls in the two weeks before my trip, pleading with Richard for payment of my debts that had accumulated from our work together. And I bombarded him with requests to arrange payment for my years of service—Critical to understanding my predicament, in those days, Assets got paid at the end of a project, in order to make sure that objectives got finished, not dropped mid-way. As my handler, making arrangements for compensation would be Dr. Fuisz's responsibility. Indeed, provision for the welfare of our team fell under his "command responsibility" as our group leader. That's a time honored tradition of the military, known as "Jus in Bello."

On Capitol Hill, Congress made glorious pronouncements, in grand speeches and press conferences, that I would receive spectacular rewards for my work on Lockerbie, securing the hand over of the two Libyans— Indeed, I qualified for a number of rewards— for Lockerbie, the U.S.S. Cole, the 1993 World Trade Center Attack, and my contributions to anti-terrorism overall.

Only the TV cameras had gone away. So what did promises matter? Didn't I understand those speeches on Capitol Hill were only to glorify themselves?

Their perpetual promise of "outstanding leadership support for anti-terrorism" had nothing to do with me, after all.

Hearing the FBI agent's whisper as I got shackled to go back to my cell, I understood that Dr. Fuisz was afraid of a Trial, too. He probably told his own spymasters at CIA that I never requested payment for my work—so he could keep all that operations money for himself. Which is what he did. After 9/11, Congress appropriated a huge, special "black budget" for the 9/11 investigation that Dr. Fuisz got to draw from—$13 million. And rightfully so, if he had applied the federal monies to our field work.

Only he didn't.

I was making one of my weekly visits when Dr. Fuisz jubilantly delivered the news. Money from the Feds had come through. And he had $13 million to build his house in Virginia. No, no, he couldn't give any of that money to me. His architect would need all of it for their great design!

Richard Fuisz was a creature of the Black Budgets alright, and he kept the whole pot of gold for himself. He hoarded American tax dollars like a miser.

I saw none of it.

My Iraqi source in Baghdad, ready to identify terrorists playing hide and seek in Iraq—worth a King's ransom for what he could do for us— got none of that money, either—though let's face it, the success of the 9/11 investigation depended on us—not our managers in Washington.

Otherwise, in all ways, Dr. Fuisz functioned as an outstanding handler.

Tragically, however, that one black mark on our relationship brought us to a tragic crossroads. Dr. Fuisz's unwillingness to hand over any of that money forced me to improvise in Baghdad to arrange payment for my friend.

And I got thrown in jail for it—though my crime turned out to be practicing extreme resourcefulness in the face of extreme deprivation. It breaks my heart even now.

For all of that, my defense strategy was fairly simple. My victory did not depend on proving Hoven's connection to DIA—except to demonstrate the legality of our team's work in New York. To satisfy the Court, we only had to prove Dr. Fuisz's CIA credentials. Thanks to Lockerbie, we could do that quite easily, with or without Dr. Fuisz's direct cooperation. But Hoven's bona fides are fascinating, too, and added to my confidence as an Asset. Bottom line: I worked with two extraordinary men, fully qualified to oversee my contacts with diplomats from the Middle East.

Cumulatively, I met Hoven and Dr. Fuisz between 700 and 800 times. I calculated it once during those lock downs at M.C.C. We understood each other's strengths and weaknesses, and I loved them both, regardless of our differences.

Oh yes, I adored these men. I had a life that seized me up, pounded my spirit with adventures, and used up my exuberance on the causes that I loved. From our first days together, I applied my peace activism to the cause of non-violence in the Middle East. Dr. Fuisz and Hoven gave me a chance to put my values into action, and accomplish something real for my values in the Middle East, of all places. It was an extraordinary opportunity! No matter what it cost me on a personal level, looking back on our projects—and the wonderful things we accomplished— I see that Arabs benefited as much as the West.

I'm a huge believer in back channel dialogue. It's not a pipe dream. Our projects achieved solid results. Sadly, if Washington had only listened to us on Iraq, the world would be looking at a wholly different landscape of prosperity and stability for the Arab region today. Despite my obvious disappointments, I remain convinced that diplomacy offers a way out of the world's downward spiral. There Is Hope that we can get it right next time.

That's what I thought about on lock downs at M.C.C.

At least in the beginning, Hoven and Dr. Fuisz proved willing to claim me.

Within weeks of my arrest, a freelance journalist for the New York Times Magazine, David Samuels, interviewed both men for a profile about me.

Both men freely volunteered that I gave advance warnings about the 9/11 attack in the summer of 2001—and the first attack on the World Trade Center in February, 1993.

Likewise, Hoven and Fuisz quickly corroborated that our team started back-channel talks with Libyan diplomats for the Lockerbie Trial. Later on, we conducted preliminary talks to resume the weapons inspections with Iraq's Ambassador at the United Nations, Dr. Saeed Hasan.

The New York Times confirmed my bona fides in May, 2004.

It was David Samuels again, who told me that Hoven and Fuisz denied receiving advance warning of my arrest. Samuels said both men got very angry at me for getting arrested. But they were caught by surprise when the strike came against me.

On the contrary, Hoven and Fuisz quickly rushed to grab me back, so the intelligence community could correct the imbalance of the mistake made by the Justice Department.

The New York Times had an exclusive alright.

But they had not printed the story. They'd taken a serious matter, and fudged the details for reasons that nobody outside of that newsroom could understand. It made no sense.

The only conclusion seemed to be that David Samuels was possibly too young and inexperienced to handle such a sensitive assignment. Unhappily for me, it exceeded his reach.

If the New York Times had acted as a proper media watch dog, given the stature of the newspaper, there would have been enough leverage to squash my indictment. The spooks could have moved swiftly to kill the whole affair. U.S. Intelligence would have controlled the conditions for dropping the charges, and very probably, I would have been forced to accept a hefty non-disclosure agreement. They would have come out on top, no question.

Instead, the New York Times Magazine published an amateurish profile on my life and legal tribulations, on par with high school level journalism. I was surprised and disappointed.

Afterwards, friends protested that they had tried to help me. It was my fault, they griped, for choosing an ingénue journalist, who botched it. I would have to agree.

By example, Samuels telephoned me a few days before publication to say that Dr. Fuisz got quite distressed after talking to fact-checkers at the Magazine. Dr. Fuisz wanted to change his quote —which surprised me. Immediately after the interview, Samuels told me that Fuisz described me as "one of the top Assets in the 1990s." According to Samuels, Fuisz said that I was "uncanny in my level of perception and accuracy." I was quote, "the smartest, smartest, smartest woman he'd ever met." Fuisz called me a "genius dealing with the Arabs."

Heavens I loved those quotes! How marvelous! Before publication, I imagined any quote by Dr. Fuisz and Hoven would be stellar. I was shocked when I saw what Samuels chose instead!

Other friends told me Samuels cobbled together obscure statements from their interviews, and twisted them out of context to draw conclusions that were not discussed.

So much for the New York Times throwing sunlight onto the situation.

This was sort of an intelligence war, and they played right into it. But I wasn't the only casualty. The Intelligence Community got smashed pretty hard by Republican leaders for dissenting from its War Policy. Ironically, the bloodbath to punish opposition gutted the infrastructure of the intelligence community, to the lasting detriment of national security and anti-terrorism policy.

Vice President Cheney wasn't the only wrecking ball, either. The Republican leadership as a whole demanded that intelligence reporting should reflect the GOP message. Congress wanted to pick and choose truth, and hide unhappy intelligence, so as to make their leadership look more successful in the public's eye than their actions warranted.

In the Republican mindset, intelligence exists to protect politicians from embarrassment or criticism for their mistakes. It should shield them from responsibility.

That's anathema to intelligence field work, which exists to protect the people and the community of the nation before all else. And it's grievously offensive to the principles of democracy, which we serve. Nobody reputable does intelligence work to protect political figureheads, or shield leaders from accountability. That's genuinely despised.

By attacking me so viciously, these Republicans—like John McCain and Trent Lott, and their cohorts on Capitol Hill— exposed something ugly about their position.

Despite all of their campaign rhetoric at election time, Congress really doesn't understand how anti-terrorism gets done on the ground, at a practical level. They don't recognize it when they see it. And they don't appreciate the men and women who do it.

In other words, they've never provided "outstanding leadership support" for Assets.

Quite the contrary, they blamed and bullied us. They arrested us when our knowledge threatened the story they wanted to invent for the people. It's a pattern of insult and injury that belies any token of support from Capitol Hill.

Any politician in Washington claiming otherwise would be lying.

CONCEALING A DEFENDANT'S INNOCENCE ON THE PATRIOT ACT

Many times I have been asked why, if my Asset work was authentic, the FBI did not discover as much during its investigation.

Ah, but who says they didn't?

Chalk it up to the Patriot Act.

My indictment was loaded up with all the bells and whistles of that atrocious law. I mean it, I tripped all the wires. For openers, I'd been subjected to at least two "warrantless searches" before my arrest. The first time, federal agents ransacked my home office for documents on the Lockerbie Trial, breaking a filing cabinet in the process. I found the Lockerbie papers laid out on my desk. During the grand jury investigation, the Feds conducted a second "warrantless search," looking for evidence to justify the indictment.

They got zilch. Nada. Nothing to support the indictment. The Prosecution was left with a lunch receipt for $35 discovered in Baghdad, suggesting that I ate a cheeseburger with an Iraqi diplomat after 9/11.[543] Plus video from a hidden camera at the Al Rashid Hotel in Baghdad a year before the Invasion,[544] on the last day of my trip to Iraq. The video captured my meeting with a senior Iraqi official— and, most critically, my special Iraqi source who was going to help the FBI identify terrorists playing hide and seek with Iraqi intelligence.

The video was red hot alright, just not the way my Prosecutor wished to claim. I could hardly wink at the camera: (It was their camera, after all.) However the tape provided startling evidence of the success of our peace framework, including Iraq's cooperation with anti-terrorism efforts, and the ability of U.S. corporations to return to Baghdad in key sectors, post-sanctions.[545] It was awesome!

I recognized at once the CIA could never play that tape to a jury. The House of Cards to justify this dreadful war would fall in a day.

Given the lack of evidence, the second warrantless search was sinister indeed. The FBI was looking for anything to hang me with. Ordinarily, you don't convene a grand jury until *after* there's proof of a crime. Under the Patriot Act, the Justice Department faces no such burden.

The second search was especially obnoxious. The feds broke my front door during their forced entry. Days before my arrest, I had to barricade the door with a piece of plywood.[546] That stumped the FBI when they showed up to arrest me. When they threatened to break the door down, I shouted back— "What? You guys already broke it! You're going to break it again?"

The FBI did not think that was funny. I guess you had to be there.

My second attorney, Shaughnessy believed the lack of incriminating evidence probably explained why the Justice Department resorted to "secret evidence" and "secret charges" to persuade the grand jury that I'd broken the law.

"Secret charges" backed by "secret evidence" implied that I had engaged in some diabolical international conspiracy too terrible to expose!

My defense was only informed of the approximate dates of my alleged offenses— and nothing more. In other words, "sometime in October, 2001," I engaged in some unidentified action that violated some unidentified law. That could mean anything—

But had I really committed some awful crime?

Shaughnessy and I suspect that I stood accused of gathering health statistics on cancer rates and birth defects in Iraq, caused by depleted uranium left behind by the United States in the first Gulf War. "Sometime in October 2001," I received a book from an Iraqi diplomat, Salih Mahmoud, describing those health risks and the devastating rise of cancer and birth defects in for Iraqi children. The book on depleted uranium carried an English-Arab translation. And the Justice Department argued that I broke the law by accepting it.

Mind you, this was a book! Yet the Justice Department argued that I should spend 5 years in federal prison, as punishment.

That health information would be highly relevant to American soldiers serving multiple tours of duty in Iraq, by the way, since it forecast serious long term health problems for them, too.

We speculated the government designated it "classified evidence," because they don't want Americans knowing about possible health risks confronting American soldiers—or possibly demanding better long term health benefits for veterans and their unborn children, when they get sick down the road. There's also strong possibility that the United States would bear financial responsibility to the Iraqi people who suffered serious damage to their health from U.S. weapons.

The second "secret charge" gave a very precise date for my alleged crime, October 14, 1999, five years prior to my indictment. No further information was provided. But I was struck by the precision of that day. Indeed, I know very well what I was up to right then.

We suspect that I got indicted for *blocking the Iraqis* from making financial contributions to the 2000 Presidential Campaign of George Bush and Richard Cheney.[547] Two of my Andy Card letters had described Iraq's enthusiastic efforts to bless George Bush and Dick Cheney with loads of campaign cash— and my efforts to stop any illegal campaign financing.

Iraq's efforts would have embarrassed the GOP, if revealed, since it illustrated poignantly how Baghdad desired so deeply to restore its former alliance with the United States. Baghdad wanted desperately to show its loyalty to America's priorities in the Gulf Region. And I had to stop them. How my actions rose to the level of criminal activity is not clear—but it sort of explains why the Justice Department labeled it a "secret charge," based on "secret evidence." They wanted to hide the question of campaign financing from scrutiny.

Alas, under the Patriot Act, it's doubtful the grand jury was allowed to hear the accusations against me, while they debated my indictment. They were persuaded to accept evidence of my wrongdoing "on faith," sight unseen.

See the danger? And the legal absurdity of it?

It was a nightmare you'd expect from China or Iran or Mynamar or some African potentate. Only the worst dictators refuse to disclose an individual's crimes in filing accusations, or otherwise deny transparency in court prosecutions. That's what distinguishes the integrity of the U.S. system of justice from other nations in the world.

Not any more, though. The Patriot Act has leveled the field.

The concept of "secret evidence" had more serious consequence for my Defense that I would not discover until the indictment got dismissed.

Shockingly, my defense strategy had been impacted by a "secret attorney debriefing" at the Justice Department on February 10, 2005, three weeks before Dr. Drob declared me "incompetent to stand trial" on February 28.

After I got shipped off to prison, the Justice Department argued that I should be detained "indefinitely," without a trial, something allowed on the Patriot Act. They definitely tested the waters to see if the Patriot Act could be designated as a major crime under the competency laws, which requires maximum detention. Regardless, my "indefinite detention" would continue until Carswell decided that I was "cured" of claiming that I worked as an Asset in Pre-War Intelligence and the 9/11 investigation. That would be years.

Adding insult to injury, after my imprisonment without a trial, I'd been threatened with solitary confinement on the SHU, citing the Patriot Act, when I got shipped out of Carswell on "Con Air", though I'd never caused a disciplinary problem in prison before.

I'd suffered all of those legal complications because of the Patriot Act.

And yet, waiting in prison at Carswell and M.C.C., I discovered something arguably worse that trumped all those other abuses of my rights, if that could be possible.

To my greatest unhappiness, the Patriot Act apparently creates a special exemption for "classified evidence," which authorizes the Justice Department to conceal exculpatory evidence that would prove a Defendant's innocence, as well. That covered grand jury testimony and the findings of the FBI investigation, including alibis and witness testimonials that validated my work as an Asset and my close relationships with Hoven and Dr. Fuisz.

All of that was off limits as "secret evidence," too.

Oh, we know what witnesses told the FBI. My defense team, spearheaded first by Ted Lindauer and later by Shaughnessy, interviewed many of the same people. Those individuals faithfully repeated what they told the FBI.[548]

As Shaughnessy put it tactfully, at the start of my indictment, the FBI might not have understood the full scale of my Asset work. But they certainly learned of it within a few short weeks after my arrest. And yes, we're convinced the FBI had full knowledge of my history before my arrest. They would have done a poor investigation indeed, if they didn't know who I was. Irregardless, after my arrest, Shaughnessy assured me those special factors and relationships would have come to light at warp speed, once the FBI started its formal investigation.

Incidentally, those findings from the FBI investigation should have resulted in the immediate dismissal of the major charges against me.

Yet when my Defense raised the issues, they flat out denied it.

Under the Patriot Act, the US Attorneys Office, the FBI and the Bureau of Prisons made a decision, individually and collectively, to deny my status as an Asset. They simply declared it "classified" information. On that basis, they claimed to have no obligation to acknowledge the extraordinary facts of my personal history to the Court, when challenged. Ted Lindauer and Shaughnessy, my second attorney, were highly aggressive on my behalf.

In regular court proceedings, that's called "withholding exculpatory knowledge" from the court, and it's considered gross "prosecutorial misconduct."

If a prosecutor discovers evidence that even partially exonerates a defendant, he is required to hand that over to a defense attorney, and acknowledge it to the Judge, as soon as it's available. A prosecutor could face disciplinary action for withholding that sort of information from the Court.

Not so on the Patriot Act.

All three federal agencies involved in my case at the Justice Department—the U.S Attorneys Office, the FBI and the Bureau of Prisons—received independent corroboration of my work relationship with Dr. Fuisz and Hoven, and my 9/11 warning. Witnesses confronted each agency head on, leaving no room for "deniability."

Nevertheless, those agencies adopted such a broad interpretation of the rules of "classified evidence" on the Patriot Act that exculpatory information was off limits to the defense. Worst by far, after omitting confirmations of my identity from their reports to Judge Mukasey, they sought to imprison me *indefinitely* and forcibly drug me with Haldol, so that I could be "cured" of believing what all three agencies at the Justice Department recognized to be fully truthful.

That's the Patriot Act for you.

Welcome to the New America. Franz Kafka would be appalled

Oh yes, I was fighting for my life.

AMNESTY INTERNATIONAL MOMENT:

They might have succeeded, if not for the unflagging perseverance of JB Fields and civil rights activist and radio journalist, Janet Phelan, now living in Toronto.

One morning at M.C.C, a few weeks after the hearing on forcible drugging, I was unexpectedly roused by guards at 5:30 a.m. for an unscheduled court appearance. Inmates going to Court have extra time for a shower and breakfast. It took my by surprise. I had no idea why Judge Mukasey had called us, and I feared the worst.

In my cell, I wept inconsolably, believing the Judge was about to issue a decision on forcible drugging. I imagined that I would get seized up and forced back to Carswell. A few days before, my cellmate got a six year sentence for heroin trafficking from Brazil, and she was left to comfort me that morning. I was in worst shape than she was.

When I got to the holding cage outside the courtroom, my attorney rushed in.

I was prepared for anything except what he came to say!

"Somebody has started a blog on your case, Susan! People are writing the Judge!"

In a single beat, my heart bounded from absolute terror and despair to sheer elation and joy!

"They've sent him papers from that psychologist you were seeing in Maryland. Judge Mukasey's so angry that he's called a court meeting to discuss it."[549]

"You better tell your friend to stop! He better not write that blog anymore."

Well, this was truly an Amnesty International moment! In my heart, I cried thank you, God! Thank you, God! Thank you!

In a powerful rollercoaster of emotion, I seized the bars, overwrought with relief.

I cried back: "MY FRIENDS WILL NEVER STOP! YOU ARE GOING TO STOP! THIS IS AMERICA! WE ARE FIGHTING TO PROTECT THE RIGHTS OF ALL DEFENDANTS UNDER THE CONSTITUTION!"

"YOU WILL NEVER GET AWAY WITH THIS! DO YOU HEAR ME?"

"TELL THAT DIRTY, CROOKED PROSECUTOR, O'CALLAGHAN, WE WILL NEVER STOP FIGHTING TO PROTECT THE CONSTITUTION!"

"YOU ARE BREAKING THE LAW!"

That's what I shouted at him: "You are breaking the law."

It was a watershed moment! A turning point in the dynamic of my case. I understood immediately who was responsible for that blogging, and what it meant that the Court had been forced to confront the blowback from these unconscionable actions.

I could not wait to thank JB Fields and Janet Phelan! The blogs saved my life that morning!

When the mainstream media blacked out my story, the Justice Department banked that I would be forcibly silenced while they did their worst.

They didn't count on JB Fields and Janet Phelan!

My precious friends refused to give up. JB and Janet took my story to the "New Media" on the internet. The blogs were just starting to flex their muscle, and discover their power to break through the barrier of media silence. Nowadays everybody takes that for granted. But my story broke at a critical moment when the corporate media had fallen behind the curve, and the blog media emerged to fill that void of knowledge for the public.

They just might save our democracy!

In desperation, on his blog, JB posted all of the session notes from my court-ordered meetings with Dr. Taddesseh at Family Health Services in Maryland. The session notes explicitly declared that I suffered "no depression," "no mood disturbances," "no symptoms of psychosis," "no delusions," and that there was "no reason for further or additional psychiatric intervention."

Then JB and Janet Phelan made the rounds on alternative radio—Michael Herzog, Cosmic Penguin, Greg Szymanski, the Genesis radio network, Derek Gilbert. Republic Broadcasting. Liberty. Oracle. They're awake and vigilant in defending our liberties. JB and Janet Phelan urged their listeners to contact the Court.

Janet Phelan is particularly eloquent on the abuse of women by psychiatry, and the treachery of the Patriot Act, as it seeks to deprive Americans of our natural rights under the Constitution.

Well, some wise and independent thinking soul decided the Judge really ought to see those session notes from my psych meetings in Maryland. That wonderful person—who is nameless to me today— recognized that somebody who observed me for a year in Maryland should have a lot more credibility than a prison psychiatrist on a Texas military base. And wasn't it interesting that no symptoms of "mental illness" showed up in real life? Only when politics got introduced to the equation?

Judge Mukasey was livid! To his great credit, he demanded to know why those papers were available on the internet—but not in his courtroom? Why had my attorney not brought those favorable psych observations to the Court's attention, given that I was fighting for my life against forcible drugging, for what I called "non-existent conditions?"[550]

Here was a credible source in psychology, who observed me for a full year, and agreed.

And what could explain the stark contrast between the session notes from Maryland and the sworn testimony by Dr. Vas, Dr. Kleinman and Dr. Drob?

Judge Mukasey demanded a formal explanation. Of course there was no explanation. It made no sense, except to prove that psychiatry invents a rationalization for itself in the courtroom.

As the guards shackled me to leave the Court, I turned to the U.S. Attorney, Edward O'Callaghan, and declared loudly:

"This is a crooked prosecution. My witnesses prove everything is true. You can't let them into Court because all of your lies would be exposed. You're a dirty prosecutor, Mr. O'Callaghan. You're nothing but a God damn crook!"

Hearing that, Judge Mukasey bowed down, and winced, and shook his head.

But he knew it was true, and he knew that truth would not stop coming.

LIFE AT M.C.C.

After that court meeting, I waited for Judge Mukasey's decision. I wish I could say that I was calm and collected through that hot, humid summer in New York City.

But fear soon washed over me again.

On the women's floor of MCC, the hypocrisy of the Justice Department's demand to drug me did not go unremarked. My fellow prisoners considered it grossly unfair that they should be sentenced to many years in prison for trafficking in narcotics. But the Justice Department could refuse to release me from prison for *refusing to use drugs that had worse side effects than anything they were caught holding. As far as inmates are concerned, there's no difference in the effects of these drugs and what they're taking. It's just another pill.*

All of us recognized that prison inmates provide a captive market for the pharmacology business that manufactures these mind-altering psychotropic drugs. There are big profits for these drug companies, with only limited benefits for prisoners. (Junkies love that stuff, mind you; it keeps them supplied with drugs in prison. They also trade pills for commissary.) But these drugs would destroy the quality of my life back home. My functioning would be wrecked worse than if I was shooting up heroin or smoking crack. There would be no hope of functioning at all. At least heroin has a withdrawal. This stuff gets in your body, and it doesn't stop messing you up.

I doubt that hypocrisy was lost on Judge Mukasey—but I didn't know it yet. All I could see was that everybody was lying to him. The bolder the lie, it seemed, the better its chance of success.

On that note, I settled into the routine at M.C.C. What else could I do?

Prison food was ghastly. Cells were over-crowded. There was an antiquated law library for trial preparation. Pages of the law books were torn out, or crumpled and faded. M.C.C needed a new set of law books quite badly, since all inmates were either pre-trial or pre-sentencing.

Outdoor recreation was limited to the roof-top every other day. There were volley ball nets, basketball hoops, and a hand ball court. But mostly we walked in laps around the rooftop. Women prisoners got outside for one hour 3 times a week, because all of the men's floors shared the same recreation space. Male prisoners might have enjoyed more recreation and library access, but only because of the criteria for segregation. It's impossible to put male and female prisoners together. Really though, women inmates need to get outside every day, too. It makes a huge difference to emotional strength and the ability to handle the pressures of trials and sentencing.

And yet, to be honest, MCC was a paradise compared to where I'd come from. Oh yeah, the food was much better at Carswell. Recreational opportunities and the outdoor track made Carswell a vastly more "comfortable" prison. On the other hand, the poor quality of medical care for chronically ill prisoners—and the frightening abuses of women on M-1— made Carswell a much more dangerous and sinister lock up.

Good staff at MCC made a big difference, too. Ms. Eldridge balanced furious control over our daily life with an equally ferocious determination to make sure women prisoners got mammograms, and lived safely amidst our fellow inmates.

Hey, I played pool with a bank robber, who kicked my butt with every set.

But I tell you proudly that the women's floor at M.C.C. had to be the cleanest in America. Women scrubbed their cells all day long. They even tacked wash cloths to the end of mop sticks, and scrubbed down the walls and the ceilings, something that astonished me at first. But hey, it kept everybody busy through the day. Me, too. And our walls sparkled bright.

Another improvement over Carswell, for the next four months, I could meet my attorney face to face and talk strategy, something impossible locked up 1600 miles away in Texas. And I could look Judge Mukasey in the eye, thank God.

Happily again, New York was close enough to Washington that my wonderful friend, JB Fields, could visit me on weekends and holidays. Now we could meet on visiting days, and talk together, a huge relief.

To my last day, I will cherish the beauty care/ hair salon set up by women prisoners, so that we could look attractive for visitors and court dates. Prison hair salons teach job skills, so inmates can find work after their release. Several times those ladies pulled me out of my cell, and styled my hair. They tried so hard to cheer me up. There were some good people at M.C.C. Those women might have done some stupid things, probably some criminal things. They would have to pay for their bad judgment, but mostly they were not bad to the core. A lot of them would not repeat those mistakes again—if they got jobs after their release.

An absolutely wonderful prison chaplain from Rykers Island appeared faithfully every Saturday, urging women inmates to give God a chance to support us through our personal crises. He was inspired. And he revitalized our strength. He brought the faith of God right into that hell, and I saw women prisoners studying the bible together in little groups through the rest of the week. He was a source of redemption that all of us ached for. A number of inmates changed totally because of the spirit and wisdom that he brought into that prison.

As impossible as it sounds, I felt a serious presence of God inside those prison walls, which truly surprised me. This was not pervasive serenity, not mildly.

It felt like a few seriously determined angels had staked out the corners. And they weren't going anywhere. If the prisons are a battleground for the soul, in the spiritual fight for good and evil, than I will share my testament that the promise of redemption shall be kept. I get criticized for talking about my faith. But some intense spiritual work goes on at MCC and Carswell. It's surprising to behold in such a place. It does not imply that prisoners are innocent of their crimes. On the contrary, it involves a process of responsibility and deep transformation. A lot of prisoners carry the bible. And they study it. And it changes them. You can feel an extra presence that is actively pulling them. And it comes from outside of our lives and beyond the harsh physical world of the prison, which is so restrictive. It's quite striking, because it's undaunted.

All of that proves that even in the worst situations, it's possible to discover something extraordinary and good that you would never experience otherwise.

Strikingly, in all of the confusion created by psychiatry, it has gotten lost that I was perfectly content with my thoughts, my choices and priorities. I chose my life actively. I accepted responsibility for all parts of it. I had not suffered from my lifestyle. Even in prison, I never considered that I had lost the better parts of myself. I was never paralyzed. I worked every day, in some way, to win my freedom. Advice from my Franciscan friend that I should view prison as a monastic experience gave me a way forward. I looked at all the women around me as contributing to my understanding of the world.

That's how I coped. It's what stopped me from becoming bitter.

Locked up with these women, I saw more evil outside of that prison than in it. Which brought us full circle, to the corruption of psychiatry.

Under federal law, I was entitled to a hearing on my competency as a matter of procedure.

Unhappily, psychiatrists had made themselves experts in the loopholes of the law, and sought to defy the most basic legal protections for defendants at every turn.

These psychiatrists understood that they had lied to the Court. Now they banded together to protect their group against exposure.

In my opinion, they exhibited a form of "group psychosis." They fought to eradicate external factors of reality, and afterwards, to create a "non-reality" that would accentuate their power. They understood that the mirage of psychiatry requires the suspension of truth. In my situation, their construct of "non-reality" would be smashed in the first minutes of participatory testimony. Their power would be gone. Their authority would collapse in the space of a moment.

External factors of reality threatened them terribly. So they grouped together to fight against any presentation of those external facts. They adopted a single consensus of non-reality—which I pictured them constructing in some dark closet without a light bulb. And together they rejected any outward factors or available witnesses, in order to shield their group in its isolation.

The end result was deceptive testimony sworn under oath in a federal court of law.

If any ballistics expert or DNA expert falsified testimony on the results of gun tests or blood testing, they would be shunned forever. They would never be permitted to testify in a court of law again. Professionally, they would be disgraced.

Psychiatry carries no such ethical burdens. They can falsify and fabricate to their hearts' content. They freely embellish. They require no behavioral evidence to support their conclusions. In my case, they freely acknowledged that in 7 months of observation at Carswell, they saw no symptoms of any kind. That didn't matter. They face no burden of culpability if they get caught in a major court deception. They go forth to the next defendant, without sanctions or penalties.

These sorts of fraudulent actions demonstrate why psychiatry should be restricted in the Courts, in my opinion. It's strictly pop culture, the fad of the moment. There's nothing scientific about it. It's a matter of legal convenience.

Change the attorney, and you change the psychiatric "diagnosis."

Even now, when I remember this nightmare, I am appalled by it.

I am appalled because, in its zealous quest for authority, psychiatry allowed itself to be used to promote a political agenda, as a weapon to punish independent thinking in the United States of America. My values support non-violence and non-aggression in U.S. foreign policy. For that, I was locked in prison without a trial. That contradicts everything our democracy stands for, as far as encouraging a pluralism of voices in the public debate.

Psychiatry prostituted itself for politicians. And worthless politicians at that.

This attack was straight out of the Soviet Union and the Cold War, from the gulag age when psychiatry punished intellectual dissidents, using shock treatments and drugs to correct political thinking. It was a miserable and selfish game plan. It relied on the amorality of its practitioners, the willingness to sell out their credentials for financial gain.

It should never have been possible.

To my horror, this was not Moscow or Leningrad in 1953.

It was New York City in 2006.

And I was petrified.

CHAPTER 29:

THE LAST MAN

Throughout those steamy summer days, on lock down at M.C.C. I pondered the insanity of my predicament. Indeed, it perplexed me.

I sat in prison, declared "incompetent" for "believing that I had a 95 percent chance of acquittal, based on the inadequacy of the evidence against me."[551] On that basis, two psychiatrists—who confessed to observing no actual symptoms of mental illness in my behavior— agreed that I lacked sufficient appreciation for the gravity of the charges, which would be necessary to contribute to my defense.

Not surprisingly, I had a very different perspective.

If anybody suffered from "psychosis" or any sort of "delusional disorder," I believed it was Congress itself, fighting aggressively to deny the reality of their choices before the War, and their responsibility for those choices. In angrier moments, I questioned the guards if Congress should be forcibly injected with Haldol, until they developed some integrity in their decision making.

At M.C.C, I watched on prison television, helpless, as Republican leaders blistered the intelligence community with criticism for failing to develop options before the War, or warn about the likely catastrophic outcomes of an Occupation. And wouldn't you know, my progress reports to Andy Card detailed a comprehensive peace framework, which would have accomplished all major U.S. policy objectives without costing the life of a single Iraqi child or American soldier. The success of our peace option could not have been more threatening to GOP leaders. It spotlighted the waste of this War, the cost of human lives thrown away for no reason, and the unnecessary destruction of Iraqi communities. And I got indicted for sharing that peace framework with Andy Card, Colin Powell and other Congressional leaders.

There was no ambiguity about it. While Congress tore its hair, I sat in shackles and chains, on lock down at M.C.C. for doing exactly what they demanded that I should have done.

We Assets got scapegoated, for sure. It was a real dog and pony show of false outrage in Washington. Genuine political theater. I steamed in fury for it.

Alas, they had power, and I did not. At MCC, I was right where Republican leaders wanted me—locked up tight, so they could huff and puff without challenge. It got crazier as Republicans recognized that with Iraq out of the way, they could distract angry voters with boasts of their leadership success on counter-terrorism. Only once again, the Republican record of achievement was much less grand than they acknowledged.

What did that matter? If I could be forcibly drugged, the GOP endgame would be perfected. They could feed the country's fever for national security forever. And I could never get out of prison and expose them— which, let's face it, would have to happen eventually.

How did Republicans rationalize such a vicious attack?

Through simple logic: *Intelligence exists to protect the leadership—not the community. Assets are supposed to make leaders look good— whether they deserve it, or not. Truth is what we sacrifice for our country. It's the politicians who matter, not the people!*

So much for national security, folks.

As a former Asset for nine years, I had to ask:

How exactly does Congress contribute to counter-terrorism? I really don't know. Seriously, from where I sat as an Asset, Congress doesn't participate at all. They never contributed anything to my field work, dealing with Iraq and Libya. They provided lousy oversight. Black budgets blocked any meaningful scrutiny of spending on intelligence operations. Congress had no idea whether financial resources reached the field—or built fancy houses in McLean, Virginia in the back yard of CIA headquarters. Congress had no clue. They made grand promises to Americans after 9/11. But other than hiring thousands of new bureaucrats in Washington for Homeland Security, not much happened.

Anti-terrorism had deteriorated into showmanship and spectacle—color coded threats. It made for triumphant grand standing. Congress got to be like circus performers, acting out a thrilling illusion. But as far as results, anti-terrorism policy proved awfully empty—like the failure to shut down the financial pipeline for Al Qaeda, what I call "happy cash," since the bulk of revenues comes from heroin trafficking. Why not kill two birds with one blow?

As for "outstanding leadership support" for men and women engaged in anti-terrorism, my arrest and imprisonment made a lie of that promise. Actions speak louder than words—except in Washington, where it's all hot air.

Unhappily for me, this was about majority control of Congress and the White House. How would the balance of power fall, in favor of the GOP or the Democrats? Any action that protected the Republican marketing image on national security would be justified. Locking up Assets in prison and threatening to forcibly drug me would be an expedient strategy for holding onto power. That was the critical objective. I would be sacrificed to safeguard their ambition.

Let's face it: Their lie was much more helpful than my truth. It served much better for their efforts to control the government.

That was the constant problem for my case.

In our drama, Judge Mukasey was the X factor. The inscrutable. The unknown. All of my fate rested on his shoulders. To him fell the responsibility for making sense of this mess of conflicting reports. Ordinarily, the defendant would lose. I knew that. And it frightened the hell out of me.

We expected the decision to take a few weeks.

Instead, we waited four months.

Judge Mukasey was retiring. It looked like mine would be the final decision of his illustrious career as one of the United States' pre-eminent Justices in the federal courts.[552]

Mercifully, my old handlers had not left me in the lurch. Years before, they told me what to do if I ever got arrested, always a possibility given my close proximity to terrorism investigations. They commanded that I should tell the Judge everything. From their perspective, I should have spoken up sooner. Except that I did. I expected my attorney to talk for me. I expected these idiot psychiatrists to portray my story with a degree of accuracy. Above all, I exercised my right to demand a trial. I always believed that I would have my day in court.

By this time, Dr. Fuisz and Hoven must have thought I had truly lost my wits. They must have thought I forgot everything they told me. But when I moved to action, it was an avalanche. Judge Mukasey received a vast amount of debriefing while I was locked up at Carswell and M.C.C. By now the Court had a clear picture of my side of the story.[553]

Judge Mukasey could see the powerful forces arrayed against me. He could see the ugliness of their fear, and the powerful motivation to destroy me, so as to hold onto power.

But none of us could figure out how he would end this game. Or if he would feel compelled to go along with the government, taking the path of least resistance. That's what I feared most.

A lesser Judge could not have figured a way out of this steel trap.

A lesser Judge could not have developed a strategy for stopping the drugging—and getting me out from under the indictment and the Patriot Act, all at the same time. A great Judge like Mukasey thinks about those precedents, and how his decisions will set the pace for future cases. But not all Judges do.

Thank God I had Judge Mukasey.

That summer in New York was hot and humid. While I waited, I paced the roof top recreation yard, my anxiety off the charts, praying with all of my heart for his decision to go my way.

Some of my fellow inmates turned out to be great people.

My best friend at M.C.C., Sarah Yamasaki from Japan had trained as an opera singer. She blessed us with roof-top performances, regaling us with arias and popular songs. She was an ebullient woman, always trying to keep our spirits up, helping us all transcend the brutal conditions of our imprisonment.

As I recall, the rooftop yard was fifteen stories above the side walks of Manhattan. All of the women prisoners longed for grass and flowers and freedom. One afternoon, one of the really spiritual women announced that she was praying hard for God to send us flowers!

"God can do it!" she laughed. "Just watch now, I tell you, God can do it!" She was so joyful that we all laughed with her. And wouldn't you know, the wind whipped up, blowing strong. From somewhere far off, a cloud of soft pink and white petals from a dogwood tree, wafted high up in the sky, fluttering over the prison yard and landed on the roof. Hundreds of soft petals swirled at our feet blowing back and forth across the rooftop.

All of us felt joyful now, like we'd all received a great blessing. All of us laughed. I remember that afternoon as one of the rare moments when all of us were so happy. And the woman turned to us, and she said, "I told you God could do it! I told you God would send us flowers!"

And she looked at me, and I remember what she said: "Susan, God's protecting you. God won't let these people hurt you. You need to strengthen your faith. And try not to be so afraid."

That was easier said than done.

When you're locked up in prison, four months feels like eternity, especially waiting for such a critical decision that impacts the rest of your life. It's like four months waiting for a jury verdict, when you don't know if you'll be released or locked up for years, and forcibly drugged on top.

By now, all of the women and the guards understood that whenever that decision came, I expected them to hunt me down any time, anywhere, interrupting any activity.

Early that afternoon, my psychic radar exploded off the charts. I was at the MCC library, returning a spy thriller from the 1970s, about a spook who gets carted off to a nut house and heavily drugged by CIA psychiatrists to stop him from talking about some operation at the Soviet Embassy, during the Cold War. The plot felt awfully familiar. I tell you, Robert Ludlum and I would have enjoyed a good tea party together, scones and crumpets all round.

In the library that afternoon, a vibrant energy suddenly suffused me, like a powerful electrical current. I felt a rush of excitement, like I hadn't experienced in months.

I rushed to the guards to ask if my attorney had sent for me. They said no, not yet.

They'd heard me ask many times over the summer. Always, they calmed me down. And they'd patiently promise to come get me as soon as anything happened. Not yet, though.

Later that evening, I jumped into the shower after dinner, trying to escape the hordes of prisoners for a moment of privacy.

That's when the message came, at the least expected moment. Suddenly, there was a pounding at the door, and one of my cellmates stuck her head in the shower room. My attorney was waiting downstairs. A guard had come to take me.

That kind of news travels fast, and several inmates hovered outside the shower room.

I was soaking wet, with a towel over my shoulders. I didn't stop to comb my hair. I just ran for the guard. The visiting office wouldn't stay open much longer. I wasn't taking any chances. I had to know the answer that night.

When I got to Sam Talkin, both of us stood in shock, looking at each other. And he said, very quietly, "Judge Mukasey ruled in our favor. You're going home."

Talkin looked as stunned by the ruling as I was.

With one stroke of a Judge's pen, my nightmare was over.

Victory was mine.

After 11 agonizing months at Carswell and M.C.C, I was saved, mind, body and soul. I fell on my knees, thanking God for it. Yes I did!

Oh, my reputation was destroyed, as Republican leaders intended. But my intellect and my creativity, my daily functioning and spirituality—what mattered most of all to my life—that was saved. What was most precious to me would be preserved.

I was deliriously happy. Ecstatic. Elated. Bounding in joy.

It was night-time. There was one guard left to share my happiness. I would be off to Court in the morning before Ms. Eldridge arrived to hear my exquisite news. But in my heart I knew she would be happy for me. All the staff understood what this meant to me. They'd been anxious, too. These were good people.

Prisoners are always happy—and somewhat jealous—when somebody goes home. It doesn't happen often. Mostly prisoners get transferred to other facilities after sentencing. But those are your friends for life. They're the ones who have helped you survive through a living hell. You don't forget them.

That night, my closest friend on the women's floor, Sarah Yamasaki, my opera singer friend, made a farewell card for me, with a gorgeous Madama butterfly. I have saved it on my bookcase.

"Now, however, there remain faith, hope, love, these three; but the greatest of these is love," she wrote, citing 1st Corinthinians 13: 4-13. My favorite bible verse.

Sam Talkin had already phoned JB Fields, who swore that he would drive to New York in the morning to take me home!

The next morning at 11 a.m. we appeared in Court to make it official.

On September 8, 2006, his very last day as a federal Judge, Chief Justice Mukasey rejected the Prosecution request to forcibly drug me, and released me on $500,000 bail.[554]

I waved my arms wildly in thanks to Judge Mukasey, who had a great big grin on his face, as bailiffs ushered me out of the courtroom.

Without question, Judge Mukasey saved my life.

People are always surprised when I describe Judge Mukasey as my hero. He's a man of fierce integrity and devotion to the law. In my case, he was surrounded by scoundrels, who brazenly lied to his Court at every turn. Forever, I will give thanks for my life to his fierce, eagle-sharp acumen. If not for that shrewd aptitude, I would have been physically and intellectually destroyed. He became my secret champion in this twisted legal scheme.

The degree of corruption that confronted him on all sides was terrifying to behold. A lesser Judge would have fallen for the trap. Carswell expected to catch him. Except for his brilliance in the law, and his ferocious determination to protect due process in the courts, they probably would have succeeded.

In the Courts, Justice is portrayed as a bronze statue of a blindfolded lady holding a scale of weights, signifying how truth hangs in the balance of the court. That blindfold over the lady's face took on sinister implications in my case. With the Prosecutor and these looney psychiatrists boldly violating legal traditions that required them to acknowledge the truthfulness of my background, that blindfold took on frightening connotations, indeed.

Psychiatry shocks me to this day for the contempt it showed this great Judge and our judicial system. Something has gone terribly wrong when psychiatry could lie so recklessly and irresponsibly before one of the pre-eminent judges of our country. It betrayed a total lack of integrity in the courtroom. I believed it should be disqualified as "expert" testimony, on par with DNA, ballistics or forensics. They can't meet standards of reliability.

It's worthy of a John Grisham novel alright.

Here was the crux of the problem: Throughout my imprisonment, clearly I had no effective legal representation that cared for the outcome. The Prosecutor tried to seize advantage from it. Psychiatry recognized Talkin's inadequacy, too, and played to it, unforgivably. The second problem was that Judge Mukasey could not re-craft my attorney's defense strategy. He could offer to schedule a competence hearing, which I believe he did, several times in fact. But he could not compel Talkin to accept the hearing to check the accuracy of my story. Afterwards, I believe he was caught by surprise when the Prosecutor pushed into the vacuum of court knowledge, with this request for forcible drugging and indefinite detention.

Ah, but this was "extreme prejudice," after all. It was a bloodless execution.

Despite all of that cunning amassed against him, Judge Mukasey accomplished something more clever than I would have dared to hope. He outfoxed the psychiatrists, and crafted an outstanding decision against forcible drugging, which should help protect other Americans in the Justice system. If it protects more Americans from this sort of abuse, then it's worth what I had to sacrifice. It was absolutely worth four extra months in prison after the hearing on forcible drugging. I have no regrets that he took longer to craft it right.

As a critical prologue to his decision, Judge Mukasey expressed frustration that he was asked to rule on the question of my authenticity without access to rebuttal witnesses, who participated in the events and could put those questions to rest with integrity. He saw the legitimacy of my grievance, and in his own way, he complained with me. He lamented that he was forced to rely on the subjective opinions of individuals who were strictly guessing about my work as an Asset, and who could not possibly enlighten the Court with the truth.[555]

Then, very cleverly, Judge Mukasey used the U.S. Attorney's own arguments in favor of forcible drugging to shoot down the continued prosecution of my case. If the Prosecutor was correct, he said, those arguments meant that I could not have committed this crime. Indeed, Judge Mukasey questioned whether my actions rose to the level of criminal activity at all. It looked doubtful, from where he sat. If the Prosecution arguments were correct, it was impossible.[556]

That's the only way he could protect me.

Judge Mukasey's outstanding decision against forcible drugging hinged on three points—that I was not threatening to myself or others in my daily life. Secondly, drugs would not improve the quality or functioning of my life. Achieving some improvement to the quality of life would be necessary to justify forcibly drugging a defendant—something I support wholeheartedly. And thirdly, Judge Mukasey doubted the prosecution was serious about trying the case. Restoring my competency would not lead to a trial, because it appeared doubtful the Prosecution intended to go forward.[557]

It was a brilliant decision. It's especially subtle if you understand the day by day blows of our legal fight.

He took all of the Prosecution arguments, and turned them back on the Justice Department, in a hard push to kill my case.

A lesser Judge could not have defeated the indictment or the Patriot Act, so effectively.

I wanted to stand up and cheer. I recognized immediately that he'd executed a brilliant move, like a chess expert who studies the board for a long time, then executes a blitzkrieg to win.

There was a downside. Judge Mukasey upheld the finding of incompetence against me—which was necessary to squash the case, unfortunately. And his decision relied on some of my spiritual viewpoints, my belief in God and angels and prophecy, and my exploration of religious mysticism, which I enjoy very much. And I have never recanted.

Candidly, in one of my summer letters, at 2 a.m. I told Judge Mukasey that he would not offend me one iota, if he cited my religious viewpoints in ruling on my competence. He would not prick my faith, or undermine my spirituality. By that time, the only thing I cared about was avoiding forcible drugging. Incompetence insulted me, but I refused to allow psychiatry to define me, which took the sting out of it. In fact, Judge Mukasey acted consistently with what I told him I could accept. He can't be criticized for that. I understand he's a religious man himself.

In my heart, I believe that Judge Mukasey thought that liberating me from prison and continued prosecution of a bad indictment would be worth accepting the finding of incompetence. From a legal standpoint, other attorneys after Carswell have told me that he made a generous ruling in favor of my defense—though outside the Court system, the finding of incompetence still raises eyebrows. I believe that Judge Mukasey allowed the finding of incompetence to stand as a vehicle for killing the case.

That's what the Patriot Act has brought us to. A choice between incompetence of a long-time Asset, or shredding the Constitution and due process of law in our Courts, tearing down the most cherished rights of all defendants in the legal system.

Given that I was in prison at the time, without hope of a trial, many hot summer nights on lock down, I and most defendants would probably agree with his choice, even if it's appallingly unfair. Psychiatry should have had more integrity than to have meddled in my case.

Bottom line: Judge Mukasey stopped the Prosecutor from physically torturing me with Haldol. And he guaranteed that the Justice Department would have to stop persecuting me for knowing the truth about our advance predictions about 9/11 and our threats against Iraq, from May 2001 onwards. At the same time his decision acknowledged the Government's fear of my intelligence background.

He split the baby down the middle. He struck a legal balance that was partially unpleasant to me. More importantly, in this perverse game of the Patriot Act, using what tools a Judge has, Judge Mukasey saved my life and my freedom.

Like I said, the man's my hero.

CHAPTER 30:

ILLEGTIMUS NON CARBORUNDUM EST

(Don't let the bastards get you down!)

Staggering out of the lock up at MCC felt like a surreal experience, putting it mildly. One moment I was getting strip searched, shackled for court and thrown into a holding cell by tough bailiffs. The next, I was waving good bye to Judge Mukasey.

After 11 months fighting like the devil to detain me "indefinitely," the process of releasing me took less than 10 minutes at the inmate center. They pointed to a door. And I crossed over into freedom land. When that steel door clanged shut, I left behind sterile linoleum and shabby prison chic for modern Manhattan.

In all, I had been held in prison 11 months, without a trial or hearing to prove the authenticity of my story. That's seven (7) months in excess of the 120 day maximum allowed by federal law for competence detentions that involve no violent actions or threats.[558]

I felt light-headed. JB Fields gave me a bear hug, as I reeled from the shock of it.

Then another gentleman stepped forward. Without giving his name, he identified himself as the former legal counsel for Panamanian dictator, Manuel Noriega and Edwin Wilson, that other black angel of the covert CIA crowd, who got nailed for running a black op involving Libya in the 1970s. Ed Wilson spent 27 years in prison, mostly in solitary confinement, until he got released on appeal, his attorney reminded me, shaking his head sadly. And the whole time the CIA disavowed knowledge that he'd got sent up for running a covert intelligence operation.

Sort of like me.

I got lucky. Wilson's attorney winked at me, sharply. Thought I had it rough? I didn't know how rough the boys could play when the CIA really wanted to. They gave me a break.

When I asked for a business card, the gentleman shook his head with a grin. He swore he just happened to be in Judge Mukasey's court that morning, tying up loose ends for another client on the Judge's last day on the bench. He wanted me to understand that Judge Mukasey had dealt with me quite generously. He shared a great story about interrogating General Noriega, playing the strong man himself in a dark room, with a single lamp on the table. He was the real thing, alright.

Call me paranoid if you like, but it's a truth universally acknowledged that there are no coincidences in the intelligence business. If you choose to believe that a high level spook attorney for General Noriega and Ed Wilson just happened to visit Judge Mukasey's courtroom that morning of my release, without some sort of design, I won't argue with you. But you don't have a functional grasp of how intelligence works.

On the intelligence side, I'm sure everybody hoped this attack on me would stop now.

Trouble was, my legal drama wasn't finished. Despite a year in prison, and two and a half years under indictment, I was still pre-trial. Little did anyone guess that I was only at the halfway mark of my ordeal. My attorney made (another) fateful mistake, by failing to seize the opening provided by Judge Mukasey's outstanding decision to move for dismissal. That decision gave us everything we needed to demolish the indictment, but Talkin took no action to push it through.

Meanwhile, a few fiercely independent thinkers on the blogs came out for a look-see to find out what the heck the GOP was hiding behind my indictment.

A surprising number of "awake" Americans had the smarts to question why the government refused to grant my requests for a trial. Roping me on the Patriot Act set off alarms.

They kept my story alive.

Before I could resume my fight, however, I had to draw back my strength. And my little family in Maryland had to recuperate. My beloved 19 year old cat, Midnight was waiting by the gate when JB Fields and I drove up to my house in Takoma Park. At Carswell, I had felt heart-sick to hear that Midnight waited by that front gate every afternoon since I left a year earlier. Midnight looked stunned, but recognized me immediately. With profound relief, my little family was reunited. My precious dachshunds, Raqi Bear and Mahji Bear performed dachsie races around the yard in honor of the occasion.

Outside of Carswell, reality swept over my life again. Friends phoned to cheer my courage for standing strong in the Courts. They couldn't believe the government questioned my competence, much less tried to forcibly "cure" my confidence as a woman Asset. Again and again, friends and colleagues swore that they had never seen signs of mental illness or instability in my life. Everyone agreed that it was awfully convenient for the pro-war camp that I got shipped off to a Texas military base for a bogus psychiatric evaluation. Their verdict was unanimous. I must know something that politicians didn't want my fellow Americans to hear.

ILLEGTIMUS NON CARBORUNDUM EST

Within days of my homecoming, some of my old gang from the Hunan rang up to assure me that while the debate on forcible drugging raged, they had contacted Talkin, vouching for my close relationship with Paul Hoven and his murky ties to U.S. Intelligence. That wasn't "in my head," they assured him.

Some of those friends invited me to speak before the Sarah McLendon Society at the National Press Club in Washington, dedicated to the former first lady of Washington journalism.

That speech, two weeks after my release from prison, turned the wheels of fate again.

In the small audience of sophisticated Washington insiders, there sat an illustrious silver-haired gentleman, with a deep Rhode Island accent, among the smattering of Congressional staffers, Washington journalists, think tank executives and the like, including reps for Naval Intelligence and the State Department.

His name was Mr. Brian Shaughnessy, and he looked mighty perplexed.

Shaughnessy was former Chief of the Fraud and Public Corruption Division at the federal court in Washington. The founding partner of an exclusive law practice,[559] Shaughnessy, Volzer & Gagner, in his former career at the Justice Department, he served as a senior federal prosecutor assigned to the Court of Chief Judge John J. Sirica. Nicknamed "Maximum John" for his tough sentencing, Judge Sirica catapulted to fame handling the Watergate cases against G. Gordon Liddy and members of the Nixon Administration. As one of the regular prosecutors in Judge Sirica's court, Shaughnessy convicted two Congress members, among a stellar load of major corruption cases. Today he handles a range of complex domestic and international security cases.

Behind his congenial and gentlemanly demeanor, Shaughnessy boasts a formidable and incisive legal mind. Listening to my address at the National Press Club that evening, Shaughnessy posed a question from the audience that cut to the crux of the problem immediately:

If the Prosecutor had any sort of real evidence against me, why for heavens sake, would he not force the case to trial? Why would any prosecutor allow my attorney to use an "incompetence defense," without protest? Why not attack it?

As Shaughnessy put it bluntly, "When I worked as a prosecutor, I wanted people competent, so I could convict them and send them to prison! I would never allow a defense attorney to make those claims without a serious challenge. I would fight it. That's what a Prosecutor does in this situation. We don't like it! If it was me, I'd be madder than heck that you got declared incompetent."

If there was real evidence that I broke the law.

Shaughnessy smelled a rat.

A senior law practitioner, who frequently takes the most complicated domestic and international cases for sport and personal challenge—and wins, Shaughnessy requested very politely if he might review the evidence in my case.

We struck up quite a conversation after my talk. Afterwards, I returned to Shaughnessy's office for a longer discourse on my ordeal, along with another man who would become extremely important in resurrecting my legal reputation from the ashes, Mr. Thomas J. Mattingly.

Mattingly proved to be an esoteric genius, a philosopher activist in his own right, with an amazing wealth of knowledge on a vast array of domestic and international issues. A veritable encyclopedia of knowledge, he could debate every issue with finesse and thoughtful detail.

With a twinkle in his eyes, Mattingly turned to Shaughnessy. "You really should take over this case, Brian. You could knock down the Patriot Act— At least punch a few good holes in it. Would that be enough of a challenge for you?"

It was as if the fates clicked everything into place at last. And so it came to pass that two weeks after my release from prison, my case took on a new attorney, as a back stop to Talkin. It marked a critical transition for my defense. Because shockingly, my ordeal was not over yet.

Happily, in Brian Shaughnessy, I found legal counsel who understood how all the pieces of the intelligence world and Washington policymaking fit together. It was a pivotal moment. In a single evening, his involvement with a helpful push from Mattingly reconfigured the dynamic of my battle at all levels.

The night had greater significance that I was yet to discover.

The Sarah McClendon Society had a comfortable and familiar feel to it, which might be explained by the cross over from our old Thursday night crowd at the Hunan.

The chief organizer of the Sarah McClendon Society is John Edward Hurley, a Civil War historian on the Confederate side. A southern gentleman from Virginia and an absolute delight in conversation, Hurley was an original member of the Hunan crowd. Most famously, he took on Oliver North and his cabal years before, ousting him from the Confederate Hall, where North was holding meetings as a front, according to Hurley. He was also close friends with Pat Wait, who introduced me to Hoven. And Hurley had personally observed my close relationship with Hoven, throughout our many years of clandestine conversations.

Hurley delighted in reminding me that spooks often dropped by our Thursday night gatherings, because we made up such an interesting crowd. And they were often invited by Paul Hoven. He offered to testify to that in Court.

Kelly O'Meara was another member of the Sarah McClendon society, who crossed over from our Thursday nights at the Hunan. A former investigative journalist and congressional Chief of Staff for Rep. Andrew Forbes, O'Meara had just published a cutting edge book, "Psyched Out: How Psychiatry Sells Mental Illness and Pushes Pills that Kill."[560]

O'Meara, too, protested that she'd known Hoven for 20 years.[561] She declared that she had always known the two of us were very close, because Hoven "talked about (me) all the time." She described Paul as an "intelligence passer," and reminded me that some of Hoven's closest friends are legendary in the intelligence community. Hoven used to take her shooting at the farm of Bill Weisenberger, a famous spook with longstanding ties to Middle East operations involving Libya and Edwin Wilson. And Hoven bragged about outing Oliver North on Iran-Contra, along with Gene Wheaton. Those sorts of bona fides say a lot.

O'Meara offered to testify to all of that in Court, too. If Hoven told the FBI something different, then he lied and obstructed the FBI investigation. In which case, Hoven broke the law.

The force of truth would not go away for the comfort and convenience of leaders in Washington.

I recall it as an extraordinary moment.

ILLEGTIMUS NON CARBORUNDUM EST

In prison, the Justice Department had isolated me—and my public attorney, Sam Talkin, whined that nobody wanted to help me. Yet here at the National Press Club, I sat with supremely credible individuals who freely vouched for me.

So where did psychiatry find the gall to attack me?

A highly respected author and former journalist herself, O'Meara showed how my case marks a frightening trend in psychiatry today. It's becoming the norm to attack healthy, functioning Americans, while fighting to limit the rights of individuals to repudiate psychiatric opinions.

Her book, "Psyched Out" exposes the dangers of mind-altering psychiatric drugs, and the links of prescription drug use to school shootings by teenagers and killing rampages by adults.[562] O'Meara documents that a startling number of these killers, who snap suddenly, share one commonality. They started taking anti-depressants, particularly Prozac, days or weeks before their murder spree. According to her research, Prozac leads the industry in serious adverse effects—like killing family members or school classmates. But drug companies like Eli Lilly are powerful enough to suppress media reports of the extreme social consequences of these adverse drug effects. As a result, ordinary Americans are largely ignorant of the links between anti-depressants and sudden violent behavior, including murders. Suicides also rise dramatically after starting anti-depressants.

"Psyched Out" goes on to examine how psychiatry contrives to create "diseases of the brain." Citing medical sources, O'Meara argues that there's no scientific proof that imbalances in brain chemicals occur at all, something that psychiatry doesn't like to admit.[563]

Leading medical experts agree.

"Although a physician may tell a patient that a chemical imbalance causes their depression, the physician would be hard pressed to provide any evidence to support this claim. There is no test available that would demonstrate that any patient has a 'biological depression' as opposed to any other type, or even that such biological depressions exist—" Dr. Antonuccio. Psychiatric Times. [564]

"At present, there are no known bio-chemical imbalances in the brain of typical psychiatric patients—until they are given psychiatric drugs." Dr. Peter Breggen, M.D "Brain Disabling Treatments in Psychiatry." [565]

"There are no external validating criteria for psychiatric diagnoses. There is neither blood test nor specific anatomic lesions for any major psychiatric disorder."[566] Dr. Loren Mosher, M.D former chief of the National Institute of Mental Health Center for the Study of Schizophrenia.

"There are no tests available for assessing the chemical status of a living person's brain." [567] Elliot S. Valenstein, PhD, "Blaming the Brain."

"Psyched Out" was illuminating to say the least, a wonderful breath of fresh air after my ordeal at Carswell.

Of course psychiatry predicates its medical authority on the treatment of these so-called "chemical imbalances," for the purpose of "curing" them. I learned the hard way myself how psychiatry has learned to maneuver cleverly through the Courts, denying individuals the right to question the medical basis for their "diagnosis." According to O'Meara, efforts to block court testimony by family and friends, who would throw cold water on psych opinions, has become an increasingly common method for defending the illusion of their medical authority.

It's a frightening trend, and it's happening more and more often. What's more, ordinary behaviors and reactions to life events—like adolescent angst, grief for a death, anxiety over job loss or a divorce—are typed as mentally defective responses, indicating the presence of long term mental "disease" that requires some sort of drug intervention. Adolescents and young adults, particularly, can face significant school pressure to comply with drug "treatment" plans, only to suffer adverse reactions to the drugs. When that happens, psychiatry seeks to cure those bad effects by prescribing additional drugs to cope with problems created by the first set of drugs. As a result, Americans are all doped up, affecting behavior and coping mechanisms—and not for the better.

I saw first-hand myself how the number one way that Carswell restores competence was to take pre-trial defendants off these drugs. After a short detox, 9 times out of 10 they'd be just fine, and ready for trial. Carswell would report back to the Court that somewhere along the way, the women got mis-diagnosed for non-existent conditions, and they would function very well without drugs in their systems. And I saw myself that Carswell was right. There was nothing wrong with these women. I listened to women thank Carswell for showing that they were mentally okay.

Finally, "Psyched Out" raises serious questions as to whether women are getting targeted by psychiatry, particularly.

By example, Eli Lilly has been marketing Prozac under the name, Sarafem, for women suffering pre-menstrual tension. The two drugs are identical in composition, except that Prozac is a green pill, while Sarafem has a pink and purple color. The color choice affects "how women react to the drug," according to Eli Lilly.[568] Women taking Sarafem have no idea that they're actually ingesting Prozac, the most powerful anti-depressant on the market.

Would women still want the drug, if they had the facts? And since when has menstruation become a mental illness anyway?

Psychiatry's attacks on women are hardly subtle.

In my case, confidence, motivation and pride for my achievements got stigmatized as "grandiosity," and condemned as a mental defect.[569] That's the new language of psychiatry to attack a woman's strength, though the same qualities in a male colleague would be praised for reflecting ambition and perseverance. Citing its "medical authority," psychiatry argued that as a lowly woman, I could not possibly have engaged in anti-terrorism work. I must be suffering a "mental disease" for believing that I had done so (for nine years). And I must suffer myself to be "cured," in order to unlearn my beliefs and confidence in my abilities. That was the fundamental premise of the psychiatric evaluations against my competence.[570]

It was blatant sexism, without any sort of "clinical" link to reality—since I could prove that I did these things. It should be a red flag that psychiatry exalts women who are submissive and dependent—and coincidentally, more needy for approval, and thus more easily persuaded to accept instruction, as part of the "doctor-patient" relationship. My situation exemplifies how psychiatry punishes women who deviate from social weakness, and challenge their authority.

In their way of thinking, we are disobedient little girls who need to be punished with drugs.

Those attitudes did not change after my release from Carswell, unfortunately. Now psychiatry demanded that I must submit to "treatment," a process of re-education that would "cure" my strength, independence, and decision-making skills. I would be cured when I no longer exhibited "symptoms" of confidence and self motivation, when I stopped believing that I have led a meaningful and productive life.

When I stopped feeling empowered and goal-oriented, when I learned self-doubt, insecurity and weakness, then at last I would be a "real woman." I would be healthy once more.

If that sounds seriously disturbed, it is.

If I had not fought back, those arguments would be continuing against me today.

Bottom line: psychiatry is big business with big profits. And the courts are a marketplace for clients. Psychiatry and pharmacology are looking to build market share together, in a quest for revenues. That's what it all comes back to. Making money.

And so my nightmare was not over, though I had defeated psychiatry on the critical issue of forcible drugging.

On that basis, Pre-Trial Services now demanded that I report to Counseling Plus in Silver Spring, Maryland for yet another psychological evaluation, followed by counseling services.

Only now, at the community level, politics was removed from the "diagnosis," as Ted Lindauer and I expected it would be. And what did the evaluation find? That I suffered Post Traumatic Stress Disorder (PTSD)—caused by my experiences at Carswell.[571] And nothing else.

The Maryland evaluation by Counseling Plus reported that I was fully grounded in reality in all my sensory faculties. I showed no signs of mood disturbances. The only thing I suffered was anxiety and tension caused by my false imprisonment at Carswell. There was no other source for my PTSD symptoms.[572]

In other words, according to this "diagnosis," if I had not got shipped off to prison without a trial or hearing, and threatened with forcible drugging, I would not suffer symptoms of any kind at all. I showed no signs of other "mental defects."

Like Dr. Taddesseh at Family Health Services before Carswell for the next year, Counseling Plus reported that I suffered "no depression or bipolar disorder, and no signs of psychosis or psychiatric symptoms of any kind. (Lindauer) is fully oriented to her surroundings times four."[573]

Even so I was forced to undergo "counseling" for 9 months, until I refused to go back.

So what did we talk about? Why, the corruption of psychology, of course, and how much I despised it. How it deprived me of my legal rights and my reputation. What else? I had nothing else to say to these people. Every Saturday got ruined by forced recitations of the awful conditions at Carswell, and the horrific abuses of prisoners, or how psychiatrists knowingly and deliberately lied in my case. It explains why my awful memories are so vivid to this day.

Beyond that, Dr. Tressa Burton, the court psychologist, surfed the internet looking for clothes and weekend entertainment for her daughter, while I was forced to sit in her office, bored out of my mind. She surfed the internet constantly during our meetings. A couple of times she handed me women's magazines, like Good Housekeeping and Cosmopolitan, and asked if I saw any articles that I'd like to discuss. We had nothing to chat about to each other.

I saw with blinding clarity that psychology is about pop culture. It's the fad of the moment. Pretty much you have to turn off your brain, and blather from your mouth. I'd look at the clock, and ten minutes would have gone by. And I'd think to myself, oh God, how dull! How much more of this can I take?

It was a huge waste of my time and your tax dollars. It contributed nothing to the quality of my life. But I had to stay the full hour, so that Counseling Plus could make money off the feds. I learned very quickly that even the sub-section of psychology that recognized the corruption in my case, lacked the integrity to turn down federal tax dollars. They used defendants as an ATM machine to make cash withdrawals off the state and federal budgets. Counseling Plus could have cut back the number of meetings I was forced to attend, since it had no value to my life. But Burton could not make money if she did. And it was always about the money. Psychology doesn't want clients to be strong or independent. They can't keep those clients. That's why they try to focus all of your energies on bad things. It doesn't surprise me that people who participate in long-term counseling have unhappy lives.

Psychology did teach me one very important thing: Focusing all of your energies on bad experiences is a stupid and unproductive activity. There's no benefit to reliving your worst nightmares over and over again. On the contrary, it's a fairly destructive past-time.

As proof, my meetings with Burton started in October, and got interrupted mid-December, when she suffered a series of seizures that forced her to cancel meetings for the next two months until late February.

Well, I was deliriously happy. I hated those meetings. I was delighted that she had to cancel them for so long. I regarded it as two full months of freedom, sans fascist efforts to control my thinking and lifestyle choices.

And what happened to my life without her "guidance" and "instruction?" How did I "cope" with my Post Traumatic Stress Disorder, without her presence for two whole months?

Immediately my quality of life improved.

My moods on Saturday afternoons picked up dramatically, carrying over throughout the week. I was much happier. I stopped ranting and raging at my friends, who were exhausted by my stress, by this time. My reminisces of my suffering decreased a hundred fold. Immediately I was more productive in my life, and the quality of my thinking and confidence in my decision-making started to rebound. My natural resilience kicked in.

Without her presence, I refinanced my house, paid off my credit card debts, and redesigned my kitchen in total. Without psychology pulling me down, I stopped feeling like an infantilized victim of my circumstances. I became empowered and functioned as a fulfilled woman again. I started taking control of my life, and acting as a goal oriented individual.

Getting away from her was the best thing for my state of mind—and my Saturday afternoons!

By the end of February, Burton got her seizure disorder under control, and started her practice again. Immediately, I crashed back into unhappiness. I was forced to suffer through Carswell all over again. I had nothing else to say to this woman. Our conversations became a tape replaying all of my anger for how the corruption of psychology had robbed my reputation for my life's work. How psychology was so selfish as to interfere with my Constitutional rights to prove my innocence in a court of law. How psychology was terrified of reality, which beat them every time.

Every conversation fed my rage. Every weekend that Burton cancelled a meeting, my happiness improved throughout the following week. When I would go back to her office, it would pull me down like the undertow of a tidal wave.

On that basis, I would seriously question why anybody should attend counseling meetings at all. Certainly when it comes to Post Traumatic Stress, fixating on the harsh experience that caused the trauma intensifies spiritual pain, instead of healing it. That's probably the worst thing you could do.

Having said that, PTSD is a real condition. It's not linked to some imaginary imbalance in brain chemicals. It's caused by real traumatic events, and *it shows itself through intensive stress and anxiety, which grows worse by reliving the moments of original distress.*

Based on my own experiences, anybody who suffers PTSD would be helped *by practicing how to refocus their thoughts onto something entirely different than the original stress.* I think of Post Traumatic Stress as a wave that builds like an ocean tide. First it laps at your feet, then it crashes at your waist. Psychology might be valuable if it helped recognize when that tide is coming on, so that you can kick your mind to a different zone. Meetings might be useful if they helped identify activities that create a new emotional space to draw your concentration. You've got to invest new energy into new experience, so that the intensity of the activity pulls your mind and your concentration onto the other area. The energy needs to be consuming, so that you're totally focused on the new moment—not wallowing in the past.

Physical exercise provides more relief than psychology, even if you've got a tread mill tucked in a corner of your office. Outward Bound for returning soldiers would be an awesome investment by the military. Therapy in a physical setting would make a difference, not sitting in a room chatting. That's how to beat post traumatic stress. Some kind of community service, in a totally different area than the stress source, makes a difference. In my own life, I turned to animal rescue work. Playing soccer or basketball, even with a child, makes a difference. Taking up musical instruments—the guitar, the saxophone, the piano. Biking or hiking on the weekends.

Any of those activities make more of a difference to PTSD than attending psychology meetings. Build that activity into your schedule, and you will get better. Essentially, your mind will create a fresh, positive area to focus its energies on, and your body will burn off excess tension through intense physical exercise. That's how you move past it. Any traumatic experience stays part of your life. *The critical thing is to learn not to focus energy on it.*

That's how to heal Post Traumatic Stress Disorder. Unfortunately, that's not what psychology allowed me to do.

If that wasn't bad enough, the Prosecutor, O'Callaghan, was not happy with the non-political findings of Burton's "diagnosis" of Post Traumatic Stress Disorder caused by the effects of Carswell. It failed to impugn my competence, especially because her evaluation freely acknowledged that there was no reason for prescribing drugs to "cure" me of anything.

So a few weeks later, O'Callaghan demanded that I submit to a second psych evaluation in Maryland, on the grounds that Burton was a psychologist—like Shadduck at

Carswell, not a certified psychiatrist. Burton was astonished by the prosecutor's request. Pre-Trial Services, which had to pay for it, protested that it was a waste of their budget. And you could be damn sure I wasn't going to pay for this. All of this was taxpayer financed.

Hearing my story, the second evaluator, who was a psychiatrist, demonstrated a modicum of wisdom. He filed a report assuring the court in New York that Dr. Burton was reliable and trustworthy in the state of Maryland, and he would not second guess her findings.[574] Pre-Trial Services denied my request for a copy of that report, but Burton told me what it said.

Post Traumatic Stress was consistent with what he saw. And so the second court evaluation in Maryland successfully sidestepped the whole business. He didn't want any part of this.

That's not what the Prosecutor wanted to hear a second time, either. At the rate I was racking up non-political psych evaluations, there would be nothing left of the bogus finding of incompetence.

So, once again, a few weeks later, O'Callaghan demanded that I submit to a Third Psychiatric Evaluation after Carswell, this time with the original psychiatrist, Dr. Stuart Kleinman, who declared me incompetent in the first place. O'Callaghan argued to Judge Loretta Preska, who took over from Judge Mukasey that the Maryland psych community didn't understand my history. It would take too much time to educate them.—Ergo, they weren't sufficiently corruptible.

Amazingly, Judge Preska granted O'Callaghan's request. That's how it came to pass that six months after Carswell, I was forced to undergo no fewer than three additional psych evaluations.[575]

The Prosecutor was shopping for what he wanted to hear. And he couldn't get it outside of politicized psychiatry. Only now, through hard experience, I'd learned a few things about how to protect myself from corrupt psychiatric practices. Too many "doctors" had laughed in my face when I said my story was truthful, and voiced my desire to prove myself in court.

More than once I'd been told, "It doesn't matter whether it's true or not. I'm going to tell the Judge you made it all up. Who do you think they're going to believe? You or me? I am a doctor."

After Carswell, I found the way. I strongly urge any individual who's forced to undergo a court ordered evaluation for any reason, even a custody dispute, to follow this method for self protection. I could have saved myself so much pain—and a year in prison—if I'd done it sooner.

Other Americans can learn from my ordeal. It's simple.

Bring a tape recorder.

Get a recording. Save the record. You will protect yourself from serious threats of psychiatric fraud, if you can prove what you said, versus what they want to pretend that you said.

You must not presume that because you have engaged in a rational conversation that these people are likewise rational. Quite the opposite. Their purpose appears to be twisting everything you say into a convoluted schematic that showcases themselves. There's nothing rational or logical about psychology. You've got to protect yourself.

Which explains why I showed up for my third psych evaluation post-Carswell with a tape recorder. From that moment, when Dr. Kleinman made inaccurate statements to the Court, we had a record of it. My new attorney, Shaughnessy promptly filed a Motion for Reconsideration on the Competence Decision[576] by Judge Preska, along with a supporting affidavit that I prepared citing parts of the transcripts.[577] Our court papers demonstrated multiple inaccuracies in Dr. Kleinman's statements. And from that moment, I started kickin' some ass!

And let me show you why. This is part of the transcript from that meeting with Dr. Kleinman on June 8, 2007.[578] It's nothing like what you'd expect.

LINDAUER: "This is Susan Lindauer in the office of Sam Talkin. I am formally requesting that he attend this meeting. I have been summoned here at the request of the court. It is with Mr. Kleinman who is guilty of perjury in my case. The FBI has already verified my story. Mr. Kleinman is on record lying to a federal judge. This tape is being taken for legal purposes in a potential lawsuit against Mr. Kleinman."

DR. KLEINMAN: "Good morning. Uh I must say that first of all, I am Dr. Kleinman. And I have been retained by the United States Attorneys Office to do a psychiatric examination on your mental state. Particularly as it relates to the charges that are pending against you and your understanding and appreciation of them."

LINDAUER: "Yes. I have already declared that I am innocent of those charges, and I have asked for trial. The Prosecutor who's so convinced that he's got a strong case has, for three years, refused to give me a trial."

DR. KLEINMAN: "OK. We'll talk about that all for a moment. First, do you know who this person is to my right and your left."

LINDAUER: "My attorney."

DR. KLEINMAN: "What is his name?"

LINDAUER: "I just announced it on the tape. His name is Sam Talkin. We are in his offices at 40 Exchange Place close to the Wall Street metro in downtown Manhattan."

DR. KLEINMAN: "Do I have your permission to speak with you?"

LINDAUER: "I am here at the order of the court."

DR. KLEINMAN: "If at any point you decide that you don't want to speak with me, please communicate it."

LINDAUER: "I am here at the order of the Court. So I expect you to ask your questions. I left my house this morning at 6:40 in the morning, and I have arrived in New York at a prompt hour. I expect this meeting will ask questions rapidly, so this can be concluded. And I refuse to answer questions about legal strategy. Except to say that I will not be using a headfucker defense at my trial. I will be using a government defense."

"And I know very well that the Prosecution has no right to dictate that defense. I shall be calling witnesses, some of whom have already been interviewed by the FBI, who will easily confirm that they have already verified the authenticity of my work, which has been questioned by Mr. Kleinman here, who pretended it was delusional. That was the word you used."

DR. KLEINMAN: "How do you think anybody listening to you right now would respond to how you—"

LINDAUER: "I don't care."

DR. KLEINMAN: "What's your opinion?"

LINDAUER: "I don't care."

And shortly after that exchange:

LINDAUER: "I will be delighted to provide a copy of this tape to you. That's not a problem.

DR. KLEINMAN: Well, I'm going to ask actually is when you're done, you'll give the tape to Mr. Talkin."

LINDAUER: "No, no, no, no."

DR. KLEINMAN: "Let me finish. And that Mr. Talkin make a copy for the following reasons.

LINDAUER: "No. No. I have an attorney in Washington [Mr. Brian Shaughnessy] who is preparing a lawsuit against you. You are guilty of perjury in a courtroom. I spent a year in prison because you lied to a federal judge, mister. You want to say you're a doctor? Well, real doctors have malpractice insurance. You have wrongly pretended that I am incompetent. You have wrongly pretended that I am delusional. You have actually advocated forcibly drugging me to cure me of the history of my life, which is true. I think you are a Despicable."

DR. KLEINMAN: "Well, here are the conditions under which I will. This is my position. I'm going to ask that the original of the tape be given by you to Mr. Talkin before you leave today."

LINDAUER: "No."

DR. KLEINMAN: "That's OK."

LINDAUER: "I will not do it. I will, however, guarantee that you have a copy of the tape. I have no trouble doing that."

DR. KLEINMAN: "That's fine, but since I want to make sure that there is only one version of the tape."

LINDAUER: "I don't trust Mr. Talkin to do it. Mr. Talkin has repeatedly refused to interview witnesses. Mr. Talkin has repeatedly refused to get subpoenas that I asked for. Unfortunately, Mr. Talkin has proven that he is not reliable."

DR. KLEINMAN: "You don't trust him."

LINDAUER: "Absolutely not."

DR. KLEINMAN: "What do you think he would do with the tape?"

LINDAUER: "Lose it."

An arrangement was made for a paralegal to make a copy of the tape at Talkin's law offices that afternoon. I took the originals home with me that evening. A simpler way would have been to buy a second tape recorder for $20 at Radio Shack, WalMart, Target or any electronic store. They're not expensive. No defendant can afford not to have a recording device at this sort of meeting. My case provides ample evidence as to why.

My decision to hold onto those tapes would become vital to my next court battle. One year later, there would finally be a competency hearing. As it happened, Dr. Kleinman would base his entire testimony on this meeting. Only now we had a record of our conversation.[579, 580]

Apparently Dr. Kleinman did not realize that I kept those tapes, instead of handing them over to Talkin, as instructed. Or else he imagined that I had lost them. Whatever his thinking, when Dr. Kleinman incorrectly described our conversation to Judge Preska,

Shaughnessy surprised everyone with a Motion for Reconsideration that shattered several major inaccuracies in Dr. Kleinman's testimony.[581]

The moral of the story is for each individual to hold onto your own tapes. Get them transcribed immediately. And always save the tapes. That's critical. Psychiatry has the ability to twist and pervert even the most innocuous conversation. That's their "contribution" to the court proceedings. They will not hesitate to make mischief.

Here's another example:[582]

DR. KLEINMAN: "So let me go back. You said when we met previously, the purpose was to cover up Iraqi Pre-War Intelligence. Do you believe that I have any role in that?"

LINDAUER: "Yes."

DR. KLEINMAN: "And did I knowingly have that role?"

LINDAUER: "Yes."

DR. KLEINMAN: "OK. So tell me what role I had in knowingly covering it up?"

LINDAUER: "You deliberately lied to a federal judge. I told you in very clear terms that I was an Asset working in Iraqi Pre-War Intelligence. You lied and pretended that I was delusional for thinking that I had done this work. Which I did for NINE YEARS."

DR. KLEINMAN: "Okay."

LINDAUER: "You got me declared incompetent, which is a joke. I mean, it's so the politicians don't have to take responsibility for what they did. And their decision-making in Baghdad. They can blame the Assets and pretend that we failed to bring them good quality intelligence. And by the way, the Senate already has investigated the January, 2003 intelligence." [The date cited in my indictment for my approach to Andy Card and Colin Powell.] "And they found it 'chilling and prophetic.' That's what they called it."

DR. KLEINMAN: "So? Let's go back. See my understanding is that I was asked by the government to evaluate you regarding your competency to stand trial. That's my understanding."

LINDAUER: "That's right. But in the course of doing that, I very clearly and carefully explained to you that I was an Asset. That I had been doing this for years. And you went to the Court, and you said, Oh, your honor. Nobody can verify her story."

"Nobody except everybody who's talked to the FBI, my friend."

LINDAUER: "This is easy to prove. Very easy to prove."

DR. KLEINMAN: "Very easy to prove. Have you given that information to your attorney?"

LINDAUER: "Absolutely. And my attorney did nothing to interview these people. So my Uncle Thayer Lindauer, who is an attorney with 40 or more years of experience, he interviewed these witnesses. He located them."

DR. KLEINMAN: "So this is your uncle who interviewed them?"

LINDAUER: "My uncle, who is an attorney, has interviewed them. They responded to his phone calls immediately."

DR. KLEINMAN: "So have you provided this information to Mr. Talkin?"

LINDAUER: "Of course."

DR. KLEINMAN: "You have?"

LINDAUER: "Of course. Of course."

DR. KLEINMAN: "So then he has—"

LINDAUER: "The whole thing has been bullshit."

And later on:

DR. KLEINMAN: "Let me speak about trial for a moment. Let's take a step back. What are the charges pending against you? What are they?"

LINDAUER: "You already know the charges. I've been accused of acting as an Iraqi Agent in conspiracy with the Iraqi Intelligence Service. Which is just the stupidest thing I've ever heard in my life. I want to hear this Prosecutor tell the people of New York that working on an anti-terrorism investigation is against the law."

"And by the way, I'm one of the people who warned about 9/11. I do not appreciate what you did in the slightest!"

DR. KLEINMAN: "How did you know about 9/11?"

LINDAUER: "We had been watching for an attack for months."

DR. KLEINMAN: "Who's we?"

LINDAUER: "Richard Fuisz had been instructing me for several months. From after the Lockerbie Trial. OK, the Lockerbie Trial ends in January. In approximately March and April, Richard Fuisz is beginning to aggressively ask me, over and over again, if there is any intelligence that I'm hearing about any attack. Specifically I am to pump my sources for information on airplane hijackings and airplane bombings. I am to tell Iraq and Libya – Iraq PARTICULARLY—that if anybody bombs the United States, and we find out that they knew about it, we will blow them fucking back to the stone age."

DR. KLEINMAN: "Did you tell Iraq and Libya that?"

LINDAUER: "Yes. And by God, Richard Fuisz did his job. Richard Fuisz did exactly what he is supposed to do. He is proactive. He is strong. He is thinking. He is working to protect this country. And he has nothing to be ashamed of. And I don't either. This is how we do it."

DR. KLEINMAN: "Let's talk about Iraq for a moment. I believe that you told me that you were once, in fact, in Iraq."

LINDAUER: "Yes. I'm not going to discuss answers to any charges against me."

DR. KLEINMAN: "I'm just asking—Do you understand that there is a charge against you?"

LINDAUER: "I understand, and I'm going to kick their fucking ass in court about it."

DR. KLEINMAN: "But what's your knowledge of the charge? The charge exists. I'm just checking to see if you know what the charge is?"

LINDAUER: "The charge is that I took a trip to Baghdad."

DR. KLEINMAN: "And?"

LINDAUER: "My answer is that they knew I was going to Baghdad. And I can prove that in a court of law. I can prove I asked for permission to go. I was doing exactly what I thought I was supposed to do. It was totally in good faith. That's my answer. I did not go off to Baghdad without anybody knowing about it. If they didn't want me to go, they just had to say so."

DR. KLEINMAN: "Fine."

LINDAUER: "Anything they wanted me to do. I'd jump up and down five times, and turn in circles for them. Seriously."

In reality, I filed a written request for permission to travel to Iraq in March, 2001, containing a description of Iraq's invitation by the Foreign Ministry. I promised to meet any U.S. official before or after the trip. I also agreed to delay the trip, at their request. The U.S. Attorney had a copy of this paper. So did Talkin.[583]

Following that exchange, Dr. Kleinman inquired about a videotape made by the Iraqis of my final meeting in Baghdad. Critically, the tape involved my Iraqi friend who had agreed to act as a valuable liaison to an FBI Task Force, once it got to Baghdad. This required extraordinary courage on his part.

LINDAUER: "There is a videotape, which I'm not even remotely moved by."

DR. KLEINMAN: "So what's your interpretation of it?"

LINDAUER: "I expected [the Iraqis] to tape the meeting. I'm an Asset. You don't wink at the camera. I'm an Asset. I'm working my ass off to persuade the Iraqis to give us information about terrorism. I am expecting them to tape that meeting."

DR. KLEINMAN: "Okay."

LINDAUER: "I expect that there is a tape recorder somewhere. Whether it's video or audio, that's the difference that I didn't know. But I expected them to tape it."

DR. KLEINMAN: "Because you're an Asset?"

LINDAUER: "They know. They know. This is a game. This is how the game works."

This sort of exchange was typical:

LINDAUER: "Applying present situations to yesterday—If you tell me today that I should have done something yesterday doesn't work for me. Because I asked for instructions. And I promised to obey the instructions. And I specifically sought instructions. And I said that "I will obey you to the letter. Just tell me what you want me to do."

"I can prove that in any court of law."

DR. KLEINMAN: "That's fine."

LINDAUER: "None of this mattered until the Presidential Commission on Iraqi Pre-War Intelligence was formed. I was their chief asset working in anti-terrorism dealing with the Iraqis. It would have been obscene. I mean, my God, you should take me out and hang me from the Stock Exchange or the Empire State Building, if I didn't help after 9/11. The whole reason my contacts existed was so that there would be somebody with deep contacts inside the Iraqi government, so whenever there was a terrorist attack of any kind there would be a back channel source to get it."

"If I had refused to get that information after 9/11, THAT would have been traitorous. That would have been treason. That would have been ugly. That would have gone against every single thing I believe in, and everything everybody else I know believes in."

Most of the conversation with Dr. Kleinman, however, focused on the possibility of a plea bargain floated by the prosecutor.

Over and over, Dr. Kleinman badgered me to plead guilty on tax charges. Steadfastly I refused, while he tried a number of approaches to persuade me that I should change my mind and accept the deal..[584] We caught it all on tape.

Notice that I was not indicted for tax charges.[585] I did not owe back taxes, and would not have owed any additional taxes if I accepted a guilty plea. It merely provided a vehicle for ending the case, if I chose to do the Justice Department another favor—not likely after Carswell. Floating a guilty plea for something not on my indictment incidentally reinforced Shaughnessy's opinion that the Prosecutor recognized that he could not get a conviction on the original charges. There really was no case against me. They knew it, and they had to find something else.

However an interesting thing happened, once Shaughnessy finally got me a hearing. Under oath, Dr. Kleinman testified that I was the one who suggested to him that the Prosecutor had floated a plea bargain. In court testimony, Dr. Kleinman told Judge Preska that he had no personal knowledge about such an offer.[586] Upon checking with the Prosecutor, Dr. Kleinman said that he discovered I was wrong. My "mistake" in believing the Prosecutor had floated a possible deal proved that I continued to be "incompetent to stand trial."

Was that actually true? Thanks to the tapes of this meeting, we could prove that Kleinman himself interjected questions about a plea bargain over and over again,[587] which I repeatedly shot down. He continued to raise the question for a good two hours of this interview time—all on tape. Another interesting point is that few of Dr. Kleinman's questions had anything to do with psychology. For example, Dr. Kleinman devoted a good half hour to exploring my finances.[588]

DR. KLEINMAN: "So, do you still own a house?"

LINDAUER: "Yes."

DR. KLEINMAN: "Do you have a mortgage on the house?"

LINDAUER: "Yes."

DR. KLEINMAN: "Do you pay the mortgage on the house?"

LINDAUER: "Yes."

DR. KLEINMAN: "How often do you make the mortgage payments?"

LINDAUER: "Every month. Like everybody else."

DR. KLEINMAN: "What is your monthly mortgage payment?"

LINDAUER: "About $2500 a month approximately. I just refinanced. That includes taxes."

DR. KLEINMAN: "Did you use any kind of mortgage broker to refinance?"

LINDAUER: "Well, yeah. Of course."

DR. KLEINMAN: "I'm not an expert, but one could do it directly with a bank. Or you can use a mortgage broker who helps?"

LINDAUER: "Yeah, yeah."

DR. KLEINMAN: "So did you do it with the bank or with the broker?"

LINDAUER: "A broker. YES."

DR. KLEINMAN: "What was the purpose of refinancing?"

LINDAUER: "Uggh! My God! To get a better interest rate. To pay off my debts. And to make some improvements to my house."

DR. KLEINMAN: "So you got a loan in other words? What did your interest rate go to? From what to what?"

LINDAUER: "That's none of your business."

DR. KLEINMAN: "It's OK if you don't tell me. I'm just asking your reasoning."

LINDAUER: "It has nothing to do with you."

DR. KLEINMAN: "Does that seem intrusive?"

LINDAUER: "Yes."

DR. KLEINMAN: "What's intrusive about it?"

LINDAUER: "It's none of your damn business."

DR. KLEINMAN: "Do you have a checking account?"

LINDAUER: "I'm not going to answer any of these questions. You're full of shit."

DR. KLEINMAN: "Am I?"

LINDAUER: "Yeah, I think you're desperate. I just refinanced my house, got a better interest rate, paid off all my debts, remodeled my kitchen and put in new windows."

DR. KLEINMAN: "What am I full of shit about?"

LINDAUER: "You're looking for some excuse to harass me."

DR. KLEINMAN: "I'm not looking for anything. It's more relevant to your mental state."

LINDAUER: "Oh yeah, right. Tell them that I'm SOOO DEPRESSED that I paid off all my debts!! I'm SOO worried because all my debts are gone. What garbage. Make sure that you say that's garbage. (Sarcastic laughter)."

DR. KLEINMAN: "What's garbage? But it relates to your competence?"

LINDAUER: "You're desperate—"

See what a difference a tape recording makes? Not what anybody expected, I'll bet! Probably you expected some emotional floss about childhood trauma, or some deep secret feelings about life. Some deeply sensitive emotional concerns that poignantly depict a wounded "inner child."

I defy anyone to explain how that conversation reflects on my "emotional well being" at all. Or how it would substantially demonstrate my inability to contribute to my defense at trial?

And yet, following this conversation, Dr. Kleinman reported to Judge Preska that I continued to be "unfit for trial." He declared that I "could not assist in my defense."

Only now Brian Shaughnessy waited for me in the wings.

From that first auspicious evening at the National Press Club, Shaughnessy became fully engaged in my defense. Without further delay, he began interviewing witnesses and examining evidence and alibis.[589] He wanted to be fully prepped for any conversation with O'Callaghan to end the case, or move it forward out of this stalemate. By now it was obvious to everyone that Talkin couldn't handle that sort of discussion on my behalf. Shaughnessy took over the role filled by Ted Lindauer at Carswell. Talkin continued to appear with me, and sit at the table. But Shaughnessy began traveling to New York for all of my status meetings in Court. He made a point of introducing himself to Judge Loretta Preska, who had taken over from Judge Mukasey.[590]

Dr. Kleinman's second declaration of my "incompetence" whet Shaughnessy's appetite. Because of these forced psych interviews, the Justice Department had my defense strategy—and Shaughnessy recognized that they most desperately did not want me to use it. The fraud of the indictment would be exposed, and the government would suffer deep embarrassment for the lies they told about me—and about Iraqi Pre-War Intelligence and the 9/11 investigation.

I would win. And they would lose big time.

To his credit, Shaughnessy recognized this was a truth that people really needed to hear.

By May 2007, I told Sam Talkin that I would not attend meetings at Counseling Plus much longer. Shaughnessy guided me skillfully. He urged me to give the Court a reasonable opportunity to achieve closure, before we reopened the question of my competence. Over that summer, he had several conversations with O'Callaghan. Above all, we reminded the Court that psychiatry had forced this finding of incompetence on me without a hearing, in strict violation of my rights under the law. If this case didn't go away, Shaughnessy would take over my defense and move for Trial.

From that point on, psychology would get tossed in the dust bin where it belonged.

In August, Shaughnessy, who's a congenial and shrewd fellow, approached O'Callaghan and gave him one final chance to drop my case. Shaughnessy reminded him of the promise that he made to Sam Talkin before I left for Carswell that he would drop the charges if I cooperated with the incompetence findings. It was now a year after my release from prison.

O'Callaghan said he had changed his mind. He intended to hold the charges against me for another year, and possibly two years.

Shaughnessy thanked him politely, and retreated to our corner of the boxing ring to prepare for another fight round. Clearly O'Callaghan had not learned the lesson of an intelligence war: He had power over his actions. He did not have power over mine.

And so, consistent with my pledge, in August, 2007 I refused to go back to Counseling Plus after 10 months of worthless psychology meetings, financed by hard working American taxpayers.[591]

I told the Court that I refused to play this game any longer. My days as a campaign contribution to Republicans on Capitol Hill was over.

But it wasn't over for O'Callaghan. His backer on Capitol Hill was now campaigning for the highest office in the land. John McCain wanted to be President. In a short time, O'Callaghan would land a plum campaign job in McCain's inner circle. O'Callaghan's internet bio boasts that he "advised McCain's campaign on terrorism and national security policy."[592]

Now that was an interesting twist. I'd been arrested after phoning McCain's Senate office, requesting to testify before the Presidential Commission on Pre-War Intelligence, which McCain spearheaded for the Republican leadership. The Justice Department's refusal to grant my request for a trial stopped me from exposing McCain's wrongful claims about 9/11 and Iraq. Any sort of public hearings would have exposed McCain's deceptions on a host of national security issues.

For years, I always suspected that some faction attacking me at the Justice Department had ties to John McCain. Now I got my proof.

Only now there was a sea-change that O'Callaghan had not expected.

Now a top Washington attorney was championing my defense. Brian Shaughnessy had my back. And he fully agreed that my case should go to trial.

CHAPTER 31:

AMERICAN CASSANDRA

"Apologies must be made, O Athenian men!"
–Plato, on the death of Socrates

I wasn't supposed to rise from the dead. I was supposed to know that I was beaten and disgraced.

Obviously they didn't understand me very well. The Justice Department profiling couldn't have been more off the mark. I dare say it lacked any insight to my personality whatsoever.

Unhappily for Republican leaders, I am nothing if not resilient.

Oh they'd smashed me up pretty good. They beat my heart with two by fours, and trashed my reputation. I would carry some ugly eggplant bruises on my soul for a long time.

Despite all of that hurting, I began to rally. I'd fought so hard to defend myself as an Asset that I almost forgot that I'm also an activist. A tenacious and persevering activist at that! That's why I could haggle with Libya and Iraq for something so impossible as the Lockerbie Trial and the weapons inspections. I'm a fighter to the end.

Now a life-time of experience kicked in. Just as Assets know how to create strategies to run a blockade, so activists know how to nurture a cause from the position of an underdog. So in a sense, after recuperating from Carswell, I returned to my natural starting position. I got up off the floor and checked for broken bones. Then I got ready to rumble.

Only now I was fighting mad. And thanks to JB Fields and Janet Phelan rallying for my cause while I was locked up, I no longer stood alone. Word of my ugly nightmare on the Patriot Act, had reached the blogs and alternative radio audiences, piquing the interest of independent thinking Americans.

From Toronto, Janet Phelan had launched her own show, "One if by Land," on Liberty News Radio and Republic Broadcasting Network. Dedicated to the spirit of Paul Revere's ride that launched (the first) American Revolution, Phelan aspired to expose stealth attacks on civil liberties in the United States, with hyper-attention to the nefarious creep of the Patriot Act, which has ambushed free thinking Americans in the Courts. She's also highly savvy to psychiatry's propensity for fraud, and its abuses of creative women who buck the system. She was my sister, alright, on many levels.

Alternative radio hosts like Greg Syzmanski, Cosmic Penguin and Derek Gilbert had made the winning difference to my freedom. While I was locked up, JB Fields talked about Republic Radio, Liberty and the Oracle Networks like a life-line. What they lack in size, they make up with heart. They have passion for America's traditions of freedom, and the urgency to protect those values. Their rallying has pricked the walls of silence around many issues. On my case, they stirred enough of a gale-force to incite blowback on the Justice Department, so that my grievances could not be ignored. When I got out, I was astonished by who had heard of the abuse I suffered, because of these cutting edge blogs and internet radio networks.

Whoever says one person's voice can't make a difference should turn on the radio.

My all time favorite radio host, Michael Herzog, championed my cause on Oracle Broadcasting and Republic, when I renewed my fight for a trial.

He asked the best opening question on-air, of all time: "So tell us, Susan Lindauer, why are you still alive?"

To which I replied: "I refuse to die until I get my trial. At this rate, I will probably live forever!"

Every show with Herzog was lively and fun, just a delight for guests. Mike's an extremely sharp and versatile host on a wide front of issues, and he brings all of that perspective to each show. He's incredibly dynamic. And during my legal drama, he proved that he's got rapid timing, I mean, lightning speed. If Pre-Trial Services threatened to revoke my bail in the morning, Mike would rework his radio schedule and get me on his show that afternoon. That's what it took to save me, and Herzog and Phelan made it happen. They refused to back down for me.

Up to that point, I must confess that America was looking kind of shabby to me. By now, I was pretty disgusted with the media. I had to question if the American people were getting exactly what they deserve.

Herzog and Phelan and Dr. Shirley Moore—and all the other blogs and alternative radio shows— got me feeling empowered again, like a revolution was starting to take back our country. And their audiences had front row seats.

In fact, all of these radio hosts have amazing tentacles of knowledge, reaching deep below the surface on many different issues. They have the depth that I'd been aching for, and missing so much in the mainstream media. I'd pretty much given up finding it, and all of a sudden, there it was— Vigilant, awake and free.

Most of all, JB Fields and the "New Media," as everybody called it, gave me the confidence, and the hope, to tell my story again. They championed my resurrection with such enthusiasm that I felt like a phoenix rising from the ashes.

Like a lot of Americans, I started looking for America in some different places.

That's when I found an investigative blog journalist who proves that the New Media possesses every bit as much "class" and journalistic quality as the old media. And a darn sight more curiosity and devotion to investigative reporting.

It was Michael Collins, one of the truly cutting edge blog journalists today.[593] I call him the Johnny Depp of blog journalism, because of his amazing versatility.

Michael Collins changed the whole dynamic of my fight.

Judge Michael Mukasey retired from the bench on the day of my release from M.C.C. Now Mukasey received the nomination for U.S. Attorney General, taking over the Justice Department from Alberto Gonzales, author of the infamous torture memos and the Guantanamo prison concept. Michael Collins took a fresh look at my case, as part of a round up of Judge Mukasey's formidable career on the bench. Pointing to Mukasey's final decision saving me from forcible drugging, Collins argued that Mukasey appeared to have a soft spot for the underdog in a fight, and might turn out to be a strong defender of individual liberties, a breath of integrity after the corruption of Alberto Gonzales and his cabal of anti-Constitutionalists at the Justice Department.

Well, the subtlety of Collins' understanding impressed me. I read his article on SmirkingChimp.com, and decided to approach him through Jeff Tiedrich, publisher of the blog.

Michael Collins did me the favor of responding immediately. He wanted to know what the hell was going on. Like Brian Shaughnessy, he smelled a rat.

He took the time to find out. We sat down for three lengthy interviews at a Lebanese bistro near my home in Maryland. Michael Collins took special care to analyze my history overall, starting with Lockerbie. He also reviewed the evidence against me. Collins was the first journalist who asked to see my letters to Andy Card, White House Chief of Staff, which resulted in my indictment. He was aghast at what he saw was supposed to convict me.

It was Collins who nicknamed me "American Cassandra," for my tragic prophecies about the outcome of this War.[594] The lack of illegal weapons in Iraq. The rise of Iran. The rise of Islamic fundamentalists through democracy. The $1.6 trillion war budget that would rob domestic programs and throw Wall Street and the Middle Classes into a downward spiral. The emergence of charismatic terrorist cells inside Iraq to fight the Infidel Occupation. The Iraqi people's bitter hatred of the United States for the misery of sanctions.

Like Cassandra, I foretold it all with clarity.

And like Cassandra, I suffered the contempt of our leaders, who did not wish to hear the truths that I forecast—

When Michael Collins got hold of my story, finally a critically thinking journalist connected the dots, and was capable of drawing connections to events on Capitol Hill. Collins recognized the aspects of a major cover up immediately.[595]

Collins cried foul on the Justice Department for faking claims of my incompetence to protect Republican leaders running from the hellacious fall out of their poor decision making. He was doubly appalled when he read the papers, and saw what I'd actually done.

Collins had the integrity to be outraged.

By now, I'd lived under the storm of indictment for three and a half bitter years. I'd spent a year in prison. And all of a sudden, there was sunshine on my story. Where the

New York Times had botched it so badly, the "New Media" now excelled. Truly it felt like a changing of the guard. It was exciting to be part of that.

Michael Collins took my story to "Scoop" Independent News, Op-Ed News, Atlantic Free Press, American Politics Journal, Intelligence Daily, Smirking Chimp, and the Agonist, to name a few of the provocative, cutting edge blogs that have established themselves as a vital source of information for the public.

His articles reach 400 blogs in a typical week, and my story posted on all of them.

With a single key stroke, Michael Collins obliterated the corporate media black out on my story. And he proved the pen is still mightier than the sword, when it comes to championing the rights of democracy and freedom.

For my own esteem, it was God-sent.

As the months rolled on, Phelan and Herzog's radio shows and Michael Collins' blog articles flagged all the breaking developments in my case, blow by blow.[596] It would be a battle to the last day. Only now, thanks to the New Media, blog readers and radio audiences started to get some facts. And wouldn't you know, those facts contradicted everything they'd been sold— not only about my life, but also about Iraq and 9/11 and the weakness of U.S. anti-terrorism policy—which had been concealed from public scrutiny, gratis of the Patriot Act. Now they started asking some tough questions.

There was still confusion for awhile, as people had to absorb the vast differences of how the Justice Department portrayed me versus new revelations about the horrific abuses that I suffered on the Patriot Act. But I was no longer standing alone in the dock. Michael Collins, Michael Herzog and Janet Phelan showed me that America cared.

Thinking people cared. "Awake" people cared. That strengthened my confidence to face down the insults from my opponents, as I pushed forward with Brian Shaughnessy and Tom Mattingly towards a trial.

Those insults—and threats on my freedom— got much worse, not better. Republicans thought they had me in a box. And they did not want me coming out of that box. My enemies camped out on Wikipedia, a useful tool for spreading false information that bastardized my reputation every chance they got. Despite multiple efforts at correction, for a couple of years Wikipedia insisted on giving me the wrong name, wrong age and birthday, and they wrongly identified the allegations against me, upping my crimes to espionage. It went downhill from there.

Happily, notoriety does not scare me. I've got an incredibly tough skin. I'm a big believer that you can tell a lot about a person by the strength of (her) enemies. Mine included Dick Cheney, John McCain, Andy Card, John Ashcroft, Colin Powell and Alberto Gonzales. So maybe I'm not so bad after all! Hey, they're big and I'm small. That doesn't make them right.

Above all, the White House was in play. And my prime arch enemy, John McCain was running for President. His staff desperately wanted to keep me silent.

Unfortunately, as McCain's poll numbers got tighter in the race with Barak Obama, there were constant threats to take me into custody. Several times, Pre-Trial Services in New York threatened to revoke my bail, ostensibly because I phoned my Supervisor *after hours* to report my whereabouts, at the instruction of my attorney, so there would be no chance of confrontation between us.[597] I taped every phone call to Pre-Trial Services for my own protection.[598]

It was incredibly dirty, of course. I was not some parolee convicted of a crime, now on probation. Three and a half years had passed, and I was still demanding my rights to a trial. By now, I had another year's worth of psych observations from Counseling Plus, documenting that nothing was wrong with me, except Post Traumatic Stress caused by my ordeal at Carswell.[599] I hardly qualified as a flight risk, since I'd already surrendered to prison once. I'm not a drug user, who might indulge in substance abuse. In five years I never committed any crime, which could have justified revoking my bail.

This was more like high stakes poker. Shaughnessy and I kept agitating for a trial, so we could shoot down the allegations against me. My very mediocre public attorney was gone. The Prosecutor squirmed with dread that he would have to play his cards, and show his lack of evidence to the Court. O'Callaghan would be forced to admit that he had knowingly concealed the facts of my identity. He would get busted for prosecutorial misconduct that resulted in false imprisonment of a known Asset, with threats of forcible drugging to shut me up. Clearly O'Callaghan did not relish that confession.

I used to joke that the Judge should post a $500,000 bond on O'Callaghan's house— identical to mine—so that the Defense could require him to come to Court.[600] He was the one avoiding the Judge, not me. I used to taunt Pre-Trial Services that I was ready. Just name the day, and I'd be happy to kick the Justice Department's ass.

Ominously for me, polls showed that support for Republicans was sinking fast. Fighting to keep a death grip on power, the GOP's worst nightmare was now coming true: I was talking on the radio about the real facts of Iraq, 9/11 and the weakness of anti-terrorism policy.

And some independent minded Americans were starting to listen. The Justice Department let me know they would not stand for it.

In September, October, November and December 2007, Pre-Trial Services mounted an aggressive effort to revoke my bail and ship me back to Carswell, with a series of false complaints.[601]

In one court deception, I was astonished when Pre-Trial Services accused me of "bursting in on another individual's session at Counseling Plus."[602]

It was a flagrant, audacious lie. Aggravating the ridiculousness of the accusation, I despised "counseling" so much that I would never dream of interrupting anybody's session. I was always happy to sit in the lobby, if Burton was running late. I had nothing to say to the woman. The longer I waited, the shorter the time I would have to waste in her office, while she surfed the internet scheduling weekend entertainments with her daughter.

The upshot was that somebody else wearing a blue coat, similar to mine, "burst" into her office, while she finished up with another client. Heavens, I was probably entering a stage of brain death at that very moment, tucked in a corner of the lobby. Astonishingly, Pre-Trial Services never bothered to check with Burton before reporting this incident to Judge Preska. They hauled me to New York for an emergency appearance, and argued vigorously that I should get shipped back to Carswell that very night. When I scorned the suggestion that I would burst into any session, given my contempt for psychology, Pre-Trial Services had to back down. Even the Judge had to acknowledge it sounded preposterous.[603]

But Shaughnessy didn't play. He confronted my Pre-Trial Supervisor in Greenbelt, and demanded a retraction.

When they got caught, do you think Pre-Trial Services had the integrity to admit to Judge Preska they made a mistake? Hardly. They pulled something else from their bag of dirty tricks. Something really dirty, even for these guys.

It got so bad that in December, 2007, Pre-Trial Services forced me to appear in Court without Brian Shaughnessy, in the company of my old attorney, Sam Talkin, while the Feds fought to revoke my bail yet again.[604] This occurred after I had paid Shaughnessy's legal fees, and he personally assured the Court that he had taken my case. The court meeting was scheduled for the only day that entire week that Shaughnessy could not travel to New York. It was particularly outrageous, since the court meeting was scheduled for 5 o'clock in the afternoon, and Shaughnessy offered to appear by 8 o'clock the next morning. He offered to travel overnight so that he could do so.

My outgoing attorney, Talkin—who'd been replaced by this point—seized the opportunity to make one final pitch to the Judge that he disputed my competence, and would agree to whatever O'Callaghan wanted to do with me. He declared in open court that if he had his way, I would never be declared competent until O'Callaghan said so![605]

Much worse, Talkin argued that I should be forced to undergo a 3 day in-patient psych evaluation, in lieu of getting sent back to Carswell, as a requirement for challenging the competency finding.[606] Never mind that a year's worth of session notes from Counseling Plus faithfully recorded that nothing was wrong with me,[607] and I suffered no personal crises in Maryland—something a faithful attorney would have emphasized in Court to help preserve my freedom. Not Talkin. Knowing that Shaughnessy was proceeding in a fully different direction, Talkin tried to inflict as much damage as possible to our efforts on his way out, even to the point of costing me my freedom.[608]

Thankfully, Brian Shaughnessy got Talkin's request overturned. He went the extra mile, soliciting opinions from the chief psychiatrists at Georgetown University, George Washington University and the Washington Psychiatric Institute, the last whom he tracked down on vacation in Israel. All swore my competency evaluation could be handled on an out-patient basis, and that hospitalization should be strictly limited to individuals in crisis, which I was clearly not. To their credit, every one of those Psychiatry Departments refused to admit me, or submit to being pawns of political leaders. They flat out refused.[609]

Instead, Shaughnessy arranged for a leading Washington psychiatrist, Dr. Richard Ratner to do the evaluation for our competency challenge at his private office.

But it struck me as shocking misconduct. At the court session in December, I was compelled to declare for the court record that I had no attorney present. Sam Talkin no longer represented me, and my real attorney, Shaughnessy had to be absent, because of prior commitments. I scoffed that anything in my life justified a 3 day in-patient evaluation for a competency review, insisting there was a huge disconnect between Pre-Trial Services' fanciful inventions and the real facts of my life in Maryland, which was going very well, thank you.[610]

Looking back, it's difficult to believe that anybody could have tried to do this. But the threat was quite real. Every time we headed to New York, Shaughnessy would tell me honestly that he had no idea if I would make it home that night, or if the Judge would take me into custody.

One thing probably saved me. Shaughnessy warned that if the Court took me into custody, we would file an emergency appeal to the 2nd Circuit Appellate Court challenging the procedures by which my incompetence had been accepted. Then we would push for trial.[611]

The fear that Shaughnessy would use any bail revocation to force a trial probably saved me. Taking me into custody would have advanced my rights to a trial dramatically, especially since Shaughnessy intended to dispute the original arguments for my incompetence. We had prepared an emergency appeal should the Court grab me, on any day. And we expected to win.

Does that sound like I don't know the law? That I'm stumped in court? Hardly.

My case was non-stop legal fraud. That's how desperately they wanted to shut me up.

They succeeded for so long because of the Patriot Act, and because I had no attorney willing to fight for me—except for my marvelous uncle, Ted Lindauer and the brilliant Brian Shaughnessy, after Carswell. Alas, the Patriot Act handicapped even the most senior attorneys.

The Patriot Act changed the equation of power in the courtroom, such that all transparency in the proceedings got erased. It emboldened the Prosecutor to misrepresent the caliber of evidence against me, when the charges should have been dropped as frivolous. As time went on, protecting the lies invented by the Justice Department required yet more abuse of my rights, and more lies, to safeguard various Republican officials from exposure.

It's why I call the Patriot Act the foundation for all future dictatorship in the United States. It's a very dangerous law. My case demonstrates several critical reasons why the Patriot Act should be repealed immediately. Every leader who supported the Patriot Act should be removed from power, Democrat or Republican, without exception. The Patriot Act should be a litmus test for judging who's qualified to protect the best traditions of democracy in our country, and who's unfit for leadership. It's that bad.

Through every blow, Collins, Herzog and Phelan stayed right by my side. Many times, we would end a radio show with a reminder that I might get carted back to prison in the next few days, because of one attack or another. That's no exaggeration, unfortunately. For several months, I prepared myself mentally and emotionally to get shipped back to Carswell. I expected to get seized at any moment.

It got so bad that U.S. Marshals telephoned Shaughnessy, threatening to take me into custody 2-3 weeks before the November election, as the battle hardened between Barak Obama and John McCain. Those sorts of phone calls almost always indicate a defendant is about to get seized. Sure enough, that warning coincided with a heavy round of radio interviews, telling listeners the truth about our 9/11 warning and the facts about Pre-War Intelligence.

To his great credit, Shaughnessy backed me a hundred percent, and never cautioned me or Michael Collins to back down. He told us to keep fighting, and fight harder!

That's where my opponents hit a wall.

Republican loyalists inside the Justice Department could deny me a trial on the most frivolous and absurd grounds. But they could not stop me from demanding my day in court.

They could scorn my "incompetence" as an Asset. But for all their speeches, Republican leaders on Capitol Hill could not reinvent my contributions to Pre-War Intelligence, or the reality of my team's 9/11 warning throughout the summer of 2001.

They faced a serious quandary that John McCain played a leadership role in both the 9/11 investigation and the Iraq Investigation—and both reports contained outrageous inaccuracies that McCain spoon fed to the American people, as key spokesperson for both Commissions.

If McCain had won the Presidency, I would have fought for his impeachment from his first day in office. He would have deserved it, too.

Some Americans have taken hard blows for questioning the official version of events about 9/11. They have possibly speculated in some wrong directions. But they are quite correct that a substantial body of facts has been concealed, like the essential truth that parts of the U.S. Intelligence Community urgently anticipated a 9/11 style of attack, with uncanny accuracy as to the method, target and timing of the attack, described as "imminent" in August, 2001. Or that urgent requests for intra-agency cooperation to pre-empt the strike were made in August, 2001 to U.S. Attorney General John Ashcroft's private staff and at their suggestion, the Office of Counter-Terrorism at the Justice Department.

I made some of those calls myself. And I am positive that I was not the only alarmist.

Finally, the 9/11 Truth community is absolutely correct that the 9/11 Commission was a white-wash. Can anybody blame them for being angry and frustrated? I don't.

Some things really are unforgivable in a democracy. Allowing thousands of your own citizens to suffer horrible deaths, in order to rationalize an unnecessary War should be judged the most terrible crime of all.

Most Americans still can't believe that some of the Republican leadership did that to all of us. But it's true. The people around John McCain understood exactly what it would mean if my story exposed those deceptions. McCain's entire campaign platform on national security would have crashed to the ground.

Very soon, my own prosecutor, Edward O'Callaghan would get appointed senior adviser on the McCain campaign, assigned to Sarah Palin in Alaska, handling the Trooper-gate fiasco. Time would show that O'Callaghan's ties to McCain ran very deep.

All of that explains why, after Carswell, the louder I spoke out, the more furiously the Justice Department tried to send me back to prison.

The final shot to revoke my bail came two weeks before Barak Obama's historic triumph over McCain at the voting booth. The attacks never stopped until McCain lost the White House.

When McCain lost, the attacks ended overnight.

If that doesn't demonstrate the power of democracy and the voting booth to thwart tyranny, I don't know what could. *Vote, people!*

My fight was definitely not for light hearts or weak stomachs.

Only now I had a powerful and effective attorney who cared what happened to me. Shaughnessy stayed ahead of the curve at all times, so that my defense would be ready for trial once the Court acknowledged my competence. Tom Mattingly assumed the role of paralegal, and together they developed a strategy for managing what would come next.

Fellow activist, Karin Anderson of Takoma Park, agreed to pony up my legal fees from her savings. This grandmotherly animal rescue activist finds a penny on every street corner, and always stops to pick it up because it reads: "In God we trust."

It was many thanks to Karin Anderson that my home and beloved pets had been safe, while I was locked up at Carswell. Now, thanks again to Karin, I could carry on my legal battle.

Alas, my beloved friend, JB Fields was suffering a mysterious illness that would prove to be lymphoma cancer. Shortly after my release from M.C.C, he started experiencing bouts of extreme exhaustion. Many months would go by before doctors discovered that his body had stopped producing blood platelets of any type.

JB Fields died in April, 2008, and was buried at Arlington National Cemetery, a worthy resting place for a proud Navy man, who trawled the ocean floor on naval submarines, a man who dedicated his life to protecting the rights of Americans under the Constitution.

Without the devotion of JB Fields, and his efforts to expose my travesty at Carswell, my legal resurrection would have been unthinkable. JB's commitment to protecting the freedoms of ordinary Americans is one military tradition that the United States cannot afford to lose.

Sadly he would not live to see my vindication or the dismissal of the charges. But he understood it was coming. Thanks to the planning skills of Shaughnessy and Mattingly, everything was ready in place when we launched our counter-attack on the Justice Department.

Now the battle resumed in earnest. Only a whole new dynamic was in play.

Thanks to blog journalist Michael Collins, the "New Media" on the internet tracked my case intensely. Front page coverage in "Scoop," American Politics Journal, Op-Ed News and Intelligence Daily, among others, guaranteed the Justice Department could no longer foist its defamation of my competence on unquestioning Americans.

Shaughnessy was like a new Sheriff in town, a congenial fellow with a South County Rhode Island drawl, and the confidence and ease of a life-time practicing law at extremely high altitudes. He swore that he had never heard of any case during his career, in which a defendant had been declared "incompetent" over the objections of her own attorney.

Shaughnessy took the fight straight to the Prosecutor. If Judge Preska wanted proof of my story, Shaughnessy promised that we would have no difficulty delivering it.

The Court hemmed and hawed for months. Clearly they wanted to avoid a positive finding that would result in a trial before the presidential election. They wanted to keep McCain and the Republicans safe through November.

No matter! The stage was set. My supporters had an under-dog mentality for this fight.

The way I saw it, they were big, but we were small. They were bulky, trapped by their deceptions. We were nimble, protected by our honesty.

And woe to the wicked!

Like Assets, we peace activists never surrender!

CHAPTER 32:

VINDICATION

Veritas vos Liberabit.
And the truth shall set you free.

On a lovely day in June, the Court could delay no longer. Facing pressure from my new, upstanding, high-power Washington attorney, Judge Preska was forced to grant our request for a hearing to challenge the bogus finding of incompetence.

This would be my first and only evidentiary hearing in the four years since my arrest. Ostensibly it would determine my "fitness" to stand trial— almost two years after my release from prison.

I would be allowed to present just two witnesses, who could authenticate key parts of my story during one morning of testimony. At trial, there would be a dozen witnesses. But for this pre-trial hearing, my Defense was forced to strip it down. The Prosecutor fought to block these participatory witnesses as well.

Shaughnessy and I believed that we had chosen wisely.

Our first witness, Kelly O'Meara spent 17 years on Capitol Hill, rising to become Chief of Staff for Rep. Andrew Forbes of Long Island, New York. She played a lead role in the congressional investigation of the mysterious crash of TWA 800 over the Long Island Sound. O'Meara cranked up the heat for months, until the Pentagon finally admitted that three submarines were performing a training exercise off the coast of Long Island that night, and appear to have fired upon the airplane, accidentally.[612]

After Capitol Hill, O'Meara turned to investigative journalism and published a book on psychiatry, "Psyched Out: How Psychiatry Invents Mental Illness and Pushes Pills that Kill," examining the correlation between the use of anti-depressants, like Prozac, and shooting rampages by teenagers and adults.[613]

Finally, O'Meara had known my former intelligence handler, Paul Hoven, for more than 20 years. Like me, she was introduced to Hoven by Pat Wait, the chief of staff for Rep. Helen Bentley, a staunch Republican from Baltimore, Maryland. She was also a regular at the Hunan for several years.[614]

O'MEARA: "I met Paul when I was investigating the death of Irana San Salvador, who was a U.S. embassy guard in San Salvador. Anyway he was killed, and I was investigating that. I was telling this friend of mine, this chief of staff about it, and she said, oh, you need to meet Paul Hoven. He can probably help you with that. So I did. I met Paul."

"He's a likeable fellow. We became friends. Paul's the one that first took me to the Hunan, or told me I should come over to the Hunan on Thursday nights, because it is a group of Capitol Hill staffers, and some Pentagon people showed up every now and then, some lobbyists. Basically it was just you know, after work, have a drink and talk shop."

O'Meara's testimony went on to describe the quirky habits of the intelligence community. Shaughnessy was determined to prove that Hoven had longstanding relationships within the intelligence community, whether he chose to acknowledge formal ties to the Defense Intelligence Agency or not. Whereas my previous attorney failed utterly to grasp the nature of intelligence work, Shaughnessy had an iron grip on its functionality. As a conversation, it would have been fascinating, if the circumstance of O'Meara's testimony wasn't so frightening.

SHAUGHNESSY: "Did you learn, as the years went along, what sorts of things he did for a living?"

O'MEARA: "I didn't know what Paul did as far as a living. I never knew Paul to have a job like everybody else. I mean, I never saw him get up and go to work, nine to five, at least when I knew him. I know beforehand, apparently, he was involved in military things on the Hill. But when I knew him, I didn't know him to have a job."

SHAUGHNESSY: "Now, did there come a time when you met a fellow named Joe Harvey?"

O'MEARA: "Yes."

SHAUGHNESSY: "How did you meet him, and what did your relationship become with Harvey?"

O'MEARA: "I was the lead investigator for TWA 800, the crash off of Long Island [in July, 1996] for Congressman Forbes. Anyway, Paul Hoven knew I was investigating that crash. And he said, "Oh, you need to talk to Joe Harvey." So he introduced me to Joe Harvey because Joe was a former Navy SEAL. That was what I was told. I met Joe. He's a very nice guy, and we had about a four-year friendship, you know."

SHAUGHNESSY: "Was there a particular term that Mr. Hoven used with respect to your relationship with Joe Harvey?"

O'MEARA: "Well, that came at the end of the relationship. During the whole time I knew Joe, even when I left the Hill and became an investigative reporter [at the Washington Times], Paul never said anything to me. It was after I was working on a story on the Oklahoma City bombing. And I remember Joe gave me some information, and I wasn't clear on it, so I e-mailed him and asked him to clarify something."

O'MEARA: "Joe Harvey wrote back, and said, "I don't ever want to talk to you again."

THE COURT: "Never?"

O'MEARA: "I never want to talk to you again." I didn't know why. I was kind of shocked because I always thought we were just really good friends. And I didn't understand what had happened."

"So anyway, when I saw Paul, I told Paul, and I showed Paul the e-mail. And Paul looked at me, and he goes, "Well, he's not your handler anymore, Kelly." Which kind of upset me, because Paul was the one that introduced me to Joe. And I had no idea that I had a handler."

SHAUGHNESSY: "What did you take the term "handler" to be?"

O'MEARA: "Well, what do you take it to be?"

SHAUGHNESSY: "You have to say."

O'MEARA: "OK. Somebody who kept an eye on me, passed information that I might have given to him, you know."

SHAUGHNESSY: "To whom?"

O'MEARA: "Intelligence. That's what I thought. I could be wrong, but that's what I thought."

SHAUGHNESSY: "With respect to Mr. Hoven, did you understand in any way that he was involved in intelligence work?"

O'MEARA: "This is just an opinion, OK."

SHAUGHNESSY: "Yes. Did you believe Mr. Hoven to be a member, or involved with intelligence?"

O'MEARA: "Yes."

SHAUGHNESSY: "Why?"

O'MEARA: "Because I always thought from the time I met Paul, that Paul was an information passer. For people who don't live in Washington, or aren't involved in investigations and stuff, maybe you don't understand that. But Paul always had interesting information. He was always asking you about what you knew. I know that I told him something once on TWA 800 that actually ended up in a newspaper the very next day."

"I always just felt Paul passed information. Add that with all of the people he introduced me to, the fact that he never had a job that I knew of, I thought that's what he did."

SHAUGHNESSY: "Do you know a gentleman named Dr. Richard Fuisz?"

O'MEARA: "I have met Dr. Fuisz."

SHAUGHNESSY: "How did you meet Dr. Fuisz?"

O'MEARA: "Through Paul Hoven."

SHAUGHNESSY: "Would you please explain what happened?"

O'MEARA: "Paul wanted me to meet his good friend, Dr. Fuisz, and we drove out to Dr. Fuisz's office. I was sick the day that we drove out there, so Paul ended up driving my car. I thought it was in Vienna, Virginia, but I understand now it's actually in Chantilly. Anyway, we went to his office and kind of just chitchatted for a while. I wasn't impressed."

SHAUGHNESSY: "Did you later find out whether or not Dr. Fuisz had any relationship to the intelligence community?"

O'MEARA: "I was told by Paul Hoven. And this is what actually got me hooked up with Susan after all these years. I read her Lockerbie deposition."

SHAUGHNESSY: "What does that mean, Lockerbie deposition?"

O'MEARA: "She wrote a deposition for the Pan Am 103 Lockerbie trial."

SHAUGHNESSY: "What was the nub of the deposition that caught your attention?"

O'MEARA: "Her deposition was actually almost to the letter what Paul Hoven told me about Lockerbie."

SHAUGHNESSY: "What was that?"

O'MEARA: "That it wasn't the Libyans that shot it down. It was the Syrians. And Dr. Fuisz was there. He knew. There was supposed to be some secret meeting that was set up between a member of Congress in Switzerland, but something happened where it didn't work out. So the Syrians were going to take the – I mean the Libyans were going to take the fall for this."

SHAUGHNESSY: "All right."

O'MEARA: "When I saw Susan's deposition on Google– I didn't even know she did a deposition until just recently. That's when I called her. I said, Susan, I had no idea that Paul had told you the same thing that he told me."

SHAUGHNESSY: "How was Dr. Fuisz related to this?"

O'MEARA: "Paul said that Dr. Fuisz was there. He knew."

SHAUGHNESSY: "There? Where?"

O'MEARA: "I assumed it was in Syria. He was in Syria."

SHAUGHNESSY: "He knew what?"

O'MEARA: "That it was the Syrians, and not the Libyans."

SHAUGHNESSY: "That is essentially what the –"

O'MEARA: "That's what Susan wrote in her deposition, and I was very, very shocked to see it, because I didn't know she had wrote a deposition, and I had no idea that anybody had told her the same thing that Paul had told me."

SHAUGHNESSY: "When did this come in relation to your meeting Dr. Fuisz?"

O'MEARA: "I don't remember the dates. I have been away from the Hill since '97."

SHAUGHNESSY: "Was it after or before your meeting with Dr. Fuisz?"

O'MEARA: "It was after my meeting with Dr. Fuisz."

SHAUGHNESSY: "And have you met Dr. Fuisz again?"

O'MEARA: "Yes. Paul contacted me, asking me to do an article (when I was a reporter) for Dr. Fuisz, about some contractor trouble he was having with a house he was building. I didn't do the article, because they never gave me the documentation that I needed."

SHAUGHNESSY: "Getting back to the deposition concerning Lockerbie and Libya, were you present, or did you observe conversations between Hoven and Susan?"

O'MEARA: "All the time."

SHAUGHNESSY: "All right."

O'MEARA: "At least every Thursday at Hunan, when I was at Hunan. I mean, sometimes you know, you have hearings or whatever, and you are not able to make it. When Susan was there and Paul was there, they were talking."

SHAUGHNESSY: "Did they talk about Lockerbie with some frequency?"

O'MEARA: "I don't know. I have no idea. I didn't go and listen to their conversations. I just know that when they were there together, they were talking to each other. And I heard about Susan all the time from Paul."

SHAUGHNESSY: "What did you hear?"

O'MEARA: "You name it. I mean, I'm sorry to say I'm embarrassed. I used to get tired of hearing about Susan frankly."

SHAUGHNESSY: "Did he speak well of her?"

O'MEARA: "Yes. Sure. I mean, I think this has already been in the press, but Paul nicknamed Susan "Snowflake," and he used do say she was dingy."

THE COURT: "She was what?"

O'MEARA: "Dingy. I never thought much of it, but Paul spoke about Susan a lot to me. I met with Paul I would say three or four times a month, you know, for years, dinners—"

SHAUGHNESSY: "Did he explain sometimes what she was doing, and –"

O'MEARA: "Sometimes."

SHAUGHNESSY: "And what was that?"

O'MEARA: "I just listened to Paul tell me the stuff."

SHAUGHNESSY: "All right. Did you talk with Paul Hoven at about the time he was interviewed by the FBI?"

O'MEARA: "I got a call from Paul after the FBI interviewed him. Yes."

SHAUGHNESSY: "Did he talk with you about the substance of the interview?"

O'MEARA: "Yes."

SHAUGHNESSY: "What was the substance according to Paul?"

O'MEARA: "It was a strange phone call. I hadn't talked to Paul for awhile. Paul left town – again, I'm guessing – I think it was right after Susan was arrested. It was very quickly. Paul left town and went back to Minnesota."

"Anyway, so I was angry at Paul for not saying goodbye to me, because I knew him for so long. So then, when I got this call, that he had been interviewed by the FBI, that was kind of interesting that he took the time to call me."

"Basically he was saying to me in Paul's fashion—Oh, Susan said I am defense intelligence and she's f'ing crazy and she doesn't f'ing know what she's talking about. I mean, that's the way Paul talks."

"I said, Paul, I said, you know, Susan was always kind of ditzy, but I never thought she was crazy. It was just this really intense phone call. I have to say that I had a feeling Paul wanted me to agree with him that she was crazy, and I couldn't. I said, Paul, I don't think she's crazy."

SHAUGHNESSY: "Well, did Paul say that Susan was incorrect or inaccurate when she described him as being intelligence, or did he say she's crazy for having said it? What was your impression?"

O'MEARA: "Paul never denied during the telephone call that he was defense intelligence, or whatever she was claiming. But he just kept saying, oh, she's crazy."

SHAUGHNESSY: "All right. Had he ever expressed the notion that Susan was crazy before this?"

O'MEARA: "No. Not to me."

On cross examination, O'Callaghan, my prosecutor, sprung a huge surprise on O'Meara.

According to O'Callaghan, Paul Hoven told the FBI he hardly knows O'Meara at all. Hoven claimed that he only met her "a couple of times."

It was a stunning moment, a whopper of a lie that caused O'Meara to visibly shake in her seat in front of the Judge.

O'CALLAGHAN: "Thank you. Now, you talked about the meetings that you had at this Hunan restaurant in Washington, D.C., correct?"

O'MEARA: "Right."

O'CALLAGHAN: "How long did these dinner meetings or dinner get-togethers take place? How many years?"

O'MEARA: "Years. I did it for years. Ten – I won't say ten. Five. Five years."

O'CALLAGHAN: "Five to ten years?"

O'MEARA: "I think I did. I mean, it was a long time that we were there. I think I was involved in it maybe five years, and I was like late to the group, I think. All I know is I went to them for a long time."

O'CALLAGHAN: "Was Paul Hoven at some of these dinner get-togethers that you described?"

O'MEARA: "Yes."

O'CALLAGHAN: "Do you think you met Mr. Hoven at these dinners quite frequently?"

O'MEARA: "Yes."

O'CALLAGHAN: **"Would it surprise you if Mr. Hoven told the FBI that he only met you once or twice at these dinner get-togethers?"**

O'MEARA: "I would be insulted to hear that."

O'CALLAGHAN: "So it would surprise you?"

O'MEARA: "Very surprising."

O'CALLAGHAN: "Now, you testified that you came to know Paul Hoven through these dinner get-togethers and conversations with him fairly well, correct?"

O'MEARA: "I knew Paul before those dinners, years before those dinners."

O'CALLAGHAN: "So, years before the dinners and then through the dinners, you got to know him through the beginning of the 1990s?"

O'MEARA: "Yes."

O'CALLAGHAN: "You never came to know what Paul Hoven did for a living, however?"

O'MEARA: "No. As I said, I never knew Paul to have a nine-to-five job or – I knew that he tinkered with voice recognition. But I didn't ever really – I was never told that he was getting paid for that, or it was a job. It was something he kind of tinkered with."

O'CALLAGHAN: "So you never came to find out that Mr. Hoven acted as a press agent for ABC News, is that right?"

O'MEARA: "While I knew Paul? Never."

O'CALLAGHAN: "And that he did freelance press work for 60 Minutes?"

O'MEARA: "That was before I met Paul. That was years before. He did a Panama story and got sick [with a heart virus]. He told me about that. I never knew Paul to do any press work while I knew him."

O'CALLAGHAN: "OK. Now, Paul Hoven never told you, did he? That he ever worked for the CIA?"

O'MEARA: "No."

O'CALLAGHAN: "He never told you that he worked for the DIA, the Defense Intelligence Agency, correct?"

O'MEARA: "That's correct. I mean nobody comes out and says they're a spook."

O'CALLAGHAN: "If I could set your time frame from 1999 to 2003, OK? Are you with me?"

O'MEARA: "Yes."

O'CALLAGHAN: "Do you know where you were working at about approximately during those years?"

O'MEARA: "1999 to 2003, I was at the Washington Times."

O'CALLAGHAN: "How often during '99 and 2003 would you speak with Paul Hoven?"

O'MEARA: "All the time. I mean, Paul and I were friends. I considered Paul a friend."

O'CALLAGHAN: "As a friend, approximately how many times a month do you think you would talk to him?"

O'MEARA: "At least once a week."

O'CALLAGHAN: "This was generally telephone conversations?"

O'MEARA: "Sometimes we went out to dinner."

O'CALLAGHAN: "Now, during those years, 1999 to 2003, did Paul Hoven ever discuss with you Susan Lindauer?"

O'MEARA: "I'm sure he did."

O'CALLAGHAN: "Do you recall any specific times that Paul Hoven discussed Susan Lindauer?"

O'MEARA: "Paul talked about Susan all the time."

O'CALLAGHAN: "I'm specifically asking you from 1999 to 2003. Did Paul Hoven's discussion about Susan Lindauer diminish in comparison to the early to mid 1990s?"

O'MEARA: "No. I would say it was more."

O'CALLAGHAN: "During the times that you did speak with Susan Lindauer, did you ever get the impression that she was exaggerating her base of information, with respect to what she was talking about? In the 1990s. Whenever you spoke to Susan, did you have a sense that she was exaggerating her role?"

O'MEARA: "No."

O'CALLAGHAN: "Have you ever had concerns about Ms. Lindauer's mental health?"

O'MEARA: "No."

O'CALLAGHAN: "Do you think you're qualified to express any opinion about her mental health?"

THE COURT: "Are you able to answer the question, as it's phrased, ma'am?"

O'MEARA: I think I'm qualified insomuch as I can, you know, read the DSM [diagnostic symptoms manual] just like any psychiatrist, and look at a list of behaviors."

O'MEARA: "As somebody who knows Susan for many, many years, not as a good friend, but as an acquaintance at meetings, at the Hunan, and from hearing about her from Paul, I never got a sense in all that time that Susan was mentally unstable."

On redirect with Shaughnessy, for the Defense:

SHAUGHNESSY: "With respect to Mr. Hoven, this fellow who maybe met you "a couple of times," approximately how many times did you meet with him from, let's say the mid '90s to the present?"

O'MEARA: "I haven't seen him in a couple of years since he went back to Minnesota, but Paul was a regular fixture in my life. I considered him a close friend. He had dinner at my family's homes many, many times. All of my – I mean, I met with Paul a lot."

SHAUGHNESSY: "Just a moment. Where does your family live?"

O'MEARA: "In northern Virginia."

SHAUGHNESSY: "Would he come over to dinner at your family's house?"

O'MEARA: "Yes."

SHAUGHNESSY: "About how many times?"

O'MEARA: "Well, he was very welcome at my sister's home. He used to love – he thought it was from Better Homes and Gardens. He went swimming in the pool there. He was you know, he was part of my life. He was a good friend. I considered him a very good friend. And we met often for dinner, talked on the phone all the time."

"In fact, Paul threatened a reporter one day for being rude to me when I was on the Hill. He called me, and told me. I told him I would kill him if he ever did that again. I mean Paul. We were very close friends."

SHAUGHNESSY: "So when he says he maybe met you a couple of times –"

O'MEARA: "He's lying."

SHAUGHNESSY: "Have you recently had brought to your attention, writings or matters that relate Paul to the intelligence community?"

O'MEARA: "Yes. I started doing some research on Google, and Paul is very evident in a blog. I actually printed out his responses. They are on my chair over there. He's responding to other people asking questions about other spooks, or other intelligence-type people like Gene Wheaton [one of the key figures who exposed Oliver North and the Iran-Contra Scandal] and Ed Wilson [a covert CIA operative who served 27 years in prison for running a black operation in Libya]."

"Paul is going into some explanation about some of these people. How Paul knew them, and so forth and so on."

"Paul also introduced me to Bill Weisenberger and Alice Weisenberger. And Bill is former CIA [heavily engaged with Ed Wilson in former CIA operations involving Libya]. I used to go shooting with Paul at Bill's farm. Paul would take me there, shooting guns."

SHAUGHNESSY: "Paul Hoven?"

O'MEARA: "Paul Hoven took me there. We used to call them Big Bill and Alice. And we would go to dinner a lot with Big Bill and his wife, Alice."

"So, I mean, is it in the realm that Paul knew people in intelligence? Yes. Certainly Bill Weisenberger was in the CIA, and it's written about all over Google. You can read it. I mean, he doesn't deny that he was in the CIA."

From the defendant's chair, I sat back and let out a long sigh. A deep breath that I'd been holding inside me for four years, anticipating this moment.

Did Paul Hoven have deep affiliations inside the murky world of intelligence?

Gracious, yes!

And did he have strong ties with me? For many years?

Indisputably.

Imagine that moment for me, as the "accused Iraqi agent."

For four years, I had begged and pleaded for this one simple pre-trial evidentiary hearing, so that I could present testimony authenticating these relationships. All of my requests got denied.

Instead, I had been incarcerated for one year in prison on a Texas military base. Labeled "incompetent." Insulted. Threatened with forcible drugging and needle injections of Haldol to "cure me" of believing in the truth of my own life. I had to listen to crazy psychiatrists argue as to whether my relationship with Hoven and Dr. Fuisz existed at all.

At one point at Carswell, the psych crowd speculated that these men might not be real people! Maybe I invented them!

It had got that crazy.

Now after four years under indictment, it was finally confirmed. I had been telling the truth all along. Would supremely credible witnesses support my cause? Absolutely.

My witnesses had been available from day one. The difference was that now I had a superior attorney capable of addressing the subtleties of my case.

That's what changed everything. One attorney's determination to advocate for my rights.

The psychological evaluations got smashed from the opening moments of Kelly O'Meara's testimony. All that speculative conjecture got debunked in minutes flat.

Consider the irony: Psychiatry had sworn that Courts have no need for participatory witnesses, their "medical insight" would be sufficient to know the "truth" about my activities and relationships. Participatory witnesses would be superfluous and unnecessary.

Except they got it all wrong.

Psychiatry failed the reality test. That morning of testimony proved psychiatry had been vainglorious and empty of insight, exactly as I told Judge Mukasey two years earlier, when I pleaded against forcible drugging. The "diagnosis" had been fraudulent and devoid of reality contact. Their opinions collapsed utterly when confronted with external factors of reality.

Sadly, for the first time, Shaughnessy and I confronted hard proof that some of Hoven's statements to the FBI must have been duplicitous—like telling the FBI that Hoven only met Kelly O'Meara "a couple of times," when they were incredibly close friends for 20 years. Hoven was close to me for 9 years.

O'Meara and Hoven attended church together. Her sister invited Hoven to family dinners and pool parties. Hoven took her shooting at the home of Bill Weisenberger, a legendary spook.

One has to wonder if Hoven scrubbed O'Meara from his life, just like he scrubbed me. He no longer needed us anymore. So he obliterated us both, erasing all the warm memories and good wishes that we shared together for so many years. O'Meara and I are baffled by it.

But those who watch the intelligence community should recognize familiar patterns in his behavior. Just like Joe Harvey dumped O'Meara after four years of close contact, once his responsibility as her handler finished, so Hoven cut me and O'Meara off entirely, too. We were used up as sources. He moved on.

Intelligence watchers would also recognize the familiarity of the lifestyle. Intelligence folk frequently appear to have no formal occupation. Dr. Fuisz used to joke that there would be "no business cards" at his meetings. Another inside joke is that you can identify the spooks according to who's mowing the lawn on a glorious Tuesday afternoon, when everybody else is tied down at an office. My neighbors gossiped about me, too. It's part and parcel of the culture.

Hoven would often hide behind his heart disease and his disability retirement to avoid explanations about his employment. In truth, his heart ailment never interfered with supervising my contacts with Libya and Iraq. He was my handler, and both of us stayed busy.

And don't forget that he showed up at my door in 1993 knowing that I had warned the Tunisian Embassy about the first terrorist attack on the World Trade Center by Ramzi Youssef.

My closest friends and family had no idea that I gave that warning. Yet Hoven had been fully debriefed in all particulars. At the beginning of our relationship, he frequently berated me that we would have no relationship at all, on account of the serious differences in our political perspectives, except for the government's desire to keep an eye on me after my warning about that attack.

Yes, he called me "goofy." Hoven was a hard right conservative, who attended "Soldier of Fortune" events in Washington. I was a progressive democrat and a peace activist. We were an odd couple, for sure. We had very different motivations for doing this work. And yet Hoven was one of my closest friends for a decade. I called him my "big brother." I described Richard Fuisz as "my uncle." I loved these men, and I considered it a privilege to share adventures with them. I considered that I had the best life I could have hoped for. I wonder if they wrongly imagined that I had complained to these crazy psychiatrists about our past. Nothing could be farther from the truth. I spoke very highly about our work together.

And what about his link to the Defense Intelligence Agency, as a double blind, through all of our years together? Hoven was adamant that our projects in New York did not break the laws against CIA operations or surveillance inside the United States, because the Defense Intelligence Agency had authorization from Congress to run domestic counter-terrorism operations. His ability to liaison with Defense Intelligence was described *by Hoven* as critical for the legitimacy of our work in New York. That's how his affiliation came up. Hoven was officially retired on disability. Yet whatever the technical definition of his relationship to DIA, Hoven always stipulated that his actions—and our team's actions—were entirely legal, because he kept the Defense Intelligence Agency in the loop. That was a big deal.

At trial, other witnesses like Ian Ferguson, a Scottish journalist and investigator for the Lockerbie Appeals, would testify that senior members of the Intelligence Community identified Hoven as the Defense Intelligence Agency's liaison for Lockerbie. I was not the only individual who believed that. A lot of intelligence people thought so, too.

When it came to identifying fellow travelers and spooks that I might encounter on my path, Hoven said it best.

"Susan, if it waddles like a duck, and quacks like a duck, it's a duck."

"But Paul!" I'd say. "How can I be sure?"

"Susan," he'd say firmly. "It's a duck."

After four years, waiting for my day in Court, I heard the testimony with a satisfied heart.

Kelly O'Meara was an outstanding witness. We had one shot at proving the authenticity of my relationship with Hoven and his wide range of intelligence contacts before trial. O'Meara knocked it out of the ball park.

But my competence defense wasn't finished yet.

Shaughnessy was determined to prove the authenticity of my 9/11 warning, as well. We intended to show that the FBI, the U.S Attorneys Office and the Bureau of Prisons had always known the truthfulness of it throughout the debate on forcible drugging, while I was locked up at Carswell and M.C.C.

That would force the question of prosecutorial misconduct out in the open. It would also keep open the question of whether Hoven lied, as O'Callaghan suggested most adamantly to Judge Preska. We could not be sure if O'Callaghan was relying on Hoven's absence to mislead the Court again. That remained a distinct possibility, given all of what had come before.

Either way, authenticating my 9/11 warning would prove O'Callaghan had told a terrible lie to Judge Mukasey, when he denied the independent validation of my 9/11 warning, during the debate on forcible drugging. That deception officially made it a cover up. The Justice Department had officially attempted to "cure me" of knowing that inconvenient truth behind two of the most tragic government cover ups in the last decade— Iraq and 9/11. It was despicable.

My second witness would shed light on that matter.

Parke Godfrey is an Associate Professor of Computer Science and Engineering at York University in Toronto, Canada's third largest university. A scientist and mathematician who does calculus algorithms for fun, like a game, Godfrey presents a calm, studied demeanor. He's a precise and methodical thinker who chooses his words carefully. During difficult court questioning, he would pause to give an accurate, thoughtful response.

The two of us had become close friends in 1990, while Godfrey worked on his PhD in artificial intelligence and deductive databases at the University of Maryland in College Park. He has taught on the faculty of York University since 1999, with a two year sabbatical at William and Mary College in Virginia.[615]

Godfrey and I met through an old friend from Smith College, my alma mater in Northampton, Massachusetts, shortly after I arrived in Washington.

SHAUGHNESSY: "With what frequency did you see Susan?"

GODFREY: "Until I moved to Toronto in '99, I probably saw Susan on an average of twice a week. I probably spoke with her on an average of two to three times a week."

SHAUGHNESSY: "So you came to know her pretty well, is that correct?

GODFREY: "Yes."

SHAUGHNESSY: "Now, were you aware that she was concerned with, perhaps, antiwar activity and peace-type activity?"

GODFREY: "Yes. I was."

SHAUGHNESSY: "Did she speak with you about certain activities that she had become aware of, that is, certain dangers that she believed were facing us?"

GODFREY: "She did, yes."

SHAUGHNESSY: "Would you please describe them?"

GODFREY: "The first way I found that she was quite an antiwar activist is probably early on. We and other friends went to a number of the demonstrations that were happening in the early '90s downtown, the marches and such."

"One, if I'm remembering correctly, was an antiwar rally during the Gulf War, and a couple of others were rallies for abortion rights."

"Then, in the mid 90s, I was aware that she was involved in a number of things that she described as peace activism. She also did quite a bit of extracurricular activity and traveling to New York to talk with different groups, in particular, always, with a very keen interest in Middle Eastern problems."

SHAUGHNESSY: "Did there come a time when she was concerned about a possible attack on the United States?"

GODFREY: "She had described that."

SHAUGHNESSY: "What did she describe?"

GODFREY: "In particular, she warned me when I was job hunting and considering potential work in New York, because I liked New York City, that New York City was dangerous, and in particular she was predicting that there was going to be a massive attack here. In particular in southern Manhattan. This was before 9/11."

"So when I was looking for the job at William and Mary, *which was late 2000* – I was at York University, but was looking at other universities – *she warned [me] not to consider New York because she thought an attack was imminent here.*"

SHAUGHNESSY: "Continue, please."

GODFREY: "I asked her about the nature of it. She said that she thought it would be something very, very big. I asked her, "Well, what do you mean?" She said that it would involve airplanes and possibly a nuclear weapon. She said that what was started in '93, she thought was going to come back."

SHAUGHNESSY: "What was that she referenced as having started in '93?"

GODFREY: "Well, the attempt on the World Trade Centers at the time."

SHAUGHNESSY: "Did she believe, or was she telling you that very shortly there was likely to be another attack of that nature?"

GODFREY: "She did. *She said that it would complete the cycle of that attack. And she said that there would be an attack in late summer, early fall.*"

"In August, she told me that she thought it was some time imminent."

SHAUGHNESSY: "Now, did you know any of the things that she was doing that might have given her access to information, that might lead to a prediction of that nature?"

GODFREY: "Well, I had known that she was active in trying to prevent escalation with what turned out to be the war in Iraq. She had been making trips to New York to talk to people there. But nothing in my mind ever connected that she would have any access to information or intelligence that would give any indication of an attack."

SHAUGHNESSY: "You said she was visiting New York periodically. Do you know who, not necessarily the names, but the nature of the people she visited in New York City?"

GODFREY: "I don't know directly, no. Only afterwards have I found out – well, I have learned that she supposedly was talking with people at the Iraqi consulate, although she had always described that she was meeting with consulate folks with different Middle Eastern countries."

SHAUGHNESSY: "Did she mention any of those countries?"

GODFREY: "Not directly, no. Not to me."

SHAUGHNESSY: "Now, sir, did she ever mention a person named Paul Hoven?"

GODFREY: "Yes."

SHAUGHNESSY: "In what respect?"

GODFREY: "Our socializing was with a group of friends. We all lived in Maryland. And in particular, it's hard to live in the Washington, D.C. area and not be somewhat political. And we were quite a tight group of Democrats. Very often a lot of our socializing revolved around some political issue or another."

"I remember a party we had at our place, the time of the [Democratic] convention, where Bill Clinton was nominated. When I talked to Susan about other things that she did, and other socializing she did, she described a group that she got together with on a weekly basis, down on Capitol Hill, and other times down on the Virginia side. And she used to laugh and say it was about as opposite from our social group as possible. A lot of these people were very, very much Republican. And also that these people that she knew, and talked with quite a bit, were involved in policy, and in particular in the Intelligence Communities."

"One of the persons that she described as being a member of that group, who was a good friend of hers, was Paul Hoven."

SHAUGHNESSY: "Did she explain anything that she may have done with Paul Hoven, or was it simply as part of the group there?"

GODFREY: "Not anything, to my knowledge, as to her political activism or peace activism. I think he was one of the first people she met in that group. As best I knew, that group was primarily a social group. They invited her in, because she had become friends with Paul Hoven, and also because of the connections with her father, who is a Republican, who had run at one point for governor of Alaska."

SHAUGHNESSY: "Did there seem to be any hostility, acrimony, hard feelings or anything of that nature between her and Paul Hoven?"

GODFREY: "Not that I am aware of, no."

SHAUGHNESSY: "You talked about Susan going up to meet with Middle Eastern, people from the Middle East, in the embassies, or whatever. Did she mention any particular countries that stand out in your mind that she went to see?"

GODFREY: "Actually, no. Whenever she did speak of such things, she always spoke of those activities in a vague way, and told me on purpose. These were activities that she was doing, to my understanding and I fully believe, as part of her peace activism. But it wasn't something that I was involved with. And she said, a lot of these talks that I am having and all, well, she just felt it was better not to go into the details."

Godfrey's exchange with the Prosecutor on 9/11 amused me. The Prosecutor tried to dismiss my 9/11 warning as "a premonition."

Godfrey adamantly corrected him that it was "a prediction— not a premonition." And he stuck by it, never deviating from the word.

For the sake of further clarity, he submitted an affidavit on the 9/11 warning,[616] which cuts through the Prosecutor's attempts to deflect the impact of my warning. (See Appendix)

GODFREY: "Ms. Lindauer's original warning to me in 2000 was somewhat vague, describing her opinion that a terrorist attack would occur in New York City. I recall that by the spring and summer of 2001, her warning became much more emphatic and explicit. She got much more agitated about the likelihood of the attack."

"Ms. Lindauer confided in me on several occasions her concern that the next terrorist attack would involve airplane hijackings and/or airplane bombings."

"In the spring and summer of 2001, on several occasions, Lindauer expressed heightened concern that a terrorist attack was in the works that would strike the southern part of

Manhattan. She claimed it would reprise the 1993 attack on the World Trade Center. She described the attack as completing the cycle started in that first attack."

"She definitely tied the threat of airplane hijackings to, what she said, would be some sort of strike on the World Trade Center. That's what she was predicting."

"In August, 2001, Ms. Lindauer told me the attack was "imminent. She warned me to stay out of New York City. She told me the situation was very dangerous, and that a lot of people would get killed in this attack. She expected heavy casualties."

Shockingly, Godfrey testified that he told the FBI about my 9/11 warning in September 2004, *four years before this hearing in New York*— and twelve months before I was incarcerated at Carswell, and subjected to the nightmarish threat of forcible drugging.[617]

GODFREY: "In September, 2004, I was interviewed by the FBI in Mississauga (adjacent to Toronto), in the presence of the Royal Canadian Mounted Police. The RCMP insisted on this, as the interview was in Canada, and I was a Canadian resident. I spoke with FBI special agent Suzan LeTourneau."

"While the interview focused on mundane details of Ms. Lindauer's life and acquaintances, the conversation did touch on her indictment and her predictions. *I told LeTourneau that Ms. Lindauer had predicted the 9/11 attack throughout the spring and summer of 2001, and that her prediction was very specific. It involved airplane hijackings and a strike on the World Trade Center.*"

Everything I said before turned out to be truthful. Within a few months of my arrest, the FBI, the US Attorneys Office—and the Royal Canadian Mounted Police— were fully aware that a private citizen—not associated with the Intelligence Community—stood ready to authenticate my 9/11 warning in a Court of Law.

Notably, Godfrey's testimony could not be suppressed by secrecy laws. In all likelihood, his revelations would have created serious blowback for Congress, which in September 2004, was getting ready to publish the 9/11 Commission Report. The 9/11 Commission issued strong denials that the Intelligence Community had advance expectation of the attack, and could have taken action to prevent the strike, or substantially cripple its impact.

Some serious shortcomings in the 9/11 Commission Report would have been exposed. Some would have denounced it as an egregious public fraud. And the truth would be out in the open.

That provided a strong motivation for the Justice Department to fight my demands for a trial.

The FBI was not the only agency at the Justice Department to speak with Godfrey, however.

In his affidavit, Godfrey discussed how he spoke with Dr. Shadduck at Carswell about my 9/11 warning, too.[618]

GODFREY: "In early December 2005, I believe, a few months after Ms. Lindauer had been sent to Carswell Prison, I spoke with the psychologist handling her competence evaluation for the Court. During our conversation, I attempted to confirm with him that Ms. Lindauer had made predictions of a terrorist attack in Manhattan to me and others prior to the 9/11 attack. He seemed to have no interest in hearing this. Our conversation was brief."

GODFREY: "While she was still detained in prison, I offered to travel from Toronto and testify at any competency hearing, as a character witness, on her mental competence, on what I knew of her political activities before her indictment, about warnings of terrorist attacks, and any other aspects for which the Court might be interested."

"I attended the hearing on forcible drugging in May, 2006. I offered to testify on that day. In fact, I arrived at the Court, assuming that I was to testify. However, her attorney, Mr. Sam Talkin, did not call me that day. In conversation that day, I told him that she had made warnings of a terrorist attack to me and others, in advance of 9/11. I told him that I was mortified by what the Court seemed to be doing."

Yet despite all of Godfrey's best efforts to authenticate my 9/11 warning in interviews with the FBI and the Bureau of Prisons—I continued to suffer taunts in Court—for years—that I was "delusional" for suggesting I gave advance warning about the 9/11 attack.

A whole crew from the Justice Department—the FBI, the US Attorneys Office, and the Bureau of Prisons deliberately lied to a senior federal judge, when I spoke up to defend myself.

If not for Judge Mukasey's superior vigilance, the deception would have succeeded. I would have been "detained indefinitely" under the Patriot Act, and shot full of Haldol— until whatever time I could be "cured" of claiming to know the facts of my life, and the truth about 9/11 and Iraq.

It was grotesquely corrupt. And legally fraudulent.

Godfrey discussed it further in his affidavit.[619]

GODFREY: "I consider Ms. Lindauer fully competent in all ways, and devoid of any mental illness or instability."

GODFREY: "Ms. Lindauer has an artistic and mercurial temperament. She is passionate as an activist supporting her causes. She is a creative writer and former journalist. I have never observed mental instability or mental illness in her behavior."

He expressed concern for the legal competence of my attorney, Mr. Talkin as well.

GODFREY: "I made myself available to speak with the investigator working for her defense attorney. I was prepared for a lengthy conversation, including a discussion of Ms. Lindauer's 9/11 warning. I was surprised when the defense investigator cut short the conversation after only five to ten minutes. His questions seemed far inadequate for the scope of the indictment against Ms. Lindauer, and for what I felt I had to share with her Defense Attorney."

GODFREY: "Several months later, I contacted Ms. Lindauer's uncle, Ted Lindauer, and spoke with him at greater length about several issues in her case. I can verify that Ms. Lindauer felt compelled to seek her uncle's assistance interviewing witnesses for her case, before she got sent to Carswell."

In conclusion, Godfrey disputed the notion of my incompetence whole heartedly, and roundly castigated the Justice Department.

GODFREY: "In my opinion, contrary to the Justice Department lawyers, Ms. Lindauer is now, and always was, competent to stand trial. The decision to accuse her of incompetence was baffling to myself and many others. I was forced to conclude that it was likely politically motivated to block her request for a trial."

"Throughout this entire ordeal, Susan Lindauer has suffered harassment. She faced inexcusable delays in setting a trial date, (or in dropping the charges). She was repeatedly questioned in court over the reliability of her terrorist warnings, despite that they had been corroborated by me and by many others in affidavits, and under oath in spoken testimony. She was incarcerated in a mental facility, within a federal prison for 7 months, 1,300 miles from her home for supposed observation. And then held in confinement for months afterwards."

"The FBI and the US Attorneys Office's behavior in Ms. Lindauer's case were abhorrent. It is quite clear that much more was going on."

The Old Gray Haired Lady Suffers Dementia.

Well, I was elated by our success. I thought we'd won the day.

Until I read the New York Times.

The article by Alan Feuer,[620] buried in the Metropolitan Section of the Times, made no mention of Godfrey's testimony confirming my 9/11 warning, throughout the summer of 2001, nor any mention of Kelly O'Meara's confirmation of my lengthy relationship with Hoven or his close involvement with intelligence matters.

Ground Zero stood 1,000 yards from the Federal Courthouse on Pearl Street where my hearing took place. But the New York Times apparently saw no reason to inform readers in New York City about the uncanny accuracy of my 9/11 prediction. The article also failed to provide any solid description of my status as an Asset involved with Pre-War Intelligence, though it rebutted the accusations against me.

Instead, in his opening lead, New York Times journalist, Alan Feuer, falsely reported that I "stuck my tongue out at the Prosecutor."[621]

I had to read it several times. I couldn't believe what I was seeing. It was an outrageous lie, not even close to the mark.

I never stuck my tongue at children in the 3rd grade. That's not my style. I might have flipped the guy a finger! But I had a broken molar tooth that day, which scraped my tongue painfully. Sticking out my tongue at the prosecutor was simply not possible. Feuer could not see my face anyway. I was seated directly in front of him, facing the Judge.

The invention was disgraceful, a gross lack of journalistic integrity. Real tabloid trash. Yet because the New York Times printed it, ordinary people would believe it.

I was aghast. Why did Feuer do it? Why? I felt so betrayed. Here I had waited four years for a chance to tell my story to the people of New York. All I got was one morning and the chance to present two outstanding witnesses. And this was how the New York Times covered my story?

Ah, but America has come a long way since the days when the New York Times served up the only source of hard news for the people.

Robert Redford would have shared my disappointment in this bitter sequel to "Three Days of the Condor." But like me, Redford would have saluted his champions in the New Media on the internet. Because in fact, the blogs carried the day! They were on the ball, ready to expose the corruption that the New York Times tried to bury, for whatever reasons.

Thank heavens for the blogs! Michael Collins had traveled to New York for my hearing that morning. He was in the courtroom, and caught it all for posterity, with careful attention to details and nuance. He reported it all. My 9/11 warning. The validation of my relationship to Hoven and his murky ties to U.S. Intelligence.

That truth was not lost, though the "gray haired lady" of journalism clearly suffered from dementia not to print it.

It was blog journalist, Michael Collins who sat up and paid attention. Collins who alerted the blogging community. Collins who told America: "9/11 Prediction Revealed at Susan Lindauer Hearing on Competence."[622]

That felt so sweet and so good. Collins posted my 9/11 warning dead center for the changing of the media guard, the rise of a new watch dog for the people.

And what about Feuer, that New York Times' hack? He got flamed on the blogs.

Damning headlines all over the internet taunted: "From the People Who Brought Us Judith Miller: The NYT "Covers" Susan Lindauer hearing."[623] Just a friendly reminder of the dishonesty of the New York Times' reporting on Pre-War Intelligence and its unchecked "facts."

It was a good lesson for the editors in New York. They can't pull this on the people anymore. It won't be tolerated.

Like everything else, it was a bittersweet validation, after so many years of harassment.

There was another surprise coming that would blow us away.

A few short weeks after Godfrey's and O'Meara's testimony, O'Callaghan left the US Attorney's Office in Manhattan.

O'Callaghan joined the upper echelon of John McCain's Presidential Campaign,[624] as part of the top circle of advisers. He was assigned to Sarah Palin's campaign in Alaska, handling "Troopergate." His on-line bio boasts that he guided McCain's Presidential Campaign "on national security and anti-terrorism policy."

It was enough to know that O'Callaghan was on McCain's payroll.

This was a political hit, like I'd always sworn it was. All the players were politically motivated. And the outcome was fixed.

I rest my case.

. . .

CHAPTER 33:

"OFF WITH HER HEAD," THE RED QUEEN SAID

I won the battle and carried the day with flying colors. It was a tremendous victory by any standard. I had one morning in court. But in that small window, I proved my declarations had been truthful from the first days of my indictment.

Ah, but did I win the decision? Did the Court accept my competency?

On September 9, 2008, lame duck President Bush nominated Judge Preska to serve on the 2nd Circuit Appellate Court, a major promotion in her career.[625]

On September 15, 2008, Judge Preska declared me incompetent to stand trial for the second time—six days after receiving her appointment to the higher court.[626]

Neither my 9/11 warning or the accuracy of my Pre-War Intelligence mattered a single iota. Assurances from O'Meara that my relationship with Hoven and his intelligence background were fully authentic made no difference. Godfrey's testimony that he observed no signs of mental instability in almost 20 years proved irrelevant.

Judge Preska declared that because of my "belief that (I) had a 95 percent chance of acquittal," I "could not appreciate the gravity of the charges against" me. Therefore, she declared that I "could not adequately assist in (my) defense," though my own attorney swore otherwise. My advanced understanding of judicial proceedings and high level of daily functioning were also irrelevant, according to Judge Preska.[627]

Judge Preska announced her decision minutes after Dr. Kleinman concluded his testimony against me. Notably, Dr. Kleinman declared that I wrongly informed him at one of our interviews that the Prosecution had floated a plea bargain. Dr. Kleinman told the Court that I had been mistaken. He cited that example as proof that I could not understand the proceedings, or participate effectively in my own defense—even if my own attorney swore otherwise.[628]

Only now, thanks to my foresight, my Defense had tape recordings of our interview.[629]

We had hard proof that Kleinman devoted two hours trying to cajole and manipulate me into pleading guilty to tax charges, something I was not indicted for.[630] Dr. Kleinman pushed hard for my agreement, while I steadfastly urged him to move on to different topics. He would come right back to it. My reply, captured on tape, was that I didn't owe any taxes, and if there had been a mistake in my filing, I would have amended my return—and still not owed a dime to the IRS.

When I rejected the plea bargain, Dr. Kleinman denied the conversation took place.

Ah, what a difference a tape recorder makes! Shaughnessy was appalled. We filed a Motion for Reconsideration, but Judge Preska ignored our appeal.[631]

By this time, no fewer than five independent psychologists and psychiatrists in Maryland had filed evaluations reporting that nothing was wrong with me. They included Dr. Taddesseh and his partner, Dr. Kennedy at Family Health Services; Dr. Tressa Burton at Counseling Plus, who observed me on a weekly basis in Maryland; a second psychiatrist hired by Pre-Trial Services to evaluate me after Carswell, who's name I don't know; and Dr. Richard Ratner, retained by Shaughnessy for the competence hearing. Burton observed that I suffered post traumatic stress caused by my ordeal at Carswell, and nothing else.

That was an unusually high number of psychiatrists for any case—and they all reported that they saw no evidence of "psychiatric symptoms" in my behavior.

Even Carswell admitted that I showed no signs of depression, delusions or hallucinations. In observation logs, prison staff on M-1 documented that I "functioned well on the unit." They called me "cooperative and pleasant," and noted I had "zero behavioral problems."

Once, when confronted about the fraud of psychiatry in the courtroom, Tressa Burton at Counseling Plus tried to wheedle an excuse. "Maybe they like your politics. If they're lying, maybe they're lying to save you. Don't you want them to save you?"

"That's the jury job," I told her. The Jury's job, indeed. And no others.

CHAPTER 34:

DIALOGUE! DIALOGUE! AND DEMOCRACY!

A friend asked what defines me more—my achievements, even if I carry them alone — or my tragedy, which has been public and excoriating.

There's a story that I like very much, about a woman who arrives in Heaven, exhausted and dispirited, after a long journey on the earth marked by many challenges and disappointments.

The Lord takes her to a stained glass window. "Look," he says. "These are the pieces of your life that broke off on your journey. You thought that your soul was fragile like glass. You thought these broken pieces of you were lost forever."

"But here, you see, I have saved them all for you. I have taken these broken pieces, and made a picture of your life in the colors of the glass. Look how the colors form a mosaic that illustrates the story of who you are. All of those dark fragments of glass come from the hard times. But now you can see how those dark colors create shadows around the bright reds, the greens, and the blues from your happier days. And so the darkness accentuates the joyful moments of your life. The darkness calls attention to your light."

"And together, all of it is beautiful."

My friend, John Edward Hurley told me that story, and I think it's lovely.

I tell that story, because I believe that whatever price I paid for my journey, it was fully worth the cost. It was a hellacious fight, however. The men and women who did this tried to destroy my confidence, my sense of identity, my pride for my achievements, and my quiet spirituality.

Most days I think they failed. I take satisfaction that I have never regretted my actions or my choices. I never recanted my political or spiritual beliefs, no matter how badly I felt threatened.

I do believe, however, that what happened to me should send a warning shot across the bow that our democracy and liberties are not so strongly protected as Americans want to believe.

The attack on my activism was irredeemably corrupt from start to finish. Yet nothing stopped it. None of the civil rights in our Constitution had any impact slowing its momentum. Except for one shrewd and perceptive Judge, I would have been destroyed.

That's the Patriot Act for you.

Franz Kafka would have been appalled by the deja vu.

Why go to so much trouble? What were Republican leaders hiding that they had to silence me under false indictment for five years without a trial?

I believe that answer is important—and surprisingly hopeful for our future.

Republican leaders wanted to hide the success of dialogue before the Iraqi war, because it showed the capability of diplomacy to achieve results that would have defrayed the conflict. They wanted to persuade us all that War was the only way forward.

They were wrong. Dialogue and engagement created a strong opportunity for peace.

I believe it's important for all of us to know that, perhaps more important today than ever before. With conflicts on every horizon, pecking at us in every direction, there's a sense of foreboding as if our global community is racing to the edge of a cliff. And what of us then?

For myself, I believe that we are ignoring a powerful tool that offers the possibility of ratcheting down those conflicts. It is simple. It is communication. Dialogue and engagement offer a way forward. That is not idealistic or ineffectual. It can be vigorous and demanding, as Libya and Iraq have shown us already.

Changing the dynamic of Libya and Iraq started with one woman walking calmly into one embassy, and sitting down with diplomats, and sharing a cup of tea and friendly conversation. From that simple action, we created a back channel for discussion on the issues. That's how the Lockerbie Trial happened. That's how Libya stopped acting as a sanctuary for terrorists and embraced the concept of nuclear disarmament. Breaking through the isolation of sanctions, we found common ground. And we discovered that our two sides could adopt some measures of friendship. We identified a few common areas of agreement, and we built out from there.

Today Libya has been totally transformed. And it's because of dialogue.

It was the same with Iraq. Most critically, the success of back-channel dialogue made War with Iraq avoidable and unnecessary. All the objectives for War had been achieved in the two year time-frame before the invasion.[632] Once international loathing of Iraq's humanitarian crisis in 2000-2001 strongly indicated the collapse of sanctions, a faction of U.S. Intelligence adopted an ambitious agenda for securing the maximum interests of the United States in any post-sanctions period. And we succeeded to a degree that would have astonished Russia and France on the Security Council.

The results of our dialogue were outstanding.

Through a period of intense back channel talks, lasting 17 months from November 2000 to March 2002, this faction of the CIA forced Iraq to accept the return of U.N.

weapons inspectors, "with no conditions," such that Iraq agreed to the most rigorous standards of compliance and maximum transparency ever imposed in history.

Iraq agreed quite readily. In December, 2000, Iraqi Ambassador Dr. Saeed Hasan vowed "it would be a short conversation, because Iraq was ready to prove its sincerity on all known U.S. demands."

Back channel dialogue won guarantees that U.S. corporations could hold major reconstruction contracts, post-sanctions, in all sectors desired by the United States. American corporations would have the right to return to Baghdad at the same level of market share they enjoyed before the first Gulf War, barring military sales or dual-use production. U.S. corporations would have enjoyed priority status for reconstruction contracts in telecommunications, health care and pharmaceuticals, and transportation.

Iraq was keen to agree in all sectors. In fact, Baghdad offered to buy one million American manufactured automobiles every year for 10 years.

With regards to oil exploration and development, as of November 2000, Iraq agreed that the United States would enjoy full rights to participate in oil exploration and development in all future oil concessions. Furthermore, Iraq offered the U.S. the rights to second and third tier oil concessions for current contracts already granted to France and Russia, as a way to guarantee U.S participation. There was no danger of the U.S. getting cut out of Iraqi oil production.

Nor was there danger that Iraq would renege on its existing contractual commitments to Europe or Asia. No country lost any contracts, under this arrangement..

Iraq embraced the United States, and encouraged Washington to consider its vast market potential across all sectors in weighing the future of their relationship. Various senior diplomats assured the U.S. through my back channel that Baghdad hoped the United States would become a major trading partner after sanctions. Frequently, diplomats reminded me that before the 1990 Gulf War, Iraq had been a strong ally of the United States. That friendship could be renewed, they said. Iraq would show its appreciation.

From my own vantage point, some of the greatest success in back-channel talks involved Iraq's cooperation with global anti-terrorism policy. Baghdad agreed that the FBI or Interpol (or Scotland Yard) would have authority to establish a Task Force inside Iraq, with authorization to conduct investigations, interview witnesses, and make arrests of terror suspects. The FBI could have interviewed Mr. Al Anai, the Iraqi diplomat who allegedly met Mohammad Atta in Prague, Czechoslavakia, per the demands of Senator John McCain and Vice President Richard Cheney.

Moreover, Iraq offered to hand over a trove of documents identifying the financial network used by terrorists. Baghdad freely offered to provide evidence of a Middle Eastern link to the 1993 World Trade Center attack and the Oklahoma City Bombing in 1995.

Finally, on my trip to Baghdad in March 2002, I developed an Iraqi source willing to act as a covert liaison to the FBI or Interpol, who would identify terrorists who had entered the country, when, where they lived, who they met, and their activities. So the FBI Task Force could have tapped a local source for assistance, as well.

It was a phenomenal achievement—and the Justice Department prosecuted me for it. As they say, no good deed goes unpunished in Washington.

The help of that Iraqi source was icing on the cake, really. If the United States and Britain cared about shutting down terrorist networks and sanctuaries after 9/11, Iraq's cooperation would have produced a substantial windfall.

These were practical actions—not propaganda. My project took the policy speeches in Washington and London, and turned them into something alive and meaningful. Our team understood the practical elements of successful terrorism containment. We'd done this work for years, and we understood the necessary structure required to implement it. I was proud of what our team accomplished. Our blueprint was outstanding.

The opportunity for advancing key democratic reforms in Iraq—suggested by Iraqi officials themselves—surprised even me. It was tremendously exciting. Baghdad itself had developed a highly creative platform for enacting substantial democratic reforms that would have integrated Iraqi exiles into the political system. Iraq suggested that foreign embassies—which qualify as sovereign territory—could house returning Iraqi exiles, backed by embassy security. That would guarantee the safety of the exiles' return, while they absorbed back into Baghdad society. Returning exiles would have enjoyed the rights to organize free political parties, complete with party headquarters, in competition with the Baathist Party, and full access to media, including the rights to create free opposition newspapers and apparatchik.

That was Iraq's proposal in March, 2002—one year prior to the invasion. It was highly innovative and creative. I think it's an idea worth exploring in other conflict zones, where there's a large exile population seeking to establish itself back in the home country.

In total, the United States and Britain, could have achieved every single objective that leaders demanded from Iraq, without deploying a single soldier to occupy Baghdad, or dropping a single missile to damage the country's infrastructure. Not a single Iraqi mother or child had to suffer and die. Nor a single U.S. soldier.

Weapons disarmament. Cooperation with global anti-terrorism. Economic reconstruction contracts. Oil contracts for the United States. Major democratic reforms. It's hard to imagine what more the U.S. and Europe could have required. If my team had thought of it, we would have demanded it from Baghdad, shamelessly. At the risk of sounding crass to an international audience, this faction of U.S. intelligence was determined to control the agenda for ending the sanctions. It was determined to get everything possible from Baghdad that would maximize U.S. interests for the future, in exchange for lifting the U.N. sanctions.

I agreed to help as a back channel, because I hated that misery of sanctions for the Iraqi people. The pre-eminence of the United States was unchallenged at that time. I believed that it would be necessary to satisfy U.S. demands in order to resolve the conflict, and so I accepted this role. And yes, I believe the world would have been better for it. The Middle East, too. And the Iraqi people most of all, whom I have grieved for.

Instead, Iraq has imploded in a sectarian nightmare. The brutality of the Occupation has made a lie of liberation philosophy. Generations of Iraqi children will hate the West. The U.S. has lost a major regional ally in the Middle East for the future, while Iran has gained a powerful partner and neighbor, certain to check U.N. efforts of nuclear containment.

War has cost us all so much.

That's why I was held under indictment for five years—through two Presidential elections in 2004 and 2008. Pro-War leaders in Washington would stop at nothing to hide those opportunities from daylight. Republican leaders particularly enjoyed strutting about, in the circus glitz of their anti-terrorism policy, though it was mostly spectacle and showmanship, without hard achievements to support the glamour. It suited Washington to pretend that Saddam's government had been a stalwart supporter of terrorists in the Middle East, instead of a covetous western ally who despised—and in fact, persecuted—Islamic fundamentalists.

Despite all of that, given the cynicism of our time—and the thundering rage and desperation that the world now faces—I believe that it's critical for Americans and the world community to understand that dialogue with Iraq succeeded.

Diplomacy and engagement worked all sorts of wonders in Baghdad.

No matter that the conflict loomed large, and appeared hopeless, in fact, hopes for peace remained intact and undaunted until the very end.

I believe that's hopeful for the world, because it shows that peaceful outcomes can succeed in other conflicts confronting the world today. Dialogue accomplished so much, even at a back channel level. Our team kept our activities below radar, and out of media range for good reason. Yet our approach was results oriented and effective. And we accomplished each part of our objectives, which promoted U.S. interests on a broad spectrum. Those were tough standards, too.

Now more than ever, it is imperative to recognize that dialogue can be so fruitful, in what otherwise appears to be the most hopeless situations.

The greatest obstacle to peace with Iraq was the ambition of War itself, and the common belief among ordinary people that diplomacy could not achieve results, and therefore would not be worth the time to pursue aggressively.

That mentality handicapped us. It was wrong. And it needs to change. Contrary to what people think, dialogue did not fail. Our resolve for crisis resolution failed. That lack of resolve presents our greatest danger today.

In my personal experience dealing directly with Libya and Iraq—two "pariah" nations in the 1990s— there is never a point at which dialogue cannot achieve results. No matter how difficult it appears, all things are possible through communication, even negotiating a pathway through conflicts that have been declared impossible and intractable— which definitely described Lockerbie and the weapons inspections.

There are four necessary ingredients for success, I believe.

First, dialogue requires the courage of leadership to face problems head on, and to work beyond the level of propaganda. Secondly, it requires a commitment to see solutions through to the end, without giving up at the first stumble. I have conservatively estimated that I met with Libyan and Iraqi diplomats 150 times each. In both situations, the work took longer than originally expected, but accomplished much more good than we hoped to achieve at the start. By the time the United Nations jumped in, the scope of discussions was much broader and higher grade. The full scale of opportunities was much more dynamic than the public realized.

Thirdly, I believe that crisis dialogue should be handled covertly at the start, as the most effective method of exploring creative options, and building possible scenarios that have not been considered before. Public debate in the media creates a demand for change, which is necessary and good. But media grandstanding does not advance the development of complex and potentially intricate solutions to problems. Premature media exposure can kill ideas. And that's self-defeating. The goal should be to nurture an atmosphere of the possible, with a priority for exploring the most innovative strategies for achieving those goals.

Finally—and this is critical, though somewhat obvious—it's vital to communicate respect for cultural and religious differences, even for those nations who qualify as our opponents. These individuals must be treated respectfully. They must become partners in bringing about a policy shift. As Iraq's package of democracy reforms show, they too have ideas and strategies to contribute, which might surprise the most hardened cynic with the quality of their innovations. They have a stake in the success of the project. Their cooperation is vital for the end game.

That was the essence of the approach that I used. And I assure you that we accomplished much more in Iraq than we originally expected by applying that approach.

For that matter, consider what my team accomplished with Libya:

It took one woman talking to Libyan diplomats, through a back channel started in 1995 to break the impasse on the Lockerbie Trial. Today Libya has stopped functioning as a sanctuary for terrorists and renounced the development of Weapons of Mass Destruction, (both causes that I championed privately). Tripoli has also moved to develop economic ties with Europe.

As of today, Libya has embraced global relations, and filled a seat on the United Nations Security Council.

Many would like to attribute Libya's change to the United Nations sanctions. They would be wrong. Dialogue and engagement changed the dynamic with Libya, thanks in large part to my team's efforts, joined by Egyptian President Hosni Mubarak, who moved things forward in a highly effective and covert way. Our process of engagement made a deliberate point of showing respect for Libya's identity and Islamic heritage, and appreciation for the value of Libya's potential contributions to North Africa.

It was dialogue that accomplished those results. And that's hopeful for other apparently intractable conflicts looming over our world, whether it's Sudan or Iran or North Korea.

Dialogue! Dialogue! Dialogue! Communication can succeed beyond our wildest hopes at the start. Dialogue creates more opportunities by the end. The transformation of relations runs much deeper and broader than the original scope of the project.

Finally, I hope that the United Nations would embrace its fullest potential as a forum for engagement, and play a much greater role in crisis resolution in the future. When it came to Iraq and Libya, the United Nations stayed out of discussions until a structural framework for the agreement had already been reached. That meant United Nations diplomats only got involved once Libya had agreed to the concept of the Lockerbie Trial, and after Iraq agreed to resume the weapons inspections, according to the maximum standards of transparency dictated by the United States. Until an agreement was reached, the United Nations stayed out of crisis talks.

The United Nations expended no political capital to achieve those results. In fairness, with regards to Iraq, U.S. intelligence wanted to avoid U.N. input, in order to guarantee that Washington controlled the agenda. However, it is also true that the U.N. showed no inclination to engage in conflict resolution with Iraq. They were quite happy to stay out of it. The United Nations was never at the front of leadership. That role must change in future conflicts.

DIALOGUE! DIALOGUE! AND DEMOCRACY!

There was a critical exception on Iraq. Malaysia's Ambassador to the United Nations, the Honorable Hasmy Agam and his senior diplomatic staff on the Security Council, Rani Ali got involved on the sidelines from the beginning of the talks in November, 2000.

Malaysia's Embassy at the United Nations provided invaluable technical guidance, encouragement and attention to this matter. Because of their input, we guaranteed that Iraq's commitment to weapons inspections would comport with U.N. standards for verifying disarmament, as necessary to end the sanctions.

Likewise, Syria deserves praise for its urgent actions to help avert war, as a member of the Security Council, offering to act as a back channel intermediary in the run up to the Invasion.

In that success lies hope for future conflicts. The American people and the world community need to know that engagement can be trusted to produce substantial results that can be highly innovative.

Dialogue can achieve results—with a little help from democracy.

I am a huge believer in democracy. In my opinion, it is a precious thing for ordinary people to have the right to contribute to public life and public debates. Democracy empowers the people to believe in their own contributions. Without doubt, the practice of those freedoms and the process of seeking public input are messy, argumentative and contentious. And yet it's vital for the public good. We must take special care to safeguard those civil rights, and not tolerate them to be degraded by the "lip service" of Washington politicians.

Throughout my nightmare on the Patriot Act, it struck me as unforgivable that American soldiers have been sent to die and kill for democracy in Iraq and Afghanistan, but America's leaders resent the practice of democracy at home. My crime was actively practicing freedom of speech and criticizing government policy. That my warnings about Iraq and 9/11 hit the mark with such accuracy aggravated leaders in Washington and London. But perhaps that misses the point. If I had been wrong, I should still have the right to speak.

Alas, they had power. And they used that power to make sure I understood that I had none.

In their mind, I was nothing.

Just another American.

Well, that's fine with me. I happen to enjoy being "just another American."

There's a ubiquitous saying that actions speak louder than words. In which case, all of us should sit up and take notice. The actions of Washington's leaders betrayed a conviction that the American people need to stay out of governance and policy making. If we interject ourselves into the public debate, believing in our democratic rights to contribute, believing our country belongs to us, and that our leaders should be accountable to us, then these politicians have decided we should be removed and punished until we learn to accept our disenfranchisement.

Our participation is no longer welcomed.

Worst of all, in the Patriot Act, Congress has created a tool of punishment to shut us up, if Americans don't get the message. We can be silenced through secret accusations. The government has no burden to show evidence that a crime has been committed. They don't have to show evidence to a grand jury. They don't have to show proof to a Judge. The FBI and Prosecutors have no burden to confess afterwards that a defendant had a legitimate alibi for the alleged wrongdoing. American citizens can be detained indefinitely without trial. They can lock us up on military bases, abusing the integrity of our soldiers, and deny us access to our attorneys.

All constitutional protections are formally revoked.

For those reasons, the Patriot Act endangers our entire way of life as a country, and our entire purpose as a people.

Many Americans would like to presume that George Bush did this. And he's gone. So we're safe now.

No mistake could be greater. Republican leaders as a whole orchestrated this attack on my rights, under the Patriot Act. It was primarily carried out by supporters of Senator John McCain, who reigns over the Senate to this day. My attackers, who deprived me of my rights for five long years, were petty bureaucrats and party officials of the sort memorialized by Franz Kafka. In the aftermath of this debacle, they have not gone away. On the contrary, they have burrowed more deeply into the power structure of Washington DC. They remain entrenched in Washington society at all levels. Only now I fear that they have learned how to use the Patriot Act successfully as a weapon against their fellow Americans. By their actions, they showed that they will not be dissuaded by Americans traditions of liberty and justice that they should protect.

That means this kind of thing is going to happen more and more frequently. They're going to become bolder and more vicious—until Americans demand that the Patriot Act must be repealed.

Free thinking Americans face the greatest risk of all.

I was one of the first American-born citizens targeted by the Patriot Act. I won't be the last. While I was under indictment, in Maryland where I live, State Police decided that local environmentalists campaigning to stop global warming qualified as potential "terrorists," and should be subjected to surveillance allowed by the Patriot Act, as well.

Applying the extraordinary power of the Patriot Act that equates civil disobedience with possible sedition, Maryland State police targeted anti-war leaders, opponents of the death penalty, and environmental leaders like the Chesapeake Climate Action Network, dedicated to protecting our precious earth from over-exploitation. Environmentalists who supported solar energy and wind power, recycling programs, cutting fuel emissions and controlling pollution, these advocates of non-violent environmentalism got singled out as potential threats to civil order.

Invoking the Patriot Act, Maryland State Police wire tapped their phones, and targeted activists for broad surveillance operations. At least one State Trooper infiltrated several peace groups to monitor upcoming activities and events.

In the twisted schematics of this new surveillance culture, the DC Anti-War Network, which opposes violence and killing, got designated a "white supremacist group," without explanation. Amnesty International got investigated for "civil rights violations." Animal rights activists working with People for the Ethical Treatment of Animals (PETA) were labeled "a security threat." Groups opposed to the death penalty were declared "potentially violent."

I ask myself often. How did America lose its heart? When did we lose faith in the values of liberty in our country? Because that's what happening today. We are afraid of freedom.

DIALOGUE! DIALOGUE! AND DEMOCRACY!

Unless we take action to repeal the Patriot Act, many more independent thinking Americans will get harmed. Our leaders should be forced to prove their loyalty to the people and our democracy by disavowing its terrible precepts. It is a law of treachery. There's nothing "patriotic" about tearing down the freedoms promised by our beloved Constitution. That's traitorous.

For myself, I have no regrets for what I paid to support my values. I stood up for what I love. My work gave me the greatest sense of personal satisfaction, adventures and achievement that I could have hoped for. Knowing the consequences, I would change nothing, even if I could.

These days I am a "free agent" for peace and non-violence. I still live in Takoma Park doing animal rescue work, with my little family of dachshunds and kitty cats.

My Japanese weeping cherry tree, planted the week of my arrest, still grows in my front yard, serene and undisturbed by the tumultuous times of our world.

Each spring, my peace tree blossoms in white petals again. And though all of us working together failed to stop this tragic War in Iraq, in my heart I am content to know that all of us tried so hard together.

As Odysseus Elytis wrote about the fight against fascism in Greece: "Let them stone us. Let them say that we walk with our heads in the clouds. Those who have never felt, my friend, with what stone, what blood, what iron, what fire we build, dream and sing."[633]

Five days before the inauguration of President Barak Obama, the Justice Department formally dismissed all charges against Susan Lindauer.[634] In five years of indictment as an alleged "Iraqi Agent," she was never convicted of any crime. And she never stopped demanding her rights to a trial.

417

AFFIDAVIT OF
PARKE GODFREY

I am Dr. Parke Godfrey, a tenured associate professor in the Department of Computer Science and Engineering at York University in Toronto, Canada. At the request of Ms. Lindauer, I am providing this brief affidavit describing parts of my testimony at a hearing before Judge Loretta Preska in June, 2008.

1. I have known Ms. Lindauer since 1991, while I was working on my doctoral degree at the University of Maryland, College Park. We were close friends until I moved to Toronto to accept a faculty post at York University in August of 1999.
    a. During that time, I spoke with Ms. Lindauer two or three times weekly, and we met once weekly, on average.
    b. Ms. Lindauer has an artistic and mercurial temperament. She is passionate as an activist supporting her causes. She is a creative writer and former journalist. I never observed mental instability or mental illness in her behavior.

2. Ms. Lindauer had various concerns and predictions of terrorist attacks, which she confided in me and others.
    a. In the year 2000, coinciding with the Lockerbie Trial, Ms. Lindauer confided in me on several occasions her concern that the next terrorist attack on the United States would involve airplane hijackings and/or airplane bombings. She warned me to stay out of New York City.

b. In the spring and summer of 2001, on several occasions Ms. Lindauer expressed heightened concern that a terrorist attack was in the works that would strike the southern part of Manhattan. She claimed it would reprise the 1993 attack on the World Trade Center. She described the attack as completing the cycle started in that first attack.

c. I have read articles by Michael Collins describing Ms. Lindauer's 9/11 warning, and I am satisfied that he has accurately described my testimony before Judge Preska in June, 2008.

3. I was involved in Ms. Lindauer's case in various ways after her arrest.

a. In September, 2004, I was interviewed by the FBI in Mississauga (adjacent to Toronto) in the presence of a Royal Canadian Mounted Policeman. (The RCMP insisted upon this as the interview was in Canada, and I was a Canadian resident). I spoke with FBI Special Agent Suzan LeTourneau. While the interview focused on mundane details of Ms. Lindauer's life and her acquaintances, the conversation did touch briefly upon the indictment on Ms. Lindauer, and her predictions.

b. I made myself available to speak with the investigator working for her defense attorney. I was prepared for a lengthy conversation, including a discussion of Ms. Lindauer's 9/11 warning. I was surprised when the defense investigator cut short the conversation after only five to ten minutes. His questions seemed far inadequate for the scope of the indictment against Ms. Lindauer, and for what I felt I had to share with her Defense Attorney.

c. Several months later, I contacted Ms. Lindauer's uncle, Ted Lindauer, who spoke with me at greater length about several issues in her case. I can verify that Ms. Lindauer felt compelled to seek her uncle's assistance interviewing witnesses for her case, before she got sent to Carswell.

d. In early December 2005, I believe, a few months after Ms. Lindauer had been sent to Carswell Prison, I spoke with the psychologist handling her competence evaluation for the Court. During our conversation, I attempted to confirm with him that Ms. Lindauer had made predictions about a terrorist attack in Manhattan to me and others prior to the 9/11 attack. He seemed to have no interest in hearing this. Our conversation was brief.

4. I continued to be involved in Ms. Lindauer's case, in hearings leading up to her trial, which never transpired.

a. In my opinion, contrary with the Justice Department's lawyers, Ms. Lindauer is now, and always was, competent to stand trial. The decision to accuse her of incompetence was baffling to me and many others. I was forced to conclude that it was politically motivated to block her request for a trial.

b. While she was still detained in prison, I offered to travel from Toronto and testify at any competency hearing, as a character witness, on her mental competence, on what I knew of her political activities before her indictment, about her warnings of terrorist attacks, and any other aspects for which the Court might be interested.

c.   I attended the hearing on forcible drugging in May, 2006. I offered to testify on that day. In fact, I arrived at the Court, assuming I was to testify. However, her attorney, Mr. Sam Talkin did not call me to testify that day. In conversation that day, I told him that she had made warnings of a terrorist attack to me and to others in advance of 9/11. I told him that I was mortified by what the Court seemed to be doing.

d.   In June 2008, *two years later,* Ms. Lindauer was finally allowed to have a hearing on her competence to stand trial. I testified before Judge Preska, who had replaced Judge Mukasey after his retirement, that I considered Ms. Lindauer fully competent in all ways, and devoid of mental illness or instability. I testified about the terrorist warnings, and how I had spoken with the FBI in September, 2004.

Despite my friendship with Ms. Lindauer, and my dislike and distrust of activities of the Federal Administration at the time, I tried to keep an open mind and to cooperate with the prosecution. I could only hope that the government had just cause in pursuing such a case, given the vigor and energy they put in it, despite what that would mean for Susan. Otherwise, it is a poor indictment for justice.

On the other hand, I have never had any direct reasons to believe the points of the indictment against Ms. Lindauer, or evidence myself of them. I have confidence and trust in Ms. Lindauer. Furthermore, I have been completely appalled over the way the Justice Department proceeded in its dealings with Ms. Lindauer, as I hope most anyone familiar with her case would be.

Throughout this entire ordeal, Ms. Lindauer has suffered harassment. She faced inexcusable delays in setting a trial date (or in dropping the charges). She was repeatedly questioned in Court over the reliability of her terrorist warnings, despite that they had been corroborated by me and by many others in affidavits and under oath, in spoken testimony. She was incarcerated in a mental facility within a federal prison for seven months, 1,300 miles from her home for supposed observation. And then held in confinement for months afterwards. The FBI and the U.S. Attorney's Office's behavior in Ms. Lindauer case were abhorrent. It's quite clear that much more was going on.

Susan Lindauer's story should be told.

Dr. Parke Godfrey July 1, 2010

AFFIDAVIT OF
THAYER LINDAUER

I have practiced corporate law for 40 years in the U.S. and international arenas. Though my expertise lies outside criminal law, I took my degree at the University of Chicago and I have extensive legal experience. I am quite satisfied that my niece, Susan Lindauer, has accurately described my involvement in her legal fight, and the events related to her incarceration at Carswell Prison.

As she relates, six months prior to her imprisonment, I interviewed several important witnesses in her case, who forthrightly authenticated her claims. Those witnesses included Edward MacKechnie, Scottish Solicitor for the Lockerbie Trial, who validated Susan's long-time work relationship with Dr. Richard Fuisz and his known affiliation to the Central Intelligence Agency. I spoke with Paul Hoven, who admitted his role as one of Susan's handlers, and further identified Dr. Fuisz as her second, CIA handler, overseeing her activities at the United Nations. I spoke with Parke Godfrey about Susan's 9/11 warning, and other assundry issues in her case. During her imprisonment, I spoke with a number of other witnesses and friends of Susan's, including, I believe, Ian Ferguson, the Scottish journalist and expert on Lockerbie.

There is no question but that Susan's history as an Asset, supervised by members of U.S. Intelligence, would have been easily proven to the satisfaction of the Court.

For those of us who trust in the legal traditions of this country, her case marked a stunning reversal of expectations. Susan correctly relates that I have tremendous respect for Judge Michael Mukasey and the predicament that he faced. There were serious questions of prosecutorial misconduct and withholding exculpatory knowledge from the Court, since it was quite clear the Justice Department did not want to admit Susan's role in Pre-War Intelligence or the 9/11 investigation, including her 9/11 warning. To incarcerate an American citizen without a trial or due process, however, opposes all of the values that the U.S. Courts seek to uphold.

Though it might seem unlikely, Susan has accurately described the Court proceedings leading up to her prison surrender. That September day, we had no idea why the court had ordered her to appear. Her public attorney insisted the Psychiatric Report by Dr. Stuart Kleinman was still unavailable to him. Until we got to Court, we had no idea they intended to send her to prison, or deny her rights to a competence hearing, which is routine procedure.

I did instruct her to fire Sam Talkin, and name me as co-counsel of her defense, so that I could demand a hearing on her behalf. It is true that the Court clerk instructed us that if Susan tried such a thing, she would be seized immediately by U.S. Marshals, and would forfeit her bail for the remainder of the proceedings. She was advised that if she consented to delay the hearing until after the Prison Evaluation, she would have three days to get her affairs in order. Judge Mukasey amended that to 10 days.

There was no doubt that Susan wanted the hearing.

It is possible that Judge Mukasey expected Carswell's evaluation to be very brief. Normally, these sorts of evaluations take 6 to 8 weeks, for other non-political defendants. Indeed, after the court meeting, Judge Mukasey's clerk suggested to me that Susan would probably come home before Christmas.

Unfortunately, the politics of her contributions to Pre-War Intelligence and the 9/11 investigation swamped the proceedings. She has not exaggerated the threat of "indefinite" detention that she faced, or the aggressive push to forcibly drug her with Haldol.

It is absolutely correct that Carswell's psychology staff, the U.S. Attorney's Office in New York, the FBI and the main Justice Department had direct knowledge that Susan had told the truth about her Asset work. I have spoken to witnesses myself, who told me that they assured the FBI and/or psychologists at Carswell that Susan was telling the truth. I must conclude the request for forcible drugging was politically motivated.

Finally, Susan has stated correctly that I made three attempts to visit her at Carswell, driving 700 miles each way. On the first two tries, guards refused to admit me to the military base, telling me no prison was there. The second time, guards insisted the prison was closed on weekends. Only when Judge Mukasey ordered U.S. Marshals to stand by as an escort was I admitted. This occurred at a critical moment, when I was trying to broker a solution that would satisfy the Court and secure her freedom. At that point, we just wanted her home. The decision on competence was secondary to protecting her from forcible drugging and winning her release.

"Extreme prejudice" strikes me as an appropriate title, given what the government tried to do.

Ted Lindauer

APPENDIX

OFFICIAL IRAQI RESPONSE TO 9/11

5843

1. If the request had been made in different circumstances it would have been possible for us to agree or go a long with it.
2. With continuation of U.S and U.K aggression and the tense atmospher in The United State of America against Iraq any step to be taken by Iraq might be intepretated in a harmful manner to Iraqi reputation and to the keeness of Iraq to maintain its dignity.
3. Despite of that all the points proposed by you reflect the real Iraqi position.
4. If U.S declared that it intends to halt(stop) the air raid against Iraq(or such thing like this) in order to concentrate on other Matters the stuation would be different (better).
5. However we are prepared to meet any American official in a covert or incovert manner to discuss the common issues.
6. In any case Iraq has suffered from terrorism and its leaders including his excellency Mr. President has been a target to many assassination attempts in addition to the attepmt to assassinate Mr. Tariq Aziz in first of April 1980 , in fact he was injured, as well as some Iraqi leadership members who sufferd from such terrorist acts.
7. Iraq demostrated a good faith towards U.S.A in 1993 after Oklahoma trade center previous accident , and informed American government through Iraqi interest section in Washigton That it (Iraq) was prepared to provide U.S.A With Some Information about the prepetrators of 1993 accident if American would send a delegate to Baghdad , but the American side dealt with our offer improperly and they said to Us (Iraq) to deliver thes information, that means evetually They rejected to meet us.
8. This is the Iraq officiall position.

EXTREME PREJUDICE

CLASSIFIED INFORMATION NONDISCLOSURE AGREEMENT

AN AGREEMENT BETWEEN ~~SANFORD NOLAN TALLIN~~   AND THE UNITED STATES
(Name of Individual – Printed or typed)

1. Intending to be legally bound, I hereby accept the obligations contained in this Agreement in consideration of my being granted access to classified information. As used in this Agreement, classified information is marked or unmarked classified information, including oral communications, that is classified under the standards of Executive Order 12356, or under any other Executive order or statute that prohibits the unauthorized disclosure of information in the interest of national security; and unclassified information that meets the standards for classification and is in the process of a classification determination as provided in Sections 1.1 and 1.2(e) of Executive Order 12356, or under any other Executive order or statute that requires protection for such information in the interest of national security. I understand and accept that by being granted access to classified information, special confidence and trust shall be placed in me by the United States Government.

2. I hereby acknowledge that I have received a security indoctrination concerning the nature and protection of classified information, including the procedures to be followed in ascertaining whether other persons to whom I contemplate disclosing this information have been approved for access to it, and that I understand these procedures.

3. I have been advised that the unauthorized disclosure, unauthorized retention, or negligent handling of classified information by me could cause damage or irreparable injury to the United States or could be used to advantage by a foreign nation. I hereby agree that I will never divulge classified information to anyone unless: (a) I have officially verified that the recipient has been properly authorized by the United States Government to receive it; or (b) I have been given prior written notice of authorization from the United States Government Department or Agency (hereinafter Department or Agency) responsible for the classification of the information or last granting me a security clearance that such disclosure is permitted. I understand that if I am uncertain about the classification status of information, I am required to confirm from an authorized official that the information is unclassified before I may disclose it, except to a person as provided in (a) or (b), above. I further understand that I am obligated to comply with laws and regulations that prohibit the unauthorized disclosure of classified information.

4. I have been advised that any breach of this Agreement may result in the termination of any security clearances I hold; removal from any position of special confidence and trust requiring such clearances; or the termination of my employment or other relationships with the Departments or Agencies that granted my security clearance or clearances. In addition, I have been advised that any unauthorized disclosure of classified information by me may constitute a violation, or violations, of United States criminal laws, including the provisions of Sections 641, 793, 794, 798, and *952, Title 18, United States Code, *the provisions of Section 783(b), Title 50, United States Code, and the provisions of the Intelligence Identities Protection Act of 1982. I recognize that nothing in this Agreement constitutes a waiver by the United States of the right to prosecute me for any statutory violation.

5. I hereby assign to the United States Government all royalties, remunerations, and emoluments that have resulted, will result or may result from any disclosure, publication, or revelation of classified information not consistent with the terms of this Agreement.

6. I understand that the United States Government may seek any remedy available to it to enforce this Agreement including, but not limited to, application for a court order prohibiting disclosure of information in breach of this Agreement.

7. I understand that all classified information to which I have access or may obtain access by signing this Agreement is now and will remain the property of, or under the control of the United States Government unless and until otherwise determined by an authorized official or final ruling of a court of law. I agree that I shall return all classified materials which have, or may come into my possession or for which I am responsible because of such access: (a) upon demand by an authorized representative of the United States Government; (b) upon the conclusion of my employment or other relationship with the Department or Agency that last granted me a security clearance or that provided me access to classified information; or (c) upon the conclusion of my employment or other relationship that requires access to classified information. If I do not return such materials upon request, I understand that this may be a violation of Section 793, Title 18, United States Code, a United States criminal law.

8. Unless and until I am released in writing by an authorized representative of the United States Government, I understand that all conditions and obligations imposed upon me by this Agreement apply during the time I am granted access to classified information, and at all times thereafter.

9. Each provision of this Agreement is severable. If a court should find any provision of this Agreement to be unenforceable, all other provisions of this Agreement shall remain in full force and effect.

10. These restrictions are consistent with and do not supersede, conflict with or otherwise alter the employee obligations, rights or liabilities created by Executive Order 12356; Section 7211 of Title 5, United States Code (governing disclosures to Congress); Section 1034 of Title 10, United States Code, as amended by the Military Whistleblower Protection Act (governing disclosure to Congress by members of the military); Section 2302(b)(8) of Title 5, United States Code, as amended by the Whistleblower Protection Act (governing disclosures of illegality, waste, fraud, abuse or public health or safety threats); the Intelligence Identities Protection Act of 1982 (50 U.S.C 421 et seq.) (governing disclosures that could expose confidential Government agents), and the statutes which protect against disclosure that may compromise the national security, including Sections 641, 793, 794, 798, and 952 of Title 18, United States Code, and Section 4(b) of the Subversive Activities Act of 1950 (50 U.S.C. Section 783(b)). The definitions, requirements, obligations, rights, sanctions and liabilities created by said Executive Order and listed statutes are incorporated into this Agreement and are controlling.

(Continue on reverse.)

NSN 7540-01-280-5499
Previous edition not usable.

312-102

STANDARD FORM 312 (REV. 1–91)
Prescribed by GSA/ISOO
32 CFR 2003, E.O. 12356

APPENDIX

NON-DISCLOSURE FOR CLASSIFIED DEBRIEFING

11. I have read this Agreement carefully and my questions, if any, have been answered. I acknowledge that the briefing officer has made available to me the Executive Order and statutes referenced in this Agreement and its implementing regulation (32 CFR Section 2003.20) so that I may read them at this time, if I so choose.

SIGNATURE	DATE	SOCIAL SECURITY NUMBER (See Notice below)
	2/10/05	████████████

ORGANIZATION (IF CONTRACTOR, LICENSEE, GRANTEE OR AGENT, PROVIDE: NAME, ADDRESS, AND, IF APPLICABLE, FEDERAL SUPPLY CODE NUMBER) (Type or print)

SANFORD N. TALKIN
TALKIN & MUCCIGROSSO LLP
0 EXCHANGE PLACE, SUITE 180
NEW YORK, NEW YORK 10005

SANFORD N. TALKIN
TALKIN, MUCCIGROSSO & ROBERTS, LLP
40 EXCHANGE PLACE, SUITE 1800
NEW YORK, NEW YORK 10005
(212) 482-0007

WITNESS	ACCEPTANCE
THE EXECUTION OF THIS AGREEMENT WAS WITNESSED BY THE UNDERSIGNED.	THE UNDERSIGNED ACCEPTED THIS AGREEMENT ON BEHALF OF THE UNITED STATES GOVERNMENT.

SIGNATURE	DATE	SIGNATURE	DATE

NAME AND ADDRESS (Type or print)	NAME AND ADDRESS (Type or print)

SECURITY DEBRIEFING ACKNOWLEDGEMENT

I reaffirm that the provisions of the espionage laws, other federal criminal laws and executive orders applicable to the safeguarding of classified information have been made available to me; that I have returned all classified information in my custody; that I will not communicate or transmit classified information to any unauthorized person or organization; that I will promptly report to the Federal Bureau of Investigation any attempt by an unauthorized person to solicit classified information, and that I (have) (have not) (strike out inappropriate word or words) received a security debriefing.

SIGNATURE OF EMPLOYEE	DATE

NAME OF WITNESS (Type or print)	SIGNATURE OF WITNESS

NOTICE: The Privacy Act, 5 U.S.C. 552a, requires that federal agencies inform individuals, at the time information is solicited from them, whether the disclosure is mandatory or voluntary, by what authority such information is solicited, and what uses will be made of the information. You are hereby advised that authority for soliciting your Social Security Account Number (SSN) is Executive Order 9397. Your SSN will be used to identify you precisely when it is necessary to 1) certify that you have access to the information indicated above or 2) determine that your access to the information indicated has terminated. Although disclosure of your SSN is not mandatory, your failure to do so may impede the processing of such certifications or determinations, or possibly result in the denial of your being granted access to classified information.

* NOT APPLICABLE TO NON-GOVERNMENT PERSONNEL SIGNING THIS AGREEMENT.

STANDARD FORM 312 BACK (REV. 1-91)

FAX COVER SHEET

DEFENSE INTELLIGENCE AGENCY

Office of General Counsel
Pentagon 2E-238, Washington, DC 20301-7400

TEL: (703) 697-3945 FAX: (703) 697-4276

Date: ___4 Feb 05_____   Verified Time Faxed: _____

From: Mr. Schapler

To: Mr. Talkin

FAX: 212-482-1303

Telephone: __ ___ _____

Subject: Letter in response to a subpoena

1. Classification: Top Secret:____   Secret:_ _ Confidential:_____ Unclassified: __X_

2. Priority: _____ ROUTINE. (By next business day.) Verification is unnecessary.
          ___X_ QUICK. (Within 2 hours.) Verification is unnecessary.

3. Hard copy to follow? Yes: '   No:

4. Comments: *Please call our office if all pages are not received.*

   Original will be mailed. A copy of this letter will be FAXED
   to Mr. O'Callaghan

                                        Page__1__of ⟋ Pages

APPENDIX

CARSWELL OBSERVATION REPORT

Exhibit 3

Federal Medical Center, Carswell
Fort Worth, Texas
Patient Name: Lindauer, Susan
          Date: 02/22/06
          Pass: yes
	INDIVIDUAL
	EVALUATION/TREATMENT/MANAGEMENT PLAN
	Continuation Sheet

DSM-III-R WORKING DIAGNOSES: FORENSIC EVALUATION
                                 R/O DELUSIONAL DISORDER   *NONE — WITNESS PROVES IT'S ALL TRUE*

PATIENT WEAKNESSES: Impaired of no relaity contact Lacks insight into illness	PATIENT STRENGTHS: Good physical health Socializes well Good intellectual functioning

PRIMARY CLINICIAN: DR. VAS	SECONDARY CLINICIAN: DR. SHADDUCK
PRIMARY NURSE: NURSE FUERTES-ASSINI	ATTENDING PHYSICIAN:

NSG DX: Potential for Impaired Social Interaction
        Altered thought process

GOAL NO. 1: The patient has been court ordered to a **120** day forensic evaluation.

OBJECTIVES: Patient will undergo clinical interviews, behavioral observations, and
                  psychological testing.

ACTION PLAN:
orensic Evaluation (Psychology)
onitor and document behaviors (Nursing)
orrectional Counseling/Observation
risis Intervention (Counselor)

TARGET DATE:

TREATMENT REVIEW:
2/22/06 Ms. Lindauer is functioning well on the unit. A referral has been sent to the court.

X _____Susan Lindauer_____
   PATIENT SIGNATURE AND DATE

ADDRESSOGRAPH:
MC, Carswell, TX

11
0

429

| PROB 46 (1/86) | **MONTHLY TREATMENT REPORT** | | This form must be completed and submitted with each monthly billing. Additional sheets may be used. | |

1. Program		2. Contract Number	2a. Fund Control Number
Family Health Center		416-04-MHPG	CANAL, RC

| Lindauer, Susan | PACT# | 4. For Period Covering 1-1-05 / 1-31-05 | |

5. Phase	5a. Time in Phase	6. Pretrial Client	7. Client Employed
II	Since 00/00/00	false	

8. CONTACTS SINCE LAST REPORT

a. Date	b. Service	c. Procedure		d. Duration	e. Comments
6-Jan	6010	Mental Health Individual	counseling	60 Min.	
20-Jan	6010	Mental Health Individual	counseling	60 Min.	
27-Jan	6010	Mental Health Individual	counseling	60 Min.	

9. URINE TESTING RECORD

Date Collected	Scheduled	Sample Not Tested	Use Admitted	Collected by	Special Test	Test Results

10. COMMENTS REGARDING CLIENT'S TREATMENT PROGRESS

Ms. Lindauer reports for therapy as required. She appears to maintain psychological stability and shows no sign or symptom of mania or psychosis. However, she appears concerned about the outcome of her legal problem.

Signature of Counselor

Bud L_____

PhD, LCPC, CAS

Date 2/9/2005

PROB 46 (1/86)	**MONTHLY TREATMENT REPORT**		This form must be completed and submitted with each monthly billing. Additional sheets may be used.	

1. Program			2. Contract Number	2a. Fund Control Number
	Family Health Center		416-04-MHPG	CANAL, RC

			4. For Period Covering
Lindauer, Susan	PACT#		3-1-05 / 3-31-05

5. Phase	5a. Time in Phase	6. Pretrial Client	7. Client Employed
II	Since 00/00/00	false	

8. CONTACTS SINCE LAST REPORT

a. Date	b. Service	c. Procedure	d. Duration	e. Comments
10-Mar	6010	Mental Health Individual counseling	60 Min.	

9. URINE TESTING RECORD

Date Collected	Scheduled	Sample Not Tested	Use Admitted	Collected by	Special Test	Test Results

10. COMMENTS REGARDING CLIENT'S TREATMENT PROGRESS

Ms. Lindauer attended one therapy session this month. She reported that she gained a full-time employment and remained concerned about her legal problem. So far she has shown no sign of mania or depression and symptom of any psychosis that may require additional intervention.

Signature of Counselor			Date
PhD, LCPC, CAS			4/7/2005

Exhibit 2

U.S. DEPARTMENT OF JUSTICE
FEDERAL BUREAU OF PRISONS
FMC, CARSWELL

NOTICE OF MEDICATION HEARING
AND ADVISEMENT OF RIGHTS

To: Susan Lindauer   Reg. No.:   56064-054

Diagnosis: Psychotic Disorder Not Otherwise Specified

Proposed Treatment: Antipsychotics, Benzodiazepeines, Antidepressanst, Mood Stabilizers

Reason for Treatment: Restoration of Competency, Treatment of Delusions.

In order to consider whether or not you should be given psychotropic medication, you are being

referred for a hearing. The hearing will convene on   12/28/05   at   11:30 a.m.

at the following location M-1 conference room

You are entitled to be present at the hearing and to present evidence at the hearing. You are also

entitled to have a staff member represent you at the hearing and if institutional security is not

threatened, to call witnesses. You may also request that staff witnesses be cross examined.

The inmate desires to have witnesses.   Yes   No

Name

Name

Name

The inmate requests that the following staff member represent her.

Name

The Administrator of the Mental Health Division appointed the following staff member to

represent the inmate:

Name   A. Damonze

MS. LINDAUER   REFUSES   TO   SIGN

~~Date~~ X   ~~Signature~~ X

Notice of Hearing given to inmate on   12/23/05   at   12:30 p.m.

by

Staff Member Signature   COLLIN   JOHN   VAS
                                                        Printed Name

U.S. DEPARTMENT OF JUSTICE

APPENDIX

CARSWELL DRUG RECOMMENDATIONS

3.　**SUMMARY OF EVIDENCE**

　　a.　**Patient Statement:** (Summary of patient's statement regarding treatment with psychiatric medication. Attach any documentation provided by patient.)

Ms. Lindauer reported she was against medication of any kind, including psychotropic medication.

She denied the possibility of mental illness, once again reporting in detail her belief that the government is having her detained because she represents a threat to the administration due to her differing beleifs about their policies on Iraq. She states she has been a government agent for 4 years working in "anti terrorism".

Ms. Lindauer denied any wish to hurt herself or others and denied any history of aggressive behavior.

ENDNOTES FOR
EXTREME PREJUDICE

1   FBI photograph of front door barricaded by plywood
2   FBI arrest record, March 11, 2004
3   Federal Indictment for Susan Lindauer, Southern District of New York, co-defendants Al Anbuke.
4   Supreme Court Overturns Sentencing guidelines, Washington Post A-1, December 2004
5   Federal Indictment, Southern District of New York
6   FBI transcript. Meeting with Bassem Youssef, June 26, 2003
7   Television transcripts NBC News, ABC News, March 11, 2004
8   Ibid. Federal Indictment
9   Ibid. Federal Indictment
10 Andy Card Letters from December 2000 to January, 2003.
11 Iraq's response to 9/11, September 21, 2001
12 FBI charges under Federal Sentencing Guidelines
13 Ibid. Federal Indictment.
14 Ibid. Federal Indictment
15 Ibid. Federal Indictment
16 Susan Lindauer Letters to Andrew Card dated March 1, 2001 and December 2, 2001
17 Ibid. Andrew Card Letters
18 Ibid. Federal Indictment
19 Ibid. Federal Indictment
20 Susan Lindauer letter to Andrew Card, December 2, 2001

21   Susan Lindauer Letters to Vice President Richard Cheney and Andrew Card, December 20, 2000 through December 2, 2001
22   Susan Lindauer Letter to Andrew Card, January 8, 2001.
23   FBI Wire Transcripts, phone calls to Senator Lott's staff, February 2, 2004.
24   Ibid. FBI Wire Transcripts, February 2, 2004
25   Susan Lindauer Letter to Vice President Richard Cheney, December 20, 2000.
26   Ibid. FBI Arrest Report
27   Mueller Nomination to head FBI. Washington Post August 3, 2001 GET HEADLINE
28   "Syria dropped on Lockerbie," New York Times. GET HEADLINE
29   Official biography of Robert Mueller
30   Oklahoma City Bombing Revelations, Patrick B. Briley, 2007
     Third Terrorist: The Middle Eastern Connection to the Oklahoma City Bombing, Jayna Davis, 2004.
31   FBI Orders Review of Oklahoma City Bombing Case, March 2005, FBI Archives
32   "Was Nidal Behind Lockerbie Bombing?" Daily Mail, UK July, 2002
33   Intelligence Resource Program
34   Ibid. Daily Mail, UK July 2002
35   Dr. Richard Fuisz. Curriculum Vitae
36   Ibid, Fuisz, C.V.
37   Ibid, Fuisz, C.V.
38   Susan Lindauer 's Lockerbie Statement to Kofi Annan, December 4, 1998
39   Richard Fuisz Deposition, U.S. District Court of Alexandria, Virginia, January, 2000. Law firm of Butera and Andrews.
40   Ibid, Dr. Fuisz Deposition, January 2000, Scottish Solicitor Edward MacKechnie
41   [Richard C. Fuisz Civil Action: 92-0941]
42   [Richard C. Fuisz Civil Action: 92-0941
43   Letter to Edward MacKechnie, Scottish Solicitor, Lockerbie Trial, July, 2000.
44   "Lockerbie: CIA Witness Gagged by U.S. Government, by Neil Mackay and Ian Ferguson. Sunday Herald, Glasgow, Scotland, May 28, 2000
45   U.S. Congress, Oct. 18, 2002
46   History Commons
47   Washington Post, Oct. 1, 2006, History Commons
48   History Commons
49   Le Figaro, 31 October 2001
50   BayArea.Com, June 6, 2002
51   ABC News, September 11, 2001
52   Dr. Parke Godfrey, Court Testimony, Southern District of New York. U.S. vs. Susan Lindauer, June, 2008
53   Ibid. Godfrey Testimony. U.S. vs. Lindauer, June 2008
54   Ibid. Godfrey Testimony, U.S. vs. Lindauer, June 2008
55   Ibid. Godfrey Testimony, U.S. vs. Lindauer, June 2008
56   Ibid. FBI Wiretaps, Susan Lindauer's home telephone, February 2, 2004
57   BBC News, February 26, 1993
58   Wikipedia, Sheikh Abdul Rahmon and Ramzi Youssef
59   Susan Lindauer Journals. Evidence in U.S. vs. Lindauer
60   Ibid. U.S. vs. Lindauer

61 Jacqueline Shelly Lindauer Obituary, Alaska Commercial Fisherman, April, 1992

62 Congressional Testimony by Andrew Zimbalist, Robert A. Woods Professor of Economics, Smith College, House Ways and Means Committee on Economic Effects of U.S. Policy Towards Cuba, March, 1994

63 *Baseball and Billions: A Probing Look Inside the Big Business of Our National Pastime*, Harper Collins. *Business Week* listed *Baseball and Billions* as one of the top eight business books of 1992.

64 Operation El Dorado Canyon, Global Security

65 Paul Hoven bio, Spartacus Education Forums

66 Leslie Cockburn, Out of Control: The Reagan Administration's Secret War in Nicaragua, 1987.

67 Daniel Sheehan bio, Spartacus Education Forum

68 Ibid, Sheehan bio, Spartacus

69 Ibid, Hoven bio, Spartacus Education Forum

70 Spartacus "Education forum" Sept 13, 2007

71 Ibid, "Education forum" Sept 13, 2007

72 David Corn, *Blond Ghost: Ted Shackley and the CIA's Crusades* 1994

73 Ibid, Spartacus Education Forum

74 Ibid, Spartacus Forum

75 Ibid, Spartacus Education Forum, September 13, 2007

76 Susan Lindauer Lockerbie Statement to Kofi Annan, December 4, 1998

77 Ibid. Lindauer Lockerbie Statement, 1998

78 Ibid. Lindauer Lockerbie Statement, 1998

79 Ibid. Letter to Edward MacKechnie, Scottish Solicitor, Lockerbie Trial. July 2000

80 Susan Lindauer Letters to Andrew Card and Vice President Cheney, December 20, 2000 through January 2008.

81 CIA could count on one hand number of agents in Iraq, Washington Post

82 Ibid. Washington Post,
    Federal indictment U.S. vs. Lindauer and Al Anbukes.

83 Testimony of Patricia Kelly O'Meara. U.S. vs. Lindauer, June 2008

84 Susan Lindauer Letter to Andy Card, March 1, 2001

85 Susan Lindauer Letters to Andy Card and Vice President Cheney, December 20, 2000 to January, 2003.

86 Ibid, Lindauer Letters to Andy Card, December 20, 2000 to January, 2003.

87 Ibid. Federal Indictment U.S. vs. Lindauer and Al Anbukes

88 Ibid. Washington Post

89 US Delegation Says Sanctions Draining Iraqi People, Associated Press

90 Iraqis Struggle Under Sanctions." Leon Barkho, February 16, 2000

91 United Nations Accounts of Contracts on Sanctions Hold by Sector

92 Iraqis Struggle Under Sanctions." Leon Barkho, February 16, 2000

93 Ibid. Barkho February 16, 2000

94 Ibid. Barkho, February 16, 2000

95 World Health Organization, United Nations Children's Fund; Iraq Health Ministry tracking statistics

96 Ibid. United Nations Children's Fund, World Health Organization; Iraq Health Ministry

[97] Ibid. World Health Organization, United Nations Children's Fund. December, 1996

[98] Ibid. Iraqis Struggle under Sanctions. Barkho

[99] Ex UN Official Says Sanctions Destroying Iraq, Reuters

[100] Iraqis Say Sanctions Killed Over 11,000 last month, Reuters, 2/23/00)

[101] Ibid. Iraqis Say Sanctions Killed over 11,000 last month

[102] "Foreign Affairs" Journal, John Mueller and Karl Mueller, May/June 1999

[103] Ibid.Ex UN Official says Sanctions Destroying Iraq, Reuters

[104] Top UN official s urges end to trade sanctions," Feb. 8, 2000

[105] Ibid. Top UN official urges end to trade sanctions.

[106] 107 Dennis Halliday online biography

[107] Congressman: Ease Iraq Sanctions, Associated Press

[108] German plane lands in Baghdad to evacuate patient. Aug 20, 2000

[109] UN Rights Body calls for lifting Iraq Embargo."

[110] Ibid. UN Rights Body calls for lifting Iraq Embargo.

[111] TIME Magazine. Jan. 1, 1999 Vol. 153 No. 1

[112] Ibid. TIME Magazine. Jan. 1, 1999 Vol. 153 No. 1

[113] "US Refiners Buying Most of Iraq's Oil"

[114] Middle East Economic Survey, July 16 issue

[115] St Petersburg Times, LUKoil's Iraq Plans Hit by 'Politics'

[116] Letter to Andy Card and Vice President –Elect Richard Cheney, December 20, 2000.

[117] Ibid Letter to Vice President –Elect Cheney, December 20, 2000

[118] Susan Lindauer Letter to Andy Card, December 2, 2001

[119] Ibid. Letter to Andy Card and Vice President-elect Cheney, December 20, 2000

[120] Ibid. Letter to Andy Card and Vice President-elect Cheney, December 20, 2000

[121] Ibid. Letter to Andy Card and Vice President-elect Cheney, December 20, 2000

[122] Ongoing correspondence, UN reports, emails and phone transcripts of communications with Malaysian diplomat Rani Ali from 2000 through December, 2002, when he returned to Kuala Lumpur.

[123] Country Fact Sheet for Malaysia, Central Intelligence Agency

[124] Ibid. Multiple correspondence, phone calls, emails with Rani Ali, Malaysian Embassy

[125] Ibid. Letters to Andy Card from December 20, 2000 through January, 2003

[126] Ibid. Letters to Andy Card from December 20, 2000 through January, 2003

[127] Clark, Wesley, *Keynote: Texas Democratic Party Convention General Wesley K Clark*. June 9, 2006.

[129] *DOD Dictionary of Military and Associated Terms (JP 1-02)*. as amended through April 2010.

[130] NORAD had drills of jets as weapons. USA Today, Steven Komarow and Tom Squitieri April 18, 2004.

[131] Vince Canistraro, <u>CNN, May 13, 2006</u>

[132] Scott, William B., *Exercise Jump-Starts Response to Attacks*. Aviation Week, June 4, 2002.

[133] i. NORAD News Maintains Northern Vigilance Sept. 9, 2001
ii. Ibid. *Exercise Jump-Starts Response to Attacks*. Aviation Week, June 4, 2002.
iii. Complete 911 Timeline, *(6:30 a.m.) September 11, 2001: NORAD on Alert for Emergency Exercises,* Peter Jennings 911 Interviews, ABC News. History Commons, 2010.

ENDNOTES FOR EXTREME PREJUDICE

134. Aviation Week and Space Technology, 6/3/2002; Bergen Record, 12/5/2003
135. ABC News, 9/11/2002
136. From History Commons. *Complete 911 Timeline.* (8:38 a.m.-8:43 a.m.) September 11, 2001)
137. Ibid. Complete 911 Timeline, *(6:30 a.m.) September 11, 2001: NORAD on Alert for Emergency Exercises.* History Commons, 2010.
138. John Arquilla, Naval Postgraduate School, Monterey Herald, Jul. 18, 2002
139. Senate Select Committee on Intelligence and the House Permanent Select Committee on Intelligence, Congressional Reports: Joint Inquiry into Intelligence Community Activities before and after the Terrorist Attacks of September 11, 2001. Government Printing Office, December 20, 2002.
140. Ibid. Joint House-Senate Investigation
141. Ibid. Joint House-Senate Investigation
142. Ibid. Joint House-Senate Investigation
143. Ibid. Joint House-Senate Investigation
144. Ibid. Joint House-Senate Investigation
145. President George W. Bush, Florida Town Hall Meeting, Sept 12, 2001. Bush, George W., *Headline Remarks,* White House, December 4, 2001.
146. CNN.com/Inside Politics, *Bush asks Daschle to limit Sept. 11 probes.* CNN.com, January 29, 2002.
147. Washington Post, Nov. 16, 2005
148. Ibid. "CIA could count Iraqi Agents on one hand," Washington Post
149. FBI Report, U.S. vs. Lindauer and Anbukes
150. FBI Evidence, photos and video, U.S. vs. Lindauer and Anbukes
151. FBI Evidence, Anbuke brothers' pay stubs and IRS tax filings, U.S. vs. Lindauer and Anbukes
152. John McCain, ABC News NIGHTLINE, November 28, 2001
153. Vice President Richard Cheney, "Meet the Press," December 9, 2001
154. Susan Lindauer Letter to Andy Card, July 2001, Committee for Global Preservation of Trade
155. Ibid. Lindauer Letters to Andy Card December 20, 2000 through January, 2003
156. Ibid. Lindauer Letters to Andy Card.
157. Osama Bin Ladin, Jihad Fatwa, April, 1998
158. FBI Evidence, letters, U.S. vs. Lindauer and Anbukes, May 1998
159. FBI Evidence, Interview with Paul Hoven. U.S. vs. Lindauer
160. James Risen and Tim Weiner, the New York Times, October 30, 2001, "Three New Allies Help CIA in its Fight Against Terror." Subheading: "Since Sept 11, CIA officials have opened lines with intelligence officials from several nations that Washington has accused of supporting terrorism."
161. Federal Indictment, U.S. vs. Lindauer
162. FBI Evidence, visa receipts from Viand Restaurant in New York, September, 2001
163. Court testimony and Affidavit, Dr. Parke Godfrey, June 2008
164. FBI Evidence, record of file creation on computer hard drive, U.S. vs. Lindauer
165. Andy Card Letter, September 24, 2001. (ii) Federal indictment U.S. vs. Lindauer
166. Ibid. Andy Card Letter, September 24, 2001
167. Ibid. FBI evidence, restaurant receipt September 22, 2001

439

168. Official Response from the Government of Iraq and Saddam Hussein to 9/11. September 21, 2001.

169. Ibid. Official Iraqi Response to 9/11 attack. (ii) Lindauer letter to Andy Card, September 24, 2001.

170. Ibid. Andy Card Letter, September 24, 2001

171. Ibid. Andy Card Letter, September 24, 2001

172. Ibid. Federal Indictment U.S. vs. Lindauer

173. Ibid. Lindauer Letters to Andy Card.

174. Lindauer Letters to Andy Card, September 24, 2001 and December 2, 2001

175. Ibid. Letter to Andy Card and Vice President-elect Cheney, December 2000

176. Ibid. Lindauer Letters to Andy Card, Dec. 2000 through January, 2003.

177. Ibid. Official Iraqi Response to 9/11.

178. Ibid. Letter to Andy Card, December 2, 2001

179. Documentary Video: "Conspiracy? The Oklahoma City Bombing." History Channel, A & E Productions, 2001.

180. Oklahoma City Bombing Revelations, Patrick B. Briley, 2007

181. Ibid. (i) "Conspiracy? The Oklahoma City Bombing"
Ibid. (ii) Oklahoma City Bombing Revelations, Patrick B. Briley, 2007
Ibid. (iii) Third Terrorist: The Middle Eastern Connection to the Oklahoma City Bombing, Jayna Davis, 2004.

182. Ibid. Conspiracy? The Oklahoma City Bombing" 2001

183. Ibid. Conspiracy? The Oklahoma City Bombing" 2001

184. Ibid. (i) "Conspiracy? The Oklahoma City Bombing"
Ibid. (ii) Oklahoma City Bombing Revelations, Patrick B. Briley, 2007
Ibid. (iii) Third Terrorist: The Middle Eastern Connection to the Oklahoma City Bombing, Jayna Davis, 2004.

185. Ibid. Official Iraqi Response to 9/11.

186. Susan Lindauer Letter to Andy Card, December 2, 2001.

187. Ibid. Letter to Andy Card, December 2, 2001

188. Ibid. Letter to Andy Card, December 2, 2001

189. Ibid. Letter to Andy Card, December 2, 2001

190. Ibid. Letter to Andy Card, December 2, 2001

191. Ibid. John McCain, ABC News NIGHTLINE, November 28, 2001

192. Ibid. Vice President Richard Cheney, "Meet the Press," December 9, 2001

193. Ibid. Letter to Andy Card, December 2, 2001

194. Ibid. Letter to Andy Card, December 2, 2001.

195. Congressional Testimony of Dr. Fuisz on U.S. Corporation that supplied Iraq with SCUD mobile missile launcher. 1992. (ii) Correspondence of Congressman Charlie Rose.

196. Ibid. Letters to Andy Card, Dec. 2000 through Jan. 2003

197. Ibid. Letter to Andy Card, December 2, 2001

198. Federal Indictment, U.S. vs. Lindauer

199. FBI Evidence, Surveillance photos possible NSA Source, February, 2002. U.S. vs Lindauer

200. Ibid. FBI Evidence. Surveillance photos, February 2002. U.S. vs. Lindauer

201. Ibid. FBI Evidence. Fax sheets to U.N. Security Council announcing peace framework and Iraq's consent to weapon inspections 'with no conditions."

202. FBI Evidence. Collection of phone transcripts, emails, letters from Rani Ali, diplomatic adviser to Ambassador Hasmy Agam from May, 2000 through December, 2002, concluding with introduction to his successor, Mr. Norzuhdy.

203. Washington Post. March 7, 2002.

204. Ibid. Federal Indictment, U.S. vs. Lindauer

205. Susan Lindauer Letter to Kofi Annan, March 17, 2002.

206. Ibid. Washington Post.

207. Global Security, Bio of Musab Al Zarqawi

208. Ibid. "Was Nidal Behind Lockerbie Bombing?" Daily Mail, UK

209. (i) Susan Lindauer Letter to Secretary of State Colin Powell, January 27, 2003
(ii) Susan Lindauer Letter to Syria's U.N. Ambassador Wehbe, February 2, 2003.

210. (i) Susan Lindauer Letter to Secretary of State Colin Powell, January 27, 2003
(ii) Susan Lindauer Letter to Syria's U.N. Ambassador Wehbe, February 2, 2003.

211. Education for Peace in Iraq Center, schedule for meeting Congressional staff on lobby days.

212. FBI Evidence report to Defense Counsel. U.S. vs. Lindauer

213. Ibid. FBI Evidence report. U.S. vs. Lindauer

214. FBI Evidence. Phone Taps July 2002 to members of Senate Foreign Relations Committee.

215. FBI Evidence. Phone Taps. Calls to Congressional offices, July 2002 onwards.

216. Congress votes on Iraq War Resolution. SourceWatch.

217. Film Documentary, Body of War, directed by Ellen Spiro and Donahue, inter cuts the 2002 war debate with the postwar life of Tomas Young, a soldier who was paralyzed with a shattered spine within a week of arriving in Iraq. Captures his personal meeting with Sen. Robert Byrd—and his snubbing by Sen. Feinstein's staff.

218. Senator Kennedy Floor Speech, U.S. Senate. Debate on War Authorization. October, 10, 2002.

219. Barak Obama Speech against Iraq War Authorization, Federal Plaza in Chicago, October 2, 2002.

220. FBI Evidence. Wire taps of phone calls to Congressional offices from July, 2002 until March, 2003.

221. FBI Evidence. Wire taps of phone calls to Senate Foreign Relations Committee

222. Letter to President Bush, Rep. Ron Kind and Rep. Sherrod Brown. January, 2003.

223. Anti War Protests Largest Since 60s. Washington Post. October 27, 2002

224. Ibid. Washington Post. October 27, 2002.

225. FBI Evidence. Citizens for Public Integrity. Blast fax and email data base listing of Congressional staffers in all House and Senate offices. U.S. vs. Lindauer.

226. Ibid. FBI Evidence. Citizens for Public Integrity. Email Data base of Congressional staffers

227. Ibid. FBI Evidence. Citizens for Public Integrity. Blast fax of Congressional offices and U.N. Ambassadors. U.S. vs. Lindauer

228. FBI Evidence. Citizens for Public Integrity Papers. U.S. vs. Lindauer Sept. 2002 through March 2003.

229. Ibid. FBI Evidence. Citizens for Public Integrity Papers. U.S. vs. Lindauer

230. Ibid. FBI Evidence. Citizens for Public Integrity Papers. U.S. vs. Lindauer
231. Ibid. FBI Evidence. Citizens for Public Integrity Papers. U.S. vs. Lindauer
232. Ibid. FBI Evidence summary for Defense. U.S. vs. Lindauer
233. "Huge Protests for Peace," San Francisco Chronicle. January 19, 2003
234. GREEN LEFT WEEKLY: "Largest Coordinated anti-war protest in history." Feb. 19, 2003
235. Ibid. Green Left Weekly. Feb. 19, 2003
236. Ibid. Green Left Weekly. Feb. 19, 2003
237. Ibid. Green Left Weekly. Feb. 19, 2003
238. Ibid. Green Left Weekly. Feb. 19, 2003
239. Wikipedia. Biography of Andrew Card.
240. Ibid. Statistics on UN sanctions deaths cross reference (i) the World Health Organization (ii) United Nations Children's Fund (iii) Iraq Health Ministry.
241. Ibid. (i) World Health Organization and (ii) United Nations Children's Fund
242. Ibid. United Nations Children's Fund
243. Ibid. Iraqi Health Ministry
244. FBI Evidence. Email exchanged by Lindauer and Rani Ali in December, 2002. U.S. vs. Lindauer
245. FBI Evidence. Email, phone and letter correspondence from Rani Ali, Malaysian Embassy.
246. Ibid. FBI Evidence. Correspondence with Rani Ali, Malaysian Embassy
247. Russian Contracts in Iraq: Forgive or Forget, June 4, 2003, Daniel Kimmage
248. Susan Lindauer Letter to Andy Card, White House Chief of Staff, January 8, 2003
249. Letter to Andy Card, January 8, 2003
250. Ibid. Andy Card Letter, January 8, 2003.
251. FBI Evidence. Manila envelope with Colin Powell's address (next door to Dr. Fuisz)
252. Ibid. Keynote: Texas Democratic Party Convention General Wesley K Clark. June 9, 2006.
253. FBI Evidence. Correspondence to Secretary Colin Powell, manila envelope plus hand written notes on Andy Card letters dated September 24, 2001; December 2, 2001; and January 8, 2003
254. FBI Evidence. Letter to Secretary Powell. January 27, 2003, manila envelope plus signature & handwritten notes
255. U.S. Senate Intelligence Committee. Inquiry of Pre-War Intelligence from January, 2003. Released in May, 2007.
256. Barbara Walters Interview with Secretary Colin Powell, ABC's 20/20. September 8, 2005
257. FBI Evidence. Correspondence with Rani Ali, Malaysian Embassy.
258. Letter to U.N. Ambassador Wehbe of Syria. February 3, 2003.
259. Ibid. Letter to U.N. Ambassador Wehbe of Syria. February 3, 2003.
260. FBI Evidence. Email correspondence with Rani Ali, Malaysian Embassy, February, 2003.
261. FBI Evidence. Wire taps of phone conversation with Syria's Ambassador Wehbe at the United Nations, February 4, 2003.
262. "U.S. Rejected 2003 Iraqi Peace Offer: Saddam Hussein Proposed Elections, Disarmament, Health with War on Terror." Joseph Farah, G2 Bulletin, March 10, 2009. WorldNet Daily.

263. FBI Evidence. Wire tap. Fax transmission of Peace Framework to Syrian Embassy, Office of Ambassador Wehbe at the United Nations. February 3.

264. Meeting at Senate Intelligence Committee offices, February, 2009 attended by Brian Shaughnessy.

265. Ibid. SYRIA'S PEACE MEDIATION. U.S. Rejected 2003 Iraqi Peace Offer: Saddam Hussein Proposed Elections, Disarmament, Health with War on Terror." Joseph Farah, G2 Bulletin, March 10, 2009. WorldNet Daily

266. Richard Harris, "MacArthur Park." Lyrics by Jimmy Webb. Recorded by Dunhill on "A Tramp Shining."

267. British Soldiers Torture, Rape Iraqi POWS, The SUN, UK, John Scott and Michael Lea, June 3, 2003

268. Soldier Accused of Assault. European Intelligence Wire.. January 26, 2005

269. Lynndie England, Life After Abu Ghraib, January 3, 2009.

270. FBI Evidence. Susan Lindauer Letter to British Ambassador Jeremy Greenstock at the United Nations on June 4, 2003, including proof of fax transmission, courtesy of the FBI.

271. UK Troops in Iraq Torture Probe. May 1, 2004. BBC, UK.

272. FBI Evidence. Legal Project in Iraq and The Hague. U.S. vs. Lindauer

273. Ibd. FBI Evidence. Legal Project in Iraq and The Hague. U.S. vs. Lindauer

274. (i) "Meeting Resistance," Documentary film directed by Richard Horowitz. 2006
(ii) "Iraq in Fragments," Documentary film by James Longley and Mohammed Haithem. 2006.

275. Ibd. "Meeting Resistance" and "Iraq in Fragments." 2006

276. Ibid. FBI Evidence. Legal Project in Iraq and The Hague. U.S. vs. Lindauer

277. Ibid. FBI Evidence. Legal Project in Iraq and The Hague. U.S. vs. Lindauer

278. Ibid. FBI Evidence. Compilation of faxes to Congress and U.N. post-invasion. U.S. vs. Lindauer

279. Ibid. FBI Evidence. Phone tap with FBI Under Cover Agent, Bassem Yousef. U.S. vs. Lindauer

280. FBI Evidence. Surveillance and audio record. FBI Meeting with Bassem Yousef. U.S. vs. Lindauer.
June 23, 2003.

281. FBI Evidence. FBI Meeting with Bassem Youseff. U.S. vs. Lindauer. June 23, 2003.

282. Ibid. FBI Evidence. Audio record. FBI Meeting with Bassem Youseff. June 23, 2003.

283. Ibid. Federal Indictment U.S. vs. Lindauer. Charge of "Organizing Resistance to the United States.

284. FBI Evidence. Surveillance and audio record, FBI meeting with Bassem Youseff, U.S. vs. Lindauer July 17, 2003.

285. Ibid. FBI Evidence. Surveillance and audio record, Meeting with Bassem Youseff, July 17, 2003.

286. Court testimony of Dr. Parke Godfrey, Southern District of New York, June, 2008.

287. FBI Evidence. Phone tap. Conversation with Bassem Youseff. U.S. vs. Lindauer. July, 2003.

288. FBI Evidence. Phone tap. Conversation with Bassem Youseff. July 2003.

289. FBI Evidence. Phone tap. Conversation with Bassem Youseff. July 2003.

290. FBI Evidence. French Ambassador Jean Marc de la Sabliere on July 23, 2003. Wire tap captured transmission record.
291. Ibid. Federal Indictment. U.S. vs. Lindauer
292. Ibid. Federal Indictment. U.S. vs. Lindauer
293. Coalition Provisional Authority. Paul Bremer. Announcement on caucuses in Iraq, Nov. 15, 2003
294. Ayatollah Sistani, Religious fatwa demanding rights to elections. December, 2003.
295. Federal Indictment. U.S. vs. Muthanna al Hanooti. March, 2008.
296. FBI Evidence. Phone taps. Conversations between Lindauer and Muthanna al Hanooti, July 2002 through March, 2004. U.S. vs. Lindauer.
297. Ibid. Washington Post. "CIA could count Agents in Iraq on One Hand."
298. Presidential Commission on Iraqi Pre-War Intelligence. Findings. New York Times. 2005.
299. A Woman of Intelligence. Smith Alumnae Quarterly. Summer 2005.
300. IBID. A Woman of Intelligence. Smith Alumnae Quarterly. Summer 2005.
301. FBI Evidence. U.S. vs. Lindauer
302. FBI Evidence. U.S. vs. Lindauer
303. FBI Evidence. Education for Peace in Iraq Center Lobby Days. June 17, 2002. Schedule meeting staff for Senator Nickles of Oklahoma and Rep. JC Watts of Oklahoma
304. FBI Evidence. Captured fax transmissions to Congressional offices, post invasion. 2003-2004.
305. Ibid. FBI Evidence. Phone Wire Taps. Conversations with Senator Lott's staff. February 2, 2004
306. Ibid. FBI Evidence. Fax Wire Taps. Congressional letter. February, 2004.
307. Ibid. FBI Evidence. Citizens for Public Integrity papers, fax and email lists.
308. Ibid. Letters to Andy Card December, 2000 through January, 2003 (ii) Dec. 2, 2001; (iii) Letter to Colin Powell Jan. 27, 2003.
309. Washington Post, New York Times, March 12, 2004. "Susan Lindauer Arrested as Iraqi Agent."
310. Ibid. FBI Evidence. Lindauer Letters to Andy Card, Dec. 2000 through January, 2003.
311. Ibid. FBI Evidence. Lindauer Letters to Andy Card, Dec. 2000 through January, 2003.
312. Court Transcripts from March 11, 2004 through January 15, 2009. U.S. vs. Lindauer
313. 9/11 Commission Report. Released October, 2004.
314. FBI Interview of Parke Godfrey, September, 2004. (ii) affidavit of Parke Godfrey, (iii) Court testimony of Parke Godfrey, Southern District of New York, June 2008.
315. Ibid. FBI Arrest Report, Susan Lindauer, March 11, 2004. U.S. vs. Lindauer
316. Ibid. Federal Indictment U.S. vs. Lindauer
317. Ibid. Susan Lindauer letter to Andy Card, January 8, 2003.
318. Ibid. FBI Evidence. Manila envelope and hand written notes to Secretary Colin Powell on copy of Andy Card letter dated Jan 8, 2003. Also letter to Secretary Powell dated January 27, 2003.
319. Ibid. FBI Evidence. Manila envelope and hand written notes to Secretary Colin Powell on copy of Andy Card letter dated Jan 8, 2003. Also letter to Secretary Powell dated January 27, 2003.

320. Ibid. FBI Evidence Summary presented to legal defense. U.S. vs. Lindauer

321. "Lester Coleman: From Agent to Outcast." Plane-Truth.com. Ongoing blog.

322. Ibid. Lester Coleman: From Agent to Outcast.

323. Vince Cannistraro, Wikipedia bio.

324. U..S. vs. Lindauer. Court transcripts from March 11, 2004 through January 15, 2009.

324. Ibid. U.S. vs. Lindauer. Court transcripts from March 11, 2004 through January 15, 2009.

325. U.S. vs. Lindauer. Court transcripts from September 2005 through August, 2008.

326. Ibid. U.S. vs. Lindauer. Court transcripts from September 2005 through August, 2008.

327. Ibid. U.S. vs. Lindauer Court transcripts from September 2005 through August, 2008.

328. WelcomebacktoPottersville.com: "Susan Lindauer, Meet Franz Kafka."

329. Ibid. Federal Indictment. U.S. vs. Lindauer

330. U.S. Patriot Act. Federal Statute.

331. FBI Evidence. Classified Phone Calls. United for Peace and Justice. San Francisco

332. Ibid. U.S. Patriot Act. Federal Statute.

332. Ibid. U.S. Patriot Act. Federal Statute.

333. Ibid. U.S. Patriot Act. Federal Statute.

334. Ibid. U.S. vs. Lindauer Court transcripts from March 11, 2004 through Jan. 15, 2009.

335. Ibid. U.S. Patriot Act. Federal Statute.

336. Ibid. U.S. Patriot Act. Federal Statute.

337. Ibid. U.S. Patriot Act. Federal Statute.

338. Ibid. U.S. Patriot Act. Federal Statute.

339. Lindauer Letters to Andy Card, dated March 1, 2001 and December 2, 2001.

340. Ibid. Federal Indictment. U.S. vs. Lindauer

341. Judge Mukasey raised the question of whether my actions rose to a level of criminal activity in his decision against forcible drugging, Sept. 8, 2006.

342. Ibid. "Lockerbie: CIA witness gagged by U.S. Government, by Ian Ferguson. May 28, 2000.

343. Correspondence with Edward MacKechnie, summer of 2004 through summer of 2005.

344. Affidavit of Ted Lindauer that he functioned as attorney to interview witnesses, including MacKechnie in May, 2005

345. Deposition of Dr. Richard Fuisz, U.S. District Court, Alexandria, Virginia. Dec. 2000 and January, 2001. Conducted by the Washington Law Firm of Butera and Andrews for Scottish Solicitors in the Lockerbie Trial at Camp Zeist, a special Court of The Hague.

346. A large number of my witnesses were connected to Lockerbie, for the simple fact that it would be the most expeditious manner of proving Dr. Fuisz's CIA credentials. It was therefore entirely relevant. Also on our list was Dennis Hart from Butera and Andrews, who took the deposition.

347. U.S. Linked to Iraqi Scud Launchers, Seymour M. Hersh, New York Times, January 25, 1992

348. Letter from Rep. Charlie Rose to Mr. Charles Murdter, Fraud Division of U.S. Department of Justice requesting criminal investigation of a U.S. Corporation

accused of supplying SCUD mobile missile launchers to Iraq, citing obstruction of justice in a congressional investigation.

349. Ibid. Court testimony by Dr. Parke Godfrey, Southern District of New York, June 2008.
350. Court record. U.S. vs. Lindauer. Extradition hearing. Susan Gauvey, Magistrate, Baltimore, Maryland. March 11, 2004.
351. Psychiatric Evaluation Report by Dr. John S. Kennedy for Family Health Services, Hyattsville, Maryland, March 13, 2004.
352. Ibid. Psychiatric Evaluation Report by Dr. Kennedy. March, 2004.
353. Ibid. Psychiatric Evaluation Report by Dr. Kennedy. March, 2004.
354. Federal Court Transcripts, U.S. vs. Lindauer. June, 2004.
355. Monthly psychological observations from Dr. Bruke Taddesseh, Family Health Services in Maryland, filed to Pre-Trial Services in Greenbelt and New York. March 2004 to March 2005.
356. Release waiver for observation notes by Family Health Services, March 2005.
357. Classified Non-Disclosure Agreement, signed by Sam Talkin, February 10, 2005. Department of Justice, Compliance Review and Litigation Security Group, Security and Emergency Planning Staff.
358. Federal Express Receipt. Transport Law offices of Talkin & Muggruccio. January 23, 2009.
359. Ibid. Classified Non-Disclosure Agreement. February 10, 2005.
360. Personal checks from Dr. Richard Fuisz to Susan Lindauer in May, 2001 and October, 2001
361. Documents pertaining to Committee Chairman Charlie Rose's investigation of a U.S. Corporation accused of supplying SCUD mobile missile launchers to Iraq.
362. Psychiatric Evaluation by Dr. Sanford Drob in New York City reports interview dates of January 18, 2005 and February 8, 2005.
363. Professional biography of Dr. Sanford Drob, Fielding Graduate University, Santa Barbara, California.
364. Ibid. Psychiatric Evaluation by Dr. Drob for Defense in U.S. vs. Lindauer
365. Release waiver for observation notes by Family Health Services, March 2005 to be sent to Dr. Drob and attorney, Sam Talkin.
366. Dr. Taddesseh's observation reports for February, March and April, 2005.
367. Ibid. Classified Non-Disclosure Agreement. February 10, 2005.
368. Ibid. Psychiatric Evaluation by Dr. Drob for Defense in U.S. vs. Lindauer. Dated February 28, 2005.
369. Ibid. Conclusion of Psychiatric Evaluation by Dr. Drob. U.S. vs. Lindauer. Feb. 28, 2005
370. Ibid. Conclusion of Psychiatric Evaluation by Dr. Drob. U.S. vs. Lindauer. Feb. 28, 2005
371. Court transcripts. Statement of Judge Mukasey demanding explanation for discrepancy in psych reporting. June 2006.
372. Ibid. Cited in the Psychiatric Evaluation by Dr. Drob for Defense. Dated February 28, 2005.
373. Record of Subpoenas filed by Defense Counsel, Sam Talkin. U.S. vs. Lindauer
374. Ibid. Record of Subpoenas filed by Defense Counsel, Sam Talkin. U.S. vs. Lindauer
375. Response to Subpoena by Defense Intelligence Agency. U.S. vs. Lindauer, February 4, 2005.

376. Email correspondence from Eddie MacKechnie and Ian Ferguson from Jan. 2005 to June 2005.
377. Email correspondence from Eddie MacKechnie from Jan. 2005 to June 2005.
378. Affidavit from Thayer Lindauer, U.S. vs. Lindauer.
379. Ibid. Affidavit from Thayer Lindauer in Appendix.
380. Ibid. Affidavit from Thayer Lindauer in Appendix.
381. Ibid. Affidavit from Thayer Lindauer in Appendix.
382. Ibid. Affidavit from Thayer Lindauer in Appendix.
383. Ibid. Affidavit from Thayer Lindauer in Appendix
384. Ibid. Affidavit from Thayer Lindauer in Appendix
385. Ibid. Affidavit from Thayer Lindauer in Appendix
385. Ibid. Affidavit from Thayer Lindauer in Appendix
386. Ibid. Affidavit from Thayer Lindauer in Appendix
387. Ibid. Affidavit from Thayer Lindauer in Appendix
388. Ibid. Affidavit from Thayer Lindauer in Appendix
389. Ibid. Affidavit from Thayer Lindauer in Appendix
390. Psychiatric Evaluation by Dr. Stuart Kleinman for the Prosecution. U.S. vs. Lindauer Sept. 23, 2005.
391. Ibid. Affidavit from Thayer Lindauer in Appendix
392. Ibid. Affidavit from Thayer Lindauer in Appendix
393. Ibid. Affidavit from Dr. Parke Godfrey in Appendix
394. Ibid. CIA Director Could Count Agents in Iraq on One Hand. Washington Post.
395. Letters to Andy Card, March 1, 2001, September 24, 2001 and December 2, 2001
396. Ibid. Federal Indictment U.S. vs. Lindauer and Al Anbukes.
397. Ibid. FBI Evidence. Restaurant receipts for 3 lunches totaling $92.92 after September 11, 2001
398. Ibid. Psychiatric Evaluation by Dr. Sanford Drob for the Defense.
399. Ibid. (i) Affidavit from Thayer Lindauer, (ii) emails from Edward MacKechnie
400. Ibid. Affidavit from Thayer Lindauer
401. Ibid. Affidavit from Thayer Lindauer
402. Ibid. Affidavit from Thayer Lindauer
403. Federal Statute On Procedures for Deciding Competence of a Defendant. (ii) Affidavit from Thayer Lindauer.
404. Ibid. Affidavit from Thayer Lindauer in Appendix
405. Ibid. Affidavit from Thayer Lindauer in Appendix
406. Ibid. Affidavit from Thayer Lindauer in Appendix
407. Ibid. Affidavit from Thayer Lindauer.
408. Federal Court Order for Surrender to Carswell Prison, Judge Mukasey, September 23, 2005.
409. Ibid. Affidavit from Thayer Lindauer in Appendix
410. Biography of Edward O'Callaghan, Law Firm of Peabody, Nixon.
411. Barbara Walters Exclusive Interview with Secretary of State Colin Powell, "20/20," September 8, 2005.
412. Psychiatric Evaluation by Dr. Stuart Kleinman for the Prosecution. U.S. vs. Lindauer. Court documents show documents submitted September 17, 2005, with decision to

incarcerate me at Carswell. The appearance in Judge Mukasey's Chambers occurred on September 23, 2005.

413. Ibid. Barbara Walters Exclusive Interview with Secretary Powell, "20/20," September 8, 2005.

414. Ibid. Barbara Walters Exclusive Interview with Secretary Powell, "20/20," September 8, 2005.

415. FBI Evidence. Lindauer Letter to Secretary Colin Powell, January 27, 2003. Manila envelope with handwritten notes to Powell and signature.

416. Federal Indictment, U.S. vs. Lindauer, manila envelopes to Powell and correspondence therein, with handwritten messages to the Secretary.

417. Ibid. Psychiatric Evaluation by Dr. Stuart Kleinman for the Prosecution. U.S. vs. Lindauer. Court documents show documents submitted September 17, 2005, with decision to incarcerate me at Carswell. The appearance in Judge Mukasey's Chambers occurred on September 23, 2005.

418. "U.S. Prison Rate remains new one in 100 Americans: Study" AFP. March 17, 2010

419. Bureau of Prisons website, Federal Medical Center-Carswell. 2008

420. A Crack in the Carswell Wall, by Betty Brink, Fort Worth Weekly. Jan. 31, 2007

421. CNN Television News. November, 2005. Interviews with Rep. Murtha, Senator Carl Levin.

422. Ibid. Federal Indictment. U.S. vs. Lindauer and Anbukes.

423. FBI Evidence. Legal Discovery of Anbuke brothers.

424. FBI Evidence. Tax forms and pay stubs for Anbuke brothers.

425. FBI Evidence. Prison phone calls by Anbuke brothers from Metropolitan Correctional Center.

426. Ibid. CNN Television News. November, 2005. Interviews with Rep. Murtha, Senator Carl Levin.

427. Ibid. Affidavit by Thayer Lindauer (see appendix).

428. Carswell Prison Blues, by Betty Brink, Ms. Magazine, Summer 2008

429. Ibid. Carswell Prison Blues, by Betty Brink, Ms. Magazine, Summer 2008

430. Ibid. Psychiatric Evaluation by Dr. Drob for Defense in U.S. vs. Lindauer. Dated February 28, 2005.

431. Ibid. Affidavit by Thayer Lindauer (see appendix).

432. Staff notes on M-1 acquired by Subpoena, Carswell Prison, October, 2005 through April, 2006.

433. Cover Up of Convenience: The Hidden Scandal of Lockerbie. Ian Ferguson and John Ashton. 2001.

434. Ian Ferguson wrote about Lockerbie as a journalist and author. After the conviction of Megraghi in the Lockerbie case, he served as Chief Criminal Investigator for the Appeals. He's also produced a documentary film on Lockerbie. His background qualifies him as one of the foremost experts on the case.

436. Ibid. Godfrey testimony. Southern District of New York. June, 2008.

435. Ibid. Godfrey testimony. Southern District of New York. June, 2008.

440. Court papers ordering my surrender cited a release date no later than February 3, 2006, in accordance with the maximum 120 day detention allowed by federal law. Signed by Judge Mukasey

441. Notice of Internal Medication Hearing. Carswell Prison. Signed December 23, 2005.

442. Biography of Edward O'Callaghan. Law Firm of Peabody and Nixon. 2010.

443. Ibid. Notice of Internal Medication Hearing. Carswell Prison. Signed December 23, 2005.

444. Ibid. Testimony of Parke Godfrey, Southern District of New York. June, 2008.

445. Ibid. Monthly reports of observation filed by Dr. Bruke Taddesseh, Family Health Services. March, 2004 through March, 2005.

446. Participants listed as Dr. William Pederson and Dr. Colin Vas. Internal Medication Hearing. Carswell Prison. December 28, 2005.

447. Internal Medication Hearing. Carswell Prison. December 28, 2005.

448. Ibid. Internal Medication Hearing. Carswell Prison. December 28, 2005.

449. Ibid. Internal Medication Hearing. Carswell Prison. December 28, 2005.

450. Ibid. Internal Medication Hearing. Carswell Prison. December 28, 2005.

451. Court filings by Carswell Prison Staff on behalf of the Bureau of Prisons. U.S. vs. Lindauer

452. (i) Ibid. staff notes on M-1 acquired by Subpoena, Carswell Prison, October, 2005 through April, 2006. Documents repeated demands for Shadduck to interview witnesses. (ii) Ibid. Court testimony by Parke Godfrey. Southern District of New York, June 2008.

453. Decision on Internal Medication Hearing. Carswell Prison. December 28, 2005.

454. Ibid. Decision on Internal Medication Hearing. Carswell Prison. December 28, 2005. See Appendix.

455. Ibid. Decision on Internal Medication Hearing. Carswell Prison. December 28, 2005.

456. Ibid. staff notes on M-1 acquired by Subpoena show repeated demands to interview witnesses and confirm story., Carswell Prison, October, 2005 through April, 2006.

457. Ibid. Decision on Internal Medication Hearing. Carswell Prison. December 28, 2005.

458. No Mercy at Federal Prisons," by Betty Brink, the Progressive Populist

459. Ibid. No Mercy at Federal Prisons," by Betty Brink, the Progressive Populist

460. Ibid. No Mercy at Federal Prisons," by Betty Brink, the Progressive Populist

461. Ibid. No Mercy at Federal Prisons," by Betty Brink, the Progressive Populist

462. Three Arrested in Conspiracy to Smuggle Alient into the United States. Department of Justice. September 8, 2004.

463. Michigan Woman Sentenced for her Role in Smuggling Scores of Iraqis and Jordanians into the United States. Department of Justice. November 19, 2007.

464. Ibid. Michigan Woman Sentenced. Department of Justice. November 19, 2007.

465. FBI Evidence. Citizens for Public Integrity Email Data Base.

466. Ibid. FBI Evidence Citizens for Public Integrity Issue Papers.

467. Ibid. U.S. Senate Intelligence Committee. Inquiry of Pre-War Intelligence from January, 2003. Released in May, 2007.

468. Ibid. Letters to Andy Card January 8, 2003 and Colin Powell, January 27, 2003.

469. Ibid. Monthly reports of observation filed by Dr. Bruke Taddesseh, Family Health Services. March, 2004 through March, 2005.

470. Carswell Prison. Monthly Observation Reports on M-1. October, 2005 through April, 2006.

471. Carswell Prison. Monthly Observation Reports on M-1, notes by Dr. Colin Vas. October 23, 2005.

472. Carswell Prison. Staff notes on M-1 on Susan Lindauer, daily and continuous from October, 2005 through April, 2006.

473. Ibid. Carswell Prison. Monthly Observation Reports on M-1. October, 2005 through April, 2006.

474. Ibid. Carswell Prison. Monthly Observation Reports on M-1. October, 2005 through April, 2006.

475. Ibid. Carswell Prison. Monthly Observation Reports on M-1. October, 2005 through April, 2006.

476. Ibid. Decision on Internal Medication Hearing. Carswell Prison. December 28, 2005.

477. Ibid. Federal Statute on Findings of Competence. U.S. Laws.

478. Affidavit by Thayer Lindauer, see Appendix.

479. Psychiatric Diagnosis. Carswell Prison. "Psychotic Disorder, Not Otherwise Specified" Dec. 28, 2005.

480. Psychiatric Diagnosis by Dr. Tressa Burton, Counseling Plus, Silver Spring, Maryland, October, 2006. Post Traumatic Stress Disorder caused by incarceration.

481. Ibid. Federal Statute on Findings of Competence, Process of Evaluations.

482. Bureau of Prison Website. Inmate Locator citing release date, status of release.

483. (i) Court papers. Carswell filing. U.S. vs. Lindauer. Request for Indefinite Detention. February 3, 2006. (ii) Ibid. Bureau of Prison Inmate Locator. Online.

484. Court papers. Carswell filing Request for Involuntary Drugging with Haldol. February 3, 2006

(ii) Carswell Federal Medical Center. Internal Memo marked "Sensitive Limited Official Use," to Bureau of Prisons, Government Exhibit 2. Drug Recommendations by Dr. Collin J. Vas, Staff Psychiatrist, December 19, 2005

485. Carswell Opinion on Competency. By Dr. Shadduck U.S. vs Lindauer December 22, 2005.

486. Ibid. Decision on Internal Medication Hearing. Carswell Prison. December 28, 2005. Appendix.

487. Ibid. Congressional Investigation by Rep. Charlie Rose (North Carolina) into U.S. Corporation that supplied Iraq with SCUD Mobile Missile Launchers before the first Gulf War.

488. Ibid. U.S. Linked to Iraqi Scud Launchers, Seymour M. Hersh, New York Times, January 25, 1992

489. Ibid. Letter from Rep. Charlie Rose to Mr. Charles Murdter, Fraud Division of U.S. Department of Justice requesting criminal investigation of a U.S. Corporation accused of supplying SCUD mobile missile launchers to Iraq, citing obstruction of justice in a congressional investigation.

490. (i) Ibid. Court testimony. Parke Godfrey, Southern District of New York, June, 2008 (ii) Affidavit of Parke Godfrey (See Appendix)

491. Ibid. Carswell Opinion on Competency. By Dr. Shadduck U.S. vs Lindauer December 22, 2005.

Omits any and all reference to witness confirmations.

492. Ibid. Decision on Internal Medication Hearing. Carswell Prison. December 28, 2005. Appendix.

493. Carswell Request for Indefinite Detention. U.S. vs. Lindauer. February 3, 2006

494. Biography of Edward O'Callaghan, Law Firm of Peabody, Nixon. 2010

495. Affidavit of Thayer Lindauer, See Appendix. 2010

496. Affidavit of Thayer Lindauer, See Appendix. 2010

497. Affidavit of Thayer Lindauer, See Appendix. 2010
498. Affidavit of Thayer Lindauer, See Appendix. 2010
499. Affidavit of Thayer Lindauer, See Appendix. 2010
500. Affidavit of Thayer Lindauer, See Appendix. 2010
501. Affidavit of Thayer Lindauer, See Appendix. 2010
502. Affidavit of Thayer Lindauer, See Appendix. 2010
503. Affidavit of Thayer Lindauer, See Appendix. 2010
504. Federal Statute on Competence
505. Ibid. Federal Statute on Competence.
506. Affidavit of Thayer Lindauer, See Appendix. 2010
507. Psychiatric Report. Dr. Stuart Kleinman. September 17, 2005.
508. Court Transcript. Ruling on Competence. Judge Loretta Preska. September 15, 2008.
509. Oklahoma City Bombing Revelations. Patrick B. Briley. 2007
510. Court Transcript. Hearing on Forcible Drugging. Judge Mukasey, May 4, 2006.
511. Federal Statute. U.S. Patriot Act.
512. Ibid. Federal Statute. U.S. Patriot Act.
513. Ibid. Classified Non Disclosure Agreement. Signed by Sam Talkin. February 10, 2005
514. Ibid. Psychiatric Report. Dr. Stuart Kleinman. February 28, 2005.
515. Ibid. Federal Indictment U.S. vs. Lindauer
516. Ibid. Patriot Act. The whole premise of the Prosecution argument hinged on that denial. With admission, the charges would have been dismissed, and the Justice Department could never have argued for forcible drugging to cure me of what the FBI, the U.S. Attorney's Office and the Bureau of Prisons all recognized was truthful.
517. Ibid. Statutory Requirements under U.S. Patriot Act.
518. Ibid. Statutory Requirements under U.S. Patriot Act.
519. Courtroom Testimony of Dr. Collin Vas, Staff Psychiatrist. Carswell Federal Medical Center. Before Judge Michael B. Mukasey. U.S. vs. Lindauer. May 4, 2006.
520. Ibid. Courtroom Testimony of Dr. Vas. Carswell FMC. U.S. vs. Lindauer, May 4, 2006.
521. Ibid. Courtroom Testimony of Dr. Vas. Carswell FMC. U.S. vs. Lindauer, May 4, 2006.
522. Ibid. Decision on Internal Medication Hearing. December 28, 2005.
523. Ibid. Courtroom Testimony of Dr. Vas. Carswell FMC. U.S. vs. Lindauer, May 4, 2006.
524. Ibid. Decision on Internal Medication Hearing. December 28, 2005.
525. Court Decision on Forcible Drugging by Judge Mukasey. Ruling for the Defense, September 8, 2006.
526. Ibid. Decision on Forcible Drugging by Judge Mukasey. U.S. vs. Lindauer September 8, 2006.
527. Ibid. Courtroom Testimony of Dr. Vas. Carswell FMC. U.S. vs. Lindauer, May 4, 2006.
528. Ibid. Compilation of Observation Notes by M-1 Staff. Submitted as Court evidence, Hearing on Forcible Drugging. U.S. vs. Lindauer. May 4, 2006.
529. Ibid. Courtroom Testimony of Dr. Vas. Carswell FMC. U.S. vs. Lindauer, May 4, 2006.

530. Ibid. Monthly Observation Reports. Carswell Prison. October, 2005 through April, 2006

531. Ibid. Compilation of M-1 staff notes, Carswell Prison. October 2005 through April, 2006

532. Ibid. Courtroom Testimony of Dr. Vas, Carswell FMC, U.S. vs. Lindauer. May 4, 2006

533. Courtroom Testimony of Dr. Robert L. Goldstein, a Professor of Clinical Psychiatry at Columbia University. U.S. vs. Lindauer, May 9, 2006

534. Ibid. Courtroom Testimony of Dr. Robert L. Goldstein. U.S. vs. Lindauer May 9, 2006.

535. Ibid. Courtroom Testimony. Psychiatric Opinion of Dr. Goldstein. U.S. vs. Lindauer May 9, 2006.

536. FBI Evidence Summary for Defense. U.S. vs. Lindauer

537. Ibid. Courtroom Testimony. Psychiatric Opinion of Dr. Goldstein. U.S. vs. Lindauer May 9, 2006

538. Three Days of the Condor., Directed by Sydney Pollack, 1975.

539. Court Papers. Copies of my letters to Judge Mukasey requesting a competency hearing got forwarded to my attorney. February, 2006 through June, 2006.

540. Ibid. Court Papers. Copies of my letters to Judge Mukasey asking to call Paul Hoven for closed testimony. May, 2006.

541. Ibid. Psychiatry Report by Dr. Stuart Kleinman. September 17, 2005. U.S. vs. Lindauer

542. Ibid. Lockerbie Deposition by Susan Lindauer. December, 1998.

543. (i) Ibid. Congressional Investigation by Rep. Charlie Rose (North Carolina) into U.S. Corporation that supplied Iraq with SCUD Mobile Missile Launchers before the first Gulf War.
(ii) Ibid. U.S. Linked to Iraqi Scud Launchers, Seymour M. Hersh, New York Times, Jan. 25, 1992
(iii) Ibid. Letter from Rep. Charlie Rose to Mr. Charles Murdter, Fraud Division of U.S. Department of Justice requesting criminal investigation of a U.S. Corporation accused of supplying SCUD mobile missile launchers to Iraq, citing obstruction of justice in a congressional investigation.

544. Ibid. Letters to Andy Card, December, 2000 through January, 2003.

545. FBI Evidence. Fax Transmissions to United Nation Security Council, February 2003, on Iraq's agreement to resume weapons inspections "with no conditions," detailed in Dec. 2, 2001 framework.

546. (i) Court testimony by Parke Godfrey, Southern District of New York. U.S. vs. Lindauer. June, 2008.
(ii) Affidavit by Parke Godfrey, see appendix

547. FBI Evidence. Restaurant Receipts from Viand in New York City. September, 2001.

548. FBI Evidence. Video by Iraqi Intelligence Service. Al Rashid Hotel. March 7, 2002. U.S. vs. Lindauer

549. Ibid. FBI Evidence. Video by Iraqi Intelligence Service. Al Rashid Hotel. March 7, 2002.

550. FBI Evidence. Photo of Front Door barricaded by plywood on morning of arrest, March 11, 2004.

551. Ibid. Andy Card Letters dated March 1, 2001 and December 2, 2001.

552. (i) Prologue by Brian Shaughnessy, (ii) Affidavit by Thayer Lindauer (see appendix).

553. Court Transcript. Judge Mukasey demand for explanation on Discrepancies in Psych June, 2006

554. Ibid. Court Transcript. Judge Mukasey demand for explanation on Discrepancies in Psych Reports. June, 2006.

555. Court Decision by Judge Loretta Preska. Upholding finding of Incompetence. September 15, 2008.

556. Court Decision by Judge Michael B. Mukasey on Forcible Drugging, in favor of Defendant. U.S. vs. Lindauer. September 7, 2006. Date of retirement September 8, 2006.

557. Court papers. Prison Correspondence from Lindauer to Judge Mukasey. Copies supplied to defense attorney, Sam Talkin.

558. Ibid. Court Decision by Judge Michael B. Mukasey on Forcible Drugging, in favor of Defendant. U.S. vs. Lindauer. September 7, 2006. Date of retirement September 8, 2006.

559. Ibid. Court Decision by Judge Michael B. Mukasey on Forcible Drugging, in favor of Defendant. U.S. vs. Lindauer. September 7, 2006. Date of retirement September 8, 2006.

560. Ibid. Court Decision by Judge Michael B. Mukasey on Forcible Drugging, in favor of Defendant. U.S. vs. Lindauer. September 7, 2006. Date of retirement September 8, 2006.

561. Ibid. Court Decision by Judge Michael B. Mukasey on Forcible Drugging, in favor of Defendant. U.S. vs. Lindauer. September 7, 2006. Date of retirement September 8, 2006.

562. Ibid. Federal Statute. Competence Detentions. 2006.

563. Biography of Brian W. Shaughnessy. Law Firm of Shaughnessy, Volzer & Gagner. 2010

564. Patricia Kelly O'Meara. "Psyched Out: How Psychiatry Sells Mental Illness and Pushes Pills that Kill." Author House. 2001.

565. Court Testimony by Patricia Kelly O'Meara at Competency Hearing of Susan Lindauer. Judge Loretta Preska, presiding. Southern District of New York.. June, 2008.

566. Ibid. O'Meara. "Psyched Out: How Psychiatry Sells Mental Illness and Pushes Pills that Kill." Author House. 2001.

567. Ibid. O'Meara. "Psyched Out: How Psychiatry Sells Mental Illness and Pushes Pills that Kill." Author House. 2001.

568. Antonuccio et al. Psychiatric Times, 12:8, August 2000. Cited in O'Meara. "Psyched Out: How Psychiatry Sells Mental Illness and Pushes Pills that Kill." Author House. 2001.

569. Dr. Peter Breggen, MD "Brain Disabling Treatments in Psychiatry." Springer Publishing Co. New York, 1997 p. 5. Cited in O'Meara. "Psyched Out: How Psychiatry Sells Mental Illness and Pushes Pills that Kill." Author House. 2001.

570. Loren Mosher, MD, former chief of the National Institute of Mental Health Center for the Study of Schizophrenia. Cited in O'Meara. "Psyched Out: How Psychiatry Sells Mental Illness and Pushes Pills that Kill." Author House. 2001.

571. Elliot S. Valenstein, PhD, "Blaming the Brain"(The Free Press, New York, 1998) p.4. Cited in O'Meara. "Psyched Out: How Psychiatry Sells Mental Illness and Pushes Pills that Kill." Author House. 2001.

572. Ibid. O'Meara. "Psyched Out: How Psychiatry Sells Mental Illness and Pushes Pills that Kill." Author House. 2001.

573. (i) Court Testimony on Forcible Drugging, Judge Mukasey presiding. Dr. Goldstein. May 9, 2006.
    (ii) Ibid. Psychiatry Report by Dr. Stuart Kleinman. September 17, 2005. U.S. vs. Lindauer
    (iii) Ibid. Psychiatry Report by Dr. Sanford Drob, January 18, 2005. U.S. vs. Lindauer

574. (i) Court Testimony on Forcible Drugging, Judge Mukasey presiding. Dr. Goldstein. May 9, 2006.
    (ii) Ibid. Psychiatry Report by Dr. Stuart Kleinman. September 17, 2005. U.S. vs. Lindauer
    (iii) Ibid. Psychiatry Report by Dr. Sanford Drob, January 18, 2005. U.S. vs. Lindauer

575. Psychology Evaluation by Dr. Tressa Burton, Counseling Plus. October, 2006. U.S. vs. Lindauer.

576. Psychology Evaluation by Dr. Burton, Counseling Plus. October, 2006. U.S. vs. Lindauer.

577. U.S. Pre-Trial Services. Session Notes filed by Dr. Burton, Counseling Plus. October 2006 through August, 2007. U.S. vs. Lindauer.

578. U.S. Pre-Trial Services. No copy of the 2nd Psych Evaluation in Maryland, post-Carswell, has survived. My Pre-Trial Supervisor refused my request for a copy. Shaughnessy and I suspect that the Justice Department feared what my Defense might do if we got hold of two positive psych evaluations that contradicted the Court proceedings. For whatever reason, they refused to hand it over.

579. Psychiatric Evaluation for Prosecution by Dr. Stuart Kleinman, U.S. vs. Lindauer. Judge Loretta Preska presiding. June, 2007.

580. Motion for Reconsideration of Decision on Defendant's Competence and Her Right to a Speedy Trial. Filed by Brian Shaughnessy, October 1, 2008. U.S. vs. Lindauer, Judge Preska Presiding.

581. Affidavit by Susan Lindauer filed with Motion for Reconsideration, citing tracts from taped interview on June 8, 2007. Judge Preska presiding.

582. Transcript of Interview for Psych Evaluation with Dr. Stuart Kleinman, witnessed by Sam Talkin at Law Offices of Talkin & Muggruccio. June 8, 2007

583. Court Transcript. Testimony of Dr. Kleinman, Judge Loretta Preska presiding. September 15, 2007.

584. Ibid. Transcript of Interview for Psych Evaluation with Dr. Stuart Kleinman, witnessed by Sam Talkin at Law Offices of Talkin & Muggruccio. June 8, 2007

585. Ibid. Motion for Reconsideration of Decision on Defendant's Competence. Brian Shaughnessy, attorney. October 1, 2008. (ii) Ibid. Affidavit by Susan Lindauer filed with Motion for Reconsideration

586. Ibid. Transcript of Interview for Psych Evaluation with Dr. Stuart Kleinman, witnessed by Sam Talkin at Law Offices of Talkin & Muggruccio. June 8, 2007

587. Ibid. FBI Evidence. Letter to Andy Card dated March 1, 2001.

588. Ibid. Transcript of Interview for Psych Evaluation with Dr. Stuart Kleinman, witnessed by Sam Talkin at Law Offices of Talkin & Muggruccio. June 8, 2007

589. Ibid. Federal Indictment. U.S. vs. Lindauer shows no tax charges.

590. Ibid. Transcript of Court Testimony. Dr. Kleinman, Judge Preska presiding. September 15, 2007.

591. Ibid. Transcript of Interview for Psych Evaluation with Dr. Kleinman, witnessed by Sam Talkin at Law Offices of Talkin & Muggruccio. June 8, 2007

592. Ibid. Transcript of Interview for Psych Evaluation with Dr. Kleinman, witnessed by Sam Talkin at Law Offices of Talkin & Muggruccio. June 8, 2007

593. Ibid. Brian Shaughnessy. Prologue.

594. Court transcripts. U.S. vs. Lindauer. Presence of Brian Shaughnessy at proceedings. June 2007 onwards.

595. Letter to Judge Preska from Susan Lindauer, June 10, 2007 notifying Court of Brian Shaughnessy's interest in the Case. (ii) Session notes from Counseling Plus in August, 2007. End of Meetings with Burton.

596. Ibid. Biography of Edward O'Callaghan. Law Firm of Peabody Nixon

597. Michael Collins hosts ElectionFraudNews.com. His articles run on 400 blogs.

598. American Cassandra: Susan Lindauer's Story. Michael Collins. "Scoop" Independent News, Oct. 17, 2007. Republished by permission of the author.

599. "American Cassandra Series:" Michael Collins. "Scoop" Independent News.

600. Ibid. "American Cassandra Series:" Michael Collins. "Scoop" Independent News.

601. Court Transcripts. September, October, November and December 2007. Major fight to force me back to Carswell. Judge Preska, presiding, after I refused to continue psych meetings at Counseling Plus.
Thomas Marino, Jr. Pre-Trial Services, New York. Randy Canal, Pre-Trial Services, Greenbelt.

602. Tape Recordings of phone calls to Pre-Trial Services, documenting reporting.

603. Session notes from Counseling Plus. Burton. U.S. vs. Lindauer October, 2006 through August, 2007.

604. Bail Bond in U.S. vs. Lindauer set at $500,000. March 11, 2004 through January 15, 2009.

605. Ibid. Court Transcripts. September, October, November and December 2007. Major fight to force me back to Carswell. Judge Preska, presiding, after I refused to continue psych meetings at Counseling Plus. Thomas Marino, Jr. Pre-Trial Services, New York. Randy Canal, Pre-Trial Services, Greenbelt.

606. Ibid. Court Transcripts. September through December, 2007. U.S. vs. Lindauer. Judge Preska, presiding

607. Ibid. Court Transcripts. September through December, 2007. U.S. vs. Lindauer. Judge Preska, presiding

608. Court Transcripts. Pre-Trial Services' attempt to revoke bail. U.S. vs. Lindauer. December, 2007

609. Ibid. Court Transcripts. Pre-Trial Services' attempt to revoke bail. U.S. vs. Lindauer. December, 2007

610. Ibid. Court Transcripts. Pre-Trial Services' attempt to revoke bail. U.S. vs. Lindauer. December, 2007

611. Ibid. Session notes from Counseling Plus. Burton–Lindauer October, 2006 through August, 2007.
612. Ibid. Court Transcripts. Pre-Trial Services' attempt to revoke bail. U.S. vs. Lindauer. December, 2007
613. Court filing. Brian Shaughnessy. U.S. vs. Lindauer. Judge Preska, presiding. January, 2008.
614. Ibid. Court Transcripts. Pre-Trial Services' attempt to revoke bail. U.S. vs. Lindauer. December, 2007
615. Ibid. Court Transcripts. Pre-Trial Services' attempt to revoke bail. September through December, 2007. U.S. vs. Lindauer. Judge Preska, presiding
616. Court Testimony by Patricia Kelly O'Meara. Hearing on Competence, Judge Loretta Preska presiding.. U.S. vs. Lindauer, June 2008.
617. Ibid. Psyched Out: How Psychiatry Invents Mental Illness and Pushes Pills that Kill," by Patricia Kelly O'Meara. Author House. 2006.
618. Ibid. Court Testimony by Patricia Kelly O'Meara. Hearing on Competence, Judge Preska presiding.. U.S. vs. Lindauer, June 2008.
619. Court Testimony by Dr. Parke Godfrey, Hearing on Competence, Judge Preska presiding.. U.S. vs. Lindauer, June 2008.
620. Ibid. Affidavit by Dr. Parke Godfrey on 9/11 warning and the question of Lindauer's Competence.
621. Ibid. Affidavit by Dr. Parke Godfrey on 9/11 warning and the question of Lindauer's Competence.
622. Ibid. Affidavit by Dr. Parke Godfrey on 9/11 warning and the question of Lindauer's Competence.
623. Ibid. Affidavit by Dr. Parke Godfrey on 9/11 warning and the question of Lindauer's Competence.
624. Anti War Activist Returns to Court for Iraq Spy Case, by Alan Feuer, New York Times. June 18, 2008
625. Ibid. Anti War Activist Returns to Court, by Alan Feuer, New York Times. June 18, 2008
626. 9/11 Prediction Revealed at Susan Lindauer Hearing on Competence. By Michael Collins. "Scoop" Independent News. June 18, 2008
627. New York Times Covers Susan Lindauer Hearing, By Michael Collins "Scoop" Independent News," June 25, 2008.
628. Biography of Edward O'Callaghan. Law Firm of Peabody, Nixon. 2010
629. Biography of Judge Loretta Preska, Wikipedia
630. Woman Accused of Iraq Ties is Ruled Unfit for Trial Again, New York Times, September 16, 2008
631. Court Decision on Competence by Judge Loretta Preska, U.S. vs. Lindauer, September 15, 2008
632. Court Testimony. Dr. Stuart Kleinman, Judge Preska presiding. U.S. vs. Lindauer. September 15, 2008.
633. Ibid. Transcript of Interview for Psych Evaluation with Dr. Kleinman, witnessed by Sam Talkin at Law Offices of Talkin & Muggruccio. June 8, 2007
634. Ibid. Transcript of Interview for Psych Evaluation with Dr. Kleinman, witnessed by Sam Talkin at Law Offices of Talkin & Muggruccio. June 8, 2007

635. Ibid. Motion for Reconsideration of Decision on Defendant's Competence. Brian Shaughnessy, attorney. October 1, 2008. (ii) Ibid. Affidavit by Susan Lindauer filed with Motion for Reconsideration

636. Ibid. Andy Card Letters. December, 2000 through January, 2003.

637. Odysseus Elytis. Nobel Poet Laureate. On the Greek Resistance to Fascism. I have carried this poem with me for 20 years. With my thanks for a cup of tea in Athens, Susan Lindauer

638. Feds Drop Case Against Accused Iraqi Agent. Associated Press. January 15, 2009.

Made in the USA
Lexington, KY
20 September 2011